THE OXFORD HISTORY OF MEDIEVAL EUROPE

General Editors
JINTY NELSON *and* HENRIETTA LEYSER

Empires of Faith

The Fall of Rome to the Rise of Islam, 500–700

PETER SARRIS

OXFORD
UNIVERSITY PRESS

Great Clarendon Street, Oxford OX2 6DP

Oxford University Press is a department of the University of Oxford.
It furthers the University's objective of excellence in research, scholarship,
and education by publishing worldwide in

Oxford New York

Auckland Cape Town Dar es Salaam Hong Kong Karachi
Kuala Lumpur Madrid Melbourne Mexico City Nairobi
New Delhi Shanghai Taipei Toronto

With offices in

Argentina Austria Brazil Chile Czech Republic France Greece
Guatemala Hungary Italy Japan Poland Portugal Singapore
South Korea Switzerland Thailand Turkey Ukraine Vietnam

Oxford is a registered trade mark of Oxford University Press
in the UK and in certain other countries

Published in the United States
by Oxford University Press Inc., New York

© Peter Sarris 2011

The moral rights of the author have been asserted
Database right Oxford University Press (maker)

First published 2011

All rights reserved. No part of this publication may be reproduced,
stored in a retrieval system, or transmitted, in any form or by any means,
without the prior permission in writing of Oxford University Press,
or as expressly permitted by law, or under terms agreed with the appropriate
reprographics rights organization. Enquiries concerning reproduction
outside the scope of the above should be sent to the Rights Department,
Oxford University Press, at the address above

You must not circulate this book in any other binding or cover
and you must impose the same condition on any acquirer

British Library Cataloguing in Publication Data
Data available

Library of Congress Cataloging in Publication Data
Data available

Typeset by SPI Publisher Services, Pondicherry, India
Printed in Great Britain
on acid-free paper by
MPG Books Group, Bodmin and King's Lynn

ISBN 978–0–19–926126–0

1 3 5 7 9 10 8 6 4 2

General Editors' Preface

The only traditional thing about this series is that its volumes will form a chronological sequence. Each volume will be single-authored and cover one or two centuries. Beyond coverage of the medieval time-span, the editors have shied away from insisting on uniformity of presentation, which can have a stultifying effect and lead to dissimilar periods finding themselves shoe-horned into common patterns. Instead, authors are encouraged, within whatever geographical frame they choose for their volume (and those will vary), to treat 'Europe' as broadly as possible, to break away from narrowly Eurocentric perspectives, and to range, as and when desirable, beyond Europe (e.g. to the Near East or North Africa). Each author will be free to emphasise, and connect, themes that they consider significant, in light of their own work and of contemporary trends in historiography. While we expect a concern with beliefs and ideas, values and sentiments to reflect history's cultural turn, authors will offer individual interpretations of their chosen periods, reflecting as they consider appropriate on interdisciplinary approaches, especially via consideration of material culture. The editors' intention is that each author's distinctive voice should be heard loud and clear, and we expect each volume to have its own unity and pace.

Our authors have been liberated from the need to produce a standard authoritative account—always a rather chimerical concept—and we trust them to write with the energy and bravado such freedom unleashes. Every historian reflects the concerns of their own times: our series will be different only in so far as this will be an explicit aim. The editors will encourage authors to address twenty-first-century controversies when they think that their work offers useful connexions, comparisons and points of departure—for in this way the volumes will, we hope, contribute to better understandings of our own contemporary world.

Jinty Nelson and Henrietta Leyser

To my mother
Patricia Sarris
for her many years of love, labour, and support

Contents

List of Maps	xiii
List of Figures	xv
Introduction and Acknowledgements	1

1. The World that had been Rome — 4
- 1.1 Roman Imperialism from Augustus to the Third Century — 4
- 1.2 The 'Crisis' of the Third Century — 8
- 1.3 The Age of the Soldier Emperors — 14
- 1.4 Diocletian, Constantine, and the Consolidation of the Late Roman State — 17
- 1.5 The Late Roman Empire: Society and Institutions — 25
- 1.6 The Demise of the Western Roman Empire — 33

2. The Formation of Post-Roman Society — 41
- 2.1 Introduction — 41
- 2.2 The Decline of the Western Empire: Chronology and Facts — 44
- 2.3 'Romans' and 'Barbarians' in an Age of Transition — 55
- 2.4 'Romanitas' and its Limits — 68
- 2.5 Continuity and Discontinuity in the Post-Roman Economy — 73

3. The Romano-Germanic Kingdoms: The Era of Theoderic and Clovis — 83
- 3.1 Introduction: The Building Blocks of the Romano-Germanic Kingdoms — 83
- 3.2 Identity, Lordship, and Kingship — 84
- 3.3 The Vandal Kingdom of Africa — 89
- 3.4 The Kingdom of Odoacer in Italy — 97
- 3.5 Theoderic and the Ostrogoths — 99
- 3.6 The Struggle for Mastery in Italy — 101
- 3.7 The Consolidation and Nature of Theoderic's Regime — 102
- 3.8 The Kingdom of Theoderic: Signs of Growing Tension — 109
- 3.9 The Fall of the Ostrogothic Kingdom — 112
- 3.10 The Roman Reconquest of Italy — 115
- 3.11 The Frankish Expansion — 120
- 3.12 Clovis' Conversion — 122

4. The View from the East: Crisis, Survival, and Renewal — 125
- 4.1 Introduction: Surviving the Fifth Century — 125
- 4.2 The Limitations and Frailties of the East Roman State — 127

4.3 The Roman Response under Anastasius and Justin	134
4.4 Justinian, Khusro, and Imperial Renewal	145
4.5 The Resumption of Hostilities	153
4.6 The Advent of the Plague	158
4.7 The Emperor and the Church	160
5. Byzantium, the Balkans, and the West: The Late Sixth Century	**169**
5.1 Introduction: Death of an Emperor	169
5.2 The West Eurasian Steppe in the Mid-Sixth Century	170
5.3 The Balkan Context to Justinian's Avar Policy	171
5.4 The Consolidation of Avar Power and its Consequences	177
5.5 Francia and Hispania	182
5.6 The Consolidation of Power in Lowland Britain	195
6. Religion and Society in the Age of Gregory the Great	**205**
6.1 Royal Conversion and the Consolidation of Roman Christianity	205
6.2 Royal, Imperial, and Episcopal Authority	208
6.3 Asceticism and Authority	210
6.4 Gregory the Great Between East and West	215
6.5 Discordant Voices	220
7. Heraclius, Persia, and Holy War	**226**
7.1 Justin II, the Court Aristocracy, and the Eastern Front	226
7.2 Roman-Persian Relations from Tiberius to Maurice	232
7.3 Mounting Social Tensions and Military Revolt	236
7.4 The Persian Advance	242
7.5 Heraclius' Rebellion and Coup	243
7.6 The Fall of the Roman Near East	245
7.7 'Persia Burning'	249
7.8 The Prophet Amongst the Saracens	258
7.9 The 'Abode of War'	268
7.10 Reasons for Arab Success	272
8. The Age of Division	**275**
8.1 The Fragility of the New World Order	275
8.2 The Near East in the Balance	279
8.3 'The day of their destruction is close'	286
8.4 New Constantines, New Justinians, New Davids	292
8.5 A World Transformed	302
9. The Princes of the Western Nations	**307**
9.1 Byzantium and the Balkans in the Seventh Century	307
9.2 Society, Identity, and Law in Langobard Italy	310
9.3 The Visigoths and the Catholic Monarchy of Toledo	317
9.4 Kings, Nobles, and Councils	321
9.5 The Crisis of the Visigothic Realm	326

9.6	The Merovingian Commonwealth of Kingdoms	329
9.7	Kingship and Consensus	333
9.8	The Frankish Nobility: Consolidation and Entrenchment	338
9.9	The Mayors of the Palace and the Rise of the Noble Faction	343
9.10	Controlling the King	347
9.11	The Age of the *Bretwaldas* and the Era of Marchland Expansion	353
9.12	The Dynamics of Power in Seventh-Century Britain	361
9.13	Bishops, 'Bookland', and the *Gens Anglorum*	370

Epilogue 377
Abbreviations 380

Select Bibliography and Further Reading 381
Index 413

List of Maps

1. The Growth of Roman Rule (J. Boardman, J. Griffin, and O. Murray, *The Oxford History of the Classical World*, pp. 534–5) — 5
2. The Roman Empire c.AD 390 (C. Mango, *The Oxford History of Byzantium*, p. 33) — 35
3. Europe c.526 (R. McKitterick, *The Short Oxford History of Europe: The Early Middle Ages*, pp. 280–81) — 116
4. The War Zone between Byzantium and Persia (C. Mango, *The Oxford History of Byzantium*, p. 41) — 136
5. Justinian's Empire in 565 (C. Mango, *The Oxford History of Byzantium*, p. 52) — 161
6. Pre-Islamic Arabia (C. Mango, *The Oxford History of Byzantium*, p. 120) — 262
7. Theme Commands in Byzantine Asia Minor c.720 (J. D. Howard-Johnston, *Witnesses to a World Crisis*, p. xxxii) — 305
8. Europe c.732 (R. McKitterick, *The Short Oxford History of Europe: The Early Middle Ages*, pp. 282–3) — 375

List of Figures

1. Execution of Barbarians on the Column of Marcus Aurelius (B. Ward-Perkins, *The Fall of Rome and the End of Civilization*, Oxford 2005, p. 26) — 7
2. Ivory Diptych of Stilicho and Family (C. Mango, *The Oxford History of Byzantium*, p. 37) — 33
3. The Theodosian Land Walls (C. Mango, *The Oxford History of Byzantium*, p. 67) — 53
4. Reconstruction of Seal-Ring of Childeric (reproduced by kind permission of the Ashmolean Museum, Oxford, and the Bridgeman Art Library) — 72
5. Gold Medallion with Bust of Theoderic (B. Ward-Perkins, *The Fall of Rome and the End of Civilization*, Oxford 2005, p. 73) — 106
6. Mosaic Panel Depicting Justinian, San Vitale, Ravenna (C. Mango, *The Oxford History of Byzantium*, p. 60) — 142
7. Exterior of Hagia Sophia, Constantinople (C. Mango, *The Oxford History of Byzantium*, p. 47) — 152
8. St Albans Cathedral and Shrine Viewed through the Walls of Verulamium (photograph reproduced by kind permission of James Cridland, esq.) — 201
9. Silver Hexagram of Heraclius and Heraclius Constantine (by kind permission of the Fitzwilliam Museum, Cambridge) — 251
10. Arab Mock-Byzantine Solidus (C. Mango, *The Oxford History of Byzantium*, p. 127) — 278
11. 'Standing Caliph' Solidus (C. Mango, *The Oxford History of Byzantium*, p. 127) — 300
12. Solidus of Justinian II (by kind permission of the Fitzwilliam Museum, Cambridge) — 301
13. Helmet from Sutton Hoo (by kind permission of the British Museum, London) — 367
14. The Staffordshire Hoard (by kind permission of the Birmingham Museum and Art Gallery) — 368
15. Anglo-Saxon *sceatta* bearing image of Christ (by kind permission of Lord Stewartby and the Royal Numismatic Society) — 373

Introduction and Acknowledgements

The starting and finishing dates for this volume, *c.* AD 500 and 700, are not in themselves significant. No major cataclysm, crisis, or foundation event detailed in this work occurred in either 500 or 700; neither do these dates constitute obvious 'book ends' to a specific era, movement, or regime. However, it is my contention, in the pages that follow, that the period from the late fifth to the early eighth century witnessed a series of crucial developments that were to do much to define the 'medieval world' as commonly understood: in the west, these centuries saw the demise of the power of the Roman state and the emergence to the fore of social relations of a martial elite and a culture of military lordship; to the east, the period witnessed the economic, cultural, and administrative recasting of the surviving Eastern Roman Empire and its transformation into the society known to us as Byzantium; whilst across the eastern and southern shores of the Mediterranean (and beyond) these years were associated with the formation and ascendancy of a sophisticated Islamic rival and foe, whose presence would do much to give sharper definition to an embryonic 'Christendom'.

The period detailed in this work is one that holds an abiding fascination for me, the origins of which can be traced back to the summer vacation of 1990 when I was preparing to go up to Balliol College, Oxford, to begin my first term as an undergraduate reading Modern History. The first paper we were obliged to study was entitled 'The History of England from the Beginning to 1330'. In practice, in those days at least, 'the Beginning' meant the coming of the Anglo-Saxons. I began by reading Sir Frank Stenton's *Anglo-Saxon England* (Oxford, 1943) alongside Sir Richard Southern's *The Making of the Middle Ages* (London, 1953) and the English translation of Marc Bloch's *Feudal Society* (London, 1961), with a view to understanding English developments in a broader medieval context. After I had finished Stenton and began to move on through the other medieval volumes of the *Oxford History of England* (in order to get to grips with the Normans and their successors), I found myself drawn ineluctably back to the questions that Stenton had first raised in my mind concerning the transition from Roman rule and the emergence of a new social order, which every page of Bloch seemed to bring to life with vivid immediacy.

Thus it came about that, although, as a schoolboy imagining university, I had idealistically planned to specialise in the history of the French Revolution, or perhaps of Chartism and British labour, I ended up hooked on the Middle Ages (and the early Middle Ages in particular), studying Anglo-Saxon, English, and early medieval European history with Maurice Keen at Balliol and Patrick Wormald at

Christ Church. As my interests became increasingly social and economic in focus, I was led eastwards to the late-antique eastern Mediterranean and the world of Byzantium, which I studied with James Howard-Johnston (who subsequently supervised my doctoral dissertation on 'Economy and Society in the Age of Justinian')—whilst also attending lectures on medieval and Byzantine history by Cyril Mango, Marlia Mundell Mango, Bryan Ward-Perkins, James Campbell, and Thomas Charles-Edwards, amongst others. The intellectual debt to these scholars that I accumulated during my time at Oxford will be evident in the chapters that follow. In particular, from Maurice Keen and James Howard-Johnston I learned the importance of warfare as an agent of historical change, and as both a shaper and a sharpener of social and political identities. One result of the combined influence of first Bloch and then Keen was a particular interest in the role of military lordship in medieval society.

At the same time, however, other currents—both historical and political—alerted me to the extent to which history was about much more than the study of kings, battles, and elites. Attempting to come to terms with the totality of social and economic relations in a given society has always struck me as central to the purpose of historical research. Accordingly, the roles played by social conflict and economic competition and exploitation in the transformation of the late-Roman and post-Roman worlds, and the impact of late-Roman and post-Roman developments on the peasantry and in the construction of social and gendered identities, are fundamental issues. In order to keep this book to a manageable size, many of those issues have only been touched upon in the following pages, but when they appear they do so for a reason.

In terms of my early influences, therefore, this is unashamedly an 'Oxford' book, and in thinking about medieval economic history I also learned much in Oxford from Rosamond Faith and Peregrine Horden. But others who were not then, are not now, or never have been based in Oxford have also had a profound influence on my approach to the early Middle Ages. Foremost amongst these are Jairus Banaji, John Haldon, Michael Maas, Rosamond McKitterick, and Chris Wickham. Indeed, when writing this book I had to make the express decision not to read Wickham's *The Inheritance of Rome* (London, 2009) in order to prevent myself from simply paraphrasing it. Gerald Bevan, Geoffrey Brown, and Nigel Williams, all of whom taught me as a boy, are amongst several others to whom I owe much.

Inevitably, I have also learned a great deal from some of the many students, first in Oxford and now in Cambridge, who have studied early medieval and Byzantine history with me over the years. I am grateful above all to have worked with an extraordinarily gifted coterie of Cambridge graduate students: first of all Philip Booth and Matthew Dal Santo; more recently, Alyssa Bandow, Danielle Donaldson, Matthew Geddes, Michael Humphreys, and Louise Nixey. My former Cambridge colleagues Teresa Shawcross and Richard Payne have also provided much inspiration and assistance through their own work; Turlough Stone read the whole of this book in draft and made a number of helpful suggestions for its improvement.

The writing of this book would not have been possible without the support of the Master and Fellows of Trinity College, Cambridge, to whom I tender my thanks, and the History Faculty of Cambridge University. Lastly, I should express my gratitude to Henrietta Leyser and Jinty Nelson for being such careful and considerate series editors and readers, to Emma Barber and Stephanie Ireland at Oxford University Press, and to my copy-editor, Richard Mason, for his remarkable efficiency and helpfulness.

Almost all that is of interest in this book I owe to others. All that is wrong with it is ascribable entirely to myself alone.

Peter Sarris
Willow Cottage

April 2011

1

The World that had been Rome

1.1 ROMAN IMPERIALISM FROM AUGUSTUS TO THE THIRD CENTURY

Towards the end of the first century BC, in Book Six of his epic poem the *Aeneid*, the Roman poet Virgil sought to remind his compatriots of what he regarded as their imperial mission. Led by the guiding shade of his father Anchises, the hero Aeneas—fictional progenitor of the Romans—is introduced to a panoply of his descendants who would go on to establish the glory of Rome. Anchises brings his celebration of future Roman might to a magnificent climax:

> *Remember, Roman, that it is for you to rule the peoples beneath your sway!*
> *These shall be your arts: to impose peace and the rule of law;*
> *To spare the conquered and battle down the proud.*[1]

When Virgil wrote these words Rome already ruled over a vast empire that embraced the entirety of the Mediterranean world and its appendages, from the Pillars of Hercules in the west to the Syrian desert in the east, and from the Rhine and Balkans in the north to the Atlas mountains and the distant reaches of Upper Egypt in the south (Map 1). Many of these conquests and their consolidation had been the work of Julius Caesar and his adopted son and eventual successor Octavian, who upon establishing his sole rule of the Roman state in 31 BC, took up the hitherto unheard-of name of *Augustus*—meaning 'something between "venerable" and "super-human"'.[2] To the east and, to some extent, to the west, Rome's reach was to be further extended after the death of the first Augustus: within a few decades of the *Aeneid*'s composition, much of Britain would come under Roman control, and whilst attempts to extend Roman power beyond the Rhine and Danube ultimately faltered, at the end of the second century AD the Romans would make significant gains in the Transcaucasus at the expense of the Persian Empire of Parthia.

Ruling over so vast an empire inevitably posed enormous logistical, political, and military problems. Accordingly, from an early date the empire had sought to co-opt into the imperial system the indigenous elites of those over whom it ruled.[3] Roman society, like that of the Greeks before it, was essentially city-based.[4]

---

[1] Virgil, *Aeneid*, tr. C. Day Lewis (Oxford, 1986), 6.851–3.
[2] J. Griffin, 'Introduction' in Virgil, *The Aeneid*, tr. C. Day Lewis (Oxford, 1986), p. x.
[3] G. Woolf, *Becoming Roman* (Cambridge, 1999).
[4] G. E. M. de Ste Croix, *The Class Struggle in the Ancient Greek World* (London, 1981), pp. 9–18.

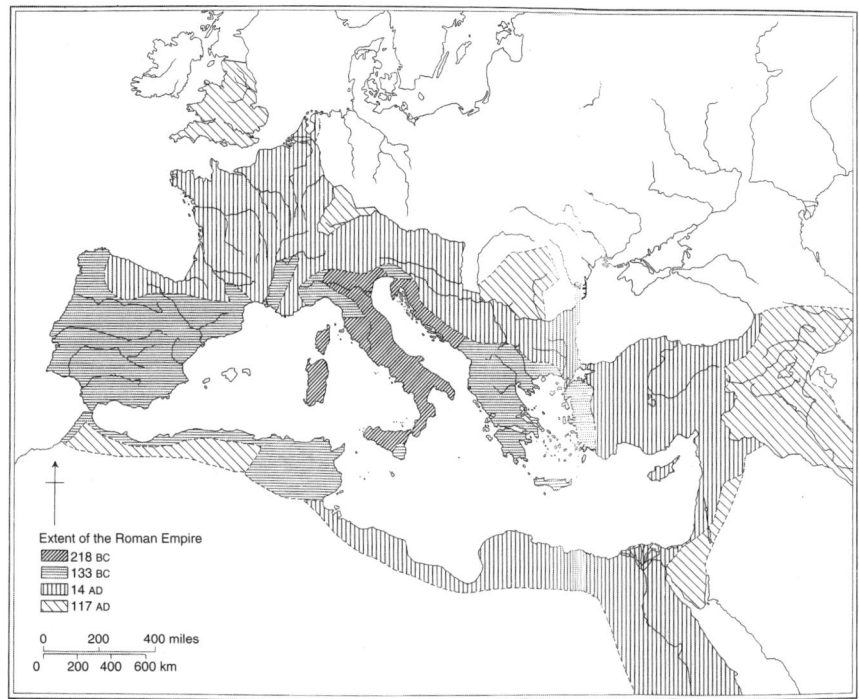

Map 1 The Growth of Roman Rule (J. Boardman, J. Griffin, and O. Murray, *The Oxford History of the Classical World*, pp. 534–5)

Although the vast majority of the inhabitants of the Roman world lived in the countryside, Roman government and governors operated from grand urban centres termed *civitates* in Latin or *poleis* in Greek. Where, as in much of the West, such cities did not exist when the Romans arrived, the Romans set about constructing them. The imperial authorities made strenuous efforts to draw the elites of the conquered regions into these cities, enrolling them onto the city councils or *curiae* (Greek *boulai*) that were entrusted with much of the governance of the territories in which they were situated. This gave local elites a stake in Roman rule. Crucially, it also exposed them to Roman cultural and political values, and soon, in the West, members of these families were adopting Latin as their preferred language and aspiring to Roman citizenship. Without the resultant acculturation and cooperation of the indigenous elites of the Western provinces, Roman imperialism would have been unsustainable.

In the Eastern provinces, matters were slightly different. Here (with the exception of Egypt, where civic institutions were generally introduced only in the early third century AD) cities were already the basis of political identity and administration well before the Romans arrived; these cities had long ago been established either by the Greeks (as in Greece itself and much of Asia Minor) or by the Greek-speaking 'Hellenistic' kings—the Macedonian generals who had shared out the territorial spoils of Alexander's great empire and had themselves used cities to acculturate, incorporate, and, in this instance, Hellenise the leaders of local society. Here too, however, effective Roman rule required the reconciliation of local interests, and the Roman emperors sought to present themselves as the guardians and protectors of existing civic identities and cultural traditions, not least by taking warfare to the ancient enemy of the Greek-speaking world: the empire of Persia to the east.[5]

Whether such acculturation and incorporation is what Virgil meant when he wrote of 'sparing the conquered', it should not be forgotten, however, that to him and to many of his compatriots 'empire' also very much meant 'battling down the proud'. At no point in its history was governing the Roman Empire simply a matter of finding and crystallising in administrative form the lowest common denominator of interest between the demands of the Roman state and the aspirations of provincial elites. The empire had largely been established by military force; everywhere the expansion of Roman rule had elicited armed resistance (even in Italy, where a major uprising against Roman domination had occurred in the 90s BC), and ultimately the maintenance of the *Pax Romana* ('Roman Peace') rested on the projection and reality of military might. This was a point that was constantly reiterated to Rome's citizens and subjects, both in the imperial capital and the provinces: it was established by means of imperial edicts and pronouncements circulated throughout the empire advertising Rome's military triumphs, and was repeated by propagandistic literature such as the writings of Virgil himself. The point was also reinforced by periodic acts of brutality in the face of local revolts, such as the savage destruction of Jerusalem in AD 70. Military power was monumentalised in stone in imperial commissions such as the Circus Maximus—constructed with booty garnered from the crushing of the Jewish Revolt—or the Column of Marcus Aurelius built in Rome at the end of the second century AD, which displayed bloodthirsty scenes of captured barbarian warriors being beheaded, and their women and children being massacred or led into slavery (Fig. 1).

As we are reminded by the *Book of Revelation*, however, with its fevered anticipation of how Rome ('the Whore of Babylon'), 'drunk with the blood of the saints and with the blood of the martyrs', would 'come into remembrance before God', not all of Rome's subjects were co-opted into Roman rule or quiescent under imperial control, and some at least dreamt of a world in which they would once more be free of Roman domination.[6] Nevertheless, it is clear that by the end of the second century AD the incorporation and acculturation of indigenous elites had reached an advanced stage, and in the year 212 the so-called *Constitutio Antoniana* ('Antonine Constitution', also known as the 'Caracallan Edict') granted Roman citizenship to virtually all free (i.e. non-slave) inhabitants of the empire. For many contemporaries the importance of this development must have been more symbolic than real, but it is significant historically in that it indicates that the Roman Empire was gradually evolving into something with at least the outward appearance of more

---

[5] S. Price, 'Gods and Emperors: The Greek Language of the Roman Imperial Cult', *JHS* 104 (1984), pp. 79–85.
[6] *Revelations* 17.6 and 16.19; Ste Croix (1981), pp. 441–2.

Fig. 1 Execution of Barbarians on the Column of Marcus Aurelius (B. Ward-Perkins, *The Fall of Rome and the End of Civilization*, Oxford 2005, p. 26)

than a mere 'Italocracy'—the imposition of Roman or Italian dominance on an alien provincial landscape.[7] Moreover, the overwhelming geographical concentration of Roman military units along the frontiers of the empire by this time (especially in Britain and along the Rhine) would also indicate that Roman rule within the provinces had become sufficiently hegemonic to be self-sustaining without too frequent a recourse to armed force. It was at the fortified military frontier zone or *limes* that Roman might was at its most conspicuous.

1.2 THE 'CRISIS' OF THE THIRD CENTURY

At its apex, however, the Roman Empire of the late second and early third centuries AD remained dominated by an essentially Italian-rooted senatorial aristocracy. This elite invested much in the traditional republican (and thus anti-monarchical) ideology of Rome, regarding the Emperor, or *Augustus*, as 'chief magistrate' rather than overlord of the Roman world, although in the provinces of the Greek-speaking east a more autocratic language of power had been inherited from the Hellenistic monarchies.[8] Yet the interests and ambitions of members of this elite—not least in the economic sphere—necessarily spanned a horizon that stretched well beyond Rome and the Italian peninsula. Many of the grandest senatorial estates were concentrated in the province of *Africa Proconsularis*, for example.[9] The imperial office was closely conjoined to the traditional senatorial aristocracy, from whose ranks the Emperor was generally appointed, but was itself subject to broader cultural currents—such as the ideological pull of the East. Over the course of the period from the first century AD to the third, it is possible to trace a growing distancing of the person of the Emperor from both the institution of the Senate and the physical location of the city of Rome.[10] Beneath the level of the Senate, the Emperor, and his entourage, stood the governors whom they appointed and whose task it was to keep a beady eye on the city councils of the empire on whose shoulders effective imperial administration ultimately rested. This was a highly devolved system of government which, conjoined with the threat of savage and violent retribution should cooperation not be forthcoming, facilitated rule over so wide an area.

In the mid-third century, however, this inherited system came under mounting pressure.[11] The primary cause for this was a change in the balance of power along Rome's northern and eastern frontiers. Up until that point the empire's outlook on these frontiers had been a relatively favourable one. To the north of the Rhine and

---

[7] P. Garnsey, *Social Status and Legal Privilege in the Roman Empire* (Oxford, 1970).
[8] F. Millar, *The Emperor in the Roman World* (London, 1977), and Price (1984).
[9] C. Wickham, *Framing the Early Middle Ages: Europe and the Mediterranean, 400–800* (Oxford, 2005), pp. 17–21.
[10] Each of these developments is addressed in great detail in Millar (1977).
[11] J. Drinkwater, 'Maximus to Diocletian and the "crisis"', in A. K. Bowman, P. Garnsey, and A. Cameron (eds.), *The Cambridge Ancient History*, 2nd ed., vol. XII: *The Crisis of Empire – A.D. 193–337* (Cambridge, 2005), pp. 28–66.

Danube, Rome had faced a series of atomised threats from a number of generally quite primitive Germanic and, in the Danubian zone, nomadic Sarmatian groupings.[12] Whilst these individual tribes could, on occasion, cause localised difficulties for the Roman authorities, they were in little position to mount a concerted challenge to Roman supremacy, and the 'barbarians' were regarded with considerable condescension by Roman authors and the imperial authorities. To the east, Rome's main rival was the relatively quiescent Arsacid dynasty of Persia, which, though capable of resisting Roman expansion, did not go out of its way to take the empire on.[13]

By the middle of the third century much of this had changed, largely—ironically—as a result of the success of Roman policy. To the north, the relatively egalitarian social structures of the Germanic tribes appear to have been corroded and undermined by economic contact with the Roman Empire and also, crucially, by Roman diplomatic activity. Trade across the frontier zone had led to a socially destabilising flow of money and goods northwards, which gave rise to ever greater social differentiation within the Germanic tribes, catalysing the (archaeologically highly visible) emergence of a warrior elite.[14] Members of this elite were able to use their enhanced wealth and authority to draw ever larger numbers of warriors into their retinues, and to cajole or coerce more and more of their inferiors and neighbours to acknowledge their overlordship. Roman diplomacy in the frontier zone had similar consequences. The Romans were eager to identify useful clients amongst the tribes and tribesmen to their north, who could be used as effective agents of imperial influence or manipulated by the imperial authorities to wage war against other barbarian groupings, thereby maintaining a pro-Roman balance of powerlessness in the northern world. These client kings and chieftains received much by way of subsidies, gifts, and payments from the empire. The net result of these economic and diplomatic developments was the emergence of more clearly articulated social hierarchies amongst the Germanic tribes, more powerful military lordships, and larger tribal confederations, which were in a much stronger position to challenge Roman mastery of the frontier zone. These included the Franks ('the Brave') and the Alamanns ('All Men') beyond the Rhine frontier, and the Goths (likewise meaning 'the Men', a migrant group from the Ukraine) along the Danube.[15]

Concurrently, from the Roman perspective, the early to mid-third century witnessed an ominous transformation in the nature of the threat posed from the east.[16] The last decade of the second century had seen the Roman Empire extend its eastern frontier at the expense of the Arsacids, with the Romans conquering a

---

[12] F. Millar, *The Roman Empire and Her Neighbours* (London, 1967).
[13] M. Brosius, *The Persians* (London, 2006), pp. 79–138.
[14] M. Todd, *The Early Germans* (Oxford, 1992).
[15] M. Todd, 'The Germanic Peoples and Germanic Society', in Bowman, Garnsey, and Cameron (2005), pp. 440–60; H. J. Hummer, 'Franks and Alamanni: A Discontinuous Ethnogenesis', in I. Wood (ed.), *Franks and Alamanni in the Merovingian Period: An Ethnographic Perspective* (Woodbridge, 1998), pp. 9–20; M. Kulikowski, *Rome's Gothic Wars* (Cambridge, 2007).
[16] R. Frye, 'The Sasanians', in Bowman, Garnsey, and Cameron (2005), pp. 461–80, and J. D. Howard-Johnston, 'The Great Powers in Late Antiquity: A Comparison', in A. Cameron (ed.), *The Byzantine and Early Islamic Near East: States, Resources, and Armies* (Princeton, 1995), pp. 157–226.

significant portion of the traditionally Persian-dominated region of Armenia. This expansion of Roman power dealt a body blow to the prestige of the Arsacid dynasty, resulting in a protracted and bloody civil war with different aristocratic interests and affinities vying for control of the Persian state. In the year 205–6 there occurred a major revolt led by an aristocrat by the name of Papak, son of Sasan. This Papak appears to have died around 208, but by 224 his son and successor Ardashir had fought his way to supreme overlordship of the Persian world. In September 226, at the palace of Ctesiphon, within striking distance of the Roman frontier, Ardashir was crowned first shah of the Sasanian dynasty. The new ruler sought to unite the fractious military aristocracy of Persia by launching a prestige-garnering offensive against the Romans. This policy of aggression on the part of the Sasanians was pursued even more resolutely by Ardashir's successor Shapur I, who in 260 launched a daring raid deep into northern Syria, sacking the magnificent city of Antioch and capturing and humiliating the Emperor Valerian. After his death, we are told by a Roman source, Valerian 'was flayed, and his skin, stripped from the flesh, was dyed with vermilion, and placed in the temple of the gods of the barbarians, that the remembrance of a victory so signal might be perpetuated, and that this spectacle might always be exhibited to our ambassadors, as an admonition to the Romans'.[17]

The fall of the Arsacids and the Sasanian ascendancy thus heralded the emergence to Rome's east of an aggressive, belligerent foe that posed a more direct threat than hitherto to the security of Rome's wealthy Eastern provinces. It was the great misfortune of the Roman state in the mid-third century that the period of maximum Persian aggression coincided with a series of large-scale incursions into Roman territory by the northern barbarians. Critically, this was a situation with which the existing Roman military and administrative system was ill-prepared to deal. The Roman army, as we have seen, was primarily garrisoned and stationed in the frontier zones of the empire where it policed the tribes and peoples of the lands beyond.[18] Roman military strategy was predicated on the concept of holding the frontier against a marauding foe.[19] By virtue of the change in the balance of power that had occurred by the middle of the third century, however, Rome's enemies were now in a position to break through the frontier zone and strike at the largely undefended provinces that lay beyond.

Moreover, the highly devolved system of government upon which the administration of the Roman Empire had come to depend—and the associated weakness of anything approximating a central imperial bureaucracy over and above the level of the city and the province—meant that when a province, region, or *civitas* found itself under attack, there was little that could be done to reallocate resources between those regions which remained untouched and those that were suffering

---

[17] Lactantius, *De mortibus persecutorum* 5, translated in M. Dodgeon and S. Lieu, *The Roman Eastern Frontier and the Persian Wars A.D. 226–336: A Documentary History* (London, 1991), p. 58.
[18] P. Southern and K. R. Dixon, *The Late Roman Army* (Guildford, 1996), pp. 4–33.
[19] G. Greatrex, 'Roman Frontiers and Foreign Policy in the East', in R. Alston and S. Lieu (eds.), *Aspects of the Roman East: Papers in Honour of Professor Fergus Millar* (Turnhout, 2007) (*Studia Antiqua Australensia* 3), pp. 103–73.

the most. Nor could one Emperor, resident primarily in Rome and drawing upon the assistance of an essentially civilian aristocracy, provide effective military leadership in the face of simultaneous military challenges across geographically widely separated frontiers. In this sense, by virtue of the military situation in which it now found itself, the Roman Empire of the mid-third century began to suffer the consequences of what might be termed a crisis of under-governance.

These consequences could be severe. Whilst it is true that in aggregate terms much of the empire, including *Africa Proconsularis* and Egypt—far and away Rome's wealthiest provinces—remained largely unaffected by the invasions and raiding activities, there is every sign that in those areas which did bear the brunt of such incursions—Gaul, the northern Balkans, Pontus, and Syria—damage was very substantial indeed. The archaeological evidence clearly indicates, for example, that the cities of northern Gaul were never to recover from the damage inflicted on them in the mid- to late third century.[20] Nor should we underestimate the destruction wrought in Rome's wealthy Eastern provinces by the Persians, who were able to mobilise military resources on a massive scale. As Shapur's high priest, Kirder, boasted of his master's rampages in Syria: 'the provincial capital of Antioch and the provinces of Syria and Cilicia . . . these were plundered and burnt and laid waste by Shapur, King of kings, along with his armies'.[21]

The increased military pressure of the mid-third century thus brought to the fore key weaknesses in the inherited Roman system of government. In particular, the inability of individual emperors to provide effective military leadership or to find their way towards a solution to the empire's military difficulties increasingly led to political instability, as one ineffectual Emperor after another was deposed and murdered, typically by members of the army's officer corps, desperate to extricate Rome from the predicament in which it now found itself. This wave of political bloodletting was inaugurated in 235 when the Emperor Severus Alexander was overthrown and executed by the leaders of the field army in the West, apparently in response to the Emperor's lacklustre Persian campaign.[22] Almost every Emperor from 235 until the accession of Diocletian in 284 died violently, and the average reign of emperors was to be only two or three years.[23] Objective military conditions served to raise the political profile of the Roman army and its high command. Paying and supplying the army with the cash wages it expected, however, was rendered increasingly difficult by the administrative and fiscal disruption caused at a provincial level by enemy invasion. Accordingly, the imperial authorities were increasingly obliged to debase existing stocks of coin, reducing the high-value silver content of the imperial coinage, in order to stretch shrinking resources to meet burgeoning military demands. The result was further military unrest, considerable

---

[20] B. Ward-Perkins, 'The Cities', in A. Cameron and P. Garnsey (eds.), *The Cambridge Ancient History*, vol. XIII: *The Late Empire, A.D. 337–425* (Cambridge, 1998), pp. 371–410.
[21] 'Inscription of Kirdir at the Kaaba of Zoroaster', taken from Dodgeon and Lieu (1991), p. 65.
[22] See Drinkwater (2005), p. 28.
[23] A. H. M. Jones, *The Later Roman Empire*, 3 vols. (Oxford, 1964), vol. I, pp. 23–4.

price inflation, and an associated destabilisation of the more monetised and commercialised sectors of the Roman economy.

At the same time, foreign invasion and political disruption also brought to the fore social tensions in the frontier zones. In the mid-third century, in the region of Pontus in northern Asia Minor, for example, the Christian bishop Gregory 'the Wonder-Worker' (*thaumatourgos* in Greek) angrily rebuked members of his congregation for 'going over to the barbarians' at a time of Gothic invasion, aiding them in the murdering of their compatriots, and pointing out to the barbarians the 'houses most worth plundering'.[24] A similar settling of social scores amidst military chaos and political crisis was also to be a feature of life in Rome's Western provinces: around the year 284–5, there occurred in Gaul the first known uprising by a group of armed peasant insurgents known as *bacaudae*. Although this insurgency was ultimately crushed by the Emperor Maximian, such *bacaudae* would continue to re-emerge at times of political dislocation and weakening social control through to the late fifth century.[25] As already noted, Roman imperialism had always met resistance, and we must assume that peasant insurgents such as the *bacaudae* enjoyed considerable local support, for such was the assumption of the Roman authorities themselves: as the jurist Ulpian commented, a bandit (*latro*) could never operate for long without local sympathisers (*receptores*).[26]

The provincial elites, however, proved more reliable. Indeed, perhaps the most striking feature of the period from *c.*235 to 285 is the extent to which, when faced with the objective reality of military crisis and the inability of the Roman high command to counter it, the response of many of the leading members of local society—the city councillors, or *curiales*—was to defend Roman society and Roman cultural values for themselves by taking up arms and taking on the barbarians. In response to imperial weakness, we see attempts made not so much to break away from Roman control as to establish more regionally focused Roman regimes better placed to counter barbarian pressure and to provide more effective localised leadership on the ground. The clearest example of this was the 'Empire of Gauls' of the general Postumus, which came to embrace much of Britain, Gaul, and Spain between 258 and 274, and the leaders of which took warfare forthrightly and effectively to the 'barbarian' enemy.[27]

The Gallic 'Empire' was eventually brought back under central imperial control by the Emperor Aurelian. The crucial point to note, however, is that although politically it constituted a separate regime cut off from the senatorial institutions of Rome itself, it was not 'separatist' ideologically. Rather, Postumus and his successors—Victorinus and Tetricus—regarded themselves as Roman rulers defending Roman civilisation, not the heads of a newly carved out successor kingdom. Such

---

[24] Gregory Thaumaturgus, *Canonical Letter* 7: written at some point in the mid-250s.
[25] The classic study of this elusive topic remains E. A. Thompson, 'Peasant Revolts in Late Roman Gaul and Spain', *Past and Present* 2 (1952), pp. 11–23. See also the highly suggestive Chinese parallels noted by R. Collins, *Visigothic Spain 409–711* (Oxford, 2004), pp. 27–8.
[26] *Digest* I.18.13 pr.; Ste Croix (1981), p. 477.
[27] C. P. Wormald, 'The Decline of the Western Roman Empire and the Survival of its Aristocracy', *Journal of Roman Studies* 66 (1976), pp. 217–26.

men claimed the title of 'Caesar Augustus', and did much to preserve the administrative and fiscal infrastructure of the Roman state, minting and distributing coins, for example, bearing their own image.[28] The support lent to regimes such as that of the empire of the Gauls thus not only illustrates how fully Romanised the leading members of Western provincial society had become by the 250s, but also reveals an ambition on their part to exercise active political leadership.

A similar pattern can be observed in Rome's Eastern provinces, although here certain important details differed. First, as we have seen, the Persians had long been the totemic enemy of the Greek-speaking elites of the cities of the east. The re-emergence of an aggressive Persian foe is thus likely to have inspired a great deal of trepidation, if not sheer panic, which would have induced many to cling ever more tightly to Rome. Yet here, once again, Roman military initiatives were largely ineffectual, particularly in the 250s and 260s. Instead, the Romans became increasingly reliant on the military services of the general Odenathus, the king of the wealthy frontier client state of Palmyra.[29] As one later Roman source recorded: 'under Gallienus the Persians invaded Mesopotamia and would have begun even to lay claims to Syria, except that . . . Odenathus, the Palmyrene decurion, collected a band of Syrian country folk and put up a spirited resistance. On a number of occasions he routed the Persians and not only defended our border but even as the avenger of the Roman empire, marvellous to say, forced his way to Ctesiphon.'[30]

The more the Roman imperial authorities came to rely on Odenathus for the defence of the east, the more ambiguous his status became. From a local perspective he served a role and fulfilled a need very similar to that of Postumus and the other leaders of the Gallic 'Empire' to the west. At the same time Odenathus was careful to make symbolic gestures to reassure Rome of his loyalty—and was in turn accorded an imperial title of some distinction.[31] After the murder—or assassination—of Odenathus in 267, however, and the succession of his young son Vaballathus (whose mother Zenobia acted as regent), relations between Palmyra and the authorities in Rome became strained. The titles accorded to Odenathus were withheld from his son, causing Zenobia to rise in revolt against Rome in 269 and establish a Palmyrene *imperium*. In the year 272, under Aurelian (r.270–75), direct Roman rule was re-imposed after Palmyrene forces were decisively defeated outside Antioch. Zenobia was led in chains to Rome, ultimately ending her days imprisoned in a villa in Tivoli.[32]

On one level, the Palmyrene revolt was the straightforward result of Roman client mismanagement. We should note, however, that at the (albeit brief) height of its power, this kingdom, perched on the edge of Rome's desert frontier, had been able to carve out for itself an empire that embraced much of Egypt and Syria. The rapid ascendancy of Palmyra might be taken to suggest that there was a core

---

[28] 'Is This the Face of Britain's Forgotten Emperor?', *The Times*, Wednesday, 25 February 2004, pp. 1 and 4: coverage by D. Alberge and P. Sarris.
[29] Dodgeon and Lieu (1991), pp. 69–110.
[30] Festus, *Breviarium* (dating from c.369–70), in Dodgeon and Lieu (1991), pp. 71–2.
[31] Drinkwater (2005), p. 45.
[32] R. Stoneman, *Palmyra and its Empire: Zenobia's Revolt Against Rome* (Michigan, 1994).

structural weakness in Rome's strategic position to the east, rooted in the vulnerability of the empire's extended southern desert flank where Roman Syria met the Arabian steppe.

If, in certain respects, the support given by the elites of the Roman provinces to regimes such as that of the empire of the Gauls in the West, or the rallying behind Odenathus in the East, demonstrated a core ideological commitment to the survival of the Roman Empire (or at the very least to the defeat of its enemies), a similar positive gloss can and probably should be put on the various military coups and usurpations that characterised the period. Beyond the ranks of the Roman Senate and the upper echelons of provincial civic society, it was perhaps to the officer corps and elements of the rank and file of the Roman army that 'being Roman' was likely to have meant the most. It was their lot, after all, to fight and die for Rome. Accordingly, an abstract, ideological commitment to Rome and her survival is likely to have been closely bound up with military social identity. The readiness of members of the officer corps of the Roman army to depose those emperors whom they felt were not up to the job, and their attempts to provide the empire with better, more effective military leadership, if necessary drawn from their own ranks, provide vivid testimony as to the core ideological commitment to the concept of empire on the part of these men.

The result of this was to be a series of soldier emperors, characterised by their willingness to innovate in the face of pressing military need, but who, at heart, were deeply conservative in ambition and world view. At the same time, by virtue of the fact that—since the days of Marcus Aurelius in the second century—the officer corps of the Roman army had increasingly been a 'career open to talent', these soldier emperors of the mid- to late third century were typically men of humble social background. The rise of these military hard-men to the acme of imperial power thus signalled a major and highly significant change in the social profile of those exercising political authority in the Roman world, and a sidelining of traditional senatorial interests. In many ways it heralded a social revolution that was both to save and to radically recast the Roman state.

1.3 THE AGE OF THE SOLDIER EMPERORS

From the 260s onwards the military fortunes of the Roman Empire's enemies began to falter. Initially at least, this had relatively little to do with the efforts of the authorities in the city of Rome itself, and was chiefly the work of Postumus in the West and Odenathus in the East. Within what remained of the 'directly managed' empire (Italy, Africa, the Balkans) it is possible to trace the contours of an ongoing power struggle between claimants to the imperial title who possessed primarily military backing and were generally from outside traditional senatorial circles, and emperors of a more aristocratic background closely associated with the interests and attitudes of the Roman Senate. The death of Gallienus in 268 marked the effective eclipsing of the senatorial faction. Instead there emerged a series of ever more effective and innovative soldier emperors, such as Claudius II (r.268–70), Aurelian (r.270–75), Probus (r.276–82), and Carus (r.282–3), who were able to re-establish both the political contours of the *imperium Romanum* (by reabsorbing the empire of the Gauls and that of Palmyra) and its military frontiers against the Persians and the invaders from the north.[33]

This consolidation of empire in the period from the late 260s through to the early 280s was achieved by more than mere brute force, however. Rather, as already suggested, these military hard-men of provincial origin (with the exception of the Gallic Carus, all came from the mountains and highlands of the Balkans) brought to the task of restoring Rome's fortunes new perspectives, insights, and solutions. Over the course of the period it is possible to chart the emergence of a series of imaginative and novel responses to the objective military, political, and administrative challenges that confronted the empire. Broadly speaking, these can be summarised as follows.

First, there was a growing realisation that one Emperor, resident primarily in Rome, was not sufficient to meet the multiplicity of threats the empire faced along its extended frontiers. What was needed was more devolved and flexible military leadership. So, for example, in 282 the Emperor Carus declared his sons Numerian and Carinus to be his duly appointed imperial deputies (or *caesars*) whilst initially reserving the title of *Augustus* for himself. Carinus took charge of the Western provinces while his father and brother marched east to face down Persia. Second, this more devolved leadership also needed to base itself closer to the major sources of military danger—Rome's turbulent foes to the north and east. Postumus had led resistance to the barbarian invaders from the frontier city of Trier, and this policy of rulers establishing themselves closer to the frontier zone at what have been termed 'sub-capitals', such as (in addition to Trier) the cities of Milan, Sirmium, and Antioch, was followed by a number of later third-century rulers.[34]

The ability of emperors to make use of these frontier capitals and to move themselves and their armies between them was enhanced by the introduction of and growing reliance upon mobile field armies with a strong cavalry presence—perhaps modelled on the so-called *clibanarii* or heavy cavalry on which the Sasanians depended.[35] The physical absence of the person of the Emperor from the city of Rome was also greatly facilitated by the growing readiness of soldier emperors such as Carus simply to leave Rome and its Senate to its own devices. The city was not neglected as such—the Emperor Aurelian provided it with a splendid set of defensive walls, sections of which stand to this day—but politically the traditional senatorial institutions of Rome were rendered a 'busted flush' by the new political and military realities of the age; and emperors now had less reason to pay empty homage to the fossilised remnants of a distant constitutional era.

The administrative corollary to this sidelining of the senatorial aristocracy was the abolition of a number of senatorial privileges (the imperial office itself officially ceased to be a senatorial preserve from 268) and a growing reliance upon the

---

[33] Drinkwater (2005).
[34] Drinkwater (2005), p. 64.
[35] Southern and Dixon (1996), pp. 9–14.

sub-senatorial aristocracy of so-called *equites* or 'knights' (a terminological hangover from the military origins of the Roman Republic). Effectively this meant drawing into the entourage of the Emperor and appointing to governmental and administrative posts more men of provincial, curial background. In other words, the emperors harnessed and increasingly gave tangible meaning to the aspiration to effective leadership of Roman society that the provincial elites had manifested at the nadir of Rome's third-century fortunes.

However, the sidelining of traditional social elites and political practices posed the soldier emperors of the late third century one problem of enormous complexity: how were such low-born military adventurers as Claudius II, Aurelian, or Probus to consolidate their authority and project to their subjects a sense of legitimacy? How could they look anything other than opportunistic usurpers alongside an Emperor as blue-blooded as Severus Alexander or an aristocrat as well-connected as Gallienus? At a more fundamental level, the military defeats, coups, usurpations, and civil wars of the third century had evidently done much to devalue the currency of the imperial office: how was its credibility to be restored?

It is instructive that over the course of the late third century we witness two significant phenomena which make sense primarily in the context of this crisis of legitimacy on the part of the imperial office in general, and of individual soldier emperors in particular. First, emperors surrounded themselves with increasingly elaborate ceremonies. If the Emperor could not rely upon dignity of ancestry to establish the requisite degree of social distance between himself and his leading subjects, then that distance might perhaps be re-established through symbolic, ceremonial means. Second, growing emphasis was placed on the personal, direct relationship between individual emperors and individual deities. Thus Aurelian is reported to have advocated the cult of a single unifying supreme deity, that of *Sol Invictus* or the 'Unconquered Sun', whose vicegerent on earth the Emperor claimed to be.[36] This cult was already popular with many of Aurelian's fellow soldiers from the northern Balkans, where such 'solar henotheism' (or worship of a supreme Sun god, from the Greek *henos* 'one' and *theos* 'god') was a long-standing feature. It is instructive that as the social profile of those who came to exercise mastery over the Roman world began to change, so too did new cults and religions become more conspicuous in the empire's public life.

It should be noted that, in a sense, many of the trends and policies commonly associated with the soldier emperors of the late third century can be traced back well before the period of crisis to the origins of the imperial office itself.[37] From an early point there was a tendency for emperors to surround themselves with courtiers and to neglect the Senate—such 'new men' (*novi homines*) and the influence they could wield were the constant horror of Roman authors of a conservative mindset. Likewise, under the gravitational pull of the political culture of the Hellenistic East, there was an inbuilt tendency for Roman emperors to become more autocratic in style and their courts more elaborate in terms of ritual and ceremony. The crucial

[36] Zosimus, *New History*, tr. R. T. Ridley (Canberra, 1982), 1.59.
[37] As argued by Millar (1977).

point, however, is that amid the enormous military, political, and administrative pressures that came to bear down upon the Roman state in the mid-third century, and by virtue of the loosening of social and political relations occasioned by the ascendancy of the soldier emperors, this evolutionary process on the part of the imperial office was dramatically and explosively catalysed. Over the course of the fourth century, the full ramifications of this catalysis would become apparent.

1.4 DIOCLETIAN, CONSTANTINE, AND THE CONSOLIDATION OF THE LATE ROMAN STATE

In 283 the Emperor Carus led his army out from Antioch and struck deep into Persian territory. In a signal victory, he succeeded in capturing the capital of the *shahs* at Ctesiphon, before suddenly being struck dead by a bolt of lightning, 'ending a life', as one Roman account puts it, 'which was like lightning itself'.[38] A bloody struggle for power ensued, which was only resolved by the assassination of both of Carus' sons, and the acclamation as Emperor in 284 by the Eastern field army of an Illyrian soldier by the name of Diocles, or 'Diocletian' as he became known upon his accession. Faced with rebellions and uprisings from Gaul to Egypt, Diocletian set about forcibly restoring order, and, in 285, named his friend and colleague Maximian his deputy or *caesar*, dispatching him to Gaul to crush a series of peasant revolts, while Diocletian himself faced down a revived Persian menace and an uprising in Egypt centred on the city of Alexandria.[39] The following year, Maximian too was granted the title of Emperor (*Augustus*), with Diocletian appointing him to rule in the West. In 293 Diocletian proceeded to nominate a certain Constantius as deputy or *caesar* to Maximian, whilst appointing a soldier by the name of Galerius as his own deputy in the East.

This arrangement came to be known as the 'Tetrarchy' or 'rule of four'. In essence it combined two important responses to the military and political predicaments of the Roman Empire in the mid- to late third century. On one level, it represented the most coherent and fully worked-out expression of the dawning realisation that the empire needed more devolved and flexible leadership. At the same time, it demonstrated an acute awareness that one of the major causes of political instability within the empire had been uncertainty as to succession to the imperial title. The system introduced by Diocletian sought to address this by making it clear that those who had been appointed as *caesars* were expected to succeed their respective *augusti*.

In this sense, Diocletian's period of rule witnessed a consolidation of the *ad hoc* political and administrative arrangements that had emerged under his predecessors. It is instructive that under Diocletian (as with Carus), the senior ruler based himself

---

[38] Sidonius Apollinaris, *Carmina* 23.91–6, from *Letters and Poems*, tr. W. B. Anderson, 2 vols. (Cambridge, Mass., 1936–65).

[39] Aurelius Victor, *de Caesaribus*, 39.17: translated in R. Rees, *Diocletian and the Tetrarchy* (Edinburgh, 2004), p. 93; S. Williams, *Diocletian and the Roman Recovery* (London, 1985).

firmly in the East, where he faced down the civilised, prestige foe of Sasanian Persia, whose rulers claimed what the Roman emperors had come to believe was theirs by right: legitimate dominion and mastery of the entire settled world (what in Greek was known as the *oikoumenê*, or in Latin the *orbis terrarum*).[40] Thus, according to the ancestral religion of the *shahs*, 'Zoroastrianism', the rulers of Persia were the unique heirs to the first divinely ordained king who had held sway over all mankind, and the Sasanian shah was the lord of the Middle Kingdom—set at the heart of creation—to whom all other rulers owed obeisance and tribute.[41]

There are other respects too in which Diocletian's reign witnessed the consolidation of policies, tendencies, or trends associated with his fellow soldier emperors of the years of 'crisis'. The senatorial aristocracy of Rome continued to find itself largely sidelined as the Emperor came to rely on men of provincial background and equestrian status; a greater element of 'defence-in-depth' was added to the fortification and defence of the frontier zones to north and east; and the reliance on rapidly deployable field armies and cavalry units continued apace. Both Diocletian and Maximian also sought to emphasise their close and personal relationship with individual deities: Hercules in the case of Maximian, and Jupiter (father of the gods) in the case of the senior *Augustus* Diocletian. It is under Diocletian's rule in particular that we catch our clearest glimpses of the growing ceremonialisation of the imperial office. As Aurelius Victor declared of the Emperor: 'He was a great man, but with the following habits: he was the first to want a robe woven with gold, and sandals with plenty of silk, purple, and jewels; although this exceeded humility and revealed a swollen and arrogant mind, it was nothing compared to the rest, for he was the first of all the emperors after Caligula and Domitian to allow himself to be called "master" [Latin *dominus*] in public, to be worshipped and addressed as a god.'[42]

The relative peace and internal security that Diocletian and the Tetrarchy brought to the empire also facilitated the introduction, consolidation, and development of a series of highly significant administrative reforms, which sought to address the crisis of under-governance and weakness of central imperial control that had caused Rome's invaded provinces so many problems during the incursions of the third century. The Tetrarchic system of power-sharing itself led to a wider and more effective distribution and diffusion of imperial power across the provinces of the empire through the establishment of the *augusti* and their *caesars* at 'Tetrarchic' capitals such as Trier or Milan to the west, Sirmium in the Balkans, or Nicomedia and Antioch to the east. At the same time, the provincial administrative and governmental structure was overhauled to facilitate tighter supervision of

---

[40] G. Fowden, *Empire to Commonwealth: Consequences of Monotheism in Late Antiquity* (Princeton, 1993).
[41] I owe this point to Dr Richard Payne of Trinity College, Cambridge, who has transformed my understanding of Sasanian ideology. He develops it more fully in his essay 'Cosmology and the Expansion of the Iranian Empire in Late Antiquity' *(forthcoming)*. See also M. P. Canepa, 'Technologies of Memory in Early Sasanian Iran: Achaemenid Sites and Sasanian Ideology', *American Journal of Archaeology* 114.4 (2010), pp. 563–96.
[42] Aurelius Victor, *de Caesaribus* 39.2–4: see Rees (2004), p. 93.

provincial life. The size of provinces was reduced and their number accordingly multiplied. Within these new provincial structures, military and civil responsibilities were separated, thereby effectively doubling the number of centrally appointed officials whose job it was to oversee the self-management of the city councils and the maintenance of provincial order. Crucially, there emerged an additional tier of government over and above the level of these new, smaller provinces: that of the so-called 'diocese' (Latin *dioecesis*) placed under the command of officials termed vicars (Latin *vicarii*).[43] A centrally appointed imperial bureaucracy of some size and scale was thus beginning to take shape. At the same time the size of the army was significantly increased.[44]

There was necessarily a human and social dimension to these administrative reforms. The high-ranking governmental and military posts now created had to be filled. To do so, the imperial authorities turned to the dominant families within the city councils of the provinces, whose ambitions were thus further harnessed to bind the empire together. The result was to be the emergence of a new trans-regional imperial aristocracy of service characterised by its members' strong provincial roots, but also by a close relationship with the central organs of the Roman state and the imperial court.[45]

These new administrative structures and personnel also had to be paid for. Indeed, perhaps the most striking feature of Diocletian's reign is the evidence it provides for the development of something approximating to a state budget that sought to reconcile the fiscal requirements of the Roman state to the productive resources of taxpayers.[46] The fiscal system that emerged was based on two principles: predictability and proportionality. From the perspective of the state, what mattered most was that there be a steady and reliable flow of tax revenues. This the imperial government sought to achieve by two means. First, it attempted to register taxpayers in fiscal communities—their 'homes' (Latin *origines*)—to which they and their descendants would henceforth be bound. Thus for city councillors the appointed *origo*, or home, was their native city and its *curia*. If a councillor (*curialis*) fled the territory of his native city and neglected the fiscal charges to which he was liable, these would be redistributed amongst his fellow councillors. Likewise the majority of peasants were registered for fiscal purposes as belonging to the village communities in which or near which they dwelled: the village was thus their legally designated *origo*. Again, flight from the village community would lead to a redistribution of fiscal obligations amongst the absent farmer's neighbours and fellow villagers. By virtue of such fiscal registration and the introduction of a regular *census*, the imperial government was able to arrive at some understanding of where its taxpayers were (or at least were supposed to be)—the first requirement of effective tax collection.

---

[43] Williams (1985).
[44] W. Treadgold, *Byzantium and its Army* (Stanford, 1997).
[45] P. Heather, 'New Men for New Constantines?', in P. Magdalino (ed.), *New Constantines* (Aldershot, 1994), pp. 11–44.
[46] Jones (1964), vol. I, p. 65, and M. Corbier, 'Coinage and Taxation: The State's Point of View AD 193–337', in Bowman, Garnsey, and Cameron (2005), pp. 327–92.

Second, for taxes to be collectable on a regular (preferably annual) basis, they had to be levied at a reasonable level that took account both of the needs of the state and the ability of taxpayers to pay. Accordingly, from c.287 we find evidence for the reckoning of the so-called state 'indiction' or fiscal period—initially, it would appear, on a five-year basis (and from the year 312 on a fifteen-year 'indictional' cycle). At every indiction, each unit would be assessed in terms of the number of taxpayers (Latin *capita*, 'heads') and the quality and extent of the acreage of land (Latin *iuga*, 'yokes') contained or subsumed within it. Having calculated its budgetary needs, the state could then issue locally calibrated tax demands accordingly. As Lactantius described the indictional survey of 298: 'the fields were measured sod by sod; the vines and fruit trees were counted; the number of animals of all kinds was set down in writing, and the humans were counted one by one.'[47]

Placing the finances of the imperial government on a surer footing was the necessary precursor to addressing the currency crisis and associated price inflation. However, this goal could not be achieved overnight. Given the enormous logistical difficulties faced by the Roman state and the practical problems posed by governing and marshalling the resources of so vast an empire, it would necessarily be many years before the new fiscal arrangements bore fruit. In the meantime, the imperial government attempted to meet the requirements of the military by circumventing the monetary system and falling back on supplying the army directly in kind.[48] This was clearly only meant as an interim measure. It was in the evident interests of the imperial government, military officials, and the soldiers themselves to revert to payment in coin as soon as was practicable: from the perspective of the government, payment in coin was ultimately less cumbersome; from that of the military, it was much more directly lucrative.

Diocletian's reign thus served to consolidate and stabilise the Roman Empire's emergence from crisis. In the year 305, elderly and perhaps ailing, he retired to a palace on the Dalmatian coast and, we are told, devoted himself to his garden. Maximian, his fellow *Augustus*, abdicated along with him and accordingly the emperors were replaced by their respective *caesars*: Galerius in the East and Constantius in the West. The following year, however, Constantius died at York, on his way to campaign against the Picts who were menacing Britannia's northern frontier. Instead of acknowledging Severus, the recently appointed Western *caesar*, Constantius's field army instead proclaimed his son Constantine as *Augustus* and, to strengthen their young protégé's bid for power, headed for Gaul. Other would-be emperors soon followed Constantine's lead and rival *augusti* emerged in both Africa and Italy, where Maximian's son Maxentius emerged as the figure of real authority, overcoming his African rival Domitius Alexander and establishing control over the central Mediterranean. In 310 Maxentius drove back the armies of the Eastern *Augustus* Galerius, who died the following year. In 312, however, Constantine achieved the success that had eluded Galerius, and prised Rome from Maxentius's grip, thereby establishing himself as sole ruler in the West. In 313, in a parallel

---

[47] Lactantius, *de mortibus persecutorum* 23.2.
[48] Southern and Dixon (1996).

move, the general Licinius liquidated the last of his Eastern rivals and established his regime at Nicomedia, a location that enabled him both to keep watch on the empire's Persian and Danubian frontiers whilst also permitting him to marshal his armies in force in the Balkans should Constantine decide to march east. After a series of military skirmishes, Constantine eventually took his chance in 323, defeating Licinius first on land at Adrianople and finally in a sea battle off the coast of Chrysopolis, near Nicomedia, in 324.[49] The historian Zosimus records what ensued: 'so Licinius was besieged by Constantine in Nicomedia, whereupon he gave up hope.... Going out of the city, therefore, he threw himself before Constantine as a suppliant, and bringing him the purple, acclaimed him as Emperor and Lord.' Zosimus goes on to report that accordingly, 'Constantine sent Licinius to Thessalonica as if to live there in security, but not long after broke his oath, as was his custom, and had him hanged. The whole empire now devolved on Constantine alone.'[50]

In celebration of his victory, Constantine gave orders that the ancient Greek settlement of Byzantium (Greek *Byzantion*), located on the European shore of the Bosphorus that connected Europe to Asia, and in the near vicinity of Nicomedia, be rededicated in his honour under the name of Constantinople. The Emperor further decreed that the city be adorned with the grand civic monuments and amenities befitting an imperial foundation. Within five years or so, much of the initial construction work was deemed to be satisfactorily complete and the 'city of Constantine the New Rome' was formally consecrated on 11 May 330. The Emperor was to remain in his city for much of the time until his death in 337.

As the passage concerning the execution of Licinius quoted above makes clear, the historian Zosimus, writing around the year 500, provides the reader with hostile testimony with respect to Constantine, in spite of the fact that he himself would appear to have been resident in the city Constantine founded. The reason for this is that Zosimus was a 'pagan', a believer in the traditional gods of Greco-Roman antiquity and a vehement defender of their cult. Constantine, however, was the first Roman Emperor to become a 'Christian'—a devotee and proponent of what in the fourth century had been the religion of only a very small minority of the empire (especially in the West). Christianity was an offshoot and mutation of the ancestral cult of the empire's Jewish subjects, which advocated the exclusive worship of one 'true' God, whose Son, it was claimed, had been made man in the form of an itinerant Palestinian preacher known as Jesus Christ (Greek *ho Christos*, 'the anointed one'), who had been executed by the Roman imperial authorities under the Emperor Tiberius. The followers of this religious movement had been subjected to official persecution as recently as the reign of Diocletian by virtue of their refusal to sacrifice to the imperial cult.

Constantine had ascribed his stunning victory over Maxentius at the battle of the Milvian bridge in 312 to his recent conversion to this religion: a conversion that he

---

[49] A. Cameron, 'The Reign of Constantine, A.D. 306–37', in Bowman, Garnsey, and Cameron (2005), pp. 90–109.
[50] Zosimus, *New History* 2.28–9.

later ascribed to a divine vision revealed to him in the heavens. When entering Rome he refused to do what was expected of an Emperor and sacrifice at the Altar of the Capitoline Jove, and from 312 onwards he had publicly declared his support for the Christian community or 'Church' (Greek *ekklêsia*), favouring it and its priests with ever greater largesse.

As so presented, and as still sometimes interpreted by modern commentators, Constantine's conversion looks like a sudden and inexplicable event that was to alter inexorably the course of human history. In many ways, it clearly was, and arguments to the contrary sit uncomfortably alongside the fact that the end result of Constantine's conversion was to be the official Christianisation of the Roman state and the subsequent transmission of Christianity as a powerful institutional force, forger of identities, and body of beliefs to the post-Roman and early medieval world. It is true, however, that Constantine's adoption of Christianity was perhaps less dramatic a break with the religious sensibilities of many of his third-century predecessors than is sometimes supposed. The soldier emperors of the third century—notably Aurelian, Diocletian, and Maximian—had frequently and deliberately associated themselves with specific individual divine patrons whose power they sought to tap. Constantine's relationship with the Christian God was essentially of a type with Aurelian's relationship with *Sol Invictus* and Diocletian's with Jupiter. Thus the Christian bishop and courtier Eusebius, for example, expounded a vision of Constantine as the Christian God's vicegerent on earth, one that seemingly reflected the similar claims that had been made with respect to *Sol Invictus* and Aurelian.[51]

The case of Aurelian and *Sol Invictus* is also instructive for a second reason. The cult of the 'Unconquered Sun' was, as has been noted, one of a number of 'henotheistic' solar cults that appear to have had a considerable following amongst elements of the Roman army. From an early date, however, Christianity had circulated in very similar social milieux and was itself characterised by a strikingly solar imagery and vocabulary: in the New Testament, for example, Christ was described as 'the light of the world' or 'the day-spring'.[52] Moreover, the line of demarcation between these various 'henotheistic' cults (advocating the worship of a supreme God) and 'monotheism' (a belief in the existence of only one God) was highly permeable.[53] Like Aurelian, Constantine's father Constantius was a devotee of the 'Unconquered Sun'. In 310 Constantine himself is described by a panegyricist as having seen a vision of Apollo, who was often identified with the Sun God Helios.[54] Evidently, the Emperor was brought up and moved within circles in which solar henotheism played an important role. When this is taken into account, Constantine's religious migration around the year 312 from solar henotheism to a monotheistic cult with strong solar associations was perhaps less dramatic than has

---

[51] T. D. Barnes, *Constantine and Eusebius* (Cambridge, Mass., 1981).
[52] John 8:12–32; Luke 1:78—drawing upon solar language in the Old Testament such as that in Malachi 4:2 ('the sun of righteousness') and Psalms 84:11 ('The Lord God is a Sun and Shield').
[53] P. Athanassiadi and M. Frede (eds.), *Pagan Monotheism in Late Antiquity* (Oxford, 1999), for various relevant studies.
[54] *Pan. Lat.*, VII (6).

appeared to posterity. Certainly, as late as 323, Constantine continued to mint coins dedicated to the 'divine companion the Unconquered Sun' and in Constantinople he erected a statue of himself as Helios-Apollo.[55] In his public imagery and propaganda, Constantine continued to use forms, expressions, and motifs that, whilst not exclusively 'pagan', could nevertheless appeal to a non-Christian audience whilst being read in an allegoricised Christian way by his co-devotees. There may well have been an element of *Realpolitik* to this: Constantine had to be careful not to offend the powerful pagan elements within the governing classes of his empire, whose cooperation and support he needed. On the other hand, it may well be that the multivalent message of Constantine's public imagery itself accurately conveyed the nature of the Emperor's own personal religiosity at this time and the initial nature of his attachment to a faith that, at first perhaps, he only dimly understood.

As the centre of Constantine's power shifted eastwards, however, and as he came under the influence of the leaders of larger and more firmly rooted Christian communities, his attitude towards other religions hardened, and his exposure to Christian theology became increasingly pronounced. For, in spite of superficial similarities, the doctrinal and psychological substructures of Christianity as expressed by the leaders of the Christian Church were fundamentally at odds with the religious attitudes of the other cults and religions that circulated within the Roman Empire, with the sole exception of Judaism. Like Judaism, Christianity advocated only one true God to whom veneration and obedience were due. The price of failing to worship or obey the laws of the one true God, however, was not just ignorance: it was damnation, as it was only to those who believed in Him and obeyed His laws that God offered life after death through resurrection on the Day of Judgement.

Indeed, it was not only the observance of other cults or belief in other deities that led to damnation; so too, to the leaders of the Christian Church, did inaccurate belief as to the nature of Christian doctrine or the Christian God. In other words, Christianity possessed concepts that were utterly alien to traditional Greco-Roman religion, namely 'orthodoxy' and 'heresy'. The problem from a Christian perspective, however, was that from the religion's very inception Christian communities had been characterised by two conflicting features: an intense aspiration to unity on the one hand, but, on the other, wild disparities of actual opinion and belief.[56] What Christianity lacked, and what the leaders of the Christian communities cried out for, was a political structure to facilitate the definition of orthodoxy, the exclusion of heresy, and the fulfilment of the Church's redemptive mission.

Once established in the East, and with his authority as *Augustus* unchallenged, Constantine began to respond to the demands and needs of the Church leadership.

---

[55] J. Maurice, *Numismatique Constantinienne*, vol. II, p. 236, plate vii, no. 14. The statue stood on the Column of Constantine—see C. Mango, *Byzantine Architecture* (London, 1986), p. 28, and G. Fowden, 'Constantine's Porphyry Column: The Earliest Literary Allusion', *JHS* 81 (1991), pp. 119–31.

[56] H. Chadwick, *East and West: The Making of a Rift in the Church from Apostolic Times to the Council of Florence* (Oxford, 2003), pp. 1–19.

He did this partly through material patronage: after defeating Licinius in 324, Constantine authorised the leaders of the Christian communities to draw from imperial coffers whatever sums they needed to expand, embellish, or construct places of worship. At the same time, however, he responded to the religious and theological ambitions of the Church. Public acts of pagan sacrifice, for example, were banned (a measure, admittedly, that probably only applied to the East and is likely to have been only sporadically observed).[57] In particular, the establishment of Constantine's rule over both East and West marked a milestone in attempts to define and unify the Christian faith. Emperors had long felt under a duty to settle religious disputes amongst their subjects; Constantine's conversion meant that the coercive powers of the Roman state could now be deployed to help define and enforce Christian 'orthodoxy'.

The turning point occurred in May 325, when, in response to the petitions of his Christian bishops, Constantine presided over the first universal or 'Ecumenical' Council of the Church held at Nicaea, not far from Nicomedia. This Council busied itself with important matters of Church organisation and discipline.[58] In theological terms, however, the main focus of the Council was a dispute of largely academic origin over the relationship between God 'the Father' and God 'the Son' that had broken out within the Church in Alexandria between Bishop Alexander, who argued that the Father and the Son were co-eternal and thus that the Son had existed prior to Christ's Incarnation; and his presbyter Arius, who held that this was illogical.[59] Interestingly, a few months prior to the Council the Emperor had written to Alexander and Arius asking why they could not simply agree to differ over what he termed 'this very silly question' after the manner of philosophers.[60] This once again illustrated the extent to which Constantine did not quite understand the psychological substructures of his adopted faith: of course Alexander and Arius could not simply agree to differ, for erroneous belief closed the pathway to salvation. At the Council at Nicaea, Arius was essentially wrong-footed by his opponents, overstated his case rhetorically, and accordingly the ranks of many of the bishops closed against him. Under the presidency of the Emperor, Arius' theology was condemned (technically 'anathematized'): his books were ordered to be burnt and Arius himself was sent into exile.[61]

For twenty-five years from 312 until his death in 337 the Emperor Constantine lent the Christian Church and its leaders concerted support. The same policy was pursued by his three sons (Constans, Constantine II, and Constantius II), between whom the empire was divided upon his death. In 361 the imperial title passed briefly into the hands of the pagan Julian (reviled by Christians as 'the Apostate' for having cast aside the God of Constantine), but he reigned for little more than eighteen months, dying on campaign against the Persians. In any case, by that point

---

[57] Barnes (1981), pp. 210–11.
[58] N. P. Tanner, *The Decrees of the Ecumenical Councils*, 2 vols. (Washington DC, 1990), vol. 1.
[59] R. Williams, *Arius: Heresy and Tradition*, 2nd ed. (London, 2001).
[60] Eusebius, *Life of Constantine*, tr. A. Cameron (Oxford, 1999), vol. II, pp. 63–73.
[61] Barnes (1981).

the Christian Church had enjoyed almost fifty years of uninterrupted imperial patronage and largesse which had, in equal measure, been denied to the increasingly fragmented, localised, and vulnerable pagan cults of the Roman world.[62] Although attempted usurpations by self-declared pagans did take place—suggesting that non-Christians remained a potentially important political constituency—the imperial title was thereafter to remain firmly in Christian hands.[63] As a result, no matter how many non-Christians continued to revere the old gods in the cities and villages of the empire, at an official level the Roman state became ever more obviously and aggressively Christian; emperors began to legislate not only to Christianise the public sphere (by constructing churches or banning public acts of pagan sacrifice), but also to legislate on the domestic sphere (by seeking to prohibit long-established patterns of behaviour —most obviously marital and sexual—that the leaders of the Christian Church found objectionable).[64] By the end of the fourth century it was clear that Christianity was not just the favoured cult of the Emperor (as it had been under Constantine): it was now the official religion of the Roman state.[65]

1.5 THE LATE ROMAN EMPIRE: SOCIETY AND INSTITUTIONS

The administrative and governmental structures that had taken shape during the rule of Diocletian essentially remained in place until the fifth century in the West (which, as shall be seen, witnessed the demise of Roman power there) and the sixth century in the East, when the Emperor Justinian initiated a major programme of provincial reform. The essential building blocks of imperial government continued to be the cities of the empire and their associated territories. In this sense the city councils and the activities of the city councillors themselves remained fundamental: in 458, for example, the Emperor Majorian described the *curiales* as 'the sinews of the commonwealth and the vitals of the cities'.[66] However, these city councils came under increasing supervision from the administrative offices (Latin *officia*, Greek *taxeis*) and bureaucrats of the separate military and civil provincial governors appointed over them—in Latin typically known as the *dux* and *praeses* respectively. From the fourth century one begins to hear of an official known as the 'defender of the city' (*defensor civitatis*), who was meant to act as an interlocutor and potential arbiter of disputes between the city councils and the provincial authorities.[67]

---

[62] G. Fowden, 'Polytheist Religion and Philosophy', in Cameron and Garnsey (1998), pp. 538–60.
[63] For the revolt of Julian's pagan cousin, Procopius, for example, see Ammianus Marcellinus *Res Gestae* XXVI.5.8.
[64] J. Goody, *The Development of the Family and Marriage in Europe* (Cambridge, 1983); G. Clark, *Women in Late Antiquity: Pagan and Christian Lifestyles* (Oxford, 1993).
[65] P. Brown, 'Christianization and Religious Conflict', in Cameron and Garnsey (1998), pp. 632–64.
[66] *Nov. Maj.*, 7 pr.
[67] A. H. M. Jones, *The Greek City from Alexander to Justinian* (Oxford, 1940), p. 150.

Within the cities of the empire, the figure of the bishop also began to play an ever more important role.[68]

The provinces themselves continued to be organised into dioceses under the watchful care of the *vicarii*. Under Constantine, these dioceses were further divided up into (depending on the period) three or four 'praetorian prefectures': Gaul, Italy, Africa, and 'the East'. The praetorian prefect (initially a military officer) became a powerful figure in the civil administration directly answerable to the Emperor and responsible for the effective collection of taxes. The praetorian prefect had his military counterpart in the Master of Soldiers (Latin *magister militum*).[69]

The continued expansion of the central imperial bureaucracy, and the rewards associated with governmental service, served to draw men of ability and ambition away from the provinces and towards the new imperial capitals. This began to cause the imperial government administrative headaches. Service on the staff of the praetorian prefect (to take but one example) was necessarily both more interesting and more lucrative than a lifetime of service on one's native city council, and trying to persuade an imperial official in Constantinople to continue to meet his share of civic responsibilities in distant Syria or Egypt was no easy matter. Accordingly, strenuous efforts were made to attempt to ensure that the sons of such administrators inherited—and met—their fathers' curial obligations. But if (as was of course likely) the sons of such administrators themselves chose to make a career in the upper echelons of the imperial bureaucracy, the problem simply repeated itself. Increasingly the practice began to emerge, therefore, whereby specific civic responsibilities were allocated or assigned on what appears to have been an essentially perpetual basis to the estates of such administrators and—ultimately— large landowners in general.[70] It also became increasingly apparent that it was easier for these estates to transmit the taxes they owed directly to the offices of the local governor rather than for them to be handled via the intermediate offices of the local *curia*.[71] Thus whilst city councils remained the basic building blocks of Roman government, both their autonomy and the extent of their supervision and control at the grassroots of provincial society were increasingly curtailed over the course of the fourth and fifth centuries.[72]

The taxes collected at a local level, one should note, were increasingly collected in coin rather than kind. Under both Aurelian and Diocletian attempts had been made to restore the silver content of the *denarius* so as to render it more stable and reliable as a unit of account and medium of exchange. Under Constantine the silver coinage was displaced from the pinnacle of the Roman monetary system and its place taken by a new gold coinage, the *solidus* (the metallic content of which was partly obtained through confiscating the treasuries of pagan temples).[73] The minting and dissemination of these *solidi* served to transform fiscal and economic

---

[68] C. Rapp, *Holy Bishops in Late Antiquity* (Berkeley, 2005).
[69] A. H. M. Jones, *The Later Roman Empire*, 3 vols. (Oxford, 1964).
[70] P. Sarris, *Economy and Society in the Age of Justinian* (Cambridge, 2006), pp. 157–9.
[71] ibid., pp. 150–54.
[72] J. H. W. G. Liebeschuetz, *The Decline and Fall of the Roman City* (Oxford, 2001).
[73] M. Hendy, *Studies in the Byzantine Monetary Economy* (Cambridge, 1985).

relations across the entire Roman world in the fourth century. Imperial officials and soldiers pressed for the 'adaeration' (or rendering into gold) of their stipends and salaries, which meant the re-monetisation of the tax system at both a local and central level.[74] This in turn meant that peasants, landowners, and farmers were increasingly obliged to sell a larger proportion of their produce at market in order to get hold of the cash required (either in gold or small-denomination copper) to meet the fiscal demands of the state. In any case, none of these groups (least of all the larger landowners) was blind to the opportunities opened up by re-monetisation: cash gave those who were able to obtain it greater economic choice, power, and autonomy. The result was a major wave of monetary expansion and a dramatic increase in the volume of trade.

The one element of the Roman fiscal framework that remained substantially non-monetary (although it was reckoned in monetary terms) was the collection of grain to feed the empire's urban populations—above all grain from Africa and Egypt, the two 'bread-baskets' of empire. These grain supplies were transported at long distance and at high cost to feed the populations of the greatest of the imperial *metropoleis*: Rome and Constantinople respectively. The grain conveyed to Constantinople was also partly diverted en route to feed the population of Alexandria, and similar systems of imperial subvention and support are likely to have been in place to maintain the populations of the larger cities throughout the empire.[75] Just as, in many places, urbanism had been established by imperial *fiat*, so too was its continued survival dependent to a great extent upon the ongoing existence of the fiscal structures of the Roman state.

The final element of the administrative and governmental system established under Diocletian that remained largely intact was the delegation of imperial power and the maintenance of systems of joint rule: rarely did only one Emperor hold sway over the entirety of the Roman Empire. Rather, a system emerged whereby there tended to be one *Augustus* (typically the senior) and his court resident in the East, and another in the West, a situation that continued to make sense militarily. From the 360s, the Eastern Emperor usually resided at Constantinople, which became the sole capital of the Eastern Roman Empire. By virtue of the fact that the major threat to the West continued to be from along the Rhine frontier, the Western Roman Emperor and his entourage typically resided in Gaul, initially at Trier, later at Vienne. At the very end of the century the court relocated to Italy for military reasons that will be examined shortly. The division of the Roman Empire into East and West took on an increasingly formal aspect, with the line of demarcation between the two being clearly established at Illyricum in the western Balkans in 395 when Theodosius I was succeeded by his sons Arcadius and Honorius.

---

[74] J. Banaji, *Agrarian Change in Late Antiquity: Gold, Labour, and Aristocratic Dominance*, 2nd ed. (Oxford, 2007).
[75] A. J. B. Sirks, *Food for Rome: The Legal Structure of the Transportation and Processing of Supplies for the Imperial Distributions in Rome and Constantinople* (Amsterdam, 1991); J. Durliat, *De la ville antique à la ville byzantine* (Rome, 1990); Sarris (2006), p. 11 and n. 10 for references to the Egyptian grain supply.

The period from the third century to the fifth was also significant in terms of the social evolution of the Roman world. In the Roman Empire of the first and second centuries AD, there had essentially existed three key markers of status: the distinction between free and unfree (i.e. slaves); between Roman and non-Roman; and, amongst the Roman free, the distinction between the three 'orders' of society (senatorial, equestrian, and plebeian). To these three markers of status one might also add a fourth—that of gender. Certainly, Roman society always had been and always would be a patriarchal society in the fullest sense of the word; according to Roman law, the head of the family (the *pater familias*) was invested with extraordinarily extensive authority over the members of his *familia*, comprising not just his wife and children but also his slaves and freedmen.[76]

There were interesting overlaps between the way in which genders were socially constructed and presented in Roman society, and the manner in which social distinctions more generally were drawn and justified. According to Roman medical authors, what differentiated male from female was that the male foetus had literally cooked for longer in the womb.[77] If an adult man was to maintain his masculinity, therefore, he had to maintain his unique 'heat'. This involved avoidance of excess of any kind—rage, sexual frenzy, drunkenness—anything that involved that dangerous loss of self-control whereby heat was sapped. Indeed, it was ultimately the self-control (Greek *enkrateia*) of the elite male, acquired by means of the education and training (*paideia*) he received as a young man, that distinguished him both from women and from lower-class males, who were governed by their animal passions and were thus in a constant state of progressive emasculation.[78]

The emphasis on education in the Roman construction of the ideal male was also important in terms of what distinguished Roman society. As already noted, the elite of the Roman world was typically an urban elite. It was also essentially civilian in culture, even if some of its members periodically adopted military careers. At the same time, it was bound together by a high culture rooted in study of the classical texts of Latin and Greek literature.[79] So powerful were these traditions and so important were they as a force for cohesion within elite society that even the leaders of the Christian Church—whose core texts in the Gospel narratives were written in the street-Greek of Palestine—were obliged to conform to the 'high style' of the classical authors and devise elaborate justifications for the continued study and imitation of pagan literature.[80]

In terms of the literary and civilian character of the elite, and in terms of the construction of gender relations, the period from the third century to the fifth was

---

[76] R. Saller, *Patriarchy, Property, and Death in the Roman Household* (Cambridge, 1994); J. F. Gardner and T. Wiedemann, *The Roman Household: A Sourcebook* (London, 1991); S. Treggiari, *Roman Marriage* (Oxford, 1991); Clark (1993).

[77] P. Brown, *The Body and Society: Men, Women, and Sexual Renunciation in Early Christianity* (London, 1988), pp. 9–12.

[78] P. Brown, 'Late Antiquity', in P. Veyne (ed.), *A History of Private Life*, vol. 1: *From Pagan Rome to Byzantium* (Cambridge, Mass., 1987), pp. 239–50.

[79] R. A. Kaster, *Guardians of Language: Grammarians and Society in Late Antiquity* (Berkeley, 1988).

[80] N. Wilson (ed.) *Saint Basil on Greek Literature* (London, 1975).

one of continuity. The distinction between 'free' and 'unfree' also remained fundamental to Roman legal and social thought.[81] In other respects, however, dramatic change took place. Firstly, the *Constitutio Antoniana* or 'Caracallan Edict' of 212 rendered the distinction between Roman and non-Roman largely redundant with respect to the non-slave population of the empire. Instead, the legal texts record the emergence of a new distinction within free society between the 'more respectable' (Latin *honestiores*) and the 'more humble' (*humiliores*), which probably served to entrench the privileges of indigenous provincial elites in the broader context of the extension of Roman citizenship. The category of *honestiores* essentially comprised *curiales* and senators, that of *humiliores* peasants and the urban poor. Over time, each group came to possess ever more clearly defined privileges and rights.[82] This was at its most evident with respect to the penal system, which spared *honestiores* from the most degrading or agonising of punishments. In terms of execution, for example, miscreant *honestiores* could look forward to decapitation and a relatively rapid death. Their social inferiors, by contrast, could be burnt alive, crucified, or thrown to the beasts in the amphitheatre (until, that is, crucifixion was abolished under Constantine). The legal testimony of *honestiores* was, on point of principle, preferred over that of *humiliores*. Any crime committed by a *humilior* was automatically regarded as more serious and was punished more vigorously than the same crime committed by a member of the upper classes. During civic celebrations and ceremonies, free distributions of money and gifts were awarded disproportionately to the privileged.[83]

The third to the fifth centuries also witnessed major developments within the ranks of *honestiores* and *humiliores* themselves. As has been seen, the era of the soldier emperors of the third century, and the emergence of the more bureaucratised Diocletianic state, witnessed a sidelining of the authority and influence of traditional senatorial interests associated with the city of Rome. This process went hand in hand with a dynamic process of elite formation across the Mediterranean world as a whole, whereby elements from amongst the ranks of the dominant elites within the city councils of the provinces (termed *principales* in Latin, or *propoliteuomenoi* in Greek) were drawn into and prospered from new careers in the expanded imperial civil and military bureaucracy.[84] Members of this new imperial aristocracy of service progressively won mastery of local landed society, forcing aside their social competitors, accumulating ever larger reserves of land, and taking advantage of the new monetary conditions in order to invest in and derive benefit from increasingly commercialised forms of agriculture.[85] From the reign of

---

[81] P. Garnsey, *Ideas of Slavery from Aristotle to Augustine* (Cambridge, 1996).
[82] Garnsey (1970).
[83] Ste Croix (1981), pp. 456–62.
[84] Heather (1994), Banaji (2007), and Sarris (2006), pp. 177–99.
[85] Banaji (2007), and P. Sarris, 'Rehabilitating the Great Estate: Aristocratic Property and Economic Growth in the Late Antique East', in W. Bowden, L. Lavan, and C. Machado (eds.), *Recent Research in the Late Antique Countryside* (Leiden, 2004), pp. 55–71. For the West, see P. Sarris, 'The Origins of the Manorial Economy: New Insights from Late Antiquity', *English Historical Review* 119 (2004), pp. 279–311.

Constantine onwards, members of this new elite—those holding the higher civil and military ranks—were themselves accorded senatorial status and were increasingly enrolled in the Senate of Rome or that of Constantinople.[86] The senatorial order thus once again became politically significant, but only by virtue of a radical change in its sociological composition. The new holders of senatorial rank—styled *honorati* ('the honourables') or *clarissimi* ('most renowned')—became figures of enormous influence both in the provinces and at court, the most important of them becoming members of the imperial *sacrum consistorium* ('sacred' or 'imperial consistory'), an inner circle within the Senate that the Emperor was expected to consult.

This process of elite formation, and in particular the reconfiguration of rural society and patterns of landholding that resulted from it, necessarily carried enormous implications for the peasantry. A series of imperial laws from the middle of the fourth century onwards records growing imperial concern at the phenomenon of peasant freeholders either selling up their land to aristocrats, or fleeing their village communities in order to work on the emergent great estates of the new aristocracy. The problem from the imperial perspective was that well-connected aristocratic landowners were regarded as a less reliable source of tax revenues than more easily cajoled or intimidated peasant proprietors. Moreover, the flight of peasants from the village communities in which they were fiscally registered necessarily increased the tax burden on those villagers they left behind. Yet there was only so much that such villagers could reasonably be expected to pay. As a result, the imperial government attempted to legislate to prevent peasants from deserting their legally appointed home or *origo*. These laws, however, failed to stem the tide. Accordingly, the imperial authorities increasingly reached an accommodation with the owners of the great estates. Peasants who had fled to or been drawn onto such estates in order to work were henceforth to remain in service on the estates, in perpetuity, along with their descendants: they could be registered on the tax roster of their landowning employer, and the estate was henceforth to be regarded as their *origo*. Such registered estate labourers became known in the East as *coloni adscripticii* ('registered farmers') and in the West as *originarii* (from the fiscal term *origo*).[87]

In theory this arrangement benefited the Roman state in that, once again, it offered some means of making the flow of tax revenues more predictable and reliable. It was certainly to the benefit of landowners, who now found many of their agricultural workers bound to them not only by private contract but also by public law. What is less clear is what, if anything, the peasants themselves gained. Initially the owners of the great estates had offered a source of protection and patronage against the workings of the Roman fisc and a measure of support when times were hard, but the realignment of the interests of landowners with the interests of the state perhaps rendered such protection

---

[86] Heather (1994).

[87] P. Sarris, 'Aristocrats, Peasants, and the State in the Later Roman Empire', in P. Eich, S. Schmidt Hofner, and C. Wieland (eds.), *Der wiederkehrende Leviathan: Staatlichkeit und Staatswerdung in Spätantike und Früher Neuzeit* (Heidelberg, 2011), pp. 377–94.

increasingly uncertain. It is true that the landowner offered paid employment, but this too appears to have been turned to the disadvantage of the workforce. In Roman law there had long been a tendency to associate the sale of one's labour with a loss of legal status, akin to self-sale into slavery.[88] Accordingly, those drafting the imperial legislation on the *coloni* of the great estates modelled the relationship between landowner and labourer on that between master and slave in the classical Roman law of persons. Like the slave, the *colonus* was placed within the *familia* of his master, who thus came to exercise total control of the peasant's *peculium* or working capital.

With respect to society at large, the *colonus adscripticius* or *originarius* remained, in theory, free. With respect to the landowner, however, his position was deemed to be analogous to that of a slave. That this descent into servile status should be regarded as meaningful rather than metaphorical is strongly suggested by the fact that there is every sign agricultural slavery continued to be a widespread reality in late antiquity.[89] As a result, the attribution of slave-like status to the tied *coloni* of the great estates is likely to have carried with it genuine implications for conditions of labour, treatment, social perceptions, and morale. For many of these agricultural workers and their families, it has been argued, the political, economic, and fiscal reconfiguration of the late Roman Empire was a disaster—this in spite of the fact that the growing monetisation, increased commodification of agrarian production, and rising population levels of the fourth century meant that the period as a whole is likely to have witnessed both aggregate and *per capita* economic growth.[90] The fruits of that growth, however, primarily filled the coffers of the wealthy.[91]

If the 'Caracallan Edict' rendered the distinction between Roman and non-Roman largely redundant with respect to the inhabitants of the empire, the distinction between Roman and 'barbarian' remained fundamental to how the elites of the Roman world continued to view others. In a sense, like members of the lower classes, the barbarians were characterised by their lack of culture (in terms of a literary high culture comparable to that of the Greeks and Romans) and a corresponding lack of self-control. To some extent a distinction was sometimes drawn between the Persians and the rest. In the Persians the Romans faced a culturally and politically sophisticated rival ruling over a settled and highly urbanised population. It is instructive that, in the fourth century, the Roman historian Ammianus Marcellinus pointedly did not apply the term 'barbarian' to Sasanian Persia.[92] By contrast, no such ambiguity appears from Roman accounts of the northern world. Occasionally Roman authors, such as Tacitus in the first

---

[88] ibid.
[89] K. Harper, 'The Greek Census Inscriptions of Late Antiquity', *Journal of Roman Studies* 98 (2008), pp. 83–119.
[90] As argued by J. Banaji, 'Late Antiquity: What Kind of Transition?' in (idem), *Theory as History* (Leiden, 2010).
[91] Sarris (2004), and Banaji (2007).
[92] G. Halsall, *Barbarian Migrations and the Roman West 376–568* (Cambridge, 2007), pp. 48–53, with p. 52 for Ammianus.

century or Salvian of Marseilles in the fifth, highlighted what they regarded as the admirable courage or laudably rigid sexual morals of the Germanic tribes they described. They did so, however, primarily as a means of passing unfavourable comment on their own compatriots. For the most part, the barbarian was viewed as representing the exact inversion of the acme of human development embodied in the figure of the sophisticated, self-restrained, Roman elite male.

As with members of the lower classes, who were similarly lacking in 'humanity' (Latin *humanitas*—a concept that combined the biological and the cultural), this justified considerable cruelty. In 393, for example, the great Roman aristocrat and man of letters, Symmachus, purchased a group of Saxon prisoners of war and brought them to Rome with a view to exhibiting them in the gladiatorial games that he had arranged in honour of his son. Theirs would, no doubt, be a suitably entertaining death. Prior to their planned entry into the arena, however, twenty-nine of them took their own lives by strangling one another. As a recent commentator has noted: 'For us, their terrible death represents a courageous act of defiance. But Symmachus viewed their suicide as the action of a "group of men viler than Spartacus," which had been sent to test him. With the self-satisfaction of which only Roman aristocrats were capable, he compared his own philosophical response to the event to the calm of Socrates when faced with adversity.'[93] Likewise, Ammianus Marcellinus frequently records without comment the wholesale slaughter of any barbarians—men, women, and children—unfortunate enough to find themselves in the path of the imperial army on campaign.[94] Such acts of extermination were clearly regarded as routine.

What is striking about such behaviour is that it persisted in spite of the fact that, by the late fourth century (when Ammianus was writing), many of the highest military commands of the empire, including that of *magister militum* itself, had passed into the hands of individuals who were themselves 'barbarian' by birth but who had acquired Roman citizenship through pursuit of a military career, as a result of which they had clearly become thoroughly Romanised in outlook. The most famous of these was the general Stilicho, who was the key power behind the throne at the court of the young Emperor Honorius (*r*.395–423). An ivory diptych of Stilicho survives (Fig. 2) in which he is depicted in the company of his Roman wife Serena and their toga-clad son, holding the codicils of his appointment to the honorific office of 'tribune and notary'. Yet however Roman Stilicho regarded himself, it did not save him from falling victim to an anti-barbarian backlash at the Western court that would claim his life, in 408.[95]

---

[93] B. Ward-Perkins, *The Fall of the Roman Empire and the End of Civilization* (Oxford, 2005), p. 24.
[94] Ammianus Marcellinus, *Res Gestae*, tr. J. C. Rolfe (Cambridge, Mass., 1935), XVI, xi.9; XVII, viii.3–4; XVII, xiii.13–20; XIX, xi.14–15; XXIV, iv.25; XXVIII, v.4–7; XXX, v.14; XXX, vii.8; and XXXI, xvi.8.
[95] J. Matthews, *Western Aristocracies and the Imperial Court AD 384–425* (Oxford, 1976), p. 281.

Fig. 2 Ivory Diptych of Stilicho and Family (C. Mango, *The Oxford History of Byzantium*, p. 37)

1.6 THE DEMISE OF THE WESTERN ROMAN EMPIRE

However much members of the Roman governing classes disdained the barbarian peoples to the empire's north, as the events of the third century had demonstrated, their own military security was critically sensitive to developments beyond the Rhine and Danube. The tribes of these regions were in turn vulnerable to any threat from the area known to the Romans as *Scythia*—the plains and grasslands that swept from the east of the Danubian basin, across the region to the north of the Black Sea, onwards to the distant marchlands of China. Instability on the Eurasian steppe could lead to the westward migration of tribes of highly mobile and militarily formidable nomadic horsemen who had the ability to cast into turmoil the northern barbarian world, either by establishing their own mastery of the region or by propelling the tribes already resident there deep into Roman territory.[96] At some time around the early part of the second half of the fourth century, a group

---

[96] T. Barfield, *The Perilous Frontier: Nomadic Empires and China* (Oxford, 1989); P. Heather, 'The Huns and the End of the Roman Empire in Western Europe', *English Historical Review* 110 (1995), pp. 4–41.

of nomadic horsemen known in the Roman sources as 'Huns' (Latin *Huni* or *Hunni*—Greek *Chounoi*—a name of unknown etymology) began just such a westward migration. This was to have major and irreversible consequences for the Roman Empire.[97]

By the mid-370s the Huns had seemingly established themselves to the north of the Black Sea and the east of the Carpathian mountains, first subduing the Alans and then displacing the Gothic tribe of the *Tervingini* ('Tervingian Goths'). In 376 large numbers of Gothic refugees arrived on the northern bank of the River Danube and asked to be permitted to settle on Roman territory in return for military service (a strategy that the Romans had employed intermittently in the frontier zone since the days of Octavian).[98] The Eastern emperor Valens agreed to this request and the Goths were settled in the northern Balkans, receiving supplies and support from the imperial authorities. In 378, however, relations between the leaders of the Goths and the Roman military commanders in the region broke down (largely, it seems, as a result of mistreatment on the part of the Romans). Accordingly, in 378, a major uprising of the Goths took place under the leadership of their warlord Fritigern. On 9 August the Roman and Gothic armies clashed to the north of the city of Adrianople. The result was a crushing and humiliating defeat for the Romans, during the course of which two-thirds of the Roman field army (which had numbered some forty thousand men) fell, as too did the Emperor Valens.[99]

A carefully targeted campaign of destruction aimed at members of the Roman governing classes ensued. The archaeological evidence, for example, records the widespread destruction—by fire—of villa sites in the northern Balkan zone in the late fourth century.[100] Interestingly, the sources suggest that (as with the Goths in Pontus in the third century) the barbarians were expressly aided in this by members of the Roman lower classes: Ammianus Marcellinus records that those who surrendered to the barbarians or were captured by them 'pointed out the rich estate settlements, especially those where ample supplies of food were said to be available'.[101] Likewise the Goths were joined by local gold miners 'who were unable to bear the heavy burden of taxation. These were warmly welcomed and proved to be of great service as they traversed this strange country by directing them to concealed stores of grain and hidden corners where people had taken refuge.'[102] Perhaps the Emperor should have listened when the court orator Themistius had warned him just months earlier that 'many of the nobles who have held office for three generations made their subjects long for the barbarians' (Map 2).[103]

---

[97] Heather (1995), and D. Sinor 'The Hun Period', in D. Sinor (ed.), *The Cambridge History of Early Inner Asia* (Cambridge, 1990), pp. 177–205.

[98] Ste Croix (1981), Appendix III, pp. 509–18.

[99] Ammianus Marcellinus, *Res Gestae*, XXXI, ii–XXXI, xvi.9; P. Heather, *The Fall of the Roman Empire: A New History* (London, 2005), pp. 176–81.

[100] A. Poulter, 'Cataclysm on the Lower Danube: The Destruction of a Complex Roman Landscape', in N. Christie (ed.), *Landscapes of Change: Rural Evolutions in Late Antiquity and the Early Middle Ages* (Aldershot, 2004), pp. 223–54.

[101] Ammianus Marcellinus, *Res Gestae*, XXXI, vi.4–5.

[102] ibid., XXXI, vi.6–7.

[103] Themistius, *Orationes*, VIII, 115.

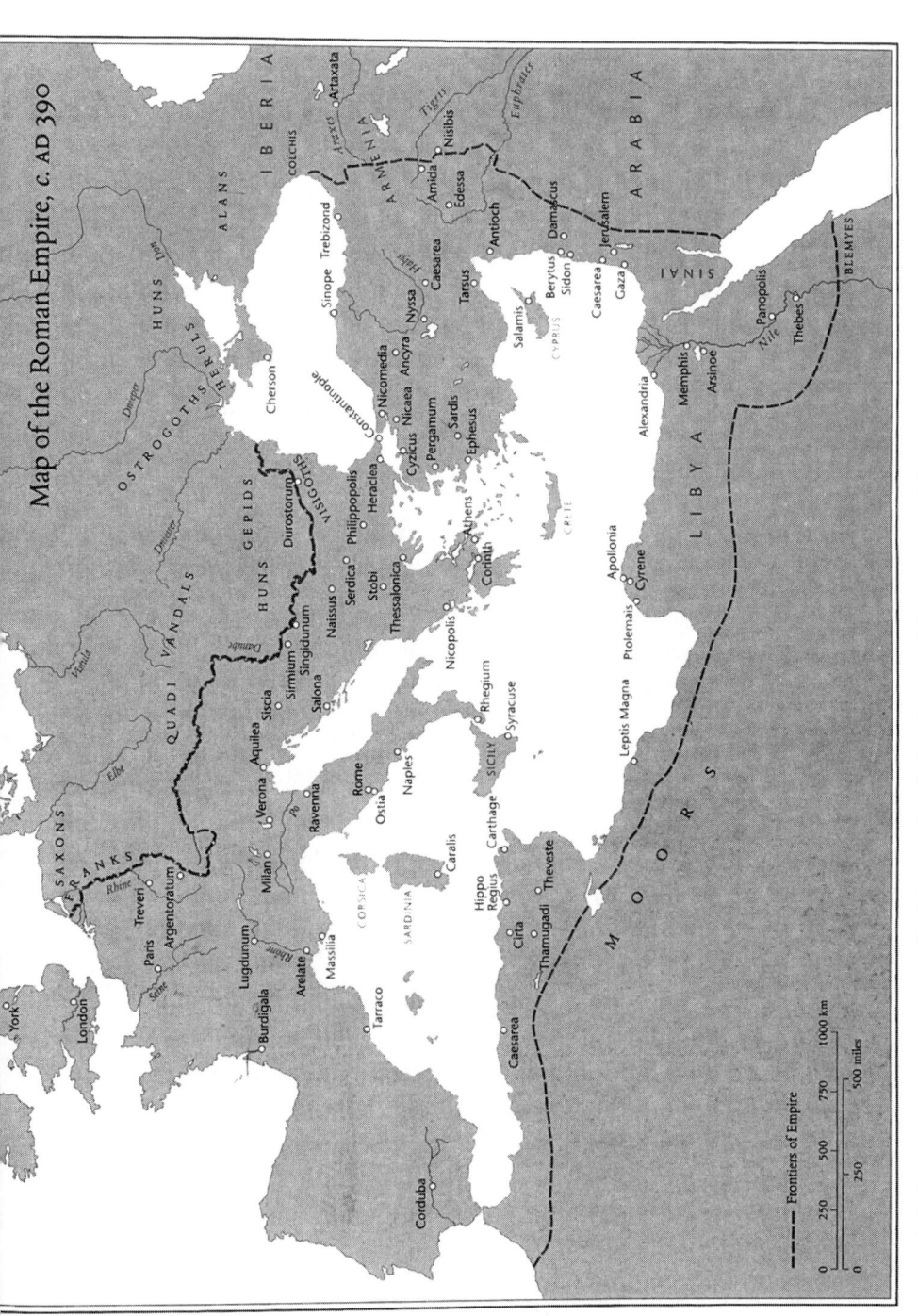

Map 2 The Roman Empire, c.AD 390 (C. Mango, *The Oxford History of Byzantium*, p. 33)

Valens' successor as Eastern Emperor, Theodosius, was eventually able to negotiate terms with the Gothic leadership, and the Goths were once more settled under treaty in Dacia and Thrace.[104] Between 395 and 410, however, relations again deteriorated and, under the leadership of their new warlord, Alaric, the Goths sought both to increase pressure on the Roman authorities and to extract ever more favourable terms and conditions from them. They attempted to play off the Western court against its Eastern counterpart and launched periodic attacks on Roman positions in both the Balkans and also, increasingly, Italy. In 410 Alaric led his Goths deep into the Italian peninsula and, as negotiations with the Senate foundered, sacked the city of Rome. Although Rome had long since ceased to be the effective seat of power within the empire, the event nevertheless sent reverberations throughout the Roman world. In distant Palestine, the translator of the Bible into Latin and biblical commentator Jerome famously declared: 'the brightest light of the whole world is extinguished; indeed the head has been cut from the Roman empire. . . . Who would have believed that Rome, which was built up from victories over the whole world would fall . . . that it would be both the mother and the tomb to all peoples?'[105]

The Tervingian Goths (or 'Visigoths' as they have come to be known) were not the only barbarian people to enter Roman territory at this time. By the early years of the fifth century the Huns appear to have established a power base for themselves to the west of the Carpathian mountains. This meant that the sort of pressure that they had previously applied to the inhabitants of the trans-Danubian world now came to bear down on the tribes to the north and east of the Rhine.[106] In 405/6 Radagaisus, the chief of yet another (hitherto unheard of) Gothic host, emerged from across the Alps and led his warriors into Italy.[107] Likewise, on New Year's Eve 405, the frozen River Rhine was traversed across a broad arc by a tumult of barbarian peoples including Vandals, Sueves, and Alans, their advance only briefly held in check by resistance to them from the Franks—another barbarian people who had been settled in the frontier zone after their defeat by the Emperor Julian in the mid-fourth century.[108]

Once the area of Frankish settlement had been broken through, the raiders from across the Rhine extended their reach until, by 409, they were able to strike into Spain. In 412 the Tervingian Goths, under the leadership of Alaric's successor Athaulf, migrated out of Italy and established themselves in southern Gaul. By the second decade of the fifth century much of the Western Empire was in the grip of a severe military paralysis. Barbarian armies were rampaging through Gaul and Spain and some were heading towards Africa, the capital of which, Carthage, finally fell in

---

[104] P. Heather, *The Goths* (Oxford, 1996).
[105] Jerome, *Commentaries on Ezekiel*, Preface to Book 1.
[106] Heather (1995).
[107] Heather (2006), pp. 194–5.
[108] For the date (normally given as 406) see W. Goffart, *Barbarian Tides: The Migration Age and the Later Roman Empire* (Philadelphia, 2006), p. 74. The best introduction to early Frankish history remains E. James, *The Franks* (Oxford, 1988), although see also G. Halsall, *Settlement and Social Organization: The Merovingian Region of Metz* (Cambridge, 1995).

439 to a joint Vandal and Alan force under the leadership of the Vandal king Geiseric.[109] Between 407 and 410 the Roman mobile field army had been withdrawn from Britain, obliging the Romano-British elite to look increasingly to their own defence, which they did, at least in part, by employing Saxon mercenaries, who began to settle in force in eastern Britain along with their wives and children.[110]

The violence and destruction associated with these military events should not be underestimated. As we shall see in Chapter Two, contemporary sources, such as the *Chronicle of Hydatius* for Spain or the writings of Salvian of Marseilles for Gaul, paint a vivid picture of closely fought battles and perhaps localised but nevertheless brutal acts of recrimination and revenge of precisely the sort recorded archaeologically for the northern Balkans in the late fourth century.[111] There is little reason to believe that the Goths had mellowed since Adrianople, or that their Vandal cousins were any more eirenic. As with the barbarian invasions of the third century, there is evidence of social upheaval and the re-emergence of groups of armed peasants again styled *bacaudae*.[112]

Although the imperial authorities were able to inflict localised defeats on the barbarians, what is most striking about the military crisis in the West of the early fifth century is the inability of the Roman army successfully to meet the barbarian challenge to the same extent that its third-century predecessor had been able to. The activities of Alaric and his Goths in Italy in the first decade of the fifth century necessarily meant that the imperial authorities were too preoccupied with events in the Italian peninsula to concentrate substantial military resources on the situation in Gaul. On good 'tetrarchic' principles, so as better to meet the Gothic challenge, in 395 the court had moved out of Gaul into Italy—initially to Milan and then subsequently to Ravenna. Accordingly, as with Britain, the imperial authorities in Spain and Gaul were increasingly obliged to fall back upon their own atomised resources.[113] The retreat of the imperial court across the Alps problematised and hindered concerted and well-coordinated resistance.

The imperial authorities also seem to have had growing difficulties raising the revenues required to finance a sustained military response. Barbarian invasion and military dislocation necessarily hindered the effective collection of the tax revenues on which the Roman army depended. Certainly, it is widely acknowledged that the fall of Africa to the Vandals and their Alan allies, and the resultant loss to the Western Empire of the tax revenues of its wealthiest province, crippled the finances of what remained of the West Roman state.[114] Thus the Emperor Valentinian III complained in 444 of the 'exhausted circumstances and afflicted condition of the state' and went on to relate that 'neither for those who are bound by new oaths of military service, nor even for the veteran army can those supplies seem to suffice

---

[109] Heather (2006), pp. 300–04.
[110] D. Mattingly, *An Imperial Possession: Britain in the Roman Empire* (London, 2004).
[111] Ward-Perkins (2005).
[112] Salvian, *On the Governance of God (De Gubernatione Dei)*, tr. Fr. O'Sullivan, *Fathers of the Church*, Series 3 (Washington DC, 1947), V, 22, 24–6; Thompson (1952).
[113] Wormald (1976).
[114] Forcefully argued in Heather (1995).

that are delivered with the greatest difficulty by the exhausted taxpayers, and it seems that from that source the supplies that are necessary for food and clothing cannot be furnished'.[115]

Even prior to the invasions of 405–6, however, the imperial authorities were facing mounting difficulties in extracting tax revenues from the brimming coffers of the emergent imperial aristocracy of service. Aristocratic tax evasion was the subject of a steady stream of imperial laws from the 360s through to the early fifth century aimed at curtailing illicit 'patronage' (or *patrocinium*) engaged in by the owners of the great estates.[116] Such tax evasion necessarily carried military consequences, as the Roman army was the main recipient of imperial tax revenues.[117] Ongoing tax evasion on the part of aristocratic landowners is described in detail for Gaul in the second quarter of the fifth century in the writings of Salvian of Marseilles, who complains that it served to intensify the tax burden on the peasantry and the poor.[118] Both Salvian and the fifth-century historian Orosius describe defections to the barbarians on the part of the poor as a direct result of this.[119] Salvian was a moralising author who presents his reader with a damning critique of Roman morals. As a result, his testimony is commonly rejected by modern scholars. Yet precisely the phenomenon described by Salvian is recorded in contemporary imperial legislation. A law of Valentinian III, for example, explains the state's dependence on tax revenues, but complains that 'the continuity of such tax payments cannot be sustained if a few exhausted persons find imposed on them a burden which the more powerful man declines, which the richer man refuses, and which, since the stronger reject it, only the weaker man assumes'.[120]

As a result of a combination of aristocratic tax evasion and the administrative dislocation caused by enemy invasion, therefore, the imperial authorities in the West increasingly lacked the resources required to maintain an effective defence. Accordingly, imperial officials and military commanders were obliged to cut deals with the leaders of the barbarians in their midst in order to bolster the military resources available to them or to achieve some measure of security. So, for example, in *c.*418, the Visigoths were settled in Aquitaine in southern Gaul, establishing a kingdom at Toulouse, in return for agreeing to protect the region on behalf of the Emperor from the depredations of other, potentially still more destructive, barbarian groups. By the end of the 440s similar settlements had been negotiated with groups of Vandals and Sueves in Galicia, with the Alans in Valence and Gallia Ulterior, and the Burgundians in Sapaudia (Savoy).[121]

---

[115] *Nov. Val.*, 15.1.
[116] Sarris (2006), pp. 149–99.
[117] Wickham (2005), pp. 73–4.
[118] Salvian, *De Gubernatione Dei*, IV, 20–21, 30–31; V, 17–18, 25–6, 28–32, 34–44.
[119] ibid., V, 21–3, 27–8, 36–8; Orosius, *History Against the Pagans (Historia Contra Paganos)*, tr. R. Defarri, *Fathers of the Church*, Series 50 (Washington DC, 1964), VII, 41.7; Ste Croix (1981) p. 481.
[120] *Nov. Val.*, 10.1.
[121] I. Wood, 'The Barbarian Invasions and First Settlements', in Cameron and Garnsey (1998), pp. 516–37.

The terms of these settlements, and their implications for social and economic life, will be revisited in the next chapter. Here, however, two points are worth noting. The first is that, as a result of such settlements, at a local and provincial level, the courts of the barbarian leaders increasingly came to serve as the main focus for the hopes and ambitions of the leading members of provincial society, who desperately craved security for themselves and their dependants. As a result, the imperial court gradually receded from sight.[122] By the 470s only Italy remained under direct imperial control. Yet even in Italy the military situation was highly precarious. In 452 the leader of the Huns, the infamous Attila, led an army into the peninsula that was, to all intents and purposes, unopposed. Only malaria drove Attila's forces back from Rome. The city's respite was, however, to be short-lived, and in 455 Rome was sacked once more, this time by the Vandals.[123]

The second important implication of the settlement of barbarians in return for their military service was that Roman society in the West became increasingly dependent for its defence on barbarian warriors, organised within their own groupings rather than recruited individually into Roman legions, and bound to the authority of their own barbarian leader rather than to a Roman commander or general. This was a significant development. As noted earlier, what had essentially extricated the Roman Empire from the 'crisis' of the mid-third century was the ruthless commitment to the ideology of empire of members of the Roman army's officer corps. Over the course of the fifth century, by contrast, the Western Empire came increasingly to rely upon outsiders whose loyalty and commitment were not to Rome but rather to their own warlords and kings.

As the Western court became increasingly emasculated, so too did the very concept of the Western *imperium* come to seem expendable. In 467–8, when the Western crown passed to an Eastern placeman by the name of Anthemius— referred to contemptuously in Western sources as the *Graeculus*, or 'Greekling'— the imperial prefect in Gaul, Arvandus, advised the Visigothic king Euric to reject the new Emperor and divide Gaul between himself and the king of the Burgundians.[124] Similarly, in a palace coup in 476, Romulus 'Augustulus', the last of the Roman emperors in the West, was deposed by his barbarian general Odoacer. Odoacer set himself up as king in Italy and informed the authorities in Constantinople that there was now no longer any need for a separate emperor in Rome or Ravenna.[125] Titular authority in the region could pass instead to the Eastern *Augustus*—a legal fiction that marked the emergence in the West of autonomous Romano-Germanic kingdoms which were now the heirs to Rome.

The Roman Empire survived in the East, however. This fact was primarily due to the greater military security of the Eastern Empire at this time.[126] Crucially, from the perspective of Constantinople, the fifth century witnessed a détente in Roman-

---

[122] Wormald (1976).
[123] Heather (2006), pp. 300–48.
[124] Sidonius Apollinaris, *Epistolae*, I, 7.
[125] *Anonymus Valesianus, Pars Posterior*, 10.
[126] Ward-Perkins (2005).

Persian relations. Both empires were fully aware of the grave threat posed to each of them by the disturbed nature of conditions on the West Eurasian steppe—to which Persia in particular was highly vulnerable by virtue of its strategic geography. Moreover, the migration of the Visigoths into Italy, combined with the increasingly westward-looking nature of Hunnic military ambitions, meant that the barbarian question was ultimately of less urgency in fifth-century Constantinople than in contemporary Ravenna or Rome. Nevertheless, the Huns did pose a major threat to the imperial position in the Balkans, a fact that prevented the emperors in Constantinople from being able to make any major contribution to the defence of the West.[127] After the death of Attila in 453 and the subsequent collapse of Hunnic power, the East Roman authorities were obliged to permit the settlement in the northern Balkans of a large and potentially dangerous 'Ostrogothic' confederation made up of former subjects of the Huns.[128] Eventually, in 488–9, the bulk of the Ostrogoths, under the leadership of their king Theoderic, were persuaded to march west to depose Odoacer from control in Italy. There, as will be discussed in Chapter Three, Theoderic set up a new regime, one that paid intermittent lip service to concepts of continued imperial suzerainty, but which, in fact, operated with a dangerous degree of independence. In Italy, Africa, Britain, Spain, and Gaul, therefore, a 'post-Roman' world was now beginning to take shape.

[127] Heather (1995).
[128] S. Barnish and F. Marazzi (eds.), *The Ostrogoths from the Migration Period to the Sixth Century* (Woodbridge, 2007).

2

The Formation of Post-Roman Society

2.1 INTRODUCTION

Therefore, as the oracle truly says, while all this [i.e. the imperial sacrifice at the temple of the Capitoline Jove] was observed according to direction, the Roman empire was safe and Rome remained in control of virtually all the inhabited world, but once this festival was neglected after Diocletian's abdication, the empire gradually collapsed and was imperceptibly barbarised. The facts themselves show this, as I will prove from chronology. (Zosimus, *New History*, II, 7)

As the epigram above demonstrates, to the pagan historian Zosimus, writing in Constantinople around the year 500, both the fact and cause of the demise of Roman political and military power in the fifth-century West were clear enough. What was far less clear to Zosimus, however, as indeed to many modern historians, was quite *how* this process of 'gradual collapse' was articulated on the ground. This problem stems partly from the indefatigable self-assurance of members of the Roman governing classes, whose voices and attitudes dominate the pages of our literary sources. At the turn of the fifth century, the Roman aristocracy was brimming with confidence. It was inconceivable to its members that Roman power could be overthrown, let alone by the barbarians of the northern world who were so evidently inferior in every sense. As the Christian poet Prudentius had declared:

> *As beasts from men, as dumb from those who speak,*
> *As from the good who God's commandments seek*
> *Differ the foolish heathen, so Rome stands,*
> *Alone in pride above barbarian lands.*[1]

It was no easy matter to persuade such men that the world was, in fact, changing and that it was no longer they who automatically held the whip hand. Even the sack of Rome by Alaric and his Goths in 410 could not dispel the confidence of some. The Christian apologist Orosius, for example, writing his *History Against the Pagans* from Roman-held Africa in the year 417–18, sought to counter the claims made by pagans (and which pagans such as Zosimus would continue to make) that the rise of Christianity was responsible for the stark decline in Rome's fortunes evident from recent military events. Rather, Orosius argued, the pagan past had witnessed far

---

[1] Prudentius, *Contra Symmachum*, II, 816–19, translation from M. Grant, *The Fall of the Roman Empire* (London, 1976), p. 132.

worse calamities, from which Rome had nevertheless emerged triumphant. In particular, he attempted to downplay the actual destructiveness of barbarian assaults. Although the fall of Rome in 410 had been associated with considerable bloodshed, at least Alaric's Goths, Orosius emphasised, had spared the city's churches and holy men. Moreover, he had even heard reassuring rumours that the current Gothic king, Athaulf, whose followers were now established around the city of Narbonne in southern Gaul, no longer sought the destruction of the Roman Empire, but rather its preservation. Orosius knew this because he had overheard someone who claimed to be a close friend of Athaulf tell St Jerome that:

> He ... had often heard what [Athaulf], when in good spirits, health, and temper was accustomed to reply to questions. It seems that at first he ardently desired to blot out the Roman name and make all the Roman territory a Gothic empire in fact as well as in name, so that, to use the popular expression, *Gothia* should take the place of *Romania*, and he, Athaulf, should be all that Caesar Augustus once had been. Having discovered from long experience that the Goths, because of their unbridled barbarism, were utterly incapable of obeying laws, and yet believing that the state ought not to be deprived of laws without which a state is not a state, he [Athaulf] chose to seek for himself at least the glory of restoring and increasing the renown of the Romans by the power of the Goths, wishing to be looked upon by posterity as the restorer of the Roman Empire. (Orosius 7.43.2–3).

On the basis of this third-hand hearsay of the witticisms of a barbarian king in his cups, Orosius, in distant Africa, looked forward to a future of peaceful cooperation between Romans and barbarians. At around the same time, the aristocratically minded author of a treatise on divine law (*de Divina Lege*) felt able to dismiss the 'common opinion' (*vulgi sententiam*) that 'the whole world has perished' (*totus mundus perit*).[2] It was such self-confidence that permitted Roman authors and propagandists to present even the slightest stabilisation of the Western Empire's military fortunes, such as occurred *c*.418 in southern Gaul or under the leadership of the general Aetius in the 430s, as heralding a restoration of imperial glory. It is all too easy for the modern student of the late-Roman world to be taken in by such rhetoric or to be overwhelmed by the effortless self-confidence of the Roman governing classes. It is perhaps rather more significant that there *was* a 'common opinion' in the early fifth century that the world had ended, or that there *existed* a 'popular expression' that '*Gothia* should take the place of *Romania*', than it was that Roman aristocrats and churchmen felt able to dismiss such idle chatter on the part of the masses.

Indeed, a further disorientating factor is that even as Roman arms faltered, Roman propagandists excelled. In particular, Roman commentators and panegyricists were especially adept at presenting almost any reversal inflicted on the Roman state, or any concession extracted from the imperial authorities by the leaders of the barbarians, not as a defeat but as a victory for Rome. In 439, for example, as noted in Chapter One, the barbarian king Geiseric, at the head of a joint Vandalic and

---

[2] J. Morris, 'Pelagian Literature', *Journal of Theological Studies* 16 (1965), pp. 26–60, 37.

Alan host, had dealt a body blow to the fortunes of the Western Roman Empire by conquering the fantastically wealthy provinces of Roman north Africa—Numidia, Byzacena, and *Africa Proconsularis*—and seizing the regional capital of Carthage.[3] These provinces were the bread basket of the Western Empire, supplying Rome with its corn supply and furnishing many members of the senatorial elite with highly profitable estates. In the following year, the Eastern and Western imperial governments responded by amassing a vast fleet and sizeable army in order to evict Africa's new masters. This effort was abandoned, however, when the detachments of the Eastern field army had to be withdrawn in response to an intensification of the Hunnic threat to the imperial possessions in the Balkans. As a result, it very suddenly became an overriding imperative for the imperial government in the West to come to some sort of accommodation with Geiseric and his Vandals, both to ensure the security of the Italian coastline and to attempt to restore the grain supply to Rome. Accordingly, Roman diplomacy went into overdrive. In 442 control of Numidia, Byzacena, and *Africa Proconsularis* was formally ceded to Geiseric, who was accorded the title of *rex socius et amicus* ('client-king and friend'). Huneric, Geiseric's son, was sent as a 'diplomatic hostage' to the imperial court at Ravenna, where he was betrothed to Eudocia, daughter of the Emperor Valentinian III, thereby providing Geiseric with an interest in the imperial succession. The formal recognition of Vandal rule in Africa, the acquisition of a Roman imperial bride for his son, and thus the reasonable expectation that a grandson of his might sit on the imperial throne, served to crown Geiseric's African triumph. Yet to Aetius' court panegyricist Merobaudes (Aetius at this point being the real power behind the throne), the treaty of 442 represented a victory for Aetius, who had managed to tame even the most presumptuous of barbarians:

> The occupier of Libya [Geiseric] had dared to tear down by exceedingly fated arms the seat of Dido's kingdom [Carthage], and had filled the Carthaginian citadels with northern hordes. Since then he has taken off the garb of an enemy, and has desired ardently to bind fast to the Roman faith by more personal agreements, to count the Romans as relatives for himself, and to join his and their offspring in matrimonial alliance. Thus, while the leader [Aetius] regains the peaceful rewards of the toga and orders the consular chair, now at peace, to abandon war trumpets, these very wars have given way everywhere in admiration of his triumphal attire. (*Panegyric*, 2.25–33)

So Aetius and Rome were the driving force behind events after all, and Geiseric no more than a suppliant doing their bidding. Yet it is worth remembering that this 'taming' of Geiseric and the Vandals did not prevent them from inflicting on the city of Rome in 455 a second and still more destructive sack than that perpetrated by Alaric in 410; nor did the formal recognition of Vandal control in Africa and the diplomatic integration of the Vandals prevent the imperial authorities from seeking forcibly to restore direct rule over the region in 461 and 468. The 'triumphal attire' of imperial propaganda and rhetoric should not be allowed, as was its aim, to mask the reality of imperial contraction and of military and political retreat.

---

[3] Heather (2005), pp. 251–99.

2.2 THE DECLINE OF THE WESTERN ROMAN EMPIRE—CHRONOLOGY AND FACTS

Given the tendency of many (although, as shall be seen, by no means all) Roman authors to put a highly optimistic and occasionally eirenic gloss on the military and political developments of the fifth century, it is worth pausing to appreciate how brutal, violent, and tightly fought the military history of the late fourth and fifth centuries actually was. It is true that in 376 the imperial authorities had permitted the settlement under treaty within the empire's Danubian provinces of the various Gothic tribes that were subsequently to revolt in 378. The authorities in Constantinople only acceded to these demands, however, because the imperial field army was busy campaigning against the Persians to the east, thus preventing the Roman government from adopting a more aggressive stance with respect to the defence of the Danubian *limes*.[4] In every other recorded instance, we should note, barbarian armies and their followers entered Roman territory by force. As seen in Chapter One, the barbarian crossings of the Rhine and the subsequent invasions of 406–9 appear to have been primarily catalysed by a westward expansion of Hunnic power, the invasions resulting either from a sort of 'domino effect' within the lands of *Germania*, or as a result of a deliberate policy on the part of individual Hunnic leaders to force frontier peoples into Roman territory as a means of testing out the empire's forward lines of defence. Over the course of the fourth century, the emergent elites of these frontier peoples had seemingly become ever more dependent on the wealth and status that could be derived from contact with the Roman world through trade, ties of clientage, and military service.[5] The withdrawal of the imperial court from Gaul into Italy in 395, primarily in response to the emergence of the Gothic threat from the Balkans, but also as a result of political struggles within Italy, is likely to have disturbed and dislocated such ties, dangerously destabilising the frontier societies and creating a power vacuum in Rome's north-western provinces, to which the invasions of 405–9 were also partly a response.

Around the year 410, some sort of stiffening of Roman resistance to the barbarian invaders is identifiable but, as in the dark days of the third-century crisis, this was primarily achieved through the self-help of the leaders of local society in the north-western provinces. Perhaps the first sign that a military crisis was imminent in the West, for which the central imperial authorities were not felt to be a sufficient match, was that a series of revolts had occurred in Roman Britain just prior to the Rhine crossings. By 407 power in the region was concentrated in the hands of a certain Constantine III, who led Roman forces stationed in Britannia across the Channel to Gaul where, prior to his downfall in 411, he coordinated resistance to the barbarian invaders, just as Postumus had done before him.[6] This may,

---

[4] Heather (2005), pp. 145–90.
[5] G. Halsall, 'The Barbarian Invasions', in P. Fouracre (ed.), *The New Cambridge Medieval History, Volume I, c.500–700* (Cambridge, 2005), pp. 35–55.
[6] Heather (2005), p. 210; Mattingly (2006), pp. 237–8 and 529–31.

perversely, have simply had the effect of pushing these invaders further south, thereby extending the carnage to other hitherto unaffected regions.

In straightforwardly military terms, the warfare of 406–18 seems to have inflicted a heavy toll on the ranks of the Roman army: careful analysis of the *Notitia Dignitatum* (a document detailing the distribution of civil and military officials at the disposal of the late-Roman state) reveals that, between 395 and 420, the Western field army seems to have lost almost half of its regiments. Not surprisingly, it was the army of the Rhine that suffered the most, losing some two-thirds of its original units. The imperial authorities attempted to redress these losses by replacing elite field army troops (*comitatenses*) with soldiers derived from the frontier garrison armies (*limitanei*). There is no sign that these garrison troops, however, were in their turn replaced, indicating an overall decline in the total number of troops under arms, as well as a critical deterioration in the quality and institutional cohesion of the crack troops on whom the empire most relied.[7] This, it should be emphasised, is a 'best case scenario' reading of the *Notitia*. The information it records may already have been severely out of date by the 420s—'a nostalgic statement of what had once been available to the emperor'.[8]

Faced with a meltdown in political leadership, some units of the imperial army responded by acting with ever greater independence, until they effectively acquired an autonomous political status and identity of their own. At the Battle of the Catalaunian Plains in 451, for example, we hear of a group described as 'Olybriones—once Roman soldiers and now the flower of the allied forces'.[9] Similarly, according to Gregory of Tours, Syagrius, 'the King of the Romans', maintained a kingdom centred on Soissons, which the Frankish king Clovis would conquer in the 480s.[10] This kingdom, based on and behind the Rhine, had initially been carved out in the early 460s by Syagrius' father Aegidius (the commander of the Roman forces in Gaul), in response to the assassination of his patron, the Emperor Majorian; faced with an uncertain future, he had chosen simply to go it alone. The final deracinated remnants of the Roman army on the Rhine were thus ultimately incorporated into the expanding Frankish *regnum*, and are likely to have made a significant contribution to the future military development of the Frankish state.[11]

Even had the frontier troops been replaced *c.*420, it is a moot point as to where, by then, the effective Roman frontier would have stood. In 412 the invaders from across the Rhine had divided up the provinces of Spain amongst themselves, the main body of the imperial field army having been withdrawn the preceding year. Around the same time the Emperor Honorius was obliged to inform a delegation

---

[7] Heather (2005), pp. 246–50, and Jones (1964), Appendix III.
[8] I. Wood, 'The Barbarian Invasions and First Settlements', in A. Cameron and P. Garnsey (eds.), *The Cambridge Ancient History*, vol. XIII, *The Late Empire, A.D. 337–425* (Cambridge, 1998), pp. 516–37.
[9] Jordanes, *Getica*, 36.
[10] Gregory of Tours, *Decem Libri Historiae*, 27.
[11] B. S. Bachrach, *Merovingian Military Organization 481–751* (Minneapolis, 1972).

from Britain that the empire could no longer provide troops for the island's defence and that its inhabitants would have to look after themselves. A sixth-century account written by the British historian Gildas records that they did so through a combination of two strategies. They clustered around the protection that could be afforded by a number of indigenous militarised lords, especially in those lands abutting the upland zones of west and north Britain, where long-standing traditions of military tribal lordship had survived alongside or just beyond the reach of Roman political structures; and they negotiated terms with assorted warriors from continental *Germania* comprising Angles, Saxons, Jutes, and Franks, who initially settled on the island as federate troops before rebelling against their masters c.440.[12] Although in 416–18 a joint Visigothic-Roman alliance was able to defeat the Vandals and Alans in Spain (thereby precipitating the Vandalic-Alan crossings into north Africa that began in c.422), in much of the Iberian peninsula a situation not dissimilar to that discernible in Britain appears to have pertained. Provincials responded to chronic military insecurity by looking to their own defence and, in the Asturias and the high plains of the northern Meseta at least, adopted an increasingly martial culture, such as had continued to exist in the tribal highlands of the neighbouring Basque country.[13] A similar situation is discernible in Armorica (modern Brittany) in north-western Gaul.

Across Gaul as a whole, the evidence would suggest that by c.420 the effective frontier of Roman military and political power had retreated to the banks of the Loire. It is instructive, for example, that between 413 and 418 the Visigoths under Athaulf had negotiated with the imperial authorities their settlement in Aquitaine, just as in c.436–7 the Burgundians would negotiate their settlement in Savoy (Sapaudia). In neither instance, however, were these negotiations entirely peaceful affairs, and warfare between Roman commanders and the Visigothic and Burgundian leadership continued to flare up intermittently until imperial suzerainty was finally cast off in the 460s and 470s. In earlier centuries, the settlement of such 'federate troops' (*foederati*) under their own leadership in Roman territory had been carefully limited to the empire's frontier zones: *prima facie* the settlement of the Visigoths in Aquitaine and of the Burgundians in Savoy should be taken as pretty fair indicators as to where the frontier zone had come to rest following the military events of 406–18.[14] It should also be noted that when, in 418, the Emperor Honorius convened a 'council of the Gauls', no representatives were received from the north Gallic provinces.

So what was going on north of the Loire? Suggestive evidence is provided by an exchange between two characters preserved in a comic play entitled *Querolus* written in Rome c.414–17. The leading character, the eponymous anti-hero of the work, prays to his household god (the *lar familiaris*) to become 'a private man of power' (*privatus et potens*). The following dialogue then ensues:

---

[12] Gildas, *De Excidio Britanniae*. For the geography of military lordships, see Wickham (2005).
[13] Wickham (2005), pp. 338–9.
[14] Halsall (2006), p. 49.

Lar:	What sort of power do you want?
Querolus:	The power to rob those who owe me nothing, to kill strangers, and to both rob and kill my neighbours.
Lar:	Hahaha! That's not power you're after, but brigandage! Well well well, I don't know how to make that wish come true for you. . . . Now I've got it—how to get you what you want: go and live beyond the Loire!
Querolus:	Eh?
Lar:	There men live according to the law of the jungle; there there are no signs of rank; there men bring forth death sentences by sheer brute strength and record them in bones; there even peasants plead as advocates and private men act as judges; there anything goes; and if you're a rich man they will call you a wretch!¹⁵

Extrapolating social and political conditions in Rome's north-western provinces on the basis of a comedy apparently written and (one might imagine) performed in Rome at the time is of course far from unproblematic. But a similar picture of political chaos, endemic violence, and social disaffection is also recorded in other disparate and unrelated sources. We possess, for example, a number of theological tracts written in the early years of the second decade of the fifth century by an enigmatic and extraordinarily arresting author, possibly of British or north Gallic extraction, who had come to reside in Sicily. There he had been drawn into Pelagian circles by a woman of senatorial rank who had dissuaded him from his original intention of travelling on pilgrimage to the East.¹⁶ In spite of this aristocratic connection, our author (sometimes referred to in scholarship as 'the Sicilian Briton') was an acute social critic who lambasted the social and spiritual pretensions of the late-Roman aristocracy. Interestingly, the 'Sicilian Briton' describes a world in which criticisms of the powerful were being popularly aired, apparently by itinerant preachers, to the great indignation of the wealthy: 'Listen to your rich man calling your poor man "wretch", "beggar", "rabble", because he dares to open his mouth in "our" presence, because in his rags he reproaches "our" morality and behaviour, because he disturbs "our" comfortable conscience by his reasoned argument and his recognition of the truth. As if the rich man alone had a right to speak, as if the understanding of truth were a function of wealth, not of reason.'¹⁷ Still more revealing, however, is the fate suffered by members of the self-same governing classes as described in the author's contemporaneous treatise 'On the Christian Life' (*de Vita Christiana*), in which he consoles a widow for the fact that her virtuous husband had died when so many of the unjust continued to live. Apparently describing the world of the troubled North, the 'Sicilian Briton' reminded his correspondent that:

> We see before us plenty of examples . . . of wicked men, the sum of their sins complete, who are at this present moment being judged, and denied this present life no less than the life to come. One can easily understand it if, through changing times, one has been waiting for the end of successive magistrates (*iudices*) who have lived criminally. . . . Thus it is fitting that those who had no man to fear when they

---

[15] *Querolus*, tr. C. Jacquemard Le Saos (Paris, 1994), 2.28–34.
[16] Morris (1965), p. 37.   [17] ibid., p. 47.

gave vicious judgement should feel God as judge and avenger.... Those who freely shed the blood of others are now forced to spill their own. Some... lie unburied, food for the beasts and the birds of the air. Others who unjustly killed vast numbers of people have individually been torn limb from limb.... Their judgements killed many husbands, widowed many women, orphaned many children. They made them beggars and left them bare... for they plundered the children of the men they killed. Now it is their wives who are widows, their sons who are orphans, begging their daily bread.[18]

If Christian apologists such as Orosius and Roman panegyricists such as Merobaudes were inclined to understate the degree of chaos, dislocation, and bloodshed resultant from the events of the early fifth century, Christian moralists such as the 'Sicilian Briton' or Salvian of Marseilles (encountered in Chapter One) naturally tended to adopt an exaggerated and apocalyptic tone. There is good reason to believe, however, that it was those who sought to downplay violence, warfare, and destruction who were the most guilty of abusing and distorting reality.

To take the question of 'enemy numbers', for example: it is clear that the Roman Empire in the West in the fifth century was not (as some once thought) simply swept away by an enormous wave of mass migration by clearly articulated protonational tribes from beyond its frontiers. The barbarian peoples that entered Roman territory, such as the Goths of 376, or the Vandals, Suevi, and Alans of 405–6, seem initially to have operated in groups of relatively modest size—although it is far from impossible that, in certain instances at least (such as in parts of northern Gaul and lowland Britain), these initial invaders were then followed by successive and archaeologically invisible waves of peasant migrants.[19] Once within Roman territory, however, the disparate and differing groups of invaders had a natural incentive to band together either against other 'barbarians' or, more commonly, against the Romans. The Romans in turn sought to respond to this by themselves mobilising against the invaders and other barbarian groups, such as the Huns, who were drawn ever more deeply into the military and political life of the Western Empire. Indeed, even before the period of the invasions, such 'barbarian peoples' had long possessed a highly composite and federative character, coalescing and dispersing according to the renown and fortunes of individual leaders.[20] As a result, the composite barbarian armies that crossed into Roman territory and then formed larger confederations once within it were capable of posing a real and effective challenge to the imperial army and of inflicting an enormous amount of damage, as the Goths clearly did in the northern Balkans. It is instructive, for example, that in the wake of Alaric's descent on Rome, the Emperor Honorius felt obliged in the year 412 to instruct the Praetorian Prefect of Italy to reduce to one-fifth of their customary amount the taxes reckoned on the provinces

---

[18] Morris (1965), p. 34. I see no reason to accept Morris' suggestion that this description need record a specifically British reality associated with the revolt against Constantine III of 410–11.

[19] P. Heather, *Empires and Barbarians: Migration, Development, and the Birth of Europe* (London, 2009), pp. 266–332.

[20] Wood (1998), p. 516.

of Campania, Tuscany, Picenium, Samnium, Apulia, Calabria, Bruttium, and Lucania for a period of five years.[21]

But how large were these composite barbarian armies? The Visigoths of Alaric and Athaulf represented one such group, made up of members of those Gothic tribes who had crossed into imperial territory in 376 (the 'Tervingi' and 'Greuthungi') as well as the remnants of Radagaisus' defeated Gothic host of 405–6. Radagaisus' army seems to have comprised something in the order of twenty thousand fighting men, twelve thousand of whom were enrolled into Roman service after his death. Including non-combatants (women, children, slaves), this would suggest that initially he had probably entered Roman territory with some one hundred thousand or so followers.[22] Alaric and Athalaric are unlikely to have led any fewer; potentially they led many more. In 408, we are told, Alaric's army in Italy, consisting of both Goths and Huns, found its numbers swelled by Roman slaves eager to take vengeance on their masters. As Zosimus records: 'day by day almost all the slaves that were in Rome poured out of the city to join the barbarians, who now numbered about 40,000'.[23] At the time of their crossing the straits to Africa in c.422, the Vandals and their Alan allies (who had originally come together in response to the joint Visigothic and Roman offensive against them) were estimated to have numbered some eighty thousand, indicating a core fighting force of perhaps fifteen thousand or so men. This may not sound that many given the tens of thousands of Roman soldiers under arms, at least on paper, in the West at this time (seventy thousand or so would perhaps be an optimistic estimate); but it was very rare indeed for the imperial government in the West ever to be able to raise, mobilise, and concentrate more than fifteen thousand men for the purpose of a single campaign. Fifteen thousand, for example, was roughly the number of troops deployed against Radagaisus in Italy in 406: there are likely to have been far fewer troops available to defend north Africa.

Of course, as the *Querolus*, with its talk of peasants administering justice, or the servile defections to Alaric in 408 remind us, it was not just barbarians who threatened the established order. As noted in Chapter One, the period 406–18 also witnessed a number of uprisings, especially in Spain and north-western Gaul, on the part of so-called *bacaudae*, some at least of whom appear to have been peasants attempting either to defend their own families and communities amidst the unsettled conditions of the age, or to take advantage of the social dislocation resulting from warfare to settle social scores and shake off deeply resented aristocratic control. Contrary to common assertion, this claim rests on more than mere wishful thinking on the part of armchair Marxists: as the writings of the Sicilian Briton and his talk of 'common' preachers in rags lambasting the wealthy reveals, social criticism of the elite was a genuine feature of the period. Sources written by

---

[21] Heather (2005), p. 246.
[22] Heather (2005), p. 198.
[23] Zosimus, *New History*, V.42. For Huns, see ibid., V.37: Alaric summoned his brother-in-law Athaulf out of Pannonia with his 'considerable army of Huns and Goths' to join him in his Italian campaign.

members of the elite themselves reveal, moreover, that peasants had indeed taken advantage of uncertainty and strife to seek to overturn social norms. Around the year 417, for example, the Gallic statesman and poet Rutilius Namatianus lauded what he saw as an anticipated restoration of imperial fortunes by describing in his poem 'On His Return' (*de Reditu Suo*) how a certain Exuperantius was currently engaged in 'teaching the shores of the Armorican provinces to love the return of peace:/he restores laws and returns liberty/and no longer permits servants to make slaves of their masters' (I, 212–16).

It has been suggested that Rutilius Namatianus' journey from Rome to Gaul, which he describes in his poem, was motivated by a desire to be present at the 'Council of the Gauls' that Honorius had summoned, and to secure the contours of his estates against the settlement of the Visigoths in Aquitaine which the council may have been convened to discuss and arrange.[24] The peace negotiated between the Roman Empire's western commander-in-chief, or *magister militum*— Flavius Constantius—and the Visigoths was probably the key to our author's optimism. Certainly, there is evidence that, as the invaders of 405–6 had been drawn closer to the Mediterranean core of the Western Empire, especially in southern Gaul, their ferocity had dissipated and the imperial authorities had achieved greater success in terms of inflicting localised defeats upon them, or at least of avoiding defeat themselves. Although the circumstances are unclear, the settlement of the Visigoths in Aquitaine, for example, appears to have been precipitated by three factors: first, Flavius Constantius is reported to have successfully cut off their food supplies and forced them from Narbonne into Spain; second, an attempted Visigothic crossing into Africa was scuppered by an unexpected storm; and third, Flavius Constantius was able to take advantage of a crisis of leadership amongst the Goths occasioned by the subsequent, and presumably related, murder of Athaulf in 415.[25]

Taking advantage of the Visigoths' momentary weakness to draw them into alliance with the imperial authorities, Flavius Constantius had then, as we have seen, mobilised them in a joint campaign against the Vandals and Alans in Spain, who subsequently joined forces and successfully crossed into Africa. Likewise, the settlement of the Burgundians in Sapaudia (Savoy) *c.*436–7 had been preceded by a significant defeat that was inflicted on them by a force consisting of Romans and Huns pieced together by Aetius, who had himself been a diplomatic hostage at the Hunnic court and so knew their ways well.[26] After this victory, Aetius had even been able to re-establish control over the *bacaudae* of Armorica (Brittany) with the aid of an army substantially made up of Alans.[27] In return for their assistance, these Alans had then been settled *c.*440, first around the city of Valence, and subsequently in the region of *Gallia Ulterior*.[28] It may well have been this temporary restoration of Roman control over Armorica, combined with an escalation of Pictish, Saxon, and

---

[24] Wood (1998), p. 531. [25] ibid., pp. 530–1.
[26] ibid., p. 519. [27] Heather (2005), p. 287.
[28] Wood (1998), p. 519.

Irish aggression at home, that induced members of the Romano-British leadership to appeal to Aetius for military assistance at some point between 446 and 452.[29]

These negotiated settlements of Visigoths, Burgundians, and Alans stand in marked contrast to the situation that had prevailed in many of Rome's north-western provinces in the period c.406–16, when landowners had suffered confiscation of property, or worse, at the hands of invader and peasant alike. However, it would be a mistake to assume, as Rutilius Namatianus clearly did, that the beast—be it barbarian or bacaudic—was now firmly under control. Flavius Constantius had provided the imperial army in Italy and Gaul with energetic leadership, and in 421 he himself became Emperor. His death the same year, however, heralded a renewed struggle for power in Rome and Ravenna, which opened the way to further barbarian territorial encroachment, above all the joint Vandal-Alan takeover of Africa. From 432 Aetius was similarly able to restore some sort of order in southern Gaul, but, as we have seen, only by inciting barbarian against barbarian: his successful harnessing of the power of the Huns against the Burgundians, for example, was effectively achieved only at the price of ceding control of Roman territory along the River Save in Pannonia, thereby intensifying the potential Hunnic threat to Roman positions in the Balkans.[30] It was, in turn, the realisation of this threat that, as noted earlier, undid the joint attempt by Ravenna and Constantinople to reconquer Africa in 440–41. Nor were the Roman authorities entirely in control even of these 'negotiated' settlements. In *Gallia Ulterior*, for example, resistance on the part of local landowners to the settlement of the Alans there simply induced the barbarians to take what they wanted by force.[31]

The common thread that unites the period between the limited military revivals of Flavius Constantius around 420 and Aetius in the 430s and 440s is the growing invisibility of the Roman field army. Increasingly, it is clear that Roman success came to depend upon the empire's diplomatic ability to mobilise barbarian against barbarian and, especially in the period of Aetius' ascendancy, its ability to secure the support of the Huns. In 431, for example, Aetius received a request for military assistance from the cities of Gallaecia in north-western Spain. In response, the imperial government dispatched a single officer, who was meant to enter into negotiations with the Suevi.[32] Increasingly constrained by the administrative and political dislocation of the Roman state and, especially after the loss of Africa, a haemorrhaging of the crucial tax revenues upon which the empire depended militarily, the Roman army effectively 'delegated itself out of existence'.[33] As a result, even in the core Mediterranean provinces, the balance of power began to shift remorselessly and irreversibly against Rome. After c.440 we hear no more of negotiated barbarian settlement anywhere outside Italy. Aetius' settlement of the Burgundians in Savoy in c.442, to protect the Alpine approaches to Italy, was to all

---

[29] T. Charles-Edwards, *After Rome* (Oxford, 2003), pp. 25–9, for elucidation of the chronology. For the Saxon threat, see *Chronicon ad annum 452 s.a*, 441–2.
[30] Heather (2005), p. 287.
[31] Wood (1998), p. 523.
[32] Hydatius, *s.a.*, 431.
[33] R. Collins, *Early Medieval Europe*, 3rd edition (London, 2010).

intents and purposes the end of the policy of deliberately settling barbarians in the Western Empire. Thereafter, concessions to the barbarians tended to be little more than official recognition of barbarian takeovers (akin to the treaties with the Vandals in Africa).[34]

This phenomenon is especially evident with respect to Aetius' great showdown with the Huns in 451. United under the leadership of Attila and his brother Bleda, the Huns in 441–2 had launched a massive and unprovoked assault upon Roman positions in the northern Balkans, an act that was repeated in 447 (under Attila alone) amid much bloodshed. In response to this, the authorities in Constantinople were obliged to hand over significant sums of tribute.[35] Such tribute played an important role in the internal cohesion of the Hunnic Empire, which was by this point made up of subject peoples from the Rhine to the Black Sea, whose loyalty to the Hunnic leadership was ultimately ensured by means of a precariously balanced combination of booty and fear.

Since the Gothic uprising of 378, however, the economic resources of the northern Balkans in particular had been seriously depleted, and Attila showed little sign of being able to storm the formidable Land Walls of Constantinople that Theodosius II had erected in response to the Hunnic threat (Fig. 3). The cities of the southern Balkans, moreover, were not particularly wealthy, and were in any case protected by a densely mountainous terrain that posed a major obstacle to Attila and his mounted warriors. Cavalry warfare and mountains do not go together. As a result, by the late 440s, Attila seems to have realised that he had probably extracted all he could from the Eastern Empire and so made the decision to head west, leading his armies, made up of his Hunnic followers and non-Hunnic subjects, on the war trail to Gaul. As the near-contemporary Gallic statesman and aristocrat, Sidonius Apollinaris, wrote: 'Suddenly the barbarian world, rent by a mighty upheaval, poured the whole of the North into Gaul. After the warlike Rugian comes the fierce Gepid, with the Gelonian close by; the Burgundian urges on the Scirian; forward rush the Hun, the Bellonotian, the Neurian, the Bastarnian, the Thuringian, the Bructeran, the Frank.'[36]

At the battle of the Catalaunian Plains in 451, at an unknown location in Gaul, Aetius faced down his erstwhile Hunnic allies. Against the Huns, he too had assembled a vast coalition, very similar in composition, in fact, to that led by Attila. As Jordanes was to describe the scene in his sixth-century *Gothic History*:

> On the side of the Romans stood the Patrician Aetius, on whom at that time the whole of the Empire of the West depended; a man of such wisdom that he had assembled warriors from everywhere to meet them [the Huns] on equal terms. Now these were his auxiliaries: Franks, Sarmatians, Armoricians, Liticians, Burgundians, Saxons, Ripuarians, Olybriones (once Roman soldiers and now the flower of the allied forces), and some other Celtic or Germanic tribes. And so they met in the Catalaunian Plains, which are also called Mauriacian. . . . That portion of the earth accordingly became the

---

[34] A point made forcefully by Wood (1998), p. 520.
[35] Heather (2005), p. 307.
[36] Sidonius Apollinaris, *Carmina*, 7.

Fig. 3 The Theodosian Land Walls (C. Mango, *The Oxford History of Byzantium*, p. 67)

threshing-floor of countless races. The two hosts bravely joined battle. Nothing was done under cover, but they contended in open fight. What just cause can be found for the encounter of so many nations, or what hatred inspired them all to take arms against each other? It is proof that the human race lives for its kings, for it is at the mad impulse of one mind that a slaughter of nations takes place, and at the whim of a haughty ruler that that which nature has taken ages to produce perishes in a moment.[37]

In the bloodbath that ensued, Aetius and his allies were able to inflict a notable defeat on the Huns and their followers, although amongst the fatalities on the 'Roman' side was the Visigothic king Theoderic I. Yet what is most striking about this encounter is the conspicuous absence from this grand anti-Hunnic coalition of any significant component of the West Roman field army. Indeed, rather than a life or death struggle between Attila and his Huns on the one hand, and Aetius, fighting on behalf of the Emperor on the other, in many respects the Battle of the Catalaunian Plains has all the hallmarks of a struggle between a Hunnic-dominated coalition and a Visigothic-dominated one as to who would enjoy the lion's share of

[37] Jordanes, *Getica*, 36.

the spoils of Roman disintegration. Frank fought against Frank, Goth against Goth, and Burgundian against Burgundian. Contrary to the Roman slant of our sources, Aetius may have been little more than a bit-player in an epic struggle from which the Visigoth Theoderic might well have emerged the real victor, had Fate not instead cast him as the fallen hero. It is instructive that when, in 455, the Western emperor Valentinian III was assassinated, the candidacy of his short-lived successor, Avitus, seems to have been sponsored by Theoderic's son, Theoderic II, with the support of some tame Gallo-Roman senators. It was the Goths who now had the upper hand.

Rather, for Rome, the real showdown came in 452, when Attila led his forces into Italy. He again here encountered negligible resistance on the part of the surviving Roman field army and, as we have seen, was only forced back from Rome itself by the onset of malaria. Nevertheless, his failed campaigns of 451 and 452 evidently did much to dent Attila's reputation for invincibility; when he died unexpectedly in 453, his empire soon began to enter into a rapid process of fragmentation, as one subject people after another broke away from Hunnic domination.

In many ways the collapse of Attila's empire served only to tilt the balance of power in the Western Empire's core territories ever further against a restoration of imperial control. For, unlike in the 430s, from the 450s onwards the Huns could no longer be looked to as a counterweight to burgeoning barbarian pressure closer to home. First the Emperor Majorian, who reigned from 458 to 461, then the Eastern general Anthemius, who ascended the Western throne in 467, sought to remedy this situation by restoring Africa to imperial control in 461 and 468 respectively. Each effort, as we shall see in Chapter Three, was to end in ignominious failure, serving only to further bankrupt and emasculate a Western court that was palpably teetering on the brink.

Anthemius was widely mistrusted by members of the Gallo-Roman aristocracy, who regarded him as little more than a puppet of the Eastern Emperor. Certainly, his accession in 467, and the failure of his attempt on Africa in 468, heralded an era of renewed aggression on the part of the Visigoths. In 467–8, as noted in Chapter One, the new Visigothic king Euric was advised by the Praetorian Prefect of Gaul, Arvandus, to divide the province between himself and the king of the Burgundians, casting aside any notion of imperial overlordship. Euric probably did not need any encouragement: as Jordanes records, 'now Euric, king of the Visigoths, perceived the frequent change of Roman emperors and strove to hold Gaul by his own right'.[38]

In response, Anthemius summoned assistance from a certain Riothamus, a Romano-British warlord who had carved out an autonomous enclave for himself in Armorica (Brittany). Not surprisingly, this Riothamus has often been associated with the King Arthur of legend. As Jordanes continues: 'the King Riothamus came with twelve thousand men ... Euric, king of the Visigoths came against them with an innumerable army, and after a long fight he routed Riothamus, king of the

---

[38] Jordanes, *Getica*, 4.45.

Britons, before the Romans could join him.'[39] Riothamus fled to the king of the Burgundians, but Euric emerged from the engagement in control of the cities of Tours and Bourges, before finding any further northern advance checked by the king of the Franks, Childeric, supported by remnants of the Roman army of the Rhine under the command of a certain Count Paul.[40]

Euric now bore down on what remained of the Roman Empire in southern Gaul: in 471 he defeated an army sent against him from Italy led by Anthemius' son, Anthemiolus. Anthemius was assassinated by his son-in-law Ricimer, having, as Jordanes put it, 'worn out Rome'. Euric now began to apply steady pressure on Arles, the capital of Roman Gaul. The imperial authorities attempted to buy him off by ceding the Auvergne to the Visigoths in 474–5. In 476, however, his armies took control of Arles and Marseilles, the only two cities of any significance still in Roman hands. That same year his forces completed their conquest of the Iberian peninsula, which had been initiated in 473 with the capture of Tarragona and the cities of the Mediterranean littoral. Only a rump Suevic kingdom now survived beyond Visigothic control in the peninsula's mountainous north-west.[41] A failed Visigothic attempt to initiate the conquest of Italy coincided with the deposition of the last Western Roman Emperor—Romulus 'Augustulus'—at the hands of his Gothic general Odoacer. By the end of 476, the 'gradual collapse' and 'imperceptible barbarisation' of the Roman realm in the West perceived by Zosimus were, to all intents and purposes, now complete. Change, however, had been the result not just of the weakness of the Romans, but also and above all, the strength of their enemies—a fact that ran contrary to every presupposition that the Roman governing classes had held.

2.3 'ROMANS' AND 'BARBARIANS' IN AN AGE OF TRANSITION

With respect to the Christianisation of the Roman Empire, Saint Augustine had declared that it was 'easier to remove the idols from the temples than it was to remove them from men's hearts'.[42] Likewise, it was of course easier to disable and dismantle the Western Roman Empire as a politically and militarily effective power structure than it was to eliminate deference, reverence, or loyalty to the idea of Rome or to the ideology of empire, on the part of members of its old governing classes. As we have seen, belief in the innate superiority of the Roman elite male over the rest of humanity, and, above all, over the barbarian, was fundamental to the mentality and self-perception of men such as Paulinus of Pella and Sidonius Apollinaris, Gallo-Roman aristocrats whose writings enable us to chart the course of the Roman Empire's political fragmentation in southern Gaul from the 430s to the 470s. It is a sign of the intensity of the political and military crisis that characterised

---

[39] ibid. [40] Heather (2005), p. 416.
[41] Heather (2005), p. 417. [42] Augustine, *Epistolae*, 232.

much of the period from 406 to 476, however, that, from a very early date, we begin to see signs of such attitudes giving way to a more pragmatic mindset.

Of course, one should not overstate the ease or smoothness of any such transition. The initial instinct of many landowners when faced with barbarian invaders was to fight, making use of their own private militias or personal retinues.[43] As noted earlier, this phenomenon was particularly evident in Britain or in parts of Spain, where landowners rapidly adopted a more martial aspect to defend their interests. As early as 408–9, for example, we see the Emperor Honorius' Spanish relatives, Flavius Verenianus and his brothers, mobilising an army composed of estate workers and slaves to confront the forces of the 'usurper' Constantine III. Strictly speaking, such private armies were illegal. However, given the objective military circumstances, even the imperial government was obliged to turn a blind eye to such manifest breaches of the civil law; indeed, in 440, in response to the threat posed to Italy by the Vandal fleet, the government had lifted the prohibition on private citizens bearing arms in the hope that the coastline could be defended 'by means of a loyal conspiracy and a joining together of shields'.[44] When, in the early 470s, the Auvergne was ceded to Visigothic control, some of the Roman landowners determined to fight on: Sidonius Apollinaris, for example, praised his brother-in-law Ecdicius (a son of the Emperor Avitus) for raising a modest military retinue with which he managed to lift the Visigothic siege of his native city of Clermont: 'At the mere mention of your name and the sight of your person a well-seasoned army was so utterly astounded that the enemy generals in their amazement could not realise how many were their followers and how few yours. The whole army was at once withdrawn to the brow of a precipitous hill, and, though previously employed in a storming assault, was not deployed for an encounter after sighting you.'[45]

Such 'self-help' on the part of members of the Roman provincial aristocracy was, of course, a high-risk strategy. The use of agricultural workers and slaves as private armed retainers can only have served to focus the attention of barbarian warlords on villa complexes: controlling estates thus became the key to pinning down terrain and consolidating conquest.[46] It is instructive, for example, how many of the earliest Anglo-Saxon settlements appear to have been located on Romano-British villa sites.[47] Moreover, when it came to mounting such resistance, some landowners were in a stronger position than others: as noted earlier, in parts of upland Britain, Armorica, and Spain, traditions of militarised tribal leadership had long persisted alongside, or beyond reach of, Roman social institutions. The mainstay of the Roman provincial aristocracy, however, was primarily civilian in character. Sidonius Apollinaris, who served briefly as Urban Prefect of the city of Rome in the 460s, was a man of letters rather than a man of war: any attempt on his

---

[43] Sarris (2006), pp. 162–73.
[44] *Nov. Val.*, 9.1.
[45] Sidonius Apollinaris, *Epistolae*, III.3. See also Gregory of Tours, *Decem Libri Historiae*, II, 16.
[46] I owe this insight to the important work of Leif Petersen, whose study of the subject is eagerly anticipated.
[47] K. Dark, *Britain and the End of the Roman Empire* (Stroud, 2000), p. 58.

part to break through the serried ranks of the Visigothic host would have come to an inglorious end. His brother-in-law Ecdicius, by contrast, probably had a background in the imperial army: in 474–5 he was appointed commander-in-chief, or *magister militum*, of the remaining (essentially vestigial) imperial forces in Gaul, before being recalled to Italy and dismissed.

For those who could not, or would not fight, there were essentially two options. The first was to take flight. Realistically, only those who also possessed property beyond the most severely affected provinces, in Italy or, better still in Constantinople and the East, were in a position to make this choice. In the 410s Paulinus of Pella considered abandoning his native Aquitaine to take up residence on his family's estates in Greece.[48] He would go on to regret his failure to do so.[49] In the aftermath of the Vandal conquest of Byzacena and *Africa Proconsularis*, where the estates of many of the grandest senatorial families were concentrated, the Emperor Valentinian III attempted to compensate landowners for the losses they had incurred, while African émigrés in Constantinople complained bitterly of their fate.[50] Flight, therefore, was primarily the reserve of members of the upper echelons of the Roman senatorial order, with access to far-ranging and trans-regional estates. For their more provincially focused neighbours and cousins, by contrast, there was a pressing imperative to attempt to come to terms with the barbarians in their midst.

To some extent, their ability to do so was facilitated by aspects of the political and administrative evolution of the late-Roman world. By virtue of the separation of military and civilian career structures associated with the 'Diocletianic' reforms, and the recruitment of non-Romans into the imperial military, over the course of the fourth century the Roman army had come to develop an increasingly distinct and distinctive subculture which was in many respects closer to the martial ethos and lifestyle of the 'barbarian' leadership than the civilian *mores* of men such as Sidonius Apollinaris. In 361, for example, when Julian had been acclaimed emperor by the field army in Gaul, his men had raised him up upon a shield. This was a practice of Germanic or Celtic origin, utterly alien to 'Roman' tradition. The high command of the Roman army in the West, moreover, had long been dominated by *magistri militum* of barbarian origin, such as Arbogast, Stilicho, or Ricimer. In that sense, irrespective of the prejudices of ideology, doing business with an Athaulf, a Theoderic, or a Euric may not have been that different from doing business with the local *dux*, or the *magister militum* at Vienne, Ravenna, or Milan.

Crucially, as early as the 410s, members of the Gallo-Roman aristocracy in northern Gaul had begun to identify in the barbarian warlord at hand a surer guarantor of their physical security than the ever more distant person of the Emperor. The settlement of the Visigoths in Aquitaine *c.*418 as imperial federate troops (*foederati*), or of the Burgundians in Savoy *c.*442, can only have extended and intensified such sentiment. The more local society came to depend for its security upon the locally preponderant Frankish, Gothic, or Burgundian warlord,

---

[48] Paulinus of Pella, *Eucharisticon*, pp. 271–3.
[49] ibid., pp. 408–25.   [50] See *Nov. Val.*, 34.1.

the more pressing became the need for local members of the Roman governing classes to reconcile themselves to the new political realities and engage with the barbarian leadership in a more constructive manner.

Relations were potentially at their most sensitive when it came to issues of land.[51] In the late-Roman world, as in all pre-industrial societies, land was the safest investment for wealth and offered the most reliable return. Accordingly, it is only natural that the invaders of the late fourth and early fifth centuries, many of whom had previously been sedentary agriculturalists, should have regarded prime agricultural land as constituting the spoils of war *par excellence*. In this respect groups such as the Goths, the Burgundians, and the Vandals were fundamentally different from the tribute-hungry nomadic Huns (although even the nomadic Alans clearly appreciated the benefits of acquiring landed estates). When the imperial authorities wanted to make peace with these barbarians, it was land that they offered them. The hard-line Eastern bishop Syncsius of Cyrene, for example, was contemptuous of how Theodosius I had bought peace with the Goths in the aftermath of the Battle of Adrianople. 'The same blond barbarians,' he declared, 'who in private life fulfil the role of domestic servants now give us orders in public life. The emperor, by excess clemency, treated them with gentleness and indulgence, gave them the title of allies, conferred upon them political rights and honours, generously made them gifts of lands. But they did not understand and appreciate the nobility of this treatment. They interpreted it as weakness on our part, and that inspired in them an insolent arrogance and boastfulness.'[52]

If land was not offered, the invaders were more than willing to take it. In Spain, for example, Hydatius records that in *c*.411 the invading Alans, Vandals, and Suevi 'apportioned to themselves by lot parts of the provinces to inhabit' (*sorte ad inhabitandum sibi provinciarum dividunt regiones*).[53] 'The Vandals,' he continues, 'occupied Gallaecia, and the Suevi that part which is situated on the western edge of the Ocean. The Alans were allotted (*sortiuntur*) the provinces of Lusitania and Carthagiensis, and the Vandals, known as the Silingi, Baetica.' The focus here was on territory and occupancy—'parts of the provinces to inhabit'—but what was being carved up here almost certainly also included shares in whatever tribute could be extracted from local civic communities or landowners. A similar emphasis on the mastery of soil is evident in the division of Roman territory into shares or allotments (*sortes*) in the aftermath of the Vandal conquest of Africa. Here Victor of Vita records the persecution of Catholics 'on the Vandal portions' (*in sortibus Vandalorum*), indicating that such shares must have had a physical dimension, and

---

[51] Halsall (2007), pp. 422–46, and 'The Techniques of Barbarian Settlement in the Fifth Century: A Reply to Walter Goffart', in *Journal of Late Antiquity* 3.1 (2010), pp. 99–112; W. Goffart, *Barbarian Tides: The Migration Age and the Later Roman Empire* (Philadelphia, 2006), pp. 119–86—summarised in his 'The Techniques of Barbarian Settlement in the Fifth Century: A Personal, Streamlined Account with Ten Additional Comments', in *Journal of Late Antiquity* 3.1 (2010), pp. 65–98; I. Wood, 'Appendix: The Settlement of the Burgundians', in H. Wolfram and W. Pohl (eds.), *Typen der Ethnogenese* (Vienna, 1990), pp. 65–9; Jones (1964), pp. 248–53.

[52] Grant (1976), p. 131.

[53] Hydatius, *Chronicon s.a.*, 411.

were not simply shares of tax revenues, as some have suggested.[54] He also records that Catholic priests were forcibly turned into tied agricultural labourers, or *coloni originarii*, presumably to serve their new Vandal masters.[55] As we shall see in Chapter Three, the Greek historian Procopius paints an evocative picture of the idyllic lifestyle of the nouveau riche Vandal aristocracy that emerged as a result of this takeover of land.

After assisting Aetius against the Armoricans in the 430s, a contemporary chronicle records that the Alans were rewarded with land that had been abandoned by its owners (*rura deserta*, presumably signifying the *agri deserti* of imperial legislation) around the city of Valence. As we have seen, however, when Roman landowners in the region of *Gallia Ulterior* baulked at the prospect of handing over more territory to them, the Alans simply seized it. As the chonicler records, 'the Alans, to whom lands in farther Gaul had been assigned by the patrician Aetius to be divided along with its inhabitants, subdued those who resisted by force of arms, and ejecting the owners, took possession of the land by force.'[56]

In Spain, Africa, and parts of north-central Gaul, therefore, land was seized, although one should not imagine that there occurred a uniform or blanket confiscation of estates. Rather, lands belonging to the imperial government and the wealthiest members of the senatorial aristocracy, whose careers and trans-regional interests drew them away from the provinces or who were in the best position to flee, are likely to have been the first to be expropriated. The acquisition of entire functioning estates, however, emerges as a major objective of the barbarian leadership: the Alans, as mentioned, had been promised 'lands to be divided up along with their inhabitants' (*terrae . . . cum incolis dividendae*). Land also featured prominently in the negotiated settlement of the Visigoths and Burgundians in Aquitaine and Savoy. Hydatius, for example, records how the Goths were 'summoned back to Gaul by Constantius, and accepted an abode in Aquitaine from Toulouse to the Ocean'—effectively the Garonne valley.[57] The later legal evidence contained in the *Codex Euricianus* refers to the existence of a Roman 'third' (*tertia*), implying a division of certain estates two-to-one in favour of the Gothic settlers.[58] On face value, this ties in well with the early sixth-century legal evidence for Savoy contained in the 'Book of Constitutions', or *Liber Constitutionum*, collated by the Burgundian king Sigismund *c.*517, which refers to 'our people' (meaning the Burgundians) receiving two-thirds of the land, one-third of the bondsmen, and half of any assarted (or cleared) woodland in certain of the areas where they had settled.[59]

That there should have been broad similarities between the negotiated settlements in Aquitaine and Savoy would seem logical, and these arrangements in turn are likely to have served as a model for the settlement of barbarian troops in Italy

---

[54] Victor of Vita, *History of the Vandal Persecution*, tr. J. Moorhead (Liverpool, 1992), 2.39.
[55] ibid., 3.20.
[56] *Chronicle of 452, s.a.,* 440–43.
[57] Hydatius, *s.a.,* 418.
[58] *Codex Euricianus,* 277 = *Lex Visigothorum,* X, 2, 1.
[59] *Liber Constitutionum,* 54.

under first Odoacer and then Theoderic the Ostrogoth. The Greek historian Procopius, for example, who saw active military service in Italy, states that Theoderic rewarded his Goths with 'that portion of the estate villages (*chôria*) which Odoacer had given to his own followers'.[60] A panegyric written by Cassiodorus expressly records a transfer of landed property from Roman civilian to Gothic soldier:

> It is my delight to mention how, in the assignment of thirds, he [the civil servant Liberius] united both the possessions and hearts of Goths and Romans. For though men usually quarrel when they are neighbours, here the sharing of rights in estates seems to have produced concord. For the result has been that both peoples, while living together, have achieved accord. Behold an unprecedented and wholly praiseworthy accomplishment: division of the soil has joined its title-holders in goodwill: the friendship of the people has grown through loss, for the cost of a part of the land, a defender has been purchased, and property preserved secure and intact. A single and just law embraces all. For sweet affection must develop among those who always share fixed boundaries.[61]

In each instance, however, the process whereby the Gothic or Burgundian settlers came to acquire full ownership over such lands appears to have been more gradual and varied than has sometimes been supposed.[62] Nor were boundaries anywhere near as 'fixed' as Cassiodorus attempted to reassure his Roman senatorial audience they would be. Under the euphemistic and socially acceptable language of hospitality (*hospitalitas*), Gothic and Burgundian retainers acquired interests in and rights over land. The precise nature and chronological duration of those rights, however, may initially have been left deliberately vague. Certainly, there is evidence from the Burgundian kingdom of the early sixth century to suggest that Roman landowners sought to claim that the rights held by Burgundian settlers on parts of 'their' estates were essentially usufructuary (that is, granting them rights to the produce of such lands), potentially limited in duration to the lifetime of the beneficiary. Attempts on the part of Roman landowners to reassert control over such property may have been one of the factors that induced the Burgundian king Sigismund to collate previous legislation, consolidating and confirming full rights of ownership for the descendants of the initial generation of Burgundian settlers over most of the land that they now occupied.[63] In the early fifth-century Balkans, East Roman aristocrats had been allowed to turn barbarian prisoners of war into tied agricultural labourers (*coloni adscripticii*) on their estates.[64] From the perspective of the surviving Roman landowners of early sixth-century Savoy, a similar solution would, no doubt, have been highly satisfactory. Sigismund could not allow that: in the Burgundian legislation, and elsewhere, the warrior-settlers and their descendants were referred to by the Germanic term *faramanni*—'the fellow travellers'—

---

[60] Procopius, *Wars*, V, 1.28.
[61] Cassiodorus, *Variae*, tr. S. Barnish (Liverpool, 1992), 2.16.
[62] M. Innes, 'Land, Freedom, and the Making of the Medieval West', *TRHS*, Sixth Series, 16 (2006), pp. 39–74.
[63] ibid., p. 65.
[64] *Codex Theodosianus*, 5.6.3.

free men united and dignified by the joint adventure of migration and conquest.[65] Their economic autonomy was to be safeguarded at all costs. As the *Liber Constitutionum* declared: 'Since we have learned that the shares of Burgundians can be pulled apart far too easily, we believe this measure must be added to the law as it stands: namely that no one be allowed to sell his land unless he owns a share or a property elsewhere.'[66]

The provisions contained in the *Codex Euricianus* and the *Liber Constitutionum* primarily concern the 'rank and file' of the Visigothic and Burgundian host and are relatively late in date. The barbarian leadership, by contrast, is likely to have acquired extensive landed property far earlier. In the 430s, for example, Paulinus of Pella records that a Goth purchased an estate from him in the region of Marseilles, while in the early sixth century, Procopius wrote of how the land-hungry Ostrogothic Prince Theodahad had 'become master of most of the estate properties in Tuscany and was eager by violent means to wrest the remainder from their owners ... to have a neighbour seemed to him a kind of misfortune'.[67] As both the writings of Paulinus and Procopius and the Burgundian legislation reveal, transfers of property were always fraught and could only serve to heighten social tensions. Nevertheless, at the end of the day, mindful of the chronic military insecurity, violence, and political dislocation that had characterised so much of the period from 406 to 476, Roman landowners had little choice but to face up to the shifting balance of power on the ground. If they failed to do so, they risked losing everything.

In those areas, such as Aquitaine and Savoy, where barbarian settlement was negotiated, the acquiescence of Roman landowners in the process whereby barbarian invaders became first settlers and then landowners in their own right was, in all likelihood, further facilitated by its comparative gradualness. This is at its most evident in the Burgundian legislation. With respect to barbarian landownership, the most important piece of legislation, contained in the *Liber Constitutionum*, is a law of King Gundobad of uncertain date, but most likely dating from the early years of the sixth century. The great evidential advantage of the comparative lateness of this law is that it alludes to successive earlier acquisitions of landed property by the king's Burgundian followers. The law is headed 'Concerning Those who Usurp a Third of the Bondsmen and Two-Thirds of the Estate contrary to the Public Prohibition', and the first paragraph of the text is worth quoting *in extenso*:

> Granted that at that time when our people received a third of the bondsmen (*mancipia*) and two-thirds of the estates, the instruction was issued by us such that whoever had already taken possession of an estate with bondsmen by virtue of Our generosity or that of Our forebears, should not demand either a third of the bondsmen nor two-thirds of the estate from that place in which he had had hospitality (*hospitalitas*) assigned; nevertheless, since we have learned there to be many who, mindless of the risks they run, have gone beyond the rules that had been set.... We order, therefore, that whatever can be shown to have been encroached upon of the estate of their host,

---

[65] Innes (2006), p. 62.   [66] *LC*, 84.1.
[67] Paulinus of Pella, *Eucharisticon*, 570–75; Procopius, *Wars*, V, 3.1–2.

contrary to the public prohibition, by those who have already acquired ownership through Our munificence, they are to return without delay.[68]

The reference in the law to estates and places at which the Burgundians had had 'hospitality' assigned probably reaches back to the very origins of the Burgundian settlement in the 440s. As we have seen, the Burgundians and the Visigoths were initially settled as imperial federate troops to defend the frontiers of the empire as they now effectively stood. The payment of federate and frontier troops with land was a long-standing Roman policy and is likely to have informed Burgundian expectations. Initially, however, the Burgundian rank and file appear to have been billeted or stationed on certain estates (*agri*) enjoying the 'hospitality' (*hospitalitas*) of the owner and, as a result, was granted or conceded little more than a right of occupancy.[69] As with other soldiers in imperial service, the Burgundians were probably able to demand supplies and maybe even stipends from such landowners. Certainly, the issuing of charges on landowners in order to support soldiers stationed in their vicinity is recorded in the imperial legislation from the 390s contained in the Theodosian Code: such troops bore documents authorising the delegation of tax revenues (*delegatoria*) in cash or kind, which they were to present.[70] Likewise, the papyrological record from Egypt reveals late-Roman landowners to have maintained troops on their estates as a public obligation (*munus*), and to have issued such soldiers and their officers with stipends and rations at their own expense.[71]

As an interim measure to support the rank and file of the Burgundian host, therefore, such an arrangement would have made sense, and there existed good Roman precedent for it. However, life as the billeted occupant of an estate would have held little appeal to the Burgundian leadership, and probably from the very inception of the Burgundian settlement the king and his companions-in-chief are likely to have received full-blown estates (*agri*) in their own right, along with the slaves and tied agricultural workers (*coloni originarii*) associated with such properties. It is these that the Burgundian legislation lumps together under the term *mancipia*, translated in the previous extract as 'bondsmen'. Such estates, as suggested earlier, were probably derived for the most part from absentee or fugitive landlords and from the extensive estates of the Crown.[72] That some *agri cum mancipiis* ('estates with bondsmen' or 'estates along with their dependent tenancies') were transferred into Burgundian ownership at the initial point of settlement is further suggested by the testimony of the fifth-century chronicle of Prosper, which records that in *c.*443 'Sapaudia was given to the remnants of the Burgundians to be divided along with its inhabitants' (*cum indigenis dividenda*).[73]

---

[68] *LC*, 54.1.
[69] For *hospitalitas* as 'occupancy', see Goffart (2006), p. 133.
[70] *Codex Theodosianus*, 7.4.22.
[71] Sarris (2006).
[72] M. Decker, *Tilling the Hateful Earth: Agricultural Production and Trade in the Late Antique East* (Oxford, 2009), p. 17 and pp. 31–3.
[73] Prosper, *s.a.*, 443.

In what we might think of as 'phase two', the law suggests that Gundobad or his father, King Gundioc, had then in turn rewarded certain of their more important followers or favoured retainers with *agri cum mancipiis*.⁷⁴ The recipients of such estates, however, were nevertheless obliged to remain associated with those Burgundians who continued to be primarily reliant on the 'hospitality' of Roman landowners (presumably to prevent the 'officer class' from becoming cut off from the rank and file). As this situation dragged on, there is likely to have been mounting pressure from the Burgundian soldiery to have their occupation, and use of those portions of Roman estates on which they had settled, put on a more permanent and secure footing. Such pressure may have become irresistible in the aftermath of the Burgundian civil war of *c*.500, and may well have been brought to bear directly upon landowners, now compelled simply to hand over land as a once-and-for-all solution to the endless cycle of requisition and supply that the Roman system of *delegatoria* had presupposed. Eventually, Gundobad resolved such tensions by sanctioning a transfer into Burgundian ownership of two-thirds of the land and one-third of the bondsmen of such properties as had continued to offer *hospitalitas*. This land was to be divided up amongst the *faramanni*, but the king expressly excluded from this redistribution those (presumably higher-ranking) Burgundians who had already received entire estates by way of royal gift, some of whom, the law records, nevertheless attempted to stake a claim. The shares of the estates so acquired could be bequeathed to male heirs 'by right of division' (*iure sortis*).⁷⁵ This was 'phase three'.

Any such division need not have been a terribly complicated affair: Roman law had prescribed that there be maintained detailed registers or 'descriptions' (*descriptiones*) of estates, listing the number of slaves, *coloni*, or oxen employed.⁷⁶ Such documents would have greatly facilitated partition. In associated legislation, the *Liber Constitutionum* goes on to detail arrangements whereby other 'barbarians' invited into Burgundian communities could come to acquire possession of such Burgundian 'shares' (*sortes*) as had been established from the division of Roman estates.⁷⁷ However, no doubt in response to Roman complaints, and in accordance with Roman law, land assarted by Burgundian 'guests' had to be shared equally with their Roman 'hosts', whilst the Roman landowner was granted a right of pre-emption should a Burgundian wish to sell his share. Even if the Roman landowner declined to exercise his option, the land could not be sold to anybody outside of what might be termed the 'community of the estate', thus preserving the landholding's contours prior to partition.⁷⁸

Over the course of the period from *c*.443 to 516, therefore, a plausible scenario is that the *hospitalitas* arrangement, whereby a connection was established between

---

⁷⁴ For the grant of entire estates to retainers, see *LC*, 55, *[agrum] quem barbarus ex integro cum mancipiis publica largitione perceperit*, and *LC extrav.*, XXI.14—estates granted by licence from the king—paralleled in the Visigothic provision, *Lex Visigothorum*, 10.1.8.
⁷⁵ See *LC*, 14.5, *tertiam . . . quam pater eius sortis iure possidens mortis tempore dereliquit*.
⁷⁶ *Codex Theodosianus*, 9.42.7.
⁷⁷ *Leges Burgundionum—Constitutiones Extravagantes*, 12, and *LC*, 79.
⁷⁸ *LC*, 54.2 and 84.

Burgundian warriors and individual estates, gradually slipped out of the control of Roman landowners as Burgundian political clout and military strength intensified on the ground. The Burgundians may initially have been settled in a position of relative military weakness vis-à-vis Aetius and his Hunnic allies, but they did not remain in that position for long. The *Liber Constitutionum*, for example, forbids Romans from acquiring Burgundian advocates in legal disputes and thereby benefiting unfairly from the Burgundians' greater social weight, or *patrocinium*: by the early sixth century it was the Burgundians who were the big men.[79]

A similar pattern is discernible with respect to the Visigothic settlement in the Garonne valley and its subsequent expansion. An initial transfer of agricultural land, presumably to the Visigothic leadership, is indicated by a surviving fragment of the fifth-century Greek historian Olympiodorus, who refers to the Goths being given Gallic lands to farm (*tôn Galatôn chôras eis geôrgian*).[80] As already mentioned, Paulinus of Pella, writing in the 430s, records that a Goth bought an estate from him, presumably investing either the fruits of war or of military service. The presence of Goths enjoying *hospitalitas* on estates, however, is recorded for Aquitaine in the early fifth century and the Auvergne in the 460s. Paulinus of Pella records that, alone amongst those of his neighbours, only his estates in the Garonne had 'lacked a Gothic host' (*hospite tunc etiam Gothico quae sola careret*), whilst later on his sons went to the family estates in the Bordeaux region, where they thought they would enjoy greater freedom 'although in company with a Gothic farmer' (*Gothico quamquam consorte colono*).[81] On these properties in the Bordelais, therefore, land was already coming under Gothic cultivation.

In a letter to Ecdicius in the late 460s, Sidonius Apollinaris complains that the governor or prefect, Seronatus, was in the process of jam-packing the estates of the Auvergne with 'guests' (*implet cotidie . . . villas hospitibus*), presumably barbarian.[82] Sidonius goes on to provide a vivid (if satirical) description of Burgundian 'guests' on his own estates, whom he was obliged to supply prior to the Visigothic takeover (when the Roman authorities in the Auvergne were evidently relying militarily upon Burgundian *foederati*).[83] In a verse to his friend, Catullinus, he wrote:

> Why—even supposing I had the skill—do you bid me compose a song dedicated to Venus . . . placed as I am among long-haired hordes, having to endure Germanic speech, praising oft with wry face the song of the gluttonous Burgundian who spreads rancid butter on his hair? Do you want me to tell you what drives away poetry? Driven away by barbarian thrumming, the Muse has spurned the six-footed verse ever since she saw these patrons seven-foot tall. I am minded to call your ears and eyes happy, happy too your nose, for you don't have the reek of garlic and foul onions discharged upon you at early morn from ten breakfasts, and you are not invaded, even before dawn, like an old grandfather or foster-father, by a crowd of giants so many and so big that not even the kitchen of Alcinous could support them.[84]

---

[79] *LC*, 22. [80] Olympiodorus, fr. 26.2.
[81] Paulinus, *Eucharisticon*, 285 and 502.
[82] Sidonius Apollinaris, *Epistolae*, II, 1.3.
[83] Sidonius Apollinaris, *Epistolae*, III, 4.
[84] Sidonius Apollinaris, *Carmina*, XII.

After the surrender of the Auvergne to Euric, the Burgundians on Sidonius' estates were seemingly replaced by Goths: Sidonius complains, for example, that after returning to his abode, his 'drooping eyelids scarcely got a wink of sleep; for a din would immediately arise from the two old Gothic women near the skylight of my bedroom, the most quarrelsome, drunken, vomiting creatures the world will ever see.'[85]

As in Burgundian Savoy, in the expanding Visigothic realm of the 460s and 470s, a system of *hospitalitas* was giving way to land transfers, and land transfers to new titles of ownership based on barbarian 'shares' (*sortes*) and Roman thirds (*tertiae*). In 468 the Visigothic king Euric decreed that 'Gothic shares and Roman thirds, which have not been revoked after fifty years, are in no way to be challenged.'[86] On the face of it this was a generous measure: fifty years was an unusually long period for appeal in Roman law. Appearances, however, can be deceptive. The time span of fifty years takes one back to the initial Gothic settlement of Aquitaine of 416–18; this decree was Euric's way of signalling that whatever the Goths had acquired, they would now keep, irrespective of any earlier agreement, or under whatever title they had acquired it. It should be noted that this legislation coincides with Euric's adoption of a much more militarily aggressive stance with respect to the remnants of the West Roman state.

A further parallel to the Burgundian situation is found in *Lex Visigothorum*, 10.1.8. This law records both the subsequent establishment of a boundary of demarcation between Visigothic and Roman 'thirds', and the mechanism by which the entirety of an estate could be gifted to a Visigothic retainer by the king. The measure is headed 'Concerning a Division of Lands Made Between a Goth and a Roman', and continues:

> once a division (*divisio*) has been made between a Goth and a Roman concerning a quantity of land or woods, it shall on no account be disturbed, so long as it can be proved that this division actually took place; provided, however, that no Roman shall take or claim for himself any of the two parts of the Goth, or that no Goth shall dare to usurp or claim any of the 'third' of the Roman, unless it has perchance been granted him by Our [*royal*] generosity.[87]

The various sub-regions of Spain, Gaul, and Italy experienced divergent fates and varying levels of violence in the troubled years from 406 to 476. As a result, one should be wary of imposing upon them too uniform a schema of barbarian settlement and land acquisition. In all of these areas, however, invaders and the descendants of invaders were landowners by the year 500. The acquisition of land is likely to have been at its most immediate where the Romans were at their weakest militarily, and where, as a result, land was seized by force: Vandal Africa or Alan *Gallia Ulterior* would be cases in point. In other regions, a transition towards

---

[85] Sidonius Apollinaris, *Epistolae*, III, 8.
[86] *Codex Euricianus*, 277; see also *Codex Euricianus*, 276.
[87] For *divisio* as physical division, see E. Levy, *West Roman Vulgar Law* (Philadelphia, 1951), pp. 84–5.

rewarding barbarian settlers with land, even where their settlement was negotiated, is also discernible from a relatively early date. The reasons for this are clear enough: the military and political dislocation of the Western Roman Empire, as we have seen, is likely to have posed the imperial authorities near insurmountable problems when it came to paying the standing army, and the Roman state had a long tradition of rewarding *foederati* and *limitanei* with land. In such circumstances, providing barbarian warriors, or their leaders, with land in return for military service made good sense. Indeed, as we shall see in Chapter Eight, the East Roman state would resort to a very similar solution when faced with military collapse in the mid-seventh century. This, in essence, is the Visigothic or Burgundian model.

Elsewhere, as in Italy under Odoacer and Theoderic the Ostrogoth, where imperial administrative traditions were at their most firmly rooted, late-Roman techniques of assigning locally collected tax revenues, or distributing supplies and rations derived from local estates to a now 'barbarised' military, are likely to have persisted for longer. Such procedures (out of which the Visigothic and Burgundian *hospitalitas* arrangements had emerged) clearly operated, however, alongside the military landholdings established by Odoacer and Theoderic, perhaps based on Burgundian or Visigothic models.[88] It is presumably because, as Procopius and Cassiodorus record, the settlement of barbarian troops in northern Italy immediately took the form of a distribution of land, that the word *hospitalitas* does not occur in the Italian sources.[89] From the start, these soldiers received a wage in the form of land, which was then supplemented by means of a cash donative. As the Ostrogothic king Athalaric informed his men: 'allotments of your own (*sortes... propriae*) feed you. Our gifts, God helping, enrich you'.[90]

It is significant that a system of assigned tax revenues is discernible in later Byzantine fiscal treatises, which record taxes from estates and estate settlements inhabited by *coloni* (Greek *paroikoi*) being allotted or diverted to beneficiaries nominated by the imperial government.[91] Such arrangements probably reflect earlier Roman practice. In Byzantium too, it should be noted, such a system was capable of existing alongside an emergent network of military landholdings supporting soldiers and their families. In that sense, Ostrogothic Italy in the early sixth century probably resembled parts of Byzantine Asia Minor in the eighth. In any such system, however, there would inevitably have been strong assimilative tendencies whereby those who had come to acquire assigned rights over estates or their revenues would seek to translate such rights into full ownership. As a result, no matter how varied the speed or rate of change, everywhere in the post-Roman West men of war were increasingly becoming men of property. Importantly, throughout this world, landholdings granted to soldiers and military retainers were exempted

---

[88] Jones (1964), p. 250 and p. 1,115 for references. For the possibility of a similar situation with respect to the Franks, see Halsall (2007), p. 447.
[89] Goffart (2006), p. 163.
[90] Cassiodorus, VIII, 26.4.
[91] Described in the Middle Byzantine 'Marcian Treatise'.

from taxation and other public burdens: consequently, the sources reveal the emergence of 'a new social order of landowners whose freedom was exemplified by the absence of tax and expressed through public military action'.[92]

It is sometimes asked why, if late-Roman landowners found themselves progressively denuded of portions of their estates, we have so little by way of a literature of complaint? Two solutions to this have already been signalled. First, imperial estates, and those of absentee landlords and fugitives, are likely to have been the first to be sequestrated. Certainly, in the Frankish north, imperial estates seem to have formed the core of those properties that would come into the possession of the Merovingian kings.[93] Nowhere was there a uniform programme of expropriation, and many estates are likely to have escaped intact. We can even identify well-connected Roman landowners in Vandal Africa who successfully weathered the storm.[94] Second, in some places, such as Burgundy, the process was sufficiently gradual that many Roman landowners may not have fully realised what was happening until it was too late. Traces of the complaints that emerged as a result are in a sense preserved in the legislation with which the Burgundian king Gundobad, or the Visigothic king Euric, responded to them.

Two further points need to be made, however. It is possible, and with respect to Italy it seems highly likely, that landowners who divested themselves of portions of their estates in favour of barbarian warriors saw an overall, and perhaps proportionately greater reduction in their tax assessment. Barbarian neighbours were, in other words, tax-deductible. But perhaps most importantly, having barbarian warriors on their land, or abutting their estates, potentially offered Roman landowners security. Given the chronically unsettled conditions through which many had lived, this consideration is not to be underestimated. The legislation for the more settled East Roman Empire in the fifth and sixth centuries records that landowners were positively eager to draw soldiers onto their estates in order to deploy them against their neighbours, rivals, and employees.[95] In the world of Rome's fragmenting western provinces, the need to acquire such assistance can only have been more pressing. Paulinus of Pella, for example, looked back to the 410s and 420s as a period of unmitigated disaster for himself and his family. One reason why his estates in the Auvergne had suffered so much from the effects of invasion and warfare, he felt, was because, unlike his neighbours, he had 'lacked a Gothic guest'. 'This circumstance,' he continues, 'was followed not long afterwards by a disastrous result, namely that, since no particular authority protected it, my estate was given up to be pillaged by the retiring horde; for I know that certain of the Goths most generously strove to serve their hosts by protecting them.'[96] We will

---

[92] Innes (2006), p. 73, citing Frankish evidence. Even in Vandal Africa, however, the picture was the same: see Procopius, *Wars*, III, 5.12. For Visigothic Spain, see *Lex Visigothorum*, 10.1.16.
[93] Jones (1964), p. 249, and Gregory of Tours, *Decem Libri Historiae*, V, 48, VI, 45, and V, 3. See also discussion in Halsall (2007).
[94] Such as, for example, Victorianus of Hadrumetum, whom Victor of Vita describes as the wealthiest man in Africa: Jones (1964), p. 249, and Victor of Vita, III, 27.
[95] Sarris (2006).
[96] Paulinus, *Eucharisticon*, 286–90.

never understand the actions or attitudes of members of the late-Roman aristocracy in the West unless we appreciate their intense and overriding yearning for security amid the troubled military conditions of the age. It was this desire, above all, that compelled them to enter into more cooperative and symbiotic relations with the barbarians with whom they found themselves confronted.

2.4 'ROMANITAS' AND ITS LIMITS

Certainly, although men such as Sidonius Apollinaris in the 460s and 470s were long to prove themselves capable of deploying anti-barbarian rhetoric or of falling back on the long-established literary *topoi* of the uncouth barbarian, his appetites tamed neither by reason nor breeding, such literary tropes were typically deployed in response to specific political circumstances. When Sidonius or his allies found themselves in conflict with individual barbarian leaders, or when Sidonius' rivals amongst the Gallo-Roman aristocracy were deemed to be benefiting from cooperation, the barbarians were presented as ravenous monsters bent on the destruction of all that Rome stood for. When, by contrast, Sidonius or his friends, relatives, or allies were seeking Visigothic or Burgundian assistance, or profiting from the very cooperation he denounced in others, the barbarian leadership is presented in a much more favourable light. So for example, Sidonius provides a highly positive description of the court of the Visigothic king Theoderic II at Toulouse: 'To sum up: you can find there Greek elegance, Gallic plenty, Italian briskness; the dignity of the state, the attentiveness of a private house, the ordered discipline of royalty.' Sidonius goes on to describe how he deliberately lost to the king at backgammon, in order to advance his cause in a property dispute: 'I lose my pieces,' he confesses, 'to win my case.'[97]

A further case in point is Sidonius' highly variable attitude to Theoderic's successor, Euric, and his regime. As the Goths bore down on the Auvergne and Sidonius sought to rally the landowners of the region against him, the Visigothic king was represented as the epitome of barbarism, and a godless heretic to boot. As Sidonius wrote to the Catholic Bishop Basilius, 'I must confess that, although the said king of the Goths is justly feared for his armed might, I dread less his designs against our Roman city-walls than those against our Christian laws.'[98] Yet, once Euric's regime was established in the Auvergne, Sidonius penned a panegyric in his honour, hoping to obtain access to the new king's court similar to that which he had enjoyed under Theoderic II at Toulouse.[99]

It is quite clear what men like Sidonius had to gain from entering into closer relations with the barbarian leadership. First, they obtained a measure of physical security that the forces of Rome had shown themselves less and less capable of delivering. Second, they gained access to a court, close at hand, in which they could

---

[97] Sidonius Apollinaris, *Epistolae*, I, 2.
[98] Sidonius Apollinaris, *Epistolae*, VII, 6.
[99] Sidonius Apollinaris, *Epistolae*, VIII, 9.

advance themselves and their interests. It was increasingly at the courts of barbarian kings that members of the Gallo-Roman aristocracy deployed the skills that they and their forefathers had honed at the tetrarchic capitals. As Paulinus of Pella confessed back in the 430s: 'It was peace with the Goths that I pursued, which... though purchased at a price, remains unregretted, since already in our state we see full many prospering through Gothic favour, though many first endured the full range of suffering, not least of whom was I, seeing that I was stripped of all my goods and outlived my fatherland'.[100] Others were less sentimental: when the Visigothic army massed before the walls of Arles in the early 470s, amongst their number was a certain Calminius, a Roman youth of good birth, whose father Eucherius had delved deep into his pockets to help pay for the city's defence.[101] Sidonius, a friend of the father, wrote to Calminius feigning to believe that he had been forced into this by Euric, and guaranteeing him a warm reception should he ever choose to return to Arles. The letter reeks of insincerity and reads more like a carefully calculated threat than a genuine 'olive branch'. Given the objective military and political circumstances of the era, not all roads now necessarily led to Rome.

The development of more cooperative relations with members of the Roman provincial aristocracy was also in the interests of the barbarian leadership. As members of the late-Roman aristocracy of service, men like Paulinus of Pella or Sidonius Apollinaris had behind them long traditions of leadership of local society and vast amounts of accumulated 'know-how'. It was they who could best advise the Athaulfs, Theoderics, and Eurics of this world how best to rule over the territories that they were now in the process of acquiring: which lands were most profitable, which villages and villagers were the most trouble, how to get the most out of the governmental infrastructure and rural properties that they had inherited. Crucially, such men could also convey to the barbarian leadership how to make their brute authority appear more legitimate by representing it in terms that chimed with the political expectations of their Roman subjects. Consequently, a key legacy of the late-Roman aristocracy of service to the Romano-Germanic successor kingdoms of the sixth and seventh centuries would be the transmission of *Romanitas* ('Roman-ness') as a language of power and a style of rule.[102]

We see this already in the late fifth century in the legislation issued by Gundobad and Euric: the *Liber Constitutionum*, the *Lex Romana Burgundionum*, and, most grandiloquently of all in terms of title, the *Codex Euricianus*, presenting itself as an updated version of the *Codex Theodosianus* promulgated by the Emperor Theodosius II in 438. These would soon be joined by the *Lex Salica*, probably collected and promulgated by the Frankish king Clovis.[103] With the exception of the *Lex Salica*, the laws contained in these collections drew overwhelmingly upon Roman law, and would have been inconceivable without the active assistance of men familiar with the technicalities of Roman jurisprudence.[104] All of the laws, moreover, were

---

[100] Paulinus of Pella, *Eucharisticon*, 303–10.
[101] Sidonius Apollinaris, *Epistolae*, V, 12. See also Heather (2005), p. 420.
[102] Wormald (1976).
[103] C. P. Wormald, *The Making of English Law*, vol. 1 (Oxford, 1999), pp. 29–51.
[104] Wormald (1976), p. 222.

written in Latin, the language of imperial power *par excellence*. All, save the *Lex Salica*, bear the hallmark of having been written by Romans present at the royal court. The Burgundian legislation, for example, has been identified with a correspondent of Sidonius Apollinaris by the name of Syagrius, whom Sidonius teases for having learned Burgundian so thoroughly that he knew it better than the Burgundians themselves. Sidonius praises him as 'the new Solon of the Burgundians—learned in laws': a reference to the great lawgiver of ancient Athens.[105] The Visigothic legislation may have been drafted by the Roman courtier and scholar Leo of Narbonne, whom Sidonius describes as the king's spokesman.[106] A more likely candidate, however, is Sidonius' bête noire Seronatus, of whom he wrote that 'he tramples on the laws of Theodosius and issues laws of Theoderic.'[107]

For the rulers concerned, such legislation inevitably served a number of purposes—not least of which, as we have seen with respect to the Burgundian or Visigothic legislation, was the resolution of disputes over landownership between their Roman and non-Roman subjects. Most importantly, perhaps, the very act of issuing such laws, written in the prestige language of Latin, was a quintessentially imperial one. It made the kings appear more imperial—and thus authoritative—in the eyes of their subjects. Therein, no doubt, lay much of its appeal.[108]

The reception and appropriation of Roman political culture on the part of barbarian elites over the course of the fifth century was a phenomenon of the utmost significance for the future development of the emergent Romano-Germanic successor kingdoms. It is important to remember, however, that the encounter between a Visigothic, Frankish, or Burgundian king on the one hand, and a Gallo-Roman or Hispano-Roman aristocrat on the other, consisted of more than the mere Romanisation of the former. The cultural exchange went both ways. In spite of the prejudices of Roman authors, for whom the barbarian was, by definition, a man without culture, the barbarian elites (as we shall see in Chapter Three) often had a very strong sense of identity and tradition of their own. Ethnic identities may have been fluid, or relatively recent, but they existed. Sidonius Apollinaris, for example, wrote to his friend Agricola that the Visigothic king Theoderic kept 'the tips of his ears hidden by the wisps of hair that train over them, according to the custom of his race (*sicut mos gentis*)'.[109] The Burgundian legislation on land settlement, as we have seen, speaks of the Burgundians as 'our people' (*populus noster*)—the 'fellow travellers' (*faramanni*) united by the joint venture of conquest. A sense of pride in people, history, and identity shines through. The *Lex Salica* may have been

---

[105] Sidonius Apollinaris, *Epistolae*, V, 5, as identified by Wormald (1976).
[106] Sidonius Apollinaris, VIII, 3, as suggested by Wormald (1976).
[107] Sidonius Apollinaris, *Epistolae*, II, 1. Alternatively, this might indicate that Seronatus was associated with a legal codification (of uncertain date) known as the *Edictum Theoderici* ('Edict of Theoderic'), attributable either to the Visigothic Theoderic II or to Theoderic the Ostrogoth.
[108] P. Wormald, 'Lex Scripta and Verbum Regis', in P. Sawyer and I. Wood (eds.), *Early Medieval Kingship* (Leeds, 1977), pp. 105–38.
[109] Sidonius Apollinaris, *Epistolae*, I, 2.

written down in Latin, but its provisions were rooted in Frankish custom, not Roman jurisprudence. In all of our early 'barbarian' law codes, those who share in the king's ethnicity are accorded a higher legal status than their Roman equivalents. In Roman law terms, to be a Roman in the Frankish, Visigothic, or Burgundian kingdoms, or, ultimately, to be a Briton (or *Wealsc*) under the Anglo-Saxons, was to be of 'inferior condition' (*inferior/deterior condicio*). Under the *Lex Salica*, for example, the blood-money due as compensation in the event of the murder of a Roman was precisely half that due with respect to a Frank.[110]

Crucially, the culture of the barbarian elite, unlike that of much of the Roman provincial aristocracy, was fundamentally martial in character, although not all Romans were entirely unappreciative of it. As Sidonius wrote to his friend Domnicius of a Visigothic procession he had witnessed:

> You, who are so fond of looking at arms and armed men, what delight, I think, you would have felt had you seen the young royal Sigismer, decked out in the garb and fashion of his race . . . the princelings and retainers who accompanied him presented an aspect terrifying even in peacetime. . . . Barbed lances and missile axes filled their right hands; and their left sides were protected by shields, the gleam of which, golden on the central bosses and silvery white round the rims, betrayed at once the wearers' wealth and ruling passion. The fine show lacked only one thing—you . . . seeing the sights your eye delights in.[111]

As a result of this cultural difference, there was an inbuilt limitation to the extent to which any barbarian king could afford to become Romanised. No barbarian king could risk compromising his martial identity. At the same time as representing his power to his Roman subjects in a manner that they could understand and appreciate, he also had to convey to the leaders of his own people that he was an effective and reliable custodian of their traditions and culture and, above all, that he remained a warlord worthy of admiration and respect. Without the support of his own people, he was nothing. At the end of the day men like Paulinus or Sidonius were only willing to work with the barbarians in their midst because they offered protection; a barbarian king who was not respected by his army, or not feared by his neighbours, was of no use to anyone. It is true that we find examples of Frankish or Gothic lords in the fifth and sixth centuries who display an interest in Latin literary or Roman 'high' culture: Sidonius Apollinaris, for instance, corresponded with the Frankish Count Arbogast, of whom he declared 'you have drunk deep from the spring of Roman eloquence and, dwelling by the Moselle, you speak the true Latin of the Tiber'. Yet even Arbogast remained primarily a man of war: the most that Sidonius could claim of him was that he was 'wont to handle the pen no less than the sword'.[112]

The careful balancing act in which barbarian kings needed to engage is exemplified by the grave-goods of the late fifth-century Frankish king Childeric, copies of which survive. In one sense, these items reveal a very Roman side to Childeric's

---

[110] *Pactus Legis Salicae*, XLI.
[111] Sidonius Apollinaris, *Epistolae*, IV, 2.
[112] Sidonius Apollinaris, *Epistolae*, IV, 17.

rule. He was interred with a Roman military belt-buckle, or *fibula*, by which Roman officers designated their rank. Also buried with him was a seal-ring bearing the Latin inscription CHILDIRICI REGIS ('belonging to King Childeric')—indicating both the use of written documents at his court and of Latin as the prestige language of power. Yet surrounded by this inscription on the ring is an image of Childeric bearing arms, and wearing the long hair that later authors inform us was characteristic of the folk kings of the Franks. Around the king's burial mound, moreover, have been found the graves of horses, a feature of elite burial sites associated with the Huns and other peoples of the Eurasian steppe. These Roman, Frankish, and Hunnic aspects to Childeric's burial convey much of the composite nature of his kingship (Fig. 4).[113]

If anything, in terms of the cultural encounter between Roman and barbarian elites that took place in the fifth and sixth centuries, it was with respect to the Roman provincial aristocracies that the pressure to assimilate was at its most pronounced. Men like Sidonius Apollinaris had not cultivated their literary skills for the sheer pleasure of it, but rather to gain advancement in imperial service and the Roman bureaucracy. As the bureaucratic structures of empire faded away, the less these literary skills mattered, beyond, that is, the ranks of the Church. As a result, over the course of the sixth century, Latin literature became an increasingly ecclesiastical preserve. By contrast, the more that Roman landowners were obliged to focus their ambitions on the courts of barbarian kings in order to advance their interests or defend their dependants, the more vital it became that they acquire the skills that these kings most valued—those of the warrior. Increasingly, favour and

Fig. 4 Reconstruction of Seal-Ring of Childeric (Reproduced by kind permission of the Ashmolean Museum, Oxford, and the Bridgeman Art Library)

[113] E. James, *The Franks* (Oxford, 1991), pp. 58–64.

preferment at court came to depend not so much on the elegance of one's Latin verse compositions as on one's dexterity with sword, swiftness on horseback, or warlike demeanour. It tells us everything we need to know of the fate of the Roman aristocracy in the post-Roman West that whereas Sidonius, former Urban Prefect of Rome, retired to his estates and to the life of a bishop, his son, Apollinaris, died fighting in battle on behalf of his Visigothic lord against the king's Frankish, Catholic enemies.[114]

The pressure to assimilate would have been further intensified by the greater social status and legal privilege that the Frankish, Visigothic, or Burgundian retainers of kings enjoyed in comparison to their Roman equivalents. As a result, it became a matter of urgency that members of the Roman provincial aristocracies consolidate or bolster their increasingly vulnerable social standing by acquiring the ethnicity of their rulers. Over the course of generations, through intermarriage, acculturation, and militarisation, this was possible. The late sixth-century Frankish historian Gregory of Tours, for example, although regarding himself as coming from 'senatorial stock', could nevertheless look back in his bloodline to a great-uncle Gundulf. Indeed, during the sixth and seventh centuries, the assimilation of Roman provincial aristocracies to new ethnicities is perhaps at its most manifest with respect to changing patterns of elite nomenclature: the naming practices of the late-Roman aristocracy died away, as men increasingly came to name their sons after weapons or those animals that were deemed to embody the ferocious qualities that a warrior society now admired—Lupus, 'the wolf', or Hildebrand, 'battle sword'.[115] In certain contexts there was linguistic assimilation too: as we have seen, Sidonius' correspondent, Syagrius, learnt Burgundian. In most places, however, Latin and its derivatives would hold out. The great exception was lowland Britain, where a lowest common denominator of the various West Germanic dialects spoken by the invaders, typically known as *Anglisc* or *Theodisc* ('the language of the people'), came to predominate and ultimately became a badge of rank.[116]

2.5 CONTINUITY AND DISCONTINUITY IN THE POST-ROMAN ECONOMY

As seen in Chapter One, the administrative and political structures of the late-Roman Empire had supported a trans-regional imperial aristocracy epitomised by the self-assured super-rich of the Roman Senate. It is the voices of this group above all that resound from the pages of our literary sources. In the late fourth century, for example, Ammianus Marcellinus recorded how members of this body would 'hold

---

[114] Wormald (1976).
[115] C. P. Wormald, 'Kings and Kingship', in Fouracre (2005), pp. 571–604.
[116] J. Hines, 'Society, Community, and Identity', in Charles-Edwards (2003), and T. Charles-Edwards, 'The Making of Nations in Britain and Ireland', in R. Evans (ed.), *Lordship and Learning: Studies in Memory of Trevor Aston* (Woodbridge, 2004), pp. 11–37.

forth unasked on the immense extent of their family property, multiplying in the imagination the annual produce of their fertile lands, which extend, they boastfully declare, from furthest east to furthest west'.[117] The historian Olympiodorus of Thebes provides estimates for the annual incomes of western senatorial families in around the year 400. He records that the grandest senatorial households received incomes from their (apparently rented out) landholdings of more than four thousand *centenaria* of gold a year, not including the wheat, wine, and all the other goods in kind, derived from the directly managed portions of their estates, which would bring in a third as much again in gold if marketed.[118] These were fortunes reckoned in terms of hundreds of thousands of *solidi* in a world in which the annual income of an agricultural worker might be just four or five.

Crucially, at the same time, the trans-regional structure of the Roman Empire served to support high levels of economic sophistication and complexity.[119] The system of roads and maritime communication that the Roman state maintained served to reduce dramatically the transactional costs associated with inter-regional trade; the impetus and assistance given by the state to urbanism required that curial landowners exchange the produce of their estates for cash in order to maintain an urban lifestyle, leading to a broader commodification of production, whilst a concentration of population in cities also served to create a market for commercialised agriculture from which members of the late-Roman aristocracy, with their extensive estates, were well placed to profit.[120] Within the cities, artisanal skills could also be fostered and advanced.

Above all, as we have seen, by minting and circulating vast quantities of coinage—especially in high-value gold and small-denomination copper—with which to pay the army and civil service, and by demanding that taxes be paid in coin, the late-Roman state catalysed a much broader and deeper monetisation of economic activity. Not only curial landowners but also peasants had to acquire cash with which to pay their taxes. With any surplus cash, they could invest in their own farms, purchase agricultural tools, or acquire the late-Roman equivalents of 'consumer durables'—high-quality storage jars, ceramics, waterproof tiles, and such like. The industrialised production and widespread dissemination of such goods is a remarkable feature of the archaeological record that survives for the late-Roman world. As one historian and archaeologist has noted, 'research has revealed a sophisticated world, in which a north-Italian peasant of the Roman period might eat off tableware from the area near Naples, store liquids in an amphora from North Africa, and sleep under a tiled roof. Almost all archaeologists, and most historians, now believe that the Roman economy was characterised, not only by an impressive luxury market, but also by a very substantial middle and lower market

---

[117] Ammianus Marcellinus, *Res Gestae*, XIV, 6.10.
[118] R. C. Blockley, *The Fragmentary Classicising Historians* (Liverpool, 1981–3), 41.2, pp. 204–5. For Olympiodorus' testimony with respect to estate structure, and how it makes sense against a broader background, see P. Sarris, 'The Origins of the Manorial Economy: New Insights from Late Antiquity', *EHR* 119 (2004), pp. 279–311.
[119] Ward-Perkins (2005).
[120] See Banaji (2007), and Durliat (1990).

for high-quality functional products.'[121] The re-monetisation of the Roman fiscal system associated with the minting and circulation of the Constantinian gold *solidus* in the fourth century sparked off a wave of economic growth that enabled the late-Roman world to achieve levels of economic sophistication, complexity, and urbanism that would not be seen again in parts of Western Europe until the seventeenth century.[122] This phenomenon acquired a momentum of its own, such that the dramatic expansion in commercialised and monetised exchange that occurred at every level of society obliged the imperial authorities to release ever more coinage into circulation, so as to maintain the liquidity of both the public and private economies. New coinage had to be repeatedly added to the old (which remained legal tender).[123] So, for example, it has been estimated that, between 346 and 386, the amount of monetised gold in circulation increased by a factor of twenty.[124]

In Rome's northern and western provinces, the political and military dislocation of the fifth century meant an end to much of this, and parts of the Roman West entered into a period of stark and rapid economic decline, perhaps unprecedented in recorded human history. This is at its most evident with respect to lowland Britain, where the archaeology reveals that the withdrawal of Rome's legions and the chronic insecurity caused by the Saxon invaders led to systemic collapse. Although many Roman villa sites were occupied by the invaders, and (as will be seen in Chapter Five) there are signs of the continued inhabitation of certain urban centres such as Verulamium (modern St Albans) into the sixth and perhaps even seventh centuries, a pronounced shift is discernible in the fundamental structure of the economy. Extensive arable agriculture—the large-scale raising of cereal crops and suchlike to feed settled populations—effectively disappeared: fields and farms were too vulnerable to the depredations of war-bands. Rather, farmers increasingly became pastoralists, scraping a living by raising sheep and cattle that could be rapidly moved upland to escape an invading foe.[125]

Coinage, without which the sophisticated networks of exchange that characterised the late-Roman economy were entirely unsustainable, became increasingly scarce, leading to a return to a barter economy.[126] Advanced building techniques associated with Roman material culture disappeared: evidence of the continued quarrying of building stone is absent, as is that of the preparation of mortar and the manufacture and use of bricks and tiles.[127] It seems that all new buildings, both in

---

[121] Ward-Perkins (2005), pp. 88–9.

[122] Banaji (2007); R. Alston, *The City in Roman and Byzantine Egypt* (London, 2002).

[123] J. Banaji, 'Precious-metal Coinages and Monetary Expansion in Late Antiquity', in F. De Romanis and S. Sorda (eds.), *Dal denarius al dinar: l'oriente e la monetà romana* (Rome, 2006), pp. 265–303, 265–70.

[124] ibid., p. 20.

[125] R. Faith, 'Forces and Relations of Production in Early Medieval England', *Journal of Agrarian Change* 9.1 (2009), pp. 23–41, with additional comments by P. Sarris, 'Introduction: Aristocrats, Peasants, and the Transformation of Rural Society, c.400–800', ibid., pp. 3–22.

[126] Ward-Perkins (2005), p. 112.

[127] Ward-Perkins (2005), p. 108.

Anglo-Saxon and unconquered British areas, employed more basic materials such as wood, drystone walling, and thatch. Whereas late-Roman Britain had supported a thriving pottery industry, by the sixth century the knowledge of how to produce wheel-turned pots had been entirely lost.[128] In short, there is evidence of massive economic and cultural dislocation and, in terms of material culture and economic complexity, a return to prehistoric levels.[129]

Lowland Britain provides the most vivid and extreme example of post-Roman collapse: within a century its economy was effectively de-urbanised, de-monetised, and predominantly pastoral. But Britain was not alone in this: in parts of northern Gaul, for example, we see a similar reorientation of the agrarian economy towards pastoralism. As a result, by c.600, economic conditions in lowland Britain and the northern Frankish territories would appear to have been broadly similar. A disappearance of industrially produced and traded ceramics is also evident with respect to parts of coastal Spain.[130] Essentially, where barbarian invasion was at its most destructive, the social and economic impact was correspondingly at its most pronounced. In each of these areas we also witness a 'tribalization' of political structures.[131] To a certain extent, chronic military insecurity seems to have pushed these economies and societies down a developmental path along which other forces and factors were already leading them. There is some evidence, for example, that the fifth and sixth centuries may have witnessed a significant drop in temperature in north-western Europe. An associated increase in levels of precipitation may have served to make arable agriculture considerably more difficult—especially in river valleys—meaning that peasants already had an incentive to move towards mixed farming with a greater emphasis on pastoralism, and also to migrate into upland zones so as to avoid floodlands. Barbarian invasion and warfare, however, provided a still more pressing incentive to do so, just as it would in Byzantine Anatolia in the seventh and eighth centuries.[132]

A far higher degree of continuity is discernible around the Mediterranean core of the old Western Empire. Here, much of the late-Roman social and economic infrastructure survived the political and military demise of imperial power substantially intact, buoyed by on-going economic contact with Constantinople and the East. Even here, however, with the exception of the Mediterranean coastal zones, there is evidence of progressive de-monetisation, de-urbanisation, and an associated ruralisation of aristocratic culture. On one level, the reasons for this are pretty simple: the high degree of inter-regional integration that had characterised the Roman economy at its height meant that the breakdown of Roman political control could have major economic consequences. The more dependent on the trans-regional imperial system a region was, the more potentially vulnerable it was to

---

[128] ibid., p. 104.   [129] ibid., p. 118.
[130] ibid., p. 104.   [131] Wickham (2005).
[132] F. L. Cheyette, 'The Disappearance of the Ancient Landscape and the Climatic Anomaly of the Early Middle Ages: A Question To Be Pursued', *Early Medieval Europe* 16 (2008), pp. 127–65; A. England et al., 'Historical Landscape Change in Cappadocia (central Turkey): A Palaeoecological Investigation of Annually Laminated Sediments from Nar Lake', *The Holocene* 18 (2008), pp. 1,229–45.

the effects of imperial fragmentation. This was most obviously the case with respect to those frontier zones (such as Britain or northern Gaul) that were major net recipients of imperial investment or subsidy. By contrast, areas such as north-central Gaul (the 'Paris basin'), where local patterns of supply and exchange had long been of comparatively greater significance, were better placed to prosper in a more fragmented political landscape. It was precisely this region that was to serve as the economic springboard for the Merovingian monarchy in the sixth and seventh centuries.[133] Likewise, Africa, which (through the state-administered grain trade) had been a net exporter of fiscally extracted resources, would appear to have achieved sufficiently high levels of internal economic development for it to be able to continue to prosper (in the medium term at least) in spite of the dislocation to Rome of the fiscal axis.[134] Instead, here the fading away of the state's demand for fiscal grain may initially have opened up new opportunities for diversification and investment. Such would certainly be the case with respect to Egypt in the seventh century, when the *annona* route to Constantinople was cut off by Persian and Arab invaders.

But economic change was also the result of processes closely tied up with the terms of 'barbarian' settlement, and as a result, change is discernible in every area where such settlement took place. As discussed, one of the driving forces for economic 'sophistication' in the late-Roman Empire had been the fiscal machinery of the Roman state, and especially the high levels of monetisation that the late-Roman fiscal economy had generated. The basis of Roman taxation was the land tax. The state demanded for the most part that fiscal dues be paid in coin, so as to support the salaried civil service but also, above all, to pay the army. Assessing, collecting, and recording the payment of the land tax was an exercise of enormous administrative complexity that required great effort, and which was associated with no small measure of brutality. Not for nothing, as one historian of the period has noticed, did the author of the early medieval hymn the *Dies Irae* conceive of the Day of Judgement in terms of the arrival of the late-Roman tax collector.[135]

The more provincial society in the late-Roman and post-Roman West became dependent for its security on bands of barbarian warriors, rewarded with land in return for their military service, the less reason there was to maintain this cumbersome fiscal system. The collection of taxes also became increasingly problematic politically, as militarised landowners came to associate tax exemption with elite status. The less need there was to maintain the Roman fiscal system, the less reason there was to go to the enormous administrative lengths required to mint and circulate coinage in vast quantities. The less coinage there was in circulation, the less feasible it became for aristocrats to reside in cities, away from their estates, and the less sustainable urbanism itself became, as the commercialised and monetised exchanges on which town life depended were progressively constrained by a now ever-diminishing money supply.

---

[133] As argued by Wickham (2005).
[134] A. H. Merrills and R. Miles, *The Vandals* (Oxford, 2010).
[135] P. Brown, *The World of Late Antiquity* (London, 1971), p. 36.

This process was not necessarily a rapid one, and only in the most extreme cases did it ever near completion, but everywhere the developmental trajectory was the same. With respect to coinage, for example, the numismatic record reveals that although many of the rulers of the Romano-Germanic successor kingdoms of the fifth and sixth centuries minted their own gold coins, typically conforming to the model of contemporary Constantinopolitan coinage, small-denomination copper coins, on which the most basic of day-to-day transactions depended, began to disappear in the West from the start of the fifth century: the last ruler to strike them there in any significant number was the Emperor Theodosius I (r.379–95). Copper coins were minted in Vandal Africa and Ostrogothic Italy, as also in the Burgundian kingdom, but seemingly in much reduced volume.[136] Locally produced copper coins have also been identified around Seville, Merida, Malaga, Valencia, and Cartagena in southern Spain, and Marseilles in Gaul (the subject of this coinage will be returned to in Chapter Five).[137] By the seventh century, however, it was only in the areas ruled by Constantinople (and in immediately neighbouring zones) that small-denomination coins continued to be minted and used.[138] This assertion holds true even if one assumes (as is likely) that older stocks of coin remained in circulation: the only areas of the West for which there is evidence of an abundant copper coinage by the end of the seventh century are the imperial enclaves of Sicily and Rome.[139] Moreover, given that much of the Mediterranean commerce surviving into the late sixth century appears to have been driven by a desire on the part of Western elites for Eastern goods, there is likely to have been a marked tendency for the remaining stock of gold coinage in circulation in the West to drain eastwards.[140] Likewise, over the course of the sixth and early seventh centuries, references to the land tax effectively disappear from our Western sources, save, once more, with respect to areas under Constantinopolitan control. According to Gregory of Tours, when, in 579, the Frankish king Chilperic attempted to revive the land tax, the people of Limoges rose up in revolt, burnt the tax registers, and hanged the king's tax collector.[141]

---

[136] Ward-Perkins (2005), p. 112; P. Grierson and M. Blackburn, *Medieval European Coinage: The Early Middle Ages (5th–10th c.)* (Cambridge, 1986); C. Morrisson, 'The Re-Use of Obsolete Coins: The Case of Roman Imperial Bronzes Revived in the Late Fifth Century', in C. N. L. Brooke, B. H. I. H. Stewart, J. G. Pollard, and T. R. Volk (eds.), *Studies in Numismatic Method Presented to Philip Grierson* (Cambridge, 1983), pp. 95–112; J. Lafaurie and C. Morrisson, 'La penetration des monnaies byzantines en Gaule', *Revue Numismatique* VI (29) (1987), pp. 38–98. For a more positive spin on this, see A. Rovelli, 'Coins and Trade in Early Medieval Italy', *Early Medieval Europe* 17 (2009), pp. 45–76, and G. Berndt and R. Steinacher, 'Minting in Vandal Africa: Coins of the Vandal Period in the Coin Cabinet of Vienna's Kunsthistorisches Museum', *Early Medieval Europe* 16 (2008), pp. 252–98. See also M. F. Hendy, 'From Public to Private: The Western Barbarian Coinages as a Mirror of the Disintegration of Late Roman State Structures', *Viator* 19 (1988), pp. 29–78.

[137] M. Crusafont, *El sistema monetario visigodo: cobre y oro* (Barcelona and Madrid, 1994).

[138] Ward-Perkins (2005), p. 113.

[139] ibid.; A. Rovelli, 'La circolazione monetaria a Roma nei secoli VII e VIII. Nuovi dati per la storia economica di Roma nell'alto medioevo', in P. Delogu (ed.), *Roma medievale. Aggiornamenti* (Florence, 1998), pp. 79–91; C. Morrisson, 'La Sicile byzantine: un lueur dans les siècles obscurs', *Numismatica e antichità classiche* 27 (1998), pp. 307–34.

[140] M. Lombard, *L'Islam dans sa première grandeur* (Paris, 1971).

[141] Gregory of Tours, *Decem Libri Historiae*, V, 28: see discussion in Wickham (2005), p. 107.

The much more limited scale of the minting of coins and of the use of money in even the most sophisticated of the Romano-Germanic successor kingdoms is a point that cannot be emphasised enough. As a result, over the course of the fifth, sixth, and early seventh centuries, commercialised agriculture and commodified exchange became harder and harder: an urban existence became ever more impracticable, and landowners increasingly retreated from *civitas* to *villa* to live directly off the produce of their estates. The cities themselves, denied the supporting hand of the Roman state, became ever more run-down and shambolic. In some places, such as northern Italy, they remained important seats of power; in others, such as Frankish Gaul, they primarily became associated with episcopal residences, the Church being, in effect, the last 'Roman' institution left.

This was to be true even with respect to regimes, such as those of Odoacer and Theoderic in Italy, that were the most committed to maintaining or facilitating the traditional Roman way of life on the part of indigenous elites, or where the imperial system was most deeply rooted. In Italy, as we have seen, a fiscal system survived the transition to Ostrogothic rule, but both it and the monetary economy were nevertheless becoming increasingly marginal.[142] There is clear evidence for an ongoing (and presumably associated) aristocratic migration to the countryside: as Theoderic the Ostrogoth's successor, the boy-king Athalaric, declared in the year 526–7:

> Let the landowners and city councillors of Bruttium return to their cities: those who ceaselessly till the fields are the peasants. Those to whom I have granted honours, whom I have approved and entrusted with public affairs, should accept that they are cut off from the life of a yokel.... Let the cities return, then, to their original glory; let no-one prefer the delights of the countryside to the public buildings of the ancients. How can you shun in a time of peace a place for which wars should be fought to prevent its destruction? Who does not welcome a gathering of noblemen? Who does not enjoy conversing with his peers, visiting the forum, looking on at honest crafts, advancing his own cases by the laws, or sometimes playing at draughts, going to the baths with his fellows, exchanging splendid dinner parties? He who wishes to lead his life in the constant company of his slaves will assuredly lack all these things.[143]

Athalaric thus provides a picturesque evocation of *la dolce vita* of the late-Roman aristocrat, a lifestyle that, in spite of his regime's best efforts, was becoming a thing of the past.

It was probably in the countryside that there occurred the least change. Again, a high degree of regional variation is evident. Most currently available evidence would suggest that in lowland Britain and north-western Gaul the old agrarian order was swept away. Elsewhere too, there are indications that the military dislocation of the fifth century opened up opportunities to peasants, slaves, and other more humble members of society to escape aristocratic domination, either by joining the barbarians, attacking the landowner, or taking advantage of his

---

[142] Ward-Perkins (2005), pp. 112–13.
[143] Cassiodorus, *Variae*, VIII, 31.

flight.¹⁴⁴ There may also have been a general tendency, informed by climatic change, towards mixed farming.¹⁴⁵ In the central Frankish domains around the Paris basin, by contrast, imperial estates appear to have passed substantially intact into the hands of the Merovingian kings, such as Childeric and his son Clovis. Here, as a result, a high degree of continuity on the ground is likely to have characterised agrarian social relations, such as facilitated the survival of large estates.¹⁴⁶ The Burgundian and Visigothic legislation, as noted earlier, records entire estates, along with their dependant workforces, having been granted by way of gift to royal favourites, and in parts of Spain there is evidence for late-Roman villas passing directly into Visigothic ownership.¹⁴⁷ Even in Vandal Africa, as we have seen, it is possible to identify not only estates but even their Roman owners surviving the transition from Roman rule. The grandest of the aristocratic families, those with far-flung properties, had the most to lose from the fragmentation of imperial rule. Those landowners whose possessions were more geographically concentrated, however, could hold on. For much of the rural population of these regions, the demise of the Western Roman Empire appears to have meant little more than a change of master—and sometimes not even that.¹⁴⁸ Indeed, given that the Romano-Germanic successor kingdoms of the fifth and sixth centuries were effectively built on the emergence of mutually supportive relations between members of the Roman provincial aristocracy, and members of the barbarian elite, there is little reason to assume that, in much of the West, members of the peasantry gained all that much.

Rather, it is possible that conditions actually deteriorated for some. As noted in Chapter One, there is considerable evidence for rural slavery on large estates in late antiquity.¹⁴⁹ Alongside such slaves, as we have seen, worked bodies of tied agricultural labourers styled *coloni adscripticii* or, in the Western sources, *coloni originarii*. These workers and their families were described as being in a legal status with respect to their masters analogous to that of slaves, although they were not slaves, and remained legally free with respect to society at large. In spite of this, landowners had long sought to do away with what they evidently regarded to be an irksome and unnecessary distinction between *colonus* and slave: in the early fifth century, for example, Saint Augustine took legal advice as to whether it was permissible for landowners simply to turn their *coloni* into slaves or to enslave their workers' children. Only the legal conservatism of the Imperial Chancery stood in their way.¹⁵⁰ In the legislation of the Romano-Germanic successor kingdoms, however, we see many landowners effectively getting what they wanted, with both *coloni* and

---

144 For post-Roman peasant autonomy, see Wickham (2005).
145 Cheyette (2008).
146 Wickham (2005), p. 195.
147 For references and bibliography, see A. Chavarría Arnau, 'Churches and Aristocracies in Seventh-Century Spain: Some Thoughts on the Debate on Visigothic Churches', *Early Medieval Europe* 18 (2010), pp. 160–74, p. 171 n. 55.
148 As argued in detail in Sarris (2004).
149 Harper (2009).
150 J. Banaji, 'Late Antiquity to the Early Middle Ages: What Kind of Transition?', in *idem.*, *Theory as History* (Leiden, 2010); P. Sarris (2011).

slaves gradually coming to form part of an undifferentiated mass of servile labour.[151] As already mentioned, in the Burgundian legislation of the *Liber Constitutionum*, both groups are subsumed under the title of *mancipia*, which in Roman law had initially been reserved for slaves. In the Edict of Theoderic (*Edictum Theoderici*) we find the formulation *colonus aut servus*—'colonus or slave'.[152] In the later Visigothic legislation, the category of *colonus* simply disappears: all are henceforth *servi*.[153] A sixth-century Merovingian will refers to *mancipia 'tam servos quam et ingenuos*'—'*mancipia* . . . "be they slave or free"'.[154] In the absence of the public institutions of the Roman state, the distinction between tied agricultural worker and slave effectively melted away, leaving only the power of the master securely in place. The key difference between the estates worked by post-Roman *mancipia* and the great estates of the late-Roman period was that in the increasingly de-monetised conditions of the sixth and seventh centuries, estates that had originally been geared towards production for the market became ever more closed, self-sufficient, and autarkic entities.

It is true that many individual estates are likely to have been broken up, especially to facilitate 'barbarian' settlement. Although the division of estates recorded in the legislation must necessarily have had the effect of altering the social profile of landownership in the societies concerned, bolstering the overall significance of medium-scale landowners and farmers at the expense of their wealthier Roman neighbours, here too, however, there are significant signs of continuity. The great estates of members of the late-Roman aristocracy had been characterised by an emphasis on the direct management of estates, rather than the simple parcelling out of estate properties amongst tenant farmers. The late-antique agricultural treatises that we possess, for example, take such regimes of direct management entirely for granted.[155] The documentary papyri from Egypt, moreover, record an essentially bipartite or bilateral structuring of many such properties.[156] On the one hand, the papyri record the existence of a directly cultivated estate demesne, sometimes referred to as the *autourgia*, worked by *coloni adscripticii* and, most probably, slave labour. The estate workers were then in turn housed in estate properties or labour settlements, known in Greek as *epoikia* or *chôria*, where they had access to allotments of land termed *ktêmata* on which they paid rent. This bipartite division of estates is attested elsewhere in the Eastern Empire, and is indicated for the late-Roman West in the writings of Olympiodorus of Thebes, where he suggests a typical ratio of two to one between the cash rental incomes derived from estate

---

[151] J. Banaji, 'Aristocrats, Peasantries, and the Framing of the Early Middle Ages', in *JAC* 9.1 (2009), pp. 59–91. See also O. Schipp, *Der weströmliche Kolonat von Konstantin bis zu den Karolingern (332 bis 861)* (Hamburg, 2009), p. 286, and p. 335 for the Ostrogothic equation of *coloni* and *mancipia* ('*mancipium originarium*').
[152] Banaji (2009), p. 74.
[153] ibid., p. 74.
[154] Sarris (2004). For the survival of *originarii* as a vestigial category in the Romano-Germanic legal sources, however, see Schipp (2009).
[155] J. Teall, 'The Byzantine Agricultural Tradition', *Dumbarton Oaks Papers* 13 (1959), pp. 35–59.
[156] Sarris (2004), and Sarris (2006).

allotments or *ktêmata* (a word he himself uses) and the marketable value of the produce of the directly cultivated demesne.¹⁵⁷

This ratio of rental income to demesne would make sense of the two-to-one division of estates in favour of the settlers recorded in the Burgundian and Visigothic law codes, as also the two-to-one division of 'bondsmen' (*mancipia*) in favour of the Roman landowner. Essentially, what appears to be envisaged is a situation whereby Roman landowners were left in control of the directly managed demesne, whereas the estate labour settlements—known in Latin as *vici*—and their associated allotments were distributed amongst the 'barbarians'. It is such estate settlements, or *chôria*, for example, that Procopius records Odoacer and Theoderic to have shared out amongst their troops. The Roman landowner, however, was granted a proportionately larger share of the workforce so as to maintain levels of cultivation on what was the most labour-intensive and labour-hungry portion of the estate. Of course, his share of the *mancipia* would now need to be rehoused. As a result new allotments and residences had to be carved out within the demesne itself for the *mancipia* to live on, holdings that in the seventh-century Frankish sources would be described as *mansi*.¹⁵⁸ In spite of this reconfiguration of large estates, however, with the creation of an estate demesne or 'inland . . . crowded with the dwellings of the workers and tenants who lived there', traditions of direct management and of the direct exploitation of labourers lived on.¹⁵⁹ This was a phenomenon that was to have major implications for the lives of the peasantry as, over the course of the sixth century, social, political, and military conditions in much of the West began to stabilise in the aftermath of the break-up of Roman power. It is to that process that we must now turn.

---

¹⁵⁷ Blockley (1981–3), pp. 204–5.
¹⁵⁸ Banaji (2009), p. 69, for references.
¹⁵⁹ Banaji (2009), p. 70, taking the phrase from R. Faith, *The English Peasantry and the Growth of Lordship* (Leicester, 1997), p. 69, where a similar situation is described.

3

The Romano-Germanic Kingdoms
The Era of Theoderic and Clovis

3.1 INTRODUCTION: THE BUILDING BLOCKS OF THE ROMANO-GERMANIC KINGDOMS

It should be apparent from Chapter Two that the demise of Roman military and political power in the empire's northern and western provinces over the course of the fifth century had led to the emergence of a highly fractured and fragmented social and economic landscape, characterised by growing regional diversity. In Britain, parts of northern Gaul and in much of the Iberian peninsula, a structural shift in the nature of the economy and a militarisation of social relations are discernible from an early date. Here, too, de-monetisation was rapid. Elsewhere, however, the waning of the fortunes of the Roman state left much of the Roman world's social and even, to some extent, economic infrastructure substantially intact. Around the Mediterranean core of the old Western Empire (southern Spain, southern Gaul, Italy, and the African littoral), a survival of Roman levels of economic sophistication was to some extent facilitated by ongoing contact with the Eastern Empire ruled from Constantinople, which continued to give cohesion and support to a broader Mediterranean economy. Indeed, it is a striking fact that if one were to chart on a map those areas in the West where, by the late fifth century, a functioning monetary economy using both high-value gold and small-denomination copper coinage had survived, they would (with the sole exception of the region around Marseilles) correspond to those areas over which Constantinople would reassert direct imperial control by the middle of the sixth century.

Likewise, although directly managed great estates were everywhere becoming increasingly autarkic, they remained a basic fact of life in much of the post-Roman West. Certainly, such archaeological and documentary evidence as we have would point to the continued survival of extensive concentrations of landholding both in the Mediterranean 'core territories' and the Paris basin further north.[1] Naturally, many of these estates, or portions of them, are likely to have fallen into the hands of new masters: indeed, the repeated references to barbarians receiving shares of the land (*sortes*) in return for their military service presupposes as much, but in structural terms, and from the perspective of the peasantry, in the Mediterranean territories and the Paris basin at least, continuity would appear to have been more pronounced than the sudden change discernible elsewhere.

---

[1] Sarris (2004), and Sarris, 'Continuity and Discontinuity in the Post-Roman Economy' (2006).

If, in these regions, many of the landed estates of the late-Roman aristocracy survived the barbarian invasions substantially intact, so too, it should be noted, did members of that aristocracy itself. As we have seen, those who suffered the most in political and economic terms are likely to have been members of the great senatorial families of the empire whose fortunes were most closely bound up with those of the Roman state and whose far-flung inter-regional property portfolios were the most vulnerable to processes of political and military disintegration. Beneath the level of this 'super-aristocracy', however, a high degree of survival on the part of elites is evident. Those whose interests had always been primarily provincial or regional frequently remained in place, seeking to cling on to such land as they could and to safeguard and protect their families and dependants. This was important not only in social and personal terms but also in cultural and ideological ones: for members of these Roman aristocratic lineages, whether acting in a secular context or (as was often the case) as bishops, became the crucial point of contact between the Roman past and what might be termed the 'medieval future'—transmitting to the leaders of the barbarians in their midst Roman modes of thought, styles of rule, and political and cultural ambitions.

As we have seen, however, these 'barbarians' themselves were more than mere passive recipients of Roman 'high culture'. The groups that entered Roman territory possessed their own social institutions and cultural norms, which in many crucial respects remained intact throughout the period of their migration and settlement and which were to play a vital role in shaping the societies that were to emerge on what had been Roman soil. This was particularly the case with respect to the culture of military lordship, which lay at the heart of early medieval conceptions of kingship and which constituted the key binding-agent of post-Roman society by providing a measure of security and defence that had hitherto been guaranteed by the manpower of the Roman army and the institutional framework of the Roman state. This feature of the post-Roman world invites closer examination, as it provides the key to understanding the variegated political and military fortunes of the Romano-Germanic successor kingdoms of the sixth and seventh centuries.

3.2 IDENTITY, LORDSHIP, AND KINGSHIP

The groups that had entered into and settled Roman territory over the course of the fourth and fifth centuries—above all the Goths and the Vandals—are known to posterity, and were recorded by Roman authors at the time, by ethnic designations that connected them to the historically attested tribal configurations of the eastern Germanic world of the first and second centuries AD (as we have seen, a period of major social evolution in *Germania*), which continued to serve as regional or tribal designations in medieval Scandinavia and the Baltic.[2] Thus, for example, the

---

[2] W. Pohl, 'The Vandals —Fragments of a Narrative', in A. H. Merrills (ed.), *Vandals, Romans, and Berbers: New Perspectives on Late Antique North Africa* (Woodbridge, 2004), pp. 31–48.

Goths, or *Gothi*, who defeated the Emperor Valens at the battle of Adrianople in 378, bore a name that we find recorded in an only slightly different form (*Gutones*) amongst the East Germanic tribes of the first century AD and which was clearly connected in some way with the region of Gøtland in what is now southern Sweden. Amongst many of the barbarians themselves a folk memory existed of a distant Scandinavian and then East Germanic origin. For example, Jordanes, a Gothic convert to Catholic Christianity writing in Constantinople in the early 550s, recorded in his *History of the Goths* that his forebears had originated in the far north from the island of *Scandza*.[3] Likewise, at about the same time, the Greek historian Procopius wrote that the Heruls (by this point resident in Italy), unhappy with their king, chose to send ambassadors to the distant north—as far as the semi-mythical land of *Thule*—to find for themselves a new ruler of their original bloodstock. A large number of claimants supposedly responded to this summons, causing the Heruls further difficulties.[4] Naturally, the barbarian peoples who settled in Roman territory were nowhere near as ethnically distinct as these connections might imply. Rather, these groupings consisted of composite hosts and confederations, made up of warriors and their families of often disparate geographical and ethnic origin, whose identity was capable of altering and evolving according to that of the military lord or lords whom they now served. Thus a Roman provincial who took up arms under a Gothic warlord might very soon come to be regarded (and to regard himself) as a Goth, just as in earlier centuries many a Germanic warrior had been Romanised by virtue of his military service to the Emperor and his concomitant commitment to the Roman state.[5]

That is not to say, however, that such folk memories were purely fictitious or such identities entirely constructed. Rather, the evidence would suggest that amongst the ranks of the barbarian elite in particular, but also amongst elements of the weapon-bearing free, such ethnic traditions and identities were jealously guarded and carefully maintained. Members of the barbarian elite thus came to serve as '*Traditionskerne*'—'kernels of tradition'—capable of imparting an inherited identity not only to their own kin but also to their followers as well.[6] Procopius identifies just such a group, whom he terms the *dokimoi*, or 'most esteemed', amongst the Goths at the apex of Ostrogothic society in Italy. These *dokimoi*, he tells us, served as the Ostrogothic king's companions in battle, and a group of them even publicly upbraided the Ostrogothic Queen Amalasuntha for providing her son, the boy-king Athalaric, with too Romanising an education.[7] The fourth, fifth, and sixth centuries thus witnessed considerable fluidity of personal and collective identities both within and beyond what had been the imperial frontier zone, but that fluidity was not total and the resultant transformation of identities was not

---

[3] See discussion in A. H. Merrills, *History and Geography in Late Antiquity* (Cambridge, 2005).
[4] Procopius, *Wars*, VI, 14, 38.
[5] G. Greatrex, 'Roman Identity in the Sixth Century', in S. Mitchell and G. Greatrex (eds.), *Ethnicity and Culture in Late Antiquity* (Swansea, 2001).
[6] R. Wenskus, *Stammesbildung und Verfassung: Das Werden der frühmittelalterlichen Gentes* (Cologne, 1961).
[7] Heather (1996), pp. 322–6; Procopius, *Wars*, V, 2, 13–18.

absolute. It is instructive, for example, that when Christianity was introduced to the trans-Danubian world in the late fourth century by followers of the anathematised churchman Arius (during the brief-lived rehabilitation of his theology by the imperial authorities between 337 and 381), the missionary bishop Ulfila translated the Bible into Gothic to ease his task, inventing a script so as to achieve this.[8] The Goths now had a written language ennobled by Holy Scripture. As a result, when, after 381, imperial orthodoxy once more returned to an anti-Arian position, the Goths and Gothic-speaking Vandals who had embraced the faith nevertheless persisted in their Arianism, which was now bound up with issues of language and identity, and which served as a useful signifier of cultural autonomy from Rome.

A similar stability and continuity is also evident with respect to social institutions. Indeed, what arguably served to preserve 'barbarian' identities across the vicissitudes of the migration period and the experience of settlement—and what, from the Germanic perspective, ultimately provided the link between the pre-migration and post-migration periods—was a focus by Germanic society on lordship both in the fifth and sixth centuries and in the more distant past. This was a social feature epitomised by the institution of the *comitatus*, or armed-warrior retinue, which surrounded and followed a lord and was bound to him by ties of reciprocal loyalty and devotion.[9]

It is important to note that, although Germanic society before the fifth century was 'lord-focused', it was not necessarily 'king-focused' to quite the same extent that early medieval society would be. Kings and monarchs certainly existed in early Germanic society and indeed would appear to have been a feature of early Indo-European society more generally: kings were known by very similar and evidently closely cognate terms in languages as distantly related as Old Irish (*rí*), Latin (*rex*), Old Gothic (*reiks*), and Sanskrit (*raj* for 'prince').[10] In early Irish society such kings combined a military function (thus the vast number of kings recorded in Old Irish literature and the Irish annals to have died in battle) with a cultic or religious one. The king was, in a sense, the embodiment of his tribe and its interface (or, more accurately, one of its interfaces) with the divine, responsible for the good fortune of his subjects, the fertility of the soil, and the clemency of the weather. The pre-Christian Old Irish *Testament of Morann* warns of the effects of an unjust king: 'the fruits of the earth are diminished ... (and) ... hurricanes and stormy weather forbid the earth's fertility'.[11] In early Germanic society kings may have borne a similar status: they are, at times, represented as the unique recipients of the divine *Heil* that ensured the good fortune of their subjects and their kin.[12] The king thus seemingly served as a cultic focus for tribal kindreds as well as being their political leader, hence the close etymological relationship between early Germanic words for these two terms—in Old English, for example, *cyn* and *cyning*. The crucial difference

---

[8] E. A. Thompson, *The Visigoths in the Time of Ulfila* (Oxford, 1966).
[9] D. H. Green, *The Carolingian Lord* (Cambridge, 1965).
[10] Wormald (2005).
[11] ibid., p. 586.
[12] Green (1965) and J. M. Wallace-Hadrill, *Early Germanic Kingship* (Oxford, 1971).

between Old Irish and early Germanic kingship, it is sometimes argued, was that in the latter military functions were separated from other functions: as the Roman historian Tacitus had declared of the Germanic tribes of the first century AD, 'they choose war-leaders on the basis of their manliness and kings on the basis of their ancestry' (*duces ex virtute et reges ex nobilitate sumunt*).[13] It should be noted that, on this model, not only was the figure of the king represented as a focus for loyalties, but so too was his lineage: his claim to the kingship rested, *a priori*, on his possession of the proper blood royal.

Tacitus' account of early Germanic kingship has generated much by way of romanticising historical literature, and has quite rightly been subject to criticism.[14] However, if the distinction that he identified in early Germanic society, between military leadership on the one hand and 'totemic' kingship on the other, had any basis in fact, and if this functional separation survived in at least some form between the first century and the fourth (as it seems to have done amongst East Germanic groups such as the Goths and Burgundians), then many of the barbarian invasions of the Roman Empire in the third, fourth, and fifth centuries may have been led by individuals who did not bear royal status.[15] Rather, these invasions were spearheaded by Tacitus' *duces ex virtute*—military commanders chosen, elected, or followed specifically on the basis of their military prowess. That such was indeed the case is perhaps implied by the fact that the contemporary Roman historian Ammianus Marcellinus, along with a number of other fourth-century authors, specifically did not describe the Gothic leader Athanaric as king (*rex*) of the Goths, preferring instead to accord him the rather more ambiguous title of *iudex*, or 'judge'.[16] That is to say, Ammianus chose not to ascribe to Athanaric a status that Athanaric did not perhaps claim for himself.[17]

As we have seen, however, over the course of the fourth and fifth centuries individual barbarian leaders and their retinues increasingly became the focus of new military confederations and affinities as they found themselves engaged in warfare within Roman territory, as they acquired ever more wealth and prestige, and as their successes attracted an ever larger number of would-be followers from diverse and disparate political and ethnic backgrounds. This process is evident in the emergence of the Gothic confederation known to posterity as the Visigoths, or in the ever closer relationship between the Vandals and Alans, first in Spain and then in Africa, as they made common cause against the Visigoths and Romans. By virtue of the

---

[13] Tacitus, *Germania*, tr. M. Winterbottom (Oxford, 1986), 7.

[14] See S. Dick, *Der Mythos vom 'Germanischen' Königtum* (Berlin, 2008).

[15] H. J. Hummer, 'The Fluidity of Barbarian Ethnic Identity: The Ethnogenesis of Alemanni and Suebi, AD 200–500', *Early Medieval Europe* 7.1 (1998), pp. 1–27, 9–10; H. Wolfram, 'The Shaping of the Early Medieval Kingdom', *Viator* 1 (1970), pp. 1–20, 4–5.

[16] Wormald (2005); H. Wolfram, 'Athanaric the Visigoth: Monarchy or Judgeship?', *Journal of Medieval History* 1 (1975), pp. 259–78.

[17] It should also be noted that the Gothic term closest to the Latin *rex*—the Old Gothic *reiks*—tends to be used in the Gothic Bible in a somewhat pejorative manner. Rather, for a lord whose power extended over a wide expanse and a large number of peoples, Gothic preferred the word *thiudans*. This fact may have informed Ammianus and others in their decision not to apply the word *rex* in a Gothic context. I am indebted to the late Professor Dennis Green for elucidation of this point.

way in which these new confederations, alliances, and composite hosts focused their loyalty on individual war-leaders or (in Tacitean terms) *duces* and their kin—even often ultimately adopting their new leaders' ethnicity as their own—so too did these leaders and their kindreds seek to consolidate and solidify their own newfound authority by claiming royal title. As a result, *duces* increasingly turned themselves into *reges*, combining ongoing active military leadership with a more permanent claim to overarching social and political authority.

This process can be traced in the linguistic evidence. In a first stage, throughout the West Germanic dialects, versions of the word for 'war-band leader' or 'military lord' (Old High German *truhtin*) can be seen to have displaced earlier less thoroughly martial words for 'lord' (such as the Old High German *frô*, which survives in the feminine in the modern German *Frau*, and which referred primarily to the lord of the household 'in his capacity of wielding authority over those who were dependent on him', equivalent to the *pater familias* of Roman law).[18] Subsequently, as we see in Old English (which most closely exemplifies the phenomenon), the word for 'war-band leader' (*dryhten*) came to be used to designate a king, before itself being displaced by *cyning* as new king-focused ethnicities took shape.[19]

Naturally, for some, the metamorphosis of *duces* into *reges* is likely to have posed genealogical problems: as the case of Procopius' Heruls reminds us, royal blood continued to matter. However, genealogies could always be re-invented, developed or altered if there was a pressing political or military case for doing so: in his *History of the Goths*, for example, Jordanes attempted to trace back the Amal dynasty of Theoderic and his kindred some two thousand years. In reality, neither the Ostrogoths whom Theoderic led nor the Amal dynasty to which he belonged dated back much before the mid-fifth century.[20] Yet the crucial point is that, within two or three generations, a succession of militarily effective rulers could successfully create a royal bloodline (*stirps regia*), as well as impart a sense of ethnic cohesion and identity to 'their' people.

The consolidation of royal authority in the fifth and sixth centuries was, of course, greatly facilitated by Roman examples and Roman expectations.[21] Roman emperors, commanders, and aristocrats negotiating with barbarian leaders had a vested interest in ensuring the rapid consolidation of power structures and chains of command amongst the barbarians with whom they sought to deal. Crucially, as we have seen in Chapter Two, the imperial office itself offered barbarian leaders a clear model to which to aspire in terms of style of rule and a symbolic language of power through which to express their new-found authority and prestige. The rhetoric, ceremonial, and actions of Roman emperors were replicated at the courts of Gothic and Vandal kings who, through their Arianism, were nevertheless able to distance

---

[18] Green (1965), p. 29.
[19] ibid.—*kyning* likewise becoming the favoured term among the Franks.
[20] P. Heather, 'Cassiodorus and the Rise of the Amalic Genealogy and the Goths under Hun Domination', *Journal of Roman Studies* 78 (1988), pp. 103–28.
[21] Wormald (2005).

themselves from the anti-Arian imperial establishment.[22] So, for example, in 484 the Vandal king Huneric would preside over a Council of the Arian Church.[23] In doing so, he both emulated and refuted the religious authority of the Emperor in Constantinople. The recasting of kingship between the fourth century and the sixth thus drew very heavily upon Roman precedent. The social dynamic that occasioned this recasting, however, drew its energy primarily from the ethos of the war-band and the culture of military lordship which the invaders had brought with them into Roman territory and which, as noted in the previous chapter, they increasingly imparted to their subjects and allies. The Romanisation of early medieval kingship was thus ultimately more a matter of style than it was of substance.

3.3 THE VANDAL KINGDOM OF AFRICA

The centrality of the role played by effective military lordship in the construction and maintenance of royal authority in the fifth and sixth centuries emerges with particular clarity from the history of the Vandals and the fortunes of the Vandalic kingdom of Africa.[24] As we have seen, the joint Vandal-Alan conquest of Carthage and the associated provinces of Byzacena and *Africa Proconsularis* in 439 had effectively cut the fiscal and military hamstrings of the Western Roman Empire. It also opened the way to the consolidation of Visigothic power in southern Gaul and ultimately Spain. In 444 King Geiseric's control over these African provinces, along with that of Numidia, was formally recognised by the imperial authorities, but relations between the imperial government and the Vandals remained tense, and in 455 Geiseric led a fleet along the Italian coastline and sacked Rome. By the mid- to late 450s, the Vandals were successfully consolidating their military position in Africa by establishing dominance of the sea lanes and islands that controlled access to the African provinces—such as Sardinia and the Balearic Islands. A Vandal foothold was even established in Sicily, whilst the one remaining Roman outpost on the mainland—Africa Tripolitania—was formally incorporated into the Vandal realm. In 461 Geiseric successfully drove back a Roman expeditionary force led by the Emperor Majorian, which had sought to gain entry to the kingdom via Spain, and in 468 the king's fireships scuppered an imperial armada sent from the East.

From the perspective of Constantinople, the events of 468 appear to have marked a final throw of the dice, and in 474 the Eastern emperor Zeno negotiated an 'endless peace' with Geiseric and his regime.[25] Thereafter, for almost sixty years, and in spite of political pressure applied by wealthy African émigrés, Constantinopolitan policy towards the Vandal kingdom was primarily characterised by an

---

[22] See discussion in P. Heather, 'Christianity and the Vandals in the Reign of Geiseric', in J. Drinkwater and B. Salway (eds.), *Wolf Liebeschuetz Reflected: Bulletin of the Institute of Classical Studies, Supplement 91* (2007), pp. 22–47; some relevant material also in M. McCormick, *Eternal Victory: Triumphal Rulership in Late Antiquity, Byzantium, and the Early Medieval West* (Cambridge, 1986).

[23] Discussion in Merrills and Miles (2010), pp. 72–3 and 184–5.

[24] For a detailed overview of recent scholarship, see Merrills and Miles (2010).

[25] Pohl (2004).

attitude of 'positive engagement'. Irrespective of questions of legitimacy, or of the confessional divide that separated the imperial Catholic Church from the Arian, the overriding imperial aim was to render relations with the Vandals as amicable as possible. The underlying consideration informing this policy is likely to have been the strength of the Vandal fleet, which, if directed against the East, risked jeopardising the strong lines of maritime communication upon which the Eastern Empire depended. It was better to contain the Vandals through diplomacy than to aggravate them through imperial hostility.

Of all the barbarian successor states of the fifth and sixth centuries, it is in the Vandal kingdom of Africa that the evidence points most clearly and irrefutably to a policy of land settlement and estate partition on the part of the newcomers. As noted in Chapter Two, the Catholic African author Victor of Vita writes expressly of the persecution of Catholic priests *in sortibus Vandolorum*, or 'on the Vandal shares'. Attempts to interpret the phrase *sortes Vandalorum* as simply meaning 'in the Vandal realm' are entirely unconvincing and sit uncomfortably alongside the rest of Victor's account. Likewise, Procopius (who was to see active military service in north Africa as well as Italy, and so should be regarded as a primary source on Vandalic affairs) describes the Vandal settlement in terms that can only refer to the distribution of actual landholdings. So Procopius describes how Geiseric:

> robbed the rest of the Libyans [his chosen term for African provincials] of their fields (Greek *agrous*) which were both very numerous and excellent, and distributed them among the nation of the Vandals, and as a result of this these lands (*agroi houtoi*) have been called the 'divisions of the Vandals' (*klêroi Vandilôn*) up to the present time. And it fell to the lot of those who had formerly possessed these estate-properties (*chôria*) to be in extreme poverty and to be at the same time free men. . . . And Geiseric commanded that all the estate settlements (*chôria*) which he had given over to his sons and to the other Vandals should not be subject to any kind of taxation. But as much of the land (*tês gês*) as did not seem to him good he allowed to remain in the hands of the former owners.[26]

Words such as 'field' (*agros*), estate-property (*chôrion*) or land (*gê*) cannot by any stretch of the imagination here signify anything as complicated as a share of tax revenue. Rather, the evidence clearly indicates that those estates that had formerly belonged to members of the great senatorial families (who indeed, *pace* Procopius, are those individuals most likely to have possessed the best and most productive land) were divided up amongst the barbarian invaders and their heirs, with a significant portion going to Geiseric's sons.[27] Procopius had no reason to make this up.

For Victor of Vita, the advent of Vandal rule and the creation of the *sortes Vandalorum* were associated with much violence and cruelty. He writes of how 'finding a province which was at peace and enjoying quiet, the whole land beautiful and flowering on all sides, they [the Vandals] set to work on it with their wicked

---

[26] Procopius, *Wars*, III, 5.12–15.
[27] A. H. Merrills, 'The Secret of My Succession: Dynasty and Crisis in Vandal Africa', *Early Medieval Europe* 18 (2010), pp. 135–59, p. 142—although I do not entirely agree with the author's reading of Procopius.

forces, laying it waste by devastation and bringing everything to ruin with fire and murders. They did not even spare the fruit-bearing orchards.... So it was that no place remained safe from being contaminated by them, as they raged with great cruelty, unchanging and relentless.'[28] According to Victor's vivid account, as well as engaging in generalised destruction, the violence and intolerance of the Vandals was specifically directed at two groups: the Catholic clergy (of which Victor was one) and the Roman aristocracy (to which he may also have belonged). Many members of both groups, as we have seen, were obliged to flee the province. Victor continues: 'many were the distinguished bishops and noble priests put to death by them'. The persecution of the Catholic Church culminated in 484 when the Vandal king Huneric issued an edict that sought to impose the Arian intuition of the Christian faith on all his subjects.[29]

Potentially, this is significant in that such an assault on the hierarchy of the Catholic or Orthodox (that is anti-Arian) Church, and the attack on the Roman aristocracy of the provinces of Africa as described by Victor, would stand in marked contrast to the policies adopted by Arian barbarian rulers almost everywhere else in the post-Roman West. That an 'edict of persecution' was issued is without doubt; again both it and its implementation are described in the writings of Procopius, who was a near contemporary. Procopius nevertheless hints at the fact that many African émigrés exaggerated the extent of their sufferings. He describes how many devout African Catholics who had refused to recant their faith claimed to have had their tongues ripped out by the wicked Vandals, yet—once in Constantinople—were miraculously able to speak. A number of these pious men then equally mysteriously once more lost the gift of speech when caught consorting with prostitutes.[30] Procopius himself tends to adopt a stance of enlightened scepticism with regard to matters of religion, and one suspects that here he was enjoying a joke at the Church's expense. Nevertheless, there are other indications that the claims of churchmen such as Victor of Vita should be treated with caution.

The Catholic communities of north Africa prior to the Vandal invasions already enjoyed a formidable reputation as an uncompromising bastion of Latin Orthodoxy. The African Church had suffered considerably, or at least, believed itself to have suffered considerably, during the Great Persecution instituted by the Emperor Diocletian in the early fourth century, as a result of which the African Church found itself enriched with the blood of many martyrs whose memory it cherished and celebrated. Even before the Diocletianic persecution, the African Church had produced a number of notable martyrs, such as St Perpetua under the Emperor Septimus Severus, or Cyprian, bishop of Carthage, at the time of Valerian. It should also be noted that Africa was particularly productive of movements resistant not only to secular but also ecclesiastical authority, as evident from the Donatist controversy that had wracked the African Church in the reign of the Emperor Constantine.

---

[28] Victor of Vita, *de Historia Persecutorum*, V.
[29] Exemplary discussion in Merrills and Miles (2010).
[30] Procopius, *Wars*, III, 8.3–6.

The specific culture of the African Church may therefore have had far-reaching implications for the character of Vandal rule. For, if the Vandals were more resolutely anti-Catholic than were their Visigothic brethren in Gaul and Spain or their Ostrogothic kindred in Italy, this might have been primarily due to the nature of the response to the Vandals on the part of the leaders of the African Church itself. In Gaul, Spain, and Italy, Catholic bishops—even bishops of Rome—were willing to cooperate with theoretically 'heretical' barbarian warlords and kings if political and military circumstances so required; as shall be seen shortly, for much of his long reign in Italy, Theoderic the Ostrogoth enjoyed a close and cooperative relationship with the papacy, despite being an Arian. The traditions of the African Church may have precluded such pragmatism, thereby eliciting a hostile response on the part of Huneric and his followers.[31]

Even then, however, caution is to be advised. As we have seen, as a result first of the Vandal invasion and then Huneric's edict of persecution, late fifth- and early sixth-century Constantinople was home to many well-connected Africans and their sympathisers who sought to press the case for a restoration of imperial rule in the region. It is very likely that Victor of Vita wrote his account, on which we are so critically dependent for our knowledge, with an imperial, Constantinopolitan audience in mind and with a view to spurring the imperial authorities into action; as such, we might imagine that the persecution he describes was exaggerated for propagandistic and polemical purposes.[32]

If Victor exaggerates the sufferings of members of the Catholic clergy at the hands of the Vandals, the same is perhaps still more true of his depiction of the plight of members of the Roman governing classes. Members of the great senatorial families clearly lost out by virtue of the Vandal settlement. At the level of the sub-senatorial and more regionally focused elite, however, the story in Africa (as elsewhere) was one of pragmatic accommodation and survival. The archaeological evidence from Vandal north Africa—particularly that relating to villa complexes (hundreds of exquisite mosaics from which survive to this day)—reveals manifest continuity in the structuring of rural wealth and modes of elite lifestyle. Likewise, the documentary evidence of the so-called *Albertini Tablets* records the workings of African landowners, farmers, and tenants on the fringes of the Vandal kingdom, who, irrespective of the change of political regime, continued to frame their property transactions and agreements according to the niceties of Roman law.[33]

As with every other region of the post-Roman West, members of the Roman governing classes in Africa demonstrated a willingness to cooperate with their new masters and to place their skills and know-how at their disposal in return for security and opportunities. The result was considerable continuity in administration and government. As noted in Chapter Two, the Vandals continued to mint

---

[31] W. H. C. Frend, 'From Donatist Opposition to Byzantine Loyalism', in Merrills (2004), pp. 259–70.

[32] D. Shanzer, 'Intentions and Audiences', in Merrills (2004), pp. 271–90.

[33] J. Conant, 'Literacy and Private Documentation in Vandal North Africa', in Merrills (2004), pp. 199–224.

copper coins after the Roman manner, albeit in smaller volume than the Roman state had achieved.[34] Such monetary policies were inconceivable without the assistance of Roman civil servants and administrators. Even Victor of Vita noted how 'a large number of our Catholics came to church dressed in their [Vandal] clothes, since they worked in the royal household'.[35]

Indeed, for many members of the sub-senatorial, regional Roman elite, the period of Vandal rule in north Africa may have represented something of a golden age. Carthage as a city continued to prosper under the Vandal kings and remained a major *entrepôt* for Mediterranean trade, drawing in goods and merchants from both the Eastern Empire and the world to the north.[36] Relieved of the censures and diktats of prudish bishops and Catholic moralisers, north African poets were free once more to celebrate the joys of the theatre and the pleasures of the flesh.[37] Not only did a traditional classical education remain available, but the schools even flourished under Vandal patronage.[38] For many well-born Romans under Vandal rule the *dolce vita* continued uninterrupted and even drew the Vandals into its embrace. As Procopius recorded:

> when the Vandals had conquered Africa, they visited the baths daily, rejoiced in the pleasures of a richly laid table, and ate the best, the sweetest which the sea and the land brought forth. They wore gold and clothed themselves with silk garments, spent their time at theatre performances and animal-baiting and other pleasant distractions, but above all hunting. And they had dancers and actors and musicians whom they listened to. The majority of them lived in splendid parks, which were well stocked with water and trees. They had a great number of banquets and rejoiced in all types of sexual pleasures.[39]

All this may sound terribly decadent, as was Procopius' intention. The emphasis that he places on the Vandals' love of hunting is significant, however: as Roman tacticians and commanders had long appreciated, the pleasures of the hunt and the pursuit of quarry could play a vital part in maintaining essential military skills on the part of warriors who did not find themselves tested on a regular basis through frequent engagement with a hostile foe. Certainly, such was the degree of security achieved by the Vandals in their new kingdom that for much of its history they were obliged to contend with little more than raiding activity from the desert fringe and the policing of the shifting frontier between their own realm and that of the tribal zone of Mauretania, where they faced warlords ruling over joint Roman-Berber populations.[40] For those contingents of Alans in particular who had joined the Vandals in the crossing to Africa, hunting would have helped to preserve that expertise in horseback archery in which they, like the Huns and the other nomads

---

[34] Ward-Perkins (2005), p. 112; Morrisson (1983); for a maximalist reading of the evidence, see Merrills and Miles (2010), pp. 141–76.
[35] Victor of Vita, *Historia Persecutorum*, II, 8.
[36] Merrills and Miles (2010), pp. 141–76.
[37] As recorded in the *Anthologia Latina*: excellent discussion in Merrills and Miles (2010), pp. 204–27.
[38] See A. H. Merrills, 'The Perils of Panegyric', and J. W. George, 'Vandal Poets in Their Context', in Merrills (2004), pp. 145–62 and 133–44.
[39] Procopius, *Wars*, IV, 6.5–9.
[40] Merrills (2004).

of the steppe, were thought to excel. It should be noted that the rulers of north Africa repeatedly and consistently styled themselves kings 'of the Vandals and Alans' (*reges Vandalorum et Alanorum*), suggesting the survival of a specific Alan identity well into the sixth century, even if—as Procopius suggests—in common parlance, the various peoples of the kingdom became 'subsumed under the name of the Vandals'.[41]

What essentially united the settlers in Africa, however, was not so much the 'name of the Vandals' but rather loyalty to those kings, and specifically the bloodline of those kings, who had led them into the province in the first place. The 'Hasding' dynasty of the Vandal royal household provides a classic example of a kingship forged on the battlefield on the basis of effective military leadership. The first attested member of the Hasding clan was a certain Godegisel, who had led his followers across the Rhine in 405–6, but had then fallen in battle against the Romans. Godegisel had been succeeded by his son Gunderic, who had rampaged with his followers around first Gaul and then Spain, contending with both Romans and Visigoths, and drawing the Alans into his retinue, thereby consolidating the ascendancy of his bloodline through his martial prowess. In 428 Gunderic had been succeeded by his son Geiseric, who negotiated the crossing into Africa and set about establishing his kingdom by force of arms. It is after the crossing to Africa that we find the Hasdings referred to as a royal lineage (*stirps regia*).[42] By Geiseric's death in 477 the royal status of the Hasding bloodline was indisputable, and Geiseric had been able to institute a complicated order of succession (probably aimed at preventing rule by militarily vulnerable boy-kings) whereby the eldest member of the dynasty would succeed upon each vacancy to the throne. So it was that in 477 Geiseric was succeeded by his son Huneric (who at that point was something over fifty years old). Upon Huneric's death in 484 the crown passed to two of his nephews, first Gunthamund (r.484–96), who was in his mid-thirties at his accession, and then Thrasamund (r.496–523), who was in his mid-forties, before reverting to Huneric's son Hilderic (r.523–30), who cannot have been far off sixty years of age.[43] This may not sound much to modern ears, until one bears in mind that the militarily highly effective Frankish king Clovis was just fifteen when he succeeded his father in 481, and Theoderic the Amal only seventeen when he was raised to royal status in 471. Early medieval warfare was a young man's game.

In the short term, the order of succession instituted by Geiseric resolved a potentially destabilising issue. In the long term, however, it was to be a source of considerable weakness for the Vandal kingdom. On one level, it sowed discord and rivalry within the Hasding bloodline, as ambitious grey-haired cousins jockeyed for position and sought to eliminate other potential claimants to the throne. This problem could only get worse as the family grew in size with each generation and its genealogy branched out.[44] On a more insidious level, however, what might be termed the 'gerontocratic principle' threatened to corrode the very core of the Vandal kingship by raising to the throne a series of monarchs who were simply too

[41] Procopius, *Wars*, III, 5.21.   [42] Pohl (2004), p. 34.
[43] ibid., pp. 41–2.   [44] ibid.

old to fulfil the core military function of the office. Under Thrasamund, for example, the Vandals suffered an unusually severe military reversal at the hands of Berber tribesmen. Martial prowess and vigour remained central to Vandal identity. For the kingdom to continue to cohere, the Vandals needed a king who was capable of embodying their own self-image by displaying the courage and valour of a Godegisel, a Gunderic, or a Geiseric. It is this consideration, in the wake of yet another defeat at the hands of Berber tribesmen, that informed the decision of Gelimer, a great-grandson of Geiseric from the opposite bloodline to Hilderic, to rise up against the king in the year 530, deposing and incarcerating him.[45] Hilderic was already unpopular in noble circles for having alleviated the burdens placed upon the Catholic Church as a response to improving relations with Constantinople.[46] Perhaps also with imperial encouragement, he had detached the Vandal kingdom from its long-standing alliance with Ostrogothic Italy, imprisoning Amalafrida, the wife of his predecessor and a sister of the Ostrogothic king Theoderic.[47] As Procopius put it, Gelimer was 'thought to be the best warrior of his time ... [and] ... allying with himself all the noblest of the Vandals, persuaded them to wrest the kingdom from Hilderic, as being an unwarlike [Greek *apolemos*] king who had been defeated by the Moors, and as betraying the power of the Vandals into the hands of the Emperor'.[48]

The Hasding dynasty thus found itself rent apart by rivalry, ambition, and anxiety about the military effectiveness of those holding royal power. The downfall of Hilderic provided an opportunity not only for the Berbers to make further inroads, but also for others to attempt to carve out their own break-away regimes and kingdoms. So it was that 'Pudentius, one of the natives of Tripoli in Libya, caused this district to revolt from the Vandals, and sending to the Emperor he begged that he should despatch an army to him; for, he said, he would with no trouble win the land.'[49] In Sardinia, Gelimer's appointed governor Godas—'a Goth by birth, a passionate and warlike man possessed of great bodily strength'— established independent rule over the island in his own name.[50] When an imperial envoy reached Sardinia to propose an anti-Vandal alliance, he found Godas 'assuming the title and wearing the dress of an emperor'.[51] If the authorities in Constantinople wished to send troops to help fend off the Vandals, the ambassador was informed, they would be welcome: the offer to appoint an imperial governor, however, was politely but firmly rejected.[52]

The offer itself is a revealing one, for in Constantinople the implications of dynastic instability in the Vandal kingdom were grasped with alacrity. Through its diplomatic contacts with the regime, the imperial authorities had perhaps come to appreciate how militarily vulnerable such a lord-and-king-focused society might be when there was trouble at the top or dissension amongst the ranks of the king's retainers and kin. If loyalty to the person of the king held such polities together,

---

[45] Procopius, *Wars*, III, 9.3.   [46] ibid., III, 8.14.
[47] ibid., III, 9.3–5. See also Pohl (2004), p. 44.   [48] ibid., III, 9.8.
[49] ibid., III, 10.22–3.   [50] ibid., III, 10.25–8.
[51] ibid., III, 10.32–3.   [52] ibid., III, 10.34.

disloyalty could rip them apart. Accordingly, the East Roman emperor Justinian, who had himself but recently come to the throne, wrote to Gelimer to inform him that the treaty which the empire had made with Geiseric acknowledging Vandal rule in Africa was now null and void. Gelimer's violation of the terms of Geiseric's order of succession, Justinian declared, was sufficient to justify an imperial military intervention 'to avenge Geiseric with all Our power'.[53] This pseudo-legalistic bluster should not be taken seriously. It is likely that such rhetoric was aimed primarily at destabilising the Vandal leadership by dividing it into 'pro-war' and 'pro-peace' (but anti-Gelimer) factions.[54] The important point is that the Roman reconquest of Africa was now underway.

What is most striking about the Vandal kingdom is the rapidity of its collapse: the force of 5,000 cavalry and 10,000 foot that the Emperor dispatched to Africa under the command of General Belisarius (who included on his staff the historian Procopius, serving as his legal secretary or *assessor*, who thus provides a first-hand account of the campaign) was as nothing compared to the vast imperial army that had been committed to the reconquest of the region in 468. Crucially, Belisarius' forces were able to make a safe landing in the vicinity of the village of Caputvada some ten miles down the coast from Carthage, before beginning their advance on the capital. Perhaps surprisingly, this move appears to have caught Gelimer off guard: his brother Tzazo and a substantial Vandal force had been sent west to put an end to Godas' royal pretensions in Sardinia. It is possible that Tzazo had taken with him the cream of the Vandal royal retinue. Certainly, Gelimer seems to have had few experienced or battle-hardened warriors at his disposal and the Vandal army was routed in the field, permitting Belisarius to occupy Carthage without facing any substantial resistance.[55]

Gelimer attempted to regroup his forces and summoned Tzazo back from Sardinia. On 31 December 533 the decisive engagement took place at Tricamarum. The king's brother fell in the field sword in hand, whereupon the Vandals were driven back to their camp. Procopius claims that the imperial expeditionary force lost only fifty men in this battle compared to some eight hundred or so on the part of the Vandals. This defeat signalled the final demise of the Vandal kingdom. Gelimer fled to an inaccessible redoubt in the Atlas Mountains, where he sought to maintain the spirits of his followers by playing ballads on his harp, reminding them, no doubt, of the past triumphs of their kindred. Ultimately, he was obliged to negotiate his own surrender and was taken to Constantinople, where he was publicly and ritually humiliated. The king was, we are told, led as a slave through the streets of the imperial capital, along with:

> [all his family and] as many of the Vandals as were very tall and fair of body... and... when Gelimer reached the Hippodrome and saw the Emperor sitting upon a lofty seat, and the people on either side, and realized as he looked about what a terrible

---

[53] Procopius, *Wars*, III, 9.19–20.

[54] For similar uses of such rhetoric, see E. Luttwak, *The Grand Strategy of the Byzantine Empire* (Cambridge, Mass., 2009).

[55] For the narrative, see Pohl (2004).

plight he was in, he neither wept nor cried out, but kept repeating to himself the words of scripture 'Vanity of Vanities, all is Vanity'. And when he came before the Emperor's throne, they stripped off his purple garment, and forced him to fall flat on the ground and prostrate himself before the Emperor Justinian.[56]

Belisarius' successful reconquest of Africa was facilitated by two facts over and beyond that of dynastic instability. First, Geiseric had dismantled civic fortifications so as to facilitate Vandal control. Conversely, this meant that once the Vandals had been defeated in open battle, they did not have the option of holing themselves up in walled cities, thereby stiffening resistance to the Byzantine advance. Instead, as the East Roman army made ever deeper inroads, they found the Vandals thronging churches and attempting to claim asylum. Second, in a society so structurally focused on the lord and king, the defeat of the king in battle and the smashing of his retinue marked the effective end of the kingdom. Tellingly, Vandal Africa was not to be the last post-Roman Germanic state to find its fortunes sealed by a single engagement: the same fate was effectively to befall the Visigothic kingdom of Spain in 711, as well as the Anglo-Saxon kingdom of England in 1066.

3.4 THE KINGDOM OF ODOACER IN ITALY

As noted in Chapter One, sometime around the year 476 the commander of the palace guard in Ravenna, the general Odoacer, deposed the Western emperor Romulus and established his own regime in Italy, which paid lip service to the concept of ongoing imperial suzerainty in the peninsula but little more. In many respects, however, this coup had much in common with the developments and processes that had culminated in the emergence of post-Roman regimes elsewhere in the West. Over the course of the fifth century, the imperial authorities in Italy had become ever more dependent militarily on groups of Germanic 'barbarians', such as the Heruls and Sciri, organised into their own divisions and under their own leaders to whom the Romans both delegated authority and accorded title and prestige. Odoacer is repeatedly presented in our contemporary or near-contemporary sources as one such leader who was able to lay claim to or build up a sense of 'royal' authority and use this as a springboard in his bid for power. As Procopius puts it, in a characteristically insightful analysis:

> During the reign of Zeno in Byzantium, the power in the West was held by Augustus, whom the Romans used to call by the diminutive name Augustulus because he took over the empire while still a lad, his father Orestes, a man of great discretion, administering as regent for him. Now it happened that the Romans a short time before had induced the Sciri and Alans and certain other Gothic nations to form an alliance with them.... And in proportion as the barbarian element among them became strong, just so did the prestige of the Roman soldiers forthwith decline, and under the fair name of alliance they were more and more tyrannized over by the

[56] Procopius, *Wars*, IV, 9.11–15.

intruders and oppressed by them; so that the barbarians... finally demanded that they should divide with them the entire land of Italy.... Now there was a certain man among the Romans named Odoacer, one of the bodyguards of the Emperor, and he at once agreed to carry out their commands on condition that they should set him upon the throne.... And by giving the third part of the estate properties to the barbarians, and in this way gaining their allegiance most firmly, he held the supreme power.[57]

Likewise, the *Gothic History* of Jordanes describes Odoacer as a 'king of nations' (*rex gentium*), a phrase highly suggestive of the composite nature of his following, and it portrays his usurpation as an invasion.[58] A similar account is contained in the so-called *Historia Theodericiana* of the 'Anonymous Valesianus', which records that, after having occupied Ravenna and deposed the young emperor, Odoacer took pity on him, 'granted him his life, and because of his beauty he also gave him an income of six thousand gold pieces and sent him to Campania to live there a free man with his relatives'.[59]

As Procopius' account indicates, Odoacer consolidated his regime by making land grants to his soldiers. These are likely to have been concentrated to the north of the banks of the River Po, from where the Italian peninsula faced its most dangerous military challenges in the form of the barbarian tribes of the Pannonian plain and the world to its north. As the Italian bureaucrat, politician, and administrator Cassiodorus would later declare of the neighbouring region of Raetia: 'the provinces of Raetia are the bars and bolts of Italy. Wild and cruel nations ramp outside of them, and they, like nets, whence their name, catch the barbarian in their toils and hold him until the hurled arrow can chastise his mad presumption.'[60] Soon Odoacer took warfare to the main grouping in Pannonia—the Rugi—smashing their army and slaughtering members of their royal bloodline.[61] There is also evidence that Odoacer intervened militarily in Gaul, launching a joint operation with the Franks against the Alamanni, who had raided Italy from the north-west.[62] Holding the northern approaches to Italy is thus likely to have been Odoacer's primary concern, and it would have made sense to concentrate his troops there.

At the same time, such a policy would have sent out reassuring signals to members of the senatorial and sub-senatorial landowning aristocracy of Italy. First, the geographical concentration of barbarian settlement would have meant that not all landowners were directly affected. Second, Odoacer's policy signalled that he took seriously the security of both his kingdom and his newly acquired subjects. As elsewhere in the West, such security was the necessary first step in the establishment of cooperative relations between a new regime and members of the Roman aristocracy. Certainly, Odoacer is known to have gone out of his way to show generosity to the Roman Senate, funding the construction of new seats for the

---

[57] Procopius, Wars, V, 1.2–9 (abridged).   [58] Jordanes, *Getica*, 46.
[59] 'Anonymous Valesianus', *Pars Posterior*, 8.
[60] Cassiodorus, *Variae*, VII, 4.
[61] 'Anonymous Valesianus', *Pars Posterior*, 10.48.
[62] Gregory of Tours, *Decem Libri Historiae*, II, 18 and 19.

senators in their assembly chamber, whilst at the same time seeking to establish amicable relations with Constantinople.[63] To many members of the Senate, the transition from the rule of Romulus to that of Odoacer is likely to have signalled little immediate change in lifestyle or even in terms of political realities: the imperial court at Ravenna, after all, had long been dominated by generals and commanders of barbarian origin, and Romulus' own father, Orestes, was a Pannonian who had once served Attila the Hun.[64] The only difference now was that rather than simply being the power behind the throne, a barbarian warlord actually sat on it.

3.5 THEODERIC AND THE OSTROGOTHS

There is every sign that, irrespective of questions of legitimacy, Odoacer was able to establish a secure and stable regime in Italy that enjoyed the support of the Roman elite. However, events beyond his control and, indeed, well beyond the frontiers of his kingdom would eventually bring down his regime. As noted in Chapter One, the break-up of the Hunnic Empire in the wake of Attila's death in 453 had seen the migration into Roman territory in the eastern Balkans of a loose confederation of former subject peoples of the Huns known to historians as the Ostrogoths. Between the 450s and the early 480s, leadership of the Ostrogoths had been contested by different warlords, including Thiudimer (*d.*474), Theoderic Strabo (*d.*481), and Recitach (*d.*484), who had carved out their own followings. It was only upon the murder of Recitach in 484, arranged at the request of the Emperor Zeno by Thiudimer's son, Theoderic the Amal, that the Ostrogoths achieved some measure of unity.[65]

The imperial authorities in Constantinople had done everything in their power to turn the young Theoderic into an agent of imperial policy. As a boy he had been kept a diplomatic hostage in Constantinople, where he is likely to have acquired an understanding of the workings of the court, even if he did not receive much by way of formal education.[66] In order to further bind Theoderic to a pro-Constantinopolitan axis, moreover, the prince was formally adopted as the Emperor's 'son-in-arms' and, along with Roman citizenship, was accorded the office of *consul* and the rank of *patricius*. Nevertheless, the presence of Theoderic and his large and militarily aggressive Ostrogothic host in the near vicinity of Constantinople remained a significant threat to the security of the Eastern Empire and, in particular, to its control of the crucial land routes to the imperial capital that traversed the plains of Thrace. For if the king was to secure and maintain the loyalty of his followers, he would need to provide them with ongoing proof of his military prowess as well as a steady supply of booty and supplies. As a result, the imperial

---

[63] B. Ward-Perkins, *From Classical Antiquity to the Middle Ages: Urban Public Building in Northern and Central Italy AD 300–850* (Oxford, 1984).
[64] 'Anonymous Valesianus', *Pars Posterior*, 8.
[65] Heather (1996).
[66] 'Anonymous Valesianus', *Pars Posterior*, 14, describes him as *illiteratus*.

authorities needed to get Theoderic and his men as far away from Constantinople as possible.

Fortunately from a Constantinopolitan perspective, such imperial interests coincided with the scale of Theoderic's own ambitions, and it was agreed that he and his host would march west to depose Odoacer in Italy. The account of this agreement in Jordanes' *Gothic History* is particularly suggestive, in that it identifies as the main driving force behind this migration the military restlessness and material expectations of Theoderic's own followers. As Jordanes wrote:

> Now while Theoderic was in alliance by treaty with the Emperor Zeno and was himself enjoying every comfort in the city, he heard that his tribe, dwelling as we have said in Illyricum, was not altogether satisfied or content. So he chose rather to seek a living by his own exertions, after the manner customary of his race.... After pondering these matters he said to the Emperor: 'Though I lack nothing in serving your empire, yet if Your Piety deem it worthy, be pleased to hear the desire of my heart.... The Western country, long ago governed by the rule of your ancestors and predecessors, and that city which was head and mistress of the world—wherefore is it now shaken by the tyranny of the Torcilingi and the Rugi? Send me there with my race.... For it is better that I, your servant and your son, should rule that kingdom, receiving it as a gift from you if I conquer, than that one whom you do not recognize should oppress your Senate with his tyrannical yoke and a part of the republic with slavery.'[67]

From the point of view of the imperial authorities, this was a 'win-win' situation, for whether Theoderic defeated Odoacer or not, he would no longer pose a threat to Constantinople. Accordingly, Zeno 'sent him [Theoderic] forth enriched with great gifts and commended to his charge the Senate and the Roman people'.[68]

It is significant, perhaps, that Jordanes did not claim that Theoderic was sent to Italy to rule as an imperial representative on the Emperor's behalf: rather Theoderic was to receive Italy 'as a gift'. Jordanes' account appears to be based on a lost Gothic history written by the Roman statesman and bureaucrat Cassiodorus, who served under Theoderic and his heirs in Italy; his interpretation of the agreement may well represent that of Theoderic and his entourage themselves. Certainly, it chimes with the reading of the agreement between Theoderic and Zeno (drafted by Cassiodorus) that was later to be dispatched to Constantinople by Theoderic's nephew and ultimate successor as king, Theodahad: 'Consider also, O learned sovereign, and consult the archives of your ancestors. Remember how large a part of their own rights your predecessors were willing to relinquish for the sake of an alliance with Our forebears. Weigh up the gratitude with which things repeatedly asked for should be received.'[69]

A more complicated picture is conveyed in the 'Anonymous Valesianus', which claimed that after coming to terms with the Emperor, 'Theoderic stipulated with him, that if Odoacer should be vanquished, in return for his own labours in Odoacer's place, he should reign supreme (*tantum praeregnaret*) until such time

---

[67] Jordanes, *Getica*, 57.   [68] ibid.
[69] Cassiodorus, *Variae*, X, 22.

as he [Zeno] should arrive.'⁷⁰ On the face of it, however, such an agreement is doubtful, not least given the fact that the Emperor Zeno had already been deposed by a coup in Constantinople once, and might have been again had he decided to leave the capital behind.⁷¹ Whatever the precise terms agreed, however, the negotiations between Theoderic and Zeno at least meant that, as he advanced on Odoacer, the former could depict himself as the defender of imperial legitimacy. To what extent he chose to do so, however, is very far from clear. As the relative success of Odoacer's regime demonstrated, issues of legitimacy were not necessarily at the forefront of men's minds in Italy, nor indeed elsewhere in the West. Rather, as Theoderic and his 120,000 or so followers made their way from the territory of the Eastern Empire in Illyricum to the wildlands of Pannonia, where the world of the empire and the kingdom of Odoacer met the turbulent tribes of the North, Theoderic sought to rally to him the warriors and retinues of the region by representing himself as a dread warlord, the sworn foe of Odoacer, and self-appointed avenger of the royal blood of the Rugi.⁷² It was in this guise, not as a Roman patrician or an imperial envoy, that Theoderic was long to be remembered amongst the Germanic peoples of the North.⁷³

3.6 THE STRUGGLE FOR MASTERY IN ITALY

In 488, as Theoderic marched along the Roman road south of the Danube towards the ancient Roman city of Sirmium, he found his way blocked, presumably at Odoacer's bequest, by the Gepids and their king, Thraustila. Theoderic is reported to have led the charge in person, and it is possible that the Gepid king himself died in the melee. The Ostrogoths then rested in Gepid territory before resuming their march. On 28 August 489 the joint Ostrogothic-Rugi host encountered Odoacer and his army at the Isonzo Bridge (*Pons Sontii*). Odoacer and his troops were driven back, ultimately to Ravenna, where he holed himself up behind the city's formidable paludian defences, and Theoderic formally entered what he later described as the 'Empire of Italy' (*imperium Italiae*).⁷⁴

A protracted struggle for power ensued as Theoderic and Odoacer vied for control of the cities of northern Italy and the support of their inhabitants. Odoacer was able to break out from Ravenna and drive Theoderic's men from Cremona and Milan; he even paid a visit to Rome where, significantly, he had his son proclaimed *caesar*.⁷⁵ In the summer of 490, however, a force of Visigoths arrived from the kingdom of Toulouse to ease the pressure on Theoderic's flank. With their assistance, the Ostrogoths were able to drive Odoacer back to Ravenna, which

---

⁷⁰ 'Anonymous Valesianus', *Pars Posterior*, 11.
⁷¹ 'Anonymous Valesianus', *Pars Posterior*, includes a useful account.
⁷² For numbers (c.40,000 warriors and 80,000 women, children, and followers), see H. Wolfram, *History of the Goths* (Berkeley, 1988). For the avenging of the Rugi royal dynasty, see ibid., p. 280.
⁷³ Note, for example, the references to Theoderic in the *Hildebrandslied*.
⁷⁴ Wolfram (1988), pp. 279–81.
⁷⁵ 'Anonymous Valesianus', *Pars Posterior*, 11.51-3.

they subjected to a concerted but ultimately an inconclusive siege. With the war grinding to stalemate, negotiations were eventually opened. In February 493 an agreement was finally brokered by the Bishop of Ravenna whereby Theoderic and Odoacer were to occupy the city jointly and would share power. Accordingly, on 5 March 493 Theoderic entered Ravenna not as king or even imperial vicegerent, but rather as co-ruler alongside a now elderly usurper whom he had spent five years attempting to eliminate. Some ten days later, however, in an act of brutal calculation, the Ostrogoth and his entourage caught Odoacer off guard and Theoderic 'with his own hand slew him with a sword'. On the same day, the 'Anonymous Valesianus' continues, 'all of Odoacer's army who could be found anywhere were killed by order of Theoderic, as well as all of his family'. Clearly, courtiers in Constantinople had had every reason to fear this ruthless Goth.

During the lengthy siege of Ravenna, we are informed, no doubt as an attempt to gain the political upper hand over Odoacer and his surprisingly resilient regime, Theoderic had sent a delegation to the Emperor Zeno under the leadership of Festus, the 'Father of the Senate', requesting that Theoderic 'be invested by him with the royal robe'.[76] We do not know what reply, if any, Zeno made, however; by the time of Theoderic's final victory over Odoacer, Zeno was himself dead and the Emperor Anastasius now sat on the imperial throne. News of Zeno's death reached Theoderic before Festus' delegation had had time to return. Rather than petition the new Emperor, and risk getting caught up in the machinations of the Byzantine court, the Goths simply acclaimed Theoderic as king of Italy.[77]

This act was important, in that it made clear both publicly and diplomatically that Theoderic owed his new-found authority in Italy to the acclamation of the Ostrogothic army, and not to any gold-sealed letter of appointment from Constantinople. Not surprisingly, the reaction in the imperial capital was decidedly frosty. Imperial recognition of Theoderic and his government was withheld. It was only some four years later that 'Theoderic, through Festus, made peace with the Emperor Anastasius with regard to his assumption of the kingdom, and Anastasius sent back to him all the ornaments of the palace that Odoacer had transferred to Constantinople.'[78] Quite what the return of these 'ornaments of the palace' signified is uncertain. What mattered most from the perspective of those members of the Italian governing classes who had hitherto cooperated with Odoacer was that there was now a new power in the land.

3.7 THE CONSOLIDATION AND NATURE OF THEODERIC'S REGIME

It is worth emphasising how closely and bitterly fought Theoderic's struggle for Italy was, as it helps to explain the intensity of his determination to reconcile members of the Italian governing and landed classes to his new regime, not only by

---

[76] 'Anonymous Valesianus', *Pars Posterior*, 11.54.
[77] ibid., 12.57.   [78] ibid., 12.64.

emphasising continuity between it and that of Odoacer, but also by conveying to his new subjects a clear sense of his willingness to conform to the still more deeply rooted political traditions of Rome and the Italian peninsula. Accordingly, the author of the *Historia Theodericiana* would look back on Theoderic's reign with evident affection: 'Theoderic,' he declared, 'was a man of great distinction and of good-will towards all men.... In his time Italy for thirty years enjoyed such good-fortune that his successors also inherited peace.... He so governed the two races of the Goths and the Romans, that, although he himself was of the Arian sect, he nevertheless made no assault on the Catholic religion; he gave games in the circus and the amphitheatre, so that even by the Romans he was called a Trajan or a Valentinian, whose times he took as a model.' 'The Roman administration,' he declared, 'he kept on the same footing as under the Emperors.' Elsewhere, the *Historia Theodericiana* informs us that Theoderic 'was besides a lover of building and a restorer of cities', and that when in Rome he had 'met Saint Peter [i.e. paid homage to his relics] with as much reverence as if he were a Catholic'. Most importantly, however, in terms of the security of Italy and Rome, 'Theoderic was a steadfast and most warlike man (*vir enim bellicosissimus, fortis*).'[79]

Theoderic's first priority in 493 was the rapid and peaceful settlement and assimilation of his troops. According to Procopius, as seen in Chapter Two, Theoderic 'distributed among them the share of the estate properties that Odoacer had given to his own followers'. Once again, the physical settlement of barbarian troops was largely concentrated in the territories to the north of the River Po, whereas elsewhere the obligation to support the Ostrogothic army was commuted into a cash payment.[80] Second, Theoderic was eager to assure his new subjects of the security of their property rights: thus amongst his first acts as king in Italy was to address a letter to the former Emperor Romulus confirming him in his possessions.[81] In particular, Roman landowners were reassured that, once settled, Theoderic's troops would not be given free rein simply to help themselves to the lands of others: 'If any barbarian occupier,' Theoderic declared, 'has taken possession of a Roman farm since the time when, through God's grace, We crossed the stream of the Isonzo, when first the Empire of Italy received us, if he has no documentation issued by an assigning officer, then let him without delay restore the property to its rightful owner.'[82]

Third, the legal rights of his subjects in general were confirmed. Legal disputes between Romans, it was declared, would be settled according to the established Roman law by competent Roman judges (*cognitores*), whereas disputes between Goths would be settled 'according to our edicts' by an official known as 'the Count of the Goths' (*comes Gothorum*). Disputes between Romans and Goths would be settled through consultation between the Count of the Goths in a given province and a Roman legal expert: 'thus each may keep his own laws and with various

---

[79] 'Anonymous Valesianus', 12.57–60; 12.70; 12.65.
[80] Cassiodorus, *Variae*, I, 14.
[81] Cassiodorus, *Variae*, III, 35.
[82] Cassiodorus, *Variae*, I, 18.

judges one justice may embrace the whole realm. So, sharing one common peace, may both nations, if God favour us, enjoy the sweet fruits of tranquillity.'[83]

Fourth, Theoderic sought to consolidate his kingdom militarily and diplomatically. In military terms, in the 490s he extended his protection over Alaman refugees fleeing the expanding power of the Franks. These he settled in the Alps to defend the passes into Italy. In 504–5 Theoderic extended his direct rule over the territory of Pannonia and the city of Sirmium, facing down not only the Gepids but also a force of Turkic Bulgar cavalry sent by the Emperor Anastasius. This gave Theoderic control over the military highway that linked northern Italy to Thessalonica and Constantinople, preventing the imperial authorities from sending a second army in his wake to eject him from his newly established kingdom. Diplomatically, Theoderic then set about creating a network of marriage alliances to bind the dynasties of neighbouring kings and peoples to his own. Upon his accession to the throne of Italy, Theoderic took as his wife Audefleda, the sister of Clovis, king of the Frankish kingdom to the north.[84] His own sister, Amalafrida, he married off to Thrasamund, the king of the Vandals, dispatching a Gothic garrison of 5,000 men to accompany her to Carthage. Thrasamund was Amalafrida's second husband: of her children from the first, the daughter was betrothed to Herminafrid, king of the Thuringians. Of Theoderic's own daughters, the eldest, Thiudigotho, he married to his kinsman and ally Alaric II, king of the Visigoths; his second eldest, Ostrogotho, was married to King Sigismund of the Burgundians; whilst the third, Amalasuntha, was kept in Italy where she was married to a Visigothic lord of Amal descent by the name of Eutharic. Along the Danube, the king of the Heruls, Rodolf, was adopted by Theoderic as his 'son-in-arms'. By these means Theoderic attempted to establish a series of alliances and client kingdoms to protect his realm from the empire to the east and the Franks to the north.

Certainly, from the first, relations with both the Franks and the Eastern Empire were strained. Any pretence of a cooperative relationship between Theoderic and Constantinople was dispelled by the clash over Sirmium in 504–5. Around the year 506 Clovis began to menace Alaric and the Visigoths in southern Gaul. Theoderic wrote to both kings, attempting to dissuade them from conflict, as well as to the king of the Burgundians, asking him to mediate.[85] As these efforts at mediation faltered, Theoderic was obliged to write to Clovis informing him that any campaign conducted against his 'son' Alaric would necessarily bring down upon Clovis the full wrath of Theoderic himself.[86] At the same time, he attempted to piece together a grand anti-Frankish coalition, mobilising the kings of the Heruls, the Warni, and the Thuringians.[87] When, however, in 507, Clovis made his move and bore down upon the Visigothic kingdom of Toulouse, Theoderic was prevented from making any substantial effort to drive the Franks back by a series of carefully timed raids on

[83] Cassiodorus, *Variae*, VII, 3.
[84] 'Anonymous Valesianus', *Pars Posterior*, 12.63.
[85] Cassiodorus, *Variae*, II, 41, III, 1, III, 2.
[86] Cassiodorus, *Variae*, III, 4.
[87] Cassiodorus, *Variae*, III, 3.

the Italian coastline by the imperial fleet, which were evidently meant to draw away Ostrogothic forces.[88]

After the Visigoths had been decisively defeated in 507 at the battle of Vouillé, Theoderic's response, therefore, was simply to annex Provence and finally, in 511, bring the whole of Visigothic Spain within his dominion, appointing his grandson Amalaric (511–31) as king.[89] The Emperor Anastasius was sent a carefully worded letter of admonition for his unwarranted act of aggression against the Ostrogothic realm.[90] In this, Theoderic acknowledged that although Anastasius was superior to other rulers by virtue of his imperial office (which, *de jure*, was unique to him), Theoderic could nevertheless claim a comparable authority for himself because of his adoption of an imperial style of rule (which he had learned in Constantinople) and his devotion to and control of Rome. Whilst there existed what he termed only one Roman 'realm', that realm nevertheless comprised 'two republics' ruled by Anastasius and Theoderic respectively. Theoderic may not himself have been an Emperor, but both he and his subjects were thus imperial and were not to be messed with. Much of this would have gone down very badly in Constantinople—which, presumably, was the point.

So why, one might reasonably ask, did Theoderic not simply lay claim to the imperial title? One consideration might have been a desire not to exacerbate tensions between Ravenna and Constantinople unnecessarily. Although relations were strained, and even at times resulted in armed conflict, each side also had reason to cooperate with the other, at least periodically. This was particularly evident with regard to the Senate. Theoderic needed the assistance of Roman senators and those who aspired to membership of the Roman Senate for the smooth administration of his realm, which was still largely entrusted to members of the Roman educated elite. Each year, the Emperor in Constantinople appointed from the ranks of the Roman Senate a Western *consul*—typically one nominated by Theoderic. This arrangement brought honour and prestige to all those concerned, and the Ostrogothic king had no interest in disturbing it. As we have seen, in the 490s the head of the Senate, Festus, had been eager to effect a rapprochement between the imperial authorities in Constantinople and the new Ostrogothic power in Ravenna, and had scurried between the two accordingly. Likewise, as the 'Anonymous Valesianus' emphasised, Theoderic was determined to maintain good relations with the Catholic Church and the Bishop of Rome. The adoption by a resolute Arian of the imperial title, and the full panoply of religious authority that had been associated therewith since the days of Constantine, might have risked sparking off bitter and politically destabilising resistance on the part of the Catholic clergy and the Pope.

It is sometimes claimed that, in addition to the imperial title, Theoderic was careful not to infringe upon other imperial prerogatives. Although he issued edicts (*edicta*) specifically concerning the laws of the Goths, he did not issue laws (*leges*) concerning his Roman subjects, declaring instead that he would uphold *civilitas*—

---

[88] See Cassiodorus, *Variae*, I, 16; II, 38.
[89] Cassiodorus, *Variae*, I, 24; III, 16; III, 17; III, 32; III, 43; V, 39.
[90] Cassiodorus, *Variae*, I, 1.

that is, the established Roman civil law.⁹¹ Likewise, although both copper *folles* and gold *solidi* were minted in his realm, the latter bore the image of the Emperor in Constantinople. Again, some suggest, these policies might have resulted from a desire not to offend the imperial authorities abroad or conservative Roman opinion at home. The reality appears rather more complicated, however. We know, for example, that a number of Theoderic's Roman subjects in fact went out of their way to address him as *princeps* (the traditional term for 'Emperor'). One Roman senator even erected an inscription to the king describing him as *augustus*.⁹² Similarly, in a mosaic in the great church of San Apollinare Nuovo in Ravenna, Theoderic was depicted wearing the 'imperial purple', which was meant to be the sole preserve of the Emperor. Moreover, in 526, to mark the thirtieth anniversary of his leadership of the Goths, Theoderic issued a special celebratory triple-*solidus* medallion (which could serve as currency) bearing his own image and according him the titles of both *rex* and *princeps* (Fig. 5).⁹³

When looking at the coinage of Theoderic's reign, it is important to bear in mind that in the still-functioning Roman economy of the sixth-century Mediterranean, coins were not primarily a vehicle for the expression of ideology. Rather, they were a medium of exchange in the context of a world dominated by trading contacts with the East. Since the creation of the *solidus* under Constantine, the gold coinage of

Fig. 5 Gold Medallion with Bust of Theoderic (B. Ward-Perkins, *The Fall of Rome and the End of Civilization*, Oxford 2005, p. 73)

---

⁹¹ Cassiodorus, *Variae*, IX, 14.8.
⁹² P. Amory, *People and Identity in Ostrogothic Italy* (Cambridge, 1998), p. 59.
⁹³ Grierson and Blackburn (1986), p. 35.

Constantinople had acquired an unrivalled reputation as a reliable medium of exchange and unit of account. As a result, even the last Western Roman Emperor—Romulus Augustulus—had issued coins bearing the designation of the imperial mint in Constantinople. According to one late sixth-century source, as far away as Sri Lanka, merchants were loath to accept any coin that did not bear the image of the Emperor of New Rome.[94] The main reason why Theoderic—along with the other kings of the Romano-Germanic West—were disinclined to mint gold coins bearing his own image, therefore, was probably that merchants engaged in inter-regional trade would not have been willing to handle them. Only as Eastern economic dominance began to break down would this begin to change.

Likewise, the main reason why Theoderic did not simply have himself acclaimed Western Emperor was perhaps not so much Roman resistance as Gothic reluctance. The Goths, it must not be forgotten, were political agents with their own traditions and their own expectations. It is very likely that they did not want a Roman Emperor; they wanted a Gothic king. Kingship itself, after all, was a relatively recent development amongst the Goths, forged on the battlefield. At the end of the day, Theoderic owed his throne to his Gothic followers and his composite army of Goths, Rugi, Heruls, and others: if a barbarian *rex* was what they wanted, a barbarian *rex* was what they would get.

This sense is reinforced if one examines more closely the main source we have for the workings of Theoderic's government: the letters composed on his behalf in Latin by his chief legal officer and secretary (*quaestor*), Cassiodorus.[95] Many of these are addressed to the Roman Senate or to the Emperor in Constantinople, and convey a highly Romanising impression of the regime, similar to that contained in the *Historia Theodericiana*. Yet what is most striking in Cassiodorus' correspondence (known as the *Variae*) is the extent to which, in letters addressed to neighbouring 'barbarian' potentates, but above all to Theoderic's Gothic followers, a proudly and resolutely Gothic identity shines through.

When mustering the Ostrogothic host against the Franks, for example, Theoderic is recorded as declaring that 'to the Goths only a hint of war rather than persuasion to strife is needed, since a warlike race such as ours delights to prove its courage. In truth, he shuns no hardship who hungers for renown of valour.' The king goes on to exhort his warriors: 'March forth to the campaign in the name of God, sufficiently equipped, according to your old customs, with horses, arms, and every requisite for war.... Thus will you at the same time show that the ancient valour of your forefathers yet dwells in your hearts and also successfully perform your king's command.... Bring forth your young men for the discipline of war. Let them see you do deeds which they may love to tell their children.'[96]

---

[94] Cosmas Indicopleustes, *Christian Topography*, XI, 19.
[95] For the complexities of handling this collection, which Cassiodorus subsequently re-edited for publication, presumably to justify his collaboration with the Goths to a perhaps suspicious Constantinopolitan bureaucratic readership, see S. Bjornlie, 'What Have Elephants to Do with Sixth-Century Politics? A Reappraisal of the "Official" Governmental Dossier of Cassiodorus', *Journal of Late Antiquity* 2.1 (2009), pp. 143–71.
[96] Cassiodorus, *Variae*, I, 24.

Theoderic took great care to maintain regular face-to-face contact with his chief military retainers and their retinues. This he achieved through a network of lavishly decorated royal palaces located in the main areas of Ostrogothic settlement.[97] The 'Anonymous Valesianus,' for example, records the construction of palace complexes and royal amenities at Ravenna, Verona, and Pavia.[98] Theoderic and his court travelled between these palaces and throughout the Ostrogothic encampments holding sumptuous feasts, distributing donatives and rewards, and hearing grievances. As Theoderic instructed the Gothic *saio*, or commander, Unigilis: 'Load with corn from the levy all the ships you can find at the city of Ravenna, and bring them to me [in Liguria] . . . [for] the province that endures my presence should find help from many sources. For my court draws with it hordes of followers; and while benefits are swiftly bestowed, necessary supplies are demanded from the people.'[99] Cassiodorus in turn describes the culture of conspicuous consumption associated with such gatherings: 'a richly laden royal table,' he declares, 'is a credit to the state': for whilst it was fitting for a private person 'to eat only the produce of his own district', it was testament to the might of a king, and the extent of the realm over which he held sway, that he be seen to enjoy delicacies drawn from far and wide.[100] In another letter issued in Theoderic's name, the Goths settled in Picenum and Samnium were summoned to their king: 'That man is like one dead whose face is not known to his lord. . . . Come therefore by God's assistance, come all into Our presence on the eighth day before the Ides of June, there solemnly to receive Our royal largesse.'[101]

Theoderic's kingship was thus military in tone, itinerant in nature, and rooted in traditions of face-to-face lordship. He further bound his Ostrogothic followers to him by supporting the Arian Church and, through it, promoting the use of the Gothic liturgy and language. Richly adorned Arian places of worship were constructed, such as San Apollinare Nuovo in Ravenna; beautifully illuminated manuscripts, such as the *Codex Argenteus*, were produced, glorifying the Word of God in Gothic; upon his adoption as Theoderic's 'son-in-arms', the king of the Heruls was informed that 'X and Y, the bearers of these letters, will explain to you in the ancestral tongue (*patrio sermone*) the rest of our message'.[102] To his leading Roman subjects Theoderic may have presented himself as 'a new Trajan or Valentinian', defending *civilitas*, the Senate, and established ways of life against the 'barbarians' of the world beyond; at the same time, however, he was careful to maintain the loyalty of the Goths, conveying to them a strong sense of active military leadership, generous lordship, and commitment to the traditions of his people.

---

[97] See map in Heather (1996), p. 238.
[98] 'Anonymous Valesianus', *Pars Posterior*, 12.70.
[99] Cassiodorus, *Variae*, II, 20.
[100] ibid., XII, 4.
[101] ibid., V, 26.
[102] ibid., IV, 2.

3.8 THE KINGDOM OF THEODERIC: SIGNS OF GROWING TENSION

Theoderic was to be regarded by posterity as a manifestly successful ruler. Procopius wrote of the king that 'love for him among both Goths and Italians grew to be great... and when he passed away, he had not only made himself an object of terror to all his enemies, but also left to his subjects a keen sense of bereavement at his loss'.[103] Likewise, Jordanes declared that 'there was not a tribe in the West that did not serve Theoderic while he lived, either in friendship or by conquest'.[104] When Theoderic died in 526, he was buried within the mausoleum that he had constructed to perpetuate his memory. The 'Anonymous Valesianus' describes it as 'a monument of squared blocks of stone, a work of extraordinary size' capped by 'a huge rock'.[105] In its outward appearance, Theoderic's mausoleum (which still stands) in many ways epitomises the nature of his rule, for it drew its architectural inspiration from two distinct sources: the Mausoleum of Augustus in Rome on the one hand, and on the other the *yurt*, or domed tent, of the steppe nomad.[106] It should not be forgotten that, to Roman ethnographers, the Goths were a Scythian race.

Even prior to Theoderic's death, however, there were signs of an emerging crisis. In the first instance, these were the result of tensions that were primarily religious in character. Although a committed Arian, Theoderic had worked hard to pursue a policy of religious toleration within his kingdom: 'no man,' he declared, 'can be forced to believe against his will' (*nemo credat invitus*).[107] Relations between Theoderic and the Catholic Church were undermined, however, by a fundamental shift in the plate tectonics of religious diplomacy that took place in around 520. Theoderic's ability to work with the Catholic hierarchy and the Bishop of Rome had been greatly facilitated by the fact that, during the reigns of both Zeno and Anastasius, the ecclesiastical relationship between Rome and Constantinople had to all intents and purposes broken down. Both Emperors were desperate to reconcile to the imperial Church those members of the Eastern congregations—above all in Syria and Egypt—who rejected the definition of the relationship between the Human and Divine in the person of Christ formulated at the Ecumenical Council of Chalcedon in 451 (to which we shall return in Chapter Four). In 482 the Emperor Zeno had issued a *henotikon*, or 'statement of unity', that sought to address anti-Chalcedonian concerns. In Rome the rigorously pro-Chalcedonian Papal authorities rejected this document as heretical and cut off relations with the imperial capital. This state of affairs persisted under Anastasius, who was suspected of anti-Chalcedonian sympathies. The resultant and ongoing breakdown in

---

[103] Procopius, *Wars*, III 1.29–31.
[104] Jordanes, *Getica*, 58.
[105] 'Anonymous Valesianus', *Pars Posterior*, 16.96.
[106] I owe this suggestion to the late Patrick Wormald.
[107] Cassiodorus, *Variae*, III, 45.2.

relations made it much easier for Theoderic to negotiate and deal with successive Bishops of Rome in good faith, for it meant that he was able to do so without harbouring the suspicion that they were in reality agents of the Emperor in Constantinople.

In 518, however, Anastasius died, to be replaced as Emperor by Justin, who had previously been captain of the palace guard. Unlike Anastasius, Justin was a Latin speaker from the empire's Balkan provinces. He was also a staunch defender of Chalcedonian Orthodoxy. Accordingly, the way was cleared for a rapprochement with the ecclesiastical authorities in Rome, which Justin rapidly effected. By 519 all outstanding matters had been resolved. This necessarily cast relations between Theoderic and the Catholic hierarchy in a new light. Still more significantly, the Emperor Justin took advantage of the re-establishment of communion with Rome to attempt to destabilise relations between Arians and Catholics in Ostrogothic Italy. In 525, for example, he instigated the concerted persecution of 'heretics' in Constantinople; his targets included Gothic Arians, many of who were induced (one might imagine with some violence) to accept the Catholic intuition of the faith. This measure was clearly meant as a provocation to Theoderic. The king responded by ordering Pope John to lead an embassy to Constantinople, where he was to plead that recent Gothic converts be permitted to return to the Arian fold. Justin seized upon the opportunity to further humiliate Theoderic. 'The Emperor Justin', we are told, 'received the Roman bishop on his arrival as he would have received Saint Peter, gave him audience, and promised that he would do everything *except* that those who had become reconciled and returned to the Catholic faith could by no means be restored to the Arians.'[108]

When Pope John returned to Italy, therefore, he had failed to alleviate the sufferings of the Arian community in Constantinople and was also regarded as having endorsed and given his public blessing to the Emperor and his policies. Theoderic had the pontiff arrested and held in Ravenna, where he soon died. As a result, John rapidly became a martyr and rallying point for the Catholic cause.[109] In response to events in Constantinople, Theoderic ordered that Catholic churches be handed over to Arian congregations.[110] The instruction was eventually rescinded, and we know that there was sufficient rebuilding of bridges between the Catholic hierarchy and Ostrogothic authorities for Pope John's successor, Felix IV (r.526–30), to have been appointed with royal consent.[111] Nevertheless, a spirit of mistrust had entered into relations between king and papacy.

Growing tensions were also evident between the king and elements within the Senate. In 523 Theoderic was informed by one of his high-ranking Roman civil servants, Cyprian, that the Senator Albinus 'had sent to the Emperor Justin a letter hostile to Theoderic's rule'. Albinus was accompanied to court by his cousin, the senator Boethius, who had agreed to serve as his advocate. In addition to being a philosopher and scholar of great renown, Boethius had also held office as Theoderic's 'Master of Offices' (*Magister Officiorum*); in effect, his 'Permanent Private

---

[108] 'Anonymous Valesianus', *Pars Posterior*, 15.91. [109] ibid., 15.92–3.
[110] ibid., 16.94. [111] *Liber Pontificalis*, 56.

Secretary'. Boethius protested to Theoderic that 'the charge made by Cyprian is false, but if Albinus did do it, then so also did I and the whole Senate with one accord; it is false my Lord King.'[112] Theoderic was neither convinced nor impressed. Cyprian then proceeded to bring forward charges against Boethius. Both he and Albinus were found guilty, and Boethius was then executed, as was his father-in-law Symmachus. Boethius, we are told, was first 'tortured for a long time with a cord bound about his forehead so tightly that his eyes cracked in their sockets, and finally, while under torture, he was beaten to death with a cudgel'.[113]

Theoderic was not short of well-born Romans to replace either Boethius or Symmachus. Indeed, Boethius' successor as 'Master of Offices', Cassiodorus, was a relative.[114] Nor is there any evidence to suggest that the executions poisoned relations between Theoderic and the Senate *per se*, as opposed to a particularly well-connected faction within it. What is perhaps more revealing, however, is Theoderic's evident sensitivity to contacts and communications between members of the Senate on the one hand and the Emperor Justin on the other.

The reasons for this were bound up with questions pertaining to the royal succession. By 518, when Justin came to the throne, Theoderic was already in his late sixties. Whilst the king had produced many daughters, whom he had put to good diplomatic use, he had notably failed to father a son capable of stepping into his war-boots and providing the Gothic host with the sort of leadership it expected. Theoderic's nephew, Theodahad, was a man unsuited to kingship both in temperament and lifestyle. The prince was notorious for his cupidity and consequently (according to Cassiodorus) had been publicly upbraided for it by the king.[115] Procopius describes Theodahad as 'a man who abhorred to have a neighbour' and who willingly robbed the properties of others.[116] Such greed might have been forgivable had Theodahad had a reputation as a warrior. Instead, he was a Goth who had gone native: a devotee of the philosophy of Plato and a lover of Latin literature, deeply versed in biblical and theological scholarship, but entirely unaccustomed to war.[117]

Accordingly, Theoderic had been obliged to nominate as his heir apparent Eutharic, the Visigothic lord to whom he had married his youngest daughter Amalasuntha. Although a formidable soldier, Eutharic was nevertheless regarded with considerable suspicion in Catholic circles: the 'Anonymous Valesianus', for example, describes him as 'an exceedingly rough man and a sworn enemy of the Catholic faith'.[118] In 522/3, however, Eutharic died, once more casting the succession into doubt. The only hope now lay in the fact that in c.516–18 Amalasuntha had given birth to a son, Athalaric, although it would be a number

---

[112] 'Anonymous Valesianus', *Pars Posterior*, 14.85.
[113] ibid., 14.87.
[114] As noted by Collins (1992), p. 111.
[115] Cassiodorus, *Variae*, IV, 39: although on Cassiodorus' representation of the reign of Theodahad, note Bjornlie (2009).
[116] Procopius, *Wars*, V, 3.2–3.
[117] ibid., V, 3.1; Cassiodorus, *Variae*, X, 1.
[118] 'Anonymous Valesianus', *Pars Posterior*, 18.80.

of years before he would be old enough to provide the Ostrogothic host with effective military leadership. The execution of Boethius in 523 thus coincided with a renewed bout of anxiety as to the succession to Theoderic, which understandably rendered the king suspicious about relations between his leading subjects and neighbouring powers.

Such suspicions are likely to have been further fuelled by the fact that many members of the great families of Rome had close personal connections to the Eastern Empire. Cassiodorus, for example, had relatives in the Senates of both Rome and Constantinople.[119] In such circumstances, it is far from inconceivable that as the 520s progressed, and as doubts about the succession mounted, members of the Roman Senate had indeed, as the king suspected, begun to consider what a world after Theoderic might look like and put out feelers to Constantinople.

At the same time, as we have seen, the imperial authorities in the east were successfully disengaging the Vandals from their long-standing Ostrogothic alliance by courting their new king Hilderic, who had come to the Vandal throne in 523. Theoderic was in no doubt that Hilderic and Justin were mobilising against him. Consequently, as a matter of urgency he began to construct a fleet with which to defend his kingdom: now that the Goths had their fleet, he announced, 'there is no need for the Greek to fasten a quarrel upon us, or for the African to insult us'.[120] This was bluster, however, primarily intended to reassure an anxious domestic audience as much as to ward off external aggression. Fleets took years, not months, to build up and train, and at the time of Theoderic's death in 526 his kingdom remained highly vulnerable to attack by sea.

3.9 THE FALL OF THE OSTROGOTHIC KINGDOM

The accession to the throne of the (probably) nine-year-old Althalaric in 526 necessarily meant a period of regency under the tutelage of the boy's mother, Amalasuntha. From the first, however, all edicts and communications were issued in the king's name, perhaps indicating a deep sense of unease, not least on the part of the Goths, at the prospect of a woman holding sway. As was mentioned earlier, members of the Gothic leadership—the old king's principal retainers—were soon expressing discontent at the manner in which the young king was being raised, and, in particular, his 'Romanising' education. As Procopius records:

> All the notable men among them gathered together, and coming together made the charge that the king was not being educated correctly. . . . For letters, they said, are far removed from manliness, and the teaching of old men results for the most part in a cowardly and submissive spirit. Therefore, the man who is to show daring . . . ought to take his training in arms. . . . And they asked her to reflect that her father Theoderic before he died had become master of all this territory, and had invested himself with a kingdom, which was his by no sort of right, although he had not so much as heard of

[119] Cassiodorus, *Variae*, I, 4. [120] Cassiodorus, *Variae*, V, 17.

letters. 'Therefore, O Queen', they said, 'have done with these tutors now, and give to Athalaric some lads of his own age to be his companions, who will pass through the period of youth with him and thus give him an impulse towards that excellence which is in keeping with the custom of the barbarians.'[121]

Those around Athalaric initially attempted to consolidate their hold on power by reminding the young king's Gothic subjects that the Amal blood that flowed through his veins had been their surest guarantee of success in years gone by. Athalaric was represented as declaring 'to the Goths settled in Italy': 'Receive then a name which has ever brought prosperity to your race, the royal offshoot of the Amals, the sprout of the Balts, a childhood clad in purple'.[122] They also exacted oaths of loyalty to the new monarch from his leading retainers in the provinces. This affirmation of the king's authority on the part of his Ostrogothic retainers enabled him to declare to the Senate that 'the hope of Our youth has been preferred to the merits of all others, and not unjustly, on account of the glory of the Amal race... the chiefs, glorious in council and in war, have flocked together [to recognise Us] without demur'.[123] The king's Roman subjects were likewise reassured that 'the person of the king only is changed—not his policy'.[124]

In spite of the rhetoric of continuity and consolidation, the king's subjects and neighbours nevertheless smelled weakness. In 527, as noted earlier, the Vandal king Huneric arrested and executed Athalaric's great-aunt Amalfrida. A menacing rebuke was dispatched to Carthage on Athalaric's behalf: 'Our Goths,' it warned, 'feel the insults conveyed in this deed, since to slay the royal lady of another race is to despise the valour of that race and doubt its willingness to avenge her.'[125] Ostrogoth and Vandal alike, however, would have noticed that no such vengeance was forthcoming. In Gaul, Athalaric was obliged to cede to the Franks those territories that Theoderic had incorporated into the Ostrogothic realm, 'as the Franks put no confidence in the rule of a child and furthermore held him in contempt, and were also plotting war'.[126]

Within the kingdom of Italy, there is evidence for growing lawlessness at a provincial level in response to the increasingly fragile and delimited nature of royal authority. For many in this lord-and-king-focused society, the absence of an active and effective ruler meant the absence of restraint. Petitioners flooded to court reporting maltreatment and abuse. The high-ranking Goth Cunigast, for example, was informed that 'Our Serenity has been moved by the grievous petition of Constantius and Venerius, who complain that [the Goth] Tanca has wrested from them the farm which is called Fabricula which belonged to them in their own right together with the stock upon it, and has compelled them... to allow the worst of all—the condition of slavery—to be imposed upon them';[127] the Governor of Sicily was lambasted for his misgovernment of the region, which threatened to alienate the population of this strategically vital island;[128] judges were ordered to restrain Gothic commanders (*saiones*) and other officials from wronging city

---

[121] Procopius, *Wars*, V, 2.4–18 (abridged).   [122] Cassiodorus, *Variae*, VIII, 5.
[123] ibid., VIII, 2.   [124] ibid., VIII, 3.
[125] Cassiodorus, *Variae*, IX, 1.   [126] Jordanes, *Getica*, 59.
[127] Cassiodorus, *Variae*, VIII, 28.   [128] ibid., IX, 14.

councillors (*curiales*) and illegally acquiring their property.¹²⁹ 'Frequent whisperings,' the king declared, 'have reached Our ears that certain persons, despising the rule of law (*civilitas*) affect a life of beastly barbarism, returning to the wild beginnings of society.'¹³⁰

In 534, having just attained manhood, Athalaric died. This unforeseen event left Amalasuntha vulnerable and isolated in Ravenna. In a desperate attempt to shore up her authority, she wrote to her nearest male kinsman, the land-hungry devotee of Platonic philosophy Theodahad, inviting him to rule jointly alongside her. Theodahad had evidently been plotting a bid for the throne and he accepted the queen's invitation with evident delight: 'Your whispers in my favour,' he informed the Roman Senate, 'might have been a source of danger, but now your openly expressed acclamations are my proudest boast.'¹³¹ As with the death of Hilderic in 530, however, the death of Athalaric in 534 presented the imperial authorities in Constantinople with the perfect opportunity to begin to meddle in Italian affairs. Neither Amalasuntha nor Theodahad were suited to exercise royal authority: neither could provide the Ostrogothic host with the active military leadership it had received from Theoderic and that it had anticipated in Athalaric, and without the sense of security that such leadership provided, the loyalties of the leading Roman senatorial families were up for grabs. Amalasuntha was able to write to the Roman Senate commending Theodahad for his erudition, but the one thing she could not praise him for was his valour in battle.¹³²

United only by their weakness, Amalasuntha and Theodahad were soon manoeuvring and plotting against one another, and drawing Constantinople into their machinations. We know that in 534–5 a dispute arose as to the taxes owed to the royal authorities by a Catholic monastery. The monastery in question made the significant decision of petitioning the Emperor Justinian to intervene on its behalf. Theodahad in turn wrote to Justinian informing the Emperor that he had done his bidding.¹³³ Amalasuntha attempted to court the Emperor Justinian's wife, the former actress and sometime supposed prostitute Theodora. In an indelicately phrased letter, she revealed to Theodora that 'We approach you with the language of veneration, because it is agreed on all sides that with every day your virtues increase.'¹³⁴ It might be inferred that—given her alleged past—they could hardly have decreased.¹³⁵ Faced with her cousin's plotting, Amalasuntha's agents ultimately approached Justinian asking whether she could place herself under his protection, an entreaty to which the Emperor seemingly agreed.¹³⁶ In response, the Emperor's wife Theodora incited Theodahad and his spouse Gudelinda, to assassinate the troublesome queen.¹³⁷ Whether or not on Theodora's prompting,

---

[129] Cassiodorus, *Variae*, IX, 2.   [130] ibid., IX, 18.
[131] ibid., X, 4.   [132] ibid., X, 3.
[133] ibid., X, 26.   [134] ibid., X, 10.
[135] Or do we perhaps here see Cassiodorus' later editorial pen at work, playing to the animosity with respect to Theodora expressed by critics of Justinian's regime such as Procopius?
[136] Procopius, *Wars*, V, 4.20–2.
[137] Procopius, *Secret History*, 16.5; Cassiodorus, *Variae*, X, 20 (letter from Gudelinda to Theodora suggestive of machinations against Amalasuntha).

Theodahad 'had [Amalasuntha] taken from a palace at Ravenna to an island of the Bulsinian lake where he kept her in exile. After spending a very few days there in sorrow, she was strangled in the bath by his hirelings.'[138] In ordering this act, Theodahad had fallen into Justinian's trap: he had provided the Emperor with the moral pretext to launch an invasion of Italy and an opportunity to divide opinion within the kingdom. In a desperate flurry of diplomatic exchanges Theodahad and his wife sought to dissuade Justinian from going to war, whilst in Dalmatia tension between the Ostrogothic garrison and nearby units of the imperial army led to violent clashes.[139] In 535 a joint Papal-senatorial embassy was sent to Constantinople to plead for peace. Once in Constantinople, the head of the senatorial delegation, the patrician Liberius, who had previously served under the usurper Odoacer and whose responsibility it had been to settle Theoderic's troops on the land, took the first opportunity to defect. For Theodahad, Liberius' move was an ominous example not only of the extraordinary pragmatism and fluidity of loyalties that characterised members of the late-Roman aristocracy in post-Roman conditions, but also of the way in which opinion in such aristocratic circles was hardening against him (Map 3).

3.10 THE ROMAN RECONQUEST OF ITALY

As with the imperial African campaign, we are much assisted in tracing the course of Justinian's reconquest of the Italian peninsula by the fact that the mission was initially entrusted in 535 to Belisarius, the hero of the Vandalic war, accompanied by his secretary, the historian Procopius, who provides a detailed eyewitness account. Unlike the Vandal adventure, however, the Italian war was to be a long drawn-out affair. This fact was partly the result of the imperial authorities' failure to commit sufficient troops to the campaign—the initial force sent with Belisarius in 535 perhaps consisted of some seven thousand five hundred men. It was also partly because, by invading Italy from south to north using first Sicily and then Naples as a base, the imperial expeditionary force was obliged to advance through often difficult and inhospitable terrain (a problem that also bedevilled the Allied forces in Italy in 1942). Geographically, as we have seen, Italy was at its most vulnerable from the north; it was only in 552–3, with Justinian's decision to send some thirty thousand additional troops from the empire's Balkan frontier along the ancient military highway that led into northern Italy, that the final remnants of Ostrogothic resistance were crushed.

The advance of the East Roman army was also impeded by the relative alacrity with which the Ostrogothic leadership—the royal companions and chief retainers of the kingdom—responded to the presence of imperial troops on Italian soil by deposing and murdering the devious but bookish Theodahad and replacing him

---

[138] Jordanes, *Getica*, 59.   [139] Cassiodorus, *Variae*, X, 20–6.

Franks
Byzantium
0
500
1000 km
0
500 miles
ATLANTIC OCEAN
NORTH SEA
PICTS
Scots
British
Anglo-Saxons and British
British
KENT
WESSEX
SUSSEX
Northmen
Scandinavians
Finno-Ugric peoples
Volga
Baltic peoples
Don
Saxons
Cologne
Thuringians
Elbe
Oder
Vistula
Slavs
Dnieper
Turkic peoples
Dniester
Danube
Lombards
GEPIDS
Rouen
Paris
Rheims
Seine
Nantes
Orléans
Tours
Rhine
KINGDOM OF FRANKS
Loire
Limoges
KINGDOM OF THE BURGUNDIANS
Lyon
Geneva
Milan
KINGDOM OF THE OSTROGOTHS
Verona
Dalmatia
Ravenna
Genoa
Spalatum
Toulouse
Arles
Marseille
Basques
KINGDOM OF THE SUEVES
Douro
Ebro
Ceasaraugusta
Tagus
KINGDOM OF THE VISIGOTHS
Toledo
Valentia
Cordoba
Corsica
KINGDOM
Sardinia
Balearics
OF THE
Rome
Naples
Bari
MEDITERRANEAN SEA
Sicily
Malta
Hippo Regius
Carthage
VANDALS
Berbers
Chersonesus
BLACK SEA
LAZICA
Trebizond
Serdica
Philippopolis
Adrianople
Constantinople
Salonica
EASTERN ROMAN EMPIRE
Athens
Smyrna
Crete
Cyprus
PERSIAN (SASANIAN EMPIRE)
Euphrates
Tigris
LAKHMIDS

The Romano-Germanic Kingdoms: The Era of Theoderic and Clovis 117

with a new leader, an Ostrogothic nobleman named Witigis. Although not of Amal blood, Witigis nevertheless possessed all the crucial military attributes expected of an effective king. As he declared to the Goths of Italy upon his accession in 536:

> Returning humble thanks to our Maker, We inform you that our kinsmen the Goths, placing me on a shield among the swords of battle, in the ancestral way, have conferred on me the kingly office by God's gift. Thus arms bestow an honour based on reputation won in war. For you must know that I was chosen not in the corner of a palace presence-chamber, but in wide-spreading plains; and that not the dainty discourse of flatterers, but the blare of trumpets, announced my elevation, so that the Gothic race of Mars [i.e. war], roused by such a din, and longing for their native courage, might gaze upon a soldier-king. . . . He who succeeds in imitating the deeds of Theoderic ought to be considered as belonging to his line.[140]

Witigis was evidently known to imperial circles in Constantinople and had visited the imperial court.[141] Accordingly, he not only sought to negotiate peace with Justinian, but also attempted to mobilise other contacts and connections in Constantinople to achieve the same result.[142] At the same time, he was able to rally at least elements of the Italian senatorial aristocracy behind him, with men such as Cassiodorus remaining in his service to the end of the day. Accordingly, in those areas that remained under Ostrogothic control, at least a semblance of the established administrative system remained in place, even if, in response to pressing military crisis, taxes were increasingly exacted in kind rather than coin and defensive ditches had to be dug around Ravenna.[143] In spite of the challenges posed by the terrain, by the time Witigis ascended the throne, Belisarius and the East Roman expeditionary force had reached Rome, having previously encountered little by way of coordinated resistance. The accession of Witigis, however, changed all that, and for over a year, from the summer of 537, the new king besieged the increasingly beleaguered East Roman forces. The imperial authorities responded by landing an additional 5,000 men at Naples. Advancing up the Adriatic coast, this second imperial army was ultimately able to break the Ostrogothic siege of Rome by cutting the lines of communication and supply between the besieging army and its high command. By 540 Witigis himself was under siege, holed up in Ravenna, just as Odoacer had been almost fifty years earlier.

The Ostrogothic leadership decided to sue for peace: their offer to surrender all of Italy south of the Po, whilst maintaining a kingdom in the north centred on Ravenna, was rejected by Belisarius, although representatives of the Emperor who had been sent to formulate terms with the Ostrogoths had been minded to accept it. Instead, Belisarius opened a second, secret round of negotiations with the Ostrogoths. It appears that in these negotiations Witigis and the Ostrogothic leadership agreed to hand over their capital to Belisarius on the condition that he would then pronounce himself Western Emperor. Belisarius agreed to these conditions, and Ravenna, Witigis, and the Ostrogothic royal treasury were formally

---

[140] ibid., X, 31.   [141] ibid., X, 32.
[142] ibid., X, 33.   [143] ibid., XII, 22 and XII, 17.

surrendered. Belisarius' coronation, however, never took place. Whether by virtue of a failure of nerve on his part, a lack of support amongst his officer corps, or a genuine sense of commitment to the Emperor Justinian and the regime in Constantinople, Belisarius made no attempt to revive the Western *imperium*. Instead he secured the city for the Emperor, and, later in 540, obeyed the summons back to Constantinople where, it was felt, his services were now required elsewhere.

It is testimony to the formidable defences of Ravenna that neither in 493 nor in 540 had the city actually been taken by force. Rather, on both occasions, negotiation and deception had proved the key to the city's capture. That the imperial authorities' victory in 540 was primarily due to opportunistic sleight of hand rather than overwhelming military might was not, however, lost on those Ostrogothic commanders and their Gothic, Gepid, and Rugian followers and allies who continued to hold much of northern Italy, including such strategically vital cities as Pavia, Verona, and Milan. Accordingly, the 'leading men' of the Ostrogoths gathered at Pavia and elected a new king by the name of Ildebad. The following year Ildebad died and was succeeded by his son, Baduila ('the fighter' in Gothic), who took war to the enemy in a concerted and bloody fashion.

After defeating the imperial field army at Faenza south-west of Ravenna (a victory that he owed to his personal leadership of a crack elite corps of 300 mounted warriors), Baduila struck south, scattering the imperial forces in his wake, cutting off the imperial supplies to Rome, and successfully besieging Naples. It is clear that during the course of these victories a considerable number of Roman troops of both Gothic and non-Gothic descent defected to Baduila's standard; whilst the Frankish king Theudebert was induced to accept peace in return for the surrender of the Veneto in north-east Italy and the acknowledgement of conquests he had secured at the Ostrogoths' expense in the Alpine region. Baduila then proceeded to invest Rome, which fell to him on 17 December 540.

This was a startling series of victories that demonstrated the core resilience of the Ostrogothic kingdom; if provided with skilful military leadership, the Ostrogoths remained a formidable fighting force. In addition to rallying the Goths, Baduila also attempted to garner support for the Ostrogothic cause amongst the Italian population. Here, however, he focused not so much on members of the senatorial aristocracy, who had been carefully wooed by the imperial authorities, but rather the slaves and peasants of the Italian countryside, to whom he promised freedom if they would join his cause. The representatives of the empire responded by declaring that all runaway peasants would be returned to their masters and by setting in place a system whereby governors would be elected by corporations of local landowners. As a result, the struggle for Italy increasingly took on the appearance of a social war.

Baduila opened negotiations with the representatives of the imperial government, threatening to destroy Rome, execute all members of the Senate and their families, and invade Illyricum if the empire did not come to terms. The Emperor prevaricated. Accordingly, Baduila marched north to Ravenna, presumably to prepare for his proposed assault on imperial territory in the Balkans, a decision that enabled the imperial army (once more headed by Belisarius) to reoccupy Rome. Furious at news of this, Baduila returned south determined to recapture the 'Eternal City'; at the same time, in the far West, his Visigothic great-uncle, Theudis, who held power in Spain, launched an attack on imperial territory in Africa, striking into Mauritania across the Straits of Gibralter. Theudis' Mauritanian venture ended in disaster, and as a result of the humiliation that he suffered in defeat, he lost his throne. In Italy, however, his kinsman was more successful. In 549 a Gothic fleet crossed the Adriatic and raided the coastline of Illyricum. On 16 January 550 Baduila once more secured the capture of Rome, which was betrayed to him by a band of soldiers from the mountainous highlands of Isauria on the grounds that their pay was in arrears.

At this point Justinian sought to sow confusion and dissent in the Gothic ranks by entrusting command of the Italian campaign to his nephew Germanus, who had taken as his wife a granddaughter of Theoderic by the name of Matasuntha. The son (also called Germanus) whom Matasuntha bore the Emperor's nephew in 551 thus possessed the Amal blood royal and was represented in propaganda composed on behalf of the Justinianic regime as the true heir to Theoderic. The Ostrogothic elite, however, were not to be fooled so easily: the disastrous reign of Theodahad had taught them that in the appointment of kings, martial prowess (*virtus*) was to be preferred over royal descent (*nobilitas*).

In 552 Justinian finally agreed to commit sufficient troops to the Italian campaign to complete the task. His general Narses led the imperial field army out of the Balkans into northern Italy accompanied by several thousand barbarian Langobard warriors who had agreed to fight on the empire's behalf. Circumventing both Frankish garrisons and Ostrogothic defences, and overcoming the marshy terrain by means of portable pontoon bridges, Narses marched on Ravenna, which, on 6 June 552, he successfully prised from the grip of the Ostrogoths. Baduila was once more obliged to head north from Rome, this time to meet a numerically massively preponderant foe. In late June or early July 552 the armies met on the plain of *Busta Gallorum*. Baduila attempted to fortify his men's spirits by riding out before his warriors 'to show to the enemy what manner of man he was'. The scene is vividly described by Procopius:

> the armour in which he was clad was abundantly plated with gold and the ample adornments which hung from his cheekplates as well as from his helmet and spear were not only of purple but in other respects befitting a king, marvellous in their abundance. And he himself, sitting upon a very large horse, began to perform the dance under arms skilfully between the armies. For he wheeled his horse round in a circle and then turned him again to the other side and so made him run round and round. And as he rode he hurled his javelin into the air and caught it again as it quivered above him, then passed it rapidly from hand to hand, shifting it with consummate skill, and he gloried in his practice in such matters, falling back on his shoulders, spreading his legs, and leaning from side to side, as one who had been instructed with precision in this art since boyhood.[144]

The martial skills that the Ostrogoths had learned from the horsemen of the steppe clearly remained central to their identity and their pride. Baduila gave his men the

---

[144] Procopius, *Wars*, VIII, 31.18.

order to charge the imperial lines on horseback, lances arrayed for the melee. Amid a hail of arrows, however, the elite Ostrogothic cavalry, some six thousand strong, was cut down almost to the last man. The body of the dying king was rushed from the battlefield by a small band of loyal retainers, who accompanied it to Caprara (Caprae) where it was buried. The Gothic commander at Verona, Teia, attempted to rally the remnants of Gothic resistance, but within three months he too was dead. The slaughter of the Ostrogothic elite on the blood-soaked plain of *Busta Gallorum* marked the end not only of the Ostrogothic kingdom but also of the Ostrogothic people, whose traditions and customs 'the most esteemed' lords of the Goths had embodied and kept alive.

3.11 THE FRANKISH EXPANSION

The breakdown of authority in Italy under the boy-king Athalaric epitomised the problems faced by any king who was incapable of providing effective military leadership. The contemporary Frankish world to the north, by contrast, reveals how rapidly the power and prestige of a series of militarily successful lords could snowball, and how dramatically their realm could expand as neighbours and rivals alike jostled to place themselves under their protection.

Over the course of the fifth century, as we have seen, the provinces of northern and western Gaul had found themselves divided up between a series of competing barbarian leaders and Roman commanders who had sought to carve out their own spheres of authority in the wake of the collapse and fragmentation of imperial power. Foremost among the groups operative in the region were the Franks, detachments of whom had been settled to the west of the Rhine in the mid-fourth century and whose kindred continued to inhabit the lands further east, thus permitting the emergence of what might be thought of as a loosely defined trans-Rhenish 'greater Francia' as the Roman frontier zone, or *limes*, disintegrated. By the late fifth century a Frankish 'count' by the name of Arbogast ruled from the ancient Roman frontier capital of Trier, while the Roman commander Aegidius had carved out a kingdom for himself centred on the city of Soissons: his son—Syagrius—would bear the title 'King of the Romans' (*rex Romanorum*). To the north-west, the territory of the former Roman province of *Belgica Secunda* had come to be dominated by a Frank called Childeric, who had consolidated his rule in the area with the support of his wife's kin, the Thuringians, whose power base lay to the east of the Rhine.[145]

As noted in Chapter Two, Childeric's grave-goods dating from *c*.481 reveal a hybridised Romano-Germanic kingship (with certain traces of the steppe). Certainly, as elsewhere in the post-Roman West, Childeric's regime appears to have been able to rely upon the support and cooperation of the local Roman elite, motivated by a desire for security in a highly volatile military world. This is

---

[145] Gregory of Tours, *Decem Libri Historiae*, II, 12.

suggested not only by the survival of Latin as a language of power and the written word as its instrument (as manifested by Childeric's seal-ring), but also by the early sixth-century *Lex Salica*, the law code of the Salian Franks over whom Childeric ruled, which set out the blood money that was to be paid as compensation for the murder not only of 'a Roman who was obliged to pay tribute' but also of 'a Roman who eats in the king's palace... a landed proprietor and table companion of the king'.[146]

It is also evident that cooperation was forthcoming even from the leaders of the Catholic Church in northern Gaul in spite of the fact that Childeric himself appears to have been a pagan (or certainly a non-Catholic). So, for example, upon Childeric's death in *c*.481, his son and successor Clovis (or Chludovicus) received a letter from Bishop Remigius of Rheims, congratulating him in highly Romanising terms on 'having taken over the administration of the Second Belgic Province'. Remigius took the opportunity to remind the new king of his moral responsibilities, advising him to 'defer to your bishops and always have recourse to their advice. For if you are on good terms with them, your province will be better able to stand firm.'[147]

In a series of startlingly successful military campaigns, Clovis set about eliminating his neighbouring rivals and foes, both Roman and Frankish. The first to face the full might of Clovis and his retinue was probably the 'king of the Romans', Syagrius. Clovis also took warfare to the Alamans. By the year 500 he had aligned himself with the Burgundian king Godigisel against the latter's brother, Gundobad. Through a series of lightning campaigns and carefully orchestrated conspiracies, he overcame and incorporated a series of Frankish kingdoms and lordships centred on Cologne, Cambrai, and Le Mans, whilst in 507, as we have seen, he took warfare to the Visigoths, defeating them (this time with the aid of Gundobad) at the battle of Vouillé. As a result of this victory, in 508–9 Clovis was able to extend his control over most of the Visigothic territories in southern Gaul, with the sole exception of Provence, which Theoderic the Ostrogoth annexed in 508. These victories provided Clovis not only with much booty with which to reward his followers but also considerable reserves of land to support the royal household and its retainers. In particular, he came into possession of extensive estates in the Paris basin, where, as noted in Chapter Two, large-scale patterns of landholding and a high degree of regional economic integration had survived from the late-Roman period. Accordingly, Clovis was able to derive both popularity and prestige by overseeing a rapid accumulation of wealth on the part of the Frankish elite.

In 511 Clovis met a fate that he had afforded few of his royal neighbours: a natural death. The kingdom that he had created was subsequently divided amongst his four sons—Theuderic (*r*.511?–33), Chlodomer (*r*.511?–24), Childebert I (*r*.511?–58), and Clothar I (*r*.511?–61)—who now had to prove their own prowess in battle and acquire enough land and booty to reward their own followers. As a result, further campaigns of aggression were waged against the Franks' neighbours. In 523 Chlodomer, Childebert, and Clothar launched a series of joint attacks on

---

[146] *Pactus Legis Salicae*, XLI, 7, 6, 5.
[147] P. J. Geary, *Readings in Medieval History* (Peterborough, Ontario, 1989), p. 157.

the Burgundians, against whom Chlodomer fell in battle in 524. This potential blow to the prestige of their dynasty (known as the Merovingians after Childeric's supposed father, Merovech) was remedied when Childebert and Clothar murdered their fallen brother's children and divided up his kingdom between themselves.

At the same time, the eldest of Clovis' sons, Theuderic—who dominated the kingdom's eastern territories—extended his lordship and control to the east of the Rhine, conquering and incorporating Frisians, Jutes, Saxons, and Thuringians. His son and successor Theudebert I ($r.533$–48) was able to take advantage of the Justinianic invasion of Italy to intervene in the peninsula, receiving Provence from the Ostrogoths in 536, launching an invasion of Italy and briefly seizing Milan in 539, and thereafter, as noted earlier, acquiring control over sections of the Veneto, where the Franks blocked the advance of the empire's Langobard allies in 552.

3.12 CLOVIS' CONVERSION

One of the ways in which Clovis had managed to achieve his series of victories was by means of the careful manipulation of a string of military alliances with his neighbours, fellow potentates, and potential rivals. One of his greatest diplomatic coups was to acquire the recognition and support of the Emperor Anastasius in Constantinople, who, as we have seen, had dispatched the imperial fleet to harry the Italian coastline, thereby preventing Theoderic from intervening militarily on behalf of the Visigoths as Clovis and the Franks bore down upon them.

It is conceivable that imperial envoys had enjoyed access to the court of Childeric; they are known to have had an entrée at the Burgundian court, a line of diplomatic communication that Theoderic the Ostrogoth had gone to great pains to disrupt. Relations between Clovis and Constantinople were, however, eased immeasurably by the former's decision, probably around the time of the Visigothic war of 507, to accept Christianity in its Catholic form.[148] As a result, the Emperor in Constantinople found himself in communion with a barbarian king who could now be drawn by him into an anti-Arian axis. As Bishop Avitus of Vienne wrote to Clovis upon hearing news of his baptism: 'Let Greece [i.e. Constantinople] indeed rejoice it has elected an Emperor who shares our Faith; but it is no longer alone in deserving such a favour. For your sphere now also burns with its own brilliance, and in the person of a king, the light of a rising sun shines over the western lands.' 'Do not doubt, most flourishing of kings,' Avitus went on to declare, 'that the soft [baptismal] clothing will give more force to your arms: whatever Fortune has given up to now, sanctity will bestow hereafter.'[149]

---

[148] D. Shanzer, 'Dating the Baptism of Clovis: The Bishop of Vienne vs. The Bishop of Tours', *Early Medieval Europe* 7.1 (1998), pp. 29–57.
[149] P. Geary (1989), p. 158.

Conversion to Christianity in its Catholic form offered tangible benefits to Clovis. On one level, it enabled him to enter into a new relationship with the Emperor in Constantinople from which both military advantage and political prestige might be derived. At the same time, it promised to draw still closer to the person of the king the bishops and leaders of the Catholic communities amongst his expanding pool of subjects. In southern Gaul in particular, it should be noted, such bishops were typically drawn from the ranks of the established Roman aristocratic families and lineages that still played an important role in local affairs.[150] Perhaps equally important, the specifically imperial associations of the Catholic faith enabled Clovis, with the Emperor's assistance, to adopt a more openly imperial style of rule in order to consolidate and enhance his increasingly trans-regional authority. This sense is conveyed very clearly by Gregory of Tours, who, writing in the late sixth century, describes how in the aftermath of his victory over the Visigoths, 'letters reached Clovis from the Emperor Anastasius to confer the consulate on him'. In response, the king staged a distribution of consular largesse: 'In Saint Martin's Church [in Tours],' Gregory writes, 'he stood clad in a purple tunic and the military mantle, and he crowned himself with a diadem. He then rode out on his horse and with his own hand showered gold and silver coins among the people present all the way from the doorway of Saint Martin's Church to Tours Cathedral. From that day on he was called *consul* or *augustus*. He left Tours and travelled to Paris where he established his seat of government.'[151]

Whether Clovis ever really styled himself *Augustus* is to be doubted. Gregory's account of early Merovingian history is frequently garbled, and it is likely that in his researches on Clovis, Gregory had confused the term for Emperor (*Augustus*) with the adjective for 'imperial' (*augustalis*), which was frequently applied to high-ranking imperial officials, such as the 'Augustal Prefect' (*praefectus augustalis*) or Governor of Alexandria. Clovis' expanding realm was sub-Roman enough for him to still be able to take advantage of the reflected glory associated with such imperial titles and Constantinopolitan connections. At the same time, however, the Frankish kingdom was sufficiently beyond Constantinople's effective military reach for such connections to be enjoyed without any hint of actual subjection to imperial authority or control. Unlike with respect to the Ostrogoths in Italy or the Vandals in Africa, no theological distancing from Constantinople was required. The king could thus draw fully upon the ideological resources and political support of the empire, the imperial Church, and the Catholic episcopacy.

Clovis was careful, moreover, not to force too much of his new religion onto his followers or to adopt too exclusively Roman a style. As with Theoderic in respect of the Goths, the king was careful to present himself as the custodian of the folk traditions of his people, and may indeed have been responsible for codifying their customary laws in the *Lex Salica*. Certainly, Procopius records a particularly bloodthirsty attachment to tradition on the part of the Frankish army as it advanced on the north Italian city of Ticenum in 539: 'upon getting control of the bridge

---

[150] Gregory of Tours, *Decem Libri Historiae*, II, 37.
[151] ibid., II, 38.

[over the River Po]', the historian relates, 'the Franks began to sacrifice the women and children of the Goths whom they found at hand and to throw their bodies into the river as the first fruits of the war. For these barbarians, though they have become Christians, preserve the greater part of their ancestral religion; for they still make human sacrifices and other sacrifices of an unholy nature.'[152] Likewise, the reason why, in 552, the Franks in the Veneto refused to let the Langobards pass was because they regarded them as their 'most bitter of foes in war'.[153] At the end of the day, it was the instincts of warriors such as these that Frankish kings needed to harness if they were to prosper. Again, like Theoderic, it was not because Clovis had attained consular rank that men followed him but rather because, as Gregory of Tours would put it, 'he was a great lord and became a famous soldier'.[154] As the rise and fall of the Vandals and Ostrogoths reveal, good lordship and feats of arms ultimately made and unmade kings and kingdoms in this new post-Roman world.

[152] Procopius, *Wars*, VI, 25.9–10.
[153] ibid., VIII, 26.18.
[154] Gregory of Tours, *Decem Libri Historiae*, II, 12.

4

The View from the East
Crisis, Survival, and Renewal

4.1 INTRODUCTION: SURVIVING THE FIFTH CENTURY

The provinces of the Eastern Roman Empire, ruled from Constantinople, had been able to surmount the crises of the fifth century substantially intact, with only the empire's Balkan territories suffering significant harm. The reasons for this had been largely military and geopolitical. In the third and fourth centuries, the main challenge to the integrity and security of Rome's eastern provinces had been posed by the empire of Sasanian Persia. In strategic terms, however, Persia was itself highly vulnerable to attack along its northern frontiers where it faced the world of the steppe. The rivalry between Persian interests and those of the steppe powers was in many ways encapsulated in the thought-world of the ancestral religion of the shahs—Zoroastrianism—according to which the cosmos was locked in a perpetual conflict between the demiurge of Order and the demiurge of Chaos. On earth, the principle of order was represented by the settled, civilised world of *Iran*, whilst its antithesis was embodied by the chaotic, lawless world of the nomad, known as *Turan*.[1]

Anxiety about the steppe was thus ingrained in both the strategic geography of the Sasanian Empire and the mindset of those that ruled over it. Unsurprisingly, the westward expansion of Hunnic power to the north of Persia in the late fourth century had occasioned major alarm on the part of the Persian authorities, who had hurriedly set about repairing relations with the Eastern Roman Empire in order to concentrate on the Hunnic challenge. In both Ctesiphon and Constantinople there was dawning realisation that, faced with a common foe in the form of the nomadic Huns, cooperation between the two sedentary empires was imperative. Accordingly, in 387, a peace treaty was agreed.[2] As part of this rapprochement, a formal partition of the contested region of Armenia was negotiated, with the kingdom of the Armenian king Khosrov forming the core of the Persian sector and that of the Armenian king Arsaces forming the core of the Roman. The fifth-century *Epic Histories* preserve an Armenian perspective on this turn of events, recording that

---

[1] See discussion in J. D. Howard-Johnston, 'The Two Great Powers in Late Antiquity: A Comparison', in Averil Cameron (ed.), *The Late Antique and Early Islamic East*, —vol. III: *States, Resources, and Armies* (Princeton, 1995), pp. 157–226.

[2] *de Caesaribus*, 48.5.

'the portion of Khosrov was larger than that of Arsaces. And many districts were cut off from both. And the kingdom of Armenia was diminished, divided, and scattered. And it declined from its greatness at that time and thereafter.'[3] Around the year 402, in a clear sign of the extent of the détente that had taken place in Roman-Persian relations, the Emperor Arcadius appointed the Persian shah Yazdgerd as guardian over his son Theodosius (II) in order to secure the young prince's succession to the throne, which took place in 408.[4]

Although there were to be subsequent moments of tension and rivalry between the two empires over the course of the fifth century (primarily in the years 421–2 and 440), peaceful conditions largely prevailed on Rome's eastern frontier. This was vital, as it enabled the Eastern Roman authorities to concentrate both manpower and resources on fending off challenges from north and west without having to worry about any opportunistic foray into Roman territory on the part of the Persians. Theodosius II (r.408–50) was able to devote vast sums to the defence of the imperial capital of Constantinople, building the formidable (and still spectacular) triple-level Land Walls that sealed off the peninsula on which the city stood from the troubled plains of Thrace, walls that were not to be breached until the Ottoman conquest of 1453 (see Fig. 3).[5] Whilst there was little the imperial authorities could do to prevent Hunnic incursions elsewhere in the Balkans, the imperial capital remained untouched. With the break-up of the Hunnic Empire following Attila's death in 453, and the westward march of Theoderic and the Ostrogoths in 489, the Emperor Anastasius had been able not only to restore Roman control up to the Danubian frontier, but also to invest in the defensive infrastructure of a region that had effectively suffered over one hundred years of constant warfare and chronic insecurity.[6]

In the territories of Asia Minor, Syria, Palestine, and Egypt, peace meant prosperity. Everywhere, beyond the Eastern Empire's Balkan provinces, there is evidence that the fifth century witnessed rising population levels—in pre-industrial conditions the main factor conducive to economic growth. The archaeological testimony of the villages of the Syrian Limestone Massif, for example, or those on the fringes of the Negev desert in southern Palestine, points to high population densities even in relatively marginal zones where agriculture was far from straightforward.[7] Economic expansion was further catalysed during the reign of the Emperor Anastasius by the introduction of new denominations of bronze coinage, which could be used for even the most basic of daily transactions; this in turn facilitated a more full-blown monetisation of both the fiscal structures of the state and the imperial economy more generally.[8]

---

[3] *Epic Histories*, VI.1 (tr. Greenwood).
[4] G. Greatrex and S. Lieu, *The Roman Eastern Frontier and the Persian Wars: Part II AD 363–630* (London, 2002), pp. 32–3.
[5] E. N. Luttwak, *The Grand Strategy of the Byzantine Empire* (Cambridge, Mass., 2009), pp. 67–77.
[6] F. Haarer, *The Reign of the Emperor Anastasius* (Aldershot, 2006), pp. 104–14.
[7] Decker (2009).
[8] ibid., pp. 202–6; Banaji (2007).

4.2 THE LIMITATIONS AND FRAILTIES OF THE EASTERN ROMAN STATE

Nevertheless, it is important neither to exaggerate the strength, cohesion, or governmental effectiveness of the Eastern Roman Empire as it entered the sixth century, nor to overstate the self-confidence of governing circles within it. In spite of the fact that Western courtiers in the service of barbarian kings, such as Avitus of Vienne in the Burgundian kingdom, or Cassiodorus in Italy, were willing to flatter the Emperor in Constantinople by lauding both the unique authority of his office and the lustre and renown of the state over which he ruled, there was a palpable sense in Constantinople in the late fifth and early sixth centuries that a very significant contraction of imperial authority had taken place and that the Western Empire had been lost.[9] As noted earlier, the pagan historian Zosimus, writing in Constantinople around the year 500, blamed this turn of events on the Emperor Constantine's refusal to sacrifice to the gods when he entered Rome; his near contemporary, the Count Marcellinus (the author of a brief Latin chronicle), identified the downfall of Romulus Augustulus as the key turning point; Procopius, as we have seen, identified a more gradual but cumulatively devastating barbarisation of the Western Roman army and state. From an imperial perspective, the fact that legitimate Roman emperors had been replaced by heretical barbarian kings only made matters worse. Understandably, within political circles in Constantinople, anxiety as to the nature of imperial rule and speculation as to its future were rife.[10] The very existence of the barbarian successor kingdoms constituted a direct challenge to imperial authority, and no amount of rhetorical bluster or diplomatic obfuscation could hide the fact.

It should also be noted that political conditions in Constantinople could be highly unstable. The reign of the Emperor Zeno (r.474–91) in particular was punctuated by a number of conspiracies and revolts. In 475 the Emperor was briefly deposed in a senatorial coup led by a certain Basiliscus. Zeno responded by fleeing to the highlands of Isauria in Asia Minor, whence he originated, and where he was able to rally to his cause the indigenous, highly militarised (and barely civilised) populace. After negotiating an alliance with Theoderic and his Goths (then still resident in Eastern Roman territory), Zeno marched on Constantinople, where 'because the Senate and people feared Zeno, to prevent the city suffering any harm, they deserted Basiliscus, opened the gates, and all surrendered'.[11] Basiliscus and his family fled to a church where they sought sanctuary, out of which Zeno attempted to coax them by swearing on oath that he would not shed their blood.

---

[9] W. Kaegi, *Byzantium and the Decline of Rome* (Princeton, 1968), pp. 3–58 and 99–145; W. Goffart, *Rome's Fall and After* (Princeton, 1989), pp. 81–110; P. Amory, *People and Identity in Ostrogothic Italy* (Cambridge, 1997), pp. 135–40.

[10] A. Cameron, *Procopius and the Sixth Century* (London, 1985), pp. 242–60; P. Bell, *Three Political Voices from the Age of Justinian: Agapetus' Advice to the Emperor, Dialogue on Political Science, Paul the Silentiary's Description of Hagia Sophia* (Liverpool, 2009).

[11] 'Anonymous Valesianus', *Pars Posterior*, 9.42.

True to his word, when they surrendered, Basiliscus, his wife, and sons were 'shut up in a dry cistern where they froze to death'.[12] Thereafter Zeno was careful to buy support for himself and his regime by showing generosity to the Senate and the inhabitants of the imperial capital (although another revolt would occur later in his reign).[13]

What lay behind Basiliscus' antipathy to Zeno is far from clear, but the very fact that a reigning Emperor was felt to be challengeable suggests a core crisis of authority at the heart of the imperial office. Any such crisis is likely to have been intensified by three additional factors. First, as we have seen, ever since the Ecumenical Council of Chalcedon in 451, the imperial Church had found itself racked by disputes as to the nature of the relationship between the human and divine in the person of Christ. The definition of this relationship as established at the Council, that Christ existed 'in two natures without confusion, change, division, or separation—the difference of the natures being in no way destroyed by the union, but rather the distinctive character of each nature being preserved and coming together into one person and one *hypostasis*'—met bitter and sustained resistance from the leaders of the Church in Egypt and Syria. They would have preferred the formula that Christ existed 'from two natures' (the reasons for this will be addressed shortly).[14] The Patriarch of Alexandria, who led Egyptian opposition to the Chalcedonian formula, was denounced as a 'New Pharaoh' by his opponents, so overbearing and imperious was his attitude perceived to be. The refusal of large sections of the Church in two of the empire's wealthiest and politically most significant regions to accept the Christological definition set down at Chalcedon constituted a direct challenge to the authority of the imperial office, as the decrees of such Ecumenical Councils carried the status of imperial law. The emperors of the late fifth and early sixth centuries attempted to respond to this challenge by a combination of limited persecution, arm-twisting of a more gentle variety, and compromise, none of which had any lasting impact. Then, when the Emperor Anastasius (r.491–518) began to reveal his sympathies with the anti-Chalcedonian party, he excited the antipathy of the pro-Chalcedonian faction. The dispute over Chalcedon cast into stark relief the practical limitations that constrained the effective workings of the imperial office. However autocratic and omnipotent in tone the orders emerging from the imperial court, there was little that emperors could do to coerce so many over so vast an empire. It was with good reason that, in Italy, the pragmatic Theoderic had declared he did not believe in compulsion in matters of religion.[15]

Second, although the urban and agrarian economy of the Eastern Roman Empire was flourishing, there is evidence that an ongoing expansion of the estates of members of the imperial aristocracy was both undermining the state's fiscal access to the resources of its subjects and also having an increasingly corrosive effect

[12] 'Anonymous Valesianus', *Pars Posterior*, 9.43.   [13] ibid., 9.44.
[14] *Acts of the Council of Chalcedon*, tr. R. Price and M. Gaddis, 3 vols. (Liverpool, 2005), 5.34.
[15] J. Meyendorff, 'Justinian, the Empire, and the Church', *Dumbarton Oaks Papers* 22 (1968), pp. 43–60.

on the structures of secular government. As noted in Chapter One, the reconfiguration and rearticulation of the political structures of the Roman state that had taken place in the fourth century had sparked off a dynamic process of elite formation in both the western and eastern provinces of the Roman world, catalysing the emergence of a new imperial aristocracy of service drawn from the upper echelons of curial society.[16] Members of this new elite, many of whom acquired senatorial status, had not only come to dominate the higher offices of state and the upper reaches of the civil bureaucracy and military administration, but also had increasingly deployed their new-found authority and prestige to win mastery of local landed society. Political clout and social connection had thus taken ever more tangible form in landed wealth. This phenomenon is readily discernible from the papyrological record from Egypt, which records a snowballing of aristocratic fortunes at the grassroots of Egyptian society over the course of the fifth and into the sixth century and an expansion of great estates owned by members of the new politico-administrative elite.[17]

Crucially, across the Eastern provinces, members of this elite took advantage both of the relative surfeit of labour (a consequence of demographic growth) and the new monetary conditions (resulting from the ever more widespread circulation of first the Constantinian gold *solidus* and then the Anastasian copper coinage) to introduce highly efficient and commercialised forms of agriculture, in which labourers and their families were drawn onto estates, where they were settled in tied villages (*epoikia* or *chôria*). Once resident on these estate labour settlements, in addition to working allotments of land on which they paid rent, peasants and their families were obliged to cultivate portions of land directly assigned to them by the household, or to provide the landowner with labour services focused on a directly administered estate demesne (typically known as the *autourgia*) for which they received wages reckoned in coin.[18] The surplus produce furnished by this centrally administered demesne, and such centrally assigned plots, was then sold at market by the landowner's agents.[19]

From a macro-economic perspective, the rise of such great estates appears to have been a positive development that helped to fuel economic growth within the Eastern Empire. As we have seen with relation to the West, however, matters were not so simple from a fiscal perspective. The growth of great estates threatened to undermine the cohesion of the village communities that had hitherto formed the bedrock of the imperial fiscal system, and represented a concentration of ownership in the hands of landowners who were better placed, by virtue of their official connections, social prestige, and governmental posts, to engage in acts of large-scale tax evasion than were autonomous peasant producers or other, more humble, members of provincial society. Even the decision of the imperial authorities to

---

[16] Sarris (2006), pp. 177–99.
[17] ibid., *passim*.
[18] ibid., pp. 81–5; P. Sarris, 'The Early Byzantine Economy in Context', *Early Medieval Europe* (forthcoming).
[19] Sarris (2006).

bind agricultural workers for fiscal purposes to the estates to which they had migrated as *coloni adscripticii* only partly ameliorated the situation.[20] The expansion of great estates thus became a pressing governmental concern.[21] The empire might have been getting wealthier, but the imperial authorities were finding that wealth ever harder to tap.

The expansion of aristocratic estates also caused the imperial government administrative headaches, in that, again, as we have seen, holders of the new governmental posts who were winning mastery of local landed society were also increasingly acquiring senatorial status in recognition of their services to the state. Strictly speaking, membership of the Senate in Constantinople was incompatible with membership of one's native city council, or *curia*. Accordingly, the rise of the new aristocracy of service threatened to cripple those curial institutions upon which provincial government rested by freeing from curial obligations the most wealthy, influential, and powerful members of local society.

Accordingly, between the reigns of the Emperors Theodosius II and Anastasius a series of accommodations were reached with the owners of the expanding great estates. Essentially, whilst formally exempted from curial obligations, senators and senatorial households were entrusted with specific authority to oversee curial affairs by, for instance, auditing civic accounts and effecting readjustments of the tax burden between different *curiales*. The owners of great estates were granted the right to collect taxes from their own employees and tenants, which they then paid directly to the imperial authorities free from curial scrutiny; at the same time, however, they took on the responsibility to fund certain key civic and governmental activities, such as the maintenance of imperial troops stationed in the locality or the issuing of stipends to imperial officials and ecclesiastical dignitaries. Moreover, in Egypt at least (and elsewhere, it seems) they took on the responsibility for collecting taxes from designated fiscal districts and villages. City councillors were expected to make decisions not simply on the basis of their own deliberations but, increasingly in consultation with any local senatorial landowners, as well as the local bishop.[22] Alongside (and increasingly in place of) the structures of civic government and curial self-rule, there thus emerged instead what has been described as a system of 'government by notables'.[23]

From the perspective of members of the expanding senatorial aristocracy, all this might sound rather burdensome. What it actually permitted them to do, however, was to entrust to their social inferiors within the city councils those curial duties from which least benefit could be derived, whilst monopolising for themselves key responsibilities that offered the chance of further bolstering their own social authority and opened up new opportunities for self-enrichment. The right to adjust the tax burden of one's neighbours, for example, was a potentially powerful weapon if one were minded to drive them off their land. Acting as paymaster to detachments of the imperial army similarly opened up opportunities to draw soldiers into the private service of the landowner and to deploy them to intimidate and discipline

---

[20] Sarris (2011). [21] Sarris (2006), pp. 190–91.
[22] ibid., pp. 149–76. [23] See Liebeschuetz (2001).

both rivals and employees. Likewise, fiscal subjection to the household of a senatorial landowner was often the first step in a process that eventually culminated in full-blown incorporation into his estate.[24] Each imperial accommodation with the burgeoning aristocracy only served further to entrench aristocratic power and control at a provincial level, thereby rendering effective imperial government increasingly reliant upon the goodwill and cooperation of members of the senatorial elite.

The final factor that is likely to have intensified unease and insecurity in political circles in Constantinople in the late fifth and early sixth century was the gradual dissolution of the empire's largely amicable relations with Sasanian Persia and the revival of Roman-Persian warfare. This threatened to undermine the security of the provinces of Syria and Palestine, where many members of the senatorial aristocracy owned land. As noted earlier, it was the common challenge posed by the Huns that had served to bind together the interests of the two states. From the late fifth century, however, the Hunnic threat effectively ceased to be an issue from the perspective of Constantinople, and there are indications that, as a result, the Eastern Roman authorities began to disengage from some of the key diplomatic arrangements and niceties that had come to symbolise rapprochement between the two powers. The Persians claimed, for instance, that the Roman government had helped to meet the costs of maintaining a garrison at the so-called Caspian Gates. This was the key crossing point between the steppe and the Persian realm's northern frontier, from where, long after the break-up of Attila's empire in the west, the Sasanians continued to face a major threat in the form of the khaganate of the 'Hephthalites', or 'White' Huns. In response to the demise of Hunnic power in the Balkans, the Roman authorities appear to have become increasingly reluctant to continue to make such payments, perhaps aware that, within the internal propaganda of the Sasanian Empire, these subsidies were presented to the shah's subjects as the '*bazh-i-Rum*', or the 'tribute of the Romans'—a presumption to which the Roman authorities had less and less reason to turn a blind eye.[25]

Accordingly, we are informed that the Persian shah Peroz sent a delegation to the Emperor Leo (r.457–74) asking that the Romans 'give them either money or men for the defence of the fortress at Iouroeipach [at the Caspian Gates]. They repeated what had often been said by their embassies, that since they were facing the fighting and refusing to allow access to the attacking barbarian peoples, the Romans' territory remained unravaged.' The Persians are likely to have been shocked by the Emperor's reply that 'each had to fight for his own land and take care of his own defence'.[26] Leo's successor, Zeno, was more amenable to Persian demands, whilst making it clear that the money sent to support the defence of the frontier zone 'was not by way of tribute, as many thought'.[27] In the 480s, however, the prestige of the

---

[24] Sarris (2006), pp. 104–5 and n. 21.
[25] Z. Rubin, 'The Mediterranean and the Dilemma of the Roman Empire in Late Antiquity', *Mediterranean Historical Review* 1.1 (1986), pp. 13–62.
[26] Priscus, fragment 47.
[27] Joshua the Stylite, 8 (242.23). See also ibid., 9–10 (242.23–243.2), and John Malalas, *Chronicle*, tr. E. Jeffreys, M. Jeffreys, and R. Scott (Melbourne, 1986), 18.44 (378.32–9/449.19–450.6).

Sasanian dynasty was dealt a series of near-fatal blows that made the Roman authorities even less inclined to be seen to be propping it up. In 482 a major revolt against Persian rule occurred in the Persian-held sector of Armenia.[28] Still worse was to follow: in 484 the Persian shah Peroz was defeated and died in battle at the hands of the Hephthalite Huns.[29] He was succeeded on the Persian throne by his brother Balash, of whom Christian Syriac author Joshua the Stylite noted that 'He found nothing in the territory, and his land was laid waste by the depopulation (carried out) by the Huns... and from the Romans he had no help of any kind such as his brother had had. For he sent ambassadors to Zeno... but he sent word to him, "The taxes of Nisibis which you receive are enough for you, which for many years have been due to the Romans."'[30]

In 488 Balash was deposed and replaced by his nephew Kavadh. Kavadh renewed demands that the Romans send him 'the customary gold' or 'accept war'. The new Eastern Roman emperor Anastasius decided to call Kavadh's bluff, thereby adding insult to injury. 'When the Armenians who were under the rule of Kavadh heard that he had not received a peaceful answer from the Romans', we are told, 'they took courage and strengthened themselves, and destroyed the fire-temples that had been built by the Persians in their land, and killed the Magi who were among them. Kavadh sent against them a *marzban* [commander] with an army to exact capital punishment from them... but they fought with him and destroyed both him and his army, and sent ambassadors to the Emperor, in order to become his subjects. He, however, was unwilling to receive them, that he might not be assumed to be provoking war with the Persians.'[31]

Revolts flared up throughout the Sasanian Empire like wildfire.[32] In 498 Kavadh was in his turn deposed in favour of his brother Zamasp, only to be restored to his throne the following year through the intervention of the Hephthalites, whose client and tributary he thus became. In order to pay the Hephthalites the sums they now demanded of him, Kavadh once more wrote to Anastasius, this time apparently indicating that he would be willing to accept a loan if the Emperor were not minded to provide him with the money upfront. Indeed, the idea of the loan may well have been the Emperor's.[33] In the end, however, according to Procopius, those around Anastasius 'did not allow him to make the agreement, for they declared that it was disadvantageous to strengthen the friendship of their enemies with the Hephthalites with their own money; rather it was better [for the Romans] to stir them up against each other as much as possible.'[34] In the absence of a common foe, it was decided at court, it was better to have a weak Persian neighbour than a strong one.

---

[28] Lazar, 136/193.
[29] Joshua the Stylite, 11; Procopius, *Wars*, I, 4; Lazar, 154–6/213–15.
[30] Joshua the Stylite, 18 (248.12). Nisibis had been ceded by the Romans to the Persians in 363, in the aftermath of Emperor Julian's ill-fated Persian campaign.
[31] Joshua the Stylite, 21 (249.15–23).
[32] Greatrex and Lieu (2002), p. 61.
[33] Procopius, *Wars*, I, 7.1; *Chronicle of Theophanes (annus mundi 5996)*, p. 223.
[34] Procopius, *Wars*, I, 7.2.

It is almost impossible for the modern reader to appreciate the scale of the cataclysm that befell the Sasanian dynasty in the 480s and 490s. It is conceivable that even the imperial authorities in Constantinople underestimated its severity, and might have reacted with greater generosity had they not done so. That, in 484, a Sasanian shah should die in battle at the hands of a nomadic foe, and that in 499 his son and successor was only able to regain his throne through the services of a nomad *khagan* to whom he was obliged to subject both himself and his realm, represented not only the very public humiliation of a dynasty that ultimately owed its prestige to a reputation for military success but also a nightmarish inversion of the cosmic order as intuited by the Zoroastrian faith. The world of *Iran* was now subject to the world of *Turan*. No wonder radical fundamentalist religious groups such as the Mazdakites, to whom Kavadh had previously lent his support, were now, literally, up in arms.[35] As the Romans should perhaps have realised, so dramatic a decline in dynastic fortunes necessitated an immediate and daring response. In order to restore the renown of the House of Sasan, and to rally behind him both the highly fractious and militarised Persian nobility and the leaders of those tribal groupings and subject peoples who had revolted against him, Kavadh had little choice but to revive the traditions of his forebears and engage in prestige-garnering warfare against the traditional enemy of Rome.[36]

In August 502, therefore, the shah led an army made up of Persians, Armenians, Arabs, and assorted client tribesmen deep into the Roman sector of Armenia, quickly capturing the capital of the province of *Armenia Inferior*, the city of Theodosiopolis. Kavadh then marched south, overrunning Roman positions in Armenia.[37] An embassy from the Emperor Anastasius was received, but curtly dismissed. Instead of retreating back into Persian territory, Kavadh bore down upon the heavily fortified (but only lightly garrisoned) Roman city of Amida in Upper Mesopotamia. After a bitter siege, lasting three months, the city's defenders, largely consisting of its own citizens, capitulated. A detailed contemporary account reveals that 'the gold and silver of the great men's houses, and the beautiful garments, were gathered together and given to the king's treasurers. They also brought down all the statues of the city, and the clock-towers and the marble.... The Shah sought for the notables and nobles of the city; and Leontius, and Cyrus the governor.... They clothed Leontius and Cyrus in filthy garments, and put swine-ropes on their necks, and made them carry pigs.'[38]

If Anastasius was initially slow to respond to the Persian invasion of Armenia, his response to the fall of Amida was resolute and determined. The Roman commander-in-chief in Armenia, Eugenius, took advantage of Kavadh's preoccupation with Mesopotamia to retake Theodosiopolis. Under the leadership of the general Olympius, Roman resistance to marauding Persian armies in northern Syria stiffened. A massive Roman field army of over fifty thousand men was assembled.

---

[35] P. Crone, 'Kavad's Heresy and Mazdak's Revolt', *Iran* 29 (1991), pp. 21–42.
[36] Greatrex and Lieu (2002), p. 62, and Joshua the Stylite, 24.
[37] Procopius, *Buildings*, III, 2.4–8.
[38] Zacharias of Mitylene, *Historia Ecclesiastica*, VII, 3–4 (22.22–31.14).

Of these some twelve thousand were sent to the frontier city of Dara, to advance on the Persian-held city of Nisibis. The remainder encamped against Amida 'to drive out from there the Persian garrison'.[39] Mobilising and supporting this army was a major logistical feat. We are told that an Egyptian landowner, the honorary praetorian prefect Flavius Apion, was put in charge of provisioning the troops from his base at Edessa, where 'as the bakers were not able to make (enough) bread, he ordered that wheat should be supplied to all the houses [in the city] . . . and that they should make the soldiers' bread at their own cost'.[40]

This was the largest field army the Romans had assembled on their eastern frontier since Julian's campaign of 363. Whilst the Roman advance on Nisibis faltered, the Roman grip on Amida tightened as the imperial army 'made war on the city with wooden towers and trenches and all kinds of engines'.[41] Across Upper Mesopotamia and the Transcaucasus where the war had started, the Romans were gaining the upper hand, and in Armenia in particular there were major defections from the Persian to the Roman camp. Yet, at Amida, Kavadh's garrison continued to hold out.[42] Eventually, in the winter of 504, an armistice was agreed and ratified by both Emperor and shah. In return for the payment of 1,100 pounds in weight of gold, the Persian army in Amida withdrew, although without a proper peace treaty actually being put in place.[43] Only in 506 were mutually acceptable terms agreed. Even that treaty, however, was of only seven years' duration.[44] Although Anastasius was thereby able to restore Roman rule to the eastern frontier, the empire's military prospects in the region now looked more uncertain than they had done at any stage for over a century.

4.3 THE ROMAN RESPONSE UNDER ANASTASIUS AND JUSTIN

The Emperor Anastasius and those around him had been determined not to be seen to prop up a Sasanian monarchy that was finding itself in increasing difficulties. This may be explained in part by the fact that Anastasius (himself a former *cubicularius*, or functionary at the imperial court) was in many ways the creature of the senatorial aristocracy. Certainly, his economic and administrative policies were geared to benefiting members of the landed elite, and in a number of contemporary sources the Emperor is praised for his generosity to members of the Senate (just as he is denounced for his meanness to the poor).[45] The payment of

---

[39] Joshua the Stylite, 54 (281.6–27).
[40] ibid.
[41] Zacharias, *Historia Ecclesiastica*, VII, 4–5 (30.14–31.1).
[42] Greatrex and Lieu (2002), pp. 71–2.
[43] Zacharias of Mitylene, *Historia Ecclesiastica*, VII, 5 (33.21–34.20).
[44] Procopius, *Wars*, I, 9.24.
[45] Sarris (2006), pp. 200–01: see John Lydus, *On the Magistracies of the Roman State (De Magistratibus)*, tr. A. C. Bandy (Philadelphia, 1983), 3.48; Procopius, *Secret History*, 19.5; *The Oracle of Baalbek*, tr. P. J. Alexander (Washington DC, 1967), 14.

subsidies to neighbouring powers in return for peace was a long-standing feature of Roman foreign policy, but it was one that was deeply unpopular in aristocratic and senatorial circles.[46] Landowners resented paying taxes at the best of times, even more so if they felt that the tax revenues collected from them were simply being handed over to the barbarians, amongst whom the Persians were now numbered. But perhaps as a result of the fact that peaceful conditions had prevailed on Rome's eastern frontier for so long, there seems to have been little expectation that unless Constantinople helped them out, the Persians really would go to war. Accordingly, when Kavadh had led his forces into Roman territory, he had not only found the Roman frontier defences in a state of disrepair but also the Roman army conspicuous by its absence. The frontier was open, porous, and vulnerable. This was a situation that the imperial authorities needed to address as a matter of urgency.

Almost as soon as Amida was restored to Roman control, therefore, the imperial government set about addressing the weaknesses in the empire's defensive infrastructure in the East that had been made apparent by Kavadh's initial successes. First and foremost, the cities of Upper Mesopotamia and Syria and Roman positions in the Transcaucasus had to be refortified and strengthened to render them less prone to sudden attack from the Persians or their allies. Accordingly, the cities of Edessa, Batnae, and Amida in Upper Mesopotamia were refortified, as were Theodosiopolis in Armenia, Euchaita in the Helenopontus, and Melitene. Further south, the city of Sergiopolis (Resafa), which served as a point of contact between the imperial authorities and the empire's own Arab clients and allies, was expanded (Map 4).[47]

Crucially, in Upper Mesopotamia, the Romans set about establishing a series of readily defensible military 'hard-points', each entrusted to a commander, or *dux*. Foremost among these new bases was that established at Dara, almost within sight (and certainly within striking distance) of the Persian-held city of Nisibis.[48] Through such policies, as the contemporary bureaucrat and scholar John the Lydian put it, the Emperor 'clamped down on the throat of the Persians'.[49]

In 518 the Emperor Anastasius died and was succeeded by the elderly head of the Palace Guard (or *Excoubitors*), Justin. This succession was achieved through an extraordinary display of low cunning. According to the contemporary *Chronicle* of John Malalas, the imperial chamberlain Amantius had handed over to Justin a vast sum of money which he was to distribute so as to buy up support for Amantius' chosen claimant to the throne, a well-born aristocrat by the name of Theocritus. Instead Justin, an Illyrian peasant by birth who had moved to Constantinople as a young man and been recruited to the Palace Guard on the basis of his strength, height, and good looks, used the money to secure for himself the backing of the army and the Constantinopolitan circus factions, who traditionally acclaimed the

---

[46] Sarris (2006), p. 222.
[47] Greatrex and Lieu (2002), pp. 77–8.
[48] Joshua the Stylite, 90 (309.12–310.3); Zacharias of Mitylene, *Historia Ecclesiastica*, VII, 6 (34.24–38.15); Procopius, *Wars*, I, 10.13–18.
[49] John Lydus, *De Magistratibus*, II, 47 (206.22–8).

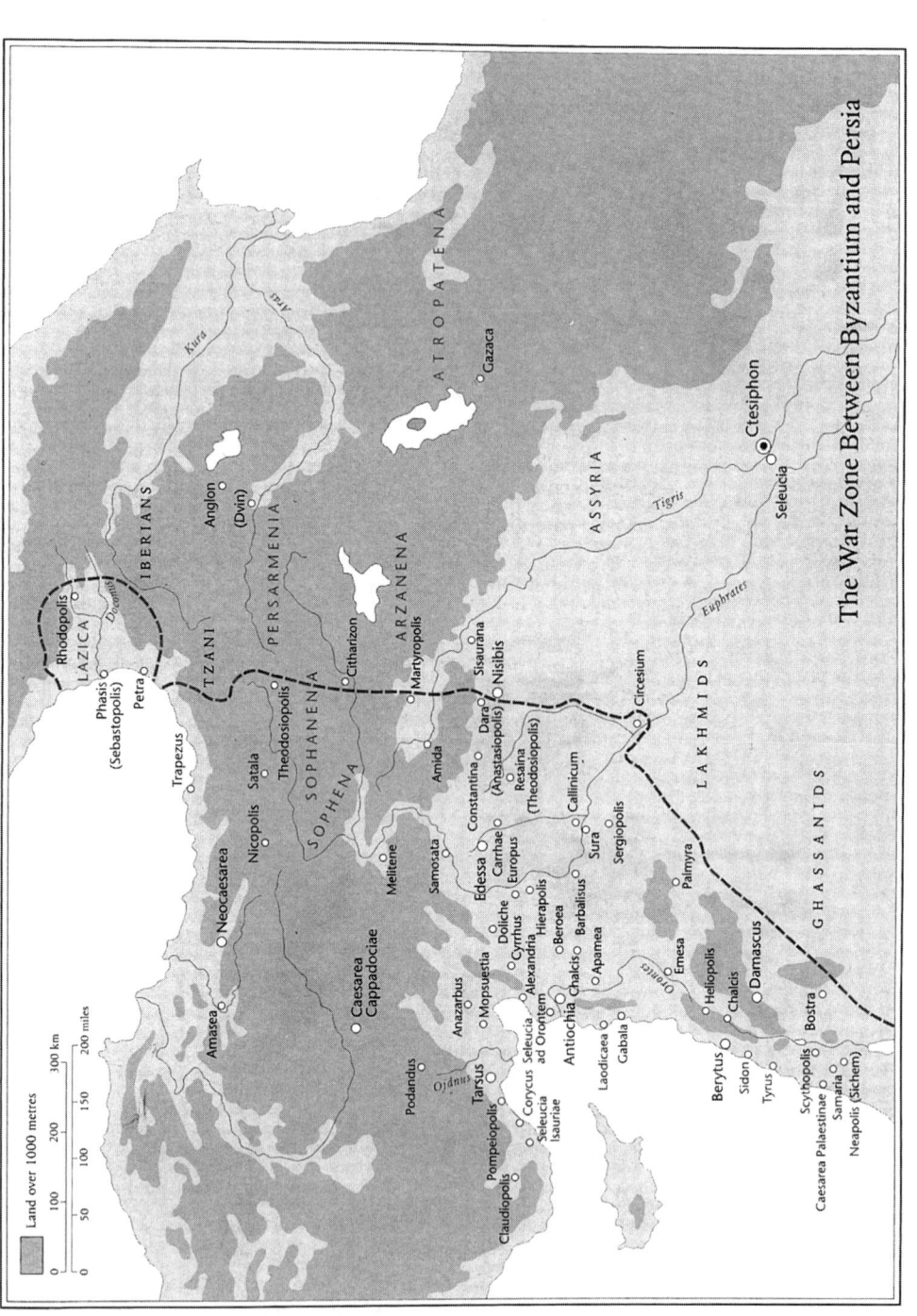

Map 4 The War Zone between Byzantium and Persia (C. Mango, *The Oxford History of Byzantium*, p. 41)

new Emperor in the Hippodrome after the Senate had announced to them its choice. Justin thus effectively managed to sideline the Senate and present its members with a *fait accompli*. As a result, after an initial (and no doubt unsightly) scuffle in the Senate House in which Justin's nephew and fellow guards officer, Justinian, was involved, the senators were obliged to acknowledge Justin's accession to the throne.[50]

As seen in Chapter Three, in theological terms Justin was resolutely pro-Chalcedonian, and he immediately set about rebuilding relations with the Church in Rome that had broken down as a result first of the Emperor Zeno's attempts to effect a compromise with the anti-Chalcedonian elements in the East, and then the Emperor Anastasius' anti-Chalcedonian sympathies. In terms of military strategy with respect to Persia, however, Justin very much followed in his predecessor's footsteps, and building work in the frontier zones of Armenia and Upper Mesopotamia continued apace. Perhaps in response to this, and to demonstrate to the inhabitants of the frontier zone that the Persians remained a force to be reckoned with, in 519–20 Kavadh mobilised his Arab clients, the Nasrids, who raided the city and military base of Osrhoene and captured its *dux*. It was only in 524 that the Emperor's representatives were able to negotiate the return of this high-ranking hostage.[51]

What had opened the window of opportunity for the Romans to engage in such major fortification work in Upper Mesopotamia and Armenia was the fact that, between *c.*504 and 520, Kavadh had been obliged to contend with the emergence of a new nomadic threat from across the Caucasus in the form of the Sabir Huns (as we have seen, from a Sasanian perspective, dealing with nomads was always the first priority) and an associated weakening of the Persian position across the Transcaucasus. In 513/14, for example, an uprising against Persian rule had occurred in the province of Persarmenia, and in 520 Kavadh appointed a *Marzban* (military commander) to the city of Mtskheta in Iberia in an attempt to restore order to the region.[52]

Essentially, Kavadh's problems in the Transcaucasus stemmed from two structural weaknesses in the Persian position. First, the mountainous terrain made the territory very difficult for any sedentary empire to control. The lords and princes of the region were bound to take advantage of any sudden interruption from outside (such as that by the Sabir Huns) to seek to regain their own autonomy by appealing for the intervention of the rival power. In that the partition of 387 had established the Persians as the dominant power in the Transcaucasus, they were naturally the ones with the most to lose from any disturbance of political or military conditions; as was evident from the readiness of Armenian lords subject to the shah to defect to the Romans in 503–4.

Second, although the Transcaucasus was traditionally a Persian sphere of influence, and it was to the Persian court that the lords and princes of Armenia, Lazica,

---

[50] Malalas, 17.2.
[51] See Greatrex and Lieu (2002), p. 79, for references.
[52] ibid., p. 80.

and Iberia had long looked for their culture, etiquette, and style, it was also a region where, since the fourth century, Christianity had made significant inroads amongst the indigenous population. The Armenian king Tiridites IV, for example, may have converted as early as 301 (although there are good reasons for preferring the year 314 as his date of conversion).[53] As the rhetoric and ideology of the Roman Empire became increasingly Christian in tone and character, so too did conversion to Christianity on the part of the lords and princes of the Caucasus draw them even further into an essentially pro-Constantinopolitan orbit. As the Sasanian authorities were fully aware, the spread of Christianity was leading to a fundamental reorientation of instinctive allegiance and cultural affinity on the part of the Transcaucasian elites that threatened to undermine Persian authority. What the Sasanians could not work out was how to address this. In 449, for example, an attempt on the part of the Persian shah Yazdgerd II to enforce Zoroastrianism on the Christian population of Persarmenia served only to unite the Armenian aristocracy behind the leaders of the Church, who, for the first time in the Christian tradition, declared a 'Holy War' in defence of the faith. The ongoing process of Christianisation meant that a measured decline of Sasanian influence in the region was perhaps the best the Persians could hope for. Yet such pragmatism was inconceivable, for without control of the crucial mountain passes across the Transcaucasus, which linked it both to the Roman Empire and the steppe, the economic heartland both of the Sasanian Empire in Mesopotamian Iraq (its most fertile and productive region) and the imperial capital at Ctesiphon could never be secure: in terms of strategic geography and natural lines of march, it was from this direction that the Iraqi (or Assyrian) territories were at their most vulnerable. The Sasanians were thus caught on the horns of a Transcaucasian dilemma.

Mounting Persian worries as to the geopolitical implications of the onward march of Christianity in the Transcaucasus were soon confirmed by a spectacular diplomatic coup on the part of the Eastern Roman Empire. Under Anastasius and Justin, as we have seen, the Romans had responded to Persian aggression by strengthening their military position in the Roman-held sector of Armenia. Justin then sought to consolidate and extend the empire's strategic advantage over the Persians in the western Transcaucasus by using representatives of the Christian Church as agents of Roman imperial influence. In 521/2, according to the contemporary *Chronicle of John Malalas*, 'Tzath, the King of the Laz, grew angry and departed from Persian territory.' This breakdown of relations was significant in that Lazica, on the Black Sea coastline of the western Transcaucasus, was of the utmost strategic and economic importance to both the Roman and Persian empires. To the Romans, the long-standing alliance between the Laz and the Persians posed a major threat to the security of their empire, because the location of Lazica meant that it could serve as a forward base for a naval assault on Roman territory, including, potentially, Constantinople itself, whilst the kingdom's wealth in mineral deposits such as gold rendered control over it an enticing prospect. To the Persians, the

---

[53] C. S. Lightfoot, 'Armenia and the Eastern Marches', in Bowman, Garnsey, and Cameron (2005), pp. 481–97, 486–7.

primary significance of Lazica was the fact that it was the one region of the Transcaucasus blessed with extensive stretches of grassland: that is to say, it alone could sustain sufficient herds of horses to supply a large cavalry force. It was thus vital for the Persians that they continue to exercise suzerainty over the kingdom, to prevent it from falling into the hands of the cavalry-dependent nomad khaganates of the north. Accordingly, we are informed, 'whenever a king of the Laz happened to die, his successor, though from the race of the Laz, was appointed and crowned by the King of the Persians'.[54]

What appears to have been behind the breakdown in relations between Tzath and Kavadh was the fact that, no doubt at the prompting of Christian missionaries, the new Laz king had recently turned aside from the traditional religion of his ancestors and:

> so as not to be appointed by Kavadh, the Persian *Shah*, and not to perform sacrifices and all the other Persian customs, as soon as his father Damnazes died, he immediately went up to the Emperor Justin in Byzantium, put himself at his disposal and asked to be proclaimed king of the Laz and to become a Christian. He was received by the Emperor, baptized, and having become a Christian, married a Roman wife named Valeriana.... He [was] appointed and crowned by Justin, the Roman Emperor, and ... won a Roman imperial crown and a white cloak of pure silk. Instead of the purple stripe it had the gold imperial border; in its middle there was a small true purple portrait bust with a likeness of the Emperor.[55]

Through his adoption of Christianity, Tzath had become the Emperor's man: he was the Clovis of the Caucasus.

Kavadh was furious, and denounced Justin for having 'appointed as king of the Laz a subordinate of mine, who does not come under the Roman jurisdiction but has from time immemorial belonged to the Persian state'. Justin's response was to retort that 'We have neither annexed nor won over any of those subordinate to your empire. Rather, a man by the name of Tzath came to us in our empire and begged us as a suppliant to be rescued from defilement and paganism, from impious sacrifices and from the errors of wicked demons, and asked to become a Christian ... it was impossible to obstruct someone who wished to enter a better way and know the true God'.[56] This was not a message calculated to put Kavadh at his ease.

Some three years later, in 525, Justin again turned Christianity to his advantage to undermine Persian influence in the Transcaucasus. In response to the conversion and defection of the king of the Laz, Kavadh seems to have attempted to bolster the Persians' grip on the important central Caucasian kingdom of Iberia (a Sasanian satellite since the fourth century) by bolstering the Zoroastrian presence in the region.[57] In response to this, Procopius states, 'Gourgenes [King of the Iberians]

---

[54] John Malalas, *Chronicle*, 17.9 (340.53–341.94/412.16–414.16).
[55] ibid.
[56] ibid.
[57] Procopius, *Wars*, I, 12.1–9. Procopius claims that Kavadh attempted to impose Zoroastrian practices on the Christian Iberians: it is more likely that he attempted to settle Zoroastrian troops in the region.

wished to go over to the Emperor Justin and he asked that he might receive pledges that the Romans would never abandon the Iberians to the Persians. And the Emperor gave him these pledges with great eagerness.'[58] Forthwith, Justin sent the Roman commander Probus to the north of the Caucasus to raise an army of Huns to place at Gourgenes' disposal. Around the same time, a similar policy was adopted with respect to southern Arabia, where the Persian-backed ruler of the kingdom of Himyar, in the Yemen (described in our Roman sources as a Jew and former slave by the name of Dhu Nuwis), was accused of persecuting Christians amongst his subjects. He is also recorded to have incited the Persians and their north Arabian allies, the Nasrids, to follow suit.[59] In response to this, the Romans sent a fleet along the Red Sea to assist the Christian ruler of the Ethiopian kingdom of Axum in launching an invasion of Himyar and driving Dhu Nuwis from the throne.

In the wake of Kavadh's assault on Amida in 503, therefore, the Roman authorities can be seen to have sought to address each and every one of the key weaknesses that had become apparent in the empire's eastern defences. Clearly, the Roman government was no longer willing to rely primarily on diplomatic means to ensure the security of its wealthy eastern provinces. Rather, Rome would look to its own defence to render itself immune to any further Persian aggression or demands for money. Initially, this change in strategic outlook took the form of refortification of the Roman positions in Armenia and Upper Mesopotamia. Increasingly, and particularly under Justin, the policy was then extended to embrace diplomatic activity amongst the tribes, kingdoms, and peoples whose territories abutted the direct Roman-Persian frontier zone to north and south, and whose support could decisively alter the balance of power between the two sedentary empires.

What to the Romans were self-evidently defensive measures, however, looked rather more sinister from the perspective of a jittery and insecure Sasanian monarchy. The Romans had already shown themselves willing to take advantage of Persian weakness to disengage from joint ventures such as the defence of the Caspian Gates, thereby undermining Sasanian authority in the eyes of their subjects; how could the Persians be sure that Roman diplomatic activities in the Transcaucasus and Arabia were not meant to destabilise and humiliate the regime further, by drawing away from the shah those who were his legitimate vassals? Did the Romans perhaps still harbour territorial ambitions towards the rich territories of Assyria between the Euphrates and Tigris rivers? The new Roman fortification at Dara, after all, looked very much like a forward base for an assault on Nisibis, which the Romans had been obliged to cede to the Persians in 363, and which the Emperor Zeno had raised as an issue at the low point of Sasanian fortunes, after their defeat at the hands of the Hephthalites in 484. As a result of the struggle over Amida, a dangerous atmosphere of mutual suspicion and anticipated violence thus descended on the lands of the Near East, whilst in Arabia and the Caucasus a

---

[58] Procopius, *Wars*, I, 12.1–9. Procopius claims that Kavadh attempted to impose Zoroastrian practices on the Christian Iberians: it is more likely that he attempted to settle Zoroastrian troops in the region.
[59] Greatrex and Lieu (2002), pp. 78–9.

version of the 'Great Game' was now underway that only promised further destabilisation and uncertainty.

By 525, however, Kavadh's thoughts were increasingly turning to his succession. The shah was now well over seventy years of age, and his chosen heir, his favourite son Khusro, faced resistance in the form not only of the rival ambitions of his brothers but also from the fundamentalist Mazdakite sect, which remained strong. In an attempt to revive the cooperative diplomatic protocols of the fifth century, therefore, Kavadh turned to Justin: the Roman Emperor might have been the Persian shah's chief military rival, but he was also the only other ruler of a settled, civilised empire which claimed for itself the sort of hegemonic status that the Sasanian monarchy did. The Emperor's support could thus be of great help in consolidating Khusro's position. Accordingly, we are informed by Procopius that Kavadh wrote to Justin asking him to accept Khusro as his adopted son.

Precisely what the details of this proposal really were is unclear. A reasonable assumption would be that Kavadh asked whether Justin would act as Khusro's guardian in the event of his father's death, just as Shah Yazdgerd I had done with respect to Theodosius II in *c*.402. Justin and his nephew Justinian (presented by Procopius as the real power in the land) are said to have been sympathetic to the shah's request, perhaps mindful of the fact that the Emperor Justin himself was by now a very old man, and that Justinian's planned accession to the throne looked far from unproblematic. Justin, as we have seen, had only acquired the purple by opportunistic sleight of hand. The aristocratic factions at court that he had outmanoeuvred might not be so easily tricked next time around, and Constantinople remained home to members of the Theodosian and Anastasian households who coveted the imperial title. Justin and Justinian may have seen in Kavadh's approach the opportunity to establish a mutually binding and bilaterally advantageous arrangement whereby each ruler guaranteed the claims of the other's intended heir.

The proposal, nevertheless, met resistance at the Constantinopolitan court, where Justin's chief legal officer (*quaestor*) expressed anxiety that any adoption of Khusro on the Emperor's part might give the former a stake in and claim to the Roman Empire. Negotiations between representatives of the two powers, which ultimately foundered on the issue of the status of the Laz, may not have been helped by the fact that the chief Roman interlocutor, Hypatius, was a nephew of the former Emperor Anastasius, and thus possibly harboured his own ambitions to the throne.[60] In 526/7, frustrated at the lack of progress, Kavadh sent his general Boes into Iberia with a large army, forcing King Gourgenes to flee to Lazica with his leading subjects. A new round of warfare appeared to be imminent.

Two factors, however, militated against an escalation of conflict at this point. The first was that Probus' attempts to raise an army on behalf of Gourgenes amongst the Huns were largely unsuccessful. As a result, the Romans were unable

---

[60] Procopius, *Wars*, I, 11.23–30.

Fig. 6 Mosaic Panel Depicting Justinian, San Vitale, Ravenna (C. Mango, *The Oxford History of Byzantium*, p. 60)

to intervene effectively in Iberia. Secondly, Justin's health was failing. Accordingly, in April 527 he named Justinian as his co-ruler and arranged for the minting and distribution of coins bearing the images of both Emperors. By advertising to the provinces in this way Justinian's accession to power, Justin once again stole a march on those who might otherwise have made a grab for the throne upon his death. In August 527 Justin died, and Justinian succeeded him as sole *Augustus* (Fig. 6).

News first of Justin's ailing health and then death was greeted with a series of raids and assaults upon Roman positions in Syria and Palestine by Kavadh's Nasrid allies. In spite of the building work of Anastasius and Justin, the empire's extended Arabian flank along the southern desert fringe remained highly vulnerable, and Kavadh once more took advantage of this to attempt to apply pressure on and obtain tribute from the Roman state.[61] In response, the Romans launched a number of retaliatory attacks on Nisibis from their base at Dara, whilst also attempting to strengthen the empire's defences in Upper Mesopotamia and along the southern *limes*.[62] Amongst Justinian's first moves as Emperor on the eastern front was the refortification of the city of Palmyra, and the bolstering of defences at

---

[61] Zacharias of Mitylene, *Historia Ecclesiastica*, VIII, 5 (77.9–24).
[62] ibid., IX, 1 (92.3–17) for assaults on Nisibis; IX, 2 (92.19–25) and IX, 5 (96.2–7) for building work to fend off Arab raids.

Thannuris, which Justin had identified as 'an advantageous place for a city to be built as a place of refuge in the desert, and for an army to be stationed'.[63]

To the north, Justinian consolidated the imperial position in Roman Armenia, by stationing a new chief commander there (the *magister militum per Armeniam*) whose responsibility it was to take charge of warfare across the Caucasus as a whole, and making the Roman army less dependent militarily on local levies and the armed retinues of members of the indigenous Armenian aristocracy.[64] The Roman position in the region of Tzanica (between Armenia and Lazica) was likewise strengthened through the introduction of a Roman garrison, the construction of a series of fortifications, the establishment of a network of Roman roads, and the introduction of Christianity to the area's recalcitrant inhabitants. Procopius' description of the extension of Roman rule to Tzanica is the best description we have of what the arrival of Roman imperialism looked like on the ground for any moment in Roman history.[65]

In spite of the building activity at Palmyra and Thannuris, it was nevertheless evident to Justinian and those around him that the empire's southern desert frontier in Syria and Palestine remained especially vulnerable to attack. The frontier zone, thus conceived, was simply too extensive to be anything but highly permeable: fortifications and towers alone would never be enough to deny the Persians' Nasrid allies freedom of manoeuvre along the desert fringe. Accordingly, around the year 529, Justinian effected a fundamental reconfiguration of imperial policy with respect to the Roman Empire's own Arab clients along the frontier zone. Rather than following in the footsteps of his predecessors, and attempting to curtail Nasrid raids by mobilising against the Persians' allies a series of competing Arab tribal chiefs and frontier lords, Justinian decided to foster a single unified client kingdom under the leadership of the Christian prince of the Jafnids, al-Harith, who received from Justinian 'the dignity of king' and the title of 'supreme phylarch'.[66]

In 528–9, however, Roman control in the east was shaken by a number of developments and chance occurrences. The winter of that year was a harsh one, leading to hunger and rising social tensions across the eastern provinces, and the cities of Laodicea and Antioch (the latter, alongside Constantinople and Alexandria, one of the most populous cities of the Eastern Roman world) were struck by destructive earthquakes. In 529 a violent uprising occurred on the part of the Samaritan peasantry of Palestine (a socially alienated but populous religious minority), which was only crushed amid much bloodshed.[67] Even before this revolt, Justinian had sent an embassy to Kavadh seeking an improvement in relations. In June 530, however, Kavadh's army struck out from Nisibis and marched on the Roman base at Dara, which was entrusted to the command of the chief Roman general in the East, the *magister militum per orientem*, Belisarius.

---

[63] ibid., IX, 2.
[64] Procopius, *Buildings*, III, 1.27–9; *Codex Iustinianus*, 1.29.5; Malalas, 18.10.
[65] Procopius, *Wars*, I, 15.24, and *Buildings*, III, 6.
[66] Procopius, *Wars*, I, 17.46–8. See discussion in I. Shahid, *Byzantium and the Arabs in the Sixth Century* (Washington DC, 1995).
[67] Malalas, 18.35.

Fortunately, as with the Vandalic and Italian campaigns, Belisarius' secretary, Procopius, was present for the engagement, and was able to write an eyewitness account of the battle that ensued.[68] With some twenty-five thousand men, Belisarius was outnumbered two to one by the Persians, but was nevertheless obliged to meet them in the field (presumably because building work at Dara was not yet complete).[69] The battle began with each side releasing its arrows upon the other; a melee was then joined as the infantry of each side met. The Persians initially had the upper hand, and the Roman army's left flank began to give way to a spirited Persian assault. Fortunately for the Romans, however, prior to the battle, Belisarius had agreed to a suggestion of the Herul commander Pharas, that he and his men should be positioned behind a hill on the edge of the battlefield, from where they might descend on the Persians and take them by surprise. Before the Persians could press home their advantage against the Romans, 'the three hundred Heruls under Pharas from the high ground got in the rear of the enemy and made a wonderful display of valorous deeds... and the Persians, seeing the forces of [the Roman commander] Sunicas too coming against them from the flank, turned to flight. And the rout became complete, for the Romans here joined forces with each other, and there was a great slaughter of the barbarians.'[70]

At the same time, Kavadh had ordered a Persian assault on Roman positions in Armenia. Here too the Romans met with considerable success, and the recently appointed *magister militum per Armeniam* proved his worth, defeating the Persians as they led an assault on the Romans' defendable 'hard point' at Satala. As a result, a number of important Persarmenian lords defected to the Roman side and the Romans gained the fortress of Pharangium, which gave them control of a major gold-producing region.[71] Although the Persians and their Nasrid allies were able to inflict a defeat on Belisarius and his army in the spring campaigning season of 531, further Persian offensives in Armenia and in Upper Mesopotamia ultimately came to little, and Kavadh was unable to claim much for his efforts either in terms of booty or fortresses captured.[72]

When, late in 531, the tribute-hungry warmonger of the East finally died, his son Khusro was eager to sue for peace in order to secure his hold on the throne. Initially, Justinian was unwilling to engage, hoping to profit from dissension and strife within the Persian realm. The Persian prince was, however, able to contain and overcome resistance on the part of both his brothers and the leaders of the Mazdakite movement with considerable rapidity. Accordingly, Justinian agreed to a three-month truce and an exchange of prisoners. Finally, in the spring of 532, full-blown negotiations began, resulting in an 'Endless Peace' by which the Romans would pay the Persians the huge sum of 11,000 pounds in weight of gold (792,000 *solidi*), supposedly for the defence of the Caucasian passes, and the Romans would withdraw their military commander (*dux*) from the forward base at Dara, whilst

---

[68] Procopius, *Wars*, I, 14.34–55. [69] Greatrex and Lieu (2002), p. 89.
[70] Procopius, *Wars*, I, 14.39–42. [71] ibid., I, 15.1–33.
[72] Greatrex and Lieu (2002), pp. 91–6.

each side would restore fortresses it had seized from the other, and Iberian refugees were to be permitted to return home unmolested.[73]

4.4 JUSTINIAN, KHUSRO, AND IMPERIAL RENEWAL

The negotiation of the 'Endless Peace' between Justinian and Khusro in 532 clearly served the interests of both rulers. In the context of the early 530s, each empire was subject to a series of geopolitical and domestic pressures and opportunities that once more rendered a period of repose in superpower relations highly desirable. It seems that Khusro was obliged to contend with a continuing Hephthalite threat along the Sasanian Empire's north-eastern frontier.[74] Certainly, he continued to face internal challenges to his authority that demanded his attention. From the perspective of Constantinople, as we have seen, dynastic instability in the Vandal kingdom of Africa and the Ostrogothic kingdom in Italy were opening up new opportunities for a reassertion of imperial might in the central and western Mediterranean, whilst much work still needed to be done to shore up Anastasius' consolidation of imperial fortunes in the Balkans. Such Western concerns were best served by peace on the Eastern frontier.

Indeed, the revival of warfare with Persia in the years since 503 may well have been the driving force behind Justinian's Western campaigns of reconquest. The Eastern Roman Empire, as we have seen, was heavily reliant upon the strong lines of communication and supply across the sea lanes of the eastern Mediterranean that helped bind the empire together, and which represented its greatest strategic advantage over the land-locked empire of Persia.[75] The existence of the barbarian kingdoms potentially threatened those lines of communication, but in the late fifth century Constantinople had been able to contain that threat diplomatically. The re-emergence of superpower warfare on a grand scale now rendered it imperative that the Romans re-establish direct control over the Mediterranean as a whole, not only to safeguard the sea lanes but also to maximise the resources at the empire's disposal by harnessing the continued prosperity of Italy, Africa, and southern Spain.

For the revival of superpower warfare had necessarily placed an enormous strain on the fiscal and administrative structures of the Eastern Roman state. The Roman army, as we have seen, was the major recipient of imperial tax revenues. Renewed conflict with Persia thus served to focus attention upon identifiable deficiencies within the empire's fiscal system. Above all, it served to highlight the significance of an issue that had been a cause of concern to the imperial government ever since the patronage legislation of the fourth century, but which had received relatively little attention under the primarily civilian and aristocratically minded administration of Anastasius and his entourage: tax evasion and fraud on the part of aristocratic landowners, provincial governors, and imperial officials. The fact that Justinian,

---

[73] ibid., pp. 96–7.
[74] G. Greatrex, *Rome and Persia at War, 502–32* (Leeds, 1998), pp. 48–9.
[75] Rubin (1986).

like his uncle Justin, was from a military background is likely to have heightened his determination to prioritise the needs of the army over and above the sensibilies of the aristocracy, amongst the ranks of whom there were signs of mounting tension and suspicion with respect to the new regime.[76] A period of introspection and internal reform was accordingly called for.

The need for internal reform was perhaps even more pressing in Persia: it is far from clear, for example, to what extent the Sasanian shahs of the period from the third century to the early sixth had ever been in receipt of sufficient tax revenues to support a free-standing bureaucracy and a professional standing army. Rather, the Sasanian dynasty seems to have been heavily reliant on the armed retinues of the Persian nobility and the Sasanians' vassals to north and south: it was for this reason that dynastic prestige was of such significance to the internal affairs of the Sasanian realm. Khusro responded to objective military conditions by seeking to extricate himself and his regime from aristocratic dominance and control. This was to be achieved by taxing his subjects more aggressively (pressing ahead, here, with earlier reforms associated with his father) and using these new revenues to support an imperial Sasanian army.[77] This necessarily excited internal opposition, which had to be overcome. Both Mazdakite fundamentalists and Persian nobles were thus once more to experience the shah's wrath.

These reforms of Khusro's do seem to have had a major effect: as a result, the Sasanian realm would experience a period of rapid fiscal, monetary, and bureaucratic expansion very similar to that which had taken place in the Roman Empire in the age of Diocletian and Constantine, and which is particularly visible in the numismatic record.[78] As in the Roman Empire of the fourth century, the emergence of a more fiscalised, monetised, and bureaucratised state went hand in hand with the rise of a new service elite, recruited from outside the Iranian nobility, from amongst the upper echelons of civic society in the densely urbanised world of Assyria (Iraq). The civic notables of Sasanian Mesopotamia were quick to grasp the advantages that service to the shah could offer, in spite of the fact that many of them were, in fact, Christian.[79] Here, unlike in the Caucasus, the prospect of material gain proved sufficient to draw Christian elites away from the political orbit of New Rome.

---

[76] Sarris (2006), pp. 203–4.

[77] J. D. Howard-Johnston, 'The Two Great Powers of Late Antiquity: A Comparison' in A. Cameron (ed.), *The Byzantine and Early Islamic Near East Volume III: States, Resources and Armies* (Princeton, 1995), pp. 157–226.

[78] J. Banaji, 'Precious Metal Coinages and Monetary Expansion in Late Antiquity' in F. De Romanis and S. Sorda (eds.), *Dal denarius al dinar: l'oriente e la moneta romana* (Rome, 2006), pp. 265–303; S. Sears, 'Monetary Revision and Monetization in the Late Sasanian Empire', in R. Gyselen and M. Szuppe (eds.), *Matériaux pour l'histoire économique du monde iranien* (Paris, 1999), pp. 149–65; A. Kolesnikov, *Denezhnoe Khozaistvo v Irane v VII Veke* (Moscow, 1998), pp. 234–47. I am greatly endebted to Dr Richard Payne for these references and for discussion of Sasanian social and economic history. See also H. Kaimian, 'Cities and Social Order in Sasanian Iran: The Archaeological Potential', *Antiquity* 84 (2010), pp. 453–66.

[79] R. E. Payne, 'Christianity and Iranian Society in Late Antiquity, ca. 500–700 CE', (Princeton D.Phil. dissertation, 2010).

In Constantinople itself, administrative and fiscal reorganisation began with legal reform. One of the factors that made imperial law of any sort difficult to impose at a provincial level, and even in the capital itself, and which the powerful are likely to have turned to their advantage, was the fact that it was often difficult to establish what the current state of law on a given subject actually was. Laws of general effect issued by emperors, *ad hoc* judgements issued by the imperial authorities and communicated in the form of official letters to provincial administrators, litigants, and petitioners, as well as the writings of legal scholars (or 'jurisconsults'), all had legal standing and could be cited in court. As a result, it was not clear how one text or authority was to be preferred over another. In the early fifth century the imperial authorities in Constantinople had attempted to remedy the situation by compiling and promulgating the *Codex Theodosianus*—notionally an official codification of all laws issued by Christian emperors since Constantine, which were deemed to be of general application or which established important legal points applicable in similar or related contexts. At the same time, a 'law of citations' was established, officially defining which jurisconsults had canonical standing and which did not. Even those jurisconsults who made it through the Theodosian pruning, however, had still bequeathed to posterity some one thousand five hundred books of opinions, and the number of imperial constitutions and rescripts had necessarily continued to proliferate.

In 528 Justinian established a law commission under the presidency of his chief legal officer, the *quaestor* Tribonian, to take this situation in hand. In a formidable editorial feat, within just six years this commission had produced a new fifty-book collation and homogenisation of the writings of the classical jurisconsults (the *Digest*, promulgated in 531); a condensed version of the same, which was meant to serve as a clear and accessible textbook for those beginning the study of law with a view to entering governmental service (the *Institutes*, promulgated in 533); and a similar collection, homogenisation, and codification of the decrees of the Christian Roman emperors (the *Codex Iustinianus*, or 'Justinianic Code', the second recension of which was promulgated in 534). It is significant that the *Digest* and *Institutes* were promulgated entirely in Latin, as too was much of the text of the *Codex*, indicating that a good Latin education was still presumed to be available in the eastern provinces, where, outside the Latin enclaves of Constantinople, Illyricum, and Berytus (Beirut), Greek remained the predominant language of the elite.

The intellectual achievement with respect to the Justinianic legal project did not lie so much in the editorial process itself. Those legal scholars commissioned to produce the *Digest*, for example, probably had to read no more than forty pages of Latin text per day and decide which twentieth part of the text read merited inclusion in the new compilation; and as a distinguished modern legal scholar and teacher of civil law has declared, 'even a law student can read forty pages in a day and highlight the 5% he thinks important'.[80] Rather, the point was that beneath a classicising veneer (which has confused historians as often as it has

---

[80] A. Weir, 'Two Great Legislators', *Tulane European and Civil Law Forum* (New Orleans, 2006), pp. 35–51, p. 40.

lawyers) Justinian's legal officers were engaged in editing, rearranging, and reworking the inherited Roman law tradition to express a single opinion and will, represented as being that of the Emperor Justinian. The codification and reform of the civil law thus served an important ideological as well as legal function: not only were the laws reworked to serve contemporary needs but also the Emperor was established, for the first time in Roman legal tradition, as the one and only legitimate source of law. The person of the Emperor was, Justinian declared, 'the law animate' (Greek *nomos empsychos*).[81] The reformed law issued in the Emperor's name was not to be altered, amended, or even further abbreviated. It is striking that law students in their second year of study were to be called *Iustiniani* ('the Justinians'); they were to be the crack troops at the forefront of the struggle to restore imperial majesty and the Emperor's control over the structures of imperial government. As Justinian declared to the 'young enthusiasts for law' to whom the promulgation of the *Institutes* was addressed:

> Imperial Majesty should not only be graced with arms but also armed with laws, so that good government may prevail in time of war and peace alike. The head of the Roman state can then stand victorious not only over enemies in war, but also over troublemakers at home. . . . Study our law. Do your best and apply yourself keenly to it. Show that you have mastered it. You can then cherish a noble ambition; for when your course of law is finished you will be able to perform whatever duty is entrusted to you in the governance of our state.[82]

For Justinian, the reform of legal education and of the body of authoritative legal texts was but the first step in overhauling the administrative structures of the Roman state more generally and in buttressing the foundations of imperial rule in the face of those vested interests (not least aristocratic) within the empire that were deemed to feed off and contribute to its decline. It should be noted accordingly that, from an early date, Justinian's legal reforms were a matter of considerable political sensitivity and occasioned mounting opposition. To Procopius (himself a lawyer by training), they epitomised the Emperor's over-centralising zeal. Procopius complains that so determined was Justinian to stamp his own authority on the constitutions he issued that he even refused to permit the person of the *quaestor* to read out the laws he had drafted, as was customary, insisting instead that he deliver the words himself.[83] Likewise, the Senate of Constantinople was left sitting 'as if in a picture': the passive recipients of imperial orders and commands rather than the active participants in deliberation and decision making that they expected to be.[84]

For some this was evidently too much. In January 532, members of the Constantinopolitan Senate sought to take advantage of an outbreak of rioting amongst the circus factions of the city's Hippodrome and so effect political change. These factions (primarily consisting of the 'Blues' and the 'Greens', but also encompassing the 'Reds' and the 'Whites' after the colours worn by the teams of chariot racers), although at core essentially bands of sporting enthusiasts, had come to play an

---

[81] *J. Nov.*, 105.2.4.   [82] *C.Imperiam Maiestatem.*
[83] Procopius, *Secret History*, 14.3.   [84] Procopius, *Secret History*, 14.8.

important part in the life of Constantinople, as well as of the other cities of the empire, in that they represented forms of association that cut across regional and class divides.[85] As such, they represented the primary collective body by which elements of the urban lower classes (including the vast numbers of migrants that thronged the great imperial cities) could be mobilised. In the Constantinopolitan Hippodrome specifically, the factions represented 'the People'. If properly manipulated, by contrast, on the streets of the imperial capital, they represented 'the Mob'. Whether through acclamations and chants at the games, or rioting and incendiarism in the porticoes, the factions were thus potentially possessed of enormous political power, and the imperial authorities curried favour with them by providing significant financial subventions.

Prior to his accession to the throne, Justinian had carefully nurtured the support of the Blue Faction, whilst his wife Theodora had lent her support to the Greens.[86] Such a balancing act was highly characteristic of the imperial couple, and was extended by them to the ecclesiastical sphere with respect to the pro-Chalcedonian and anti-Chalcedonian parties. The loyalty of the factions, however, was always precarious, not only because support amongst them could always be bought up by whatever interest group or cabal wished to flex its muscles but also because their composition was constantly being altered by the influx of new migrants into the imperial capital.

In early 532 it was the anti-Justinian party in the Senate that was eager to take its message to the streets. What began, therefore, in January 532 as a protest against the arrest of leading members of the factions in Constantinople soon escalated into what seems to have been a carefully orchestrated campaign of widespread destruction. This saw the Senate House, the *Augustaeum* (an important ceremonial square), the Great Church, and the offices of the Praetorian Prefecture burnt down, and the rioters massing in the Hippodrome and on the streets. They demanded the resignation of the chief officers of state, including the Praetorian Prefect John the Cappadocian, the Urban Prefect of Constantinople, and, significantly, the Emperor's *quaestor* Tribonian.[87] Justinian was obliged to accede to these demands. The riots nevertheless continued. Accordingly, we are informed, the Emperor decided to appear before his subjects in the imperial box in the Hippodrome, in the hope of quelling the rioters. As the *Paschal Chronicle* records:

> on the 18th day of the same month, early in the morning the emperor went up into the Hippodrome to his own box, carrying the Holy Gospel. And when this was known, all the people went up, and the entire Hippodrome was filled by the crowds. And the Emperor swore an oath to them saying, 'By this Power, I forgive you this error, and I order that none of you be arrested—but be peaceful; for there is nothing on your head but rather on mine. For my sins have made me deny to you what you asked of me in the Hippodrome.'

---

[85] P. Bell, 'Social Tensions in the Early Byzantine Empire' (Oxford University D.Phil. dissertation, 2006).

[86] Procopius, *Secret History*.

[87] Procopius, *Wars*, I, 27.17; *Chronicon Paschale*, tr. M. and M. Whitby (Liverpool, 1989), pp. 115–16.

And many of the people chanted, 'Augustus Justinian, may you be victorious.' But others chanted, 'You are foresworn, ass.' And he desisted, and the emperor himself went down from the Hippodrome; and he immediately granted dismissal to those in the Palace, and said to the senators, 'Depart, each to guard his own house'.[88]

It was now clear that a portion at least of the crowd was intent on deposing the Emperor.

According to Procopius, at this point Justinian considered taking flight from his capital, and was only dissuaded from doing so by his wife, the indomitable Empress Theodora. There are signs, however, that rather than giving up the game, Justinian instead threw caution to the wind and decided to flush out his opponents once and for all. This is perhaps suggested by the otherwise curious decision to release those senators who were in his company, whom he sent back to their own residences. For amongst those whom he had kept with him in the Palace was the *patricius* and senator Hypatius, nephew of the Emperor Anastasius, the same Hypatius who had led negotiations with the Persians earlier in Justin's reign. Justinian must have realised that those elements behind the mob who were intent on a change of regime would be on the look-out for a new Emperor to acclaim in his place, and that Hypatius, with his faultless imperial pedigree, had all the makings of an excellent candidate. Releasing Hypatius to the crowd was both a challenge to his opponents and a trap for Hypatius.

The *Paschal Chronicle* informs us that, as might have been expected:

> when they had got out, the people met Hypatius the patrician, and Pompeius the patrician; and they chanted, 'Hypatius Augustus, may you be victorious.' And the people took the same patrician Hypatius to the Forum of Constantine wearing a white mantle, and they carried him on high . . . and the people brought from the palace of Placillianae, as it is called, imperial insignia which were stored up there, and they put them on the head of the same Hypatius, and a golden torque upon his neck. And when this was made known to the Emperor, the Palace was locked up; and the masses of the people took the same Hypatius and Pompeius the patrician and Julian the former praetorian prefect and led the same Hypatius away to the imperial box [in the Hippodrome], wishing to bring out imperial purple and a diadem from the [adjoining] Palace and crown him Emperor.[89]

Even before Hypatius had been acclaimed, however, elements of the imperial bodyguard, under the command of Justinian's trusted Persarmenian general Narses, were already active distributing money and buying up elements within the crowd, whilst Belisarius and his men stood ready at the heavily fortified bronze doors that connected the inner sanctum of the Palace to the Imperial Box. When the signal was given, the suborned elements amongst the circus factions raised a chant in support of Justinian, whereupon Narses and his troops drew their swords and initiated a prodigious massacre of the rioters trapped in the Hippodrome, whilst Belisarius and his men burst into the Imperial Box from the Palace and arrested Hypatius and those around him.[90] Before the day was out, up to 'thirty-five

---

[88] ibid., pp. 120–21.
[89] ibid., pp. 121–22.   [90] ibid., pp. 124–5.

thousand citizens and visitors were slain at the Palace.... And on the next day, Hypatius and Pompeius the patricians were slain, and their corpses were thrown into the sea.'[91]

Hypatius was subsequently to receive a posthumous pardon from the Emperor Justinian, who even paid for a verse epitaph to be composed and erected in his memory.[92] His estates were nevertheless confiscated, as too were those of other senatorial households whose loyalties were under suspicion. Essentially, Justinian seized upon the 'Nika' insurrection (so named after the recorded chant of the crowd—*Nika*—'Conquer!') to clear out of the Senate a number of individuals who were felt to pose a threat to his regime. At the same time, he turned the destruction wrought by the rioters to his advantage by rebuilding the monumental heart of his capital on a scale and grandeur that served to reflect still greater glory upon himself. Foremost amongst these imperial building commissions was the domed cathedral church of Hagia Sophia ('Holy Wisdom'), which, for many centuries, was to be the largest enclosed space in Christendom. 'Solomon', Justinian is reported to have declared upon the completion of the project, 'I have surpassed you.'[93] Royal Scandinavian visitors to Hagia Sophia would later receive baptism into the Orthodox faith in the tenth century on the grounds that, in Justinian's great church, they had seen where God dwelled.[94] In a Constantinople adorned with building works funded by and glorifying aristocratic donors and patrons, it was vital that the Emperor's building commissions be pre-eminent in both magnificence and scale (Fig. 7).

In the aftermath of the Nika insurrection, Tribonian and John the Cappadocian were restored to office, and legal and administrative reform quickened. In 535, with the new corpus of legal texts established, the procedures whereby provincial litigants were able to gain audience first at the courts of provincial governors and then in Constantinople (technically known as the 'appellate procedure') were overhauled in order to render access to the reformed law more practicable on the part of the Emperor's subjects.[95] Justinian then set about the reform of provincial government itself, seeking to tighten the grip of provincial governors over the territories that they administered and the officials placed at their disposal. The stipends issued to governors were substantially increased to render them less prone to the bribes and blandishments proffered by the wealthy, and bishops and provincial administrators termed *defensores* were instructed to keep a careful eye on those appointed to the governor's residence and report any acts of corruption or venality directly to Constantinople.[96] Governors were issued with a detailed and standardised set of instructions setting out their duties and responsibilities, as well as the punishments to which they would be liable if they failed to carry out their

---

[91] ibid., pp. 125–6.
[92] *Anthologia Graeca*, VII, 591.
[93] *Scriptores Originum Constantinopolitanarum*, I, 105; Romanos, *kontakion*, 54.20.4.
[94] *Russian Primary Chronicle*, 111.
[95] M. Maas, 'Roman History and Christian Ideology in Justinianic Reform Legislation', *Dumbarton Oaks Papers* 40 (1986), pp. 17–31.
[96] See *J.Nov.*, 8 and 15.

Fig. 7 Exterior of Hagia Sophia, Constantinople (C. Mango, *The Oxford History of Byzantium*, p. 47)

orders.[97] Foremost amongst these responsibilities was that of collecting taxes. Between 535 and 539 there then followed a series of laws aimed at remedying the challenges faced by the imperial government in specific provinces, from the coast of the Black Sea to Arabia, via Egypt: throughout this legislation, mention is repeatedly made of tax evasion on the part of well-connected landowners, the seizure of property by the powerful, and their maintenance of bands of armed retainers in breach of imperial prohibition.[98] In the Lebanon, governors were ordered to restrain 'the households of the mighty';[99] with respect to Cappadocia, the Emperor declared that the lawlessness of the magnates of the region and their private armed retinues, including their encroachments into imperial estates, made

[97] *J.Nov.*, 17.   [98] See Sarris (2006), pp. 210–20.   [99] *J. Edict.*, 4.

his face go red with anger;[100] in Egypt, aristocratic tax evasion threatened 'the very cohesion of Our state itself';[101] whilst in every province, governors were to demand from the collectors of the public taxes precise details of all landholdings, individuals, and estate properties on which taxes were owed, as well as how much had actually been received. Those tax collectors who were unable to provide such figures were to have their hands cut off.[102] It is a shame that we do not have similar legal sources for Khusro's Persia: one suspects that the shah's pronouncements would have been very similar both in content and tone. In both great empires (and after a manner reminiscent of Europe during the 'military revolution' of the seventeenth century) it was the funding of warfare that ultimately set the pace of reform.

4.5 THE RESUMPTION OF HOSTILITIES

In spite of Justinian's Western preoccupations and his determination to overhaul the administrative and fiscal structures of the Eastern Roman state, the imperial authorities in the 530s continued to pay careful attention to Roman interests in the Caucasus, where the reign of the Emperor Justin in particular had witnessed such significant Roman advances. In 536, for example, Justinian ordered the systematic reorganisation of the administration of Roman Armenia, building upon his earlier military reforms in the Armenian territories. The former 'satrapies' of *Armenia Inferior* were now divided into four provinces, whilst a new Roman garrison was deployed in Lazica and a city established at Petra to serve as an administrative centre.[103] As a sign of the tightening of Roman control in the Caucasus, the Laz are reported to have complained at the trade restrictions introduced in the region by the Roman commander, and there are indications of growing unease at the extent of Roman domination on the part of elements within the Armenian aristocracy.[104] Further south there is evidence for considerable cooperation between the Roman and Persian authorities in Upper Mesopotamia, with the Persians even assisting the Romans in arresting anti-Chalcedonian clergymen whose activities were deemed to be injurious to the public good.[105] In return, Justinian is likely to have desisted from any further military building work along the Syrian frontier zone, relying instead upon diplomacy and subsidies to prevent raids into Roman territory on the part of nomadic Bedouin tribesmen.[106]

At the end of the day, however, the strategic geography of the Roman-Persian frontier zone necessarily meant that in spite of such examples of cooperation, the ongoing consolidation of Roman power in the Caucasus posed a major and intensifying threat to the military security of the economic and political heartland

---

[100] *J. Nov.*, 30.　　[101] *J. Edict.*, 13.
[102] *J. Nov.*, 17.　　[103] *J.Nov.*, 28.
[104] Procopius, *Wars*, II, 15.1–26 and II, 2–3.
[105] Elias, *Life of John of Tella*, 65.24–66.21 and 71.21–73.11.
[106] Greatrex and Lieu (2002), pp. 99–100.

of the Sasanian Empire in Iraq. This was a fact to which Khusro would have been keenly sensitive, and if Khusro was to justify his programme of internal reform to what may well have been a sceptical audience of Iranian noblemen, then he would have to roll back the juggernaut of the Roman state in the Caucasus. The pressure to demonstrate the military vitality of the Persian state is likely to have been further intensified by an awareness of Roman successes in the West; the Vandal king Gelimer's ritualised humiliation in Constantinople in 534, for instance, was witnessed by a Persian ambassador, whilst in 537 the Ostrogothic king Witigis sent an embassy to Khusro, alerting him to Justinian's lust for conquest and inciting the shah to make a pre-emptive strike against his imperial rival.[107]

Late in 539, aware of rumblings of discontent against the Romans in the Caucasus, and taking advantage of a dispute over pasturage rights between his own Arab clients, the Nasrids, and the Roman-backed Jafnids, Khusro began to make preparations for war.[108] By May 540 he was ready to strike: with the assistance of his Arab allies, Khusro and the Persian army marched along the southern bank of the Euphrates and the frontier zone's desert fringe, thereby circumventing Roman defences in the region and showing Persian banners in an area where, since 529, Justinian's representatives had been actively engaged in attempting to build up the client kingship of the Jafnid al-Harith. Khusro then led his men in a frontal assault on Antioch—the capital of the Roman East. Thanks to a weakness in the city's defences, and the fact that a newly arrived Roman garrison had not yet been able to dig in properly, the Persians were able to gain control of its walls and drive out the Roman troops. Members of the city's circus factions attempted to lead resistance to the invaders, but to little avail. At Khusro's command, the triumphant Persian army razed the city to the ground, stripped its inhabitants of their wealth and led many of them into captivity in Persia.[109] It was a devastating blow to the Eastern Roman Empire, and one that left a deep mark on Procopius, who declared after his account of the fall of the city that 'I become dizzy as I write of such a great calamity and pass it on to future generations, and I am unable to understand why indeed it should be the will of God to exalt on high the fortunes of a man or of a place, and then to cast them down and destroy them.'[110] From this point on Procopius' writings, already subtly critical of the Emperor Justinian and his regime, take on an ever more openly bitter and disillusioned tone. Khusro and his men now pressed home their advantage, spreading mayhem and slaughter throughout the cities of Syria.[111] From Antioch, Khusro marched west to the port of Seleucia, where he washed his warboots in the Mediterranean. Before returning to Persian territory, the shah led a symbolically charged assault on Dara, which was only fended off through the ingenuity of the Roman sappers and the payment of 1,000 pounds in weight of silver.[112]

[107] Zachariah of Mitylene, *Chronicle*, IX, 17; Procopius, *Wars*, II, 1.1–11.
[108] Tabari, I, 958/252–3; Procopius, *Wars*, II, 4.14–26.
[109] See the *Life* of Symeon Stylites the Younger 57 (50–2); John Lydus, *De Magistratibus*, II, 54 (216.14–22); Procopius, *Wars*, II, 8.20.
[110] Procopius, *Wars*, II, 10.4–5.
[111] ibid., II, 10.19–24. [112] ibid., II, 13.1–29.

The following year, Justinian's commanders attempted to take warfare to the enemy: a retaliatory assault from Dara on Nisibis was driven back by the Persians, but the intervention of Belisarius prevented the Roman retreat from becoming a rout.[113] The Roman client king of the Jafnids was also prevailed upon to intervene, attacking a number of Persian cities and reportedly seizing many prisoners.[114] In 542 Khusro responded by leading his forces once more into Roman Mesopotamia, striking at the lightly defended city of Callinicum.[115] In other cities of the East, the Roman authorities were busily engaged in the upgrading of fortifications: 'Up with the victory of the General Belisarius!' one inscription raised on some contemporary defensive work declared; 'Many years to Justinian the Emperor and to the Augusta Theodora', proclaimed another.[116] This programme of refortification seems to have been relatively successful, and Khusro's campaigns of 543 came to little: the Persian advance faltered outside the city of Edessa and the shah was persuaded to withdraw in return for five *centenaria* of gold (36,000 *solidi*).[117] Eventually, in 545 first an armistice and then a five-year truce was agreed and some measure of peace was restored to the frontier zone.

It is significant, however, that the truce of 545 only applied to Mesopotamia: as we have seen, it was in the Caucasus that the Romans had most markedly strengthened their position in the early sixth century; and it should be noted that Khusro's drive into Roman Syria coincided with a concerted and sustained assault upon Roman positions in the northern mountain zone that was specifically excluded from the peace negotiations of 545, and where warfare continued unremittingly for many years to come. All this would indicate that, in the 540s, it was in the Caucasus that Khusro's true strategic ambitions lay, and that his assaults on Susa, Antioch, Callinicum, and Edessa were at least in part meant as diversionary manoeuvres, calculated to distract Roman attention and draw Roman forces away from the region.[118] In 541 Khusro had received an embassy from the Laz, who were increasingly restless under Roman domination.[119] Accordingly, prior to the Roman assault on Nisibis, he led his northern field army out of Iberia into Lazica, where he received the surrender of the Laz king Gubazes. The Roman base at Petra soon fell to Khusro's forces, and the Roman garrison in the city defected.[120] At Pityus and Sebastopolis, the Roman garrisons destroyed their fortifications before withdrawing, so as to prevent them falling into enemy hands.[121]

Khusro's successful efforts to bring Lazica back within the Persian fold was a major diplomatic and military coup. It was now once more Persian dominance that

---

[113] Procopius, *Wars*, II, 18.1–26.
[114] Agapius, *P O*, 8.431.
[115] Procopius, *Wars*, II, 21.30–2; Jacob of Edessa, *Chronicle*, p. 320.
[116] *IGLS*, 145 and 146.
[117] Procopius, *Wars*, II, 26.1–46.
[118] As with so many other aspects of Roman-Persian warfare and relations, I owe this suggestion to my former tutor and supervisor, James Howard-Johnston.
[119] Procopius, *Wars*, II, 15.1–30.
[120] ibid., II, 17.1–28.
[121] ibid., VIII, 4.4–5.

the Christian lords of the Caucasus had to fear. Accordingly, a number of Armenian princes who had previously complained of the tightness of Roman control returned to Roman allegiance.[122] In order to prevent a similar defection back to the Romans on the part of the Christians of Lazica, Khusro made plans to assassinate King Gubazes and alter the religious geography of the western Caucasus by deporting the Laz. Before either plan could come to fruition, however, the feared defection took place, and Justinian dispatched some eight thousand crack troops to Lazica to bolster Gubazes' hold on power and to move against the Persians.[123] An attempt to drive the Persians out of Petra failed, but a successful ambushing of the Persian field army in the narrow mountain defiles obliged the withdrawal into Persian territory of many of the shah's forces. The conflict between Rome and Persia in the Caucasus was thus increasingly taking on the appearance of a guerrilla war, with the Persians dominating the lowland zones and the fortified cities, but with Christian insurgents inflicting losses on their enemies as they traversed the mountain passes.

The only way for the Roman forces to break out of the highland zone was for the empire to commit more resources. Accordingly, Justinian sent yet another army to the region, simultaneously inviting the Sabir Huns to attack Persian positions. Not until 551, however, did the fortified city of Petra finally fall to the Romans: that the imperial troops promptly dismantled its walls, however, demonstrated their lack of confidence in being able to hold on to the city.[124] In spite of Justinian's best efforts, Iberia, eastern Lazica, and the strategically significant kingdom of Suania to its north—effectively a listening post on the steppe—were securely in Persian hands.[125] Between 552 and 556, along this blurred zone of demarcation, warfare between the Romans and Persians for mastery of the Caucasus gradually ground to a standstill.[126]

In 551, with the ending of the Mesopotamian truce, Justinian had attempted to negotiate a general settlement with Khusro and, to this end, had sent his envoy, Peter the Patrician, to the Sasanian court at Ctesiphon. A reciprocal delegation to Constantinople agreed to renew the truce for a further five years, in return for large cash subsidies, although, once more, fighting in the Caucasus was expressly excluded from its provisions.[127] Eventually, however, the stalemate in the Caucasus obliged the Persians to come to terms, and in 557 a general armistice was agreed, whereby each side would remain in possession of such territories in Lazica as it currently held.[128] Further rounds of negotiations, however, were required before this armistice could be transformed into a full-blown peace settlement. In 561–2 the two great powers agreed three separate detailed treaties of fifty years' duration whereby, as a contemporary source records, 'Lazica should be ceded to the Romans ... [but]

---

[122] Procopius, *Wars*, II, 21.34.
[123] ibid., II, 29.1–9.
[124] ibid., VIII, 12.28–9.
[125] ibid., VIII, 16.1–5.
[126] Greatrex and Lieu (2002), pp. 118–22.
[127] Procopius, *Wars*, VIII, 15.1–7; Constantine Porphyrogenitus, *De Cerimoniis*, 89–90.
[128] Agathias, *History*, IV, 30.7–10.

the Persians would, however, receive 30,000 *solidi* per year from the Romans for the peace. It was also established that the Romans should provide in advance the amount for ten years at one go.'[129] Further Persian demands that the Romans should also pay subsidies to their Nasrid allies were, however, rejected, and neither side was able to agree as to the standing of Suania, which was traditionally subject to the king of the Laz, who was now formally acknowledged to be a Roman client.

If the armistice of 557 had simply reflected the balance of power between the Romans and Persians in Lazica as it had stood on the ground, the terms of the treaties of 561–2 heralded a very major Persian climbdown. Admittedly in return for substantial cash subsidies that were clearly meant to soften the blow to Persian pride, Khusro had agreed to withdraw Persian troops from a strategically vital, traditionally Persian sphere of influence, to which, for sixteen years and with considerable success, he had committed both men and resources. The Romans had thus been able to salvage by diplomacy what they had not been able to hold onto by military might. It was a dramatic and highly significant Persian *volte-face*.

This Persian disengagement from Lazica is principally explicable in terms of the strategic geography of the Persian Empire and the thought-world of the Iranian nobility. As the example of the Huns (Hephthalite or otherwise) had revealed, although it was to Rome that the Sasanian shahs looked for a prestige enemy, and although Roman ambitions in the Caucasus posed a genuine threat to the core interests of the Persian state, the Shahs were nevertheless obliged to keep a constant eye on the world of the steppe and the realm of *Turan*, whence they faced not only their most dangerous foe but also their ideological and cosmological antithesis. Consequently, it was the threat posed by the nomad that was always the prime concern. As late as 540, it seems, Khusro had been obliged to contend with an aggressive and vigorous Hephthalite neighbour to whom he was forced to pay tribute. After that date, the power of the Hephthalite Huns began to wane, and it was this that gave Khusro his opportunity to concentrate both manpower and resources on Lazica and the West.

This eclipsing of the Hephthalites, however, was the result of a new and, from a Persian perspective, potentially still more dangerous threat. The 540s and 550s witnessed a series of political convulsions on the Eurasian steppe, which saw a new power advance along the undulating grasslands of Manchuria and Central Asia, namely the Turk Khaganate. First scattering to east and west a group known as the Avars (to whom we shall return in Chapter Five), and then combating and ultimately subduing the Hephthalites, by the mid-550s the Turks had established themselves to the north of the Caspian Gates. It was to address this new and formidable foe that Khusro had been obliged to withdraw from Lazica; Justinian ultimately owed his Caucasian victory to the Turks.

---

[129] Menander, fragment 6.1.134–54. For the detailed treaty, see Menander, fragment 6.1.314–97.

4.6 THE ADVENT OF THE PLAGUE

Warfare was not the only cataclysm to befall the provinces of the Eastern Roman Empire in the 540s. For reasons that are not entirely clear (although a major volcanic explosion in East Asia perhaps provides the most plausible explanation), the 530s represented a period of extreme and violent climatic instability in much of the known world.[130] The impact of climate change on the delicate grassland ecology of the Eurasian steppe may well explain the dynamic shift in political fortunes there that was to result in the expansion of the Turks towards Persia and the west. Nomadic armies, after all, relied on their horses, and horses depended on pasture. In central Africa, where bubonic plague was endemic (technically 'enzootic') to the rodent population, the change in climatic conditions seems to have forced rodents to forage ever further afield for food, bringing them into more frequent contact with first the nomadic and then the sedentary societies of central-east Africa, including the Christian principality of Axum, Byzantium's satellite state on the Red Sea.[131] As a result, these rodents passed on to the human population the deadly *bacillus* that was the prime causative agent of bubonic disease.

In 541 the plague traversed the Red Sea and manifested itself at the important Egyptian entrepôt of Pelusium, from where it spread to Alexandria, the rest of Egypt, and then to Palestine.[132] A harrowing account of the immediate impact of the plague within Egypt is recorded in the writings of the contemporary ecclesiastical historian John of Ephesus, who witnessed the ravages of the disease whilst travelling from Alexandria to Constantinople via Palestine and Syria in the early 540s. John relates, for example, that 'it was told about one city on the Egyptian border (that) it perished totally and completely with (only) seven men and one little boy ten years old remaining in it'.[133] By the spring of 542 the disease had reached the imperial capital of Constantinople, where the Emperor was reported to have contracted it, although he was subsequently to recover.[134] The same year the plague reached cities in Syria, Illyricum, Africa, and Spain. By 543 the pestilence had further extended its reach to embrace Armenia, Italy, and Gaul, before eventually arriving in the British Isles and Ireland.[135]

The contemporary narrative sources available to the historian—be they from East or West, or written in Latin, Greek, Syriac, or Arabic—speak with one voice in describing the plague as having had a major and sudden impact on both urban and rural communities alike throughout the Mediterranean world. Procopius, for instance, who was present in Constantinople when the plague first struck in 542,

---

[130] D. Keys, *Catastrophe: An Investigation into the Origins of the Modern World* (London, 1999).
[131] P. Sarris, 'The Justinianic Plague: Origins and Effects', *Continuity and Change* 17.2 (2002), pp. 169–82.
[132] Procopius, *Wars*, II, 22.6.
[133] Fragment preserved in Pseudo-Dionysius of Tel Mahre, *Chronicle: Part III*, tr. W. Witakowski (Liverpool, 1996), p. 77.
[134] Procopius, *Wars*, II, 22.9–23, and *Secret History*, IV, 1.
[135] L. K. Little (ed.), *Plague and the End of Antiquity: The Pandemic of 541–750* (Cambridge, 2006).

describes how at one point it laid low 10,000 victims in a single day, with the dead being disposed of in mass graves in the sea and beyond the city walls. Likewise, John of Ephesus witnessed 'villages whose inhabitants perished altogether'. As he passed through Syria, John relates having encountered 'houses and waystations occupied only by the dead, corpses lying in the fields and along the roadside, and cattle wandering untended into the hills'. The late sixth-century churchman Evagrius, whose own family was struck by the disease, and who was himself afflicted with it as a boy, recorded that the plague, like the fiscal indiction, returned in a fifteen-year cycle to lay low each new generation. On the borders of Syria, the Arab poet Hassan Ibn Thabit described the plague as 'the stinging of the *jinn*', devastating the rural population of the desert fringe. A high rate of mortality is also recorded with respect to Gaul in the writings of Gregory of Tours.[136]

There is no good reason to gainsay these eyewitness accounts. There is considerable evidence, for example, that high rates of plague-induced mortality disrupted military operations in the early 540s by the Eastern Roman authorities in Italy and the Persians in the Caucasus.[137] A sudden loss of taxpayers resulting from the plague can also be seen to have wreaked havoc with imperial finances, obliging the Eastern Roman state to retrench expenditure on civil-service pensions and military pay, and to debase the gold coinage, issuing payments in the form of light-weight *solidi* while presumably demanding that tax collectors receive only the full-weight coin.[138] With the fiscal pressures on the Roman state occasioned by warfare remaining constant, diminishing revenues had to be spread ever more thinly. In Britain, where the arrival of the plague coincided with chronic military and political insecurity, the archaeological evidence points to a staggering demographic collapse, with the population perhaps halving over the course of the fifth and sixth centuries.[139]

Both from the perspective of those who were struck by it and the Eastern Roman state, the advent of the bubonic plague was clearly a disaster. For many of those more humble members of society who survived the disease, however, the ravages of the plague opened up new opportunities. The legal sources indicate that, within the empire, the impact of plague resulted in severe localised labour shortages, which workers and artisans were keen to take advantage of to better their lot. Thus, in April 545, Justinian issued an edict of imperial-wide effect, complaining of how, in the wake of the plague, tradesmen, artisans, and agricultural workers had 'given themselves over to avarice', and were demanding 'twice or even three times the prices and wages' that had hitherto been the norm. The Emperor decreed that those responsible for issuing wages and stipends to building workers, agricultural labourers, or any other group of workers were not to 'credit them with any more than

---

[136] Sarris (2002) for references.
[137] Procopius, *Wars*, II, 24. For Italy, see J. Teall, 'The Barbarians in Justinian's Armies', *Speculum* 40 (1965), pp. 294–322.
[138] Sarris (2002)—much of which I repeat here.
[139] Wickham (2005), p. 312, for references; the archaeologists date this collapse to the fifth/sixth centuries, or a 'long fifth century', but the sixth century makes considerably more sense given the literary and other evidence for plague.

their customary remuneration'.¹⁴⁰ The sixth-century *Life* of St Nicholas of Sion records how in Lycia, on the southern coast of Asia Minor, local farmers refused to deliver food supplies to the city of Myra in spite of the furious injunctions and demands of city councillors.¹⁴¹ At the same time, the documentary evidence from Egypt suggests that tenants took advantage of the demographic conditions around them to extract ever more favourable terms from their landlords: analysis of extant land leases from the period reveals a marked improvement in the security of tenure enjoyed by lessees around the middle of the sixth century.¹⁴²

Naturally, many of these leaseholders are likely to have been individuals of relatively high social standing, paying rent on extensive plots. Moreover, as has been seen, the extensive leasing of land would not appear to have played a central role in the domestic economy of many of the great landowning families—members of the imperial aristocracy of service, whose estates tended to be cultivated by a centrally directed agricultural workforce paid, at least in part, in coin.¹⁴³ That those owners of land who did rent out holdings, however, were obliged to do so, from their perspective, on ever more disadvantageous terms, would still indicate that, in the context of a plague-ravaged society, a new premium had come to be placed on ensuring the continuous cultivation of land.

That the demands for higher wages made by that proportion of the agricultural and non-agricultural workforce remunerated in coin may also have been successful is indicated by trends evident in the rate of exchange between the gold and copper coinage. Given that the poor were generally paid in small-denomination coinage, but prices and taxes were reckoned in gold, any devaluation of gold vis-à-vis copper inevitably benefited the more humble members of society to the disadvantage of their nominal superiors. It is therefore significant that the number of copper coins (*folles*) per gold *solidus* seems to have declined from around 210 during the period 538–42 to around 180 during the period 542–50.¹⁴⁴ This would have represented a significant improvement in the standard of living of much of the labouring population of the Eastern Empire. The plague thus served to alter the social balance of power at the grassroots of Eastern Roman society. It shook the economic foundations of aristocratic control, while curtailing still more sharply the fiscal resources upon which the state depended.

4.7 THE EMPEROR AND THE CHURCH

Of the many internal and external challenges facing the imperial authorities in the early sixth century, each and every one elicited a concerted response in the reign of the Emperor Justinian. He addressed the challenge posed by the emergence of the Romano-Germanic successor kingdoms by invading first Africa, then Italy, and ultimately, in the 550s, south-west Spain; here, as we shall see in Chapter Five, the

---

[140] *J.Nov.*, 122.
[141] *Life of Nicholas of Sion*, tr. I and N. Sevcenko (Brookline, Mass., 1984), ch. 52.
[142] Sarris (2002), p. 130.   [143] Sarris (2006).   [144] Sarris (2006), pp. 224–5.

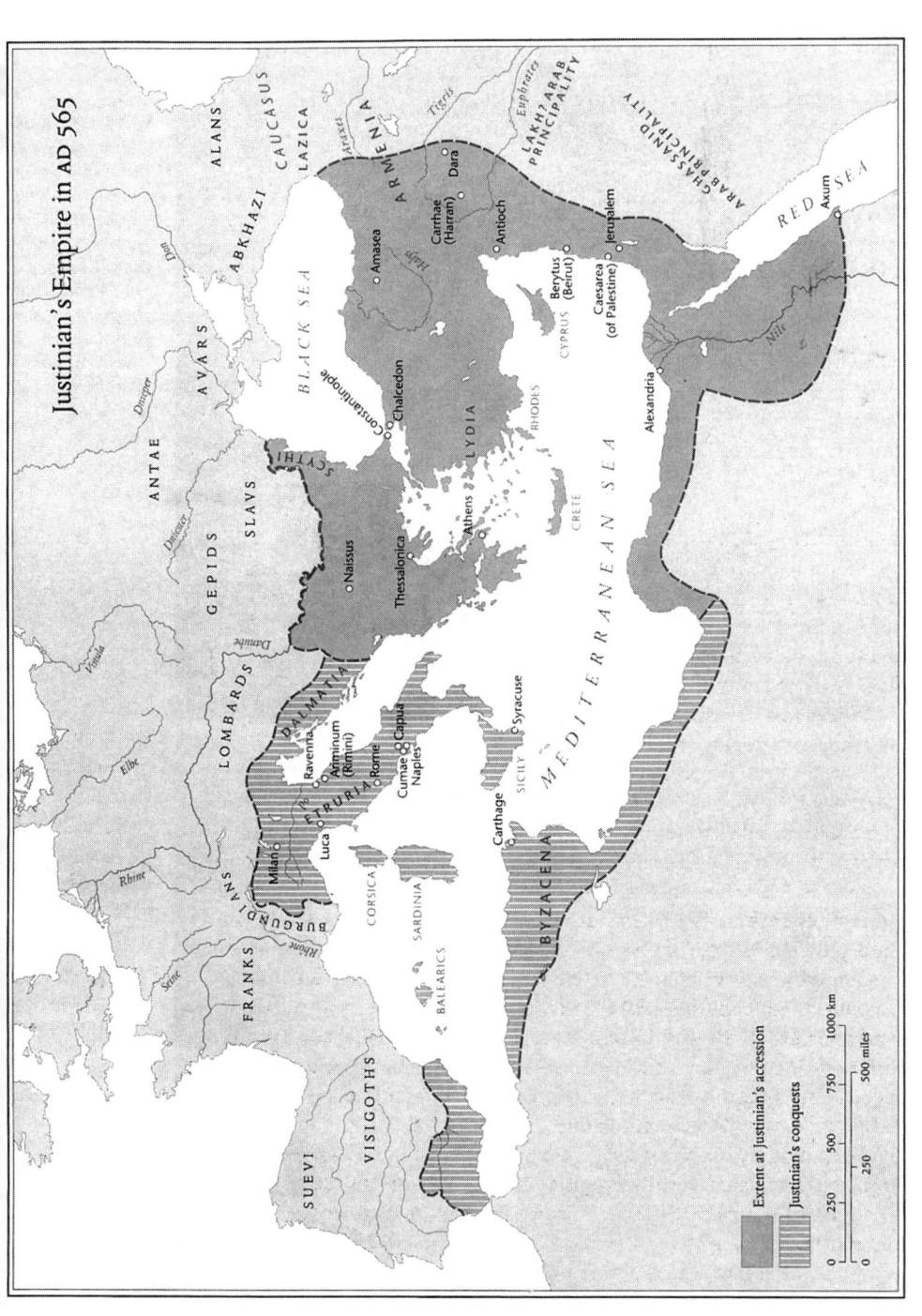

Map 5 Justinian's Empire in 565 (C. Mango, *The Oxford History of Byzantium*, p. 52)

imperial authorities again took advantage of a succession dispute to intervene militarily and establish a foothold in the Iberian peninsula. As a result of Justinian's exertions, the Mediterranean once more became a 'Roman lake' (Map 5).

The atrophying of imperial authority at a provincial level occasioned by the burgeoning influence of aristocratic landowners, and the growing difficulties faced by the imperial government in collecting tax revenues, likewise elicited root-and-branch reform of the empire's legal, administrative, and fiscal framework. Here results were more mixed. As the 'Nika' riots had demonstrated, and as the highly critical writings of both Procopius and his contemporary, the high-ranking civil servant and scholar John the Lydian, serve to remind us, resistance to internal reform within elite circles was considerable; and (as Anastasius had realised) without the active support and consent of members of the senatorial and provincial aristocracy, effective imperial government at a local level was ultimately impossible. As the years passed, opinion seems to have hardened against the Emperor's reform programme. In 541, perhaps in an attempt to head off yet another, potentially insurmountable wave of discontent, the Empress Theodora had moved against the Emperor Justinian's right-hand man in the programme of reform, the Praetorian Prefect of the East, John the Cappadocian, securing his final dismissal and exile from the capital.[145] If Theodora's aim in removing John had been to ensure that the Emperor would change course, her ambitions would have been further aided in 541/2 by the death of the *quaestor* Tribonian.[146]

Whatever the political context to the dismissal of John the Cappadocian and the death of Tribonian, the removal of the two men on whom Justinian most relied for the internal administration of the empire, combined with the recurrent impact of bubonic plague, the requirements of warfare with Persia, and an increasing concentration on attempting to draw the protracted Italian campaign to a conclusion, prevented Justinian from ever again attempting anything more than piecemeal reform; indeed some elements of his earlier provincial legislation were put into reverse.[147] Moreover, even within the newly reformed governmental structures, there are signs that members of the provincial and senatorial aristocracy were beginning to reassert their influence, perhaps responding to a loosening of their economic control at the grassroots of Eastern Roman society by seeking to tighten their grip on the institutions of the Roman state.[148] This was to become most apparent upon the death of Justinian in 565 and the accession of his nephew, Justin II, whose support was primarily senatorial, and who from the start of his reign went out of his way to advance aristocratic interests, adopting a tone highly critical of his predecessor's policies and regime.[149]

---

[145] J. A. S. Evans, *The Age of Justinian: The Circumstances of Imperial Power* (London, 1996), pp. 196–7.
[146] Procopius, *Wars*, I, 25.2.
[147] Stein, *L'histoire du Bas Empire* (Paris, 1949), II, pp. 747–56.
[148] ibid., pp. 752–3; Sarris (2006), and M. Kaplan, *Les Hommes et la Terre à Byzance* (Paris, 1992), pp. 176–80.
[149] Sarris (2006), and Cameron (1985), p. 250.

The View from the East: Crisis, Survival, and Renewal 163

If the dividends derived from Justinian's reform programme were uncertain, the Emperor's religious and ecclesiastical policies were, in the medium term at least, barely more productive. As seen earlier, the Eastern Roman Empire of the early sixth century had inherited a *damnosa hereditas* from the Theodosian Empire of the fifth century in terms of unresolved ecclesiastical disputes and theological wrangles. The core of the dispute revolved around the issue of the relationship between the human and divine in the person of Christ, a debate that had been ignited by Theodosius II's personal nominee as Patriarch of Constantinople, Bishop Nestorius.

Nestorius' main concern had been to emphasise the extent to which, behind the undivided appearance of the person of Jesus Christ, His two natures (the human and the divine) nevertheless remained distinct. The reason for this emphasis was that, to Nestorius, as also to other theologians approaching the issue from a similar perspective, a tendency to overemphasise the unity of these two natures threatened to undermine the entire theological basis upon which the concept of the salvation of mankind through the incarnation of Christ depended. As had first been acknowledged at the Council of Nicaea in 325, and then been confirmed at the Council of Constantinople in 381, for Christ's incarnation, crucifixion, and resurrection to have truly opened the path to salvation, Christ had to be not only fully consubstantial with God the Father in His divinity but also fully consubstantial with mankind in His humanity. If Jesus was not fully divine, then he could not open the pathway to salvation by atoning for our sins and redeeming our flesh; if Christ was not fully human, then once again, the way to salvation remained closed, as His resurrection and ascent to Heaven could be regarded as unique to Him. To Nestorius, and those who worried along similar lines, overemphasis upon the union, mixing, and blending of Christ's two natures threatened to produce a Jesus who was neither fully human nor fully divine, but rather a *tertium quid*, or 'third category', fundamentally unlike either God or Man, just as water mixed with wine is neither wine nor water.

Nestorius' 'two nature', or *duophysite*, emphasis nevertheless elicited concern from others who were equally anxious to uphold the traditional teachings of the Church with respect to the 'economy of Salvation', but who worried about it from a slightly different angle. To other thinkers, such as the formidable contemporary Patriarch of Alexandria, Cyril, overemphasis on distinction threatened to undermine the concept of salvation by dividing the person of Christ in such a way as to make it impossible to explain or comprehend how the human and divine within Him were able to interact, relate, and cohere; as Cyril and his followers realised, without such cohesion through the full assumption of the human by the divine, there again could be no salvation through Christ.

It should be noted at the outset that each tendency was primarily concerned with the errors that might result from overemphasis on the other's approach rather than with error itself. Although there existed both extreme two-nature and extreme one-nature (or *miaphysite*) theologians, who were widely agreed to be heretical, the theological differences between most bishops and theologians were relatively slight. Nevertheless, the escalation of this dispute had obliged Theodosius II to summon an Ecumenical Council, held at Ephesus in 449, at which Nestorius and his theology had been condemned ('anathematised').

The deposition of Nestorius and his exiling to Egypt sent reverberations throughout the Church, both East and West (and especially in the latter, where 'duophysite' sympathies were strong). Accordingly, in 451, at the Council of Chalcedon, the Emperor Marcian had attempted to mollify duophysite opinion by a Christological formula that emphasised distinction between the human and divine within Christ, whilst upholding the condemnation of Nestorius. The Council declared that Christ existed 'in two natures without confusion, change, division, or separation—the difference of the natures being in no way destroyed by the union, but rather the distinctive character of each nature being preserved and coming together into one person and one *hypostasis*'.[150] This was too much for the leaders of the Church in Egypt and Syria, who, following the logic of Cyrilian Christology, would have preferred the formula that the person of Christ had been formed 'from two natures', thus emphasising unity.

The ensuing rancour within the imperial Church can only partly be explained in terms of theology. Ecumenical Councils had never been purely doctrinal affairs; as well as thrashing out crucial areas of belief, the bishops assembled under the imperial aegis at Nicaea, Constantinople, Ephesus, and Chalcedon had also debated, discussed, and made arrangements for the political and administrative governance of the Church. So, for example, at Nicaea in 325 it had been agreed that there should be a bishop appointed to every city in the empire, and that the structure of the Church should be modelled upon the administrative structure of the state. It is instructive that, if one were simply to set the Christological debate aside, in terms of ecclesiastical politics, there were very clear winners and losers at the Council of Chalcedon. Those who lost the most in terms of political leadership and authority within the Church were also those who were to emerge the least happy with the Chalcedonian Christological settlement.

At Chalcedon two important non-theological developments had taken place. First, the full equality of the Patriarch of Constantinople to the Patriarchs of the other, apostolic sees of Rome, Alexandria, Antioch, and Jerusalem was formally and finally acknowledged. Second, within the context of the equality of the five patriarchs, the concept of the supremacy of honour of the Bishop of Rome as the heir to St Peter, to whom Christ had granted authority over His disciples, was finally and formally agreed. The episcopal authorities in Rome and Constantinople had thus emerged from the Council of Chalcedon with their political authority enhanced. It is perhaps no wonder, as a result, that subsequent bishops of these cities were to be highly resistant to any attempt to tamper with the Chalcedonian settlement, whilst the Bishops of Antioch and Alexandria, who had seen their authority proportionately diluted, were at the forefront of resistance to the Chalcedonian definition of the faith. The Patriarch of Jerusalem, by contrast, would, for the most part, do whatever he was instructed by the representatives of the Emperor

---

[150] *Acts of the Council of Chalcedon*, 5.34.

on whom he was dependent for his security, faced as he was with a large and hostile Jewish and Samaritan population in Palestine. Moreover, as the dispute over Chalcedon became increasingly engrained in the mindset of its participants, so too did it come to acquire an ever more symbolic and ritual character, such that, from the perspective of subsequent generations of Egyptian bishops, monks, and Patriarchs, for example, voicing opposition to Chalcedon effectively became an expression of loyalty to the memory of St Cyril.

What is most striking, however, in spite of these difficulties and complexities, is the extent to which Justinian's reign witnessed a concerted effort on the part of the imperial authorities to devise and propose a genuine theological solution to the Christological dispute. In 532–6, for example, Justinian opened negotiations with the leaders of the Syrian Church aimed at exploring common ground and thrashing out a formula that would address anti-Chalcedonian theological concerns while removing from office those miaphysite bishops who had most publicly gainsaid the imperial will. In 544/5 Justinian sought to convey to his miaphysite subjects the extent to which, though upholding Chalcedon, he nevertheless opposed the more pernicious extremes of duophysite thought by condemning the writings of three fifth-century supporters of Nestorius who had not been condemned at either the Council of Ephesus (which had deposed Nestorius) or at Chalcedon. Nestorianism and Chalcedonian Christianity, the Emperor wished to demonstrate, were fundamentally incompatible. This posthumous anathematising of the writings of the three duophysite thinkers Theodore of Mopsuestia, Theodoret of Cyrrhus, and Ibas (known as the 'Three Chapters') provoked a furious reaction in the West, where it was regarded as uncanonical and profoundly subversive of Chalcedonian authority.

Finally, in 553–4, Justinian himself convened an Ecumenical Council in Constantinople in an attempt to draw a line under the Chalcedonian dispute. In intellectual and theological terms, the solution that Justinian's court theologians put before the Fifth Ecumenical Council was a *tour de force* that sought to argue—and at a conceptual level did so highly successfully—that the Christological definition proposed at Chalcedon was fully reconcilable with the known writings of Cyril of Alexandria, when properly understood. In particular, it was proposed, Cyril's core contention that there necessarily existed only 'one nature of God the Word Incarnate' was fully compatible with Chalcedonian teaching, once it was realised that what Cyril meant by nature (Greek *physis*), the Chalcedonian formula more accurately described using the Greek philosophical term *hypostasis*.

The delicacy of the theological balancing act required is evident from the definition of the faith proposed at the Council, which declared that 'When we speak of one composite Christ constituted of each nature, that is of divinity and humanity, we do not introduce confusion into the union.' This rigorously duophysite statement was then tempered by the conceptually highly Cyrilian, but terminologically Chalcedonian, follow-on, however, that 'And while we know our one Lord Jesus Christ, the Logos of God, who was incarnate and became man, in each nature, that is in divinity and humanity, *we do not introduce into his one hypostasis a division or separation of parts* . . . but rather . . . we affirm that the union has taken place in the *hypostasis*.'[151]

In purely theological terms, the Christological formula proposed at Constantinople in 553 ought to have worked: in its fine detail, it addressed the soteriological concerns of all but the most extreme representatives of duophysite and miaphysite opinion with a precision that bears striking witness to the extraordinary intellectual resources at the disposal of the Emperor and his court. The Council itself, moreover, was carefully stage-managed so as to muffle dissent and browbeat and bully recalcitrant Chalcedonian hardliners, such as the Roman Pope Vigilius, into signing up to it and its repeated condemnation of the 'Three Chapters', in spite of Western qualms. Miaphysite bishops were not even invited to attend. The hope was evidently that the theology proposed would commend itself to moderate Miaphysites, while also mollifying opinion in the West through its unambiguous reassertion of the orthodoxy of Chalcedon, in spite of the earlier prevarications of Zeno and Anastasius.

That leading members of the Church in Syria and Egypt nevertheless rejected even this Cyrilian glossing of Chalcedonian Christology, however, demonstrated the extent to which the dispute was no longer (if it had ever been) reducible to purely theological debates or amenable to a theological solution. It should come as little surprise, therefore, that alongside attempts to propose a detailed doctrinal settlement to the Chalcedonian dispute, growing emphasis was placed within the imperial Church on the 'inexpressible mysteries' of the Christian faith and the limited ability of human reason to apprehend the divine (what is known as 'apophatic' theology). The Council of 553 did at least have the effect, however, of giving sharper definition to imperial orthodoxy and preventing the Chalcedonian Church from splintering within itself.[152]

Given the difficulties faced, one might reasonably ask why Justinian tried quite as hard as he did. On a basic level, the answer is straightforward: even the most hostile of contemporary sources agree that the Emperor was, in his own mind at least, a devout and committed Christian with a genuine interest in theology. Accordingly, the Emperor took seriously his moral obligation to seek to ensure unity of belief within the Church. As the 'Confession of the True Faith' promulgated by him in 551 declared:

> Seeing that nothing pleases the merciful God more than that all Christians be of one mind concerning the pure orthodox faith and that there be no schisms in God's holy Church, we deem it necessary that the confession of the true faith which the Holy Church of God proclaims be made clear by this edict by removing every occasion for scandal, so that those who confess the true faith might guard it with firmness, and those who contend against it may learn the truth and hasten to unite themselves to the holy Church of God.[153]

---

[151] K. P. Wesche, *On the Person of Christ* (New York, 1991), pp. 165–6. For the most detailed recent account of 'Neo-Chalcedonian' Christology, see *Acts of the Council of Constantinople of 553*, tr. R. Price, 2 vols. (Liverpool, 2009).
[152] Price (2009), I, p. 41.   [153] Wesche (1991), p. 162.

It should thus come as little surprise that the reassertion of imperial control over the religious and moral life of his subjects had, from the first, been one of Justinian's chief concerns. Amongst the first acts of the Emperor upon his accession to the throne, for example, had been measures instituting the concerted persecution of educated pagans, heretics, and homosexuals. The Emperor's practical efforts to restore the unity of the Church and to improve the moral character of his subjects were further associated with a determined effort to reposition the figure of the Emperor within the conceptual framework of imperial Christianity, by emphasising the unique responsibility of the Emperor to regulate the lives not only of his lay but also his priestly subjects, and declaring that both the priestly and the imperial offices derived their authority from a common divine source. Moreover, as we shall see in Chapter Six, this repositioning of the imperial office at the very centre of the religious life of his Christian subjects was increasingly mirrored representationally and ceremonially, through the growing use of the Christian liturgy in imperial ceremonial and the ever greater intrusion of religious images into public imperial contexts.[154]

The highly religious tone of Justinian's reign was informed by more than the ongoing Christianisation of the Eastern Roman Empire, however. The Emperor's religious policies also fed into and were meant to sustain Justinian's broader social, political, and economic objectives, and, in particular, the need to strengthen the structures of imperial government in the provinces. For, at a provincial level, alongside the figure of the landowner and the governor stood the bishop, whose authority, if properly harnessed, could be turned to serve the Emperor's purposes. An ever closer association between the Emperor and the imperial Church through the Christianisation of the imperial office thus offered a means of binding the institutions and personnel of the Church ever more tightly to the person of the ruler, thereby enabling the authorities to make use of the Church to disseminate the imperial will and give vocal support to the objectives of imperial policy. The Church could thus be used as a counterweight to aristocratic influence in the provinces, and the figure of the bishop could be turned into the Emperor's eyes and ears, reporting back to Constantinople examples of official or other malpractice. It is instructive, for example, that Procopius accuses Justinian of having deliberately sought to build up ecclesiastical estates at the expense of lay landowners.[155] At the same time, trumped-up charges of paganism and homosexuality appear to have been levelled opportunistically at members of the governing classes whom the Emperor and his wife were keen to get rid of for quite different reasons.[156] It was, no doubt, to Justinian's great disappointment that the imperial Church ultimately proved itself to be too theologically fractious and politically fissile to

---

[154] A. Cameron, 'Images of Authority: Elites and Icons in Late Sixth-Century Byzantium', in M. Mullett and R. Scott, *Byzantium and the Classical Tradition* (Birmingham, 1981), pp. 205–34; M. McCormick, *Eternal Victory: Triumphal Rulership in Late Antiquity, Byzantium, and the Early Medieval West* (Cambridge, 1986).
[155] Procopius, *Secret History*, 13.5–7.
[156] ibid., 11.34–6.

serve his purposes. At the end of the day there were simply too many bishops and theological partisans who, in the words of the Emperor's definition of the faith, were willing to 'separate themselves from the Holy Church of God by disputing over names or syllables or phrases rather than preserving a pious understanding'. The piety of such men, Justinian thundered, 'exists in name only and not in deed, for such a one delights in schism. He will have to render an account of himself and of those whom he has deceived or will deceive to our great God and Saviour Jesus Christ at the Day of Judgement.'[157] To the theologian-Emperor this was no idle threat, but rather a promise of eternal damnation to those whose obstinacy had further frustrated the realisation of what Justinian believed to be his providential mission to restore the fortunes of God's Empire on earth.

---

[157] Wesche (1991), p. 198. For the complexity and diversity of Christological dispute in the fifth and sixth centuries, see S. Brock, 'The Nestorian Church: A Lamentable Misnomer', in J. F. Coakley and K. Parry Bull (eds.), *The Church of the East: Life and Thought* (Bulletin of the John Rylands Library, 78.3, 1996).

5

Byzantium, the Balkans, and the West
The Late Sixth Century

5.1 INTRODUCTION: DEATH OF AN EMPEROR

On 14 November 565 the Emperor Justinian died, drawing to a close a reign that had lasted some forty-eight years. Although much contemporary reaction to Justinian's policies had been hostile, in the eyes of posterity his period of rule would be looked back to as something of a golden age. In the late eighth century, for example, Paul the Deacon, a priest, monk, and scholar from Italy, would declare of the Emperor that he had governed the Roman Empire:

> with good fortune. For he was prosperous in waging wars and admirable in civil matters. For by Belisarius, the patrician, he vigorously subdued the Persians and by this same Belisarius he reduced to utter destruction the nation of the Vandals, captured their king Gelimer, and restored all Africa to the Roman Empire after ninety-six years. Again, by the power of Belisarius he overcame the nation of the Goths in Italy and took captive Witigis their king. He subdued also the Moors who afterwards infested Africa.... In like manner too, he subjugated other nations by right of war. For this reason, on account of his victories over them all, he deserved to have his surnames and be called *Alamanicus*, *Gothicus*, *Francicus*, *Germanicus*, *Anticus*, *Alanicus*, *Vandalicus*, and *Africanus*.[1]

Paul went on to lionise Justinian for his legal reforms, and noted that 'the same Emperor also built within the city of Constantinople to Christ our Lord, who is the wisdom of God the Father, a church which is called by the Greek name *Hagia Sophia*, that is "Divine Wisdom." The workmanship of this so far excels that of all other buildings that in all the regions of the earth its like cannot be found. This Emperor in fact was Catholic in his faith, upright in his deeds, just in his judgements, and therefore, to him all things came together for good.'[2]

In spite of the rhetoric of imperial triumph, however, as the last chapter demonstrated, Justinian had in fact been a far from uniformly successful Emperor, and many of his achievements rested on what would prove to be highly fragile foundations, which the very existence of Paul the Deacon's historical account reveals. For Paul, born in Friuli in the far north of Italy, ended his days in the monastery of Monte Cassino to the far south, not as the subject of a Roman Emperor residing in

---

[1] Paul the Deacon, *History of the Langobards*, I, 25, tr. W. D. Foulke (London, 1907), pp. 44–5.
[2] ibid., p. 47.

Constantinople but rather of a Frankish king residing in Aachen. The history that he composed, moreover, detailed the genealogy and glorified the achievements of what Paul regarded as his own people, the Langobards or 'Longbeards', who, within just three years of Justinian's death, had come to settle first in northern and then in south-central Italy, thereby fracturing, dismembering, and localising what remained of East Roman control in the recently reconquered Italian peninsula. This outcome was the result of a long chain of events that reached beyond the world of northern Italy, across the Balkans, the Pannonian plain (or 'Danubian basin'), and the Ukrainian steppe, to the distant marchlands of Manchuria in the Far East.

5.2 THE WEST EURASIAN STEPPE IN THE MID-SIXTH CENTURY

As already seen, the military security of both the Eastern Roman and Sasanian Empires was critically sensitive to military and political developments on the grasslands of the west Eurasian steppe. Political and military conditions on the steppe were themselves highly sensitive to climate change. Any abnormal variation in temperature risked having a dramatic impact on the availability and quality of grassland on which the nomad powers and tribal confederations of the region depended for their military might; for these were, as we have seen, cavalry empires, their warriors famed for their swiftness on horseback and dexterity with bow, reliant on a ready supply of well-fed mounts.[3] A late sixth-century Byzantine military handbook (the so-called *Strategikon of Maurice*) noted of such 'Scythians... and others whose way of life resembles that of the Hunnic peoples', that 'they are hurt by a shortage of fodder which can result from the huge numbers of horses they bring with them. Also, in the event of battle, when opposed by an infantry force in close formation, they stay on their horses and do not dismount, for they do not last long fighting on foot.'[4] The 530s, as seen in the previous chapter, was a period of major climactic instability, and was recorded as such by chroniclers, historians, and witnesses from as far afield as Ireland, Gaul, China, and Japan.[5] This in turn opened the way to a major reconfiguration of power relations on the steppe, resulting in a renewed period of political and military insecurity for both Persia and, ultimately, Byzantium, associated with the demise of the Hephthalites and the arrival on Persia's frontiers of the Turk Khaganate.

Around the year 557–8 a group of fugitives from Turk expansion, known as the Avars, made their presence known to Roman commanders in the northern Caucasus. These commanders in turn immediately reported this intelligence to Constantinople. As a late sixth-century Byzantine historian, Menander the Guardsman, records:

---

[3] Keys (1999), pp. 27–8.
[4] *The Strategikon of the Emperor Maurice*, XI, 2, tr. G. T. Dennis (Pennsylvania, 1984; revised).
[5] See Keys (1999).

Concerning the Avars: after many wanderings they came to the Alans and begged Sorosius, the leader of the Alans, that he bring them to the attention of the Romans. Sarosius informed Germanus' son Justin, who at that time was general of the forces in Lazica, about the Avars. Justin told Justinian, and the Emperor ordered the general to send the embassy of the tribe to Byzantium. One Kandikh by name was chosen to be the first envoy from the Avars, and when he came to the palace he told the Emperor of the arrival of the greatest and most powerful of the tribes. The Avars were invincible and could easily crush and destroy all who stood in their path. The Emperor should make an alliance with them and enjoy their efficient protection. But they would only be well disposed to the Roman state in exchange for the most valuable gifts, yearly payments and very fertile lands to inhabit. Thus spoke Kandikh to the Emperor.[6]

Menander goes on to relate that Justinian discussed the matter with the Senate before deciding to commit to an Avar alliance. The Eastern Roman Empire at the time faced a number of burgeoning threats from the regions to the north of the Danube and the west of the Ukrainian steppe. Justinian's hope was clearly that the Avars would either help neutralise these challenges to imperial power or neutralise themselves in the process. As Menander put it:

The Emperor put the matter up for discussion, and when the holy senate had praised his plan and its shrewdness, he immediately sent the gifts, cords worked with gold, couches, silken garments and a great many other objects which would mollify the arrogant spirits of the Avars. In addition, he sent an ambassador Valentinus, one of the imperial bodyguard, and he urged the tribe to make an alliance with the Romans and take up arms against their enemies. This, in my view, was a very wise move, since whether the Avars prevailed or were defeated, both eventualities would be to the Romans' advantage.[7]

The Avars were thus drawn into the tribal politics of the trans-Danubian world to the empire's north and, ultimately, the internal affairs of the empire's Balkan and north Italian territories.

5.3 THE BALKAN CONTEXT TO JUSTINIAN'S AVAR POLICY

Roman territory in the Balkans in the sixth century can be divided into two broad zones. Firstly, beyond the Land Walls of Constantinople existed the plains of Thrace, and, to their west, a broad sweep of lowland territory to the south of the banks of the River Danube that eventually connected to northern Italy via Illyricum. This region was bound together by the main Roman military highway that led from Constantinople, via Thessalonica, through Illyricum to the west, and had been home to extensive aristocratic estates until the Gothic uprising of the late fourth century. The economy of the plains of Thrace and the northern Balkan zone was never fully to recover from the damage inflicted by the Goths and the chronic insecurity subsequently associated with the Hunnic threat. The plains of Thrace

[6] Menander, 5.1, p. 49.   [7] ibid., 5.1–5.2, pp. 50–51.

remained highly vulnerable to attack from the steppe, to which they were accessible by means of easily traversable land routes that led directly from the grasslands of the western Ukraine; at the same time, to the west, lines of communication across the military highway had been blocked by first the Ostrogothic and then (after 536) Gepid occupation of the city of Sirmium, which controlled access to Italy.[8] By the year 500, therefore, much of this zone had been reduced to a sparsely populated marchland, its landscape dotted by the occasional fortified town or city typically consisting of little more than a collection of military installations, storehouses, a church—and the ramshackle dwellings of the inhabitants who would often appear to have supported themselves by means of agriculture conducted behind the defensive embrace of their settlement's walls.[9] Of the north Balkan cities, only Constantinople and Thessalonica maintained their ancient contours. In the immediate environs of Constantinople, the inhabitants now primarily engaged in horse-rearing and stock-raising rather than agriculture, enabling them to flee with their property when the inevitable enemy attack came.

To the south of this northern lowland zone, and separated from it by the mountains and ravines of the Balkans proper, stood the coastal plains and seaboard agricultural pockets of the Illyrian coastline and mainland Greece. In this region urban life remained more firmly entrenched than in the north, but Greece in particular had never been wealthy: the cultivated zone on which its inhabitants depended was painfully meagre. Accordingly, the cities of Greece were critically dependent on broader networks of Aegean and Mediterranean trade and carefully directed imperial subvention and support. Lines of north-south communication across the Balkan peninsula essentially depended upon treacherous mountain passes, but what the cities of the south, such as Corinth and Athens, gained thereby by way of security was arguably counterbalanced by the disadvantages of economic isolation.

The threats that the empire's Balkan territories faced from the region to the north of the Danube in the mid-sixth century were relatively minor compared to the challenges with which the Roman authorities had been obliged to contend in the fourth and fifth centuries. Indeed, to a certain extent, the reign of Justinian can rightly be regarded as marking a high-point of Byzantine control in the region. The Gothic uprising of 378, followed by the Hunnic invasions, had forced the Byzantine authorities effectively to disengage from much of the northern Balkan zone, with the government holed up behind Constantinople's formidable defences. As we have seen, following the break-up of Hunnic power in the 450s, the Romans had been faced with a renewed period of insecurity as former subject peoples of the Huns, such as the formidable Ostrogothic confederacy, entered into imperial territory. It was Theoderic's decision to march on Italy in 488–9 that finally presented the imperial government with an opportunity to re-establish Roman control in the north and restore the Danubian *limes*. Moves to do just this were

---

[8] F. E. Wozniak, 'East Rome, Ravenna, and Western Illyricum, 454–536 AD', *Historia* 30.3 (1981), pp. 351–82.
[9] Poulter (2004).

effected under the Emperor Anastasius. The Emperor's legislation, however, reveals the difficulties faced in raising taxes even from the territory of Thrace, where imperial control ought to have been at its tightest.[10] Nevertheless, a programme of investment in the defensive infrastructure of the Balkans was initiated under Anastasius and continued under his successor Justin. It was in Justinian's reign, however, that the programme of investment and administrative and military reorganisation was most vigorously pursued.

It is sometimes suggested that Justinian's concern for the Balkans arose from the fact that the Emperor originated from the region. Certainly, in about 535 the village in which Justinian had been born in western Illyricum was renamed *Iustiniana Prima* and elevated to civic status. It should be noted, however, that this elevation did not take place, as one might have expected, upon Justinian's immediate accession to the imperial throne. Rather, the Balkans had to wait their turn. Until 532 the main focus of imperial investment remained what it had been under Justin and Anastasius—the defensive infrastructure of the eastern provinces. Between 532, the date of the Nika insurrection, and 534, resources were diverted to restore the monumental heart of Constantinople, laid waste by the uprising. From 534 onwards, however, attention shifted to the Balkans. This was probably associated with the initiation of the reconquest of Italy and a corresponding need to tighten control over the military highway that led from Constantinople to the West. In spite of the fact that Sirmium remained in Gepid hands, it was along this military highway that in 552 Narses was to lead the army that would go on to crush the final remnants of Ostrogothic resistance, mobilising the Gepids' neighbours, the Langobards, against them, thereby enabling imperial forces to drive through the territory of the Gepid king of Sirmium substantially unchecked.[11] From 534 until the advent of the bubonic plague in 542 the Balkans emerged as the main focus of imperial investment; in order to sustain the military and governmental infrastructure of the region, in 536 Justinian created the administrative unit of the so-called *Quaestura Exercitus*, whereby the tax revenues of the wealthier islands of the Aegean and Cyprus were assigned to support the north-eastern Balkan provinces of *Moesia Inferior* and *Scythia Inferior*.[12]

The imperial programme of investment essentially sought to create and sustain three broad lines of defence across the peninsula. First, from Anastasius onwards, there was clearly some attempt made to maintain a military presence along the southern bank of the Danube as well as a naval presence on the river itself. The Eastern Roman authorities also maintained outposts to the north of the Danube, presumably in order to engage in policing activity of various sorts. These were not regarded as a good posting: in 539 the Emperor Justinian warned soldiers stationed in Egypt that if they failed to show due diligence in assisting with the collection of tax revenues, they would be sent to serve 'not only along the River Ister [i.e. the Danube] but at those places beyond the River Ister'.[13] Beyond the Danube, the

---

[10] F. Curta, *Southeastern Europe in the Middle Ages 500–1200* (Cambridge, 2006), p. 44.
[11] Procopius, *Wars*, IV, 25.
[12] *J. Nov.*, 41.   [13] *J. Edict.*, XIII.

empire engaged in a carefully orchestrated campaign of client management, attempting to maintain a pro-Roman balance of powerlessness amongst the tribes resident there.

The second and third zones of defence were built up largely during the reign of Justinian, and are described in detail in the treatise *On Buildings* written by Procopius. He lists or details over five hundred buildings and fortifications in the Balkan peninsula either constructed by Justinian or restored or completed under him.[14] In the north Balkan zone, the programme concentrated on ensuring that cities were adequately fortified, and that those sections of the road network traversing the Balkans from east to west which were deemed to be most at risk from attack were provided with lateral lines of defence. Additional defences were also put in place to attempt to slow down any enemy advance along the land approaches to Constantinople, and smaller versions of the Constantinopolitan Land Walls were erected to defend vulnerable but defendable outcrops of land, such as the Gallipoli peninsula.

To the south, the programme's focus shifted somewhat. Here, emphasis was placed on fortifying the mountain passes that controlled access from north to south. In addition to this, however, efforts were made to ensure that cities as far south as the Peloponnese were walled, and, crucially, that small fortified redoubts and citadels were provided for the rural population to retreat to in times of danger. The concerted nature of this programme is itself impressive, but what is perhaps still more striking is the strategic logic that underpinned it. For Justinian's building work in the Balkans was predicated upon the assumption both that the restored Danubian *limes* could not be rendered impermeable and, moreover, that once the enemy was within imperial territory, they would be able to raid as far south as the southern Peloponnese. Throughout the Balkan peninsula, therefore, the best the imperial authorities could aim for was a state of measured insecurity. They sought to deter raiders from beyond the Danube by minimising the spoils available to them once they were within Roman territory, whilst perhaps deliberately maintaining in the northern Balkans a sparsely populated *cordon sanitaire*, so as not to attract raiders from the north by tantalising them with conspicuous displays of Roman wealth.

This strategy makes good sense when seen in the light of the nature of the threat posed to the Byzantine position in the Balkans in the early to mid-sixth century, as revealed by contemporary sources. To the north-west, the Gepid kings of Sirmium were relatively placid neighbours with whom the empire could generally deal diplomatically and with whom the imperial authorities periodically cooperated; but without Sirmium in imperial hands the Roman authorities could never feel secure. Accordingly, as seen earlier, from the 540s the imperial authorities sought to mobilise against the Gepids their western neighbours, the Langobards, a Germanic grouping that had migrated to the Middle Danube region in the early 500s, and on whom the imperial authorities had bestowed federate status.[15] To the north-east, as

---

[14] Procopius, *Buildings*, IV.   [15] Curta (2006), p. 55.

noted above, there was little that could be done to prevent various nomadic tribes of Hunnic origin, such as the Kutrigurs and Bulgars, from descending on the plains of Thrace from the grasslands of the western Ukraine. In 539 a group of such raiders even reached the suburbs of Constantinople.[16]

To the north of the Danube, however, matters were in a greater state of flux. The plains of Pannonia (or the 'Danubian basin') had in many ways been the great forcing ground of the barbarian world in the period from the third century to the fifth. A number of barbarian peoples—Sarmatians, Goths, Ostrogoths, and Huns—had established hegemony in the region before in turn either being subjugated by their neighbours or, increasingly, migrating into Roman or former Roman territory. The Ostrogothic migration had represented the last great emptying out of this region. Typically, Roman observers of the Trans-Danubian world tended to comment on the most militarily and politically sophisticated groupings that they could identify there—those that necessarily posed the most concerted threat to imperial security. As each migration took place, however, different strata of trans-Danubian society would begin to fill the gap left by those who had departed, and thus become more conspicuous in Roman accounts. By the early sixth century, Roman commentators were increasingly noting the presence of tribes and kindreds of barbarian peoples described variously as 'Sclavenes' or 'Antae', who shared many features of social and military organisation and who may well have possessed a common language.

Where the Sclavenes and Antae (or 'Slavs') came from is unclear, but it is entirely conceivable that they had not travelled far, but had increasingly come to cluster along the Danubian *limes* as their more aggressive and organised neighbours had migrated first into and then beyond imperial territory.[17] What Byzantine commentators on the Slavs frequently mention is their primitive kin-based social structure, their lack of political leadership, and their tendency to inhabit marginal lands, such as highland, woodland, and swamp. As the late sixth-century *Strategikon* records:

> The nations of the Slavs and Antes live in the same way and have the same customs. They are both independent, absolutely refusing to be enslaved or governed. They are populous and hardy, bearing readily heat, cold, rain, nakedness, and scarcity of provisions.... They live among nearly impenetrable forests, rivers, lakes, and marshes, and have made the exits from their settlements branch out in many directions because of the dangers they might face. They bury their most valuable possessions in secret places, keeping nothing unnecessary in sight. They live like bandits and love to carry out attacks against their enemies in densely wooded, narrow, and steep places. They make effective use of ambushes, sudden attacks, and raids.... Their experience in crossing rivers surpasses that of all other men, and they are extremely good at spending a lot of time in the water. Often enough when they are in their own country and are caught by surprise in a tight spot, they dive to the bottom of a body of water. There they take long hollow reeds they have prepared for such a situation and hold them to

---

[16] Procopius, *Secret History*, 18.20–21.
[17] The area to the north of the Carpathian Mountains is their most likely origin: see Heather (2009), pp. 386–452.

their mouths, the reeds extending to the surface of the water. Lying on their backs on the bottom they breathe through them and hold out for many hours.[18]

The preferred habitat ascribed to the Slavs, and the techniques of survival attributed to them, would suggest a deliberate strategy on their part of avoiding more powerful, sophisticated, or aggressive neighbours, in whose absence, from the end of the fifth century onwards, they were increasingly able to come out into the open and begin to raid imperial territory to the south.

The problem from the Roman perspective, however, was that the Slavs and Antae posed a very different type of threat to the Roman position in the Balkans from that of the Goths or Huns. On one level, due to their lack of political organisation, the Sclavenes and Antae were very unlikely to engage in concerted campaigns of conquest. On the other hand, their very lack of political organisation also meant that it was difficult for the Roman authorities to incorporate the Slavs into the empire's existing tribal policy of 'divide and rule'; there was effectively no political leadership or figure of authority with whom to negotiate or deal. The primitive social structure of the Slavs thus effectively placed them beyond—or more accurately, beneath—the reach of imperial diplomacy. More problematically still, however, the smallness of the groups in which the Slavs typically operated, their skill in crossing river networks, and their readiness to pass through and inhabit inhospitable terrain, to some extent placed them beyond the reach of the Byzantine military. This effectively rendered it impossible for the Byzantine authorities either to prevent Slav raiders from across the Danube from reaching imperial territory or to prevent such raiders from spreading further south once they were within it. It was this insidious threat that Justinian's programme of Balkan defences was designed to contain.

There are indications that from the 530s onwards, contact between the Roman authorities and the Slavs began to catalyse a process of social evolution amongst them comparable to that which had taken place in the Germanic world in the second and third centuries, whereby more clearly articulated and tightly led military and tribal groupings began to emerge. On one level, this may have been due to the socially destabilising effects of flows of wealth northward from the Roman world that resulted from raiding; on another, it may have been the product of Roman efforts to build up potential clients amongst the Slavs. The emergence of larger raiding parties under more powerful leaders may also have been a direct response to the stiffening of Roman resistance as a consequence of Justinianic policy, with the Sclavenes and Antae now having to combine to obtain what they wanted. Either way, the effects of these social and organisational changes were soon to become apparent to the Eastern Roman authorities. Procopius records, for example, that in 545 a large army of Sclavenes crossed the River Danube, ransacked Roman territory, and enslaved many Roman subjects. For the late 540s the ecclesiastical historian John of Ephesus recorded an assault on the suburbs of Constantinople itself, which was led by 'the leaders of the Antae'—a designation that would have

---

[18] *Strategikon*, XI, 4, tr. Dennis pp. 120–21.

made little sense thirty years earlier. Raids from the edge of the steppe also continued apace, with the Kutrigurs once more raiding up to the Land Walls of Constantinople in 558. It was this ongoing pressure on Byzantine possessions in the Balkans on the part of 'Hunnic' groups such as the Kutrigurs and Bulgars, combined with evidence for the emergence of more clearly articulated military leadership on the part of the Sclavenes and Antae, that probably informed Justinian's decision in 558 to invite the Avars westwards. After receiving Justinian's envoy, Menander records, 'the Avars first crushed the Unigurs, then the Zali, a Hunnic tribe, and they also destroyed the Sabirs', and, 'when the leaders of the Antae had failed miserably and had been thwarted in their hopes, the Avars ravaged and plundered their land'.[19]

5.4 THE CONSOLIDATION OF AVAR POWER AND ITS CONSEQUENCES

By the year 562 at the latest, the Avars had overcome most of the Kurtigurs and the other nomadic tribes on the edge of the west Ukrainian steppe and had reached the Danube.[20] The reports of negotiations between the Avar *khagan* Baian and the Emperor Justinian around this time indicate that the Avars were keen to settle to the north-east of the river, as they were 'unwilling to live outside Scythia'.[21] In other words, they were eager to maintain access to the grasslands and pasture of the Ukrainian steppe on which their herds—and thus their military power—depended. From an imperial perspective, however, Avar settlement to the north-east of the Balkans threatened to simply reintensify insecurity on the plains of Thrace. Rather, Justinian was keen to direct the Avars to the north-west of the Balkans, where they would be able to act as a counterweight to Gepid power, and from where Constantinople would be out of reach. Baian was eventually persuaded to do as the Emperor asked, but only after Justinian had effectively held hostage the Avar embassy to the imperial court.[22]

In 565, upon report of Justinian's death, an Avar embassy was once more directed to Constantinople to renew Baian's pact with the imperial authorities. In Byzantium, however, the political mood had turned decisively against Justinian's policy of paying subsidies to the empire's barbarian neighbours in order to induce them to wage war against one another or otherwise to buy peace. Such diplomatic subsidies had long been unpopular in senatorial circles and had occasioned acerbic comment in the writings of contemporary historians of a conservative temperament such as Procopius.[23] The new Emperor, Justinian's nephew Justin II, owed his accession to the throne primarily to senatorial support, and his policies carefully

---

[19] Menander the Guardsman, fragment 5.2–5.3: Blockley (1985), pp. 50–51.
[20] See Blockley (1985), p. 253.
[21] Menander the Guardsman, Fragment 5.4: Blockley (1985), p. 53.
[22] ibid., fragment 5.4: Blockley (1985), p. 53.
[23] Procopius, *Secret History*, 19.1–16.

reflected senatorial attitudes. In addition, in the wake of recurrent outbreaks of bubonic plague, the Emperor was also critically short of funds.[24] Accordingly, the Avar envoys received short shrift. As the ecclesiastical historian John of Ephesus records:

> after a few days they [the Avars] had an audience with Justin, and said to him, 'Give us what he used to give us who is dead; and send us away to our king'. But Justin, having been one of those who were vexed and grumbled at the amount which these barbarians received, and carried out of the empire, answered them, 'Never again shall you be loaded at the expense of this empire, and go your way without doing us any service: for from me you shall receive nothing.' And when the Avars began to threaten, he grew angry, and said, 'Do you dead dogs dare to threaten the Roman realm? Learn that I will shave off those locks of yours, and then cut off your heads.'[25]

This display of imperial bravado clearly left its mark—and the Avars decided to redirect their search for tribute westwards. As Menander records of the Avar delegation: 'they fell into great despondency and speculated upon what would be the outcome of the present situation and how their affairs would turn out. For they did not wish to remain in Byzantium to no purpose, nor did they wish to return empty-handed. But it seemed to them the better of two evils to return to their tribe, and rejoining their fellows, they all went off to the land of the Franks thunderstruck by the emperor's reply.'[26] The following year, the Avars inflicted a major defeat on the East Frankish king Sigibert, who 'immediately sent to the Avars wheatflour, vegetables, sheep, and cattle'.[27]

This increasingly westward focus of Avar ambition coincided with a period of mounting tension between the Langobards and the Gepids. In 566 warfare erupted between the Langobard king Alboin and the Gepid king of Sirmium, Cunimund, whose daughter, Rosamund, Alboin had allegedly abducted. In return for Roman support, Cunimund offered to return Sirmium to imperial control. Accordingly, the Emperor Justin ordered that the army intervene against the empire's erstwhile allies.[28] With Roman support, Cunimund was able to avenge his daughter's honour, but then failed to fulfil his side of the bargain. This left the Gepids dangerously isolated diplomatically. Having secured an imperial promise of neutrality, Alboin negotiated an alliance with the Avars in 567, declaring that 'if they joined the Langobards, they would be invincible, and when they annihilated the Gepids, they would together be masters of their wealth and land'.[29] Cunimund was obliged to renew his offer of Sirmium to the Emperor Justin. This time it was the Emperor's turn to engage in a double-cross: for the first time in almost eighty years, an imperial army re-garrisoned the city, but then failed to provide the Gepid king

---

[24] Note the Emperor's complaints in *J. Nov.*, 148.
[25] John of Ephesus, *Ecclesiastical History*, VI, 24: Smith (1860), p. 429.
[26] Menander the Guardsman, fragment 8: Blockley (1985), p. 97.
[27] ibid., fragment 11: Blockley p. 129. See also Gregory of Tours, *Histories*, 4.29. The Franks and Avars had clashed before as early as 562, on which occasion the Frankish king Sigibert had been more successful: Gregory of Tours, *Histories*, 4.23; Paul the Deacon, *History of the Lombards*, 4.10.
[28] Theophylact Simocatta, *History*, VI, 10, 7–13.
[29] Menander the Guardsman, fragment 12: Blockley (1985), p. 129.

with any support. Caught in a pincer movement between the Langobards on one side and the Avars on the other, Cunimund's fate was sealed. The eighth-century Langobard historian Paul the Deacon preserves a vivid present-tense account of the ensuing battle, an account that shows every sign of having originated in a vernacular oral epic tradition:

> A sad messenger coming to Cunimund, announced to him that the Avars had entered his territories. Although cast down in spirit, and put into sore straits on both sides, still he urged his people to fight first with the Langobards, and that, if they should be able to overcome these, they should then drive the army of the Huns from their country. Therefore battle is joined and they fight with all their might. The Langobards become the victors, raging against the Gepids in such wrath that they reduce them to utter destruction, and out of an abundant multitude scarcely the messenger survives. In this battle Alboin killed Cunimund, and made out of his head, which he carried off, a drinking goblet.... And he led away as a captive, Cunimund's daughter Rosamund... together with a great multitude of both sexes and every age. Then the Langobards secured such great booty that they now attained the most ample riches, but the race of the Gepids were so diminished that from that time on they had no king.[30]

The defeat of the Gepid king in 567 was thus to a great extent a victory of Byzantine diplomacy: the Avars had seemingly been weaned off imperial subsidy; Sirmium had been reoccupied; and for all that Paul the Deacon regarded the Langobards to have been enriched with Gepid plunder, it was to Constantinople that Cunimund's nephew, Reptila, fled with the royal treasury.[31] The establishment of Avar power in the former Gepid realm, however, soon began to cause the imperial authorities growing difficulties, with the Avar *khagan* demanding that the Romans surrender Sirmium to him, and northern Italy, which was already menaced by the Franks, now lying vulnerable to Avar assault. Faced with a shortage of military manpower (exacerbated by recent bouts of plague), the Byzantine commander in Italy, the Persarmenian eunuch Narses, issued an invitation to detachments of Langobards to settle on the military landholdings to the north of the River Po that had formerly supported the armies of Odoacer and Theoderic.[32] Faced with what was effectively a power vacuum in the region, however, what began as an orderly settlement of Langobardic warriors and their families increasingly took on the aspect of a full-blown migratory invasion, and, on a date normally identified as 2 April 568, Alboin led his followers out of Pannonia and Noricum into northern Italy, where he began to carve out an autonomous Langobardic *regnum*. Other bands of Langobards headed further south, eventually establishing themselves in the mountainous inland regions of Spoleto and Beneventum.[33]

---

[30] Paul the Deacon, *History of the Lombards*, Bk. I, ch. xxvii.
[31] John of Biclaro, *Chronicle*, 23.
[32] A seemingly garbled account of Narses' invitation is to be found in Book II of Paul the Deacon's *History of the Lombards*, for discussion of which see N. Everett, *Literacy in Lombard Italy c.568–774* (Cambridge, 2003). See also W. Pohl, 'The Empire and the Lombards: Treaties and Negotiations in the Sixth Century', in W. Pohl (ed.), *Kingdoms of the Empire: The Integration of Barbarians in Late Antiquity* (Leiden, 1997), pp. 75–134. For plague, see Paul the Deacon, *History*, II, 4.
[33] Paul the Deacon, *History*, II, 6–27.

In 571 the Langobardic king Alboin was assassinated as part of a coup orchestrated by his wife, Cunimund's daughter Rosamund—his offence supposedly having been to drink in front of her from the cup made of her father's skull.[34] Rosamund and her accomplices then fled to the court of the Emperor's representative, the Exarch, in Ravenna, but the imperial authorities still lacked sufficient military manpower on the ground to be able to take advantage of this situation. As we shall see in Chapter Seven, warfare with Persia had revived, and events on the eastern front necessarily took priority. So secure did the leading warriors, or *duces*, of the Langobards feel themselves to be, along with their kin-based retinues (*farae*), that they did not even bother electing a new king to replace their fallen lord. Instead, a series of independent Langobard 'duchies' emerged, centred upon the northern Italian cities such as Cividale, Trento, Brescia, and Turin, as well as in the Langobards' mountainous redoubts to the south.

Appeals from Rome and Ravenna to Constantinople for direct military aid produced only limited results. Rather, Justin II's successor to the throne, the former general Tiberius, reverted to the tried and tested methods of gift-giving diplomacy, with the aim of securing a gradual reassertion of Constantinopolitan control. In 574–5 he negotiated a new treaty with the Avars, agreeing to pay the *khagan* 80,000 *solidi* per year by way of subsidy.[35] In 577–8 an imperial agent was sent back to Italy with 3,000 pounds of gold with which to buy up allies from amongst the ranks of the Langobard elite.[36] As Menander records: 'the Emperor did send a small army from the men whom he had available and he made great efforts to win over some of the leaders of the Langobards by approaching them with gifts and promising them very great rewards. Very many of the chiefs did accept the Emperor's generosity and came over to the Romans.'[37]

The Emperor Tiberius' diplomatic re-engagement with the Avars enabled the imperial authorities to harness the burgeoning prestige of the *khagan* to ever greater effect against the ongoing threat to Eastern Roman security posed by the Slavs in both the northern and southern Balkan zones. In the late 570s the imperial fleet even ferried detachments of the Avar horde across the Danube to pursue Slav raiders and to facilitate the harrying of Slav settlements. In 578 the Emperor, we are told, persuaded the *khagan* 'to make war on the Slavs, so that all of those that were laying waste Roman territory would be drawn back by the troubles at home, choosing rather to defend their own lands. Thus they would cease to plunder Roman territory, preferring to fight for their own.'[38] Menander goes on to relate how the governor of the *Quaestura Exercitus* and the cities of Illyricum, the general John:

> came to the land of Pannonia, and transported Baian himself and the Avar forces to Roman territory, ferrying the multitude of barbarians in the so-called 'large transports'.

---

[34] ibid., II, 28.
[35] Menander the Guardsman, fragment 25.1: Blockley (1985), pp. 217–19.
[36] ibid., fragment 22: Blockley (1985), p. 197.
[37] ibid., fragment 24: Blockley (1985), p. 217.
[38] ibid., fragment 21: Blockley (1985), p. 193.

It is said that about sixty thousand armoured horsemen were brought across into Roman territory. From there Baian crossed Illyricum, reached Scythia, and prepared to re-cross the Danube in the so-called 'double-sterned' ships. When he gained the far bank, he immediately fired the villages of the Slavs and laid waste their fields, driving and carrying off everything, since none of the barbarians there dared to face him, but took refuge in the thick undergrowth of the woods.[39]

There are clear indications, however, that by the early years of the 580s, Roman policy with respect to the Slavs was becoming increasingly counterproductive. For, faced with such scorched-earth tactics on the part of the Avars—and indeed, in the 590s, the Romans, who emulated Avar techniques when striking to the north of the Danube—Slav tribes began to head south into Roman territory. Their intentions now were not only to raid but increasingly to settle, taking advantage of the fact that the Avars, with their dependence on cavalry, could not pass through or operate in mountainous terrain.[40] The Roman-backed consolidation of Avar power to the north of the Danube had thus led to an ominous escalation and evolution in the nature of the Slav threat. From the 580s, archaeological evidence for the proliferation of their settlements as far south as the Peloponnese begins to mount, whilst the evidence of coin finds suggests a withering of urban life in the southern Balkans amid ever greater physical insecurity. In 582 an army of Slavs even besieged the city of Thessalonica, in the hinterland of which they had apparently settled. As the *Ecclesiastical History* of John of Ephesus, written c.584, records of the year 580–81:

> that same year, being the third after the death of the Emperor Justin, was famous also for the invasion of an accursed people called Slavonians, who overran the whole of Greece and the country of the Thessalonians, and all Thrace, and captured the cities, and took numerous forts, and devastated and burned, and reduced the people to slavery, and made themselves masters of the whole country, and settled in it by main force, and dwelled in it as though it had been their own without fear. And four years have now elapsed, and still, because the Emperor is engaged in the war with the Persians, and has sent all his forces to the East, they live at their ease in the land, and dwell in it, and spread themselves far and wide, as far as God permits them, and ravage and burn and take captive. . . . And even to this day . . . they still encamp and dwell there, and live in peace in the Roman territories, free from anxiety and fear, and lead captive and slay and burn; and they have grown rich in gold and silver, and herds of horses, and arms, and have learned to fight better than the Romans, though at first they were but rude savages, who did not venture to show themselves outside the woods and the coverts of the trees.[41]

If the 580s saw the territories of the south-central Balkans slipping from imperial control, so too did the empire's grip on the plains to the north become increasingly precarious as Avar demands of the Roman state became ever more extortionate. The more Avar hegemony to the north of the Danube intensified, the more the traditional Roman policy of 'divide and rule' among the tribes of the region became less and less practicable. Avar ascendancy also led to a further deterioration of the

---

[39] ibid., fragment 21: Blockley (1985), pp. 193–5.
[40] See M. Whitby, *The Emperor Maurice and his Historian* (Oxford, 1988).
[41] John of Ephesus, *Ecclesiastical History*, VI, 25: Smith (1860), pp. 432–3.

empire's predicament with respect to military manpower, as warriors and tribesmen who might otherwise have been induced to serve the Emperor increasingly found themselves subject to the authority of the *khagan*. The Avars organised their Slav subjects into larger composite hosts which they equipped with siege equipment, directing them against Roman-held cities. It was probably the Avars who were behind the Slav siege of Thessalonica in 582. That same year the population of Sirmium was evacuated in the face of Baian's threats, and the Avars occupied the city.[42] For Baian, control of Sirmium enabled him to grasp the Roman Balkans by the jugular, intensifying or relaxing pressure on the empire as he saw fit, thereby maximising the flow of tribute on which his authority over his own followers depended. Slav pressure to the south and Avar pressure to the north thus mounted to the empire's great detriment.

In Italy, likewise, the 580s witnessed a backfiring of the Eastern Roman Empire's diplomatic attempts to roll back the Langobard threat. The initial success of the Emperor Tiberius' efforts to win over individual *duces* to the imperial cause, combined with the empire's contemporaneous mobilisation of the Franks, sparked off a political crisis within the northern duchies. In response to the dangers that they now faced, the Langobard warrior elite once more drew together and elected a king—Authari, son of Cleph. As we shall see in Chapter Nine, Authari adopted a highly Romanising style and was supported along with his retinue from a share of the wealth of the dukes who had elected him.[43] His election paved the way for a consolidation of Langobard power and a stiffening of resistance to both imperial and Frankish interventions. Paul the Deacon records that in the face of 'the entrenchment of the Langobards in their towns', the Frankish king Childebert sued for peace, while certain of those *duces* who had gone over to the imperial party were forcibly subdued along with their territories.[44] In 585–6 the Exarch of Ravenna was obliged to sign a truce. The reassertion of imperial control that the Emperor Tiberius had bankrolled in northern Italy had proved to be pitifully short-lived.

5.5 FRANCIA AND HISPANIA

If military and political fragmentation was characteristic of the history of the imperial territories in Italy and the Balkans in the late sixth century, much the same was also true of the Romano-Germanic successor kingdoms in Gaul, on face value at least. As we saw in Chapter Three, the division of the Frankish *regnum* upon the death of Clovis in 511 had witnessed escalating and expansionist warfare between the late king's sons, on the one hand, and the rulers of those peoples who bordered Merovingian territory (such as the Burgundians) on the other. It also witnessed, however, armed conflict between Clovis' sons and heirs themselves. The

---

[42] Menander the Guardsman, fragment 27.3: Blockley (1985), p. 241.
[43] Paul the Deacon, *History*, III, 26.
[44] ibid, III, 17–18.

growing involvement of rulers such as Theudebert I (r.533–47), Childebert I (r.511–58), and Childebert II (r.575–96) in the affairs of northern Italy and the territories to the east of the Rhine and Alps did little to prevent further bloodletting within the Merovingian clan in its traditional heartlands. From the 520s onwards, a series of struggles between members of the dynasty is recorded in our principal narrative source (the *Ten Books of Histories* of Gregory of Tours).[45] Theuderic I attempted to kill his half-brother Clothar I; Clothar and Childebert I slaughtered Chlodomer's sons; Childebert and Theuderic's son Theudebert I then mobilised against Clothar, who also had to face down a rebellion led by his own son Chramn.

A renewed series of internecine conflicts broke out in the 560s. Upon the death of Clothar in 561, rivalry over the division of their father's kingdom led to violent clashes between his sons, Charibert I, Guntram, Sigibert, and Chilperic I, and their entourages of aristocratic retainers, or *leudes*. In 562, while Sigibert was on campaign against the Avars, Chilperic seized control of a number of cities claimed by his brother. Sigibert struck back by attacking Chilperic's royal seat at Soissons. In 566 Sigibert also sent an army against that of his brother Guntram at Arles. The two clashed again in 573, in response to which Chilperic launched an opportunistic raid on Sigibert's territories south of the Loire. In 575 Sigibert was seemingly on the verge of eliminating his troublesome sibling Chilperic once and for all, but was himself murdered before he could put his plans into effect.

Sigibert left behind him a young son, Childebert II. Chilperic grasped the opportunity offered by Childebert II's minority to seize some of the cities nominally under the boy king's lordship. The loyalty of his father's retinue, coupled with the support of his uncle Guntram, enabled Childebert to overcome this initial crisis of his reign, however. Chilperic was soon obliged to face a revolt within his own kingdom on the part of one of his sons, Merovech, who sought to bolster his bid for power by marrying his widowed aunt, Brunhild, wife of the late Sigibert. The attempted usurpation soon foundered, however, and Merovech found death at the hand of one of his own retainers, whom he asked to kill him out of fear of the more gruesome death he anticipated courtesy of his father. Peace between Childebert II and Guntram, and the murder of Chilperic in 584, offered the prospect of some restoration of stability, but in 585 an additional supposed son of Clothar by the name of Gundevald, who had been passed over in the division of the *regnum* in 561, returned from exile in Constantinople and claimed the throne. Gundevald died in 585, but tensions between Childebert II and his uncle Guntram are discernible until the latter's death in 592.[46] As we shall see in Chapter Nine, it would be 613 before the Merovingian territories would once again be united, and then only after another phase of bloodletting between the sons of Childebert II— Theudebert II and Theuderic II—and their cousin Clothar II.

The causes of this endemic political and military instability are as complicated as the narrative itself. In broad outline, the troubled political conditions that prevailed in late sixth-century Francia can be accounted for on a number of grounds. First

---

[45] I. Wood, *The Merovingian Kingdoms 450–751* (London, 1994), p. 89.
[46] ibid., pp. 89–90.

was the fact that there existed no set order of succession within the Merovingian 'monarchy' (itself, in this instance, essentially a misnomer) and no particular territorial clarity as to the 'kingdoms' over which royal princes could hope to rule. By the 560s, Paris, Rheims, Soissons, and Orleans had each become established as seats of royal power, and it was at these centres that Charibert, Sigibert, Chilperic, and Guntram had set themselves up respectively in 561. Beyond that, however, the situation was as blurred as it was fluid. Each ruler was eager to retain a share of the rich resources of the Paris basin, where extensive estates and sophisticated networks of exchange survived at something approximating to late-Roman levels. But as with many of the military aristocrats and *leudes* who served them, and many of the bishops who attended their courts, each king was also likely to have owned estates scattered throughout the *regnum Francorum* and its appendages. The will of Bishop Bertram of Le Mans (*d*.616), for example, records him to have bequeathed lands (estimated at some 300,000 hectares) as far apart as the Seine Valley, Lorraine, Burgundy, Provence, the Pyrenees, and Bordeaux.[47] Different cities clustered under the lordship of different members of the Merovingian royal bloodline, and the bishop and notables of a given city might be minded to switch their allegiance if political conditions rendered it advantageous to do so. This fluidity of loyalties was itself highly conducive to political instability and conflict.

Such a situation was exacerbated by the fact that typically, as the case of Gundevald reminds us, there were many more potential claimants to royal power than there were thrones to fill. Merovingian monarchs proved themselves keen to take wives and concubines, and to replace them when they were murdered or died, and these new wives and concubines in turn were eager to produce sons who might become kings. If Ostrogothic Italy had suffered from a shortage of princes, Merovingian Francia in the sixth century suffered from a surfeit of them. In order to stake a claim to power, a young prince would need to win a reputation for martial prowess and for generosity to his followers. Only that way would he be able to draw to himself a military retinue of sufficient strength to secure his place on a throne. This in turn could only be achieved through the active pursuit of warfare, be it at home or abroad. As a result, many Merovingian conflicts were driven by the thirst for booty of a royal or princely retinue: Theuderic's campaign in the Auvergne in 524, for example, was effectively forced on him by his warriors after he had refused to take warfare to the Burgundians; while in the 570s Sigibert's troops were reportedly furious at the news that he had made terms with his troublesome brother Chilperic.[48] The demand of well-born warriors for good (meaning remunerative and thus preferably aggressive) lordship was therefore of itself a cause of rivalry and warfare.

Civil war and conflict within the Merovingian bloodline is very much at the forefront of our chief narrative source for late sixth-century Gaul, the moralising *Histories* of Bishop Gregory of Tours. Gregory himself was involved in certain of the struggles he recounts and so should not be regarded as a dispassionate observer.

---

[47] Bertram, *Testamentum*; see discussion in Wickham (2005).
[48] Gregory of Tours, *Histories*, III, 11, and IV, 49.

The career of a bishop could be a dangerous one amid the fluid political landscape of the late sixth century, and Gregory was keen to convey through his narrative that those kings who most prospered, through divine will, were those who showed greatest reverence not only to the saints but also to the bishops who guarded their relics. Chief among the saints, for Gregory, was St Martin of Tours, whose relics were within his care. It should be noted, however, that beneath Gregory's tumultuous narrative, it is possible to discern evidence for growing sophistication and a deepening of the roots of the Merovingian monarchy within Gaul and the wider Frankish world.

On one level, this is revealed by the evidence for growing ideological ambition on the part of Merovingian rulers themselves. Like their Gothic and Vandalic counterparts before them, Merovingian kings had long expressed their authority to their subjects through a combination of styles borrowed from Roman political and cultural traditions, and those indigenous to their non-Roman followers and retainers. As we saw in Chapter Two, for example, the grave-goods of the late fifth-century Frankish king Childeric portrayed his authority after both a very Roman and a very Frankish fashion. Likewise, it may have been during the reign of Childeric's son, Clovis, that the first recension of the 'Law Code of the Salian Franks' (*Lex Salica*) was promulgated. On one level, the issuing of this code was a very 'Roman' act: its compilation under royal auspices echoed the legislative activities of Roman emperors, and the *Lex* itself was promulgated in Latin. Yet the laws themselves were not Roman in origin; rather they were derived from the indigenous customary laws of the Franks, and were compiled by a coterie of learned Frankish elders rather than Gallo-Roman advisers.

The conversion of Clovis to Catholic (i.e. imperial) Christianity and the extension and consolidation of Frankish rule to the south, however, had brought the Merovingian monarchy within a still more markedly Romanised and imperial orbit, and from the mid-sixth century onwards Frankish kings such as Theudebert I can be seen adopting and appropriating an ever more openly imperial style; this development was further catalysed by growing Frankish involvement in northern Italy. Procopius complains in his account of the Gothic Wars, for example, not only that Theudebert (whose armies struck towards Pavia) minted gold coins with his own image on them (the first Romano-Germanic king to do so), but, moreover, that he even presided over chariot races at the Hippodrome of Arles after the imperial fashion.[49] To Procopius, such presumption sounded the death knell of even vestigial imperial authority: 'at about this time,' he declared, 'the barbarians became unquestionably masters of the whole West'.[50] Certainly, relations between Theudebert's court and that of Justinian were tense: Theudebert is reported to have reminded the Emperor, for example, that his kingdom too stretched to the Danube.[51] It was probably with an eye to the Franks as much as to the Gepids

---

[49] Procopius, *Wars*, VII, 33.6.
[50] ibid., VII, 33.1.
[51] Agathias, *Histories*, I, 4.1–4.

that Justinian chose to negotiate the settlement of the Langobards in Pannonia in the 540s.

Theudebert's emulation of imperial example clearly went well beyond the ceremonial and stylistic. Rather, there are signs that he even attempted to revive the collection of the land tax within his domains, drawing, crucially, upon the services of a minister by the name of Parthenius, who had spent time at Byzantine Ravenna. Gregory of Tours informs us that upon the king's death the citizens of Trier seized Parthenius, 'struck him with their fists and then spat at him. They then bound his hands behind his back, tied him to a pillar, and stoned him to death.'[52] From the perspective of the king's subjects, imperial imitation had clearly gone too far.

Further signs of the growing sophistication of Merovingian kingship are also discernible from the fact that, from the middle of the sixth century onwards, there is burgeoning evidence for Merovingian kings legislating and dispensing justice ever more actively.[53] This may have been in response to the prompting of the Church; much of the evidence that survives is concerned with the protection of ecclesiastical rights and privileges. Nevertheless, the indications are that late sixth-century Merovingian kings issued laws frequently and in a variety of contexts. Most striking of all, however, is the evidence for growing Roman influence over the content of that legislation. Whereas Clovis had primarily codified inherited Frankish customary law, Childebert II's legislation clearly drew upon Roman models: thus, in accordance with Roman law, Childebert granted claimants legal title to land if they could be shown to have possessed it for thirty years, whilst his legislation on rape likewise mirrored provisions contained in the Theodosian Code.[54] Moreover, by presiding over councils of the Gallic Church (such as Clovis convened in Orléans in 511), kings were able to foreground their authority in a highly imperial fashion, overseeing the maintenance of ecclesiastical discipline after the manner of Constantine, and receiving the plaudits and praise of attendant bishops and panegyricists.[55]

Both kings and bishops were eager to impose order on Frankish society and restrain those elements of Frankish custom that were deemed most conducive to civil discord. Gregory of Tours, for example, records a vivid example of conflict from within the ranks of the Frankish aristocracy of his native city. During the reign of Childebert, he relates, a certain Sichar had committed the bloody murder of the relatives of a fellow Frankish inhabitant of Tours by the name of Chramnesind. In accordance with Frankish customary law, however, Sichar had paid Chramnesind blood money by way of compensation for the slaughter of his relatives. Perhaps rather more surprisingly, thereafter, he and Chramnesind had become close friends, 'and they became so devoted to each other that they often had meals together and

---

[52] Gregory of Tours, *Histories*, III, 36.

[53] Wood (1994), pp. 102–19.

[54] *Capitularia Merowingica*, 7; *Codex Theodosianus*, IX, 24; I. Wood, 'The Code in Merovingian Gaul', in J. Harries and I. Wood (eds.), *The Theodosian Code* (London, 1993), pp. 159–77.

[55] *Venantius Fortunatus: Personal and Political Poems*, tr. J. George (Liverpool, 1995), pp. 73–80 (panegyric to Chilperic delivered at Council of Berny, 580).

even slept in the same bed'. Nevertheless, trouble was brewing: 'one day as twilight was falling', Gregory goes on to record:

> Chramnesind ordered his supper to be prepared and then invited Sichar round to eat with him. He came and they both sat down to table. Sichar drank far more wine than he could carry and began to boast at Chramnesind's expense. He is reported to have said: 'Dear brother, you ought to be grateful to me for having killed your relatives. For there is plenty of gold and silver in your house now that I have recompensed you for what I did to them. If it weren't for the fact that the fine which I've paid has restored your finances, you would still today be poor and destitute.' When he heard Sichar's remarks, Chramnesind was sick at heart. 'If I don't avenge my kinsfolk,' he said to himself, 'they will say that I am as weak as a woman, for I no longer have the right to be called a man!' Thereupon he blew out the lights and hacked Sichar's skull in two. Sichar uttered a low moan as life left his body, then he fell down dead to the floor. . . . Chramnesind stripped Sichar's corpse of its clothes and hung it from a post in his garden-fence.[56]

Chramnesind realised at this point that he could be in some trouble. Accordingly, he hastened to the king to plead mitigation. At the royal court, however, he soon discovered that the man whose blood he had shed was a protégé of the queen mother Brunhild. Accordingly, Chramnesind fled to the neighbouring territory of King Guntram, while his wife abandoned both him and their children and took herself off to her relatives, who found her a new husband.[57] Eventually, Childebert II granted Chramnesind a pardon, but the message of Gregory's account was clear: the traditional social institutions of the Franks were potentially highly destabilising. What was needed was more active and interventionist kingship, and it is precisely this that we find reflected in Childebert's legislation.

Perhaps most revealing of all, however, throughout the civil wars of the period, is the evident attachment to the Merovingian royal bloodline on the part of aristocratic retainers and local magnates, even in relatively outlying areas such as Aquitaine. A claimant to royal title, such as Gundevald, who could persuade others of his Merovingian credentials, had at least the chance of a throne. Without acknowledgement of the blood royal on the part of other members of the family or the Frankish aristocracy, however, such hopes were futile.[58] Merovingian kings were keen to convey to their subjects that there was something special about them: in the late sixth century, for example, Guntram was reputed to be capable of performing miracles, whilst in the seventh century it was claimed that the founder of the dynasty, Childeric's father Merovech, had been sired by a sea monster.[59] Generations of military success had clearly added lustre to renown.

Lastly, it should be emphasised that the experience of Merovingian kingship and Frankish overlordship can increasingly be seen to have come to frame regional

---

[56] Gregory of Tours, *Histories*, IX, 19.
[57] ibid.
[58] On the subtle politics of this, see I. Wood, 'Deconstructing the Merovingian Family', in R. Corradini, M. Diesenberger, and H. Reimitz (eds.), *The Construction of Communities in the Early Middle Ages: Texts, Resources, and Artefacts* (Leiden, 2003), pp. 149–72.
[59] Gregory of Tours, *Histories*, IX, 21; Fredegar, III, 9, the author of which chronicle clearly had his doubts: see Wood (2003).

identities within the Merovingian realm. In the writings of Gregory of Tours, for example, ethnic designations are remarkably vague. As subjugation, service, and then loyalty to Merovingian kings began to embrace an ever larger proportion of the elite population of post-Roman Gaul, so too did more and more of that elite come to think of itself as Frankish, either in absolute terms or as part of a more hybridised or composite identity. This is clear, for example, from the way in which language ceased (or failed) to operate as a marker of ethnic identity within the Merovingian kingdoms: there were Frankish lords who spoke Frankish (Latin *Teudesca*) and others who spoke forms of Latin.[60] It was perhaps this embedding of new loyalties and the progressive 'sweating away' of old identities that permitted the Merovingian dynasty the luxury of internecine strife.

A similar combination of political instability alongside growing ideological assertivenesss is also evident in the history of the Visigothic kingdom to the south during this period. If anything, the fifth century in the Iberian peninsula had witnessed even more pronounced political and military fragmentation than had occurred in Gaul. After the migration of the Vandals and Alans to Africa in 429, the Sueves had remained in the region and were settled by treaty in the region of Gallaecia to the north-west, although the Suevic kings Hermeric, Rechila, and Rechiarius soon extended the territory under their sway to include the rest of western Hispania by conquering the province of Lusitania. A foray into east-central Hispania and the region of Carthaginiensis, however, was initially contained through the efforts of the remaining Roman commanders in the field, but Suevic pressure remained a constant concern to the imperial authorities.

Accordingly, the Western emperor Avitus (*r*.455–6) had induced King Theoderic II of the Visigoths to march against the Suevic host, which he defeated in battle in 456 near the city of Asturica Augusta (Astorga). Thereafter the Sueves generally confined themselves to the west of the peninsula, periodically raiding territories in Lusitania from their Gallaecian base, where ever more symbiotic relations were forged with members of the local Roman elite. A further attempt on the part of the imperial authorities to impose a military solution on the Sueves through the exertions of the Visigoths in 460 proved unsuccessful, but the effort was nevertheless highly significant, for thereafter those regions of the diocese of Hispania that had not been directly occupied or were not ruled by the Suevic kings were now primarily dependent upon Visigothic protection. As elsewhere in the West, effective imperial government receded from sight, to be replaced, in this instance, by the expansionist kingdom of the Goths.[61]

Over the course of the early sixth century, military pressure from the Franks obliged the Visigothic kingdom to become increasingly 'Hispanised'. The Frankish victory over the Visigoths at Vouillé in 507 drove them from their capital at

---

[60] T. Charles-Edwards, 'The Making of Nations in Britain and Ireland in the Early Middle Ages' in R. Evans (ed.), *Lordship and Learning: Studies in Memory of Trevor Aston* (Woodbridge, 2004), pp. 1,314; E. Ewig, 'Volkstum und Volkbewusstein im Frankenreich des 7. Jahrhunderts' in *idem., Spätantikes und fränkisches Gallien*, 2 vols. (Stuttgart, 1976–9), II, pp. 232–6.
[61] Collins (2004), pp. 26–37.

Toulouse. Thereafter, as we have seen, what remained of the Visigothic kingdom in Gaul—primarily the region around Narbonne—as well as the Visigothic spheres of authority in Hispania were reduced to the status of an Ostrogothic protectorate. The death of Theoderic in 526, however, once more rendered the Visigothic territories in Gaul vulnerable, and in 531 the Frankish king Childebert I inflicted a major defeat upon the Goths outside Narbonne, during the course of which the Visigothic king Amalaric, last descendant of Theoderic I and the 'house of Balt' that he had founded, perished. Although Narbonne itself remained in Gothic hands, an influx of Visigothic refugees into northern Spain ensued.

During the course of the 530s, therefore, the Visigothic kingdom was obliged to undergo significant reconfiguration as the kingship passed to two aristocratic warriors of Ostrogothic origin, Theudis (r.531–48) and Theudisclus (r.548–9). Although increasingly confined south of the Pyrenees, Visigothic power within the Iberian peninsula itself intensified, above all in the region of the central plateau and the territories to the south. An attempt to consolidate the kingdom territorially by taking or restoring Gothic control of the Straits of Gibraltar and the African approaches to Spain, however, failed, with the East Roman army driving the Visigoths back from the city of Ceuta (Septem).[62]

As elsewhere in the post-Roman West, the power of the barbarian newcomers rested upon their martial prowess and their acquisition of landed wealth. The legislation that survives from the Visigothic kingdom from the seventh century, for example, still referred to 'the division of lands effected between the Goths and the Romans' and 'the woodland left undivided between Romans and Goths'.[63] Nevertheless, one should be very careful not to overstate the tightness of Visigothic control at the grassroots of Iberian society in the sixth century, beyond those areas where the Visigothic elite themselves owned estates, such as in the northern sector of the Meseta.[64] The physical geography of Hispania was not one that lent itself easily to political integration, with coastal lowland zones separated by near impenetrable mountains and semi-arid plains. Indeed, during the invasions and wars that had characterised the fifth century, much of the peninsula had effectively become self-governing, with members of the local Roman elite either taking up arms or mobilising bands of armed retainers or slaves to defend their properties and familial interests. Elsewhere, as we have seen, above all in the central zone of the Meseta and those lowland zones in close contact with mountain territories, where more primitive pre-Roman social structures had persisted, a 'tribalisation' of society occurred, effectively a reversion to a pre-Roman Iron Age norm of militarily and economically self-sufficient autonomous peasant communities.[65] For much of the fifth and sixth centuries, therefore, Visigothic power had expanded and contracted, ebbed and flowed—according to the prowess of each individual ruler—over a landscape often populated either by independent Roman *patroni* resident in cities

---

[62] Isidore, *Historia Gothorum*, 42.
[63] *Leges Visigothorum*, X, 1.8 and 9.
[64] Chavarría Arnau (2010), p. 171.
[65] Wickham (2005), pp. 338–9.

but still in possession of extensive rural estates, or the recalcitrant inhabitants of the tribal zones.

Power in the Iberian peninsula in the late fifth and sixth centuries was thus highly fragmented. This rendered Visigothic overlordship both fragile and contestable. In 496, for example, an uprising occurred in *Tarraconensis* under the leadership of a certain Burdunellus. The exemplary brutality of the latter's punishment reveals how vulnerable to rebellion the Visigothic monarchy felt itself to be: after being seized and conveyed to Toulouse, Burdunellus was placed inside a bronze bull and burnt alive.[66] In the 550s the Visigothic monarchy was further destabilised by divisions amongst the Gothic elite. In 549 Theudisclus was murdered at a banquet and succeeded as king by a certain Agila (r.549–54).[67] Agila was soon faced by an uprising in the city of Córdoba. The king marched upon the rebels but suffered a humiliating defeat: in addition to killing Agila's son, the Cordobans were able to seize the royal treasury.[68] Agila was then obliged to flee to the city of Mérida in Lusitania to the west. A second uprising then ensued, this time led by a Goth by the name of Athanagild, operating from the city of Seville.[69] Crucially, in 552, this power struggle within the Gothic elite opened the way to Byzantine military intervention in the province, with Athanagild requesting aid from Justinian.[70]

The East Roman army appears to have received widespread support on the part of members of the Hispano-Roman senatorial aristocracy.[71] This support may in part have been a response to the fact that the imperial expeditionary force was led by the patrician Liberius, who had previously served Odoacer and Theoderic in Italy and Provence before defecting to the imperial authorities in Constantinople; Justinian duly rewarded his defection by appointing him governor first of Alexandria and then of reoccupied Sicily. That Liberius was regarded as a key interlocutor and fixer is revealed by the fact that he must by this point have been in his late eighties or nineties: men of this age, one might imagine, are not usually sent on military campaign unless they are deemed to have a unique political contribution to make.[72] It should also be noted that the revived imperial presence in the western Mediterranean (and especially north Africa), resulting from Justinian's expansionist wars, would appear to have drawn the cities of southern Spain into closer economic contact with the empire, stimulating the circulation of coinage within the territories of Seville, Mérida, Málaga, Valencia, and Cartagena.[73] Byzantine merchants thus

---

[66] *Chron. Caesaraugustanorum*, s.a., 496 and 497.
[67] Isidore, *Historia Gothorum*, 44.
[68] ibid., 45.
[69] ibid., 46.
[70] ibid., 47. For the history of East Roman intervention, see S. Wood, 'Defending Byzantine Spain: Frontiers and Diplomacy', *Early Medieval Europe* 18 (2010), pp. 292–319.
[71] A. Barbero and M. I. Loring, 'The Formation of the Sueve and Visigothic Kingdoms in Spain' in Fouracre (2005), pp. 162–92, p. 182.
[72] Jordanes, *Getica*, 58; *PLRE*, III, Liberius.
[73] P. Reynolds, *Hispania and the Roman Mediterranean, AD 100–700: Ceramics and Trade* (London, 2010). I am grateful to Miss Danielle Donaldson of Trinity College, Cambridge, for discussion of these issues.

served as the advance guard for Constantinople's armies of reconquest, forging links, affinities, and alliances that would help pave the way for the restoration of imperial rule.

The extent of the zone that the Byzantines came to occupy is not entirely clear.[74] By the 550s, it is unlikely that the imperial authorities would have been in a position to commit much by way of investment in the newly conquered territories; as a result, the archaeological evidence reveals little by way of any major programme of military fortification such as Justinian had provided for the Balkans in the 530s, or such as is even discernible with respect to Byzantine-controlled north Africa.[75] Economically, culturally, and politically, the emergent frontier of the Byzantine province of *Spania* (which also included the Balearic Islands) is thus likely to have been highly porous. At an absolute minimum, the East Roman authorities controlled a coastal strip from the probable regional capital at Cartagena to the River Guadalete, along with some inland bases such as those at Basti (Baza) and Asidona (Medina Sidonia). Further inland, members of the Roman aristocracy seemingly took advantage of this situation to establish their own independent regimes, such as had already emerged at Córdoba. The nature of the relationship between these senatorial *juntas* and the newly established Byzantine administration is uncertain. It is likely, however, that the *patroni* of the region sought to play off Visigothic and Byzantine commanders against one another in order to maximise their own autonomy.

Just as Byzantine aggression with respect to the Ostrogoths in the 530s or the Langobards in Italy in the 570s can be seen to have catalysed a drawing together of what had otherwise become fractious military elites, the same was true of the Visigoths in Spain in the 550s. In 554 Agila's retinue rose up against the king and slew him. They then pledged their swords to Athanagild's service.[76] He in turn took warfare to the Byzantines in Baetica, from whom Athanagild was eventually able to wrest control of his former stronghold at Seville. This concentration on containing the Byzantine advance was achieved by buying peace with the Franks, and two of Athanagild's daughters were sent north as brides to Merovingian kings, along with a panoply of diplomatic gifts.[77]

On one level it might appear that Athanagild's achievement essentially boiled down to his having extricated his people from a crisis that was, to a great extent, of his own making. But Athanagild's revolt against Agila must be placed in the context of earlier rounds of factional infighting within the Visigothic aristocracy, especially at moments of anxiety with respect to the military effectiveness of kings. Athanagild's casting off of Agila's kingship echoes a similar revolt in 510, when, in the wake of Alaric's defeat at Vouillé, his successor, Gesalic—caught between the hostility of the Ostrogoths on the one hand and elements of the Visigothic leadership on the other—was opposed, forced from the throne, and ultimately

---

[74] Wood (2010).
[75] Merrills and Miles (2010), pp. 228–55.
[76] Isidore, *Historia Gothorum*, 46.
[77] Gregory of Tours, *Histories*, IV, 27–8.

put to death.[78] Likewise, as we have seen, Agila's predecessor Theudisclus was also assassinated; according to Jordanes, he 'met his death at the hands of his own followers'.[79] The loyalty of Visigothic military retainers to their lords and of these lords to their king was as fluid as that of their Hispano-Roman subjects to the Visigoths themselves.[80] For a ruler to unite the Visigothic aristocracy behind him, just like his Ostrogothic and Frankish counterparts, he had to demonstrate his prowess in the field. Effective military lordship remained the key to successful kingship throughout the post-Roman West. In the case of the Visigoths, however, ties of loyalty were perhaps rendered still more friable by the demise of the house of Balt, which had brought the Visigoths to Spain. After the death of Amalaric in 531, no one lineage automatically inspired respect.

According to the seventh-century chronicler of Hispanic affairs, the scholar and churchman Isidore of Seville, in the aftermath of Athanagild's death in 568 there occurred a five-month interregnum.[81] When the kingship was restored, the rulers had to face down both internal and external challenges described for us in some detail in the *Chronicle* of John of Biclaro. Liuva was acclaimed king at Narbonne, where, crucially, he remained, presumably to keep the Franks in check.[82] The following year (569), he named his brother Leovigild as co-ruler, and entrusted him with the governance and defence of the territories to the south. As with the Tetrarchy of the fourth century, this system of multiple rulership would suggest the need to contain a multiplicity of threats. In order to consolidate his authority in Hispania, Leovigild took as his wife Gosuintha, Athanagild's widow. Having thereby bound Athanagild's former followers and household to him, the king then set about crushing various revolts, as well as taking warfare to the troublesome inhabitants of the mountain zones to the north and south and the Byzantines to the south-east.[83] Leovigild is also recorded to have quelled at least one peasant revolt.[84] It was this series of campaigns that effectively reconstituted the Visigothic *regnum*, especially after 572, when the death of Liuva left Leovigild as sole ruler.[85]

From a Visigothic perspective, Leovigild was an admirably ruthless king. In 573, probably with a view to assuring an orderly succession, he set up his sons, Hermenegild (the eldest) and Reccared, as co-rulers. In 579 Hermenegild's authority took on a territorial aspect, and he was put in charge of the south (presumably Visigothic-held territory in Baetica).[86] The following year, however, Hermenegild repaid this favour by openly rebelling against his father, forging an alliance with the

---

[78] Isidore, *Historia Gothorum*, 34–7.
[79] Jordanes, *Getica*, 58.
[80] Note the provisions concerning armed retainers choosing to transfer their loyalty from one lord to another contained in the Visigothic law codes: *Codex Euricianus*, fragment CCCX, in *Leges Visigothorum: Lex Visigothorum*, 5.3.1 (*De Patronorum Donationibus*).
[81] Isidore, *Historia Gothorum*, 47.
[82] John of Biclaro, *Chronicle*, 6.
[83] ibid., 10–20.
[84] ibid., 47 and possibly 20.
[85] ibid., 24; Collins (2004), pp. 62–3.
[86] John of Biclaro, *Chronicle*, 54.

Sueves and entering into negotiations with the imperial court.[87] Possibly to curry favour with Constantinople, in *c.*582 Hermenegild chose to cast aside the ancestral Arianism of the Goths and embrace Christianity in its imperial, Catholic form.[88] Leovigild responded in 582 by invading his son's territory and conquering Seville and Córdoba in 583 and 584 respectively. Hermenegild was eventually killed, no doubt for his lack of filial piety.[89] With the royal host clearly in fine fettle, the king now unleashed it upon the Sueves, whose kingdom he conquered in 585.

This victory marked the high watermark of Visigothic Arian kingship, and it should not surprise us that, as in mid- to late sixth-century Francia, there are signs during Leovigild's reign of growing ideological confidence on the part of the monarchy and the adoption of an increasingly imperial style, possibly as an explicit refutation of Byzantine claims to authority in the region. Leovigild minted gold coins in his own name instead of that of the Emperor, for example, and broke away from the weight standard set for coinage by Constantinople.[90] Although the Vandal king Huneric had reputedly renamed the city of Hadrumentum *Unericopolis*, Leovigild is the first Romano-Germanic king we know of to have followed imperial example in founding a city, *Recopolis*, supposedly named after his son Reccared (although its original name may simply have been *Rexopolis*—'the city of the king').[91] At court he made strenuous efforts to convey a strong sense of monarchical majesty, and engaged in a concerted programme of legislative activity, possibly removing the (much flouted) civil-law prohibition on marriage between Goths and Romans. As Isidore put it: 'He was the first who met his people enthroned, covered in regal clothing; since before him, the dress and seating were communal for the people and the kings', whilst 'in legislative matters he corrected all that which seemed to have been left confused by the legislation of Euric, adding many laws, omitting and removing many superfluities'.[92] Also like the Vandal Huneric, Leovigild presided over a Council of the Arian Church, held at Toledo in evident emulation of (and perhaps rivalry to) the Ecumenical Councils of the empire.[93] Nevertheless, in spite of this, as Isidore realised, Leovigild remained above all else a man of war and a ferocious scourge of any potential foe.[94]

Hermenegild's conversion to Catholic Christianity, however, had perhaps highlighted a structural weakness at the heart of the kingdom that had been brought to the fore by the Byzantine presence: the division between Arian and Catholic amongst the king's Christian subjects. In Ostrogothic Italy, the imperial authorities had successfully played upon this potential fault-line within Theoderic's *regnum* to

---

[87] ibid., 55 and 66; Gregory of Tours, *Histories*, V, 38.
[88] ibid.
[89] John of Biclaro, *Chronicle*, 64–6, 68, 74.
[90] A. Harris, *Byzantium, Britain, and the West* (Stroud, 2003), pp. 102–3.
[91] John of Biclaro, *Chronicle*, 51; Collins (2004), p. 56, for 'Rexopolis'. For Huneric, see Merrills and Miles (2010), p. 72; L. Olmo Enciso, 'The Royal Foundation of *Recopolis* and the Urban Renewal in Iberia During the Second Half of the Sixth Century', in J. Henning (ed.), *Post-Roman Towns, Trade, and Settlement in Europe and Byzantium*, 2 vols. (Berlin, 2007), I, pp. 181–96.
[92] Isidore, *Historia Gothorum*, 51; Collins (2004), pp. 232, 234, 237 for discussion.
[93] John of Biclaro, *Chronicle*, 58.
[94] ibid. See also M. McCormick (1986), pp. 298–301.

destabilise relations between the Gothic authorities and the Catholic Church in the dying days of Theoderic's reign. Hermenegild's defection would suggest that the imperial authorities were attempting to replicate this policy with respect to Visigothic Spain. Leovigild responded by encouraging conversion to Arianism amongst his Catholic subjects, the Council at Toledo decreeing that such converts did not need to be baptised afresh.[95] 'By means of this seduction,' the Catholic John of Biclaro records, 'many of our own inclined toward the Arian doctrine out of self-interest rather than change of heart.'[96] This issue was not finally resolved, however, until after Leovigild's death in 586. The following year his son and successor, Reccared (r. 586–601), adopted Christianity in its Catholic form, and in 587 much of the Visigothic Arian clergy followed suit.[97] In 589 a council of the Church was convened at Toledo under Reccared's presidency to mark the formal conversion of the Visigoths to the Catholic faith.[98] It was a sign of the great success with which Leovigild had managed to reconstruct the Visigothic monarchy that this theological and, above all, cultural *bouleversement* elicited only a handful of revolts in the period 587–90, each of which Reccared was able to overcome with ease (in spite of the best efforts of the Byzantines to capitalise on dissent).[99] What now mattered to Visigothic kings and the churchmen around them was how to construct a Catholic identity distinct from that of the still-menacing empire of Constantinople.

The late sixth century thus witnessed a recasting of political and cultural conditions in the Frankish and Visigothic kingdoms. These changes were shaped, however, not only by military but also by economic developments. The impetus to economic integration and limited re-monetisation that the restored imperial presence in the western Mediterranean seems to have given to the cities of southern Spain, for example, was also experienced by certain of the remaining urban centres in southern Gaul. The port town of Marseilles can be seen to have profited considerably from contact with Byzantine Italy and imperial possessions further afield, and, as a result, there occurred in Provence a resurgence in the minting of mock-imperial gold coinage, and even small-denomination issues.[100] Both in Marseilles and in those cities in Hispania beyond Byzantine control, such as Merida and Barcelona, moreover, there is also evidence of urban revitalisation, epitomised by the building of new churches.[101] This regeneration of formerly Roman *civitates* may itself have been catalysed by the radiating economic influence of the expanded East Roman state. It almost certainly derived much more of its impetus, however, from the increasingly close alliance that was being forged between kings and bishops in both the Visigothic and Frankish realms.

In so far as there was regeneration and renewal on such urban sites in southern Gaul and Spain, furthermore, it was not according to traditional Roman civic or

[95] John of Biclaro, *Chronicle*, 58.
[96] ibid. [97] ibid., 85.
[98] ibid., 92. [99] Wood (2010).
[100] S. T. Loseby, 'Marseille: A Late Antique Success Story', *Journal of Roman Studies* 82 (1992), pp. 165–85.
[101] See N. Christie and S. T. Loseby (eds.), *Towns in Transition: Urban Evolution in Late Antiquity and the Early Middle Ages* (Aldershot, 1996).

aesthetic principles: once grand open monumental spaces were now filled with private dwellings, often constructed in wood, or patched up with brick and clay; the grand houses (*domus*) of the once all-powerful city councillors, or *curiales*, were subdivided and sections of them turned over to more utilitarian purposes. In parts of Gaul and Spain, the archaeological evidence would suggest, the late-antique city had become 'an administrative, trade and episcopal centre, focused on the cathedral, market, and palace of bishop or king'.[102] Similar trends are discernible with respect to those rural villas in southern Gaul and Spain that remained in use: concerns for monumentality were displaced by practicality and sidelined by an apparent lack of regard for late-Roman architectural or aesthetic norms.[103] By the late sixth century, it would seem, in even these most Romanised of former Roman territories, surviving elites had responded to new political and economic circumstances by transforming their cultural values, beginning to reinvent not only themselves but also the conceptual geography of the towns and villas in which they lived.

5.6 THE CONSOLIDATION OF POWER IN LOWLAND BRITAIN

As we noted in Chapter Two, the fifth century in lowland Britain had witnessed the militarisation and tribalisation of society after a manner very similar to that encountered in parts of the Iberian peninsula at around the same time. The inability of the Roman state to furnish the inhabitants of the province of Britain with the wherewithal to ensure their physical security had forced the Romano-British elite to fall back upon its own resources. Whilst still thinking of themselves as 'Roman', members of this elite too had experienced a 'cultural transformation', divesting themselves of the civilian culture that had most clearly signified membership of the Roman governing classes. It is not surprising, therefore, that to continental outsiders, such elite Romano-Britons appeared increasingly indistinguishable from the barbarians with whom they were obliged to contend. Thus, for example, the Romano-British settlers who arrived in the province of Armorica in north-western Gaul (modern Britanny) in the 460s clearly regarded themselves as 'Roman' and would long describe themselves as such in their law codes; however, their well-born Gallo-Roman neighbours, such as Bishop Felix of Nantes, evidently did not recognise them as such and treated them as little more than dangerous aliens.[104]

From a Romano-British perspective, the main threat in the early fifth century had come from the north and west. Just as, in the third century, larger confederations of barbarian peoples capable of mounting an ever more concerted challenge to

---

[102] T. Lewit, 'Vanishing Villas: What Happened to Elite Rural Habitation in the West in the 5th–6th c?', *Journal of Roman Archaeology* 16 (2003), pp. 260–74.
[103] ibid.
[104] Charles-Edwards (2003), p. 6.

imperial hegemony had formed along the empire's Rhine frontier, so too did a similar process take place along the Romano-British frontier over the course of the fourth century. To the west, the tribal kindreds and petty kingdoms of Ireland were slowly coalescing into more hierarchically ranked confederacies, the leaders of which were eager to profit from the raiding of those Roman territories on the other side of the Irish Sea with which they had formerly traded. In the 360s Ammianus Marcellinus mentions two such groups, which are best thought of as composite hosts, whom he describes as *Scotti* and *Atacotti*, probably originating from the south and north of Ireland respectively.[105] Similar conditions prevailed along Britannia's northern *limes*, where the fourth and fifth centuries witnessed the emergence of a new people known as the Picts (from *Picti*, 'the painted men'), who found rich pickings in Roman territory and gradually pushed the effective Roman frontier southwards. Roman Britain was also subject to seaborne raids on the part of Saxons from the east (indeed, in 367, as Ammianus records, all three groups attacked the province simultaneously), but the Irish and Picts emerge from the sources as the main concern.

Faced with this situation, as we have seen, the leading members of Romano-British society had looked to their own defence, and a series of sub-Roman or Romano-British military lordships emerged that formed the backbone of resistance to external aggression, whilst requests for intervention and support continued to be directed to the imperial authorities in Gaul. There are signs of a high degree of cooperation between the various Romano-British potentates in the early fifth century, and, indeed, for the existence amongst them of an overarching leader, who was to be remembered in the Latin account written by the sixth-century British clergyman, Gildas, as 'the proud tyrant' (probably a Latinisation of the Brittonic title accorded him by posterity—Vortigern, or 'the proud ruler'). Gildas describes, for example, how sometime between 446 and 452, 'the proud tyrant', together with 'the councillors of the Britons', wrote in vain to the general Aetius in Gaul requesting military assistance against barbarian attack.

According to Gildas, Vortigern and his advisers had responded to Aetius' failure to send reinforcements by entering into negotiations with the leaders of the Saxons, who were allowed to settle in eastern Britain in return for their military service. The treaty, however, soon broke down, leading to a Saxon uprising associated with a major onslaught on 'the neighbouring cities' and widespread destruction that engulfed almost the entire province. Gildas presents the Saxon uprising as a vast conflagration that 'devastated town and country round about, and, once it was alight, it did not die down until it had burned almost the whole surface of the island and was licking the western ocean with its fierce red tongue'.[106]

In key respects, Gildas' account of the Saxon settlement is somewhat misleading. As we have seen, Saxon raids on the eastern shoreline of Britain can be traced back to at least the fourth century, and a series of impressive Roman fortifications (of which Gildas was aware) dotted the south-eastern seaboard, built to contain the

---

[105] Charles-Edwards (2003), p. 31; Ammianus Marcellinus, *Res Gestae*, XXVII, 8.5.
[106] Gildas, *de Excidio Britanniae*, 23.

threat posed by acts of piracy and aggression from across the Channel and the North Sea.[107] Indeed, it is entirely possible that it had been the Roman authorities rather than their Romano-British successors who had first cantoned the Saxons in eastern Britain as *foederati*. Such a practice, after all, would have been entirely in accordance with Roman policy elsewhere at the time. There is archaeological evidence to suggest that, as with the Sueves in north-western Hispania, the initial phase of the Saxons' settlement was tightly controlled either by the imperial government or the local aristocracy, with the immigrants deliberately being kept at arm's length from the main concentrations of Romano-British population and aristocratic estates. In modern Sussex, for example, the earliest Anglo-Saxon cemeteries (discernible by virtue of differences in burial custom between the newcomers and the natives) are to be found well away from the most Romanised part around Chichester, in a circumscribed area with few Roman villas between the rivers Ouse and Cuckmere.[108] Nevertheless, at some time around the mid-fifth century, there occurred a breakdown in relations between the indigenous leaders of British society and the settler communities, as a result of which much of lowland Britain was lost to Romano-British control. Contrary to the impression derived from Gildas, this breakdown seems to have taken place prior to Vortigern's approach to Aetius: the *Gallic Chronicle of 452*, for example, records a major Saxon victory in lowland Britain in *c*.441.[109] It is significant that the author of this chronicle has been identified with Abbot Faustus of Lérins, himself a Briton by birth.

This collapse in the Romano-British position, although not uniform across lowland Britain, may well have opened the way to large-scale migration into eastern Britain from the Continent.[110] The possibility of such migration is sometimes challenged on the grounds that it is very hard to spot archaeologically. It is true that, in numerical terms, there are relatively few Anglo-Saxon burials in lowland Britain datable to the sixth century—but then the same is true of non-Anglo-Saxon burials too. This was, after all, a period of major demographic collapse. Moreover, peasant migrations are often invisible to the archaeological eye by virtue of the low level of material culture at which peasants operate. It is worth noting, however, that the descendants of those who settled in the British Isles at this time regarded their ancestors to have been part of a large-scale movement of peoples. In the eighth century, for example, the Anglo-Saxon churchman and scholar the Venerable Bede recorded that the region from which his own people—the 'Angles'—were said to have originated, a territory lying between that of the continental Saxons (the north-west Rhineland) and that of the Jutes (Jutland), had, as a result of the migration, remained deserted of inhabitants from that day to his. Remarkably, this claim may be verifiable archaeologically. The fifth century was a period of rising sea levels, which affected the coastline of northern Germany especially severely; in response to this, the archaeological evidence records a

---

[107] ibid., 18.
[108] E. James, *Britain in the First Millennium* (London, 2001), p. 115.
[109] *Chronicum ad annum 452*, s.a., 441.
[110] Heather (2009).

widespread contraction and abandonment of settlement sites over the course of the fifth and sixth centuries. It follows that Bede's claim is entirely plausible. There is also evidence for the settlement of Angles and Saxons in Normandy and Picardy that may well have taken place at around this time and that is likely to have been motivated by the same 'push-factors'.[111]

As Bede's account reminds us, although our Roman and Romano-British authors typically describe the invaders of lowland Britain as 'Saxons', their heirs and descendants remembered more diverse and heterogeneous roots. Bede identifies the main bodies of migrants as consisting of Saxons, Angles, and Jutes. He also refers to a pell-mell of other barbarian peoples who were represented amongst the newcomers: 'Frisians, Rugini, Danes, Huns, Old Saxons, and Boructari'.[112] Some of these supposed invaders are more credible than others. But certainly one should not think of Romano-British control in lowland Britain as having been dismantled by distinct and separate peoples, who came to settle in carefully demarcated territories under their own imported kings, whilst preserving a series of unique though interrelated customs and cultures. As we noted in Chapter Two, the linguistic evidence reveals the intermingling of various West Germanic dialects, which would soon settle at a lowest common denominator commonly known as *Anglisc* or *Theodisc* ('the language of the people'), before later acquiring dialectical structures of its own as new regional identities took shape. Interestingly, we also see evidence for an emergent sense of shared identity on the part of the diverse settlers and invaders, perhaps rooted in a common awareness of continental origin.[113] On the basis of this shared identity, regional identities were then constructed. The evidence of material culture points in the same direction: although the emergent Anglo-Saxon kingdoms were to be characterised by distinct fashions and styles of dress (most especially in terms of female costume and attire) that bear a close resemblance to identifiable material cultures in different regions of mainland *Germania*, none of these early Anglo-Saxon cultures can be directly 'sourced' geographically. Rather, each one consisted of a locally distinct amalgam of elements and signifiers of diverse origin.[114]

Indeed, it is interesting that, from an early date, the term *Anglisc* would appear to have emerged as the preferred designation with which to describe the language spoken by the Germanic inhabitants of lowland Britain (as well as its speakers), in spite of the fact that only a minority would have regarded themselves as 'Angles' by ethnicity or descent.[115] One reason may have been that this designation enabled the leaders of the Anglo-Saxons to differentiate themselves not only from the Romano-British speakers of Latin and *Wilisc* (Brittonic) but also from the continental

---

[111] James (2001), p. 110.
[112] Bede, *Ecclesiastical History of the English People* [*Historia Ecclesiastica*], ed. and trs. B. Colgrave and R. Mynors, 2 vols. (Oxford, 1969), V, 9.
[113] T. Charles-Edwards, 'The Making of Nations in Britain and Ireland in the Early Middle Ages', in Evans (2004), pp. 11–38.
[114] J. Hines, 'Society, Community, and Identity', in Charles-Edwards (2003).
[115] Charles-Edwards in Evans (2004), pp. 11–38.

Frisians and Saxons with whom they maintained close contact.[116] The word *Seaxisc* ('Saxon') would have been too multivalent, and *Theodisc* was used with respect to many speakers of West Germanic dialects (hence 'Dutch' and *Deutsch*), and not just insular ones.[117] This usage of *Anglisc* would inform the practice of others: in sixth-century Welsh poetry, the term *Eingl* is found used with respect to the Anglo-Saxons as a whole, and, probably writing in Constantinople in the 550s, the Greek historian Procopius described Britain as inhabited by *Britonnes*, *Frissones*, and *Angiloi* (pronounced *angili*).[118]

Above all, the Anglo-Saxons provide us with our clearest evidence of a world in which kingship was not only tested but forged on the battlefield. Thus, as we have seen, the word for 'king' commonly used in the earliest—or, in terms of register, most archaic—Old English sources was *dryhten*, a word that originally meant 'war-band leader'.[119] It is instructive that many of the genealogies of the Anglo-Saxon royal bloodlines that were preserved in later sources trace the royal lineages of the early Anglo-Saxon kingdoms back to Woden, the god of war and especially of war-bands.[120] Amongst the Germanic peoples of north-western Europe in the fifth and sixth centuries, it should be noted, lowland Britain was proverbial as a land of adventure and opportunity: Gregory of Tours, for example, records a dialogue between the late fifth-century Frankish king Childeric and his wife-to-be Basina. When asked by Childeric why she had abandoned her husband, the king of Thuringia, and instead come to him, she declared, 'It is because I know you to be a man capable in deed and strenuous in battle . . . be sure that if—in the parts beyond the sea—I knew someone more capable than you, I would have sought him as my husband.'[121] As a distinguished historian of the Anglo-Saxons has concluded: 'The "parts beyond the sea" sound like Britain, and the implication could be that this was where Frankish and other German adventurers were doing well in the third generation of the fifth century, providing in principle the most promising hunting-ground for this demanding lady.'[122]

Such adventurers did not, however, have things entirely their own way. Although Gildas paints a vivid picture of the havoc and destruction wrought by the breakdown in relations between the Romano-British elite and the leaders of the Germanic newcomers, at the time he wrote his account (usually dated to *c.*540) a period of peace had prevailed for a generation. This peace had been achieved by a Romano-British commander by the name of Ambrosius Aurelianus, who had inflicted a major defeat on the Saxons near a place called *Mons Badonicus*, thereby stemming their westward advance. Aurelianus was remembered by Gildas (who claimed to have been born in the same month as the famous victory) as a quintessentially Roman character, the last of the 'old school': he was, as he put it, 'a

---

[116] ibid.   [117] ibid.
[118] Charles-Edwards in Evans (2004), p. 18, n. 38; Procopius, *Wars*, VIII, 20.7.
[119] Green (1965).
[120] F. M. Stenton, *Anglo-Saxon England* (Oxford, 1943), p. 100; Wallace-Hadrill (1971), pp. 12–13.
[121] Gregory of Tours, *Histories*, II, 12.
[122] J. Campbell, 'The Lost Centuries', in J. Campbell and P. Wormald, *The Anglo-Saxons* (London, 1982), pp. 20–44, p. 37

gentleman who perhaps alone of the Romans, had survived the shock of this notable storm: certainly, his parents, who had worn the purple [i.e. the toga], were slain in it'.[123]

Quite where Mons Badonicus was situated (if the locality existed at all) is unknown, but even as far east as the Chilterns there are signs of a stiffening of Romano-British resistance in the early sixth century. Under the Romans, for example, the city of Verulamium had been an important centre of political authority in south-eastern Britain. There is evidence of ongoing habitation of the site as late as the seventh century.[124] As it was home to St Alban, the proto-martyr of the Christian Church in Britain, the Romano-British population around and within the settlement may have enjoyed a strong sense of cohesion and solidarity, focused on the shrine of the Saint, which enabled them, initially at least, to surmount the military crisis occasioned by the Saxon uprising. It is striking that no non-Christian burial sites have been identified in the vicinity of St Albans (as Verulamium became) from before the late seventh century, and that, in the eighth century, Bede declared that from the date of Alban's death in the second century until his own day, miracles had not ceased to be performed at the proto-martyr's tomb.[125] There is evidence, in short, that the region around Verulamium may have remained under Romano-British control until very late in the day, perhaps as late as the 570s (Fig. 8).[126]

The second half of the sixth century, however, witnessed major Anglo-Saxon advances both to the west and the north as Romano-British resistance weakened, perhaps as a result of the impact of plague and an associated atrophying of lines of communication and supply linking the Romano-British leadership to the East Roman state. Up until that point, Constantinople appears to have provided some measure of support, perhaps in return for tin, and the leaders of the Romano-Britons had sought to associate themselves politically with the surviving Eastern Empire.[127] Nominally at least, the Emperor in Constantinople still claimed authority over Britain as rightly Roman territory, and in Britain these claims were taken seriously: an inscription from Gwynedd in north Wales, for example (the so-called 'Penmachno stone'), is dated according to the Emperor Justinian's consulship of 540.[128] Moreover, in his *Secret History*, Procopius alludes to Justinian having paid subsidies to British rulers.[129] It is possible, therefore, that the East Roman authorities had deliberately sought to bolster and sustain the leaders of Christian Romano-British society in the early sixth century in the face of ongoing Anglo-Saxon pressure. The fiscal and demographic impact on the empire of the bubonic

---

[123] Gildas, *de Excidio*, 25.3.
[124] Hines (2003), p. 88.
[125] Bede, *Historia Ecclesiastica*, I, 7.
[126] Campbell (1982), pp. 36 and 51. See R. Niblett, 'Why *Verulamium*?', in M. Henig and P. Lindley (eds.), *Alban and St Albans: Roman and Medieval Architecture, Art, and Archaeology* (Leeds, 2001), pp. 1–12.
[127] Harris (2003), pp. 149–51.
[128] ibid., p. 157. For continuing imperial claims to authority, see Procopius, *Wars*, VI, 6.28.
[129] Procopius, *Secret History*, 19.13.

Fig. 8 St Albans Cathedral and Shrine Viewed through the Walls of Verulamium (photograph reproduced by kind permission of James Cridland, esq.)

plague, however, is likely to have severely curtailed any such assistance, and may well have been associated with a large-scale contraction in demand for whatever commodities the Byzantines derived from their British trade. Certainly, direct economic contact between west Britain and the empire is discernible archaeologically up to the middle of the sixth century, but seems to have faded away very rapidly thereafter, in a pattern that ties in very closely with the chronology of Romano-British military collapse.[130] It is also very likely that the Romano-British population itself was severely depleted by the plague, thereby opening the way to further phases of migration on the part of Germanic settlers from the Continent.[131]

---

[130] E. Campbell and C. Bowles, 'Byzantine Trade to the Edge of the World', and C. Salter, 'Early Tin Extraction', in M. Mundell Mango (ed.), *Byzantine Trade 4th–12th Centuries* (Farnham, 2009), pp. 297–314 and 315–22.
[131] Charles-Edwards (2003); Keys (1999); J. Maddicott, 'Plague in Seventh-Century England' in L. K. Little (ed.), *Plague and End of Antiquity* (Cambridge, 2007), pp. 171–214 and 215–30.

In particular (as we shall examine in more detail in Chapter Nine), the late sixth century witnessed the formation of a new Anglo-Saxon kingdom in north Britain known in the sources as *Bernicia*, initially centred on the settlements of Bamburgh and Lindisfarne. This kingdom was carved out by means of conquest.[132] Renewed waves of settlement, especially to the north of the Thames, are also discernible. The archaeological evidence, for example, bears witness to the appearance of a new elite material culture in eastern Britain at this time that bears close similarity to that found in southern Sweden. Like the west Baltic elite, this warrior aristocracy buried its dead in great barrows or earth mounds, complete with weapons, armour and other signifiers of rank.[133] It is highly suggestive in this context that it is in the world of southern Sweden that the narrative details of the great Anglo-Saxon heroic poem *Beowulf* unfold. It is also worth remarking that a series of later annals trace the origins of a number of the Anglo-Saxon kingdoms of the seventh and eighth centuries to the sixth century and not the fifth, as did the royal genealogies of their kings preserved in the *Anglo-Saxon Chronicle*. Thus the origin of the East Angles was associated with some sort of migration *c.*527, while the royal dynasties of Essex, East Anglia, and Mercia traced themselves back to 527, 571, and 585 respectively.[134] The late sixth-century origin claimed by the royal house of Mercia is particularly suggestive: Mercia, like Bernicia, was a frontier kingdom, well placed to profit from Romano-British weakness. It was the kings of these marcher kingdoms, rather than the rulers who had emerged in those territories where the Germanic warriors and their families had first settled in the fifth century, who would come to establish mastery of the Anglo-Saxon world in the seventh century.

As these developments would suggest, the late sixth century in lowland Britain was witnessing an incipient consolidation of social and political hierarchies: the archaeology reveals evidence for increasing social stratification, with the appearance of large buildings, separate, high-status settlements and planned layouts which made use of enclosures and trackways.[135] This implies the crystallisation at the grassroots of society of new structures of lordship that were imposed on the remaining Romano-British population, living alongside the settlers, by new Anglo-Saxon masters. An ethnic differentiation between different social classes is certainly a feature of the early Anglo-Saxon law codes that begin to appear from the end of the sixth century, and according to which the blood money (*wergild*) paid by way of compensation for the murder of a Briton (*wealh*) was typically half that demanded with respect to an Anglo-Saxon (a ratio that almost certainly drew on Frankish example). The same differentiation may also be visible archaeologically: study of Anglo-Saxon cemeteries, for example, has revealed that males buried with weapons and richer assemblages of grave-goods are on average between 2 and 5 centimetres taller than men buried without weapons. Both groups show signs of having suffered from malnutrition, indicating that the difference in height between

---

[132] Bede, *Historia Ecclesiastica*, I, 34.
[133] Campbell (1982), pp. 27 and 33.
[134] ibid., pp. 26–7.
[135] H. Hamerow, 'The Earliest Anglo-Saxon Kingdoms', in Fouracre (2005), pp. 263–90, p. 278.

social groups cannot be accounted for simply in terms of diet.[136] Rather, the weapon-bearing elite seems literally to have been a breed apart.

As in post-Roman Gaul, the association between preferable status and Germanic identity, which is such a marked feature of the early medieval law codes, would have provided members of the subject population with a strong incentive to divest themselves of their inherited identity and adopt the manners and customs of their masters and neighbours. Through emulation and intermarriage, over the course of several generations, the descendants of many Christian Romano-Britons thus became pagan Anglo-Saxons, acquiring a new identity through newly emergent structures of lordship. Unlike Latin-speaking Gallo-Romans who became Franks, however, Brittonic or Latin-speaking Romano-Britons who became 'Anglicised' lost their language, although pockets of Celtic in the east are likely to have persisted into at least the seventh century: according to his hagiographer, the seventh-century Anglo-Saxon royal saint Guthlac spent time in exile amongst the Britons to the west and there learned 'to understand their sibilant speech'. By virtue of this, later on in his career, he was able to understand the demons that he encountered in the wasteland of the Fens.[137]

Above the level of local military lordships, the late sixth century also witnessed the formation within the Anglo-Saxon territories of a system of ranked kingdoms and kingships very similar to that encountered in contemporary Ireland (a point to which we shall return in Chapter Nine). In the late sixth century, for example, the dominant ruler in lowland Britain was Æthelberht, king of the *Cantware*, or 'Kentings', although, as already intimated, leadership was soon to pass to members of the frontier dynasties. Likewise, as noted earlier, the emergence of these Anglo-Saxon kingdoms was associated with the formation of new regional identities that drew upon diverse roots. Certain of these roots were evidently British in origin. It is instructive, for example, that the name of the Kentings, or *Cantware*, was derived from an earlier, pre-Roman tribal designation, that of the *Cantiaci* as they were known in Latin. The name of the sixth-century kingdom of Bernicia is likewise of Brittonic etymology. Several of the royal genealogies recorded in the *Anglo-Saxon Chronicle* preserve Celtic names early on in their respective *stemmata*, whilst many of the most basic social and economic institutions upon which the oldest of the Anglo-Saxon kingdoms rested (such as those relating to patterns of landholding or tribute collection) were clearly derived from preconquest, and perhaps even pre-Roman, practices.[138] The tribalisation and militarisation of society in lowland Britain had taken place before the Anglo-Saxons had arrived *en masse*. The 'coming of the Saxons' described by Gildas and elaborated by Bede thus may have witnessed the formation and consolidation of new political and linguistic cultures, but in other respects there were deep-rooted similarities between the societies that developed under Anglo-Saxon rule and those that continued to exist beyond it to the north and west, including Ireland.

---

[136] James (2001), pp. 113–14.
[137] Felix, *Life of Guthlac*, ch. 34.
[138] James (2001).

If it is important to place the developing kingdoms of the Anglo-Saxons in their broader British context, it is equally important to understand them from a continental and European perspective. As the exchange between Childeric and Basina preserved by Gregory of Tours reminds us, there were strong links between the Germanic warrior aristocracies of lowland Britain and their kindreds and equivalents on the other side of the Channel and the North Sea. The migrants who arrived in Britain in the late sixth century, for example, appear to have included bands of continental Saxons who had served in Italy under Langobard leadership: the author of the Old English poem *Widsith* claimed to have fought there in the service of 'Ælfwine the son of Eadwine', that is, Alboin the son of Audoin.[139] Connections with the Franks were particularly close, and there are even indications that, in the sixth century, Merovingian kings claimed some sort of suzerainty over those parts of lowland Britain closest to their realm: Procopius records how the king of the Franks pointedly included Angles as part of a delegation sent to the Emperor Justinian, in order to demonstrate Frankish authority over the region, whilst, in an admittedly late Breton saint's life, it is clamed that Childebert I held sway not only in Gaul but also in *Britannia transmarina* ('Britain over the sea').[140]

To what extent such claims were exaggerated is far from clear, yet the evidence not only of such texts but also of archaeology would point to the coexistence in sixth-century Britain of an essentially sub-Roman world to the west and what could fairly be described as a sub-Frankish world to the east.[141] It is instructive that the dominant ruler in lowland Britain in the late sixth century, Æthelberht of Kent, had a Merovingian wife, Bertha. We might also wish to associate with this Frankish connection Æthelberht's own somewhat Romanised style of rule: there are hints in the writings of Bede that Æthelberht may have periodically resided in a palace built on the site of the former Roman city of Canterbury.[142] Such continental influences were to become still more pronounced, however, when, in 597 Æthelberht received a mission sent to him from Rome by Pope Gregory the Great. With the encouragement of Bertha, Æthelberht accepted baptism into the Catholic faith. Gregory took special care to remind him that the religion he was embracing was that of the Emperor Constantine and of the Roman state, whilst the Pope informed the queen that news of her husband's conversion had even reached the ears of the Emperor Maurice.[143] In accepting Christ, Æthelberht had thus acquired membership of a political commonwealth of Catholic monarchs that radiated outwards from the city of Byzantium.[144]

[139] *Widsith*, ll. 70–4.
[140] Campbell (1982), p. 38.
[141] I. Wood, *The Merovingian North Sea* (Alingsas, 1983).
[142] Campbell (1982), p. 38.
[143] Bede, *Historia Ecclesiastica*, I, 32.
[144] Gregory the Great, *Register*, XI, 35; Wallace-Hadrill (1971), p. 32.

6
Religion and Society in the Age of Gregory the Great

6.1 ROYAL CONVERSION AND THE CONSOLIDATION OF ROMAN CHRISTIANITY

In purely religious or spiritual terms, it is impossible to say precisely what Christianity had to offer Æthelberht of Kent when he converted at the invitation of the Papal mission of 597, not least because our understanding of the religious life of the pre-conversion Anglo-Saxons is so limited.[1] Certainly, the appeal was not irresistible: upon his father's death in 616, Æthelberht's son and successor Eadbald was to return to the ancestral faith of his people. Eventually, however, Eadbald too embraced Christianity and began to impose it on those of his subjects who were non-Christian, reminding us that, in a lord- and king-focused society, it was the conversion of kings that was the necessary precursor to wider processes of evangelisation. Importantly, it was through the marriage of Eadbald's sister to King Edwin of Northumbria in 625 that Christianity spread northwards, with Edwin taking the new faith as well as a new wife. That said, part of the nature of the personal and spiritual appeal of Christianity to rulers such as Æthelberht or Edwin is conveyed by some of our later Anglo-Saxon sources, such as the writings of Bede, which appear to preserve elements of what might be thought of as earlier missionary propaganda.

The world of post-Roman Britain in the fifth and sixth centuries, as also of the Western Empire's former provinces on the Continent, was one increasingly dominated, as we have seen, by the concerns and mores of a warrior elite, whose extrovert lifestyle was rooted in publicly displayed violence, conspicuous consumption, and manifest excess. The ideal of the warrior-lord may well have been a self-consciously heroic one, but it was one very much rooted in the here and now. Christian missionaries, therefore, had to persuade such lords that the teachings of the Church were compatible with the warrior ideal, and in particular, that the Christian God was one capable of delivering what all warlords craved—success on the battlefield. This was achieved, in both lowland Britain and on the Continent, by laying emphasis on the figure of Constantine and his divinely inspired victory at the battle of the Milvian Bridge in 312, and by reiterating one of the core themes of the

---

[1] Wallace-Hadrill (1971), pp. 21–46; Stenton (1943), pp. 96–102.

Old Testament: that kings who do God's will are granted success in this life and overcome their foes.[2] Both the imperial template of Constantine and the Scriptural model of Old Testament kingship feature prominently in the writings of Bede in the eighth century, just as they did in those of Gregory of Tours in the sixth.[3]

But what, our Anglo-Saxon advocates for Christianity repeatedly ask, comes after this life? What is there beyond the pleasures of the feasting hall, or the heroic death? The case is put most famously and vividly in Bede's account of the conversion of the Northumbrians. Upon hearing Edwin's exposition of his newly adopted faith, one of the king's retainers is reported to have responded:

> This is how the present life of man on earth, O King, appears to me in comparison with that time which is unknown to us. You are sitting feasting with your commanders and chief retainers in winter time; the fire is burning on the hearth in the middle of the hall and all inside is warm, while outside the wintry storms of rain and snow are raging; and a sparrow flies swiftly through the hall. It enters in at one door and quickly flies out through the other. For the few moments it is inside, the storms and wintry tempest cannot touch it, but after the briefest moment of calm, it flits from your sight, out of the wintry storm and into it again. So the life of man appears for but a moment; what follows or indeed what went before, we know not at all. If, therefore, this new doctrine brings more certain information, it seems right that we should accept it.[4]

A similar message is conveyed by the Old English poem *Beowulf*, in which the great hero, after surmounting repeated challenges and obtaining a series of spectacular victories, is finally let down by his necessarily fallible human retainers and succumbs in mortal combat with a dragon. It is presented as an inevitable conclusion: 'the wages of the hero', as Tolkien put it, 'were death'.[5] Christianity, it is inferred, offered something more. As the *Beowulf* poet declares: 'Well shall it be for him who upon his death-day is permitted to seek the Lord and ask for refuge in the embrace of the Father.'[6] It should not surprise us that these words were most probably penned by a monastic scribe eager to propagandise on behalf of the faith to his noble kinsmen.[7]

The specific appeal of imperially defined (and thus 'Catholic' or 'Orthodox') Christianity, which drew to it not only Æthelberht and Edwin but also Clovis and Reccared, is more certain. The conversion of all of these rulers to Catholic Christianity can be understood against the broader background of how post-Roman and Romano-Germanic kings and warlords sought to stabilise their rule and consolidate the foundations of their power. In particular, royal conversion to Catholic Christianity reveals the ongoing appeal of *Romanitas* and all that was

---

[2] Wallace-Hadrill (1971).

[3] For the prominence of Old Testament themes in Anglo-Saxon literature, see also D. Whitelock, *The Audience of Beowulf* (Oxford, 1951).

[4] Bede, *Historia Ecclesiastica*, II, 13.

[5] J. R. R. Tolkien, 'Beowulf, the Monsters, and the Critics', *Proceedings of the British Academy* 22 (1936), pp. 245–95.

[6] *Beowulf*, 106–8.

[7] C. P. Wormald, 'Bede, Beowulf, and the Conversion of the Anglo-Saxon Aristocracy' (1978), in C. P. Wormald and S. Baxter (eds.), *The Times of Bede* (Oxford, 2006), pp. 30–105.

associated with it as a means of conveying a ruler's authority to retainer, subject, and rival alike. Catholic Christianity was, above all else, the religion of the Emperor and the empire. Through association with Catholic Christianity, therefore, rulers were able to share in the reflected glory of the *imperium Romanum* and the renown of the Caesars. As for the first generation of 'barbarian warlords'—men such as Geiseric or Theoderic the Ostrogoth, who had carved out kingdoms for themselves in nominally imperial territory—this fact is likely to have induced them to cling ever more firmly to the Arian Christianity that their peoples had acquired around the late fourth century: as we noted in Chapter Three, adoption of imperial, Catholic Christianity would have been regarded as signifying some measure of personal or collective subjection to imperial authority that such warlords would have been loath to accept. Many of these rulers, in any case, had shown themselves to be more than capable of matching the Romans in battle. It is striking that of those 'barbarians' who entered Roman territory between 376 and 406, only the Suevi (under their king Rechiarius) are known to have converted to Christianity in its Catholic form, and even they initially passed through an Arian phase.[8]

By contrast, for those groups and kingdoms that rose to power in the late fifth and sixth centuries, or which established themselves beyond the empire's effective or potential reach, such as the Franks and Anglo-Saxons, political association with the Roman Empire through religion may well have appeared more a source of prestige than of potential danger. In spite of its fifth-century contraction, the Roman Empire continued to exist at a manifestly higher level of material culture than that enjoyed by any of the post-Roman successor states, and its rulers maintained a reputation for military prowess, probably enhanced by Justinian's western reconquests, that these second- and third-generation rulers could admire from a relatively secure distance. In a culture in which material reward and military victory were regarded as indicative of divine pleasure, and in which kings were held to be personally responsible for defeat, this sent out a strong message.

As a result, the ecclesiastical leadership soon learned to play upon imperial and material themes. Gregory the Great, for example, as we have seen, was careful to inform Æthelberht's wife, Bertha, that news of the king's conversion had reached the Emperor in Constantinople, just as Clovis, after his conversion, is recorded by Gregory of Tours to have received letters from the Emperor Anastasius conferring upon him the title of *consul*, and can be seen to have entered into military alliance with Byzantium, perhaps as a result. After his conversion, the Northumbrian king Edwin is described as having had borne before him 'the type of standard which the Romans call the *tufa*' and, as we shall see in Chapter Nine, he adopted a highly Romanised style of rule.[9] Both Pope Gregory with respect to Æthelberht, and his successor Pope Boniface with respect to Edwin, engaged in gift-giving diplomacy, thereby emphasising the superior wealth and luxury of Roman culture, whilst both Roman military and material superiority are leitmotifs of Anglo-Saxon literature.

---

[8] I. Wood, 'The Conversion of Barbarian Peoples', in G. Barraclough (ed.), *The Christian World* (London, 1981), pp. 85–98, p. 86.
[9] Bede, *Historia Ecclesiastica*, II, 16.

So, for example, the Old English poem *Elene* speaks of 'the Romans, men renowned for their victories'; the *Widsith* speaks of 'Caesar, who held sway over festive cities, over riches and desirable things, and over the empire of the Romans'; whilst another poet famously described the visible remains of a Roman city as 'the work of giants'.[10] None of these Anglo-Saxon literary sources is early, but there is no reason to doubt that they accurately reflect a mentality that would have been apparent in the sixth and seventh centuries. Through conversion, 'a barbarian entered a world in which . . . he could enjoy the idea that he actually was in some sense a Roman'.[11]

In Visigothic Spain such imperial associations were politically less straightforward. Here, as we noted in Chapter Five, conversion formed a necessary part of containing the military threat posed by the Byzantine enclave of Spania. The conversion of the Visigothic monarchy to Catholic Christianity enabled Reccared and his heirs to draw closer to their leading Catholic subjects, and so prevent them from being lured into the political orbit of Constantinople. At the same time, it allowed them to rely upon the surviving trans-regional structures of the Church, as represented by its councils, both to give greater territorial cohesion to an otherwise fragmented realm and to set about constructing a Hispano-Gothic identity rooted in a strident anti-Arianism, anti-Judaism, and anti-Byzantinism that is manifest in Visigothic legislation and in the writings of Isidore of Seville. In post-Roman conditions throughout much of the West, the Church was the only trans-regional power structure to survive, and rulers were keen to co-opt it to enhance their own authority. So, for example, in 589, on the model of emperors presiding over Ecumenical Councils, we see the Visigoth Reccared presiding over a council of the Iberian Church (Toledo III). Likewise, in Anglo-Saxon England, the role of kings such as Offa of Mercia in presiding over ecclesiastical councils would be associated with an assertion of political supremacy, or *principatus*, over the *orbis Britanniae*, or the wider realm of Anglo-British kingdoms.[12] The Catholic Church in turn sought to consolidate further the authority of Catholic rulers by sanctifying their power. As Gregory of Tours declared of Reccared: 'Having understood this verity, Reccared put an end to all dispute, submitted to the Catholic law and received the sign of the blessed cross with the unction of holy chrism.'[13]

6.2 ROYAL, IMPERIAL, AND EPISCOPAL AUTHORITY

As the actions of Reccared show, the appeal of Catholic Christianity and of the Catholic Church to Romano-Germanic kings was greatly enhanced by the fact that in much of Gaul and Spain, as we have seen, the episcopal structures of the Church

---

[10] *Elene*, 41–55; *Widsith*, 75–8; *The Ruin*, 2.
[11] J. Campbell, 'The First Christian Kings' in J. Campbell (ed.), *The Anglo Saxons* (1982), pp. 45–69, p. 67.
[12] E. John, *Orbis Britanniae* (Leicester, 1949).
[13] Gregory of Tours, *Histories*, IX, 15.

were able to survive the military events of the fifth century substantially intact; bishops often remained the last vestigial face of Roman authority as the empire faded away. From the conversion of Constantine onwards, bishops had come to play an ever greater role in imperial politics, civic life, and administration, their power enhanced by the fact that whereas a governor's term of office in a given province was finite, a bishop, once appointed, remained in office until he died or was deposed.[14] As a result, episcopal office had become an increasingly attractive career option to members of the Roman governing classes. This development became more pronounced as the decline of empire closed down other career paths, a fact that helps to explain how and why members of Gallo-Roman senatorial families, such as that of Gregory of Tours, effectively sought to monopolise episcopal office so as to shore up their own political interests and fortunes. Indeed, it was probably the demise of empire that heralded the final Christianisation of the Western senatorial elite, as Roman aristocrats found solace and refuge in the *Romanitas* of the Church. As governors, bureaucrats, and *curiales* faded from sight, the bishop was left as a figure of towering political significance—a fact perhaps reflected in the high rate at which bishops were murdered amid the factional politics of the Merovingian era.[15]

In the surviving provinces of the Eastern Roman Empire, the role and responsibilities of the bishop continued to become increasingly entwined with the workings of the Roman state. By the end of the reign of the Emperor Anastasius, bishops had come to form part of the local *collegia* of notables into whose hands fiscal administration was entrusted. By the end of Justinian's reign, as we have seen, bishops had been charged with the task of keeping a watchful eye on the activities of governors, were obliged to advertise newly promulgated imperial laws to their congregations, and were rendered responsible for appointing the *defensor civitatis*, who was meant to protect the interests of the poor, needy, or vulnerable at a civic level, as well as the *sitônes*, or overseer of the civic grain supplies.[16] During the reign of Justin II, bishops, along with the dominant local landowners in a province, were accorded the extraordinary privilege of being allowed to choose their own provincial governor.[17]

Indeed, the sources also record growing imperial political reliance on the Church more generally. As we noted in Chapter Four, the ongoing Christianisation of the Roman state played an important role in Justinian's reform programme, as the Emperor sought to secure the political loyalty of his Christian subjects by harnessing their piety. Secular symbols and images of imperial authority were increasingly supplemented by and replaced with Christian ones; images or icons of Christ, the Virgin, and saints became more visible at the court of Emperor and governor alike;

---

[14] C. Rapp, *Holy Bishops in Late Antiquity: The Nature of Christian Leadership in An Age of Transition* (Berkeley, 2005).
[15] P. Fouracre, 'Why Were So Many Bishops Killed in Merovingian Francia?' in N. Fryde and D. Reitz (eds.), *Bishofsmord im Mittelalter: Murder of Bishops* (Göttingen, 2003), pp. 13–36.
[16] Rapp (2005), pp. 263–4.
[17] Sarris (2006), p. 223.

imperial ceremonial came to adopt more elaborately Christianised ritual dimensions, and imperial rhetoric an increasingly biblicised frame of reference and tone.[18] This biblicised language of power had gained prominence in the fifth century, in the debate surrounding the Council of Chalcedon, when bishops had drawn upon Old Testament models of rulership in their appeals to the Emperor. Under Justinian, such rhetoric now began to form part of the imperial court's own rhetorical armoury.[19] As we have seen, through his reconstruction of the Cathedral Church of Holy Wisdom (Hagia Sophia), Justinian had been able to depict himself as a 'New Solomon'. In the same vein, his associated reconstruction of the monumental heart of his capital (laid waste by the Nika riot of 532) was associated with the creation of a public space in which to unite imperial and religious ceremonial. In the triumph organised for the general Belisarius in 559, the secular *adventus*, or victory procession, was combined with the saying of prayers for the soul of the emperor's wife, the long-departed Theodora. As an astute observer of Byzantine religious culture has commented, 'small hints show that a regular pattern of imperial behaviour now existed, interwoven with the religious calendar'.[20] It was upon the prayers of the pious, and especially the most spiritually committed amongst them—the monks and holy men who epitomised Christian ideals of asceticism—that the fortunes of the empire were ultimately deemed to rest. As Justinian declared in his law of 539:

> When these holy people pray to God for the prosperity of the government with pure hands, and souls free from every blemish, there is no doubt that Our armies will be victorious, and Our cities well-governed: for where God is appeased and favourably disposed towards us, why should We not enjoy universal peace, and the loyalty of Our subjects? The earth offers us its fruits, the sea gives us up its wealth, and the prayers of Our people will invoke the blessing of God upon the entire Empire.[21]

6.3 ASCETICISM AND AUTHORITY

It is worth noting that in the spiritual economy of empire as envisaged by Justinian in his law of 539, it was not the prayers of monks and ascetics alone that the Emperor believed would ensure divine favour: rather the prayers of *all the faithful* would 'invoke the blessing of God'. Yet the prayers of 'these holy people', the monks who were the main focus of the law in question, were singled out as

---

[18] A. Cameron, 'Images of Authority: Elites and Icons in Late Sixth-Century Byzantium', in M. Mullett and R. Scott (eds.), *Byzantium and the Classical Tradition* (Birmingham, 1981), pp. 205–34, p. 209.

[19] C. Rapp, 'Old Testament Models for Emperors in Early Byzantium', in P. Magdalino and R. Nelson (eds.), *The Old Testament in Byzantium* (Washington DC, 2010), pp. 175–98. Rapp sees this as a Heraclian development, but there are signs of it already under Justinian and Justin II: see R. D. Scott, 'Malalas, *The Secret History*, and Justinian's Propaganda', *Dumbarton Oaks Papers* 39 (1985), pp. 99–110, p. 104.

[20] Cameron (1981), pp. 209–10.

[21] *J. Nov.*, 133.5.

especially efficacious for the reason that, through their casting aside of the world, their constant attention to the divine, and their Christ-like (or 'Christophoric') abnegation of the ego, they stood that much closer to God. Accordingly, it was they who could most earnestly and convincingly entreat the Lord's intervention in human affairs.

The ideal of the ascetic or holy man, on which the life of the monk was based, dominated the imagination of many late antique and early medieval Christians. At the core of that ideal stood textual, and above all, scriptural models. The Old Testament template of Moses in the wilderness, and especially of Moses before the 'burning bush', presented the believer with a stark image of man in the searing and inescapable presence of God. That to focus more attentively on what God was saying, to enter into communion with one's Maker, one had to depart from society and instead seek out the actual or proverbial desert, was reinforced both by the Scriptural model of the life of John the Baptist and by the instructions of Christ Himself; Christ had advocated the stripping away of the trappings of family and society and the casting aside of property, in order to grasp 'the Kingdom of Heaven' that He declared to be at hand. At the heart of the Christian Gospels stood a profoundly eremitic impulse to which the most spiritually sensitive would always be inclined to respond: the believer was enjoined to flee the world.

The extent to which the life of the Christian holy man was essentially one generated by Scripture is discernible from the fourth-century account of our earliest recorded Christian holy man, Antony, the father of Egyptian monasticism. The author, Athanasius, Patriarch of Alexandria, describes the young, orphaned Antony as having decided one day to sell all his goods and devote himself to a life of contemplation and prayer, ever further removed from the settled, civilised world. Accordingly, Antony headed out further and further into the desert, or *erêmos*, where, undistracted, he could confront himself, his God, and the demons who sought to draw him away from his Creator. This decision was made, according to Athanasius, in direct response to the Gospel reading that Antony heard in his village church: 'If thou wilt be perfect, go and sell all that thou hast and give to the poor, and come follow Me.'[22]

In the desert, Athanasius records, Antony attracted disciples who yearned to emulate him and follow him on his spiritual journey. What begins as an account of a solitary soul seeking to draw closer to his Maker, thus becomes an account of *monachoi*, or monks: men who were alone, but alone in company. The history of an individual recluse morphed into the foundational text of a monastic movement. For, as the text of Athanasius' *Life* of Antony circulated ever more widely, and rapidly found itself translated into Latin, the ascetic, eremitic, and core monastic ideals that it described soon sparked off a second round of textually generated emulation on the part of the spiritually hungry. In response to the circulation of Athanasius' *Life*, 'soon the islands of the Adriatic and the Tyrrhenian Sea . . . even

---

[22] *Vita Antonii*, ch. 2.

escarpments washed by the treacherous eddies of the Loire, became little "deserts" for their ascetic inhabitants'.[23]

The ideal of the Christian holy man that Antony was deemed to personify was also shaped by a second, and perhaps still more powerful textual model and Scriptural impulse: a desire to emulate the life of Christ as set out in the Gospels. 'I have come . . . not to do my own will,' Christ was recorded to have declared, 'but the will of Him who sent me.'[24] It was this sense of devoted selflessness that had enabled Christ to suffer death on the Cross and thereby open the pathway to salvation for mankind. During the eras of persecution, believers had been able to emulate Christ by enduring torture and death at the hands of the Roman authorities, thereby obtaining the martyr's crown. But with the passing away of the age of state-sponsored persecution, and the growing institutionalisation of the Christian Church in the years following Constantine's conversion in $c.312$, that crown slipped ever further from reach. In response, individuals began to decide that if 'the powers of this world' were no longer willing to persecute them for their love of God, they would instead render themselves their own persecutors. Through self-mortification and fasting, the holy man, be he hermit or monk, could achieve *apatheia*—an indifference to the disorientating and distracting concerns of the flesh—and so would be able to attend ever more closely to the divine. This phenomenon was vividly epitomised in the early fifth century by the renowned Symeon Stylites the Elder, who purportedly spent thirty-seven years on top of a stone pillar near the great city of Antioch in northern Syria. Like Antony, Symeon soon attracted disciples, pilgrims, and ultimately emulators from as far afield as Constantinople and northern Gaul.[25]

Through drawing closer to God (Greek *theôsis*), the greatest of holy men were believed to be capable of acquiring spiritual power here on earth, much as we find recorded with respect to Jesus and the Apostles in the New Testament: the ability to discern and cast out demons, to cure the sick, or to perform miracles of a still more remarkable nature. As the Egyptian hermit Barsanuphius wrote to a correspondent of his in the 520s, in a justly famous passage: 'I speak in the presence of Christ, and I do not lie, that I know a servant of God, in our generation, in the present time and in this place, who can raise the dead in the name of Jesus our Lord, who can drive out demons, cure the incurable sick, and perform other miracles no less than the Apostles. . . . For the Lord has in all places His true servants, whom he calls no more *slaves* but *sons* [Galatians 4:7].'[26]

The holy man, both living and dead, was widely regarded as acquiring freedom of speech (*parrhesia*) before God—and a consequent ability to intervene or intercede on behalf of a community or individual supplicant. He also acquired a manifest authority before men, however: the *Lives* of holy men and saints depict

---

[23] P. Brown, 'Asceticism: Pagan and Christian', in Cameron and Garnsey (1998), pp. 601–31, p. 616.
[24] John 6:38.
[25] *The Life of Daniel the Stylite*; Gregory of Tours, *Histories*, VIII, 15 and below.
[26] Barsanuphius, *Correspondence*, 91: translation from P. Brown, *Authority and the Sacred* (Cambridge, 1995), p. 57.

them as intervening in disputes between urban and rural communities, between provincial society and the imperial authorities, and within rural communities themselves, in order to maintain peace or restore social order. St Symeon, for example, is described as attracting the devotion of nomadic Arab tribesmen who flocked to his pillar and whose patron he became. This picture should not be accepted entirely at face value. These *Lives*, after all, were literary texts, typically written in an official, prestige language, presumably for a literate elite audience. The emphasis that these texts place on the role of 'holy men' in the maintenance of social order, especially in the countryside, need not necessarily reflect a marked or novel social reality. Rather, such anecdotes and hagiographical *topoi* sought to play upon the social anxieties of an elite audience of absentee landowners, in order to acquire their patronage, financial assistance, and support for the religious institutions and monasteries that were often associated with the memory of the holy man whose life was the subject of the work.[27] The nomad, for example, was always a source of fear and concern to the settled populations of the Near East: that Symeon could tame even him truly was a sign from God.

The social significance of the emergent figure of the Christian holy man, therefore, probably lay far less in the role he supposedly played in intervening in potentially fraught social relations than in the spiritual revolution that he himself represented in his own person. There had, of course, existed pagan antecedents to the figure of the Christian holy man, chief amongst them being the philosopher.[28] Both holy man and philosopher are represented as engaging in a rigorous programme of training (*askêsis*) of both body and mind, whereby they achieved indifference (*apatheia*) to their bodily wants, and through contemplation (*ennoia*) came to an appreciation of the true nature of the cosmos. There was, however, one crucial difference between the pagan philosopher of late antiquity and the Christian holy man. The profound insight into the nature of the universe that the philosopher obtained required education, meaning a deep familiarity with the foundational texts of classical thought. Such an education was necessarily expensive. As a result the path of the philosopher was open only to a socially as well as intellectually select few. The insight and power that the Christian holy man obtained, by contrast, were the result of his striving to know and love God with all his heart and all his soul: it was a path open to everyone, irrespective of social background. The point was not lost on contemporaries: when, in the 380s, Augustine and his friend Alypius heard news of the spiritual exertions of the former farmer Antony, Augustine records that they 'stood amazed...hearing such wonderful works...so generally testified, so fresh in memory, and almost in our own times'.[29] The well-educated and well-born Augustine was brought to the brink of a breakdown: 'troubled both in mind and body', he had ended up crying out to his friend: 'the uneducated rise up and take heaven by storm, and we, with all our learning, here we are, still wallowing in flesh

---

[27] Brown (1995), pp. 62–4; Sarris (2006), pp. 118–21.
[28] Brown (1998).
[29] Augustine, *Confessions*, VIII, 6.

and blood'.[30] Nor was Antony alone: St Symeon the Elder in the fifth century was the son of a shepherd, whilst, in the seventh century, St Theodore of Sykeon was the illegitimate offspring of a prostitute. As a further sign of the spiritual aspirations of the poor, the imperial authorities were obliged to legislate to prevent estate workers and slaves from becoming clerics without the permission of their masters.[31]

The path to holiness was also, in theory, open to all irrespective of gender. In practice, however, fleeing the world could be far from straightforward for the would-be holy woman. A vivid example of the difficulties that could be faced is to be found in the sixth-century *Life* of the fifth-century St Matrona, founder of a nunnery in Constantinople.[32] As the *Life* informs us, Matrona had come to Constantinople aged twenty-five, with her husband, Dometianus, who probably had business of some sort in the city, and a small daughter named Theodote. Matrona took advantage of her arrival in the capital, however, to make contact with a group of pious women associated with the Church of the Holy Apostles. With their help, she ran away from her husband and entrusted her daughter to the care of a local widow. Dometianus soon realised that Matrona had left him, but assumed she had run off to become a prostitute. Matrona then disguised herself as a eunuch and entered a male monastery dedicated to Saint Bassianus. Eventually the other monks realised that something was amiss when they noticed that the ears of the newly arrived 'monk' were pierced. Accordingly, Matrona was obliged to leave the monastery, only to find both that her daughter had died and that her husband was after her. Some of her friends from the monastery managed to get her shipped out of Constantinople, and Matrona made her way to a nunnery in Syria, where she became abbess. There she performed the miracle of curing a blind man, and her fame soon spread.

In consequence, news of Matrona's whereabouts reached her husband, who headed for Syria in pursuit. Matrona in turn fled to Jerusalem, then to Mount Sinai, and thence to Beruit where she hid in a ruined pagan temple, looked after by a local cabal of wealthy women. Fearful her husband would find her, Matrona decided to double back to Constantinople where another group of wealthy women took her under their wing. At this point Matrona's husband seems either to have given up, lost her trail, or died. One wealthy patron—this time a man—presented her with an estate in the suburbs of the city, where she founded her nunnery with a group of women who had gathered around her. Secure at last, Matrona found happiness in the company of her spiritual sisters, whom she dressed, interestingly, not in the customary woollen girdles and veils typically worn by nuns, but rather in wide leather belts and men's white cloaks. As the great Byzantinist Cyril Mango has commented, 'a psychologist may make something out of that'.[33] At the end of the day, escaping the constraints of a deeply patriarchal society was no easy

[30] Augustine, *Confessions*, VIII, 8; P. Brown, *Power and Persuasion in Late Antiquity* (Madison, 1988), pp. 71–2.
[31] *J. Nov.*, 123.17.
[32] Discussed in C. Mango, 'Saints', in C. Cavallo (ed.), *The Byzantines* (Chicago, 1997), pp. 255–80, on which I rely for what follows.
[33] ibid., p. 268.

matter, and for a woman of a spiritual inclination, childless widowhood was probably the ideal state.

In the post-Constantinian Church, therefore, what might be termed 'charismatic leadership' within Christian communities can be said to have passed from the hands of the traditional guardians and overseers of those communities—their deacons, presbyters, and, above all bishop—to the holy man or monk who personified the core ideals of the faith. This could occasion tension: at the Ecumenical Council of Chalcedon of 451, for example, monasteries were placed under episcopal jurisdiction. Likewise, in the late sixth century, Gregory of Tours records an illuminating incident, when a monk by the name of Vulfolaic set himself up on a pillar outside the city of Trier. In response, the bishop emerged from the city and ordered him to get down. Vulfolaic did so, on the grounds that it was a sin to disobey a bishop. The bishop then had the pillar destroyed.[34] There was almost certainly a social dimension to such tensions. The life of the Christian holy man, as we have seen, was theoretically open to all. The public and administrative responsibilities of the bishop, however, were best suited to those who possessed an upper-class education, more akin to that of the philosopher. In the fifth century, for example, Synesius had been elected Bishop of Cyrene in Tripolitana, precisely because he possessed the rhetorical education, governmental contacts, and aristocratic bearing required to act as a good patron to his urban flock.[35]

Such tensions, however, should not be exaggerated: in the Old Testament, after all, Moses had returned from the wilderness to lead his people out of captivity. The bishop, as well as the monk or hermit, was meant to serve as a paragon of Christian virtue, and many found themselves elevated to episcopal office precisely on account of their perceived moral and spiritual qualities. Like monks, bishops were also expected to be celibate. Given that deacons and presbyters were permitted to marry, this in practice meant that, especially in the East, episcopal office increasingly came to be filled by men with a background in, or experience of, monasticism. Episcopal office could mark the pinnacle of a new, Christian *cursus honorum* that began for many in a monastic cell. Not all achieved the transition from private devotion to public responsibility smoothly. The *Life* of the sixth-century St Nicholas of Sion, for instance, records that the hero of the work made such a hash of his time as Bishop of Myra in Lycia that he was allowed to return to his monastery, the prohibition of canon law notwithstanding.[36]

6.4 GREGORY THE GREAT BETWEEN EAST AND WEST

The key paradox that bishops such as Nicholas, of monastic background and vocation but with public obligations, had to address was how to live a life that was both active and contemplative. This was a major preoccupation of Nicholas'

---

[34] Gregory of Tours, *Histories*, VIII, 15.
[35] Rapp (2005), pp. 164–5.
[36] ibid., p. 298.

fellow sixth-century bishop, Pope Gregory I.[37] In many ways Gregory's personal history, writings, and concerns encapsulate much of what was happening not only to episcopal office in the sixth and seventh centuries but also to Christianity itself. Gregory stands at the crossroads of both Eastern and Western developments and can be seen to have enunciated issues that were fundamental to the spiritual concerns of his age. Born in Rome *c*.550 to wealthy parents of senatorial rank, Gregory belonged to the final vestiges of the Roman aristocratic establishment whose interests had been so profoundly shaken and dislocated by the Gothic wars. As was appropriate to his background and rank, Gregory received a classical education as a young man, inherited his father's house on the Caelian Hill, and played an active part in the administration of the city.[38] In 573 he even served as Urban Prefect of Rome—the city's highest civil administrative post.

The following year, however, Gregory responded to a deep-rooted spiritual calling. Selling his family estates in Sicily, he used the proceeds to found a number of monasteries and to assist those in need. His family villa on the Caelian Hill he likewise turned into a monastery, dedicated to St Andrew, where Gregory himself became a monk, following a tradition of aristocratic monastic repose and contemplation that stretched back in the Latin world to Cassiodorus and Augustine. After some five years in his monastic cell, Gregory was summoned by the then Bishop of Rome to join the priesthood. Ordained deacon, he initially served in his native city, before being sent in 579 as Papal representative, or *apocrisarius*, to Constantinople, where he engaged in a public theological disputation over the nature of the Resurrection with the Patriarch Eutychius. By 587 Gregory had returned to Rome, and in 590 he was elected its bishop.

On one level, therefore, Gregory was the aristocratic bishop *par excellence*. His Gallic senatorial contemporary, Gregory of Tours, was a figure of rather lowly origins by comparison. When, as Pope, we encounter Gregory facing down the Langobardic threat, arranging for the city's food supply, or showing concern for the management of Papal estates in Sicily, Sardinia, and beyond, we see him in many ways simply returning to the sorts of duties that would previously have concerned him as Urban Prefect or as the young head of an aristocratic household. Indeed, the letters of Gregory concerning the day-to-day administration of the *Patrimonium Sancti Petri*—the great landholdings of the Roman Church—preserve some of the best evidence that survives for a late-Roman landowner at work, instructing stewards, responding to petitions, and intervening in disputes.

Gregory's palpable sense of *noblesse oblige* reveals a profoundly conservative and aristocratic mindset. That conservatism was also evident with respect to his political vision, both in terms of secular and ecclesiastical authority. Gregory's letters to emperors, kings, patriarchs, and bishops reveal a man very much at ease with the established constitution of both empire and Church. Thus it has been noted that 'whereas the emperor is always addressed as the Pope's "most supreme lord" . . . barbarian rulers, kings, dukes, and so forth are his "most excellent", or "most

---

[37] R. A. Markus, *Gregory the Great and His World* (Cambridge, 1997).
[38] G. R. Evans, *The Thought of Gregory the Great* (Cambridge, 1986).

glorious sons".[39] Gregory perceived a hierarchy of rulers over which the Emperor in Constantinople sat supreme: 'his political imagery... is the old image of the world dominated by Rome.... The Empire—the Empire of Justinian and his immediate successors—were both the major sphere of the Pope's activities and the permanent backdrop of all his thoughts.'[40]

As far as ecclesiastical politics were concerned, although Gregory was aware that at Chalcedon the Bishop of Rome had been accorded a primacy of honour amongst the leaders of the Church (as heir to St Peter), 'first among equals' alongside the Patriarchs of Antioch, Alexandria, Constantinople, and Jerusalem, his emphasis was on equality rather than primacy. When the Patriarch of Constantinople adopted the epithet 'ecumenical' (or 'world') patriarch, on the basis that Constantinople was the 'ecumenical' capital, Gregory berated him for offending the collective dignity of the apostolic Patriarchs as a whole, rather than that of Rome alone.[41] Although a man of deep theological conviction, Gregory's classical background inevitably showed through: when attempting to persuade the Emperor Maurice to intervene in the 'ecumenical' dispute, he could not help but slip in the Ciceronian exclamation *O tempora! O mores!* ('O the times! O the manners!').[42] It is perhaps true that in Gregory's correspondence we see him playing a more active role in secular affairs than some of his predecessors had done, but this was not due to any great Papal 'strategy' of world domination on his part. Rather, it was because objective circumstance demanded it: Gregory negotiated with the Langobards in the absence of imperial military assistance because he had no choice; as bishop, he increasingly had to take up the administrative slack left by the crumbling of civic institutions. He did no more, and no less, than his fellow bishops in fifth-century Gaul or seventh-century Syria and Egypt had done or would do in similar circumstances. Likewise, theologically, he was very much a churchman of his age, albeit one possessed of an exceptional mind and an especially keen sense of vocation.

Gregory's return to the world after his life in the cloister troubled him deeply. In 590, for example, he wrote to an old friend in Constantinople: 'When you described the sweetness of deep contemplation you stirred again my groans over my ruin, for I heard what I have lost inwardly; although outwardly I have ascended—undeservedly—to the high point of rule, rainclouds of sorrow blind the eyes of my mind. For I reflect, crashing down from the high point of my peace, to what a low point of outward advancement I have climbed.'[43] The point is reiterated throughout Gregory's writings, and especially his *Book of Pastoral Care* (*Liber Regulae Pastoralis*), written shortly after his accession to the See of Rome. In this work, Gregory sought to set out how the bishop should best advance the spiritual development of his congregation: how to preach, how to encourage, and

---

[39] R. A. Markus, 'Gregory the Great's Europe', in *idem., From Augustine to Gregory the Great* (London, 1983), XV, p. 29.
[40] ibid., p. 22.
[41] ibid., pp. 30–33.
[42] Gregory the Great, *Register*, V, 37.
[43] ibid., I, 6; Evans (1986), p. 123.

how to restrain, without himself falling prey to pride or vainglory. It is a work keenly aware of the moral pitfalls inherent in leadership, and one that in essence constitutes an exhortation to Christian *praxis*: the necessary unity of reading, contemplation, and action. It reveals a keen and pressing determination that the leadership of the Church should be morally fit to lead the faithful to salvation.

One of the reasons why this appears to have been such an urgent issue is that, like many sixth- and early seventh-century Christians, Gregory's thought was informed by a starkly apocalyptic sensibility. Since at least the early third century, a widespread view had established itself in Christian circles that the world would last for about six thousand years. The *Book of Psalms* had declared that a thousand years to mankind were as a day to the Lord (*Psalms*: 90.4). On the basis that the world had been created in six days, and that God had rested on the seventh, it was agreed that the world would exist for six 'cosmic days'. Christian chroniclers, tracing the generations as enumerated in the Bible, and matching them up against the history of Greece and Rome where this was possible, had come to a consensus that the world had been created, in modern terminology, *c*.5500 BC. Accordingly, the year 500 AD (*annus mundi* 6000—six thousand years since Creation) marked the dawning of the Last Day.[44] There was, therefore, a 'structural' or 'computational' reason for the ever more marked apocalypticism that we encounter from the reign of the Eastern Roman emperor Anastasius onwards. But this textually driven sense of the imminence of the *eschaton* (or 'the End') was palpably confirmed, in the eyes of contemporaries, by the violently disordered and chaotic events of the age: barbarian invasions, earthquake, plague. Mankind was confronting the vale of tears, which heralded the imminent arrival of the Antichrist as foretold in the Bible. Accordingly, it was a matter of grave urgency to Gregory that mankind be prepared for Divine Judgement. It was probably a combination of his political conservatism and this grim apocalypticism that informed what might otherwise appear an unexpected initiative on Gregory's part: his decision to send a mission to Kent (which, as we have seen, arrived in 597). From Gregory's Roman, aristocratic perspective, lowland Britain was the only part of the 'world' (meaning the Roman world) to have fallen out of the hands of the Church. The evangelisation of the region was, accordingly, imperative: it might even have been regarded as the necessary precondition for Christ's return to mankind.[45]

It is in his apprehension of the impending Apocalypse that Gregory can most obviously be seen to belong to a broader theological culture that embraced the East as much as it did the West. His engagement with debates that stretched beyond Rome went beyond that, however. As important research has revealed, in one of his other works, the *Dialogues*, or *Miracles of the Italian Fathers*, Gregory engages in a careful and highly sophisticated defence of key aspects of contemporary Neo-Chalcedonian Christian practice and doctrine (i.e. as defined at the Council of Constantinople of 553) that were being challenged both within the Church and beyond it: the belief that the soul could exist separately from the body, and that, as a

---

[44] C. Mango, *Byzantium: The Empire of New Rome* (London, 1983), p. 204.
[45] R. A. Markus, 'Gregory the Great and a Papal Missionary Strategy', in Markus (1983), XI.

result, there existed an afterlife; that, in the afterlife, the souls of Saints were active and could be enjoined to intervene with God on our behalf or to effect miracles here on earth; and that prayers for the souls of the dead could alleviate their burden in the hereafter.[46] What is interesting is that the debates that Gregory here addresses can be seen to have been taking place at around the same time, and in very similar terms, in Constantinople, Palestine, and further afield still, amongst the Christian populations of Persia.[47] Gregory's *Dialogues* thus form part of a struggle for hearts and minds that reached beyond the frontiers even of the Roman Empire at its height.

At the same time, however, Gregory was a very Latin figure. To some extent this emerges in his *Book of Pastoral Care*, a work that addresses a field—that of pastoral theology—of which there appears to have been little conception in the Greek-speaking East. This was perhaps a reflection of the divergent intellectual legacies of Greco-Roman antiquity: when we turn to the acts and decrees of the Council of Chalcedon, or of the Second Council of Constantinople, we encounter a speculative theology, informed by the vocabulary, nuances, and attitudes of a long tradition of Greek speculative philosophy. In Gregory's pastoral theology, by contrast, we see a more Latin concern for practicalities and basics, the theological equivalent of the engineering and law upon which the older Rome's intellectual credentials had ultimately rested.

Gregory's 'Latinism' is at its most discernible, however, in the praise that he lavishes upon the early sixth-century figure of St Benedict of Nursia in Book Three of his *Dialogues*. Benedict is described by Gregory as having lived the life of a Christian hermit or solitary before founding a monastery at Monte Cassino and writing a *Rule* for monks, which Gregory lauds as 'remarkable for its discretion and its clarity of language'.[48] Not least by virtue of Gregory's recommendation, the *Rule* was to go on to dominate the monastic life of the Middle Ages. Its appeal to Gregory, however, was perhaps more subtle than the *Dialogues* let on. The monastic ideal as it radiated westwards from the ascetic communities of Syria, Palestine, and Egypt was one that carried with it a strongly perfectionist message; that it really was possible, in this life, to rid oneself of the blemish of sin and so begin to regain the state that Adam had lost at the Fall. In the 540s, for example, the Egyptian Barsanuphius wrote to reassure his monks, stricken with anxiety at the first ravages of the bubonic plague, that 'There are many who are imploring the mercy of God, and certainly no one is more a lover of mankind than He, but He does not wish to show mercy, for the mass of sins committed in the world stand in His way. There are, however, three men who are perfect before God, who have transcended the measure of human beings and who have received the power to bind and to loose, to remit our faults or to retain them. . . . Thanks to their prayers, God

---

[46] M. Dal Santo, 'Gregory the Great and Debate Concerning the Cult of the Saints in the Early Byzantine Mediterranean and its Hinterland During the Later Sixth and Seventh Centuries' (Cambridge University Ph.D. dissertation, 2008).

[47] ibid.

[48] Gregory the Great, *Dialogues*, III, 36.

will chastise with mercy.'⁴⁹ In the somewhat different theological environment of Africa and Italy, such perfectionism smacked of the heresy of Pelagianism that St Augustine of Hippo, the great father of the Latin-speaking Church, had gone to such lengths to extirpate in the early fifth century. To Augustine, whom Gregory revered, such doctrines of perfectibility reeked of the sin of pride and belied an ignorance of the depth of Man's fall. Mankind could not be reconciled to God simply by an act of will.

It is instructive, then, to note that the *Rule of St Benedict* (even when compared to other *Rules* circulating in the West at around the same time), whilst acknowledging the enormous spiritual authority of the Eastern fathers, conveys a much more restrained and pragmatic sense of what could realistically be expected of those setting out on the monastic journey. Its focus, as with Gregory's *Pastoral Care*, is on getting the basics right, sorting out the practicalities of communal living, stability, and routine—the externalities that needed to be taken firmly in hand before the inner journey could begin. The *Rule* describes itself as 'this little rule for beginners' (*hanc minimam incohationum regulam*). Spiritually, its emphasis is on humility and selflessness: 'the first rule of humility is obedience without delay'.⁵⁰ The monastic life described is austere, but it is not gratuitously or ostentatiously so—spiritual pride is to be avoided at all costs. Such a life offered a path that could be followed by any man of calling, and not just the *virtuosi* whose remarkable achievements were described in the Eastern literature. In short, the *Rule* appropriates the ascetic and monastic traditions of the East, but infuses them with a strongly Augustinian pessimism. Herein, ultimately, lay its appeal to Gregory.

6.5 DISCORDANT VOICES

'Whilst other popes devoted themselves to the task of building of churches, and adorning them with gold and silver, his prime concern was the saving of souls': such, looking back from the eighth century, was the Venerable Bede's assessment of the pontificate of Gregory the Great.⁵¹ Partly by virtue of Gregory's exertions, as well as those of the imperial authorities for whom, as we have seen, missionary activity played an important role in military and diplomatic strategy, the world of c.600 was one in which an ongoing process of Christianisation was extending itself geographically, whilst at the same time sinking deeper roots in those areas where Christianity already had a presence.⁵² It was in this period, for example, that the evangelisation of rural communities in the West began in earnest.⁵³ As a result, it was a world where, as one distinguished historian has put it, there was a 'draining

---

⁴⁹ Brown (1995), p. 58—they are named as John of Rome (probably meaning Constantinople, or 'New Rome'), Elias at Corinth, and an unnamed third in Jerusalem.
⁵⁰ *Regula Benedicti*, ch. 73; ch. 5.
⁵¹ Bede, *Historia Ecclesiastica*, II, 1.
⁵² P. Brown, 'Christendom c.600' in T. F. X. Noble and J. M. Smith (eds.), *The Cambridge History of Christianity: Early Medieval Christianities c.600–c.1100* (Cambridge, 2008), pp. 1–20.
⁵³ Wood (1981), p. 85.

away' of the secular, with religious identities increasingly emerging to the fore of men's social imagination.[54]

This phenomenon was to have pronounced implications for those who came to find themselves classed as outsiders in Christian society, such as pagans, Jews, and those of whose sexual practices the Church disapproved. Over the course of the period from the late fourth to seventh centuries, for example, as the East Roman state adopted a more marked Christian identity, the large Jewish communities of the Near East began to show signs of growing alienation from the empire. In southern Arabia, as we saw in Chapter Four, the Persians pointedly sought to mobilise Jewish communities as a counterweight to Roman and Christian influence. Within the Roman Empire itself, Jewish elites progressively disengaged from the Hellenic high culture that they had previously held in common with their pagan and Christian counterparts; in its stead we see a reassertion of Jewish confessional identity.[55] In Visigothic Spain the royal authorities attempted to galvanise their Christian subjects through the promulgation of increasingly shrill anti-Jewish legislation.[56] As for classical pagans, Justinian's closure of the Academy in Athens in 529, and his crackdown on pagan elements within the governing classes (who were banned from holding governmental posts), marked the final phase in the struggle between Christianity and what had once been regarded as Rome's proper religion. In 540 the temple to Isis in Philae, southern Egypt, was forcibly closed by the imperial army.[57] Homosexuals likewise bore the brunt of the Emperor's Christianising measures, suffering forced castration and public humiliation on the streets of Constantinople.[58]

It is important to realise, however, that even by the year 700, Christianisation was by no means complete in those areas under Christian rule and there continued to be many who, in Bede's terms, were not interested in having their souls saved. Nowhere and at no social level did Christianisation go unchallenged. This is at its most evident on the level of the surviving curial elites of the cities of the eastern Mediterranean. Irrespective of the legislation of Christian emperors, so long as urban life continued in a recognisably classical form, and for so long as cities continued to serve as centres of elite residence, the great *poleis* and *metropoleis* of the eastern Mediterranean were able to continue to function as centres for the replication of classical Greco-Roman elite culture, allowing for the survival of modes of thought and traditions of sexual and moral conduct largely alien to the Christian Church.

Greco-Roman elite culture, for example, had long demonstrated itself to be perfectly at ease with the phenomenon of sexual attraction and activity between men: provided a Roman elite male did not adopt a passive role with respect to a social inferior or junior, such conduct was perfectly respectable, regardless of the

---

[54] R. A. Markus, *The End of Ancient Christianity* (Cambridge, 1998).
[55] N. de Lange, 'The Jews in Justinian's Empire', in M. Maas (ed.), *The Cambridge Companion to the Age of Justinian* (Cambridge, 2005).
[56] R. Collins, *Early Medieval Spain: Unity in Diversity* (1983), pp. 129–45.
[57] Procopius, *Wars*, I, 19, 35.
[58] Procopius, *Secret History*, 11, 34–6.

denunciations of emperors and churchmen. The Emperor Constantine's son, Constans, for example, had notoriously kept a sort of male harem of barbarian prisoners of war.[59] The sixth-century bureaucrat and scholar John the Lydian alleged that Justinian's chief finance officer, John the Cappadocian, regularly had sexual intercourse with his male slaves, in which, shockingly, he allowed himself to be penetrated.[60] Such 'liberal' behaviour persisted to the end of our period and beyond.[61]

Likewise the survival (and, in the sixth century, the revival) of classical intellectual traditions did much to hinder and curtail the Church's ability to capture men's imaginations. The great Greek historian Procopius, for example, felt able to dismiss all of the Emperor Justinian's Christologically focused religious policies with the aside that he would not discuss Christology in any detail, as to him it was 'an insane folly to investigate the nature of God': the mind of man found it hard enough to comprehend human affairs, he noted, without attempting to explain divine ones.[62] Throughout his writings, Procopius reveals an attitude of tolerant scepticism towards religion, criticising fanaticism in all its forms.[63] The Church did not have everything its own way. In spite of Justinian's closure of the Athenian Academy, for example, there occurred in the sixth century a major revival of philosophy, particularly Aristotelean thought: a phenomenon associated in the Latin West with the figure of Boethius and in the Greek East with John Philoponus, who sought to marry Aristotelean physics with Christian theology. In spite of Philoponus' best efforts, however, this revival of Aristotelean philosophy caused the ecclesiastical authorities considerable difficulty. Aristotle had taught that the human soul could not exist without the body; if that was the case, how could the soul of a man possibly survive after his death, and what was the point of praying to saints, whose mortal remains had long since turned to dust?[64] These were challenges that Gregory the Great in Rome, as well as his contemporary the presbyter Eustratius in Constantinople, were obliged to confront head-on in their writings.[65] The survival of Galenic medical traditions occasioned similar difficulties, especially when it was pointed out how many 'miracles' of healing achieved by saints and holy men appeared to be the result of prescribing herbal treatments derived from the *corpora* of Galenic medicine: behind many miracles, it was claimed, were straightforwardly material explanations.[66] Intellectually generated scepticism towards the cult of the saints was a notable feature of the age.

---

[59] Aurelius Victor, *de Caesaribus*, 41.
[60] John Lydus, *De Magistratibus*, 3.62.
[61] J. Boswell, *Christianity, Social Tolerance, and Homosexuality* (Chicago, 1981).
[62] Procopius, *Wars*, V, 3.6–9.
[63] P. Sarris, 'Introduction', in G. Williamson and P. Sarris, *Procopius: The Secret History* (London, 2007).
[64] Dal Santo (2008).
[65] M. Dal Santo, 'Gregory the Great and Eustratius of Constantinople: The Dialogues on the Miracles of the Italian Fathers as a Justification of the Cult of the Saints', *Journal of Early Christian Studies* 17.4 (2009), pp. 421–58.
[66] P. Booth, 'John Moschus, Sophronius Sophista, and Maximus Confessor Between East and West' (Cambridge University Ph.D. dissertation, 2007).

Nor did the conversion of elites run entirely smoothly in those areas where Christianity was a more recent introduction. In Britain, as we have seen, the conversion of Æthelberht of Kent was followed by the (admittedly short-lived) apostasy of his son, Eadbald. In 632 the Northumbrian Christian convert Edwin died in battle against the pagan Penda of Mercia. When, the following year, the throne of Northumbria was once more seized by a Christian, the new occupant, Oswald, had learned his faith from Irish monks, to whom he turned in preference to the representatives of the Roman mission.

Scepticism and hostility to the Church and its teachings, however, were not limited to the level of elites. Peasant attitudes to the Church in general are likely to have been shaped by its development as a landowning institution from the fourth century onwards. Through imperial grants, pious donations, and straightforward opportunism, bishops and—ultimately—monasteries had come to acquire extensive estates across the Mediterranean world and its northwestern appendages.[67] By the late sixth century, for example, the See of Rome was probably the wealthiest landowner in Italy.[68] By Gregory's day Papal estates stretched from Gaul to north Africa and included vast holdings within Campania.[69] Nor was it simply the great patriarchal sees that built up extensive property portfolios: by the sixth century, for example, the Church may have owned more land around the Middle Egyptian city of Oxyrhynchus than the regionally predominant aristocratic household of the Flavii Apiones, members of which held high office in Constantinople under Justinian and dominated local politics.[70]

The growing involvement of the Church and its personnel in agrarian social relations is likely to have had marked implications for how elements of the peasantry viewed their ecclesiastical masters. That life labouring on the estates of the Church was regarded as far from entirely optimal is strongly suggested by a letter of Gregory the Great, in which he complains of the flight of tied agricultural labourers (*coloni adscripticii*) from Papal estates in Sicily. Gregory fulminates that these peasants, though bound by their legal status (*ex condicione ligati*) to work the Church's lands, had the temerity to behave 'as if they are in control of their own lives and are free' (*quasi sui arbitrii [sunt] ac liberi*).[71]

As we saw in Chapter Two, exploitation stood at the heart of relations between landowners and peasants in late antique and early medieval society. Whether the landowner in question was a secular magnate, the Church, or the Crown, such exploitation is likely to have bred animosity and generated resistance.[72] Accordingly, it should come as little surprise that the sources record numerous examples of

---

[67] Rapp (2005), pp. 215–19. For what follows, I draw heavily on P. Sarris, M. Dal Santo, and P. Booth (eds.), *An Age of Saints? Power, Conflict, and Dissent in Early Medieval Christianity* (Leiden, 2011).
[68] Markus (1997), p. 112.
[69] Booth (2007), p. 128.
[70] E. R. Hardy, *The Large Estates of Byzantine Egypt* (New York, 1931), p. 44; Sarris (2006), pp. 17–24.
[71] Gregory the Great, *Register*, IX, 129.
[72] Sarris (2006), pp. 222–34.

peasants pointedly and violently contesting the demands of the Church as a landowning institution. Peasant resistance to what were perceived to be the unreasonable demands of the Church as landowner, for example, is chronicled in the seventh-century *Life of Theodore of Sykeon*, in which it is stated that, as bishop, Theodore:

> used to entrust the administration and the governance of the properties belonging to the Church to men of the city and injustice was done to the peasants; in one case, for instance, he had entrusted them to a leading citizen (*protikor*) of Anastasioupolis, Theodosius, by name; and he continually acted unjustly and defrauded the peasants. So they came to the servant of Christ and met him in tears, and he, moved with sympathy, grieved over them, for his holy and sensitive soul could not bear to see any one in trouble. He summoned Theodosius and with many admonitions besought him to cease his acts of injustice against the peasants. But Theodosius again invented some pretexts against the villagers and continued in his unjust treatment, whereupon in one of the villages, called Eukraous, when he was proceeding to his usual acts of injustice, the peasants of the village were roused to uncontrollable anger; they all gathered together with a common purpose, armed themselves with various weapons and swords and catapults, and took up their stand outside the village to meet him, and threatened him with death if he did not turn back and leave them.[73]

Similar evidence for hostility to the Church and its agents emerges from the West. The *Chronicle of Hydatius*, for example, records how in 449 a band of peasant rebels, or *bacaudae*, under the leadership of a certain Basilius, entered the Iberian city of Turiasso and 'killed the bishop Leo in his church'.[74] A still more revealing episode is recorded for sometime in the early eighth century in the Frankish marchlands. According to the *Passio Thrudperti*, the holy man Thrutpert was granted an estate in the region of the Sornegau by a sympathetic lord. Thrutpert proceeded, however, to work his *coloni* so hard that ultimately they could bear no more, and one of them crept up to him as he slept one afternoon and stabbed him to death.[75]

At the heart of the acts of violence depicted in the *Life of Theodore of Sykeon* or the *Passio Thrudperti* were clearly economic issues and complaints. That said, peasant hostility to the Church and its representatives in the early Middle Ages is likely to have been further fuelled by resentment at the introduction of a new religion that was, for the most part, imposed from above.[76] This is vividly illustrated by Bede, writing in the eighth century, in his *Life of Cuthbert*. In the third chapter of this work, he describes how a body of monks from a monastery near the mouth of the River Tyne, who had set off by raft to collect some timber, found themselves being pulled out to sea. Bede continues:

---

[73] *Life of Theodore of Sykeon*, ch. 76; E. Dawes and N. H. Baynes, *Three Byzantine Saints: Contemporary Biographies of St Daniel the Stylite, St Theodore of Sykeon, and St John the Almsgiver* (Oxford, 1948), p. 139.
[74] E. A. Thompson, 'Peasant Revolts in Late Roman Gaul and Spain', *Past and Present* 2 (1952), pp. 11–23, p. 16; Hydatius, *Chron.*, Sub anno, 449.
[75] *Passio Thrudperti*, ed. B. Krusch, *M.G.H. S.R.M.*, IV, pp. 352–63, chs. 4–5, pp. 358–60.
[76] B. Dumézil, *Conversion et liberté dans les royaumes barbares d'Occident* (Paris, 2005).

On the other bank of the river stood no small crowd of the common people, and he [Cuthbert] was standing among them. These were watching the rafts on which the monks [in the monastery] were sadly gazing, being carried so far out to sea that they looked like five tiny birds riding on the waves, for there were five rafts. Thereupon they began to jeer at the monks' manner of life, on the grounds that they were deservedly suffering, seeing that they despised the common laws of mortals and put forth new and unknown rules of life. Cuthbert stopped the insults of the blasphemers, saying, 'Brethren, what are you doing, cursing those whom you see even now being carried away to destruction? Would it not be better and more kindly to pray to the Lord for their safety rather than to rejoice over their dangers?' But they fumed against him with boorish minds and boorish words and said: 'Let no man pray for them, and may God have no mercy on any one of them, for they have robbed men of their old ways of worship, and how the new worship is to be conducted, nobody knows.'[77]

In the early medieval West, moreover, animosity towards holy men, monks, and clergy was given added piquancy by broader processes of cultural change and, in particular, by the militarisation of elite culture. The extrovert, military culture of the emergent elites of the Romano-Germanic successor kingdoms of the fifth, sixth, and seventh centuries, with its emphasis on martial prowess, boastful and exuberant virility, sumptuous feasting and general excess, was in many ways the exact antithesis of the concept of the ideal man embodied in the ascetic self-denial, restraint, and humility of the model Christian holy man, bishop, or monk.[78] The dissonance between such markedly divergent models of masculinity and such contrasting visions of the ideal man inevitably led to tension and, at times, conflict. The celibate bishop, in the company, perhaps, of monastic attendants, must have seemed a strange and alien sight to the eyes of many an early medieval warlord. Gregory of Tours, in the late sixth century, recounts how a certain Palladius, Count of Javols, barracked the Bishop Parthenius at the court of the Frankish king Sigibert: 'Palladius accused the bishop of being soft and effeminate (*mollem episcopum effeminatum*). "Where are all your little husbands," he declared, "with whom you live in such filthy debauchery?"'[79]

Resistance or hostility to the Church, its teachings, and representatives in the early Middle Ages was not limited, therefore, to the ranks of conservative intellectuals and classically minded *curiales*. Rather, the more the Church found itself politically institutionalised and economically embedded, the more the realities of social and economic relations on the ground are likely to have generated tension, animosity, and conflict, focused on the institution of the Church and its agents. As a result, the 'Christianisation' of the peasantry was probably a far more haphazard, piecemeal, and gradual process than is commonly supposed. Rather, there are for a long time likely to have been many who, like Bede's Northumbrians, would have been quite content to see their neighbourhood monks, and probably bishops and clergy too, drift slowly out to sea.

---

[77] B. Colgrave, (ed.), *Two Lives of St Cuthbert* (Cambridge, 1940), pp. 163–5.
[78] M. Rouche, 'Violence and Death', in P. Veyne (ed.), *A History of Private Life from Pagan Rome to Byzantium* (Cambridge, Mass., 1992), pp. 485–518.
[79] Gregory of Tours, *Histories*, IV, 39.

7
Heraclius, Persia, and Holy War

7.1 JUSTIN II, THE COURT ARISTOCRACY, AND THE EASTERN FRONT

As we saw in Chapter Five, the age of Justinian would long be regarded by commentators and kings as the apogee of the imperial office. The grandiose style of rule and autocratic language of power that Justinian and his advisers articulated were to exercise a strong influence over the ambitions of rulers not only in Constantinople, but throughout the commonwealth of Romano-Germanic *regna* that were gradually taking shape around the shores of the western Mediterranean and beyond. Justinian, in short, changed what it meant to rule.[1] Nowhere was the heightened scale of imperial ambitions (and their limitations) clearer than with respect to Justinian's ecclesiastical policies: the Second Council of Constantinople of 553 had, from the first, been a carefully stage-managed affair orchestrated by the imperial court—half Chalcedonian rally, half show-trial of the prevaricating Pope Vigilius, who had to be bullied into ratifying its decisions. Even many of the speeches of those attending the Council appear to have been penned by the imperial hand.[2] The determination of Justinian and his entourage to micro-manage the event stands in sharp contrast to the palpable chaos that had prevailed at the Council of Chalcedon just over a hundred years earlier.

Yet, as we have seen, Justinian was ultimately unable to carry the dissident congregations of Egypt and Syria with him. In spite of his most strident efforts, he bequeathed to posterity an imperial Church in which division was increasingly hardening into schism, as Miaphysite (or anti-Chalcedonian) bishops began to ordain their own 'orthodox' clergy and traditions of hostility became entrenched.[3] Justinian's legal, administrative, and provincial reforms likewise had served to heighten social tensions without curtailing the malfeasance of members of the provincial and senatorial aristocracy whose activities his legislation had targeted. At the end of the day, Justinian's regime found itself hamstrung by one insurmountable fact: at a provincial level, those whose misdemeanours his legislation sought to contain were the very same individuals on whom the Emperor was reliant for the imposition and application of his laws. As a result, contemporary East Roman perspectives on the Emperor's reign were far less admiring than later ones.

---

[1] A point first made to me by my pupil Mr Michael Humphreys of Pembroke College, Cambridge.
[2] See Price (2009).
[3] W. H. C. Frend, *The Rise of the Monophysite Movement* (Cambridge, 1972).

A plot against the Emperor was discovered as late as 562 (chiefly orchestrated by a coterie of bankers from whom he may have exacted forced loans), whilst the Church historian Evagrius noted his death with the pithy summary: 'thus indeed Justinian, after filling absolutely everywhere with confusion and turmoil and collecting the wages for this at the conclusion to his life, passed over to the lowest place of punishment'.[4]

The succession to Justinian was carefully arranged at court: the Emperor's death in 565 was initially kept secret until preparations were in place for the acclamation of his nephew, Justin II, who appears to have been strongly supported by members of the Constantinopolitan Senate.[5] Prior to the moment of coronation, before the eyes of the assembled imperial court, the Patriarch of Constantinople 'blessed [Justin] as he stood there and praying to the Lord of heaven, he asked him to sanctify the head of the Emperor with the holy diadem'.[6] This sounds very like the patriarchal prayer of coronation preserved in an eighth-century Byzantine manuscript, according to which the Heavenly Father was implored: 'Lord our God, King of kings and Lord of lords. You who, through the intermediary of your prophet Samuel, chose your servant David and, by unction, made him king of your people Israel, hear also today our supplication, look down from your holy dwelling on high on us who are unworthy, deign to anoint with the oil of grace your faithful servant ...'.[7] Justin was then cheered by the senators and led to his throne.[8]

The new Emperor was keen both to draw a line under the old regime and to shore up the primarily aristocratic basis of his support. Accordingly, from the first we see him adopting a stridently hostile tone with respect to his deceased uncle and his policies, declaring in an early law that he had 'found the treasury burdened with many debts and reduced to utter exhaustion', a situation which, he argued, threatened to cripple the empire militarily.[9] In spite of such straitened circumstances, Justin nevertheless felt able to reward great landowners with a tax rebate, repay those bankers at whose expense Justinian had amassed debts, and set his predecessor's programme of provincial reforms into reverse.[10] In an extraordinary measure that did much to consolidate aristocratic control at the grassroots of East Roman society, Justin II decreed in 569 that henceforth governors were not to be sent out from the imperial capital, to serve as the Emperor's 'eyes and ears' in the world beyond Constantinople, but rather were to be elected by the great

---

[4] Evagrius Scholasticus, *Ecclesiastical History*, tr. M. Whitby (Liverpool, 2005), p. 254. For the plot, see discussion in M. Whitby, 'The Occasion of Paul the Silentiary's *Ekphrasis* of S. Sophia', *Classical Quarterly* 35 (1985), pp. 215–28; Theophanes, *Chronicle*, tr. C. Mango and R. Scott (Oxford, 1997), pp. 349–51.

[5] Corippus, *In Laudem Iustini Minoris Libri Quattor*, tr. A. Cameron (Oxford, 1976), p. 131, n., and p. 165, n.

[6] ibid., II, pp. 160–65.

[7] Bibliotheca Vaticana, Barberini, gr. 336, fols. 176v–177r, ed. S. Parenti and E. Velkovska, *L'Euchologio Barberini gr.336 (ff.1–263)* (Rome, 1995); Rapp (2010), pp. 190–91.

[8] Corippus, *In Laudem Iustini Minoris*, II, pp. 165–6.

[9] *J. Nov.*, 148 (proemium).

[10] ibid.; Theophanes, pp. 257–8; Corippus, *In Laudem Iustini Minoris*, II, 360–404. For the heightened importance of bankers in late antiquity, see Banaji (2006).

landowners and bishops of the provinces concerned.[11] In place of Justinian's antagonistic approach to the senatorial and provincial aristocracy, Justin II deliberately courted their admiration and sought to advance their interests in a manner that had not been seen since the days of Anastasius. As Justin is reported to have declared to the Senate upon his accession, although he, as Emperor, represented the head of the 'body politic', they—the senators—constituted 'the limbs nearest to me, the great hope of our reign'. 'You,' he went on to inform them, 'are the breast and the arms of this head, whose counsels and toils the state used to subdue peoples and conquer kingdoms. The highest responsibility for everything is entrusted to me. But because it is our task to govern the subject world, we give to you the care of the earth.... Govern the lower orders, as it is fitting for the true fathers of the Empire to govern.'[12] The Emperor was taken at his word: at a provincial level, landowners, bishops, and the agents of the state combined to claw back the gains in living standards and pay that peasants and the urban poor had come to enjoy in the wake of plague-induced labour shortages.[13] It was clear that the age of Justin II was to be driven primarily by 'seigneurial' and aristocratic concerns.

In particular, senatorial attitudes at court and conservative opinion more generally would do much to shape Justin II's foreign policy. From the outset of his reign, Justinian had appreciated the merits of subsidy diplomacy; buying peace with Persia in 532 so as to free up resources for his western campaigns, or drawing the Avars into the empire's diplomatic embrace by employing them to take on the burgeoning Slav threat to imperial possessions in the Balkans. This policy, however, had elicited unswerving hostility from authors with a conservative frame of mind, such as Procopius, to whom it represented a profligate and gratuitous waste of other people's money. It was one thing to squeeze landowners for taxes, but then giving the revenues away to barbarians simply added insult to injury. Thus, in a vivid passage, Procopius lampooned the way in which Justinian had:

> never ceased lavishing great gifts of money on all barbarians, those of the east and those of the west and those to the north and to the south, as far as the inhabitants of Britain—in fact all the nations of the inhabited world, even those of whom we had never heard before, but the name of whose race we learned only when we first saw them. For they, of their own accord, on learning the nature of the man, kept streaming from all the earth into Byzantium in order to reach him. And he, with no hesitation, but overjoyed at this situation, and thinking it a stroke of good fortune to be dishing out the wealth of the Romans and flinging it to the barbarians, or, for that matter, the surging waves of the sea, day after day kept sending them away, one after the other, purses stuffed with money.[14]

Under Justin II, this policy was brought to an abrupt halt. As we saw in Chapter Five, the Church historian John of Ephesus records that the Avar embassy sent to

---

[11] *J. Nov.*, 149; Sarris (2006), p. 223.
[12] Corippus, *In Laudem Iustini Minoris*, II, 195–217 (abridged).
[13] Sarris (2006), pp. 222–7.
[14] Procopius, *The Secret History*, 19.13–16.

negotiate with the new Emperor was informed that Roman tribute was a thing of the past and curtly dismissed.[15] A similar message was conveyed to the Arab tribesmen on whom the empire depended for the security of its desert frontier to the east. As the Roman envoy John informed Shah Khusro upon Justin's accession: 'We are unwilling to give anything in future to the Saracens.... The present emperor wishes to be an object of greatest fear to all.'[16]

It was with respect to relations with Persia, however, that Justin II most strenuously sought to make his mark and distinguish his regime from that of his uncle. As we saw in Chapter Three, since the outbreak of the war over Amida in 502–3, East Roman policy towards the empire's Sasanian rivals had been characterised principally by an attitude of aggressive defensiveness: Anastasius, Justin I, and Justinian had all sought to strengthen the empire's eastern defences, minimising vulnerability to Persian assault while bolstering the empire's military and diplomatic position in Arabia and the Caucasus. Such policies clearly threatened Persian interests (in particular the prestige of the Sasanian ruling dynasty) but, although the status of Nisibis was occasionally raised in diplomatic negotiations, the emperors in Constantinople had little interest in territorial aggrandisement at Persia's expense *per se*. Unprovoked campaigns of aggressive warfare were the preserve of Persia; the Romans sought to do little more than contain them. Again, this was a policy that aggrieved conservative commentators such as Procopius, who lambasted Justinian's general Belisarius for failing to press home advantages in the field against the Persians and advance on the capital of the shahs at Ctesiphon.[17]

Justin II, by contrast, was determined to adopt a far more belligerent stance. The negotiations of 562, as we have seen, had signalled a significant consolidation of the East Roman position in the western Caucasus, with the Persians formally conceding control of the principality of Lazica. Only the status of the frontier Laz dependency of Suania remained open to question, with Khusro presumably keeping the issue alive as a face-saving measure. The Persians, after all, had not been defeated in the field. Rather, their disengagement from the western Caucasus had been dictated primarily by the core strategic geography of the Sasanian Empire and the need to prioritise containment of the new Turk threat from the north-east.

In response to the consolidation of Roman control in Lazica, as well as to Turk raids from across the mountains, in the late 560s the Persians attempted to bolster their own position in the central and eastern Caucasus by settling large numbers of Zoroastrian troops and their families in the predominantly Christian valleys of Persarmenia and Atropatene, and by locating a new military commander, or *marzban*, in the region. As seems to have happened in Iberia in the 520s, however, the settlement of Zoroastrian colonists in a predominantly Christian enclave aggravated local sensibilities and excited the ambitions of the Emperor in Constantinople. Ever since the days of Constantine, emperors had claimed an

[15] *The Third Part of the Ecclesiastical History of John Bishop of Ephesus*, p. 429.
[16] *The History of Menander the Guardsman*, 9.1, pp. 100–01.
[17] Procopius, *The Secret History*, 2, 25.

ecumenical duty to protect Christians in the Persian Empire from possible persecution. At the same time, disaffection on the part of the Persarmenian aristocracy, were it to lead to open revolt, would present Justin with the perfect opportunity for a campaign of territorial expansion, either in the Caucasus or Mesopotamia. Accordingly, when, in 570, the Armenian noble Vardan informed Justin of plans for an orchestrated uprising against Sasanian rule, and requested Roman support, he received a warm welcome and hearty encouragement.[18]

It is likely, however, that even before Vardan's embassy to Constantinople, Justin had already decided upon a major campaign in the East. A struggle for power with the Persians over control of southern Arabia had, by 570, resulted in the expulsion of the empire's Ethiopian allies from Himyar (the Yemen).[19] Most significantly of all, in late 568 or 569, a dispute had broken out between Persia and the Turk leader Sizabul over control of the highly lucrative silk route to China and the East.[20] Accordingly, the Turks had entered into negotiations with the Romans, proposing an anti-Persian alliance:[21] By 571 the Emperor was confident that a mutually beneficial Romano-Turk pact had been secured. This was to have far-reaching consequences. As Menander the Guardsman noted:

> There were many other reasons for war between the Romans and the Persians, but the Turks were the nation that most encouraged Justin to open hostilities against the Persians. For they . . . sent an embassy to Justin to urge him to fight with them against the Persians. They asked him to destroy, in concert with them, those hostile to both of them, and [so] to embrace the cause of the Turks. For in this way, with the Romans attacking from one direction and the Turks from another, the [state] of the Persians would be destroyed in the middle. Aroused by these hopes, Justin thought that the power of the Persians would easily be overthrown and annihilated. He therefore made every preparation to keep his friendship with the Turks as firm as possible.[22]

Between them, the Turks and the Persarmenians offered Justin the opportunity of inflicting real and lasting harm on Persian interests, and of covering himself and his regime with the glory that he evidently craved. It is a sign of the Emperor's confidence that, from an early stage, he set his sights on the prestige target of Nisibis.

The war opened in late summer of 571 when the Persarmenian aristocracy and the leadership of the Armenian Church rose up in revolt, receiving support from both the Romans and their Iberian co-religionists. Justin was quick to take advantage of this to reveal his wider ambitions. As the *Chronicle* of Michael the Syrian records:

> the Armenians revolted against the Persians and sought help from the Romans. And when the Romans helped the Armenians, they defeated the Persians. Khusro demanded that Justin return the Armenians to him . . . Justin replied, 'I will not deliver into your hands a Christian people which has forsaken the worship of demons and has sought refuge with me . . . and since you ask me for the country of the North [i.e.

---

[18] Greatrex and Lieu (2002), pp. 167–8.
[19] ibid., p. 137.
[20] On the economic significance of this, see Banaji (2006).
[21] *The History of Menander the Guardsman*, fragment 10.1, pp. 110–17.
[22] Greatrex and Lieu (2002), p. 137; Menander, fragment 13.5, pp. 146–7.

Armenia], so also we demand Nisibis; for it belonged to the Romans, and it was given to the Persians conditionally.'[23]

It would appear, however, that events in Persarmenia had acquired a momentum of their own, and that the revolt may in fact have broken out before the Romans were really in a position to take advantage of it. Only in the summer of 572 did the newly appointed *magister militum per Orientem*, Marcian, reach Mesopotamia, by which point it was too late in the campaigning season to initiate any significant acts of aggression.[24] It was not until the following spring that he was able to launch the assault on Nisibis that Justin had threatened. Not surprisingly, the Persians were now ready for them. 'The Persians', as one of our sources records, 'brought provisions to Nisibis and cut down the parks and gardens which were around the city, as far as a missile can be thrown. They expelled the Christians who were in the city and appraised the *shah* Khusro of the situation.'[25] As a result, the Roman siege failed and the imperial army retreated in disorder. Driving the dispirited Roman forces back, Khusro launched a rapid counter-offensive. While one division of his army struck into Syria, the shah led a second detachment against Dara, the jewel in the crown of Justinian's eastern defences. After a six-month siege, and amidst much bloodshed, Khusro's soldiers and saboteurs were finally able to overwhelm the city's defences, 'plundering the entire city and enslaving the population'.[26] Although the Romans had been able to make significant gains in Armenia and the wider Transcaucasus, Justin's Mesopotamian venture had ended in disaster. In response, we are told, the Emperor suffered a physical and mental collapse.[27]

Given how propitious the strategic outlook had appeared for the Romans *c.*570, this was a dramatic reversal of fortunes. Justin's failure may be ascribed to three factors. First, as we have seen, his ambitions were hampered by the autonomy and independence of the military lords of Armenia and the Transcaucasus, whose fluidity of loyalties had long served to destabilise Romano-Persian relations. Although Justin had been able to take advantage of events in Persarmenia, he had not been able to control or orchestrate them anything like as tightly as necessary in order to use them as a springboard for military success in Mesopotamia. Second, Justin's ideologically (and perhaps materially) driven refusal to pay military subsidies to the Arab warlords of the desert fringe was ultimately self-defeating. For it led to a rapid breakdown in relations with the Jafnid king al-Mundhir, the empire's long-standing Arab client in the region. Indeed, Justin had attempted to have the king assassinated after al-Mundhir had declined to provide him with assistance in 570. Unfortunately for the Emperor, the instructions for this assassination, which he had sent to his commander in the field, fell into al-Mundhir's hands. As a result, the Romans were denied Jafnid support in the crucial two or three years between

---

[23] Michael the Syrian, X, 1 (331–2a/282–3); see Greatrex and Lieu (2002), p. 140.
[24] Note the comments of John of Epiphania in Greatrex and Lieu (2002), p. 142.
[25] *Chronicon ad annum 1234*, 65 (Greatrex and Lieu [2002], p. 144).
[26] John of Epiphania, 5, in Greatrex and Lieu (2002), pp. 148–51, and Evagrius, *Ecclesiastical History*, V, 11.
[27] John of Epiphania, 5, in Greatrex and Lieu (2002), p. 151.

572 and 575. Although al-Mundhir might not have been able to secure the capture of Nisibis, he might have been able to prevent the fall of Dara.[28]

Third, and perhaps most significantly, in spite of the repeated promises that had been made since 568, there is no evidence of any significant mobilisation against the Persians on the part of the Turks. It is possible that the Turks were bought off with Sasanian silver. More probable, however, is that the Turks had never actually intended to mobilise in the first place. Rather, as the newly dominant power on the west Eurasian steppe, eager to consolidate and advance their position, it was in the evident interest of the Turks to encourage and initiate warfare between the two great sedentary empires to their south, locking them into a mutually debilitating state of conflict from which the Turks alone could expect to profit. The weaker their neighbours, after all, the easier it would be for the Turks to extract tribute from them; and the more preoccupied the Persians and Romans were with one another, the less likely either would be to focus their power on the Turks themselves. Precisely such a policy of predatory 'divide and rule' characterised contemporary relations between the Turks and the northern and southern kingdoms of China.[29] Correctly discerning the ideological predisposition of Justin's foreign policy, in short, it is arguable that the Turks had set him up. Their primary goal had been to engineer a balance of powerlessness between the two great sedentary empires of western Eurasia, and Justin had walked into their trap.

7.2 ROMAN-PERSIAN RELATIONS FROM TIBERIUS TO MAURICE

In 574 Sophia, the wife of the by now insane Emperor, took charge of negotiations with the Persians while the general Tiberius (who was appointed *Caesar* and regent) headed west to the Balkans to raise reinforcements.[30] The Persians were eager to have their dramatically strengthened position in Upper Mesopotamia recognised by treaty, while continuing to pursue warfare against the Romans and their allies in the Transcaucasus, where the major Roman gains of 571–3 were yet to be reversed. In the Transcaucasus both sides vied for the support of the nomad confederacies whose assistance promised to tip the balance of power towards one side or the other in what was becoming an increasingly protracted conflict. In spite of further Roman attempts to enlist the aid of the Turks in 576–7, the latter instead seized the Roman city of Bosporus in the Crimea, a vital imperial 'listening post' on the world of the steppe.

Crucially, however, in 576 the Romans and their Armenian allies were able to inflict a humiliating defeat on a Persian army led in person by Shah Khusro some

---

[28] For references see Greatrex and Lieu (2002), p.136. Al-Mundhir may also have been bought off by the Persians: see Whitby (1988), pp. 256–8.
[29] See T. Barfield, *The Perilous Frontier: Nomad Empires and China* (Oxford, 1989).
[30] Greatrex and Lieu (2002), p. 151.

distance to the west of the city of Melitene. The Armenians captured the queen, extinguished the shah's 'holy flame' which he took with him on campaign, and drowned his high priest.[31] These were potentially fatal blows to the prestige of a Sasanian ruler whose dynasty ultimately owed its legitimacy to its reputation for military prowess. As a result, Khusro passed a law that henceforth no Persian ruler was to lead an army on campaign in person.[32] The Romans took advantage of Persian disarray to launch a series of assaults on their positions in Upper Mesopotamia and finally to subdue the frontier territory of Suania, the king of which was captured by the Roman commander Romanus and led into captivity in Constantinople 'together with his treasury, his wife, and his children'.[33]

Inconclusive negotiations and repeated rounds of skirmishing in Upper Mesopotamia and the greater Caucasus continued into 579, when diplomatic endeavours were interrupted by the death of Khusro. The new Persian ruler, Hormizd IV, adopted an aggressive stance with respect to the Romans, who nevertheless just about managed to maintain the upper hand in Armenia.[34] At the same time, since 575, the Romans had been able to repair relations with al-Mundhir and the Jafnids, leading to a stiffening of resistance on the Eastern Roman Empire's southern desert flank, and some notable Jafnid victories against the Persians and their Nasrid Arab allies in 580 and 581.[35] This reconciliation, however, proved to be short-lived, and after a faltering of the Roman war machine in both Lower Mesopotamia and Persarmenia, in 582 al-Mundhir was arrested by the imperial authorities. As a result, his son, al-Nu'man, led a series of raids into Roman territory in both Syria and Palestine. Although al-Nu'man would subsequently come to heel, the Jafnids were never again to enjoy the same degree of unity and influence that they had acquired under al-Harith and al-Mundhir.[36]

In 582 Tiberius, who had become sole Emperor as Tiberius II upon Justin's death in 578, himself died, and the throne was ascended by the general Maurice, who had acted as Tiberius' commander-in-chief in the East. Unsurprisingly, therefore, the accession of Maurice heralded no significant alteration in the pattern of warfare on the eastern front. For the most part, the Romans maintained an edge over the Persians in the Transcaucasus, where the careful manipulation of Christian sentiment continued to draw many of the lords of the region into an essentially pro-Roman orbit. To the south, however, a further deterioration in the Roman position, associated with the implications of the loss of Dara and the ongoing fragmentation of Jafnid power, is discernible.[37] The imperial frontier zone stretching from Mesopotamia to the foothills of Armenia, which in about 500 had been characterised by a rough parity of power, was gradually spinning

---

[31] Greatrex and Lieu (2002), pp. 155–6.
[32] Theophylact Simocatta, *History*, III, 14.11.
[33] Greatrex and Lieu (2002), p. 158. For Suania, see John of Biclaro, *s.a.*, 576.
[34] Greatrex and Lieu (2002), p. 162.
[35] ibid., p. 153.
[36] ibid., p. 166.
[37] Michael the Syrian, X, 19; see Greatrex and Lieu (2002), p. 168.

out of control, with the Romans gaining advantage in the north and the Persians to the south.[38]

This deterioration in Rome's military position in Mesopotamia was further exacerbated in the late 580s by growing resentment in the rank and file of the imperial army at attempted economies in military expenditure. Accordingly, in 588 the garrison at the important frontier city of Martyropolis simply handed it over to the Persians, declaring that they 'would not be ruled over by a shopkeeper'. That same year, much of the imperial field army, stationed at Monocarton near Edessa, rose up in rebellion against the Emperor Maurice's proposed 25 per cent reduction in military pay. In response, the general Priscus attempted to cow the rebellious ranks into submission by revealing to them one of the holiest relics in Christendom, the *Mandylion* of Edessa, 'the image of God incarnate which the Romans call "not made by human hands" which he ordered to be carried before the troops'.[39] As the seventh-century historian Theophylact Simocatta records, however, 'the multitude was not brought to its senses thereby, but even pelted the ineffable object with stones'.[40] Only some rapid backtracking on the part of the Emperor was able to salvage the situation, and the leaders of the mutiny, though tried and convicted in Constantinople, were pointedly pardoned.[41]

However, it was political turmoil within Persia that would ultimately serve to destabilise the geopolitical situation. As we have seen, in the aftermath of his humiliation near Melitene in 576, Khusro had decreed that henceforth no Persian ruler should lead an army in person. Whilst this offered some means of shielding the person of the shah from the ignominy of defeat, Khusro's edict nevertheless posed dangers of its own. For it inevitably meant that the prestige associated with any victorious campaigns would henceforth accrue not to the Persian king but rather to the generals and commanders appointed to lead the armies in his stead. These generals were typically men of noble birth and ancient lineage, the grandest of them regarding themselves as no less royal than the Sasanians themselves. The blood of the ancient Arsacid dynasty, whom the Sasanians had overthrown in the third century, still flowed through the veins of some of these commanders, who, accordingly, may yet have harboured designs on the throne. Certainly, the Parthian princes had eyed with growing hostility the attempts of shahs since Kavad to foster a new service aristocracy drawn from the ranks of the urban elites of Assyria (Iraq). The ascendancy of this new elite threatened noble interests and inevitably had led to a heightening of tensions at court.[42]

One such prince was the general Vahram, who in 588 inflicted a decisive victory over the Turks on Persia's north-eastern frontier. From there, Vahram headed to the Transcaucasus to repel Iberian raids on Persian interests in Caucasian Albania.[43]

---

[38] For a revival of Persian strength in Albania and Persarmenia, see Greatrex and Lieu (2002), pp. 163 and 171.
[39] Theophylact Simocatta, *History*, III, 1.11.
[40] ibid., III, 1.12.
[41] Greatrex and Lieu (2002), p. 170.
[42] See P. Pourshariati, *Decline and Fall of the Sasanian Empire: The Sasanian-Parthian Confederacy and the Arab Conquest of Iran* (London, 2009).

He then marched into Roman Suania, amassing booty and defeating the Romans in open battle. As he returned to Albania, however, Vahram fell prey to an ambush prepared for him by the Roman commander Romanus and local Christian insurgents.[44] Shah Hormizd seized this opportunity to cut down to size his well-born and dangerously successful general. Sending him a woman's dress as a signal of his humiliation, Hormizd dismissed the general from his post.[45] In response Vahram and his army rose up in open revolt.[46] In the struggle for power that ensued, Hormizd was deposed and replaced by Vahram, while the former shah's son and chosen heir, Khusro II, fled to the court of the Emperor Maurice in Constantinople.[47]

A fascinating round of negotiation and counter-negotiation ensued, as both Vahram and Khusro II courted Maurice for recognition and support. The terms offered to the Roman Emperor were necessarily generous in the extreme. In return for Khusro II, Vahram offered the Romans not only the cities of Martyropolis and Dara, so recently lost to imperial control, but also the city of Nisibis, which Justin II had coveted to such disastrous effect. Khusro II likewise offered to return Martyropolis and Dara. But rather than offer up the long-standing prestige target of Nisibis, he instead offered the Romans the prospect of a dramatic extension of their power in the Transcaucasus; this would effectively reverse the partition of 387 and concede to the Romans control over two-thirds of Greater Armenia as well as of the Bitlis Pass that controlled access across the mountain range to the heartland of Sasanian territory in Assyria. The treaties were conceived of and described in precise geographical detail, recorded in the seventh-century *Armenian History*.[48]

The Emperor ultimately accepted Khusro's offer, and that choice reveals everything we need to know of the ability of the Roman authorities to think tactically and territorially. The proposed partition of Greater Armenia offered an unprecedented extension of Roman control in the most strategically vital of areas. In spite of countervailing advice from members of the Constantinopolitan Senate, who were minded to accept Vahram's more modest proposal if it meant the destruction of the Sasanian monarchy that had bedevilled Rome since the days of Ardashir in the 230s, Maurice dispatched an army of imperial troops and federates to help Khusro II regain his throne. Although Vahram was able to elude the expeditionary force, his army was not, and after a decisive victory at Ganzak, Khusro managed to fight his way back to power.[49] The new shah was swift to put his agreement with Maurice into effect: 'thus indeed,' Theophylact Simocatta noted, 'the great Persian war was gloriously brought to an end for the Romans'.[50] As a result, our *Armenian*

---

[43] See Greatrex and Lieu (2002), p. 171.
[44] ibid., pp. 171–2.
[45] Theophylact Simocatta, *History*, III, 8.1.
[46] ibid, III, 8.2–3.
[47] ibid, III, 8.12.
[48] *Armenian History*, Chapter 11 (76–80).
[49] See references in Greatrex and Lieu (2002), pp. 173–4.
[50] Theophylact Simocatta, *History*, V, 15.2.

History records, 'out of the Armenian nobles, many were in the Greek sector, and a few in the Persian'.[51]

The partition of the Transcaucasus in 591 marked an extraordinary victory for Roman diplomacy, albeit one originally rooted in the highly fractious nature of the Persian nobility. Yet, with the benefit of hindsight, Maurice's decision to throw in his lot with Khusro II, on the terms proposed, perhaps represented the Eastern Roman Empire's 'Versailles moment', when it concluded a peace which inevitably sowed the seeds of a future war greater than any that had gone before. For the territorial concessions to the Romans in Greater Armenia were on such a scale, and left the crucial administrative and economic heartland of the Persian Empire in Iraq so critically vulnerable to attack, that no self-respecting Persian shah could possibly leave the treaty in place. Accordingly, it was not so much a question of whether the Persians would attempt to roll back the frontier as established in 591, but when.

7.3 MOUNTING SOCIAL TENSIONS AND MILITARY REVOLT

In spite of the obvious temptation to go to war, external factors dictated that relations between Maurice and Khusro II remained amicable. The Emperor took advantage of the situation to redeploy significant sections of the East Roman field army to the Danube, where they were able to take battle to the Slavs and Avars with increasing success (see Chapter Five). The Roman authorities had come to appreciate that even the hardiest of their nomadic foes were obliged to make camp in the harsh Balkan winter. Accordingly, if the Roman army could extend the campaigning season into these most inhospitable of months, they had a chance of inflicting real pain on their troublesome northern neighbours. Accordingly, the 590s witnessed what one historian has described as the most impressive show of Roman force on the Danube since the days of Marcus Aurelius.[52] These campaigns, however, are likely to have done little to address the situation further south in the empire's Balkan territories, where Slav settlement continued apace, and may even have been intensified by the successful Roman campaigns to the north. Khusro, likewise, had other concerns: the final crushing of Vahram and his supporters in their traditional clan abode of Media, and the subsequent rebellion in *c*.599 of the nobleman Bestam, who drew his support from the same area, and who, like Vahram, was able to claim Arsacid descent.

The peace that ensued between Rome and Persia in the 590s was not, however, necessarily a blessing to the inhabitants of the frontier zone. The lords and princes of the Caucasus had a long-standing interest in maximising their own political autonomy by playing the two great empires off against one another, defecting from Persia to Rome and Rome to Persia as objective political circumstances demanded (as the Laz had done in the 520s, 530s, and 540s). The *Armenian History* would

---

[51] Greatrex and Lieu (2002), p. 174.
[52] D. Obolensky, *The Byzantine Commonwealth* (New Haven, 1971), p. 76.

look back on the years of 'peace' in the 590s as an age of unmitigated tyranny: Maurice is reported, for example, to have forcibly resettled Armenian men-at-arms and their households on the plains of Thrace, helping to secure the defences of the land approaches to Constantinople while taming the potentially rebellious highlands of the East.[53]

Prospects were little better for the dissident Christian populations of Syria and Mesopotamia. With greater military security on the empire's eastern frontier, the vehemently pro-Chalcedonian Maurice and his entourage no longer needed to fear the political implications of alienating the region's large anti-Chalcedonian congregations. As a result, under the supervision of the Emperor's nephew, Bishop Domitian of Melitene, large numbers of Miaphysite clergy were removed from post and their churches handed over to bishops and clerics more minded to toe the imperial line.[54] This was the closest the Chalcedonian authorities would ever come to an age of persecution. Khusro II, by contrast, was careful to court Miaphysite sentiment in the frontier zone, patronising the shrine of St Sergius at Sergiopolis, a major cultic site for the anti-Chalcedonian Arab tribesmen of the desert fringe.[55]

Rising Christological tensions were matched by mounting social tensions across the territories of the Roman Near East. At a provincial level, the expansion of large estates and the consolidation of aristocratic power continued to gather momentum. Tiberius, for example, was obliged to legislate against the practice whereby the administrators of imperial estates were effectively privatising them, incorporating them into their own property portfolios, and inflicting injustices on their inhabitants similar to those described in the earlier Justinianic legislation.[56] In Egypt the *Chronicle of John of Nikiu* describes a world where central imperial power was gradually receding from sight, leading to ever more destabilising effects.[57] Tiberius is recorded to have been dependent for the administration of the region on the services of a certain Aristomachus, the son of an Egyptian landowner and prefect, with a reputation for the brutality of his private armed retinue.[58] Likewise, two violent uprisings within Egypt are recorded in the reign of Maurice, led by local landowners.[59]

The heightening of social tensions, however, potentially carried more profound political consequences than even these revolts would suggest. As we have seen, the reign of Justin II had witnessed a drawing together of the political will of the imperial authorities and members of the senatorial and provincial aristocracies, a reconciliation evident in Justin II's reformed procedures for the appointment of governors. Moreover, at a provincial level, from the late fifth century, but gathering pace over the course of the sixth, we see the administration of local government and

---

[53] *Armenian History*, Chapter 30 (105).
[54] 'Dionysius Reconstituted' in A. Palmer and S. Brock, *The Seventh Century in the West-Syrian Chronicles* (Liverpool, 1993), pp. 117–18; and 'Chronicle of 819' in ibid., p. 76.
[55] Greatrex and Lieu (2002), pp. 176–8.
[56] Sarris (2006), pp. 192–3.
[57] ibid., pp. 230–31.
[58] *The Chronicle of John, Bishop of Nikiu*, 151–3.
[59] ibid., 157–8.

of tax collection being dominated by the locally preponderant magnate households, which took advantage of such official responsibilities to bolster their own social authority and expand their already extensive estates.[60] As a result, by the late sixth century, from the perspective of the peasantry or the urban lower classes, the private authority of the great landowner and the public authority of the Roman state had essentially become indistinguishable. Consequently, resentment and hostility towards the attitudes and actions of the wealthy were readily translatable into political sedition and discontent.

This situation was rendered still more serious by the downward pressure on the standard of living of estate workers, other more humble members of society, and the urban poor, resulting from the 'seigneurial reaction' of the reign of Justin II and continuing to the end of the sixth century and beyond. The numismatic record, for example, records a collapse in the purchasing power of the copper coinage on which such social strata depended for their daily needs.[61] Accordingly, it should not surprise us that, as in parts of the fifth-century West, members of the lower classes in the late sixth-century Syrian and Mesopotamian warzones sought to take advantage of military dislocation (in this instance generated by superpower conflict) to settle social scores and shake off much-resented aristocratic control. The great senatorial families of Antioch, for example, had long been notorious for the ruthlessness with which they exploited the urban poor and the working population of the surrounding countryside. It is revealing, therefore, that, amid the collapse of Roman defences in Upper Mesopotamia in 573, the ecclesiastical historian Evagrius records that the inhabitants of the city 'rebelled in their desire to begin a revolution, as often happens, especially at times such as these'.[62]

An escalation in violent conflict between the circus factions is also recorded in many cities of the empire.[63] As we saw in Chapter Four, these associations had received a measure of financial support from the imperial authorities. Straitened economic circumstances may, therefore, have served to intensify competition between the factions for access to the diminishing resources available from the state, leading them to flex their muscles on the street, to the clear detriment of both good government and social order.[64] As the Thessalonican *Miracles of Saint Demetrius* record:

> For you all know what clouds of dust the Devil stirred up . . . when he smothered love and sowed mutual hatred in all the East, in Cilicia, in Asia, in Palestine and the neighbouring lands up to Constantinople itself. The factions were no longer content merely to spill the blood of their comrades on the streets: they broke into one another's homes and slew the occupants mercilessly. Women and children, old and young, those who were too weak to save themselves by flight, they hurled from the windows of the

---

[60] Sarris (2006), pp. 149–200.
[61] ibid., pp. 224–7. See also F. Carlà, *L'oro nella tarda antichità: aspetti economici e sociali* (Turin, 2009), pp. 478–9.
[62] Evagrius, *Ecclesiastical History*, V, 9.
[63] Liebeschuetz (2001), pp. 249–83.
[64] A point I owe to Dr Philip Booth of Trinity College, Oxford, and his important research on circus factions in the *Chronicle of John of Nikiu*.

upper floors; like barbarians they plundered their fellow citizens, their acquaintances and their relatives, and put their homes to the flame so that not even the most wretched inhabitant could escape. And just as a fire that is not tamed spreads itself with ease throughout the whole neighbourhood, so too did the din of the eastern horrors resound throughout the cities of Illyricum, exciting within them passions of material greed.[65]

Most ominously of all for the imperial authorities, it was not just the peasantry, the poor, and the circus factions that were sensitive to the shifting economic fortunes of the late sixth century. A diminution in tax revenues caused by the demographic impact of bubonic plague and aristocratic tax evasion appears to have occasioned mounting difficulties in paying the army. It is in this context that we should understand the attempted reduction in military pay proposed by the Emperor Maurice in 588. Failure to pay the army adequately or on time, however, tended to lead to desertion, defection, or revolt, as most vividly revealed by the Eastern field army's response to Maurice's attempted cuts. Moreover, at some point in the late sixth century, it appears to have become common for the cash component of the stipend issued to garrison troops to be paid in copper rather than gold.[66] Consequently, the collapse in the purchasing power of the copper *follis* from the reign of Justin II onwards is likely to have had ever more pronounced implications for the loyalty and morale of the military rank and file, as well as of the civilian population of the empire.

Such tensions were to come to a head in the year 602/3. In accordance with what had become the preferred anti-nomad tactic, as the winter of 602 approached, the imperial field army in the Balkans was ordered to extend its campaigning to the north of the Danube into the winter months, supporting itself by means of foraging in enemy territory.[67] Maurice, as we have seen, was already unpopular in military circles for his perceived parsimoniousness, and for many, the prospect of having not only to fight but also to forage across the harsh winter landscape of the northern Balkans was too much. According to Theophylact Simocatta, even the Emperor's hapless representative, the general Peter, was obliged to admit with respect to imperial policy that 'an avaricious manner brings forth nothing good; avarice is a citadel of evils'.[68] By November, the Balkan field army had risen up in revolt under the leadership of an officer by the name of Phocas and had begun to march on the capital, where rioting directed against the person of the Emperor and his entourage immediately flared up.[69]

In response, Maurice and his family attempted to take flight, although the ship on which they embarked was held back by unfavourable winds. Within the city, rioting continued apace: 'the masses lapsed into tyranny, and spent the night

---

[65] P. Lemerle (ed.), *Les plus anciens recueils des miracles de S. Demetrius I: Le Texte* (Paris, 1979), 10, chs. 82–3, pp. 112–13—detailing the reign of Phocas, but depicting a heightening of factional violence also discernible for the reign of Maurice.
[66] Sarris (2006), pp. 233–4.
[67] Theophylact Simocatta, *History*, VIII, 6.2.
[68] ibid., VIII, 7.3.
[69] ibid, VIII, 9.4–6.

revelling in wickedness and declaiming insulting chants against Maurice'.[70] The following day Phocas was crowned Emperor by the Patriarch Cyriacus near the outskirts of the city. On 25 November the new Emperor proceeded to make a triumphal entry into the imperial capital, entering via the Golden Gate (which was opened for him by members of the Green faction) and riding in a chariot the entire length of the main monumental highway of the city (known as the *Mese*), 'with no-one at all opposing, but everyone acclaiming him' until he reached the palace.[71] The coup against Maurice was, thus far, an entirely bloodless affair.

All that was to change two days later: Maurice and most of his family were apprehended and brought back to the city of Chalcedon. There, the deposed Emperor and four of his five sons were executed, whilst his wife and daughters were packed off to convents. In Constantinople itself, Phocas moved against Maurice's chief ministers and associates. The *Chronicon Paschale* records that 'Peter too, the brother of Maurice, who was *curopalatus* was arrested and slain, and other officials were also arrested. Constantine Lardys, the former praetorian prefect, logothete, and curator of the palace of Hormisdas, and Theodosius the [remaining] son of Maurice were slain at Diadromoi, near Acritas; Comentiolus, the patrician and *magister militum*, was also slain on the far side, near St Conon by the sea, and his body was eaten by dogs.'[72] Theodosius' head, however, was not seen on public display.[73] As a result, rumours soon circulated that Maurice's eldest son had, in fact, managed to escape the cull, and had fled east to obtain support from his father's erstwhile brother-in-arms, Khusro II of Persia.

The reign of the Emperor Phocas is known to us chiefly from works derived from or associated with the court of his own eventual executioner, and successor, Heraclius.[74] Accordingly, the sources are eager to paint his reign as an age of unmitigated anarchy and chaos. It is worth noting, however, that Phocas had achieved the first successful military coup since the reign of Constantine, and, initially, his regime evidently enjoyed considerable support amongst the circus factions, the army, and the broader Constantinopolitan population, who had cheered him as he entered the capital in 602.[75] The Papal authorities in Rome were also amongst the regime's backers: in the Forum, a large column was erected in honour of the Emperor (which stands to this day). Phocas, in turn, gave the Papacy the magnificent pagan monument of the Pantheon to turn into a church. Pope Gregory the Great, moreover, had made a point of writing to Eusebia, daughter of his friend, the Sicilian *emigrée* Rusticiana, advising her senatorial husband—Flavius Apion—not to machinate against the new ruler.[76] It is possible that, as a former officer of the Balkan field army, Phocas was especially committed

---

[70] Theophylact Simocatta, *History*, VIII, 9.8.
[71] *Chronicon Paschale*, 602, p. 142.
[72] ibid., p. 143.
[73] Theophylact Simocatta, *History*, VIII, 13.6.
[74] D. M. Olster, *The Politics of Usurpation in the Seventh Century: Rhetoric and Revolution in Byzantium* (Amsterdam, 1993).
[75] W. E. Kaegi, *Heraclius: Emperor of Byzantium* (Cambridge, 2003), p. 37.
[76] Gregory the Great, *Register*, XIII, 34–5.

to the defence of Byzantine territories in the West, a fact that would help explain his appeal to Gregory as he faced down the looming Langobard threat.

By contrast, amongst members of the Constantinopolitan Senate and the upper echelons of the imperial bureaucracy, the regime was regarded with evident hostility.[77] In 603, for example, a counter-coup was attempted by Germanus, 'patrician and father-in-law of Theodosius son of Maurice'.[78] This was thwarted by the refusal of the Green faction to cooperate, in spite of the fact that Phocas was closely associated with their rivals, the Blues.[79] Relations between the government and the Green faction did deteriorate, however, and, not long after Germanus' attempted putsch, 'a faction riot occurred [and] the *Mese* was burnt from the palace of Lausus, and the *praetorium* of the city prefect, as far as the Treasury opposite the Forum of Constantine'.[80]

In 605 a second and primarily senatorial plot against the Emperor was discovered, in which Maurice's widow, Constantina, was also implicated. Phocas' response was characteristically forthright: the *Chronicon Paschale* recounts how around a dozen high-ranking officials 'were beheaded, on the grounds that they were discovered plotting against Phocas. At the same time Constantina, the former queen was also beheaded... and the surviving female children of her and Maurice... were also killed'.[81] As an eminent historian of Byzantium put it, Phocas engaged in 'a wave of indiscriminate slaughter which was particularly directed at members of the most distinguished families in order to forestall their opposition. The aristocracy answered this orgy of massacres with a series of conspiracies, all of which ended in further executions'.[82]

It was not just in Constantinople, however, that the accession of Phocas heralded a wave of bloodletting and factional violence. The seventh-century *Armenian History* describes how, after the fall of Maurice: 'Then there was no little turmoil in the Roman Empire—there in the royal capital, and in the city of Alexandria in Egypt, and in Jerusalem and Antioch. In all the regions of the land they took up the sword and slaughtered each other.'[83] The claims of the *Armenian History* are corroborated with respect to Alexandria by the *Chronicle of John of Nikiu* and for Antioch by a number of sources, including the *Chronicon Paschale*, the 'Doctrines of Jacob' (*Doctrina Iacobi*), and the *Chronicle of Theophanes*. So, for the year 608–9, the *Chronicle of Theophanes* (drawing upon a seventh-century account) records that rioters 'killed many men of property and burnt them'.[84] Theophanes identifies the rioters as Jews, the *Chronicon Paschale* as soldiers, and the *Doctrina Iacobi* as a combination of Christians, Jews, soldiers, civilians, and faction members.[85] It is

[77] *Chronicon Paschale*, p. 146, n. 410.
[78] ibid., p. 144, with discussion by M. and M. Whitby, n. 406.
[79] P. Booth, 'Shades of Blues and Greens in the Chronicle of John of Nikiu' (forthcoming).
[80] *Chronicon Paschale*, p. 145.
[81] ibid., p. 146.
[82] G. Ostrogorsky, *History of the Byzantine State*, tr. J. Hussey (Oxford, 1956), p. 83.
[83] *Armenian History*, Chapter 31 (106).
[84] Theophanes, pp. 425–6.
[85] *Chronicon Paschale*, pp. 149–50; *Doctrina Iacobi*, 1.40.

highly significant, however, that the rich were deliberately targeted. As we have seen, in Constantinople, Phocas' foes were primarily senatorial: it is possible that the chaos into which the provinces of the empire descended in the wake of the coup was fuelled by an associated—and perhaps coordinated—wave of resistance to the new regime by aristocratic retinues and affinities, to which Phocas responded by mobilising his supporters amongst the army and his chosen circus faction (the Blues), who were a major presence in the empire's cities.[86]

7.4 THE PERSIAN ADVANCE

In spite of strong military backing for the new Emperor, in late 603 the general Narses rose up in revolt against Phocas on the empire's eastern frontier and established himself at the city of Edessa, which he occupied by force, writing to Khusro II inviting him to intervene.[87] Khusro, however, probably needed little by way of encouragement. As we have seen, reversing the territorial losses of 591 is likely to have been a long-standing ambition, and the deposition and murder of his patron Maurice now gave the shah the perfect pretext to take up arms and lead his forces west. Conditions on the steppe were also favourable: the main military focus of the Turks at this point was on Mongolia, where a major revolt had obliged the *Khagan* Tardu to disengage from military machinations in northern China.[88] It is noteworthy that Khusro personally took part in the campaign that he now initiated, in spite of the law of his namesake forbidding future Sasanian rulers from doing so. Clearly, the shah was eager to be seen to expiate the taint of 591.

Khusro and his forces broke through Roman defences in Upper Mesopotamia late in the spring of 603. By the summer of 604, the fortress of Dara had fallen after a lengthy siege. With Phocas' forces having to contain both Khusro and the mutinous Narses, the effectiveness of the Roman response to Persian invasion was necessarily limited. After the victory at Dara, Khusro himself returned to Ctesiphon, but his commanders in the field initiated the systematic conquest of the major Roman military 'hard points' in Mesopotamia. This was a slow and painstaking affair, and the precise chronology of this campaign to break down the network of Justinianic fortifications is not entirely clear.[89] By 610, however, all remaining Roman cities east of the Euphrates had fallen, leading to a flood of refugees.[90] At the same time, Khusro directed a series of assaults on Roman positions in Armenia, seeking to reverse the gains that Maurice had made. Around

---

[86] Booth, 'Shades of Blues and Greens in the Chronicle of John of Nikiu' (forthcoming).
[87] For a Syriac perspective on Phocas' coup against Maurice and Narses' rebellion, see 'Dionysius Reconstituted' in Palmer and Brock (1993), pp. 118–22; Greatrex and Lieu (2002), p. 183.
[88] Barfield (1989), pp. 136–8: I am grateful to James Howard-Johnston for this point and for having made available to me in advance narrative chapters of his magnum opus, *Witnesses to A World Crisis: Historians and Histories of the Middle East* (Oxford, 2010), on which I rely heavily for the military details that follow.
[89] Howard-Johnston (2010), p. 437.
[90] Greatrex and Lieu (2002).

606–7 the Romans suffered a major defeat near the capital of Roman Armenia at Theodosiopolis, after which Roman forces were effectively driven from the province.

7.5 HERACLIUS' REBELLION AND COUP

By the winter of 609/10, therefore, Khusro II's armies had achieved two highly significant feats. First, they had systematically conquered the densely fortified landscape of Roman Mesopotamia in which Anastasius, Justin I, and Justinian had invested so much. Second, to the north of the Taurus Mountains, they had effectively managed to drive the Romans out of the Transcaucasus, forcing them back to a defensive line running from Trapezus (Trebizond) to Satala (see Map 4). According to the seventh-century *Armenian History* and a number of other sources, these conquests were to some extent facilitated by the fact that Persian forces were initially accompanied by an individual claiming to be the late Maurice's eldest son, Theodosius, who had supposedly fled east and whom Khusro had crowned and proclaimed Emperor.[91] The clear implication of the *Armenian History* is that this figure was an imposter and that, as the *Chronicon Paschale* claims, Theodosius' attempted flight to Khusro had been thwarted, leading to his execution. However, political conditions were evidently sufficiently unsettled, and lines of communications sufficiently disrupted, for claims that Theodosius had indeed survived to remain both current and credible.[92] More tangibly, the ongoing power struggle in Constantinople, and the explosion of violence across the cities of the empire, clearly did much to limit the effectiveness of Roman resistance. It is a sign of confidence on Khusro's part that at some point between 606 and 610 he abolished the Nasrid client state on whom the Persians had relied in order to raid the Roman Empire's desert fringe. The Persians were no longer in need of such assistance as their ambitions began to shift to the west of the Euphrates.[93]

As the Roman Empire's position in the east gradually deteriorated, pressure mounted on Phocas. The predictable result was a renewed round of plotting. A successful coup would need military support, and perhaps aware that such support was unlikely to be forthcoming from those units of the army most implicated in the rise and consolidation of the new regime, contact was made between members of the Senate in Constantinople and Heraclius 'the Elder', governor of *Africa Proconsularis*. The elder Heraclius had seen active service in the east as *magister militum per Armeniam*. More significantly, his family had strong roots in Cappadocia, where it appears to have possessed estates, situating it socially amid the world of the haughty Cappadocian magnates and aristocrats against whose activities

---

[91] J. D. Howard-Johnston, 'Al-Tabari on the Last Great War of Antiquity', in J. D. Howard-Johnston, *East Rome, Sasanian Persia, and the End of Antiquity* (Aldershot, 2006), VI, p. 11.
[92] *Armenian History*, ch. 31 (106); Theophylact Simocatta, *History*, VIII, 13.5.
[93] Howard-Johnston (2010), pp. 436–7.

Justinian had railed.[94] According to John of Antioch and later Byzantine sources, the chief interlocutor on the Senate's side was the Urban Prefect of Constantinople, Priscus, whose dislike of the Emperor was intensified by virtue of Phocas being his son-in-law.[95]

In 608 Heraclius the Elder and his son, also called Heraclius, launched an open rebellion against Phocas and his regime, minting coinage bearing images of the two of them with the younger Heraclius placed in the senior position—indicating that he was to be regarded as the Emperor nominate. As the younger Heraclius began work on putting together a naval fleet with which to sail for Constantinople and, presumably, negotiating a route for that fleet to take, his cousin Nicetas began the long cross-country march from *Africa Proconsularis* along the coast of Libya to Africa Tripolitania, from where he was able to take the field against pro-Phocas forces in Egypt, seizing Alexandria in 609–10.[96] The capture of Egypt in general, and Alexandria in particular, was vital, in that it enabled the rebels to cut off the grain supply on which Constantinople depended. Aware of this, Phocas had been obliged to order his general Bonosus to withdraw from Palestine into Egypt in order to forestall this eventuality, an unavoidable decision that had the inevitable consequence of further weakening Roman resistance to the Persian advance.[97] By August or September 610, however, Nicetas had driven Bonosus and his forces back to the port of Pelusium, whence they fled by sea to the imperial capital, which Nicetas was now in a position to begin starving into submission.[98]

On 3 October 610 Heraclius' fleet, with an army including numerous Berber soldiers or mercenaries, landed at a fort near the Hebdomon, just outside the city walls of Constantinople.[99] Amid the panic that ensued, Phocas' forces, under the command of Bonosus, quickly abandoned the city's seaward defences, perhaps with a view to regrouping around the palace complex.[100] If so, any such strategy was too late: Heraclius' landing at the Hebdomon gave the signal to Phocas' senatorial opponents to make their move.[101] On 5 October, as the *Chronicon Paschale* records:

> as Monday was dawning, Photius, the curator of the palace of Placidia, and Probus the patrician seized Phocas stark naked from the [church of the] Archangel in the Palace and led him off through the harbour in the direction of the mansion of Sophia; after throwing him into a skiff, they displayed him to the ships; and then they brought him to Heraclius. And his right arm was removed from the shoulder, as well as his head, his hand was impaled on a sword, and thus it was paraded along the *Mese*, starting from the Forum. His head was put on a pole, and thus it too was paraded around. The rest of the body was dragged along on the belly, and was brought in the direction of the

[94] Kaegi (2003), p. 21, n. 5.
[95] ibid., p. 43.
[96] ibid., pp. 44–5.
[97] ibid., p. 44.
[98] ibid., p. 45.
[99] ibid., p. 45 for Berbers, and p. 49 for landing. For discussion of the possible route taken by Heraclius, see ibid., pp. 46–7.
[100] ibid., p. 49.
[101] ibid., pp. 49–50.

Chalce of the Hippodrome.... And about the ninth hour of the same Monday, Heraclius was crowned emperor in the most holy Great Church by Sergius patriarch of Constantinople. And on the following day, Tuesday, while a race meeting was being held, the head of Leontius the Syrian [the former finance minister] was brought in and burnt in the Hippodrome, along with the image of Phocas which during his lifetime, foolish men wearing white robes had conducted into the Hippodrome with lighted candles.[102]

It was suggested earlier that the explosion of violence across the Roman Near East in the aftermath of Phocas' coup, although fuelled by mounting social tensions, had been ignited by aristocratic resistance to the new regime. Certainly, Phocas' eventual fall from power bears all the hallmarks of a 'senatorial coup'.[103] It is perhaps not entirely without reason that the author of the *Chronicle of John of Nikiu* in fact believed Phocas to have been seized and slain by members of the Senate.[104] On one level, his account may convey something of the truth of the Emperor's downfall, even if, on matters of detail, the version contained in the *Chronicon Paschale* is to be preferred.[105] In such circumstances, how was the empire to hold together?

7.6 THE FALL OF THE ROMAN NEAR EAST

The short answer is that it was not to hold together. Although writers and propagandists associated with the court of Heraclius later went to enormous lengths to pin the blame on Phocas, it was the Heraclian rebellion and the early years of the new Emperor's reign that marked the period of real East Roman military collapse.[106] It was over the course of the year 610, as Heraclius sailed on Constantinople and sought to establish his regime, that the Persians broke through the inner line of Roman defences along the Euphrates. The fall of the city of Edessa, long regard by the local Christian community as impregnable, must have been a major blow to morale.[107] Heraclius attempted to enter into negotiations with Khusro in order to stem the Persian advance. The shah, however, was in no mind to negotiate and simply executed the Roman ambassadors.[108]

The Persians now began to press home their advantage. In 611 the commander-in-chief of the shah's western field army—Shahvaraz—struck deep into Syria, seizing Apamea and Antioch, and securing the surrender of Emesa.[109] To the north, the Persians exploited their control of the east-west lines of communication across Armenia to strike into Anatolia, where, with the help of the local Jewish

---

[102] *Chronicon Paschale*, pp. 151–3.
[103] J. Herrin, *The Formation of Christendom* (Oxford, 1987), pp. 189–90.
[104] *The Chronicle of John, Bishop of Nikiu*, tr. R. H. Charles (London, 1916), pp. 177–8.
[105] See Kaegi (2003), pp. 50–51.
[106] Kaegi (2003), p. 48.
[107] Greatrex and Lieu (2002), p. 186.
[108] ibid., p. 188.
[109] ibid., p. 189.

population, they were able to capture the city of Caesarea in Cappadocia.[110] The fact that Persian armies were now capable of striking and operating on the Anatolian plateau compelled Heraclius to take personal charge of the army, something that no Roman ruler had done since Valens' death in battle at Adrianople in 378. In the near vicinity of Antioch, however, the Persians were able to inflict a significant defeat on the Emperor. Pursuing the retreating Roman forces and capturing Tarsus, the Persians now established Cilicia as a bridgehead for assaults on the rich cities of Asia Minor. To the south, Damascus fell, opening the way for the Persians to initiate the conquest of Palestine, the capture of which would enable them to cut the Roman Empire in two.[111]

From Damascus, Shahvaraz and his army pressed southwards to Bostra, where the defeat of the Roman army sent shockwaves throughout the world of the Arabian tribes to the south.[112] Advancing through Galilee, the Persians struck first at the great Mediterranean port town of maritime Caesarea. As Roman resistance crumbled, violent clashes broke out between Jewish and Christian communities: as in Anatolia in 611, many of the former are recorded as welcoming and assisting the Persian invaders. In 614 negotiations between the Persian high command and civic leaders led to the occupation of Jerusalem. As the author of the *Armenian History* put it:

> Then all of the land of Palestine willingly submitted to subjection to the Persian king; especially the survivors of the race of Hebrews, rebelling against the Christians and embracing ancestral rancour, [they] caused great harm among the multitude of the faithful. They went to them [the Persians] and made close union with them. At that time the army of the Persian king was encamped at Caesarea of Palestine; their general called Razmiozan, that is Khoream, parleyed with Jerusalem that they should willingly submit and be left in peace and prosperity.[113]

The loss of Jerusalem was a humiliating blow, but worse was to follow. As the *Armenian History* again records:

> At first they [the inhabitants of Jerusalem] agreed and submitted. They offered to the general and the [Persian] princes splendid gifts. They requested reliable officers, whom they installed in their midst to guard the city. But after some months had passed, while all the mass of the ordinary people were complaisant, the youths of the city killed the officers of the Persian king, and themselves rebelled against his authority. Then there was warfare between the inhabitants of the city of Jerusalem, Jewish and Christian. The larger number of Christians had the upper hand and slew many of the Jews. The surviving Jews jumped from the walls and went to the Persian army. Then Khoream... gathered his troops, went and camped around Jerusalem and besieged it. He attacked it for 19 days. Having mined the foundations of the city from below, they brought down the wall.[114]

---

[110] Greatrex and Lieu (2002), p. 188.
[111] ibid., pp. 189–90.
[112] ibid., p. 190: Qur'an, *Sura*, 30.2–5; Tabari, 1, 1007/327.
[113] *Armenian History*, ch. 34 (115).
[114] ibid., ch. 34 (115).

'For three days', the *History* informs us, 'they [the Persians] put to the sword and slew all the populace of the city. And they stayed within the city for 21 days. Then they came out... and burnt the city with fire'. Some seventeen thousand civilians, it was claimed, were slaughtered, and a further thirty-five thousand led away in captivity, as too were the remains of the True Cross, which was first trampled on before being carried off to Ctesiphon as a trophy of war.[115]

News of the sack of Jerusalem and the seizure of the True Cross was greeted with horror and revulsion throughout the Christian world. As the author of the *Chronicon Paschale* recorded:

> In this year we suffered a calamity which deserves unceasing lamentations. For, together with many cities of the east, Jerusalem too was captured by the Persians, and in it were slain many thousands of clerics, monks, and virgin nuns. The Lord's tomb was burnt and the far-flung temples of God and, in short, all the precious things were destroyed. The venerated wood of the Cross... was taken by the Persians, and the Patriarch Zacharias also became a prisoner.[116]

The Patriarch of Alexandria, John 'the Almsgiver', gave emergency assistance to refugees and went into mourning for a year.[117] As eyewitness accounts of the massacring of the Christian population by the Persians and Jews circulated, the refugee Eastern churchman Sophronius fulminated: 'O Christ, grant [us] to see Persia burning soon instead of the holy places!... May you curb by the hands of Christians the ill-fated children of impious Persia!'[118] The event was also a crushing blow to imperial prestige: renewed Visigothic pressure on the Byzantine enclave in Spain signalled that the Emperor in Constantinople was no longer regarded as a force to be reckoned with.

To make matters worse, from their base in Cilicia the Persians initiated a 'scorched-earth' policy, targeting the wealthy and densely urbanised coastal zone of western Asia Minor. Ephesus—the greatest city of Roman Asia—was stormed and its centre reduced to ash and rubble.[119] By 615 a detachment of the Persian army had reached Chalcedon, on the Asian shore of the Bosphorus and within sight of Constantinople.[120] Heraclius was desperate to sue for peace. Taking advantage of the proximity of the enemy army, the Emperor made his way towards Chalcedon and held talks with the Persian general, Shahin. Essentially, Heraclius appears to have offered the commander of the Persian forces in Anatolia a blank cheque: he would do anything required to bring the war to an end short of outright surrender. He was even willing to set aside the crown and make way for a candidate of Khusro's

---

[115] ibid., ch. 34 (116). For higher estimates of both casualties and captives, and for reference to archaeological evidence for this episode, see Greatrex and Lieu (2002), pp. 190–93, and Kaegi (2003), p. 78.

[116] *Chronicon Paschale*, p. 156.

[117] *Life of John the Almsgiver*, 9.

[118] Greatrex and Lieu (2002), p. 191.

[119] C. Foss, *Ephesus after Antiquity* (Cambridge, 1979), and 'The Persians in Asia Minor and the End of Antiquity', in *English Historical Review* 90 (1975), pp. 721–47.

[120] Greatrex and Lieu (2002), pp. 193–4: in response, a division of the Roman army was sent eastwards to draw the Persians away.

choosing.¹²¹ Shahin pulled back the Persian siege engines, while, in Constantinople, a high-ranking peace delegation prepared to head east to meet Khusro II.

The shah had never acknowledged Heraclius' imperial claims and had repeatedly refused to enter into negotiation with his representatives. Accordingly, the embassy that was sent to him in 615–16 spoke in the name of the Senate, comprised the praetorian prefect, Olympius, the Urban Prefect of Constantinople, Leontius, and a certain Anastasius, a priest on the payroll of the cathedral church of Hagia Sophia, who was presumably authorised to negotiate on behalf of the Patriarch.¹²² It is clear from the letter from the Senate that the ambassadors conveyed to the shah, the text of which survives in the *Chronicon Paschale*, that this delegation was meant to mark the beginning of the endgame.

In what is perhaps the single most humiliating document in all of Roman history, the senators of Constantinople the New Rome begged Khusro's forgiveness, excoriating Phocas as the murderer of Maurice. The senators described themselves as 'insignificant men', Khusro as their 'supreme Emperor', and the ambassadors as his 'slaves'. Begging that the senatorial delegation be received and returned in safety, they entreated Khusro to consider Heraclius as his *teknon*, or 'boy'—a word signifying both child and slave.¹²³ In short, the Senate was requesting a negotiated surrender, such as would leave in place a rump Roman state, centred on Constantinople, but subject to openly acknowledged Persian overlordship. The realm of the Caesars, empire of Christ, and heir to the fiery genius of Alexander, would henceforth be a supplicant and tributary at the feet of the Persian, Zoroastrian shah. Khusro was not interested: the ambassadors were executed and Chalcedon seized. Constantinople itself was now firmly in his sights.¹²⁴

By the end of 616 the occupation of Palestine was complete and the following year two armies were sent into Anatolia to renew the scorched-earth policy. A Persian fleet attacked Constantia (Salamis) in Cyprus, thereby signalling the loss of Roman control of the sea lanes of the Mediterranean, and presumably cutting off the grain shipments on which Constantinople depended.¹²⁵ In 618 the conquest of Egypt was initiated, and in 619 Alexandria fell.¹²⁶ By 621 all of Egypt and, with it, the whole of the Roman Near East beyond Anatolia and Asia Minor, was in Persian hands. On the Anatolian plateau itself they were applying inexorable pressure to what remained of the East Roman state. Probably in 622 they seized control of the important central Anatolian city of Ancyra. In 622–3 Rhodes and a number of other Aegean islands were subjected to attack. Persian armies and, increasingly, the Persian fleet, were spreading devastation along the coastal zone of Asia Minor, where the last functioning imperial mint (at Nicomedia) had been obliged to

---

[121] *Armenian History*, ch. 38 (122).
[122] *Chronicon Paschale*, pp. 159–60.
[123] ibid., pp. 161–2.
[124] J. D. Howard-Johnston, 'Heraclius' Persian Campaigns and the Revival of the Eastern Roman Empire', *War in History* 6 (1999), pp. 1–44, p. 3.
[125] Greatrex and Lieu (2002), pp. 195–6.
[126] ibid., p. 196.

abandon coin production in 619. What was left of the East Roman state appeared to be on the verge of collapse.

7.7 'PERSIA BURNING'

Total victory was palpably within Khusro's grasp; a total victory that would enable him to unite the resources of the sedentary populations of western Eurasia against the threat posed by the burgeoning power of *Turan* as represented by the Turks, who had now re-established control over Mongolia and whose armies had crossed the Oxus, raiding Persian territory in Rayy and Isfahan in 615.[127] In refusing to negotiate with Heraclius' regime, however, and—in particular—by seizing and executing the members of the senatorial delegation sent to him that same year, Khusro had perhaps made a dangerous miscalculation. As the reigns of Maurice and Phocas had revealed, the Roman army and the Constantinopolitan Senate had shown themselves to be more than capable of deposing emperors if they saw fit, and the first five years of Heraclius' reign had witnessed one military disaster after another. The Emperor, as we have seen, had even effectively offered to make way for a candidate more acceptable to Khusro. The shah's decision to reject even the most self-abasing of Roman overtures signalled his absolute determination to destroy the Roman state once and for all. The result, combined with the psychological impact of the sack of Jerusalem, was to galvanise the support of the Roman governing classes in what remained of the empire behind Heraclius: the Constantinopolitan Senate, the military high command, and the leadership of the Church had nowhere else to turn. Heraclius' fate was now their fate.

Consequently, between 615 and 622, Heraclius was able to draw upon this support to institute a series of crisis-driven measures aimed at maximising the resources at his disposal, introducing economising policies and cuts the like of which Justinian, Maurice, or Phocas could only have dreamt. Official salaries were halved and the free distribution of bread in Constantinople was suspended. The resources of the Church were also harnessed: according to the *Chronicle of Theophanes*, 'being short of funds, he [Heraclius] took on loan the money of religious establishments and he also took the candelabra and other vessels of the holy ministry from the Great Church'.[128] With the Church's silver plate, Heraclius minted a new silver coinage—the *hexagram*—enabling the government to maximise its gold reserves by collecting revenue in *solidi* but making payments in silver.[129] The metallic content of the copper coinage was also heavily reduced, so as to stretch depleted fiscal resources ever further, and in Constantinople even the bronze ox that stood in the Theodosian Forum was said to have been melted down to meet the needs of the military treasury.[130] Numismatic evidence reveals that, at

---

[127] Howard-Johnston (2010), p. 440; *Armenian History*, ch. 28 (101–2).
[128] Theophanes, p. 435; Howard-Johnston (1999), pp. 34–5.
[129] *Chronicon Paschale*, p. 158.
[130] ibid., pp. 158–9, n. 441, and Greatrex and Lieu (2002), p. 198.

the grass roots of East Roman society in Asia Minor, finds of copper coins at urban sites become much rarer, signalling that the wealth of the remaining provinces was being remorselessly hoovered up by the Roman state to fund its war effort.[131]

These funds were used to attempt to buy peace with the Avars to the west, and to elicit the support of the Christian population of the Transcaucasus and the occupied territories. This effort was reinforced by a religious propaganda drive (aimed at those who were amenable to it) that emphasised the horrors associated with the fall of Jerusalem in 614, and which played upon the spiralling apocalyptic sensibilities that were such a pronounced feature of the age.[132] The new silver hexagram coinage, for example, bore on it an image of the True Cross, which as noted had been seized in 614, beneath the slogan 'DEVS ADIVTA ROMANIS' ('God help the Romans!') (Fig. 9).[133] At the same time, withdrawing the remnants of the battle-hardened imperial field army from the Balkans to face down the Persian challenge, the Emperor set about organising a sort of 'New Model Army': an intensively trained infantry force versed in the tactics of guerrilla warfare and enthused with religious fervour. Crucially, a concept of Christian 'holy war' against the Persian infidel came to be enunciated. The Greek-speaking theological tradition had hitherto proven itself uneasy with respect to claims of religious justification for acts of state violence (although, in the West, St Augustine had begun to develop a doctrine of just war, and both within the empire and beyond prayers for the victories of pious rulers and their armies were a liturgical feature).[134] In Armenia, by contrast, where, in the fifth century, the leaders of the Church had spearheaded resistance to the tightening of Persian control, a more full-blown concept of holy war and of martyrdom through death in battle was already being expounded, and it was probably on these traditions that Heraclius drew.[135] As he led his new troops in training manoeuvres on the plains of Bithynia, 'rousing them with warlike cries' according to the court poet George of Pisidia, Heraclius is reported to have brandished before them the image of Christ that had been rescued from Edessa.[136] Their pockets perhaps now filled with new wages in silver, these soldiers were more responsive to the sight of the relic than Maurice's mutinous troops had been outside Monocarton in 588.

In 622 the Avars and their Slav vassals responded to the withdrawal of the Roman field army from the Balkans by launching an assault on Thessalonica.[137] The city's formidable defences withstood the siege, which lasted thirty-three days, but it may have been a close-run thing: Heraclius was obliged to disengage from his

---

[131] Revealed by the fact that the copper coinage diminishes in incidence while the gold coinage (the currency of the state) remains constant: see G. Ostrogorsky, 'Byzantine Cities in the Early Middle Ages', *Dumbarton Oaks Papers* 13 (1959), pp. 47–66.
[132] Howard-Johnston (1999), p. 37.
[133] ibid., p. 37.
[134] See, for example, Basil of Caesarea, *Canonical Letters*, 188.13.
[135] Howard-Johnston (1999), p. 40.
[136] Theophanes, pp. 435–6: on the chronicler's dependence on a lost history of Heraclius by George of Pisidia, see Howard-Johnston, 'The Official History of Heraclius' Persian Campaign' in Howard-Johnston (2005), IV.
[137] Howard-Johnston (1999), pp. 14–15, for date.

Fig. 9 Silver Hexagram of Heraclius and Heraclius Constantine (by kind permission of the Fitzwilliam Museum, Cambridge)

military exercises to enter negotiations with the Avar *khagan*, who took advantage of the encounter to attempt to kidnap the Emperor, perhaps at Khusro's bequest. Heraclius managed to escape in disguise, although the imperial baggage train and retinue were captured. An armistice was eventually purchased on the most exorbitant of terms.[138] As we have seen, when faced with simultaneous threats to the Balkans and to the Eastern Empire the first instinct of Roman emperors had long been to prioritise warfare against the prestige enemy of Persia, and, in this regard, Heraclius was no exception. The Avar assault on Thessalonica, however, had distracted the Emperor from the first phase of what appears to have been a carefully masterminded counter-strike against the Persians, upon which the very survival of the Christian Roman Empire would depend.

It was clear to Heraclius by 622 that there was little point in attempting to engage the superior Persian forces on open terrain in Anatolia or Syria. Rather, his best hope would be to head north, to Armenia and the Transcaucasus, where he would be able to request reinforcements from the Christian lords of the region, and where a small, highly mobile army might yet outwit a numerically preponderant foe. A tradition of 'holy war' against Persia was, as we have seen, already present amongst the Armenian nobility and in the collective memory of the Armenian Church: the Transcaucasus, therefore, offered fertile ground for Heraclius' religious propaganda drive. Moreover, as noted earlier, Heraclius' own father had served as commander of the Roman forces in Armenia under Maurice. It is possible that, in the highly 'feudal' world of the Armenian highlands (dominated, as they were, by local military lords and their retinues of armed retainers), there were still old companions and allies of the father who might be minded to lend assistance to his son. Crucially, the mountain passes of the Transcaucasus offered a route into Persia, allowing Heraclius to take battle to the enemy.

[138] ibid., pp. 14–15, and Theophanes, pp. 433–4.

Accordingly, in the summer of 622 Heraclius led his army from Pontus, where he raised new recruits, into Armenia, where he defeated a detachment of Arab cavalry in the service of the shah.[139] He then attempted to strike into Persia, but was prevented by its commander-in-chief Shahvaraz, who occupied the passes leading east through Armenia, blocking the Roman advance. The two armies proceeded to shadow one another uneasily until, in early August, Heraclius inflicted a morale-boosting defeat on the Persian host before being obliged to head west to deal with the Avar threat, leaving his army to winter in Armenia.[140]

In the spring of 624, once peace with the Avars was restored, Heraclius once more departed from Constantinople and headed towards Caesarea in eastern Cappadocia. Advancing up the Euphrates, Heraclius struck first at Theodosiopolis, the former capital of Roman Armenia, and then Dvin, the capital of Persarmenia, which he sacked. Drawing the Persian forces out of Anatolia through his actions, Heraclius then pressed south-east, bearing down on the 'holy land' of Sasanian Zoroastrianism in Atropatene (Azerbaijan). There Heraclius encountered an army led in person by Shah Khusro, which he drove back from the city of Ganzak, seizing and destroying the premier fire-temple of the Zoroastrians at Takht-i-Sulaiman (Thebarmaïs), thereby avenging the sack of Jerusalem. As Heraclius is reported to have exhorted his troops on the eve of battle: 'Men, my brethren, let us keep in mind the fear of God and fight to avenge the insult done to God. . . . Let us avenge the rape of our virgins and be afflicted in our hearts as we see the severed limbs of our soldiers. The danger is not without recompense: nay, it leads to eternal life. Let us stand bravely, and the Lord our God will assist us and destroy the enemy.'[141] As Khusro and his army fled, Heraclius' forces ravaged the surrounding terrain.[142] Heraclius then headed north, establishing his winter quarters in the Caucasian principality of Albania. It is from here that the Emperor is likely to have issued his summons to the Christian lords of the region, considerable numbers of whom flocked to his standard along with their men-at-arms.[143] Ominously for Khusro, Heraclius took advantage of his proximity to the steppe to direct an embassy to the *khagan* of the Turks, in an attempt to negotiate an alliance with the formidable nomad power.[144]

In the campaigning season of 625 three Persian armies were sent in pursuit of Heraclius. Outmanoeuvring and defeating each of these in turn, the Emperor headed towards the Black Sea coast and the kingdom of Lazica, stoking up the rhetoric of holy war against the infidel Persians, and promising martyrdom and eternal fame to those who died in battle: 'Be not disturbed, O brethren, by the multitude [of the enemy]', the *Chronicle of Theophanes* (drawing upon George of Pisidia) records him to have declared, 'for when God wills it, one man will rout a thousand. So let us sacrifice ourselves to God for the salvation of our brothers. May

---

[139] Theophanes, p. 436. For the raising of recruits in Pontus, see Greatrex and Lieu (2002), p. 198.
[140] Greatrex and Lieu (2002), pp. 198–9, and Howard-Johnston (1999), p. 4.
[141] Theophanes, p. 439.
[142] See Greatrex and Lieu, pp. 200–01.
[143] Howard-Johnston (1999), p. 17.
[144] ibid., p. 17.

we win the crown of martyrdom so that we may be praised in the future and receive our recompense from God.'[145] It was at this point that disturbing news reached the Emperor from Constantinople: perhaps in order to draw him out of Lazica and Armenia, the Persians were once more massing their forces in Anatolia, this time preparing for an assault on Constantinople itself, an attack that was to be coordinated with an Avar siege of the city's European Land Walls.[146] In a remarkable show of nerve, Heraclius decided to place his trust in the city's formidable defences and stay put in the East.

Rather than rush back to his capital, the Emperor led his troops into Anatolia, where he was able to harry detachments of the advancing Persian forces. In Constantinople itself, tensions were running high: a proposal by a certain John 'the Earthquake' (*Seismos*)—probably the Urban Prefect—to practically triple the price of bread from three *folles* to eight and to remove the privileges of the palatine guard almost led to a riot within the cathedral church of Hagia Sophia itself. The next day the Patriarch and the chief ministers of state presented themselves before the troops to tell them that John was to be dismissed and the public images of him destroyed: 'From now on you have a grant of bread from me,' the Praetorian Prefect Alexander informed them, 'and I hope that I may speedily make restitution as regards it.'[147] Now was no time for a mutiny.

On the Asian shore, the Persian army had returned to Chalcedon, the suburbs and churches of which the Persian commander Shahvaraz put to the torch as he awaited the arrival of the Avar *khagan* Baian and his forces.[148] Eventually, at the end of June, the Avar advance guard reached the outskirts of the imperial city, launching sallies against the defensive walls that had been built by Anastasius, and attacking Roman soldiers and civilians who were caught foraging for supplies.[149] A forward base was then established on high ground near the suburb of Galata, from where the Avar commanders were able to communicate by means of fire signals with the Persians, who had now advanced further along the Asiatic coast to Chrysopolis.[150]

By the end of July the main body of the Avar host, comprising some eighty thousand men in total, had arrived.[151] The author of the *Chronicon Paschale*, who appears to provide an eyewitness account, describes Slav infantry and siege engines being massed along the entire length of the Theodosian walls from the Sea of Marmara to the Golden Horn.[152] It was apparent, however, that the Avars still did not have either sufficient men or sufficient skill to overcome the Land Walls of Constantinople, whose gargantuan combination of ditch, moat, and tower

---

[145] Theophanes, pp. 442–3; for the relationship between the *Chronicle of Theophanes* and George of Pisidia, see Howard-Johnston (2010).
[146] See Howard-Johnston (1995).
[147] *Chronicon Paschale*, pp. 168–9. See n. 456.
[148] ibid., p. 170: see Howard-Johnston (1995) for the fullest modern account.
[149] *Chronicon Paschale*, p. 171.
[150] ibid., p. 171.
[151] For the size of the army, see J. D. Howard-Johnston, 'The Siege of Constantinople in 626', in Howard-Johnston (2006), VII, p. 137.
[152] *Chronicon Paschale*, pp. 173–4.

represented the acme of Roman military engineering. Rather, they needed Persian assistance. The Romans' best hope, therefore, lay in deploying naval resources that they had been able to pull back into the Sea of Marmara and around the Golden Horn in a concerted effort to prevent the Avar and Persian armies from joining forces. Having approached Chalcedon by land, the Persians apparently had no boats of their own to speak of: such shipping as had been in dock when the Persians had advanced on Chalcedon and Chrysopolis is likely to have been commandeered by the Roman fleet before Shahvaraz's arrival.[153] In order to remedy the situation, Baian ordered his Slav subjects to row dugouts and canoes (*monoxyla*) over to the Asiatic shore to ferry across the Persian troops.[154]

As the Slavs began to make the return journey from Chrysopolis, encumbered with their Persian charges, the Romans and their Armenian allies struck, causing mayhem amongst the enemy canoes by spreading fire amongst them off the coast at Blachernae.[155] Faced with this reversal, a number of the *khagan*'s Slav subjects, amassed before the Land Walls of Constantinople, immediately began to desert and take flight, obliging the Avars to pursue them or face a collapse of discipline within their ranks.[156] It was primarily a combination of fear and prestige that held the Avar war machine together, and as the smoke rose above the Bosphorus, Baian's forces were in palpable disarray.[157] As a result, according to the *Chronicon Paschale*, 'the accursed *khagan* retired to his rampart, took away from the wall the siege engines which had been set beside it and the palisade which he had constructed: by night he burnt his palisade and the siege towers and the mantelets, after removing the hides, and retreated.'[158] As the Avar army withdrew, the *khagan*'s forces attempted to save face by torching the suburbs and churches they passed.[159] On the Asiatic shore, Shahvaraz's army was obliged to withdraw in order to avoid entrapment by approaching Roman forces.

The failure of the joint Avar-Persian siege of 626 was regarded by contemporaries as little short of miraculous. Indeed, the Virgin Mary herself was reported to have been seen hastening to the city's defence, the slaughter of the Slav sailors and their Persian charges having taken place near the site of one of the principal Constantinopolitan churches dedicated to her honour.[160] In gratitude, the Patriarch Sergius composed a hymn to the Virgin that was given pride of place in the liturgy of the Great Church: 'Unto you O Theotokos, invincible Champion, your City, in thanksgiving, ascribes the victory for the deliverance from sufferings. And having your might unassailable, free us from all dangers, so that we may cry unto you: Rejoice O Bride Ever-Virgin!'[161]

---

[153] *Chronicon Paschale*, p. 177, n. 471.
[154] ibid., p. 178.
[155] ibid., pp. 178–9; see also the *Armenian History*, ch. 38 (123).
[156] *Chronicon Paschale*, p. 179.
[157] A fact fully recognised by the Romans: see Maurice's *Strategikon*, XI, 2.
[158] *Chronicon Paschale*, p. 179.
[159] ibid., p. 180.
[160] Howard-Johnston (1995), p. 141.
[161] *Kontakion* to the *Akathistos* hymn.

After a brief return to Constantinople to participate in victory celebrations, in 627 Heraclius hastened back to Lazica. It was now that he initiated the alliance with the Turks that his ambassadors had successfully negotiated. Already, in 626, with express Roman encouragement, the Turks had invaded the eastern Caucasian principality of Albania, receiving the formal submission of the local Christian warlords and the head of the Albanian Church.[162] Having shown his strength of arm, the Turk *khagan* reportedly sent a letter to Khusro instructing him to evacuate Roman territory:

> If you will not turn your face from the king of the Romans and yield to him all the countries and cities which you have seized through your violence, and if you will not despatch all the prisoners taken from his land, which you have at present under your control, together with the wooden cross which all Christian peoples worship and glorify, and if you will not summon outside his borders all your forces, the King of the North speaks in this way, the Lord of All the Earth, your King and King of all Kings, 'I shall set my face against you, you governor of Asorestan [i.e. Persia], and in place of one evil which you employed against him, I shall pay you back double. I shall move against all your borders with my sword in the same way that you moved with your sword against his borders. I shall not release you, and I shall not hesitate to act against you.'[163]

In 627 a large Turk army stormed Persian positions between the Caucasus and the Caspian and struck deep into the Persian-held kingdom of Iberia. Outside the regional capital of Tiflis (modern Tblisi), Heraclius and the Turk *Khagan* Ziebel came face to face. 'When Ziebel saw him', the *Chronicle of Theophanes* relates, 'he rushed forward, embraced his neck and did obeisance to him, while the Persians were looking on from the town of Tiflis. And the entire army of the Turks fell prone to the ground and, stretched out on their faces, reverenced the emperor.'[164] According to a later source, Heraclius even betrothed his daughter, Eudocia, to the *khagan*.[165] 'After picking 40,000 noble men', Theophanes continues, 'Ziebel gave them in alliance to the emperor, while he himself returned to his own land. Taking these men along, the emperor advanced on Khusro.'[166]

The Turk *khagan* proceeded to seal the alliance in blood by storming Tiflis and killing the Persians' Iberian client king, Stephen.[167] In the meantime, Heraclius and his joint Romano-Turk army marched south through Atropatene to the Zagros Mountains, gathering Armenian volunteers as he advanced. Entering the Iranian heartland of the Sasanian Empire, Heraclius followed the course of the River Tigris and, in December 627, defeated a Persian army near the city of Nineveh, scattering the shah's forces before him.[168] Advancing along the left bank of the Tigris,

---

[162] Howard-Johnston (2010), p. 443, and Greatrex and Lieu (2002), pp. 209–12.
[163] Movses Dasxuranci, *History of the Caucasian Albanians*, tr. C. F. J. Dowsett (London, 1961); see Greatrex and Lieu (2002), pp. 208–9.
[164] Theophanes, pp. 446–7.
[165] See discussion in Greatrex and Lieu (2002), p. 209.
[166] Theophanes, pp. 446–7.
[167] Greatrex and Lieu (2002), pp. 210–13.
[168] Greatex and Lieu (2002), pp. 213–14.

Heraclius bore down upon the Persian capital at Ctesiphon. Rather than risking a frontal assault on the heavily fortified city, however, the Emperor ravaged the cities and countryside to the north, emulating Khusro's commanders in Asia Minor in their 'scorched-earth' tactics, and intensifying the psychological pressure on the Persian nobility and high command by reducing to ashes the most productive of their domains.[169]

In military and court circles in Ctesiphon panic set in. A delegation was sent to Heraclius advising him of a conspiracy to depose Khusro II, replace him with his son, Kavad-Shiroe, and initiate negotiations with the Romans. On 24 March 628 notice reached the Emperor that Khusro was dead and that the arrival of a full peace delegation was imminent.[170] As the victory dispatch to Constantinople, preserved in the *Chronicon Paschale*, announced:

> Let all the earth raise a cry to God; serve the Lord in gladness, enter into his presence in exultation, and recognize that God is Lord indeed. It is he who has made us and not we ourselves. We are his people and sheep of his pasture.... Let the heavens be joyful and the earth exult and the sea be glad, and all that is in them. And let all we Christians... give thanks to the one God, rejoicing with great joy in his holy name. For fallen is the arrogant Khusro the enemy of God. He is fallen and cast down to the depths of the earth, and his memory is utterly exterminated...[171]

Political conditions within Ctesiphon remained highly volatile. In October 628 Kavad-Shiroe died and was replaced by his son Ardashir. Ardashir in turn was overthrown by the commander of the Persian forces in the West, Shahvaraz, who evacuated Roman territory in return for Heraclius' support for his bid for power. Shahvaraz himself was then overthrown and replaced by a weak council of regency headed by his daughter Boran. As one regime succeeded another, Heraclius took advantage of the situation to negotiate ever more favourable terms. Eventually, it was agreed to return the Romano-Persian frontier to that established by Khusro and Maurice in 591. On 21 March 630 Heraclius restored the True Cross to Jerusalem.[172]

Heraclius had achieved a remarkable reversal of military fortunes—one of the most striking and unexpected in the entirety of military history. This he had achieved through great personal courage, an ability to maximise the ideological and fiscal resources of the Roman state, and especially the readiness of many Armenian and Caucasian Christians to come to his aid. By taking warfare to the Transcaucasus, the Emperor had not only been able to take advantage of the gradually shifting religious plate tectonics of the region associated with ongoing Christianisation, but had also appreciated the core vulnerability of the political, economic, and cultic heartlands of the Sasanian Empire to attack from the north. But above all, securing the alliance with the Turks was the key to Heraclius' success: as seen with Justin II's disastrous campaign of 573, the dominant nomad power on

---

[169] Greatrex and Lieu (2002), pp. 213–19. See also Howard-Johnston (2010), pp. 443–4.
[170] See Howard-Johnston (1999), p. 26.
[171] *Chronicon Paschale*, pp. 182–3: the dispatch echoes Psalm 99 (100).
[172] Howard-Johnston (1999), pp. 28–30.

the west Eurasian steppe had an interest in maintaining a balance of powerlessness between the two great sedentary empires of Rome and Persia. The nightmare scenario from a nomad perspective was that either one of these powers should eclipse the other and then turn its attention to the steppe. As a result, when faced with the prospect of imminent Roman collapse, the Turk *khagan* had committed to Heraclius in a way that no nomad predecessor would have done to Justin II or Maurice. The Turks had intervened, just enough, to redress the balance, before pulling their forces back from the Zagros Mountains and leaving Heraclius to complete his task. The Emperor was fortunate in the timing of the *khagan*'s intervention: in 629 the Turks suffered a major defeat in Manchuria at the hands of the T'ang, who had managed to unite the sedentary kingdoms of China. The result was a sudden withdrawal of Turk forces from the Transcaucasus and a bloody civil war in the course of which Ziebel was assassinated.[173]

Heraclius was also helped, as we have seen, by a tendency on the part of Khusro to overplay his hand. Had the shah held his troops back at the Euphrates in 610, or accepted the senatorial plea for a negotiated surrender in 615, he would have been in a much stronger position to face down the Turks, who posed the real threat to the integrity of his realm. Instead, his rapid and opportunistic conquests in the period 610–18 risked imperial overstretch and threatened to weaken his empire's defences against the steppe and the world of *Turan*: this was manifested in the successful uprisings and assaults orchestrated by the Turks in Persia's north-eastern territories in 615–16.[174] Within the occupied territories, Khusro had very sensibly left pre-existing forms of administration and administrative personnel in place, and had sought to court anti-Chalcedonian sentiment by returning to Miaphysite control those bishoprics that Maurice had removed from the dissidents during his crackdown of the 590s.[175] Yet any reputation for toleration and pragmatism that the shah may have hoped for was wrecked by the events associated with the fall of Jerusalem and the massacring of its Christian population in 614, which was the perfect propaganda gift to the Emperor in Constantinople.

At the end of the day, religious diversity in the late-antique Near East had posed Khusro more problems than it had offered him solutions.[176] Certainly, the cold-shouldered Miaphysite clergy of Syria and Egypt were no friends of the Chalcedonian authorities in Constantinople. Khusro's ability to court and maintain Miaphysite support is likely to have been severely compromised, however, by his need to maintain the loyalty of the Nestorian clergy of Iraq—the bishops and prelates of the 'Church of the East' who stood at the opposite end of the Christological spectrum from the Miaphysites, but who were stalwarts of the Sasanian regime. The increasingly alienated Jewish populations of the Near East offered the Sasanian invaders enthusiastic assistance and support, welcoming them as liberators

---

[173] Howard-Johnston (2010), p. 444; Barfield (1989), pp. 142–5; Greatrex and Lieu (2002), p. 209.
[174] *Armenian History*, ch. 28 (101–2).
[175] 'Fragments of the Chart of James of Edessa' in Palmer and Brock (1993), p. 38 ('Notices to the Right of Chart 1').
[176] Note discussion in F. Millar, *The Roman Near East* (Cambridge, Mass., 1993), p. 434, n. 188.

from Roman oppression; but, as events in Jerusalem had revealed, too close an association with the Jews threatened to poison relations between Khusro and the many Christians serving under his rule, many of whom held high office in his own administration and army.

Both in 614 and 615, the actions of Khusro and his commanders had served merely to unite support behind Heraclius and his administration. Heraclius in 628, by contrast, had skilfully played upon the highly fissile character of the Sasanian court and the growing readiness of the Persian nobility to move against a wounded or compromised shah.[177] At the same time, he had been able to reach beyond the Christological complexities of conciliar theology to appeal to the core instincts and gut reactions of Christians across the Mediterranean and Near East to rally support to his cause; thus Heraclius turned the Eastern Roman Empire's struggle for survival into a Christian Holy War to redeem the True Cross, and to confront and confound the forces of Anti-Christ. In response to Heraclius' propaganda drive and victory, eschatological expectation scaled unprecedented heights.

In the wake of his victory, moreover, Heraclius chose to express his authority through an increasingly Biblicised language of power, following in the footsteps of his predecessor Justinian. The ceremonies associated with the Emperor's restoration of the True Cross to Jerusalem, for example, echoed David's triumphal installation of the Ark of the Covenant.[178] In a law of 629 the Emperor described himself in Greek as *basileus*—the royal title used both for the Old Testament kings, such as David (after whom Heraclius named a son born in 630), and for Christ.[179] Whereas the Biblical David had been the *basileus*, or king-Emperor faithful in God, so too was Heraclius *pistos en Christô basileus*, king-Emperor faithful in Christ. The 'faithlessness' of his Jewish subjects, who had collaborated with the Persian occupation, was thus a matter of pressing concern, and the Emperor ordered the forced baptism of all Jews within the empire.

7.8 THE PROPHET AMONGST THE SARACENS

The Eastern Roman Empire was thus restored territorially, but it was a shadow of its former self. The imperial concentration on the East had necessarily led to a further weakening of its position in the Balkans. Although the Avar confederacy was facing mounting difficulties in the aftermath of the failed assault on Constantinople in 626 (with the Romans now mobilising their enemies against them, from the Franks in the west to the Serbs and Croats to the north of the Carpathian

---

[177] See J. D. Howard-Johnston, 'Pride and Fall: Khusro II and his Regime, 626–8' in Howard-Johnston (2006), IX.

[178] J. W. Dijvers, 'Heraclius and the *Restitutio Crucis*—Notes on Symbolism and Ideology', in G. R. Reinink and B. H. Stolte (eds.), *The Reign of Heraclius (610–41): Crisis and Confrontation* (Leuven, 2002), pp. 175–90, 184–5.

[179] Heraclius, *Novel*, IV. For the role of David in Heraclian propaganda, see Spain Alexander, 'Heraclius, Byzantine Imperial Ideology, and the David Plates', *Speculum* 52 (1977), pp. 217–37. I owe much to Michael Humphreys for discussion of this and related points.

Mountains), not only the highlands, but, increasingly the lowlands of the Balkan peninsula were being settled by autonomous Slav tribes. Many of the cities of Anatolia and Asia Minor had been ransacked by the armies of the shah or exhausted by the fiscal demands of Heraclius' war effort. In Syria, Palestine, and Egypt, the reassertion of imperial control at this point must have been largely nominal.

In particular, conditions of considerable uncertainty are likely to have prevailed along the Eastern Roman Empire's extensive desert frontier. With the Sasanian occupation of Upper Mesopotamia, Khusro had set about reconfiguring the clientage arrangements among the tribes of northern Arabia upon which both the Romans and Persians had relied. As noted earlier, at some point between 606 and 610 Khusro had abolished the Nasrid monarchy based at al-Hira, on whose services the Sasanians had traditionally depended, and set about creating a new network of tribal alliances, a cat's cradle of diplomatic arrangements criss-crossing the frontier zone, drawing together the remnants of the Jafnids to the south-west, the Banu Ijl to the south-east (in place of the Nasrids), and a number of other tribes across northern Syria and Mesopotamia.[180] In response to this, the Banu Ijl had found themselves subjected to attack by the Nasrids' own former clients, who defeated them around the year 610 at the battle of Dhu Qar.[181] The sudden withdrawal of Persian patronage from the frontier zone's western sector between 628 and 630 can only have had further destabilising effects.

Arab pressure on the frontier zones of Rome and Persia intensified dramatically between 633 and 634. In 633 a number of the tribes that operated along the desert fringe of Sasanian Iraq, such as the Banu Shayban, were attacked by a war leader from the settlement of Yathrib to the south, by the name of Khalid ibn al-Walid. The city of al-Hira surrendered, its notables agreeing to pay tribute in return for the protection of their churches and palaces.[182] Early in 634, two further armies appeared from the desert, this time focusing their attentions on Roman territory. As one of these armies drew imperial forces eastwards, the other column punctured the defences of the province of *Oriens*, defeating a Roman army some twelve miles to the east of Gaza in southern Palestine. The invaders proceeded to turn their attention to the countryside, targeting the civilian population. As a near-contemporary account, written in Syriac, records: 'The Romans fled, leaving behind the *patrikios*... whom the Arabs killed. Some 4,000 poor village people of Palestine were killed there, Christians, Jews and Samaritans. The Arabs ravaged the whole region.'[183] The author of the same chronicle identifies these invaders as 'the Arabs of Muhammad'.[184] Within a year, the entirety of Palestine, including Jerusalem, would be in their hands.[185]

---

[180] Howard-Johnston (2010), p. 441.
[181] ibid., p. 438.
[182] H. Kennedy, *The Great Arab Conquests* (London, 2007), pp. 103–5.
[183] 'A Chronicle Composed in AD 640' in Palmer and Brock (1993), pp. 18–19.
[184] ibid., pp. 18–19.
[185] Howard-Johnston (2010), pp. 460–87—note his significant re-dating to 635 of the Arab occupation of Jerusalem (traditionally placed in 638).

Paradoxically, given his subsequent significance, the historical figure of Muhammad is a relatively shadowy presence in the pages of the seventh-century sources. Perhaps the earliest reference we have to him—or at least to a Prophet who had arisen amongst the Arabs—is to be found in the so-called 'doctrines of Jacob' (*Doctrina Iacobi*), a fascinating work dating from around 637. In the aftermath of Heraclius' defeat of the Persians, as noted earlier, the Emperor is reported to have ordered the forcible baptism of his Jewish subjects, presumably as punishment for Jewish collaboration with the Persian occupying forces, and also to hasten the *eschaton* by drawing to a conclusion the evangelisation of mankind. Heraclius' defeat of the shah and his restoration of the True Cross had not only sent apocalyptic expectations soaring, but had also led to a sudden and major revival in the prestige of the Emperor of Constantinople in the eyes of the rulers of the Christian kingdoms to the west: the restoration of the Cross was marked liturgically, for example, in both Rome and the Frankish Church, and the Merovingian monarch Dagobert openly acknowledged Heraclius' overlordship, receiving instructions from the Emperor in 629 to baptise his own Jewish subjects, a policy that he immediately set about putting into effect.[186]

Jacob, we are informed, was an East Roman Jew who, during the initial rounds of the Heraclian persecution, was arrested at Carthage in Byzantine-controlled north Africa, and eventually made a sincere conversion to Christianity when reading Holy Scripture in prison. After he was freed, he then began work as an itinerant preacher, attempting to convert the remnants of the Carthaginian Jewish community. The 'Doctrines' record a dialogue that ensued between Jacob and a certain Justus, as Jacob attempted to convince him that the Day of Judgement was at hand: Antichrist, he pointed out, already walked the earth, meaning that the Biblically promised 'Anointed One', or Messiah, must already have been and gone, and was to be identified with Jesus. Justus was convinced, we are told, for he had heard from his brother in Palestine that Satan—'the Little Horn'—had indeed arrived and walked amongst men. According to the *Doctrina Iacobi*, Justus declared that:

> My brother Abraham has written to me from Caesarea that a false prophet has appeared among the Saracens. 'For when the *candidatus* Sergius was killed by the Saracens', says Abraham, 'I was at Caesarea and I went by boat to Sycaminum; and they said "the *candidatus* has been killed", and we Jews had great joy. And they say that a prophet has appeared coming up with the Saracens and proclaims the coming of the anointed, the Christ who cometh. And when I Abraham came to Sycaminum, I went to the elder, a very learned man, and said to him: "What do you say, Rabbi, about the prophet who has appeared with the Saracens?" And he groaned loudly and said: "He is false, for surely the prophets do not come with sword and chariot.... But go, Abraham, and enquire about the prophet that has appeared." And I Abraham made enquiry and learned from those that had met him, that you find nothing true in the

---

[186] *The Chronicle of Fredegar*, 65. See also Kaegi (2003), p. 217. S. Borgehammar, 'Heraclius Learns Humility: Two Early Latin Accounts Composed for the Celebration of the *Exaltatio Crucis*', *Millennium* 6 (2009), pp. 145–202.

so-called prophet, save shedding the blood of men: for he says he holds the keys of paradise, which is untrue.'[187]

By c.640, as we have seen, Muhammad is mentioned by name in the Syriac sources, and a more detailed, less openly hostile account of him is to be found in the *Armenian History* written at some point after 660, which records how:

> At that time [c.619–20] a certain man from among those same sons of Ismael [i.e. the Arabs] whose name was Mahmet, a merchant, as if by God's command appeared to them as a preacher [and] the path of truth. He taught them to recognize the God of Abraham, especially because he was learned and informed in the history of Moses. Now because the command was from on high, at a single order they all came together in unity of religion. Abandoning their vain cults, they turned to the living God who had appeared to their father Abraham. So Mahmet legislated for them: not to eat carrion, not to drink wine, not to speak falsely, and not to engage in fornication.[188]

Between them, these three sources represent amongst our earliest historical attestations of the person of Muhammad, but the *Armenian History* in particular confirms certain crucial details of the Arabic traditions concerning the figure of the Prophet that would be set down in writing and codified from the mid-eighth century onwards.[189] According to this Arabic historical tradition, Muhammad was born c.570 in the settlement of Mecca in south-central Arabia, which was a major cultic site for the surrounding tribes (Map 6). As the *Armenian History* claims, Muhammad was reported to be a merchant, his family (like other Meccan families) engaged in trade with the Roman provinces of Syria to the north. According to the Arabic tradition, around the year 610 he began to receive a number of verse revelations, via the angelic intermediary of the angel Gabriel, from the one true God (*Allah*) who had previously revealed himself to the Jews and Christians. These revelations, which would subsequently be collected in the Qur'an ('recitation'), made plain to Muhammad the imminence of divine judgement and the absolute and pressing necessity for mankind to prepare for that judgement by means of submission (*islam*) to the will of God. Further, they established him as the 'seal of the prophets', the last in a series of God's messengers stretching back from Jesus via Moses to Abraham.

Subsequently, Muhammad began to preach his new religion to the inhabitants of Mecca, as a result of which, in 622, again according to the Arabic tradition, he and his followers were driven out of the settlement and took flight to the town of Yathrib (thereafter known as al-Medina) some 320 kilometres to the north, in closer proximity to the world of the great empires. In Medina/Yathrib Muhammad's prophethood was recognised by the population. Those who acknowledged his leadership and the truthfulness of his revelation were established as the *umma*, or community of the faithful, amongst whom feuding was prohibited. They engaged in armed conflict with the Meccan leadership until in 630, after victory

---

[187] *Doctrina Iacobi*, ed. Déroche: translation from Jones (1964), p. 317.
[188] *Armenian History*, ch. 42 (135).
[189] See discussion in C. Robinson, *Islamic Historiography* (Cambridge, 2003), pp. 24–30.

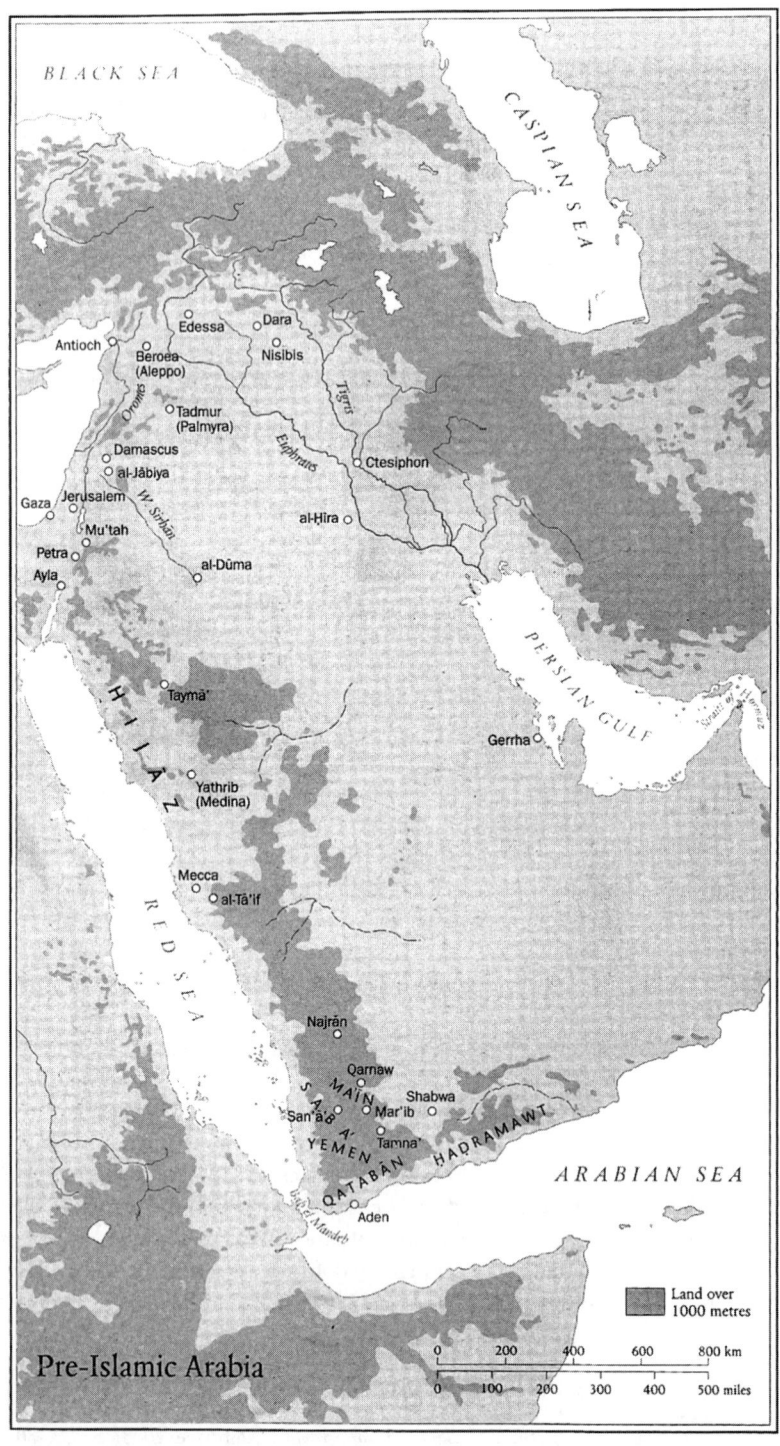

Map 6 Pre-Islamic Arabia (C. Mango, *The Oxford History of Byzantium*, p. 120)

at the battle of Badr, Muhammad and his forces returned to Mecca triumphant. According to the later Arabic sources, Muhammad died some two years later, but not before uniting much of Arabia under the aegis of his movement. After his death, a number of tribes broke away from the *umma* but were forcibly brought back within the fold by his successors to the leadership of the community, Abu Bakr (632–4) and Umar (634–44). These men were early followers of the Prophet drawn from the upper ranks of Meccan mercantile society, who also directed the initial raids on Roman Palestine that Muhammad himself had ordained.[190]

We should be careful not to accept too much of the fine detail of this later Arabic historical tradition, even if much of its broad outline can be said to be relatively secure.[191] That Muhammad came from a merchant family in Mecca, but that his *umma* (and perhaps quite a lot of the content of his religion) took shape and acquired definition in Yathrib, a town subject to much stronger external influences, may be important. For there are indications that the 'Arabs of Muhammad' that we see invading Roman territory in 633–4 may not have had quite as uniformly clear-cut a religious or indeed ethnic identity as later Muslim authors would ascribe to them. In order to understand this, however, it is necessary to appreciate the geopolitical and cultural context out of which the invaders of 633–4 emerged. In particular, it is important to place the testimony of the later Arabic sources alongside that of the more contemporary Syriac, Greek, and Armenian accounts.

As we saw in Chapter Four, the superpower conflict that erupted between Rome and Persia with the war of 502–6 had drawn both empires ever more deeply into the affairs of the peoples and kingdoms to the north and south of the Romano-Persian frontier in Mesopotamia, in the Transcaucasus and Arabia respectively. As early as the reign of Justin I, we see not only conflict between the two empires' respective client rulers along the north Arabian desert fringe, but also a struggle for control of the Yemen to the far south of the Arabian peninsula, which was finally to be resolved in favour of the Persians in 570. As a result of repeated rounds of superpower strife, therefore, the world of Arabia in the sixth and seventh centuries was disrupted and penetrated as never before by the military interventions of the great empires to the north, as well as of their allies. These included the Christian Ethiopian kings of Axum, who sought to police southern Arabia and the Yemen on Constantinople's behalf.

Crucially, military penetration went hand in hand with pronounced cultural penetration as both empires attempted to manipulate religion to advance their respective causes. As the struggle over the Yemen reveals, the Romans and their allies were eager to bolster and defend Christianity in the region, and, as in the Transcaucasus, are likely to have encouraged missionary activity as a means of

---

[190] In general, see H. Kennedy, *The Prophet and the Age of the Caliphate* (London, 1987), and *The Great Arab Conquests* (London, 2007).
[191] See P. Crone and M. Cook, *Hagarism and the Making of the Islamic World* (Cambridge, 1977). Kennedy (2007) is more sympathetic to traditional Arabic accounts. Note also F. M. Donner, *Muhammad and the Believers: At the Origins of Islam* (Cambridge, Mass., 2010).

disseminating Constantinopolitan influence. The Persians, by contrast, lent their support to the region's long-standing Jewish communities as a bulwark against Roman power, with their clients, such as Dhu Nuwis (see Chapter Four), periodically engaging in bouts of persecution of Christian minorities. At the same time, as the arteries of imperial orthodoxy hardened, and as warfare in Syria and Mesopotamia escalated, Arabia is likely to have found itself home to growing numbers of religious dissidents and refugees, from Gnostics and Nestorians to monks, Manichaens, and Messianic Jews. As a result, the main areas of settlement in Arabia in the sixth and seventh centuries are likely to have been alive with conflicting identities, beliefs, and ideas. Amongst the groups alluded to in the Qur'an and the earliest Arabic traditions are Christians, Jews, polytheists, animists, Zoroastrians, Yazidis (members of an ancient Near Eastern religion who worshipped the 'Fallen Angel'); and varieties of monotheists such as the 'Hunafa', who were thought to preserve elements of the pure religion of Abraham, and the Shabiyun, whose beliefs are entirely unknown to us, but whom the compilers of the Qur'an regarded with evident respect. In particular, in order to draw the Arabs into the Biblicised history of the Christian Roman Empire, and in emulation of the claims of earlier Jewish writers, Roman observers and missionaries projected onto the Arabs a specific scriptural genealogy: they were the sons of Ishmael, descendants of Abraham's first-born son via the slave-girl Hagar, whom Abraham had been obliged to cast out into the desert.[192]

Since the fourth century AD, Arabia had also been acquiring ever greater cultural and linguistic cohesion with the growing dissemination of a common Semitic dialect that would form the basis of Arabic.[193] Mounting superpower involvement in this increasingly homogeneous Arabian world arguably sparked off what some historians have characterised as a 'nativist reaction'—whereby the identities, ideologies, and ideas that had been introduced into the thought-world of Arabia from the outside, or projected onto the Arabs themselves, were internalised and appropriated by certain of them as a means of constructing a new, autonomous, pan-Arab identity, capable of surmounting the differences of tribe and kindred, and so better able to serve as a means of resisting imperial pressures.[194] We see elements of this, perhaps, in the appeal of Muhammad's message. For, as both the later Arabic and more contemporaneous non-Arabic sources testify, the Prophet preached the unity of the Arabs (or at least those of Mecca and northern Arabia) through Ishmael; their identity as a people of God through Abraham and through Muhammad's own revelation; and the urgency of uniting all Arabs within the embrace of the faith and overcoming the endemic feuding that beset the tribal politics of the era, and which the great powers had done so much to foster. 'We have rendered it an *Arabic*

---

[192] F. Millar, 'Hagar, Ishmael, Josephus, and the Origins of Islam', *Journal of Jewish Studies* 44 (1993), pp. 23–45.
[193] See R. Hoyland, *Arabia and the Arabs from the Bronze Age to the Coming of Islam* (2003), pp. 198–248.
[194] Crone and Cook (1977).

recitation, that you may understand,' God declared through Gabriel to Muhammad.[195] The emphasis on language and identity is telling.[196]

The nascent appeal of the religion of Muhammad as a Biblically rooted monotheism for the Arabs comes across strongly from some of the earliest Arabic traditions and accounts we have concerning the dissemination of the faith. According to one tradition, for example, Muhammad's last words were: 'Let there be not two religions in Arabia': the Prophet's message was for all mankind, but the evangelisation of the Arabs was the first priority.[197] The way in which the appeal of the religion was enhanced by a familiarity with the claims of the other great monotheistic movements is illustrated by a revealing episode preserved in the ninth-century redaction of the earliest Arabic historical account, Ibn Ishaq's 'Life of the Prophet', compiled in c.761: 'Asim b. Umar b. Qatada told me,' the author narrates:

> that some of his tribesmen said: 'What induced us to accept Islam, apart from God's mercy and guidance, was what we used to hear the Jews say. We were polytheists worshipping idols, while they were people of the scriptures with knowledge which we did not possess. There was continual enmity between us, and when we got the better of them and excited their hate, they said, "The time of a prophet who is to be sent has now come. We will kill you with his aid as Ad and Iram perished." We often used to hear this. When God sent His apostle we accepted him when he called us to God and we realized what their threat meant and joined him before them.'[198]

The same source relates how a Jewish elder had warned his flock of the imminent bearer of the message of God, 'His time has come... and don't let anyone get to him before you, O Jews, for he will be sent to shed blood and to take captive the women and children of those who oppose him.'[199] The Jews were anticipating the coming of their Messiah. But as sons of Abraham, where was the Messiah for the Arabs? They found him in the Prophet Muhammad. A similar sense of the importance of Jewish contacts, and of a concept of Abrahamic descent, as a preparation for the dissemination of Islam, is conveyed by the *Armenian History*, which records how 'the twelve tribes of all the clans of the Jews', driven from Edessa by Heraclius, 'taking desert roads went to Tachkastan [i.e. the realm of the nomadic Arabs], to the sons of Ishmael, summoned them to their aid and informed them of their blood relationship through the testament of scripture'.[200]

The religion of Muhammad as it emerges from the earliest sources was a faith deeply engaged with wider debates and concerns that were coming to dominate the religious life of the Mediterranean world into which Arabia, from the fringes of

---

[195] Qur'an, *Sura*, 43.3.
[196] On Ishmaelite genealogy, see also R. Hoyland, *Seeing Islam as Others Saw It: A Survey and Evaluation of Christian, Jewish, and Zoroastrian Writings on Early Islam* (Princeton, 1997), pp. 131–2 and p. 336; I. Shahid, *Byzantium and the Arabs in the Fifth Century* (Washington DC, 1989).
[197] Preserved in Malik's *Muwatta*, Bk. 45, 45.5.18.
[198] *The Life of Muhammad: A Translation of Ibn Ishaq's Sirat Rasul Allah*, tr. A. Guillaume (Karachi, 1955), p. 93.
[199] ibid., p. 94.
[200] *Armenian History*, ch. 41 (134).

Syria to the Yemeni littoral, was increasingly being drawn. The verses of the Qur'an reveal a preoccupation with the imminence of the apocalypse, and a determination to counter those who denied the existence of the afterlife, such as we have already encountered in the writings of Pope Gregory the Great. Like Gregory's *Book of Pastoral Care* (or the *Spiritual Meadow* of the seventh-century Palestinian monk John Moschus, who wrote under papal patronage), its verses offer an intensified but pragmatic piety whereby the core asceticism of the 'Holy Man' was available to all.[201] The vision of paradise contained in the work, and the rituals associated with prayer that we encounter in early Islam, moreover, bear a striking resemblance to those found in the early Christian Syriac ascetic tradition. The respect in the Qur'an for the Virgin Mary, but its denial of Jesus' divinity and crucifixion, chime closely with shades of contemporary Christianity, both 'orthodox' and 'heterodox'. Indeed, it is striking that a Christian heresy is precisely what the eighth-century Syrian theologian John of Damascus regarded Islam to be.[202] What Muhammad's austere monotheism cut through were the complexities and controversies of Christian Trinitarian and Christological doctrine. In that sense it was itself a fulsome response to contemporary Christian debate.

It is also worth noting that both the Arabic and non-Arabic sources record that Muhammad preached a doctrine of 'holy war', or *jihad*: he was from the start both a religious and military leader, who ultimately promised paradise to those who died for the faith.[203] As God declares to Muhammad in the Qur'an: 'Let those fight in the path of God who sell the life of this world for the other. Whoever fights in the path of God, whether he be killed or victorious, on him shall We bestow a great reward.'[204] Verse five of the Qur'an declares that 'The only reward for those who make war upon Allah and His Messenger and strive after corruption in the land will be that they will be killed or crucified, or have their hands and feet, on alternate sides, cut off, or will be expelled out of the land. Such will be their degradation in the world, and in the hereafter will be an awful doom.'[205] In a third verse we find the injunction: 'Fight against such of those to whom the Scriptures were given as believe neither in Allah nor the Last Day, who do not forbid what Allah and his apostle have forbidden, and who do not embrace the true faith, until they pay tribute out of hand and are utterly subdued.'[206]

That Muhammad should have preached a doctrine of martyrdom and holy war at precisely the time that these selfsame concepts were featuring so prominently in the official pronouncements of the East Roman state is highly suggestive, and may indicate that Heraclian propaganda was percolating into the Arabian peninsula.

---

[201] I am indebted to Dr Philip Booth for understanding this aspect of the writings of Moschus. For Gregory, see Dal Santo (forthcoming).

[202] *John of Damascus: Writings* in *The Fathers of the Church*, vol. 37 (Washington DC, 1958), pp. 153–60; J. M. Blázquez Martínez, 'Religión y Estado en el monacato oriental. Muhammad', *Gerión* 25.1 (2007), pp. 501–34.

[203] Kennedy (2007), pp. 48–51.

[204] Qur'an, *Sura*, 4.74.

[205] ibid., 5.33.

[206] ibid., 9.29.

The region around Mecca appears to have been one of the few parts of Arabia that had not come under direct Persian control by the late sixth and early seventh centuries, and thus it may have been something of a bastion of pro-Roman sentiment. Certainly, sympathy for Heraclius' cause is strongly indicated by the Qur'anic verse on 'the Greeks' (*al-Rum*), possibly recording the Persian defeat of Roman forces near Bostra in 613: 'the Greeks have been defeated in a neighbouring land. But in a few years they shall themselves gain victory: such being the will of Allah before and after.'[207]

The imprint of the world beyond Arabia is thus clearly discernible in the concerns and preoccupations highlighted by the religion of Muhammad. At the same time, however, there was a quintessentially Arabian core and structure to the faith, evident from the way in which Muhammad's teachings addressed themselves to the needs of a tribal society to overcome the divisions of feud, and the extent to which his *umma* fed off the moral economy of the kin group, establishing a sort of 'super-tribe' of the faithful. The verses of the Qur'an were rooted in the poetic sensibilities of the Arabic language and, as we have seen, much of the appeal of the religion was bound up with issues of identity. Crucially, at the end of the day, however, like the cult of the Christian 'Holy Man' examined in Chapter Six, what the movement ultimately drew its power from was the stark and awe-inspiring relationship between one man and his God, the solitary soul cut adrift amid the barren landscape of the desert, who then called his brethren to piety.

With the flight (or *hijra*) of Muhammad and his followers to Medina in 622 we have evidence for the emergence of a clearly distinguishable Muslim identity: from as early as the 640s, Arabic documentary papyri have been found that can be dated back to that crucial watershed in the history of the nascent faith.[208] It is important to note, however, that the community, or *umma*, that was established in 622 by agreement between Muhammad and his followers on the one hand, and the townsfolk of Yathrib on the other, was neither a purely Muslim nor a purely Arab affair. Rather, the *Constitution of Medina*, setting out the terms of the agreement, which is preserved in what appears to be an authentic form in Ibn Ishaq's *Life of Muhammad*, makes it clear that many Yathribi Jews were also willing to sign the covenant.[209] Conversion was not necessary to becoming part of the community: rather, one had to acknowledge the worship of the one true God, who had previously revealed himself to the Christians and Jews, accept the imminence of the Last Days, recognise the authority of Muhammad, and agree to contribute to the war effort against the unbeliever. Militant monotheism and eschatological piety were Muhammad's core demands.

These were terms that many messianically minded Jews and apocalyptically inclined Christians could well have accepted. The *Doctrina Iacobi*, after all, suggest that there were at least some Palestinian Jews willing to consider the possibility that

---

[207] ibid., 30.1.
[208] R. Hoyland, 'New Documentary Texts and the Early Islamic State', *Bulletin of SOAS* 69.3 (2006), pp. 395–416.
[209] Guillaume, trs., *The Life of Muhammad* (1955), pp. 231–3; Donner (2010), pp. 227–32.

Muhammad or his successor Umar was in fact the long-awaited 'Anointed One'. What the *Constitution of Medina* effectively established was a broad-based coalition of monotheistic fighting men united by their devotion to the 'cause of God' and the joint venture of military conquest.[210] It is important to note that, after the occupation of Mecca, it was to Roman Palestine, the Biblically ordained 'Promised Land', that Muhammad directed his forces. The *Armenian History* depicts Muhammad as declaring to his followers: 'With an oath God promised this land to Abraham and his seed after him for ever. And he brought about as he promised during that time while he loved Israel. But now you are the sons of Abraham, and God is accomplishing his promise to Abraham and his seed for you. Love sincerely only the God of Abraham, and go and seize your land which God gave to your father Abraham. No one will be able to resist you in battle, because God is with you.'[211] It is instructive that both the Arabic and non-Arabic sources concur that the armies of conquest which punctured the defences of Roman Palestine in 633–4 included non-Muslims who fought alongside their Muslim brothers.[212] The armies, in short, comprised monotheists of diverse origins as well as Arabs (clearly a majority) drawn to monotheism in an essentially Qur'anic form.[213] The military focus of early Islam was dictated by the movement's cultic orientation towards the Biblical Holy Land. It is also likely to have been informed, however, by material considerations, and a desire to profit from the opportunities opened up by dislocation and strife in the wealthy, urbanised territories of Roman Syria and Palestine to the north. As a later Arab poet declared with respect to certain members of the early armies of conquest: 'No, not for Paradise didst thou the nomad life forsake;/Rather I believe it was thy yearning after bread and dates.'[214]

7.9 THE 'ABODE OF WAR'

With the death of the Prophet Muhammad in 632, leadership of the *umma* had passed to one of his earliest followers, Abu Bakr, whose piety won him the allegiance of the new faith's followers in both Medina and Mecca.[215] Beyond this core of believers, however, as noted earlier, a series of rebellions and revolts arose amongst various of the other tribes that—whether by negotiation or conquest—had joined the Prophet's fledgling commonwealth. It was as part of the ensuing so-called *ridda*, or 'wars of apostasy', that the commander Khalid Ibn al-Walid initiated his campaign against the tribes of the Iraqi desert fringe in 633, as a concerted effort was made to bring all Arabs within the embrace of the faith.[216] By 634, as we have seen, this process was sufficiently complete for the Muslim high

---

[210] Hoyland (2006), pp. 409–10.
[211] *Armenian History*, ch. 42 (135).
[212] Hoyland (2006), p. 409.
[213] Donner (2010).
[214] Abu Hamam, *Hamasah*.
[215] For the circumstances and aftermath of the Prophet's death, see Guillaume (1955), pp. 678–90.
[216] Kennedy (2007), pp. 55–7.

command in Medina to turn its attention to the conquest of Roman Palestine that Muhammad had ordained, initiating the campaigns of that year. From the first, these endeavours were characterised by a high degree of central control of the Arab armies, which combined the warlike spirit and rapid mobility of the nomadic Bedouin with the more organised military traditions of the settled populations of the southern Arabian littoral.[217]

After the defeat of the Roman army east of Gaza in early 634, and the subsequent failure of imperial forces to contain the second, more easterly Arab column, the invaders were able to establish control of much of Palestine, focusing their attacks on villages and winning mastery of the countryside.[218] This in turn enabled them to isolate the cities of the region, a number of which began to submit to Arab rule, agreeing to pay tribute in return for security. By Christmas, Bethlehem was in Arab hands, making it impossible for the Christian clergy of Jerusalem to perform their customary pilgrimage. The Patriarch of Jerusalem, the hard-line Chalcedonian Bishop Sophronius, whose lament on the fall of the city to the Persians was cited earlier, complained of how: 'As once that of the Philistine, so now the army of the godless Saracens has captured the divine Bethlehem and bars our passage there, threatening slaughter and destruction if we leave this holy city.'[219] 'The Saracens,' he declared, 'have risen up unexpectedly against us because of our sins and ravaged everything with violent and beastly impulse and with impious and ungodly boldness.'[220] By the end of 635, not only much of the Holy Land but also probably Jerusalem itself was under Arab control.[221] The death of Abu Bakr and his succession by another of the early companions of the Prophet, Umar 'al-Faruq', or 'the Redeemer', did nothing to stem the Arab advance. Bearing the title of *amir al-mu'minin*, or 'Commander of the Faithful', Umar would eventually make a triumphal entry into Jerusalem, whence the remains of the True Cross had been spirited away to Constantinople.[222] As the *Chronicle of Theophanes* records: 'Sophronius, the chief prelate of Jerusalem, negotiated a treaty for the security of all of Palestine. Umar entered the holy city clad in a filthy camelhair garment. When Sophronius saw him he said "In truth, this is the abomination of the desolation established in the holy place, which Daniel the prophet spoke of." With many tears, the champion of piety bitterly lamented over the Christian people.'[223]

The Arab armies now pressed on to the west bank of the Jordan, advancing on Roman Syria. In a series of engagements along the northern fringes of the volcanic Hawran plain, by the River Yarmuk, the Arabs defeated a large Roman army led by the Emperor's brother Theodore.[224] As Heraclius reconfigured the forces available

---

[217] Hoyland (2006), pp. 398–9.
[218] Palmer and Brock (1993), pp. 2 and 19.
[219] Sophronius, *Christmas Sermon*, translation taken from Kennedy (2007), p. 345.
[220] Sophronius, *Synodical Letter*, translation taken from Kennedy (2007), p. 91.
[221] Howard-Johnston (2010), p. 466, moving the traditional date of the fall of Jerusalem to 635 from 638.
[222] See the *Armenian History*, ch. 42 (136). See Donner (2010) for discussion of titlature.
[223] Theophanes, pp. 471–2.
[224] See discussion in Kennedy (2007), pp. 93–5, and Howard-Johnston (2010), p. 466.

to him in southern Syria, resistance stiffened somewhat, but in a decisive encounter the Arabs broke the East Roman field army in open battle between Emesa and Damascus.[225] The remnants of the Roman forces were obliged to withdraw to defensive positions in Cilicia, the foothills of Armenia, and northern Mesopotamia.[226] An Arab raid across the Euphrates targeted the region's famed monastic communities. As one near-contemporary Syriac source records: 'the Arabs climbed the mountain of Mardin and killed many monks there'.[227] Another account relates how 'these Arabs went up to the Mardin mountains and they killed there many monks and excellent ascetics, especially in the great and famous abbey on the mountains above Rhesaina'.[228]

In response, the commander of the Roman forces in Upper Mesopotamia attempted to buy peace, leading to his dismissal by the Emperor.[229] The Roman refusal to pay elicited a concerted Arab response, and in 636 the *amir* Umar's armies advanced in force across the Euphrates into Upper Mesopotamia. The civic notables of Edessa and Harran surrendered, but first Tella and then Dara were taken by storm. In the latter, we are told, every single Roman found in the city was executed.[230] Rather than face this fate, the inhabitants of Amida and a number of other cities rapidly came to terms. Extending their control over the old Roman-Persian frontier zone, the Arabs now struck east into Sasanian territory, sweeping across the 'black lands' of the Iraqi alluvium and bearing down on the capital of the shahs at Ctesiphon. A massive Persian army was assembled to meet them under the leadership of the general Rushtam. In 637 this force, which included significant Transcaucasian contingents and which the author of the *Armenian History* reckoned at some eighty thousand men, managed to drive the Arabs away from Ctesiphon and propel them back across the Euphrates, inflicting the first significant defeat on the Arabs since their campaigns of conquest had begun.[231]

From the length and breadth of Arabia the forces of the *umma* were rallied, and in January 638 at al-Qadisiyya, near the old Nasrid capital of al-Hira, the massed ranks of the Arab and Sasanian field armies clashed. The result was a cataclysm for the Persians. Broken in open battle, a retreat rapidly became a rout. As the *Armenian History* records, 'The Persian army fled before them, but they pursued them and put them to the sword. All the leading nobles were killed, and the general Rushtam was also killed.'[232] As the Arabs once more focused their attention on Ctesiphon, in the following year a desperate attempt to evacuate the Persian high command and the royal treasury ended in disaster as the baggage train was ambushed and its precious cargo seized. Shah Yazdgerd III, a grandson of Khusro

---

[225] Howard-Johnston (2010), p. 467.
[226] ibid.
[227] Palmer and Brock (1993), p. 19.
[228] ibid., p. 150.
[229] ibid., pp. 162–3.
[230] ibid., p. 163.
[231] Howard-Johnston (2010), p. 467; the *Armenian History*, ch. 42 (137), and Kennedy (2007), pp. 105–7.
[232] *Armenian History*, ch. 42 (137).

II who had ascended the throne in 632, managed to flee east to the rocky fastness of the Zagros Mountains, but there was little he could do to save his capital, which the Arabs were now able to occupy almost unopposed.[233]

In the west, the Romans took advantage of the Arab preoccupation with Persia to launch raids on Arab-held northern Syria and northern Mesopotamia, whilst, on the Palestinian coast, the garrison at Caesarea continued to hold out, receiving supplies by sea. The Arab general Iyad was, however, able to drive back these imperial assaults, which are recorded to have done much to alienate the local population from the Roman army, and the commander of the Muslim forces in Syria, Mu'awiya, finally overcame the defences of Caesarea and put both the garrison and the population to the sword. 'The city', we are told, 'was plundered of vast quantities of gold and silver and then abandoned to its grief. Those who settled there afterwards became tributaries of the Arabs.'[234]

With the loss of Caesarea, all of Syria and Palestine was now in Arab hands. In 640 Muslim forces advanced into south-western Armenia while the general Amr ibn al-As, pursuing retreating Roman forces out of Palestine, initiated the conquest of the Nile valley.[235] Aided by reinforcements directed to him from Medina, the general was able to take first Oxyrhynchus, then in 641 the Roman military base at Babylon, where he seized abandoned siege engines, before fighting his way up towards the Nile Delta, attacking the estate complexes of the local aristocracy where resistance was seemingly concentrated.[236] In 642 the general's armies initiated the siege of Alexandria. Parleying on behalf of the imperial authorities, the Patriarch Cyrus negotiated an armistice whereby the Arabs received an annual sum of 200,000 *solidi* and the city was demilitarised, the Roman army and administration being obliged to withdraw to Cyprus. A subsequent attempt in 646 on the part of the Roman general Manuel to reoccupy the city and use it as a bridgehead for the reconquest of Egypt (to which we shall return in the following chapter) impelled the Arab army to enter the city and slaughter the garrison. Manuel and the Patriarch Cyrus fled to Constantinople.[237]

As the final remnants of Roman resistance in the Near East beyond Anatolia, Asia Minor, and the islands were snuffed out, the Arabs pressed ahead with their conquest of the crumbling Sasanian Empire. Assaults were launched across the Persian Gulf in 641 and into the Zagros Mountains. In 642 the Arabs advanced through the Zagros into the Parthian territory of Media. With the defeat there of the Persian army at Nihawand, the Arabs spread over the remaining regions of the Persian world in what was essentially a mopping-up exercise, breaking down the resistance of the regional lords and princes one by one. Finally, in 652, Yazdgerd III was assassinated as he attempted to flee to the steppe, the last son of the House of Sasan ignominiously a fugitive in the realm of *Turan*. The medieval Persian epic the

---

[233] Howard-Johnston (2010), pp. 468–9; Kennedy (2007), pp. 116–24.
[234] Palmer and Brock (1993), pp. 164–6; Howard-Johnston (2010), p. 468.
[235] On Armenia, see the *Armenian History*, ch. 42 (138); on Egypt, see John of Nikiu, 111.
[236] John of Nikiu, 111–20.
[237] Palmer and Brock (1993), pp. 158–60.

Shahnameh, or 'Book of Kings', describes how the assassin, a miller by the name of Khusro, approached Yazdgerd 'his heart filled with shame and fear ... his cheeks were stained with tears, and his mouth was dry as dust. He came up to the king like someone about to impart a secret in a man's ear and plunged a dagger beneath his ribs. The king sighed at the wound, and his head and crown fell down to the dust, beside the barley bread that lay before him.'[238]

7.10 REASONS FOR ARAB SUCCESS

What had begun as an attempt on the part of Muhammad's followers to claim and occupy what they regarded as their divinely promised patrimony in Palestine had therefore escalated into an extraordinary wave of conquests; these wiped the ancient empire of Persia off the face of the map and once more drove Heraclius and the Romans back behind the mountains of the Taurus and ante-Taurus that defended the Anatolian plateau. From their initial focus on Palestine, and on uniting all Arabs within the embrace of the new faith, the armies of Abu Bakr and Umar had acquired a momentum of their own: they would continue to march on and conquer until either they were defeated or the Day of Judgement came. The Arab armies were clearly aided in their success by the relative exhaustion of the two great superpowers that they had set about dismembering; it was the perspective of the author of the *Armenian History*, for example, that it was the destructive pride and overweening ambition of Khusro II which had opened the gates of Hell and unleashed the Saracen scourge. In Persia, as we have seen, political circles in Ctesiphon had gone into meltdown as a result of Heraclius' victorious campaign of 628. Heraclius' daring descent into Persian territory and his ravaging of the lands to the north of Ctesiphon may well have done lasting damage to the agricultural resources and administration of a region that had been the economic powerhouse of the Sasanian state. Political paralysis and administrative chaos may also have critically limited the ability of the Persian authorities to respond to the Arab threat.

Likewise, Heraclius, it should be noted, had gambled everything on his last throw of the dice against Persia. Already drained of their resources by the demands of his war effort, or reduced to ruin by Persian assault, the cities of Asia Minor simply may not have been in a position to finance and support a sustained defence of Syria, Palestine, and Egypt, where the restoration of Roman rule in the aftermath of the Persian withdrawal of 628–30 is likely, in any event, to have been largely symbolic at the time when the Arab armies began to appear: long-standing traditions of Roman control had been fractured and disrupted and were yet to be fully restored. Indeed many of the 'Roman' armies that the Arabs encountered are likely to have been little more than *gendarmes*, or local levies, hastily gathered together by civic notables and landowners to defend their cities and estates.

[238] *Shahnameh*, p. 849.

Moreover, it could be argued that the Eastern Roman Empire's extensive desert frontier was in any case its Achilles heel. The Romans had never successfully resolved the problem of how to police and defend the frontier: walling it off was impossible; maintaining security through the services of conflicting networks of client chiefs had proved untenable; and relying upon the services of a single client chief had been unworkable. At the end of the day, all that had perhaps rendered Roman imperialism practicable and sustainable in Syria and Palestine had been the absence of a concerted threat from along the desert fringe. The Palmyrene revolt of the 270s had demonstrated how fragile Roman control of the region might be if faced with such a challenge. 'Divide and rule' thus remained the key to Roman survival. Given the objective military and geographical circumstances, the unity that the religion of Muhammad provided to the tribes of north-central Arabia, and the cultic and military focus towards Roman Palestine that the Prophet ordained, may of itself have been sufficient to seal the fate of Roman power in the East. Constantinople, too, suffered political problems of its own: the death of Heraclius in 641, and the power struggle that ensued, did much to distract attention from the Arab march on Alexandria and to detract from the effective coordination of Roman resistance.[239] Likewise, disaffection on the part of Jewish and other religious minorities, and alienation on the part of the peasantry and the poor, are also likely to have played their role in encouraging communities to come to terms with the invaders in their midst.

But the triumph of the Arab armies was also the work of the Arabs themselves. The combination of Beduin mobility and the more organised military and political traditions of the sedentary populations of the southern Arabian littoral, such as the Yemenis, created a formidable war machine, whilst the wealth of the Roman and Persian territories provided a clear material incentive for military expansion (especially for tribesmen whose ability to profit from trade with the sedentary empires to the north had perhaps been disrupted by warfare). Tactically, the strategy we see at work in Palestine in 634, of Arab armies attacking 'soft targets' such as villages, engaging in conspicuous massacres of the rural population, and then offering terms to the leaders of civic communities, promising security in return for tribute, was a psychologically canny one that permitted strikingly rapid conquests and the avoidance of entanglement in lengthy sieges. When faced with resistance from cities such as Dara, the favoured Arab strategy was simply to storm them, throwing men at the walls until enough of them got in, rather than bedding down to a long drawn-out war of attrition. The brutality shown to the inhabitants of those cities that did resist sent a clear message to the leaders of other communities that it would be in their manifest interest simply to surrender and 'pay tribute out of hand', as the Qur'an directed, rather than risk suffering a similar fate. As the *Armenian History* records of the Arabs, 'then dread of them fell on the inhabitants of the land, and they all submitted to them'.[240]

---

[239] See discussion in Kennedy (2007).
[240] *Armenian History*, ch. 42 (136).

It is, however, the ability of the Arab commanders to storm cities—to order their warriors to advance and attack and advance again until a city fell, irrespective of the casualty rate—that perhaps alerts us to the ultimate factor behind Arab success: zeal. Driven on by religious fervour and certain of paradise, the Arab armies appear to have had a far higher 'pain threshold' and to have enjoyed morale superior to that of either their Persian or Roman adversaries.[241] Dead or alive, Allah would reward them. Confident in the power of their God, the authority of the Prophet, and the imminence of Divine Judgement, the forces of Islam swept all before them. Both Roman and Persian armies, by contrast, had recently experienced defeat, and, as the military theorist Carl von Clausewitz realised, in warfare it is morale that is often the decisive factor.[242]

---

[241] I owe this point to Leif Petersen.
[242] As pointed out to me in a tutorial in 1993 by James Howard-Johnston.

8

The Age of Division

8.1 THE FRAGILITY OF THE NEW WORLD ORDER

Between the initial raids into Roman Palestine in the early 630s and the death of Yazdgerd III in 652, the 'Arabs of Muhammad' and their allies had not only managed to drive the Roman forces of Heraclius back into Anatolia and Asia Minor but had also destroyed once and for all the ancient empire of the shahs of Persia. Of the two great powers that had for so long dominated the politics and culture of western Eurasia, one was no more and the other was palpably on the ropes. In 652–3 the Arabs extended their control into the Transcaucasus, exacting oaths of loyalty from the Armenian prince Theodore Rshtuni and his vassals, who had hitherto fought on Constantinople's behalf.

This was the necessary precursor to the intensification of the *jihad* against Byzantium, for it secured for the Arabs control over the lines of east–west communication across the valleys of Armenia that led onto the Anatolian plateau. As the *Armenian History* records:

> In that same year the Armenians rebelled and removed themselves from [allegiance to] the Greek kingdom and submitted to the king of Ismael. T'eodoros, lord of Rshtunik, with all the Armenian princes made a pact with death and contracted an alliance with hell, abandoning the divine covenant. Now the prince of Ismael spoke with them and said: 'Let this be the pact of my treaty between me and you for as many years as you may wish. I shall not take tribute from you for a three-year period. Then you will pay tribute with an oath, as much as you may wish. You will keep in your country 15,000 cavalry, and provide sustenance from your country: and I shall reckon it in the royal tax. I shall not request the cavalry for Syria; but wherever else I command they shall be ready for duty. I shall not send *amirs* to [your] fortresses, nor an Arab army—neither many nor even down to a single cavalryman. An enemy shall not enter Armenia; and if the Romans attack you I shall send you troops in support, as many as you may wish. I swear by the great God that I shall not be false.' In this manner the servant of Anti-Christ split them away from the Romans. For although the emperor wrote many intercessions and supplications and summoned them to himself, they did not wish to heed him.[1]

As this passage reveals, however, and as both the Arabic and non-Arabic sources agree, the tightness of Arab rule over the recently acquired territories varied enormously, and would continue to do so to the end of the seventh century and

---

[1] *Armenian History*, ch. 48 (164).

beyond. In general terms, Arab rule was at its most secure in lowland zones and inland areas, such as the *jazira* of Mesopotamia. The Arab armies of conquest were clearly at their least confident when fighting on mountainous terrain. As a result, all they were really able to acquire from Theodore Rshtuni and the Armenians was a loose acknowledgement of Arab suzerainty and a promise to provide a military levy. The Arabs would only intervene in Armenia if the Romans, under their new Emperor, Constans II, did. What the Arab commanders were effectively promising was a guarantee of Armenian autonomy, something that the princes of the region had hitherto sought to achieve by playing off the rival powers of Rome and Persia.

Likewise, at no point in the seventh century did the Arabs manage to conquer or occupy by force the mountains of the Lebanon, which, as shall be seen, were to be home to bands of Christian insurgents known as the 'Mardaites' who maintained a campaign of guerrilla warfare against the Muslims and who would periodically descend from Mount Lebanon to attack Arab forces in the plains and cities below. To the east, the Zagros Mountains remained outside direct Arab control and would provide a place of refuge for every malcontent, heretical or disaffected group that early Islam would generate. The Arabs' grip on coastal zones was similarly precarious. As noted in Chapter Seven, supplied by sea, the city of maritime Caesarea in Palestine had resisted Arab conquest for years. There are indications that many of the cities and communities along the Syrian coast drifted in and out of Arab rule over the course of the seventh century, paying tribute to the Arabs when they perceived them to be strong, but turning off the tributary tap when they sensed the power of the Muslims to be waning. In the late seventh century the inhabitants of Cyprus would pay tribute to both the Arabs and the Romans, sending cargoes of copper west to Constantinople and east to Syria.[2] In Egypt the original deal agreed between the Patriarch Cyrus and Amr ibn al-As was that Alexandria would pay tribute and the Nile Delta effectively be demilitarised with the evacuation of the Byzantine garrison. Only Constantinople's subsequent attempt to reoccupy the city had led to a more forceful assertion of Arab might.

Even within the lowland zones and inland, however, the rapidity of the Arab advance, and the willingness of the conquerors to cut deals with the leaders of provincial society, offering security and religious and property rights in return for the payment of tribute (as recorded for example, with respect to the Christian Arabs of al-Hira in 633), necessarily meant that for much of the seventh century, Muslim rule rested relatively lightly over the lands of the Near East. So long as tribute was paid to the Arab authorities, then long-established local elites could get on with running the communities they had so long dominated. A classic example of this emerges from Egypt where, according to the *Chronicle of John of Nikiu*, the first Arab-appointed Prefect, or governor of the city of Alexandria, was a certain John of Damietta, who had previously been the Byzantine general in charge of Roman resistance to the Arabs.[3] In the mid-eighth century, the great Christian Orthodox theologian John of Damascus could claim descent from a family of Roman imperial

---

[2] Theophanes, p. 506.   [3] *Chronicle of John of Nikiu*, p. 200.

administrators who had continued their mandarin lifestyle under their new Arab masters. In terms of administration, economic activity, and even, to some extent, religion, life in the conquered territories continued as it had before. Essentially, at a grassroots level, the same people were effectively collecting the same taxes in the same manner; the difference was that thereafter these taxes were being handed over to the Arabs rather than to the representatives of the Roman Emperor or the Persian shah. As in the post-Roman west, the provincial-level regional aristocracies and elites remained in place. It was at the level of the grandest families, most closely implicated in imperial rule or most heavily dependent on the trans-regional structures of empire, that discontinuity was at its most apparent, with such families either fleeing or being snuffed out.

The high degree of continuity in social and administrative structures evident in the wake of conquest was also facilitated by the fact that the Arab armies, carefully supervised by the high command in Medina, were, for the most part, cantoned separately from the populations over whom they now ruled. These armies were living in newly established garrison towns such as Fustat in Egypt (modern Cairo), or Kufa and Basra in Iraq, where they received stipends (*ata*) derived from the tribute of the local population. Only in Syria do rulers and ruled appear to have lived cheek by jowl, but here in any case there were long-standing Arab populations. The conquerors were thus able to maintain their identity, effectively living as a separate and privileged military caste feeding off the resources of their Christian, Jewish, or Zoroastrian tributaries. The conversion of subject populations was not a priority, and in order not to alienate either the subject peoples or the non-Muslims who had fought in their own ranks in the armies of conquest, the early leaders of the *umma* such as Umar (r.634–44) and his successor Uthman (r.644–56) adopted the religiously ambiguous and multivalent title of *amir al-mu'minin*—'commander of the faithful'—rather than anything more stridently or aggressively Islamic.[4]

The documentary papyri that survive from Egypt in the seventh century convey much of the paradoxical nature of this nascent 'early Islamic' world. The densely inhabited and intensively cultivated landscape of the Nile Valley ought to have been amongst the easiest terrains for the Arab conquerors to dominate. Yet they barely register in the documents we have concerning rural life. Instead day-to-day life was dominated both by members of the local Christian elite, bearing the old Roman title of 'pagarchs' (*pagarchoi*), and the personnel of the Miaphysite Church; together, these took up much of the slack left by the withdrawal of Roman governors, the flight of the Chalcedonian patriarch, and the disappearance of the great households of members of the upper echelons of the senatorial aristocracy, such as the Flavii Apiones of Oxyrhynchus.[5] Indeed, from the 'bottom up', for much of its post-Heraclian history, seventh-century Egypt would have looked very much like a Coptic Christian theocracy in which society was dominated and taxes were collected by the Church and by Christian notables—before the lion's share of

---

[4] Hoyland (2006), pp. 409–10; Donner (2010).
[5] P. Sijpesteijn, 'Landholding Patterns in Early Islamic Egypt', *Journal of Agrarian Change* 9.1 (2009), pp. 120–33, and Sarris (2009).

these revenues was then handed over to the Arab Muslim administration and its army based at Fustat, whose demands for tribute were pressing and insistent. A similar situation pertained among the Christian communities of Iraq, where the disappearance of the institutions of the Sasanian state led to a major expansion of the juridical and administrative authority of the episcopacy and city-level Christian elites.[6] In both Arab-controlled Egypt and Iraq, 'Muslim rule' paradoxically meant stronger bishops.

As the documentary evidence from Egypt and Iraq reminds us, administration was not just continued by the same sorts of people in the same manner; it continued in the same languages, above all Greek (with some Syriac and Coptic) in the former Roman provinces, and Syriac and Pahlavi (Middle Persian) in the ex-Sasanian ones. Roman gold coins and Persian silver coinage continued to circulate in their respective currency zones, with the Muslims minting mock-imperial coinage, albeit ultimately devoid in the Roman case (perhaps from the 660s onwards) of Christian religious imagery (Fig. 10).[7] It must have seemed to many that although some seismic shift had clearly occurred, the new world order looked remarkably like the old. To all intents and purposes there existed a 'sub-Roman' Arab Empire in the former Roman territories, and a 'sub-Sasanian' one in the lands hitherto subject to the shah. Indeed many clearly anticipated an imminent Byzantine counter-strike, whereby the provinces would be restored to the empire of Christ just as Heraclius had won them back after twenty years of Persian occupation in the late 620s. It was a sense shared by certain of the Arabs themselves: a proverb cautioned that 'Islam has started as a foreigner [to all lands] and may again

Fig. 10 Arab Mock-Byzantine Solidus (C. Mango, *The Oxford History of Byzantium*, p. 127)

---

[6] R. E. Payne, 'Christianity and Iranian Society in Late Antiquity, ca. 500–700 CE', (Princeton, D. Phil. dissertation, 2010); C. F. Robinson, *Empire and Elites after the Muslim Conquest: The Transformation of Northern Mesopotamia* (Cambridge, 2000); M. Morony, *Iraq after the Muslim Conquests* (Princeton, 1984).

[7] C. Foss, *Arab-Byzantine Coins: An Introduction, with a Catalogue of the Dumbarton Oaks Collection* (Washington DC, 2008); for the economic context, see Banaji (2006).

become a foreigner, folding back [on Mecca and Medina] like a snake folding back into its hole.'[8]

8.2 THE NEAR EAST IN THE BALANCE

In spite of the rapidity of the Roman military collapse in Syria, Palestine, and Egypt in the 630s and early 640s, the strategic outlook for the imperial authorities c.652–3 was not entirely bleak; there were still a number of cards that the Emperor in Constantinople could hope to play. First, although the Eastern Roman Empire of the late sixth and early seventh century does not appear to have possessed much by way of a standing navy, the Romans were far more experienced than the Arab high command in operating at sea, and could take advantage of the huge stretch of coastline that the Arabs now had to police to cause the invaders problems similar to those which Rome's extended desert frontier had posed emperors in the sixth and seventh centuries.[9] The frontier, in short, could not be defended in its entirety, and the Romans could attempt to destabilise Arab rule by striking almost anywhere along it.

Second, although the resources of Asia Minor were severely depleted, the empire still controlled extensive and economically highly productive territories in southern Italy, Sicily, and north Africa, which could be harnessed to finance a Byzantine counter-strike. Third, in spite of Christological differences between Constantinople and leaders of the Church in Armenia, Syria, and Egypt, with one or two exceptions, there was little sign of anything but hostility towards the Arabs on the part of the Christian clergy, members of which, if properly handled, might yet be turned to in order to mobilise broader bodies of support in the occupied territories, especially in the Transcaucasus. It is instructive that the authors of both the *Armenian History* and the Egyptian *Chronicle of John of Nikiu*, although rabid anti-Chalcedonians, regarded the Arab invaders with palpable animosity. Fourth, it was highly likely that the leaders of the Arab armies of conquest, flushed with tribute and the spoils of war, would fall out amongst themselves, opening the way to a restoration of Roman rule. It was thus a matter of the utmost importance that the imperial authorities remain in contact both with key figures among the inhabitants of the occupied territories in Syria and Palestine, in order to identify potential allies and clients should Arab rule begin to fragment, as well as with the lords and churchmen of the Transcaucasus, so as to be in a position to piece together a Heraclian-style 'grand alliance' capable of striking down from the north and sweeping the Arabs before them.

The imperial authorities' ability to emulate Heraclius in this respect was severely impaired, however, by the aftermath of the crisis on the steppe orchestrated by the T'ang rulers of China.[10] A newly stable nomad state, the Khazar khaganate, was

---

[8] S. Bashear, 'Apocalyptic and other Materials on Early Muslim-Byzantine Wars: A Review of Arabic Sources', *Journal of the Royal Asiatic Society* Series 3.1 (1991), pp. 173–207, 187–8.
[9] Howard-Johnston (2010).   [10] ibid., p. 444.

only just taking root to the north of the Caucasus in place of the Turks, and was yet to be fully integrated diplomatically by Constantinople. In 642 the Arabs had struck across the Caucasus and defeated the Khazar *khagan* on the lower Volga and momentarily forced him to accept Islam.[11] Although this initiated over a century of intermittent hostilities between the Khazars and the Arabs, the Romans were not yet in a position to take advantage of the situation militarily.

Constantinople also faced a number of other difficulties with respect to putting any grand strategy against the Arabs into place. A Roman counter-strike, as we have seen, would need the active support of the leaders of Miaphysite communities in both the Transcaucasus and the occupied territories. It was thus important that the imperial government adopt a pragmatic and conciliatory stance with respect to Christology. In his attempt to hold together the East, Heraclius had permitted a modification of the Christological position adopted at the Second Council of Constantinople in 553 and reached out, with some success, to Miaphysite communities. This had been done by examining ways in which one could describe the human and divine in the person of Christ to have been galvanised by a single unifying energy (a policy known as *monoenergism*) or will (*monotheletism*), thus avoiding discussion of His natures.[12] This attempted compromise had enunciated shrill condemnation from hard-line supporters of the Council of 553 (known as 'Neo-Chalcedonians'), such as the Patriarch Sophronius in Jerusalem, but, of necessity, their voices were not those to which the ear of the Emperor had inclined.

The same imperative to reconcile Miaphysite opinion was incumbent upon the regime of the young Emperor Constans II. For Constans, however, the situation was complicated by the fact that, whereas Heraclius' war effort had depended upon the resources and population of Asia Minor and Anatolia, the war machine that the new Emperor now needed to put in place was dependent upon the resources of southern Italy and north Africa; however, episcopal opposition even to Justinian's attempted engagement with the Miaphysite leadership was intense there, and had almost broken the authority of the Pope in Rome, sparking a schism with the north Italian churches that had only recently been healed. Robbing Peter while cutting a deal with Paul would be no easy matter.

Moreover, neither the imperial government nor what remained of the East Roman army appeared to be fit for purpose. Upon Heraclius' death in February 641, the throne had initially passed, in accordance with the late Emperor's will, to his eldest son, the twenty-nine-year-old Heraclius Constantine, ruling jointly with Heraclius' eldest son by his second wife (his niece Martina), the fifteen-year-old Heraclonas. Just three months later, however, Heraclius Constantine had died of tuberculosis, leaving a boy on the throne under the care of his mother, who now became regent. Many in court and ecclesiastical circles had regarded Heraclius' marriage to his niece as an incestuous abomination and the children as degenerate bastards. Rallying support around the regime of Martina and Heraclonas was thus

---

[11] P. Golden, 'The Peoples of the South Russian Steppes', in D. Sinor (ed.), *The Cambridge History of Early Inner Asia* (Cambridge, 1990), pp. 256–84, p. 265.
[12] Frend (1972).

fraught from the start, and opinion began to strengthen in favour of the late Heraclius Constantine's ten-year-old son, Constans.

The commander of the Eastern field army, Valentine, marched on Chalcedon trumpeting the young prince's claims, while rioting directed against Martina and her entourage broke out on the streets of Constantinople. In September, Valentine entered the city. Martina and Heraclonas were deposed, although, as an act of kindness, they were not executed. Instead she had her tongue slit and Heraclonas' nose was sliced open, such physical disfigurements traditionally being regarded as incompatible with imperial office. Valentine was now the dominant political figure in the empire, but as the military situation deteriorated, opinion had in turn hardened against him. In 644, as the Arabs raided deep into Asia Minor and, in Italy, as the Langobards defeated and killed the Byzantine governor, or 'exarch', and occupied Liguria, Valentine was himself strung up by an angry mob. This had secured Constans' place on the throne, but it had also left a youth of barely fourteen years of age in charge of affairs. Critically, during the political paralysis resulting from these court intrigues, the Arabs had been able to secure their grip on Egypt and Alexandria.[13]

A further round of infighting in Constantinople, of uncertain date but presumably aimed at deposing the young Emperor, is recorded in highly colourful and clearly exaggerated terms in the *Armenian History*. As in the reign of Phocas, the result was a purge of the Senate and court:

> What more shall I say about the disorder of the Roman empire, and the disasters of the slaughter from which the civil war was never free, and the flowing of the blood of the slaughter of prominent men and counsellors in the kingdom who were accused of plotting the emperor's death? For this reason they slew all the leading men; and there did not remain in the kingdom a single counsellor, since all the inhabitants of the country and the princes in the kingdom were totally exterminated.[14]

This crisis of political leadership had coincided with a crisis in the administration of the army and the state. The war-torn remnants of the East Roman field army as it had been pulled back into Anatolia and Asia Minor appear to have been in utter disarray. Maintaining and supplying the troops in the field—even billeting them— is likely to have posed near insurmountable problems, given the cash-starved nature of the state and the fact that already under Heraclius there are signs that the administrative machinery of the Praetorian Prefecture, on which the fiscal system and the army depended, was in a state of collapse and had effectively had to be dismantled.[15] In 638, as noted in Chapter Seven, a Roman counter-attack against the Arabs in northern Syria had alienated the local population by virtue of the fact that the imperial army had been obliged to forage for supplies: the units under the command of the Armenian general David, we are told, had had 'no scruples at all

---

[13] As argued for by Kennedy (2007). For the complicated court politics of the period, a sure guide is to be found in W. Treadgold, *A History of the Byzantine State and Society* (Stanford, 1997), pp. 307–10.
[14] *Armenian History*, ch. 47 (162).
[15] See J. F. Haldon, *Byzantium in the Seventh Century: The Transformation of a Culture* (Cambridge, 1993), pp. 186–91.

about plundering the population down to their last possession. They also tortured men and women cruelly to discover where hoards of treasure had been buried.'[16] By the early 640s matters would have deteriorated further. In such circumstances, the army could barely be relied upon even for the defence of Anatolia and the land approaches to Constantinople, let alone an aggressive campaign to regain lost ground. The imperial army and its system of supply needed to be dramatically overhauled, and a navy had to be put in place so as to attack the Arabs, defend Asia Minor, and secure the lines of communication and supply to the west.

There are indications that by the mid-640s those around Constans II were beginning to take matters in hand, and the boy-Emperor himself was asserting his authority to ever greater effect, demonstrating that it really was Heraclius' blood that flowed through his veins. It was on the reorganisation of the army and the piecing together of a specialised naval capability out of the empire's extensive merchant fleet that attention was necessarily focused. At some point in the early 640s, the surviving units of the Roman field army in Anatolia, presumably bolstered by local levies, had been organised into newly consolidated regiments called 'themes', or *themata*; those of the 'Anatolikon' (comprising survivors of the Eastern regiments formerly under the *magister militum per Orientem*); the 'Armeniakon' (from the forces under the *magister militum per Armeniam*); the 'Thrakesion' (from the Balkan field army); and the 'Opsikion', probably built up around a core of privately armed retainers, Transcaucasian volunteers, and men-at-arms who, like freedmen (ex-slaves) in Roman law, had an obligation of loyalty and service (*obsequium*) to their masters.[17]

Growing Roman naval confidence had been revealed when in 646, the expeditionary force under Manuel had set sail for Egypt, where a dispute between the new *amir al-mu'minin* Uthman and the general Amr ibn al-As had led to the latter's removal from office and subsequent disaffection on the part of the Arab rank and file.[18] Presumably operating out of Cyprus, Roman marines had been able to occupy Alexandria and fan out across the Nile Delta. This was a serious challenge to which Uthman had responded with forthright pragmatism: Amr ibn al-As was immediately restored to his command and, from his base at Babylon, the Belisarius of the Arabs was able to prevent any Roman advance up the Nile Valley. Defeating the Roman expeditionary force near the town of Nikiu, he retook Alexandria after a short siege. A retaliatory attack was then launched on Roman Africa where, in 647, the Exarch Gregory was defeated in battle and fell in the field. This was not entirely bad news for Constans, as in 646 Gregory had rebelled against his rule and declared himself Emperor on the pretext of imperial 'monotheletism'.[19] Amr ibn al-As then withdrew to the Pentapolis on the edge of the Libyan desert, securing the land route to Alexandria.[20]

---

[16] Palmer and Brock (1993), p. 164.
[17] Howard-Johnston (2010), pp. 483–4 with n. 64.
[18] ibid., p. 154, n. 55.
[19] Haldon (1993), pp. 56–7.
[20] Kennedy (2007), p. 162 and pp. 207–8; Howard-Johnston (2010), p. 477.

The Arabs now set about commandeering the resources and labour of the Alexandrian and Palestinian shipyards to put together a navy of their own, something they achieved with remarkable success, which may indicate that they were able to draw upon seafaring traditions on the part of Yemeni and other Muslims from the coastal zones of the Arabian peninsula.[21] In 649 a large fleet under the command of the Governor of Syria, Mu'awiya, arrived off the coast of Cyprus, where the Arab forces were able to land effectively unopposed and amass a great deal of booty. In 650 a second Arab army occupied the island.[22] That same year the small but strategically vital island of Aradus (Arwad) off the coast of Syria was attacked and, in 651, fell after an extensive siege.[23]

Although events were not entirely going the Emperor's way, we can see Constans II and his regime making concerted efforts to respond to the objective military and political needs of the day. The imperial government also began to sketch the outline of an ecclesiastical strategy aimed at undercutting the theological complexities of the interminable Christological dispute. The solution proposed by the imperial edict, or *Typos*, promulgated in 648 was disarmingly simple: henceforth discussion of how many wills, energies, or natures Christ possessed was to be prohibited. Christians were to be reminded of the core Nicene faith that all had in common. From a partisan perspective however, silence was unacceptable, as it simply provided a cloak for error and a cover for the path whereby the souls of the faithful were led to perdition. In 649 Pope Martin I convened a council in Rome, attended by the hard-line eastern Neo-Chalcedonian monk Maximus, at which the *Typos* of Constans was formally condemned. The newly appointed Exarch in Italy, Olympius, was ordered to force Martin to sign the *Typos* just as, in 553, Vigilius had eventually been compelled to sign the denunciation of the 'Three Chapters'. Instead Olympius chose to side with the Pope and, in 650, following in the footsteps of the African exarch Gregory, declared himself Emperor.

Fortunately for Constans, Olympius died of bubonic plague before he was able to reach Sicily. His replacement as governor, Theodore Calliopas, proved more reliable. Pope Martin and Maximus were arrested and sent to Constantinople. There both were tried and found guilty of treason. Condemned to death, the Emperor intervened to commute the punishment imposed on the churchmen to exile. Whilst Pope Martin was sent to Cherson, on the northern coast of the Black Sea, where he died in 656, his collaborator Maximus (remembered for his mystical theology as the last Father of the Greek Church) was mutilated and sent to the fortress of Schemarion in Lazica, where he passed away in 662.[24] Constans' actions made Justinian's humiliation of Vigilius look like child's play and spoke of the Emperor's absolute determination to extricate Constantinople from the crisis in which it found itself.

---

[21] Kennedy (2007), p. 325.
[22] ibid., pp. 325–6.
[23] L. I. Conrad, 'The Conquest of the Arwad: A Source-Critical Study in the Historiography of the Early Medieval Near East', in A. Cameron and L. I. Conrad (eds.), *The Byzantine and Early Islamic Near East*, vol. 1: *Problems in the Literary Source Materials* (Princeton, 1992), pp. 317–401.
[24] Haldon (1993), p. 58.

With the fall of both Cyprus and Arwad, military pressure on the Eastern Roman Empire was renewed and in 651 Isauria in southern Asia Minor was raided. This was ominous for the Romans because, although the new 'theme' regiments were now in existence, the reformed systems of remuneration and supply envisaged for them were not yet in place. Accordingly, the Governor of Isauria, Procopius, was authorised to travel to the high command of the Arab western field army in Damascus, where he negotiated a three-year truce in return for tribute.[25] The Arab commander in Syria, Mu'awiya, took advantage of this to direct his army to Armenia where, as we have seen, in 653 he secured the submission of Theodore Rshtuni, the commander of Roman allied forces in the region. Now in his twenties, and capable of providing real military leadership, Constans took charge of the situation. Rather than sit back and observe the collapse of the empire's client network in the Transcaucasus, on which hopes for imperial survival, let alone recovery, would depend, he led his forces east into Armenia to rally support. At Karin, Theodosiopolis, and Dvin, he secured pledges of loyalty from a number of Armenian princes and was able to send troops into Iberia. He also signed a concord with the head of the Armenian Church. Slowly, the Emperor began to piece back together a Christian alliance across the Trancaucasus, as Theodore Rshtuni lay holed up in his fortress island on Lake Van.[26]

Taking advantage of the Emperor's Armenian sojourn, and using it as a pretext for war, Mu'awiya massed his forces for a joint land and sea attack on Constantinople, greater even than that which the city had faced in 626. He reportedly wrote to the Emperor inviting him to convert and accept the status of a client and tributary: 'If you wish to preserve your life in safety, abandon the vain cult which you learned from your childhood. Deny that Jesus and turn to the great God whom I worship, the God of our father Abraham. Dismiss from your presence the multitude of your troops to their respective lands. And I shall make you a great prince in your regions and send prefects to your cities. I shall make an inventory of the treasures and order them to be divided, three parts for me, one part for you. I shall provide you with as many soldiers as you may wish, and take tribute from you, as much as you are able to give.'[27] The Emperor hastened back to Constantinople.[28]

The dockyards of the Near East and the cities of northern Syria were thronged with shipwrights, sailors, soldiers, and slaves as the forces of *jihad* were summoned from throughout the lands ruled by the *umma*. In the occupied territories the Emperor's allies attempted to thwart these ominous preparations: in the Syrian port town of Tripoli, we are told, 'two Christ-loving brothers . . . were fired with a divine zeal and rushed to the city prison. They broke down the gates and after liberating the captives, rushed to the emir of the city, whom they slew together with

---

[25] *Armenian History*, ch. 45 (147).
[26] ibid., ch. 48 (164–70).
[27] ibid., ch. 49 (169–70).
[28] For the ensuing siege (and the evidence for it), Howard-Johnston (2010) is essential reading.

his suite and, having burnt all the equipment, sailed off to the Roman state.'[29] Even such acts of sabotage, however, could not hold back the Islamic juggernaut. As Mu'awiya's Syrian armada amassed off the shore of Asia Minor, the young Emperor decided to lead the Byzantine fleet against them. A major engagement took place off the south coast in the bay of Phoenix in the summer of 654.[30] The result was a decisive Arab victory after which, we are told, 'the sea was dyed red with Roman blood'.[31] The Emperor himself narrowly avoided capture, escaping back to Constantinople in disguise. The Arabs now seized the islands of Crete, Rhodes, and Cos before sailing north towards Constantinople.

At the same time Mu'awiya's armies advanced across Anatolia. Roman resistance beyond the capital crumbled. As the *Armenian History* records: 'While he [Mu'awiya] marched to Chalcedon . . . all the inhabitants of the country submitted to him, those on the coast and in the mountains and on the plains . . . the host of the Roman army entered Constantinople to guard the city.'[32] With the arrival of a second fleet from Alexandria, Mu'awiya was ready to initiate his assault on the imperial capital: 'Behold the great ships arrived at Chalcedon from Alexandria with all the small ships and all their equipment. For they had stowed on board the ships mangonels, and machines to throw fire, and machines to hurl stones, archers and slingers, so that when they reached the walls of the city they might easily descend from the top of the towers and break in. . . . He ordered the ships to be deployed in lines and to attack.'[33]

Within Constantinople, Constans is reported to have 'lifted the crown from his head, stripped off his purple [robes] . . . put on sackcloth, sat on ashes, and ordered a fast to be proclaimed'.[34] Prayerful and sober, the Emperor and his subjects awaited the Arab onslaught. It was now that Mu'awiya ran out of luck. According to the *Armenian History* (our closest contemporary source), a sudden and violent storm blew up that first contained and then wrecked much of the Arab fleet, leaving what remained, it might be imagined, prone to Roman assault, rather as had befallen the Slavs and Persians in 626. 'On that day', the *History* declares, 'by his upraised arm God saved the city through the prayers of the pious king Constans.'[35] With no means of crossing over to the European side of the Bosphorus to assault the Land Walls of Constantinople, the Arab expeditionary force was obliged to withdraw in haste before winter set in. A second Arab army was defeated by Roman forces in Cappadocia. Driven back into Armenia, an attempt was made by the Arabs to save face by launching an assault on the Romans' allies in Iberia. The Iberians, however, held firm, and 'beset by snow', the Arabs were obliged to retreat south.[36]

---

[29] Theophanes, p. 482.
[30] See C. Zuckerman, 'Learning from the Enemy and More Studies in "Dark Centuries" Byzantium', *Millennium* 2 (2005), pp. 79–135, pp. 114–17.
[31] ibid.
[32] *Armenian History*, ch. 50 (170).
[33] ibid., ch. 50 (171).
[34] ibid., ch. 50 (170).
[35] ibid., ch. 50 (171).
[36] ibid., ch. 50 (171).

For the first time in a generation, the Arabs' foes sensed blood. 'The Armenian princes', we are told, 'from both Greek and Arab territory... came together at one place and made a pact with each other that there should be no sword and shedding of blood among them... for the lord of Rshtunik [the Arabs' client Theodore] had fallen ill and withdrew to the island of Altamar [in Lake Van]. He was quite unable to come out or form any plans. They divided the land according to the number of each one's cavalry.'[37] With Theodore isolated, Arab authority over the Transcaucasus—always precarious—collapsed. Further east, in the old Parthian territory of north-west Media, 'the Medes rebelled from submission to Ismael. They made their refuge and retreat the fastness of the land of Media, the deep forested valleys, the precipices, the rocks... and the strength of those active and intrepid peoples who inhabited them.... They began to bring together the surviving militia and to organize battalions, in the hope that they might be able to escape from the teeth of the dragon and from the cruel beast.'[38] In 655 the Romans launched an offensive in Armenia. Although this campaign was successfully contained, there was little the Arabs could do to prevent revolts from flaring up across the Transcaucasus.[39] Recriminations soon broke out amongst the Arab high command.

8.3 'THE DAY OF THEIR DESTRUCTION IS CLOSE'

Tensions and rivalries between the Arab commanders in the Transcaucasus were mirrored in Mecca and Medina. The *amir al-mu'minin* Uthman was already facing mounting criticism for advancing members of his own family, whilst the political domination of the *umma* by the Meccan clan of the Quraysh was a source of growing resentment amongst members of the army in Iraq and Egypt, who gave vent to their dissatisfaction during the *hajj*, or pilgrimage to Mecca in 655. The following year, with Mecca again thronged with Egyptian pilgrims suspicious of Uthman and his Qurayshi regime, the *amir*'s compound was stormed and Uthman killed.

The assassination of Uthman opened the way to a bitter struggle for control of the nascent Islamic Empire, which soon drew the *umma* into a bloody civil war (known as the first *fitna*, or 'division'). Muhammad's son-in-law and cousin, Ali, was proclaimed ruler by a dynastic party, which held that political and religious authority within Islam was the sole preserve of the Prophet and his bloodline. Ali's succession was opposed, however, by a widow of the Prophet, Aisha, who was also a daughter of Muhammad's first successor, Abu Bakr, and by the latter's son-in-law, al-Zubayr. This group headed a faction of early converts to the faith who insisted that the Commander of the Faithful should be elected by a council of military and tribal leaders representing the community as a whole.[40] Ali and his supporters were

---

[37] ibid., ch. 50 (172).
[38] ibid., ch. 51 (172).
[39] ibid., chs. 51–2 (172–4).
[40] W. Madelung, *The Succession to Muhammad: A Study of the Early Caliphate* (Cambridge, 1997), pp. 113–40.

regarded as usurpers who had Uthman's blood on their hands.⁴¹ Crucially, the Governor of Syria, Mu'awiya—a relative of Uthman's—threw his weight behind those hostile to Ali, demanding that his kinsman be avenged.

Soldiers loyal to Ali were mobilised against Aisha, al-Zubayr, and their followers, who had come together at the garrison town of Basra. They then turned on Mu'awiya who, in response to Ali's refusal to hand over the killers of Uthman, had proclaimed himself ruler. As the forces for and against Ali faced each other at Siffin on the Euphrates, an agreement by Ali to subject his and Mu'awiya's claims to arbitration led a group of his most radical followers, known as the Kharijites, to break away. Ali was obliged to have them hunted down and killed so as to maintain discipline in the ranks. Talks with Mu'awiya collapsed when the appointed arbiters challenged Ali's legitimacy. As the Syrian general's army began to launch raids on their opponents in Arabia and Iraq, Ali fell victim to a Kharijite assassin.⁴²

It was now that civil war broke out in earnest across Syria, Iraq, Arabia, Egypt, and Iran. Ali's cause was taken up by his sons, Husayn and Hasan, whose claim to power on behalf of the bloodline of the Prophet was opposed by a Syrian army loyal to Mu'awiya and other members of the Meccan elite. Mu'awiya's forces took on and defeated Alid and Kharijite forces first in Iraq and then in Egypt, where, in a telling diplomatic coup, the Byzantine authorities secured the conversion and defection of a major contingent of the Arab army. As the *Armenian History* records, 'the army which was in Egypt united with the king of the Greeks, made a treaty, and joined him. The host of troops, about 15,000, believed in Christ and were baptized.'⁴³ The day of liberation, Biblically foretold in the *Book of Daniel*, appeared to be at hand: 'The day of their destruction is close; the Lord has arrived upon them in readiness.'⁴⁴ Gradually, however, and amid much bloodshed, by 661 Mu'awiya had stamped his authority on the *umma* and the lands over which it ruled: 'The blood of the slaughter of immense multitudes flowed thickly among the armies of Ismael. Warfare afflicted them as they engaged in mutual carnage. They were unable to refrain for the least moment from the sword and captivity and fierce battles by sea and land, until Mu'awiya prevailed and conquered.' In the closing sentence of his *History* our unknown Armenian author concluded: 'Having brought them into submission to himself, he rules over the possessions of the sons of Ismael and makes peace with all.'⁴⁵

The crisis into which the empire of the *umma* descended between the death of Uthman in 656 and the final victory of Mu'awiya in 661 provided Constans II and his regime with a crucial window of opportunity. For the first time since the early 630s, military pressure on the empire's eastern front had eased and a series of much-needed reforms of the military and governmental infrastructure could be put into effect. It was the needs of the army that came first. The reformed regiments of the

---

⁴¹ Palmer and Brock (1993), pp. 181–2.
⁴² ibid., pp. 141–310, 183–5.
⁴³ *Armenian History*, ch. 52 (175).
⁴⁴ ibid., ch. 52 (177).
⁴⁵ ibid., ch. 52 (176).

640s were put on a firmer administrative footing: the old provincial administration was increasingly sidelined, and instead Asia Minor and Anatolia were divided up into a series of new territorial units (initially termed *stratêgiai*, or commands), each of which was appointed to a theme regiment from which it took its name—the *themata* of the Opsikion (stationed around Constantinople), the Thrakesion (in western Asia Minor), the Anatolikon (in south-eastern Asia Minor and Anatolia), and the Armeniakon (the north-east) (see Map 7). Within these territorial units, supreme military authority was entrusted to the figure of the *stratêgos*, or general, appointed directly from Constantinople. These *stratêgoi* oversaw the defence of the provinces from urban centres that were turned into heavily fortified 'hard-points'. As a result, the cities of the empire would cease to be referred to in Greek as *poleis*; rather they were increasingly known as *kastra* (from the Latin *castrum*—'military camp'). The ports and harbours of the coastal zone were also fortified, in order to withstand attack and protect the navy.[46]

Crucially, the army's system of maintenance and supply was revolutionised. State warehouses, or *apothêkai*, were established in the provinces under the supervision of requisitioning agents and purchasing middle-men bearing the title of *genikoi kommerkiarioi*, or 'general merchants', who are first attested in *c*.654–9.[47] These warehouses were probably used to supply the rank and file with weapons, armour, clothing, and such like. Second, a structural shift occurred in how the army was paid: rather than receiving wages primarily in coin, soldiers and their families were issued with military landholdings (*stratiôtika ktêmata*) that the soldiers could pass on to their heirs in return for military service to the state, for which they also received a cash donative, initially issued every five years or so. The precise dating of this reform is unclear from the literary references and is not mentioned in the legal ones: in a tenth-century law it is described as 'of unwritten custom'.[48] However, the easing of Arab military pressure can be seen to coincide archaeologically with a significant decline in finds of copper coins at a series of sites of great military significance across Asia Minor and Anatolia, indicating that it was probably at this point that the system for paying the army was overhauled and the military landholdings were introduced.[49] As a result, the material interests of a nascent soldier-peasantry were increasingly harnessed to the military interests of the East Roman state, and the rank and file of the armies of the Emperor were finally given something tangible for which to fight.[50] Subsequent events would reveal that the result was a noticeable stiffening of both morale and nerve.

---

[46] Haldon (1993); Howard-Johnston (2010); P. Niewöhner, 'Archaeologie und die Dunkeln Jahrhunderte im byzantinischen Anatolien', in J. Henning (ed.), *Post-Roman Towns, Trade and Settlement in Europe and Byzantium*, 2 vols. (Berlin, 2007), vol. 1, pp. 119–58.
[47] Haldon (1993), pp. 232–3.
[48] Zepos, *Ius Graeco-Romanum*, II, p. 222.
[49] Hendy (1985), pp. 640ff.
[50] G. Ostrogorsky, 'Agrarian Conditions in the Byzantine Empire in the Middle Ages', in M. M. Postan (ed.), *The Cambridge Economic History of Europe*, vol. 1: *The Agrarian Life of the Middle Ages* (Cambridge, 1966), pp. 205–34; Howard-Johnston (2004). For the recasting of imperial government in general, see W. Brandes, *Finanzverwaltung in Krisenzeiten: Unterchungen zur byzantinischen Administration im 6–9. Jahrhundert* (Frankfurt, 2002).

The institution of the military landholdings in Anatolia and Asia Minor, rather like the settlement of barbarians on the land in return for military service in the fifth-century west, helped to ease the financial straits in which the war-ravaged Roman state found itself. Unlike in most of the contemporary post-Roman west, however, the land tax continued to be demanded and collected in coin, and, as we have seen, a cash component to military wages persisted.[51] Importantly, Constans II was able to take advantage of the shift in the balance of power on the empire's eastern frontier to begin to exact tribute from the Arabs. As the *Chronicle of Theophanes* records, *c*.656–8, 'In this year peace was concluded between Romans and Arabs after Mauias [i.e. Mu'awiya] had sent an embassy, because of the rebellion, offering that the Arabs should pay the Romans a daily tribute of one thousand *solidi*, one horse, and one slave.'[52]

Once the reformed military structures of the empire had been established, Constans was able to begin to put into effect his 'grand strategy'. In 660 he led a large army into the Caucasus, where he received oaths of loyalty from the lords and princes of Armenia, led by Hamazasp Mamikonean, and from Juanshir, the leading Christian lord of Iberia. The latter had been wounded in battle fighting against the Arabs on behalf of the Sasanian shah Yazdgerd III in 638, and Constans appointed him ruler 'of all the eastern people', rewarding him with a fragment of the True Cross and a belt that had once belonged to Heraclius.[53] The whole Christian commonwealth of the Transcaucasus was now united in the anti-Arab cause. It was perhaps at this point that the Emperor sealed his alliance with the mutinous Christian converts of the Arab army in Egypt. We should imagine Byzantine agents at work throughout the occupied territories.

With his Heraclian-style coalition of the faithful in place, and confident in the loyalty and stamina of the provincial armies should the Arabs choose to strike, Constans headed west, to marshal the resources of the empire's wealthiest remaining provinces in Italy, Sicily, and north Africa, with which he would be able to fund his great campaign to drive the Arabs back into the desert and confound the forces of Antichrist. After a year of preparations back in Constantinople, Constans left the reins of power in the capital in the hands of the entourage around his eldest son, Constantine (then probably aged about ten), and headed across the plains of Thrace accompanied by troops of the Opsikion. From Thrace he and his men made their way down to Athens from where they set sail for Italy, landing at Tarentum in Apulia in the late autumn of 662.

After wintering at Naples and entering into negotiations with the Langobard Duke Romuald of Beneventum, in July of 663 Constans visited Rome—the first Emperor to do so since the deposition of Romulus Augustulus in 476.[54] As Paul the Deacon records, 'At the sixth milestone from the city, Pope Vitalian came to meet

---

[51] For the significance of this, see M. Whittow, *The Making of Orthodox Byzantium* (London, 1996).
[52] Theophanes, p. 484—the entry is placed in the year 657–8, but the chronicler is notoriously imprecise in matters of chronology.
[53] *Armenian History*, ch. 52 (175) and ch. 42 (137); Howard-Johnston (2010), p. 485.
[54] *Liber Pontificalis*, 343.

him with his priests and the Roman people. And when the emperor had come to the threshold of St Peter he offered there a pallium woven with gold.'[55] Just as Heraclius had melted down the gold and silver plate of the Great Church in Constantinople to fund his war effort, his grandson now set about doing the same in Rome: 'Remaining at Rome twelve days he pulled down everything that in ancient times had been made of metal to the ornament of the city, to such an extent that he even stripped off the roof of the church of the blessed Mary which at one time was called the Pantheon.'[56] Constans then set sail for Sicily, where he established his operational base at Syracuse, enabling him to communicate with his officials in both Italy and north Africa (the Byzantine presence in the Iberian peninsula having seemingly by this point been extinguished by the Visigoths), and to face down any Arab naval assault, whilst also extracting much-needed tax revenues.

According to the Roman 'Book of Pontiffs' (*Liber Pontificalis*), in Sicily the Emperor introduced a new poll tax and set about the construction of an extensive new naval fleet and the conscription and manning of its crews.[57] Having narrowly avoided capture by the Arab fleet at the battle of Phoenix in 654, the Emperor was clearly determined to regain naval superiority. Again, the resources of the Church were specifically targeted and levies of forced labour introduced. As the *Liber Pontificalis* records, Constans 'imposed such afflictions on the people, occupiers and proprietors of the provinces of Calbaria, Sicily, Africa, and Sardinia for many years by tributes, poll-taxes and ship-money, such as had never been seen before, so that wives were even separated from their husbands and sons from their parents. ... They also took away all the sacred vessels and equipment from God's holy churches, leaving nothing behind.'[58] We have records of strikingly high levels of land tax being levied on ecclesiastical estates in Sicily at around this time, with the state taking almost half of net revenues in coin.[59] Clearly, Constans was determined to maximise the resources at his disposal.

The construction of a new Mediterranean fleet from scratch was a time-consuming affair—a matter of years rather than months. The problem for Constans, however, was that the victory of Mu'awiya over his opponents in 661 meant that time was now in relatively short supply. The Emperor's prolonged absence from the imperial capital was bound to raise political tensions in Constantinople and lead to anxiety in the Caucasus. Constans must also have realised that if he did not strike at the Arabs soon, then Mu'awiya would be after him. For in distant Damascus, the *amir al-mu'minin* was busy putting into place a grand strategy of his own.

Mu'awiya had come to power on the back of a bloody civil war that had left the *umma* deeply divided and which had clearly raised hopes amongst elements of the Christian populations of the Near East that the days of Arab rule were drawing to a

---

[55] Paul the Deacon, V, 11.
[56] ibid.
[57] *Liber Pontificalis*, 344.
[58] ibid., 344; R. Davis, *The Book of the Pontiffs* (Liverpool, 2000), p. 72.
[59] Agnellus, ch. 111. See discussion in C. Wickham, *Early Medieval Italy* (London, 1981), p. 75.

close. In Egypt, moreover, his forces had shed much Christian blood.[60] The last thing his regime needed was the emergence of a determined pro-Roman 'fifth column'. It was thus urgent that the new ruler both reunite the Arab armies and reconnect with his Christian subjects. We see him trying to achieve the latter in the very earliest days of his reign, when he visited Christian pilgrimage sites in Palestine, showing due reverence.[61] Reuniting the Arabs, however, required a different tone: his regime was to be legitimised by means of active pursuit of the *jihad* against Constantinople, which would remind the Muslims of their common purpose and divine mission. Like the Sasanian shahs before them, the Arab leadership sought to surmount internal tensions by means of prestige- and booty-garnering warfare directed against New Rome. As with Constans in Sicily, this was to be financed by overhauling the fiscal structures of his empire, signs of which we perhaps see in an attempted (and failed) reform of the coinage recorded in the Syriac sources.[62] In Egypt determined efforts were made to maximise the flow of taxes into the coffers at Fustat, and demands for *corvée* labour and supplies feature prominently in the documentary papyri that survive from Mu'awiya's reign.[63]

In 662 Mu'awiya's forces began a series of what were probably yearly raids into Anatolia and Asia Minor: 'In this year', the *Chronicle of Theophanes* records, 'the Arabs made an expedition against the Roman state. They made many captives and devastated many places.'[64] Two years later, the general Abd al-Rahman 'invaded the Roman state and wintered there, devastating many lands'.[65] According to a Syriac account, the Arab army struck as far as Smyrna on the Aegean coast.[66] In 667 a large Arab force led by Mu'awiya's son Yazid marched on Melitene, in response to a request for support from the commander, or *stratêgos*, of the Armeniakon, a general of Persian origin by the name of Shapur, who had risen up in revolt. Shapur met an untimely death, but the Arabs marched on towards Chalcedon before capturing the important *kastron* of Amorium.[67] Unlike in the early 650s, however, this time there was no collapse in Roman morale. As the Arabs bedded down for winter in the captured city, a detachment of Roman soldiers scaled its walls and slaughtered the Arabs to a man.[68]

It appears to have been in court circles in Constantinople that doubts began to spread as to the wisdom of Constans' strategy. The well-placed author of a *History of the Caucasian Albanians*, tracing the reign of the Iberian king Juanshir, the 'Lord of the East' to whom Constans had entrusted his grandfather's belt prior to his

---

[60] Palmer and Brock (1993), p. 188.
[61] ibid., p. 31.
[62] ibid., p. 32. For taxation under Mu'awiya, see Hoyland (2006).
[63] C. Foss, 'Egypt under Mu'awiyya, Part I: Flavius Papas and Upper Egypt', *Bulletin of the School of Oriental and African Studies* 72.1 (2009), pp. 1–24; *idem.*, 'Egypt under Mu'awiya, Part II: Middle Egypt, Fustat and Alexandria', *Bulletin of the School of Oriental and African Studies* 72.2 (2009), pp. 259–78.
[64] Theophanes, p. 486.
[65] ibid., p. 487.
[66] Palmer and Brock (1993), pp. 34–5.
[67] Theophanes, pp. 488–90.
[68] ibid., p. 490.

western mission, records how a delegation of high-ranking Romans made their way to Damascus, where they informed Mu'awiya that a plot was in hand to assassinate the Emperor and open peace negotiations with the Arabs. There they were joined by Juanshir, who, faced with the Emperor's absence and mounting pressure from Khazars and Huns to the north of his principality, had accepted client status from the Arabs in 665.[69] In return for his role as interlocutor and broker, Juanshir was rewarded with purple robes, silks for his wife, an elephant, and a parrot ('beautiful to behold').[70] Terms were agreed and preparations put in place. On 15 July 669 Constans was accompanied into his bathhouse in Syracuse by a certain Andreas, son of a high-ranking Constantinopolitan judge. According to a near-contemporary source, as Constans reclined in his bath 'in the process of washing the king [i.e. Emperor], he [Andreas] so covered his head with soapsuds that he was unable to open his eyes. Then he took a silver bucket, which he had placed in front of the king, and brought it crashing down on his head, fracturing his skull. Hurrying out of the bathhouse he was caught by no one. They bore the king away to his royal palace and two days later he died.'[71]

As news of the murder spread, in what bears all the hallmarks of a carefully pre-prepared sequence of events (choreographed by Mu'awiya and the wily old Juanshir), units of the army in Sicily proclaimed as emperor a handsome Armenian officer and aristocrat by the name of Mzez (in Greek, 'Mizezios').[72] Rather than await the arrival of a peace delegation, as the Constantinopolitan plotters no doubt had expected him to, Mu'awiya activated the Arab army and fleet. A major assault was launched on Byzantine positions in north Africa.[73] It was perhaps at this point that the Arabs established a bridgehead on and seized part of Sicily, in an episode recorded (but misplaced) by the chronicler Theophanes and also recorded by Paul the Deacon, who places it immediately after the death of Constans.[74] Major incursions were made by land into Asia Minor, whilst Arab fleets sailed on and landed at Smyrna as well as in Cilicia and Lycia.[75] 'In this year [671–2]', the *Chronicle of Theophanes* records, 'in the month of March, a rainbow appeared in the sky, and all men shuddered and said it was the end of the world.'[76]

8.4 NEW CONSTANTINES, NEW JUSTINIANS, NEW DAVIDS

Constans II was to be remembered in the Greek and Latin sources as amongst the most reviled of Byzantine emperors. The reasons for this are clear: these accounts

---

[69] Movses Dasxuranci, *History of the Caucasian Albanians*, II, 27–8 (pp. 124–8): these important events have been brought into the light of day by Howard-Johnston (2010).
[70] *History of the Caucasian Albanians*, II, 28 (pp. 127–9).
[71] Palmer and Brock (1993), p. 193. Howard-Johnston (2010); *Liber Pontificalis*, p. 72; Paul the Deacon, V, 11. For the date, see Howard-Johnston (2010), p. 491.
[72] Theophanes, pp. 490–91, and Howard-Johnston (2010), pp. 491–2.
[73] Theophanes, p. 491.
[74] ibid., p. 487—see fn. 1 and Paul the Deacon, V, 13.
[75] Theophanes, pp. 492–3.
[76] ibid., p. 493.

were written by hard-line Chalcedonian churchmen who regarded his treatment of Pope Martin and the monk Maximus with horror. Theophanes, for example, claimed that the Emperor 'was hated by the people of Byzantium, particularly because he had brought ignominiously to Constantinople Martin, the most holy Pope of Rome and exiled him to the Klimata of Cherson, because he had cut off the tongue and hand of the most learned confessor Maximus, and had condemned many of the orthodox to torture, banishment, and confiscation of property. . . . For these reasons he was greatly hated by all.' None of the Emperor's actions could be praised; each and every one had to reveal his baseness of character. Constans' decision to head west to Italy and Syracuse, for example, was not an act of daring aimed at saving the empire and freeing the Christians of the east from their Arabian captivity: rather, 'it was out of fright' for 'he intended to transfer the seat of the empire to Rome'.[77] It is because of such bias that our Miaphysite Transcaucasian sources, such as the *Armenian History*, are so vital. Yet even the prejudices and distortions of Theophanes cannot entirely obliterate the traces of what was clearly a reign of breathtaking creativity as well as extraordinary courage and imagination.

That the Emperor did not achieve his goal of rolling back the Arab conquests may be explained on a number of counts. Chief amongst these is probably the fact that the damage done to the military, economic, and administrative infrastructure of the empire by decades of Persian and Arab warfare was such that, during the window of opportunity opened up by the *fitna* of 656–61, the Emperor's main focus had to be on consolidation and reform at home rather than aggressive warfare abroad. By the time those reforms were in place, the opportunities to strike were already receding, for Mu'awiya's victory was simply too complete and rapid. At the end of the day, aware of its members' isolation in ruling over vast subject populations of non-Muslims and non-Arabs, and sensitive to the fragility of conquest, the *umma* had pulled back from the precipice. Importantly, however, Constans II's reforms had bequeathed to the empire of New Rome the strength and will to hang on.

In spite of the grim forebodings elicited by the rainbow of 671–2, the 'theme' regiments responded to the Arab onslaught unleashed upon the death of Constans with remarkable *élan*. The coup of Mzez and the Arab assault on Roman Africa were brought to a swift conclusion by the rapid response of Constans' eldest son and nominated heir, Constantine IV (now aged eighteen or nineteen). Clearly confident of his position at home, he had sailed west without delay. Perhaps surprised by the young prince's determination to face down the Arab expeditionary force rather than remain in the capital to consolidate his hold on power, Mu'awiya pulled his forces back.[78] Mzez holed himself up in Syracuse, but was captured and executed in 672, by which point Constantine had already returned to the imperial city, having 'established order in the west'.[79]

---

[77] ibid., p. 491.
[78] Howard-Johnston (2010).
[79] Theophanes, p. 491.

In 674 a large Arab army was again landed in Lycia, in south-west Asia Minor. However, a concerted pincer movement managed to drive the Arabs back to their ships, inflicting heavy losses.[80] As the Arab fleet attempted to evacuate the remnants of the field army, it was ambushed by the Roman navy, which deployed against the Arab ships the empire's newly acquired secret weapon of 'Greek fire', a petroleum compound fired through siphons that had been introduced to the Byzantine high command by a Christian refugee from Heliopolis in Syria named Kallinikos, who, according to Theophanes, 'manufactured a naval fire with which he kindled the ships of the Arabs and burnt them with their crews'. 'In this way', the chronicler continues, 'the Romans came back in victory.'[81]

The Romans now launched a startlingly confident counter-attack. In 677–8 the imperial navy landed units of Christian tribal insurgents, or 'Mardaites', along the north Syrian coast from where they fanned out across the mountains of Syria and Palestine from the west of Antioch to Jerusalem and across to Mount Lebanon. From their highland redoubts, the Mardaites were able to make common cause with local Christian militiamen, including veterans of the Roman army, fugitive slaves, and escaped prisoners, and to attack Arab forces and populations in the cities and plains below.[82] Fearing a full-blown Christian uprising, Mu'awiya offered the Romans a thirty-year peace treaty, sealed by payment to the Emperor of a yearly tribute of gold, slaves, and horses. The Roman ambassador John was received with great honour and, having accepted Mu'awiya's proposal, returned to Constantinople loaded with gifts.[83] 'When the inhabitants of the West had learned of this,' Theophanes records, 'namely the *khagan* of the Avars, as well as the kings, chieftains and *gastaldi* who live beyond them, and the princes of the western nations, they sent ambassadors and gifts to the emperor, requesting that peace and friendship should be confirmed with them. The emperor acceded to their demands and ratified an imperial peace with them also. Thus great security prevailed in both East and West.'

The success of the Byzantine counter-strike under Constantine IV was necessarily a major blow to the prestige of Mu'awiya and his regime. He was by this point an elderly man, and as minds began to turn to the question of his succession, factions inevitably began to emerge at court and across the empire of the *umma*. Mu'awiya's decision to nominate his son, Yazid, as 'heir apparent', alienated him from the anti-dynastic sentiments of many of those who had been his supporters against the Alids: upon Mu'awiya's death in April 680, Abd Allah b. al-Zubayr, the son of a prominent anti-Alid from the days of the civil war, refused to take the oath of allegiance to Yazid and rallied support against the dynastic succession of Yazid in Mecca and Medina. A second *fitna* thus emerged as in 683 Yazid's armies marched on his enemies in Arabia. The unexpected death first of Yazid and then of his own

---

[80] Theophanes, p. 494.
[81] ibid., p. 494; J. F. Haldon, 'Greek Fire: Recent and Current Research', in E. Jeffreys (ed.), *Byzantine Style, Religion, and Civilization—In Honour of Sir Steven Runciman* (Cambridge, 2006), pp. 290–326.
[82] Howard-Johnston (2010), pp. 494–5; Palmer and Brock (1993), p. 195; Theophanes, p. 496.
[83] Theophanes, p. 496.

son, Mu'awiya II, that same year simply added to the confusion. The leaders of the army in Syria, which formed the main body of support for Mu'awiya and his family, chose the elderly Marwan ibn al-Hakam as Commander of the Faithful, but his succession too elicited mounting opposition, this time led by the general al-Dahhak.[84] The Marwanid loyalists defeated al-Dahhak, however, at a decisive encounter near Damascus in 684 and the army in Egypt was won over to their cause.[85]

In the April of 685 Marwan passed away and was succeeded by his eldest son, Abd al-Malik. The regime was rapidly destabilised, however, by a major invasion of the Caucasus by the Khazars, who had by now consolidated their position as the dominant nomad power on the western steppe. In spite of the thirty-year truce that Constantine IV had negotiated, the temptation for the Romans to seize this opportunity to strike against the *umma* proved irresistible, and the new Roman emperor, the sixteen-year-old Justinian II, directed his forces into the Transcaucasus. Roman control soon extended over Armenia, Iberia, Caucasian Albania, and into the old Parthian heartlands of Media in the east. The *stratêgos* Lentios, we are told, 'after imposing taxes on these countries, sent a great sum of money to the emperor'.[86] The *Chronicle of Theophanes* suggests that concurrently Abd al-Malik was obliged to put down an uprising in Antioch, and it is very likely that at this point the Mardaites and their Christian allies again rose up.[87] In Arabia forces loyal to Ibn al-Zubayr continued to resist the new regime, and conflict between rival factions in Iraq, including surviving Alids, was intense.[88]

It might be thought that with the *umma* divided, Roman control established over a broad arc of the Transcaucasus from Armenia to Media, and the west Eurasian steppe now dominated by a nomad power with a track record of hostility to the Arabs going back to the 640s, all the preconditions were finally in place for Justinian II to emulate Heraclius and sweep all before him. That he did not do so appears to have been due in large part to crippling manpower shortages at home, caused by the repeated ravages of the bubonic plague that had first struck the empire in the 540s, and which had returned periodically ever since. For the late seventh century, outbreaks of the plague are recorded from Britain in the northwest to Iraq in the south-east.[89] Paul the Deacon records severe episodes of the disease not only in Italy but across the Eastern Roman Empire, such that 'a heavy pestilence followed from the same eastern quarter and destroyed the Roman people'.[90]

---

[84] Kennedy (2007), pp. 88–90.
[85] ibid., pp. 90–93.
[86] Theophanes, p. 507.
[87] ibid.
[88] Kennedy (2007), pp. 93–7.
[89] For Britain see J. Maddicott, 'Plague in Seventh-Century England', in Little (2007), pp. 171–214. For plague in Italy and the Near East see D. Stathokopoulos, *Famine and Pestilence in the Late Roman and Early Byzantine Empire* (Birmingham, 2004), pp. 358–65, and *idem.*, 'Crime and Punishment: The Plague in the Byzantine Empire, 541–749, in Little (2007), pp. 99–118, p. 107.
[90] Paul the Deacon, V, 31.

Accordingly, when, in 687, in a desperate attempt to shore up his position, Abd al-Malik offered Justinian II substantially increased sums of tribute in return for peace and a withdrawal of the Mardaite guerrillas from Syria and Palestine, the Emperor accepted. As Theophanes records, 'In this year Abd al-Malik sent emissaries to Justinian to ratify the peace, and it was concluded on these terms: that the emperor should remove the host of the Mardaites from the Lebanon and prevent their incursions; that Abd al-Malik would give to the Romans every day one thousand gold pieces, a horse, and a slave, and that they would share in equal part the tax revenue of Cyprus, Armenia, and Iberia.'[91] 'The emperor', we are told, 'sent the *magistrianus* Paul to Abd al-Malik to ratify the agreement, and a written guarantee was drawn up and witnessed. After being honourably rewarded, the *magistrianus* returned home. The emperor sent orders to receive the Mardaites, 12,000 of them.'[92] Abd al-Malik was now able to concentrate his attentions on the enemy within: gradually his opponents in Iraq and Arabia were ground down and destroyed, but it was not until 692 that his army was able to prise control of Mecca from his foes, with Ibn al-Zubayr falling in battle.[93]

Justinian II's readiness to withdraw the Mardaites from Syria and Palestine and resettle them within the empire is telling. For, as we have seen, it would suggest that, in spite of the great opportunities opened up by the second *fitna*, there was a growing realisation within the imperial high command that beyond the Transcaucasus, the empire now simply did not have the military manpower required to mount a sustained campaign of territorial aggression, or perhaps even to fill the ranks of the provincial armies around Constantinople and in western Asia Minor. Just as Constans II's first priority in the 650s, therefore, had been the consolidation of such armies, Justinian II's in the 680s was on manning them. The result, as Theophanes records, was that the Mardaites were withdrawn, Slav prisoners of war captured on the plains of Thrace were enrolled in the Opsikion, a second larger levy of Slavs was organised into a new mobile field army whom the Emperor named 'the Chosen People', and an attempt was made forcibly to resettle the population of Cyprus on the Anatolian mainland.[94] The demographic pressures arising from the plague, coupled with the eventual defeat of Ibn al-Zubayr, effectively closed down the window of opportunity for the restoration of Roman rule across the Near East. Indeed, it was perhaps a sign of Justinian II's realisation of this fact that when, in 691–2, he summoned an Ecumenical Council in Constantinople (the so-called Council *in Trullo*), its deliberations and decrees were primarily concerned with issues of ecclesiastical discipline and practice and the codification of canon law. No attempt was made to reach out to the non-Chalcedonian Christian communities of the east. Their views, effectively, now no longer mattered.

By codifying canon law, however, Justinian II effectively completed the programme of legal reform that had been initiated by his great namesake, Justinian

---

[91] Theophanes, p. 506.
[92] ibid.
[93] Kennedy (2007), p. 98.
[94] Theophanes, pp. 507–11.

I, with whose now retrospectively lionised reign he was thus able to associate himself. There are signs, moreover, that the canons of the Council *in Trullo* circulated in the Frankish and Visigothic West, influencing ecclesiastical legislation there. Certainly, the Council claimed authority to legislate with respect to the Church 'in barbarian lands'.[95] It was now primarily through canon law and the structures and culture of the Church that Constantinopolitan influence was mediated westwards. Predictably, in the decrees of the Council, there was a strongly Biblicising emphasis on the nature of imperial power, and indeed, the character of the empire itself: Justinian II was addressed as a Christ-like ruler at the head of 'a holy nation, a royal priesthood', made up of all Christians from whose devotions 'any remnant of pagan or Jewish perversity' was to be expunged.[96] As the bishops declared to the Emperor: 'It was your great desire, after the example of Christ, the good shepherd, searching for the sheep lost in the mountains, to bring together this holy nation, as a special people, and to return it to the fold.'[97]

Any lingering hopes for an East Roman revival were further dashed by both the fact and focus of the campaigns of territorial aggrandisement that Abd al-Malik now initiated. Seizing upon Justinian II's attempted population transfer from Cyprus as a pretext for war, the *jihad* against Byzantium was renewed to devastating effect. An attempted Roman counter-attack on Arab forces in Armenia ended in disaster when the Emperor's Slav 'Chosen People' defected to the Arabs.[98] The princes of the region soon began to follow suit as the balance of power on the ground swung decisively towards Abd al-Malik.[99] Major incursions were once more made into Anatolia.[100] In 695 Justinian II was deposed but fled to the realm of the Khazars, from where he would eventually be able to orchestrate a counter-coup and his own return. In the interim, however, things went from bad to worse for the Romans. In 696/7 the ruler of Lazica submitted to the Arabs, whilst the general al-Walid led forces into Anatolia, returning with many captives.[101] Crucially, a major Arab offensive occurred in north Africa, where the Arabs were able to drive back the Roman forces and seize the capital of Carthage. An imperial expeditionary fleet was able momentarily to liberate the city from the grip of the invader, but this simply elicited a still more determined Arab response. As the massed forces of the *umma* advanced once more on Carthage by land and by sea, the Roman garrison chose to withdraw.[102] It was an anti-climactic end to a campaign of enormous significance. For the loss of Carthage to the Arabs in 698, like the city's fall to the Vandals in 439, effectively set the seal on Roman failure. Forced to fall back on the depleted resources of Anatolia and Asia Minor, the empire of Constantinople now faced a

---

[95] *Council in Trullo*, canon 30. I am indebted to Mr Michael Humphreys for discussion of this Council and Miss Danielle Donaldson for its echoes elsewhere.
[96] G. Nedungatt and M. Featherstone, *The Council in Trullo Revisited* (Rome, 1995), p. 53.
[97] ibid.
[98] Theophanes, p. 511.
[99] ibid., p. 512.
[100] ibid., pp. 512–13.
[101] ibid., p. 516.
[102] ibid., pp. 516–17.

long drawn-out struggle for survival that was to dominate its history for much of the eighth and ninth centuries. By the end of the seventh century it would have been clear to Romans and non-Romans, Christians, and others, that the Arabs were now there to stay, at least for the foreseeable future.

Within the lands ruled by the *umma*, the reign of Abd al-Malik and the surmounting of the second *fitna* heralded a turning point. It must have been becoming increasingly apparent to many Muslims that the Day of Judgement was perhaps not quite as imminent as the first generations of the faithful had believed. Through divine favour, they had landed themselves with a 'world empire'. They now had to get on with running it. Gradually, the authorities set about overhauling the inherited machinery of government. Instead of minting mock-Roman coins in the former Roman territory, and mock-Sasanian ones for the former domains of the shah, a single unified currency zone comprising all of the lands ruled by the *umma* was introduced, an act that, alongside the discovery and minting of vast silver deposits in the eastern territories of Khorasan in the eighth century, and an influx of gold from the Sudan, was to have major economic consequences. Through extensive inter-regional trade with the less developed areas around them, the Eastern Roman and Sasanian empires had drawn into their territories vast quantities of precious metals that the conquests of the *umma* had already placed at the disposal of an Arab elite with strong mercantile roots, and an even keener interest in commerce and trade than either the late-Roman or Sasanian aristocracies had possessed.[103] The opportunities resulting from the creation of a vast unified currency zone stretching from the Atlantic to the Indus, and a major expansion in the volume of coinage in circulation, were seized upon by members of this elite, whose enterprise and spirit would turn the Muslim Near East into the economic powerhouse of the West Eurasian world.

From the late seventh century, Arabs became increasingly involved in provincial, civic, and village-level administration and tax affairs, and the various local tributary arrangements were reorganised into a more uniform poll-tax levied on all non-Muslims.[104] As the Syriac *Chronicle of Zuqnin* records:

> Abd al-Malik made a census among the Syrians, issuing strict orders that everyone should go to his father's house, and that everyone should be registered in his own name and that of his father, together with his vineyard, olives, cattle, sons and everything that belonged to him. From this time the poll-tax [Arabic 'jizya'] began to be levied on the skulls of adult males. From this point onwards the Sons of Hagar began to subject the Sons of Aram [i.e. the Syrians] to Egyptian slavery. But this is our own fault: because we sinned, slaves have become our masters. This was the first assessment that the Arabs made.[105]

---

[103] M. Lombard, *L'Islam dans sa première grandeur* (Paris, 1971); J. Banaji, 'Late Antique Legacies and Muslim Economic Expansion', in J. F. Haldon (ed.), *Money, Power and Politics in Early Islamic Syria* (Farnham, 2010), pp. 165–80.
[104] For reflection of this in the documentary sources, see Sijpesteijn (2009).
[105] Palmer and Brock (1993), p. 60.

Crucially, it is under Abd al-Malik that we see Arabic being introduced as a language of government and administration, supplanting Greek, Coptic, Syriac, and Pahlavi. For the first time, now, the sons of local notables in the cities of the Near East would have to learn Arabic if they wished to preserve their social status or advance through governmental service. This marked a milestone in the Arabisation of the Near East: in the eastern, Persian territories especially, conversion to Islam began to gather pace.

Perhaps the most important development in the reign at Damascus of Abd al-Malik and his immediate heirs was that Islam itself was beginning to acquire a clearer identity and greater definition. As the structures of empire were consolidated, so too were the structures of faith, in a process similar to that evident with respect to Christianity in the aftermath of Constantine the Great's conversion in the early fourth century.[106] Compared to the reign of Mu'awiya, a major shift in emphasis is evident. Ibn al-Zubayr had accused Abd al-Malik and the Umayyads of being bad Muslims. His was a purist regime that had blazoned the name of Muhammad on its coinage.[107] As a result, even in victory, Abd al-Malik could not afford to seek to consolidate his regime by visiting Christian pilgrimage sites. He had to demonstrate, in the face of fundamentalist opposition, that his was a regime of Muslims, for Muslims, proclaiming the pure message of Islam. In place of the broad coalition of monotheistic fighting men that had initiated the conquests in the 630s, Muslim (and Arab) supremacy was now clearly asserted.[108] On the Dome of the Rock in Jerusalem, dominating the ancient city holy to Muslims, Christians, and Jews, Abd al-Malik constructed a magnificent place of worship that bore the triumphalist inscription addressed to his non-Muslim subjects: 'The Messiah Jesus son of Mary was only a messenger of God, and His word which He committed to Mary, and a spirit from Him. So believe in God and His messengers and do not say "three"; refrain, it is better for you. God is only one God; he is too exalted to have a son. He is all that is in the heavens and on the earth. God suffices as a defender.'[109]

When Abd al-Malik determined to rebuild Mecca, we are told, he proposed to do so with columns stripped from the Church of Holy Gethsemene, until one of his Christian officials persuaded him to accept marble columns sent from Constantinople for this purpose instead.[110] In 691 he is reported to have deliberately antagonised the Byzantine authorities by sending tribute not in mock-imperial *solidi* but in a new issue.[111] Certainly, c.692 Abd al-Malik had minted and circulated coins bearing the Arabic inscription 'In the name of God, there is no God but God alone; Muhammad is the messenger of God.' On the new coinage, either Muhammad or Abd al-Malik was depicted leading the faithful sword in hand [Fig. 11].[112] Abd al-Malik also proclaimed himself, in direct rivalry to the

---

[106] Donner (2010).
[107] Hoyland (2006), p. 397.
[108] Donner (2010).
[109] Translation taken from Hoyland (2006), p. 409.
[110] Theophanes, p. 510.
[111] ibid., p. 509.
[112] See discussion in Foss (2008).

Fig. 11 'Standing Caliph' Solidus (C. Mango, *The Oxford History of Byzantium*, p. 127)

ideological claims made by emperors in Constantinople, to be the *khalifat Allah*, or 'God's Deputy'.[113] In the Qur'an, we should note, the term *khalifat* is specifically applied to the Biblical king David, the founder of Jerusalem, whose building work (along with that of Solomon) Abd al-Malik was also perhaps seeking to emulate.[114] This necessitated a Byzantine response. Justinian II retaliated by minting and disseminating gold coins bearing a foreboding image of Christ 'King of kings' [Fig. 12], with an image of the Emperor on the reverse, described as 'servant of Christ'.[115] Drawing upon earlier Jewish criticisms of Christian practice, Abd al-Malik in turn denounced the Byzantine use of images of Christ and the Saints as idolatrous, in breach of the Second Commandment against 'graven images'. For the first time establishing hostility to images as a cornerstone of the Islamic faith, the *khalifat*, or 'Caliph', now minted his reformed coinage for the 'Caliphate' as a whole, which was entirely epigraphic and aniconic in decoration.[116] Christian sensitivity that the Arab charge of idolatry was not perhaps entirely unfounded would contribute to the 'Iconoclast dispute' in Byzantium in the eighth and ninth centuries, when emperors and churchmen attempted to regain divine favour by turning against such images or 'icons' (Greek, *eikones*) of Christ, Mary, and the Saints. The struggle for mastery of the Near East was increasingly being fought on an ideological plane and in competition over a shared symbolic universe framed by the Old Testament.[117]

It is sometimes asked why the Christian communities of the Near East did not simply rise up against their Arab masters.[118] As we have seen, sometimes they did,

---

[113] See Hoyland (2006).

[114] Qur'an, *Sira*, 38:26; see discussion in Donner (2010), pp. 210–11.

[115] P. Grierson, *Byzantine Coinage in the Dumbarton Oaks Collection*, vol. II: *Phocas to Theodosius III 602–717* (Washington DC, 1968), pp. 568–70.

[116] P. Grierson, 'The Monetary Reforms of Abd al-Malik: Their Metrological Basis and Their Financial Repercussions', *JESHO* 3.3 (1960), pp. 241–64; Foss (2008).

[117] See the magnum opus by L. Brubaker and J. Haldon, *Byzantium in the Iconoclast Era, c. 680–850: A History* (Cambridge, 2010).

[118] See, for example, Kennedy (2007).

Fig. 12 Solidus of Justinian II (by kind permission of the Fitzwilliam Museum, Cambridge)

especially when there was a realistic prospect of receiving imperial support. The early leadership of the *umma*, however, proved itself remarkably effective at co-opting local political and religious elites and implicating them in their system of rule. It was only in the eighth century, for example, when Christian notables began to find themselves sidelined in the lucrative business of tax collection, that we see revolts flaring up among the Christian population of Egypt.[119] Moreover, part of the cumulative impact of the Christological dispute on the collective psychology of Christian communities, both Miaphysite and Neo-Chalcedonian, may well have been a growing sense that 'true religion' could stand alone from the structures of empire (a realisation to which St Augustine of Hippo had come in the fifth century). The associated ability of both Miaphysite and hard-line Chalcedonian congregations, exasperated by imperial attempts at compromise, to flourish and expand in the early Islamic period is striking. This stands in marked contrast to Zoroastrianism, which had seemingly become so structurally dependent upon the Sasanian monarchy and Iranian nobility that it could not survive without them save at the level of a remembered folk religion and a religion of exile.

There may also, however, have been another factor informing the relative passivity of many Christians. Sixth- and seventh-century Christianity, as we have seen, was ever more apocalyptic in character and tone. The struggle between first Heraclius and Khusro, and then Byzantium and Islam, was understood as part of a great cosmic drama that was reaching its final act, and which generated a great deal of apocalyptic literature as a result.[120] The so-called *Apocalypse of Pseudo-Methodius*, for example, written around the time of the second *fitna*, foretold how, after much suffering for the Christian population, the 'King of the Greeks' would come to sweep the Arabs away, before in turn being attacked by the 'people of the north'. God would then intervene, sending an angel who would smite the foe. Eventually, the king of the Greeks would make his way to Jerusalem, and at Golgotha take off his gold crown and place it on the True Cross. Both crown and Cross would then

---

[119] Sijpesteijn (2009).
[120] See discussion in Kennedy (2007), pp. 346–9.

302   *Empires of Faith*

be physically assumed into heaven.¹²¹ As a vision of the preordained, such eschatological reveries may well have brought solace to the faithful, but they hardly constituted a 'call-to-arms'. Many living under Arab rule, in short, must have felt they were observers of the great cosmic drama unfolding before them rather than active participants in it. Political passivity on the part of the conquered was hard-wired into the apocalyptic mindset. Only beyond the frontiers of the Caliphate could mindfulness of the Last Days serve to stiffen resistance.

8.5 A WORLD TRANSFORMED

The wars between first Rome and Persia, and then Byzantium and Islam, that comprise so much of the history of the Near East in the seventh century, were complex in nature, tortuous in execution, and often finely balanced on the ground: had Heraclius been captured in the Caucasus in 625, or the forces of the shah been victorious at al-Qadisiyya in 638, everything might have turned out differently. Much emphasis has been placed on the details of the military narrative in the foregoing chapters, not only because they are so richly recorded in the sources (and thus can be asserted as fact) but also because the consequences of these often finely balanced struggles were to be so far-reaching, their ramifications being ones with which we still live. As a result of these years of warfare, the ancient empire of Persia was destroyed; a new religion and an associated confessional state were born; and the Roman Empire was reduced to an Anatolian rump, with sufficient ideological, political, and military resources to resist the Arabs, but seemingly not to drive them back. The growing economic, political, and military isolation of the besieged Roman Empire of Constantinople in turn set the Christian kingdoms of western Europe along new paths of development, and led to a reorientation of the post-Roman world (although Byzantine influence continued to be felt).

Within what remained of the Eastern Roman Empire, by the end of the seventh century, social, political, economic, and cultural conditions had been fundamentally reconfigured. Subjected to the ever-escalating demands of the state on the one hand, and chronic insecurity caused by warfare on the other, in much of the empire the great urban centres, with which the lifestyle and culture of the traditional civic elites had for so long been associated, can be seen to have lost much of their monumental character as well as their political role—in a process very similar to that encountered with respect to cities in parts of the sixth-century West. With political power (and physical security) increasingly confined to the imperial capital, civic notables and their families seem to have fled the provincial cities, either for Constantinople or the countryside.¹²² The cities themselves, as noted earlier, increasingly took on the appearance of shrunken fortified compounds, whilst the

---

¹²¹ Palmer and Brock (1993), pp. 222–42.
¹²² Foss (1975)—now to be read in the light of Niewöhner (2007); M. Whittow, 'Early Medieval Byzantium and the End of the Ancient World', *Journal of Agrarian Change* 9 (2009), pp. 134–53.

rural population of eastern Anatolia were provided with underground citadels and redoubts in which to take refuge during Arab raids.

The urban dislocation caused by warfare was to have profound cultural consequences, for the cities could no longer serve as the *locus* for the replication of traditional Greco-Roman literary or intellectual culture, such as had formed the sceptical, liberal, but elitist world view of the likes of Procopius of Caesarea in the sixth century. Rather, the way was now clear for the Church to emerge as the dominant force in Byzantine cultural and intellectual life. What classical Greek authors' works we possess today have primarily come down to us because Byzantine monks chose to copy them. The post seventh-century literature of Byzantium was to be overwhelmingly religious in content, focus, and source.[123] Of course, much the same was true with respect to Latin literature in the West, where recognisably Roman elites had long since faded away.

With urban dislocation, and a growing emphasis on the part of the East Roman state on supplying the army in kind and rewarding troops with land, a contraction in the monetary economy would appear to have taken place, with a decline in finds of small-denomination coinage at archaeological sites, and the reusing of old coins until they were worn away to little more than worthless scraps.[124] In the most wartorn or vulnerable parts of the empire, there is also evidence for a shift away from arable agriculture and towards pastoralism and mixed farming, after a manner again highly reminiscent of parts of the post-Roman West, and driven by the same factors.[125] Around Constantinople, and in those parts of the empire better shielded from yearly Arab raids, however, such as Bithynia and the rich coastal zone along the Aegean, much more of the economic, urban, administrative, and fiscal infrastructure of late antiquity persisted.[126] The seventh century had thus bequeathed a highly fragmented and remarkably diversified Anatolian landscape in which there were, nevertheless, important elements of continuity.[127]

This had implications for how East Roman society and the East Roman state organised itself. In many parts of what remained of the empire, the great networks of highly commercialised aristocratic estates that had characterised late antiquity are likely to have been shattered by warfare, and it may well have been from the lands of abandoned estates that the imperial government carved out military landholdings. Certainly, there is evidence that extensive estates with long-standing roots had

---

[123] See discussion in C. Mango, *Byzantium: The Empire of New Rome* (London, 1983).
[124] Grierson (1968).
[125] H. Vanhaverbeke, F. Martens, M. Waelkens, and J. Poblome, 'Late Antiquity in the Territory of Sagalassos', in L. Lavan and C. Machado (eds.), *Recent Research on the Late Antique Countryside* (Leiden, 2004), pp. 247–80; A. England et al., 'Historical Landscape Change in Cappadocia (Central Turkey): A Palaeoecological Investigation of Annually Laminated Sediments from Nar Lake', *The Holocene* 18 (2008), pp. 1,229–45.
[126] See P. Sarris, 'Large Estates and the Peasantry in Byzantium, *c.* 600–1100', in *Revue Belge de Philologie et d'Histoire* (forthcoming).
[127] See discussion in Wickham (2005). For comparatively high continuity in urbanism in western Asia Minor, see E. A. Ivison, 'Amorium in the Byzantine Dark Ages (Seventh to Ninth Centuries)' in Henning (2007), pp. 25–60, especially p. 55; for discontinuity, see A. K. Vionis, J. Poblome, and M. Waelkens, 'The Hidden Material Culture of the Dark Ages: Early Medieval Ceramics at Sagalassos (Turkey). New Evidence (*c.* AD 650–800)', *Anatolian Studies* 59 (2009), pp. 147–66.

passed into the ownership of the imperial government.[128] Within Constantinople itself, however, and around the Sea of Marmara and adjacent areas (such as Bithynia and the Aegean coastline), senatorial families and (it is probable) their property portfolios survived into the reign of Justinian II and beyond.[129] In 713, for example, the Emperor Philippikos Bardanes is reported to have dined with 'citizens of ancient lineage'.[130] At the imperial court, however, the influence of such families was increasingly supplanted or assimilated by that of a new generation of functionaries, as well as by military hardmen, often of Caucasian or Armenian origin (the mountains of the Caucasus having now replaced the Balkans as the main Roman military recruiting ground).[131] As a result, a new palatine elite took shape, more economically dependent on the state, and perhaps more ideologically committed to it. Beyond the Aegean coastline, Bithynia, and the environs of Constantinople, a higher degree of peasant autonomy is discernible, whilst in the most militarily insecure territories, along the marchlands of Cappadocia and the East, communities increasingly clustered around the protective embrace of local military warlords, who knew the terrain and were thus best placed to coordinate resistance to Muslim attack. Again, many of these lords, who invested their wealth in castles and cattle, were of Armenian, Caucasian, or even Christian Arab descent, and members of these marcher families were progressively drawn into the service of the Emperor in Constantinople (Map 7).[132]

The two great elements of continuity in East Roman society were the Church and the state. Each now found its power enhanced. With the transformation of cities, as we have seen, and the demise of the traditional educational and cultural infrastructure of the *polis*, the Church now entirely dominated Byzantine culture and, as the declarations of the bishops at the Council *in Trullo* and the coinage of the Emperor Justinian II reveal, it increasingly defined East Roman ideology and political identity. With the weakening of the old networks of aristocratic power, the imperial government could now govern the core territories of what remained of the empire around Constantinople and in western Asia Minor with something approximating to the tightness of control and intensity of scrutiny to which Justinian had aspired in the sixth century, but which the power on the ground of the late-antique aristocracy of service and senatorial elite had effectively precluded.[133] With that aristocracy now diminished or replaced, the efficient collection of taxes and supplies was perhaps more straightforwardly achieved than at any time since the days of

---

[128] See discussion in P. Magdalino, *The Empire of Manuel I Komnenos, 1143–80* (Cambridge, 1993).
[129] J. F. Haldon, 'The Fate of the Late Roman Senatorial Elite', in J. F. Haldon and L. I. Conrad (eds.), *The Byzantine And Islamic Near East*, vol. 6: *Elites Old and New* (Princeton, 2004), pp. 179–234.
[130] ibid.; Theophanes, p. 533.
[131] ibid.
[132] T. F. and A. C. D. Matthews, 'Islamic-Style Mansions in Byzantine Cappadocia and the Development of the Inverted T-Plan', *Society of Architectural Historians* 56.3 (1997), pp. 294–315; V. Kalas, 'The 2004 Survey of the Byzantine Settlement at Selime-Yaprakhisar in the Peristrema Valley, Cappadocia, *Dumbarton Oaks Papers* 60 (2006), pp. 271–93; J. F. Haldon, 'Social Elites, Wealth, and Power', in J. F. Haldon (ed.), *A Social History of Byzantium* (Oxford, 2009), pp. 168–211.
[133] Whittow (2009).

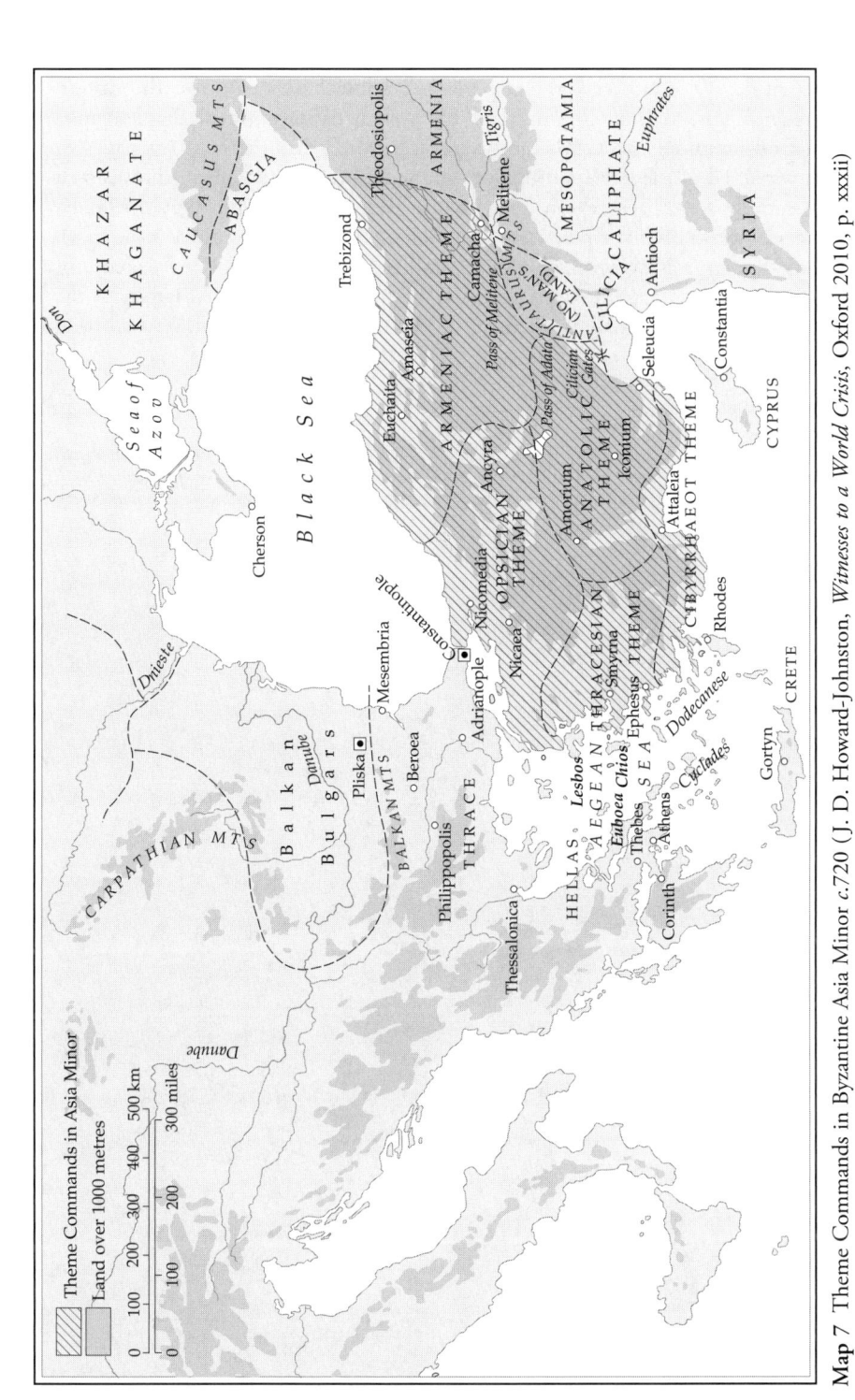

Map 7 Theme Commands in Byzantine Asia Minor c.720 (J. D. Howard-Johnston, *Witnesses to a World Crisis*, Oxford 2010, p. xxxii)

Constantine. Thus although the imperial government's control over the eastern marchlands was, at best, intermittent, the system of government that emerged from Constantinople's seventh-century crisis ensured that the core territories of what remained of the empire probably represented the most tightly administered and centrally supervised region anywhere to the west of China.[134] Accordingly, whereas in much of the fifth-century West (as also the seventh-century Near East), the late-Roman aristocracy had survived military crisis largely at the expense of the late-Roman state, in Anatolia and Asia Minor the state survived largely at the expense of the late-Roman aristocracy.[135] The core dynamics of power had been transformed.

---

[134] A. Toynbee, *Constantine Porphyrogenitus and His World* (Oxford, 1973). For the more limited writ of the state in the east, see L. Neville, *Authority in Byzantine Provincial Society* (Cambridge, 2004).

[135] C. Wickham, 'The Other Transition: From the Ancient World to Feudalism', *Past and Present* 103 (1984), pp. 3–36.

9

The Princes of the Western Nations

9.1 BYZANTIUM AND THE BALKANS IN THE SEVENTH CENTURY

As we saw in Chapter Five, it was a basic fact of the political and military geography of the Byzantine state that threats from the east had to be prioritised over those from the west. This core strategic sensibility was conveyed, for example, by the equestrian statue of Justinian that stood in the heart of Constantinople, and which Procopius describes as depicting the Emperor facing eastwards and 'stretching forth his right hand towards the rising sun ... commanding the barbarians in that quarter to remain at home and to advance no further'.[1] As a result of this inescapable reality, Heraclius had been unable to take direct military advantage of the blow to the authority of the *khagan* caused by the failure of the Avar siege of Constantinople in 626. Instead his response was diplomatic. The traditional Roman policy of 'divide and rule', which the Avar domination of the Pannonian plain had rendered less and less practicable, was now reactivated by the Emperor, but on a far grander scale than before. Bands of Croats and Serbs were induced to migrate into Avar-controlled territory from north of the Carpathian Mountains, the latter group converting to imperial Christianity and forming a firm alliance with Constantinople.[2] To the west, a Frankish merchant (*negutians ... exercendum negucium* [sic]) by the name of Samo led an uprising of 'those Slavs who are known as the Wends', over whom he went on to rule for thirty-five years.[3] Samo was perhaps an agent of the Frankish king Dagobert, who, as we have seen, acknowledged Heraclius' overlordship (although Frankish forces and Samo's Slav followers were later to clash).[4] In the north-east, on the Ukrainian steppe beyond the Black Sea, the Bulgars likewise rose in revolt and carved out for themselves a separate khaganate. As the Byzantine author Nicephorus relates: 'Koubratos, the nephew of Organas and lord of the Onogundurs, rose against the *khagan* of the Avars and, after abusing the army he had from the latter, drove them out of his land.'[5] According to Theophanes, this Kubrat was master of 'the old Great Bulgaria' stretching from

---

[1] Procopius, *Buildings*, I, 2.12.
[2] Constantine VII, *De Administrando Imperio*, tr. R. J. H. Jenkins (Washington DC, 1967), ch. 32.
[3] Fredegar, IV, 48, 68, and 87. This revolt is traditionally dated to 623/4, but a date after 626 makes considerably more sense.
[4] Fredegar, IV, 43, 68.
[5] Nicephorus, Patriarch of Constantinople, *Short History*, tr. C. Mango (Washington DC, 1990), 22.

north of the Crimea to the Sea of Azov.[6] There are some indications that he too may have been a personal ally of the Emperor.[7] The Frankish *Chronicle of Fredegar* also records a civil war breaking out within the Avar Khaganate *c.*631–2, in which Avar and Bulgar parties clashed.[8] Again, one detects the hand of Constantinople at work.

The sudden emergence of the Arab threat, however, meant that the Roman authorities were necessarily too preoccupied with events in the east to take advantage of Avar collapse by reasserting imperial control over the south-central Balkans. Instead, the result was a power vacuum that was filled by new non-Roman polities. A rump Avar state remained on the Pannonian plain, intervening periodically in the affairs of northern Italy and Istria, where the Avars were able to force various of the Langobard *duces* to submit to their rule and pay tribute.[9] Although their power was much diminished, the Avars would remain a force to be reckoned with until they were defeated in 795–6 by the Frankish ruler Charlemagne, a defeat so comprehensive that to this day Russians still use the phrase 'to be slaughtered like Avars'.[10] As the royal biographer, Einhard, noted: 'the utter depopulation of Pannonia, and the site of the *khagan*'s palace, now a desert, where not a trace of human habitation is visible, bear witness how many battles were fought in those years, and how much blood shed. The entire body of the Hun nobility perished in this contest, and all its glory with it. All the money and treasure that had been years amassing was seized, and no war in which the Franks have ever engaged within memory brought them such riches and such booty.'[11]

Over the course of the seventh century, the power of the Bulgars expanded to the north-east of the plains of Thrace, until they were capable of challenging Byzantine control of the approaches to Constantinople. One of Kubrat's sons, Asparukh, had conquered much of the eastern Balkans by *c.*670 and soon initiated raids into what remained of imperial territory, extracting tribute from the empire. A campaign against the Bulgars directed across the Danube by the Emperor Constantine IV in 680–81 culminated in a significant Roman defeat, following which the Bulgars were able to force a number of Slav tribes to submit.[12] An increasingly sophisticated and self-confident Bulgar khaganate began to take shape, characterised by the Turkic Bulgar aristocracy's domination of a Roman and Slav subject population. Traditions of urbanism and literacy in Greek appear to have lingered on amongst the former.[13] At their capital at Pliska, the Bulgar rulers drew upon these skills to advertise their authority in triumphal carvings and inscriptions blazoning their

---

[6] Theophanes, p. 498. For the location of 'Old Great Bulgaria', see discussion in Curta (2006), pp. 77–8.

[7] ibid., pp. 77–8, drawing on John of Nikiu.

[8] ibid., p. 76.

[9] Paul the Deacon, V, 21.

[10] Einhard, *Vita Karoli*, ch. 13.

[11] ibid.

[12] Curta (2006), pp. 79–81.

[13] J. D. Howard-Johnston, 'Urban Continuity in the Balkans in the Early Middle Ages', in A. Poulter (ed.), *Ancient Bulgaria*, 2 vols. (Nottingham, 1983), I, pp. 242–55.

authority and might.[14] These 'proto-Bulgar' inscriptions provide some of our best evidence for the nature of the emergent polity, with the Bulgar *khagan* adopting the Roman title of *archôn* ('governor' or 'ruler') or *ek theou archôn* ('ruler through the grace of God').[15] At the level of their formerly Roman subjects, Christianity was allowed to continue, and the Bulgars' own approach to religion was highly syncretist. Bishops, however, were treated with suspicion and banned from Bulgar territory as agents of the Emperor in Constantinople. As a result, 'popular religion' was able to evolve free from episcopal control. Perhaps not surprisingly, to the end of the Middle Ages, and long after the conversion of Bulgar rulers to Christianity in the ninth century, the northern Balkans would be regarded by the ecclesiastical authorities as a hotbed of heresy.

Prior to the consolidation of Bulgar power, Constans II had at least been able to show Roman banners in the Balkans during the course of his march west, descending from the plains of Thrace to Athens before sailing on to Italy (as we saw in Chapter Eight). By the reign of Justinian II, however, the Roman position had clearly deteriorated markedly, such that when, in 687–8, the young Emperor wished to visit Thessalonica, he had to fight his way there.[16] In the absence of any effective Roman challenge, independent Slav chieftaincies (described in our Greek sources as *sklaviniai*) had formed from Thrace down into the southern Balkans and Peloponnese.[17] Justinian II took advantage of the peace with the Arabs that he negotiated in 685–6 to take warfare to the Bulgars and the *sklaviniai* of Thrace. Although he was able to take many Slav prisoners of war, in 687–8 the Emperor and his army were ambushed by the Bulgars as they returned from Thessalonica, and Justinian barely escaped with his life.[18] In the following decades, according to a treatise attributed to the tenth-century Byzantine emperor Constantine VII Porphyrogenitus, all of Greece would be 'slavonicized and turned barbarian'.[19]

Quite what Slavonic settlement actually meant on the ground is uncertain. There are traces in both the archaeological and literary record, as well as in the evidence of place names, that Slav settlement continued to be at its most pronounced in highland, forest, and marginal zones, with a Greek-speaking Christian population probably remaining predominant in lowland areas and on the rapidly atrophying urban sites. Around the city of Patras, for example, symbiotic relations between Greek Christians and surrounding Slav communities had formed by the eighth century.[20] As elsewhere, however, aristocratic flight is likely to have been the order of the day, and many diocesan structures (which had generally survived 'barbarian invasion' in the West) simply disappeared. It was not to be until the

---

[14] J. Henning, 'The Metropolis of Pliska, or, How Large Does an Early Medieval Settlement Have to be in order to be Called a City?', and G. Prinzing, 'Pliska in the View of Protobulgarian Inscriptions and Byzantine Writers', in Henning (ed.) (2007), pp. 209–40 and 241–52.
[15] V. Beševliev, *Die Protobulgarische Inschriften* (Berlin, 1963), pp. 72–3.
[16] Theophanes, p. 508.
[17] ibid., p. 507.
[18] ibid., p. 508.
[19] Constantine VII, *De Thematibus*, 4.
[20] Constantine VII, *De Administrando Imperio*, ch. 49.

late eighth century that an easing of Arab pressure on the empire's eastern flank would once more permit the imperial authorities to concentrate minds and resources on the Balkans, and set about extending control over the world of the *sklaviniai* in a series of campaigns that would combine conquest with conversion.

9.2 SOCIETY, IDENTITY, AND LAW IN LANGOBARD ITALY

As we have seen with respect to both the Slavs in the Balkans in the sixth century, and the various barbarian *gentes* operating in the territories of the Western Roman Empire, Roman military aggression had often catalysed the emergence of larger, more cohesive military and political groupings amongst those peoples with whom the Romans came into contact. The absence of an effective Roman military response, by contrast, is probably the main explanation for the highly fragmented and independent nature of the settlement of Langobardic war leaders (*duces*) and their kin-groups and retinues (*farae*), both in northern Italy and around Beneventum to the south in the late sixth century, who secured their position by holing themselves up behind the walls and defences of the cities of the regions they had conquered: in Langobard Italy, as in seventh-century Byzantium, towns would be described as military camps, or *castra*.[21] Between 574 and 584, as we have seen, the Langobard *duces* operated without a king and with a high degree of autonomy. Only with the more aggressive stance adopted by the Emperor Maurice c.590 did the leaders of the northern Langobards once more begin to make common cause and elect a ruler. Under the energetic leadership first of Authari (r.584–90) and then Agilulf (r.590–616), peace was bought with the Franks and a number of cities along the Po were brought under or restored to Langobard control. In 593–4 an assault was even launched on Rome.[22] Agilulf then turned his attention to obtaining the submission of a number of the more independently minded Langobardic dukes. Paul the Deacon, drawing on a contemporary history written by Agilulf's courtier, the Roman Secundus of Non, relates how at least eight were either deposed or submitted (out of a supposed total, according to Paul, of thirty-five, although the latter figure is probably an exaggeration).[23] Agilulf's efforts were initially concentrated in the north, where, in 603, the most self-confident and autonomous of the duchies—that of Gisulf II of Friuli—submitted.[24] In 605 a peace treaty was agreed with Pope Gregory the Great, and by the end of his reign Agilulf's

---

[21] *Edict of Rothari*, 244, p. 100, where *castrum* appears synonymous with *civitas* or *oppidum*. On the nature of settlement in the context of the Byzantine military response, see W. Pohl, 'Invasions and Ethnic Identity', in La Rocca (2002), pp. 11–34, 21–2. On cities, see B. Ward-Perkins, 'The Lombard City and Urban Economy', in G. Ausenda, P. Delogu, and C. Wickham (eds.), *The Langobards Before the Frankish Conquest: An Ethnographic Perspective* (San Marino, 2009), pp. 95–117.
[22] Wickham (1981), pp. 33–4.
[23] Paul the Deacon, II, 32.
[24] Wickham (1981), p. 33.

control had extended over Theodahad's old stamping ground of Tuscany. Beneventum, however, remained independent under its Duke Arichis I (r.591–641).

There are distinctly Romanising overtones to Agilulf's reign. He ruled from the sometime imperial capital of Milan, where he presided over ceremonies in the city's circus. As Paul the Deacon records, in 604, he raised to co-rulership Adaloald, the son of his predecessor Authari, whose widow Theodelinda he had married. The ceremony announcing co-rulership took place 'in the circus of Mediolanum (Milan) . . . while the ambassadors of Theudebert, king of the Franks were standing by'.[25] Agilulf's court was attended by Roman ministers such as Secundus of Non, and the Langobard leadership soon began to forge symbiotic and cooperative relations with the Catholic episcopate of northern Italy, with bishops acting as spokesmen for civic communities.[26] Agilulf even adopted the title 'king of the whole of Italy' (*rex totius Italiae*).[27] There are signs, in short, that what was coalescing at the Langobard court was a regime that to all intents and purposes probably looked rather like the old Ostrogothic kingdom of Theoderic. Indeed, the political and even ceremonial institutions of the two regimes can be seen to have borne a striking resemblance: thus just as Witigis had been acclaimed king by the leading men of the Goths 'among the swords of battle in the ancestral way', so too was the Langobard king chosen in a military assembly known in Langobardic as the *gairthinx*, or the 'assembly of the lances'.[28] The Roman political classes of northern Italy would have known how to engage with such men.

That having been said, however, one should not understate the destruction and violence associated with the Langobardic settlement, and relations with the indigenous elite were far from uniformly eirenic. Paul the Deacon, for example, recounts how, soon after the initial invasions, King Cleph 'killed many powerful men of the Romans with his sword, and expelled others from Italy'. 'Many Roman nobles', he continues, 'were killed through greed.'[29] The archaeological record reveals clear signs of the economic harm and physical insecurity often associated with warfare.[30]

Much of Roman administrative culture nevertheless clearly persisted. There are indications that in the earliest phases of settlement—perhaps those negotiated by the Roman authorities—the Langobards were accommodated by means of *hospitalitas* arrangements such as were encountered in Chapter Two with respect to the Burgundians and Visigoths.[31] Those Roman nobles who did not flee or who were not put to the sword, we are told, 'were divided among the guests [*per hospites*] and made tributaries, that they should pay the third part of their produce to the

---

[25] Paul the Deacon, IV, 30.
[26] T. S. Brown, 'Lombard Religious Policy in the Late Sixth and Seventh Centuries: The Roman Dimension', in Ausenda, Delogu, and Wickham (2009), pp. 289–308.
[27] Wickham (1981), p. 34.
[28] Cassiodorus, *Variae*, X, 31; S. Gasparri, 'Kingship Rituals and Ideology in Lombard Italy', in F. Theuws and J. L. Nelson (eds.), *Rituals of Power from Late Antiquity to the Early Middle Ages* (Leiden, 2000), pp. 95–114, p. 98.
[29] Paul the Deacon, II, 31–2.
[30] Wickham (1981), p. 65, and (2005), pp. 644–56 and 730–32.
[31] W. Pohl, 'The Empire and the Lombards', in Pohl (ed.) (1997), pp. 75–134.

Langobards'.³² As in fifth-century Gaul, there is little evidence that the 'barbarian' invasions of northern Italy led to any significant impact on the underlying social structure or the organisation of the agrarian economy. Certainly large estates persisted, worked by both slave and servile labour. The former are described in the legal sources as *mancipia* and *servi rusticani*, the latter as 'half-free' *aldii*—probably the descendants of the *coloni originarii* of the fifth century.³³ Memories of the Roman fiscal system also lingered on, no doubt informed by the survival of that system in neighbouring Byzantine territory.³⁴ It does not appear, however, that taxation itself survived. Certainly, there is no mention of it in the earliest Langobard legal source, the *Edict of Rothari*, which was promulgated in 643.³⁵

Instead, the basis of royal government, as also probably of ducal power, was the 'tribute bearing estate'—the *casa ordinata tributaria*—from the proceeds of which the kings, dukes, and their military retainers supported themselves.³⁶ As Paul the Deacon noted of the re-establishment of the Langobard monarchy under Authari: 'In these times, for the restoration of the kingship, the dukes then gave one half of their property for the use of the king, in order to support the king himself, his retainers and those who were required to accompany him by virtue of the various offices which had been assigned to them. But the oppressed people (*populi adgravati*) were divided among the Langobard guests (*per hospites partiuntur*).'³⁷ At a local level, the centre of administration was the royal court (*curtis regia*)—probably initially a block of estates—overseen by a royal official termed the *gastaldus*. These were centres for both tribute collection and the administration of justice.³⁸ We also find references to ducal courts (*curtes ducales*), which again served as centres of seigneurial authority in the broadest sense. This was a world where land was power.³⁹

On the face of it, the world of highly fragmented, 'parcelised sovereignty' encountered in the Langobardic evidence might appear a recipe for political disintegration. That it did not prove to be so can probably be accounted for in two ways. First, Langobard kings such as Agilulf were successful at ensuring that their own estates, and thus sources of power, were never eclipsed by those of their dukes. So long as the 'royal demesne' prospered, royal authority remained strong. Second, Agilulf and his heirs, operating in the geographically relatively compact valleys and plains of the north, managed to establish a realm characterised by a remarkable degree of ideological cohesion focused on the royal court situated first at Milan and then at the site of the old Ostrogothic capital at Pavia.⁴⁰ It is a striking fact that although the Langobard kingdom was to suffer considerable political troubles, with coups and usurpations taking place in 626, 662, 688, and 702,

---

³² Paul the Deacon, II, 32.
³³ *Edict of Rothari*, 103 (p. 69), 132 (p. 72), and 134 (pp. 94–5). As with the *colonus originalis*, the master of an *aldius* had control of his working capital, or *peculium*—see ibid., 235 (p. 99).
³⁴ Everett (2003), p. 77.
³⁵ Wickham (2005), pp. 115–17.
³⁶ *Edict of Rothari*, 252 (p. 102).
³⁷ Paul the Deacon, III, 16.
³⁸ Everett (2003), pp. 72–3.
³⁹ Wickham (1981), p. 40.
⁴⁰ ibid., pp. 38–9.

there was no attempt on the part of any of the Langobard dukes to secede from the realm. It seems that the Langobardic monarchy and kingdom came to be taken for granted as 'establishing the parameters in which political life was conducted'.[41]

Unlike the Visigothic kingdom in Spain in the aftermath of Reccared's conversion in 587, the ideological cohesion of the Langobards was not rooted in religion; different *duces* and kings espoused 'Arian' and 'Catholic' Christianity respectively according to family tradition or personal faith, with no obviously deleterious political consequences. Rather, their cohesion resulted from a shared and carefully nurtured sense of Langobard identity, and from the ability of kings to present themselves as effective guardians and custodians of Langobardic memory and custom.[42] Upon the death of Agilulf in 616 the crown passed to his stepson Adaloald, who reigned until 626. He was then succeeded by his brother-in-law Arioald (*r.*626–36). Related to the Bavarian royal family via Theodelinda, these kings were open to international influences and cultures that perhaps contributed to their relatively Romanising style of rule.[43] In 636, however, the crown passed to Rothari, a Langobard warlord determined to stress his Langobard credentials. In his *Edict*, promulgated in 643, we encounter a carefully constructed evocation of Langobardic identity preserved and codified by royal will.

In this legal compilation, Rothari and his advisers—'the principal judges'— begin by charting the history of the Langobardic kings since 'the happy arrival of the Langobards in Italy'.[44] 'In these matters', the king declares, 'our concern for the future assures us that what we do here is useful and so we have ordered the names of the Langobard kings, our predecessors, and from what family they came to be noted down insofar as we have ascertained them from the older men of the nation.'[45] The substance of the law—presented as the orally preserved memory of the Langobards—is then conveyed:

> With the favour of God and with the greatest care and most careful scrutiny, obtained by heavenly favour, after seeking out and finding the old laws of our fathers which were not written down, and with the equal counsel and consent of our most important judges and with the rest of our most happy nation assisting, we have established the present lawbook containing the provisions which are useful to the common good of all our people. We have ordered these laws to be written down on this parchment, thus preserving them in this edict, so that these things which, with divine aid, we have been able to recapture through careful investigation of the old laws of the Langobards known either to ourself or to the old men of the army, we have put down in this lawbook. Issued and confirmed by the formal procedure according to the usage of our nation, let this be a strong and stable law.[46]

---

[41] ibid., p. 38.
[42] N. Christie, 'Pannonia: Foundation of Langobardic Power and Identity', and P. Delogu, 'Kingship and the Shaping of the Lombard Body Politic' in Ausenda, Delogu, and Wickham (2009), pp. 6–29 and 251–88.
[43] ibid., p. 36.
[44] *Edict of Rothari*, Prologue.
[45] ibid.
[46] ibid., 386 (p. 129).

There is much to this *Edict* that is highly Roman: it is written in Latin, and at one point mirrors the language of Justinian's codification of the Roman *ius civilis*, with its talk of the king having 'perceived it necessary to improve and reaffirm the law, amending all earlier laws by adding that which is lacking and eliminating that which is superfluous'.[47] However, much of the substance of the codified law of the Langobards is unmistakably Germanic; its core momentum and impetus is driven by the institution of the 'blood feud', which was entirely alien to Roman legal tradition and practice. Technical terms, moreover, are glossed in Langobardic, providing our best evidence for what remained at that point a living language.[48] What we effectively get, as a great authority on early medieval law noted, is a 'codification of traditional practice so as to give it a Roman patina'.[49]

The *Edict* delineates the contours and concerns of Langobardic society. It is king-focused, lord-focused, and kin-based. 'That man who conspires or gives counsel against the king', we are told, 'shall be killed and his property confiscated.'[50] 'He who kills his lord', it continues, 'shall be killed himself.'[51] Its ethos is that of the war-band: 'he who during a battle with the enemy abandons his comrade . . . shall be killed'.[52] The Langobards are a people in arms, the 'nation' an 'army' (*exercitus*).[53] In addition to regulating the workings of justice, the status of slaves, serfs, and freedmen, and the compensation and blood money required of a kindred if feud was to be averted, the lawbook provides fascinating insights into Langobardic values and beliefs. 'No one', it declares, 'may presume to kill another man's freedwoman or woman slave as if she were a vampire (*striga*) which the people call witch (*masca*), because it is in no wise to be believed by Christian minds that it is possible that a woman can eat a living man from within.'[54] 'If a man', the *Edict* records, 'because of his weighty sins, goes mad or becomes possessed and does damage to man or beast, nothing shall be required from his heirs. If the madman is killed, likewise nothing shall be required, provided, however, that he is not killed without cause.'[55] However, the most telling feature of the *Edict* is the sense of Langobardic pride that it conveys. To be a 'Langobard' was not just a question of ethnicity, it was a mark of status. As a result, just as there necessarily occurred an appropriation of Frankish identity on the part of many Roman aristocratic families in sixth- and seventh-century Gaul, so too in Italy did many Romans have to become Langobards if they were to protect their interests and preserve their social status. Accordingly, whilst the disappearance of identifiable and self-identifying 'Roman' aristocrats in northern Italy at this time almost certainly reflects actual flight on the part of some, it also suggests a readiness on the part of others to

---

[47] ibid., Prologue.
[48] D. Green, 'Linguistic and Literary Traces of the Langobards', in Ausenda, Delogu, and Wickham (2009), pp. 174–94.
[49] Wormald (1999), p. 40.
[50] *Edict of Rothari*, 1.
[51] ibid., 13, p. 55.
[52] ibid., 7, pp. 53–4.
[53] ibid., 386, p. 129.
[54] ibid., 376, pp. 126–7.
[55] ibid., 386, p. 129.

remould their identity and values around the contours of a now dominant Langobard ideology.⁵⁶

The *Edict of Rothari* effectively constructed the king as the custodian of the folk traditions and identity of his people, and thus served an ideological function and symbolic purpose. As the charter evidence and later legal sources reveal, however, royal law was also put into effect on the ground.⁵⁷ The administration of justice through royal and ducal *curtes* may appear to have been in some sense a private affair, but it was primarily to royally codified Langobardic law that people turned. There are indications that the king's subjects had a right to choose whether they wished to operate under Roman or Langobardic legal procedures.⁵⁸ This could cause difficulties, and a growing territorialisation of law within the kingdom is evident. The *Laws of Grimoald*, promulgated in 668, for example, suggest that estate workers (*aldii*) were claiming a right available to *coloni adscripticii* under Roman law as amended by Justinian, to acquire their liberty after thirty years' service to a landowner.⁵⁹ King Grimoald strenuously forbade this, declaring that an *aldius* should 'continue to render obedience to his patron' irrespective of the number of years served.⁶⁰

Under Rothari we see renewed military aggression against Byzantine territories in Italy, reminding us that beneath the veneer of such law-giving, martial prowess remained the primary attribute that Langobards looked for in their king. In 652 Rothari was succeeded by his son Rodoald before, in 653, the crown reverted to the 'Bavarian' dynasty of Theodelinda, with the rise to power of her son by Agilulf, Aripert I (r.653–61). A civil war between Aripert's sons then opened the way for Grimoald, the *dux* of Beneventum, to seize the northern throne in 662, leaving Beneventum itself under the charge of his son Romuald. Grimoald successfully faced down a Frankish invasion from the north, an Avar assault on Friuli, and the presence in Italy of the Emperor Constans. Again, burgeoning military pressure, not least from the Byzantines, contributed to the greater cohesion of the Langobardic kingdom. With the death of Grimoald in 671, and the minority of his young son Garibald (671–2), the throne was secured by Perctarit, one of the sons of Aripert whom Grimoald had deposed in 662, who had lived as an aristocratic exile amongst the Avars, Franks, and Anglo-Saxons. His son Cunicpert (r.679–700) took an Anglo-Saxon bride, reminding us of the persisting ties of kinship and allegiance between the Langobards and the Saxons to the west. At his capital at Pavia, Cunicpert built a monumental palace gate through which to celebrate his triumphs.⁶¹

Over the course of the seventh century, there are indications of a growing stratification of Langobard society. By the early eighth century the evidence for

---

⁵⁶ Wickham (1981), p. 72.
⁵⁷ See discussion in Everett (2003).
⁵⁸ ibid., p. 173.
⁵⁹ On this legislation, see A. J. B. Sirks, 'The Colonate in Justinian's Reign', *Journal of Roman Studies* 98 (2008), pp. 120–43.
⁶⁰ *Laws of Grimoald*, 1, p. 132.
⁶¹ Paul the Deacon, IV, 36.

this is unmistakeable. According to a law of Liutprand, promulgated in 726, the freemen of Langobard society—those whom the *Edict of Rothari* had spoken of as 'folk free'—were divided into two groups: those who owned a warhorse and those who did not.[62] The latter were known as the 'little men', or *minimi homines*. A law of 724 likewise distinguished higher-ranking members of the Langobardic host from those soldiers (*exercitales*) who were 'little people' (*minimae personae*).[63] By 750 we find a tripartite division within which the two richest groups were still distinguished by the possession of horses.[64] The sorts of assets at the disposal of members of the lower aristocracy within Langobardic society at around this time are revealed in the family archive of a woman by the name of Ghittia from Pisa. The inventory of this archive, comprising some eighty-eight charters, records that in addition to landed property, the family had acquired *mundium*—judicial authority—over their social inferiors, enabling them to profit from the proceeds of justice. In terms of moveable wealth, the members of the family possessed two gold rings, a pair of earrings, a piece of gold, a belt with a silver-gilt buckle, a silver bowl, and silver spurs.[65] Such were the accoutrements of conspicuous consumption and display expected of the Langobard military elite.

The evolution of the Langobard kingdom thus encapsulated many of the key changes that were taking place across much of the West in the sixth and seventh centuries; in particular the militarisation of society and the growing dominance within that society of a martial aristocracy living directly off the produce of their own estates in the context of an economy in which urbanism and monetisation were in decline. In Byzantine-controlled parts of Italy, by contrast, where the fiscal structures of the Roman state persisted and where levels of monetisation were correspondingly higher, greater economic sophistication prevailed. One should be wary, however, of imagining too sharp a contrast between Langobard 'primitivism' and Byzantine 'sophistication'. The Justinianic reconquest had momentarily re-integrated northern Italy into a broader Mediterranean imperial economy, and this is likely to have had implications for urbanism, economic activity, and cultural life.[66] Of themselves, the Langobard invasions did not entirely undo what, on a substructural level, Justinian's commanders had achieved. Although Langobard cities were in decline, the levels of urbanism in the Langobard north were probably higher than anywhere else in the post-Roman West. Likewise, by virtue of the role of Roman courtiers such as Secundus of Non and the Catholic bishops of the northern cities, significant elements of the region's cultural infrastructure remained intact, as suggested by the comparatively high levels of Latin literacy within lay society revealed by the evidence of eighth-century charters.[67] In particular, Lango-bard kings were obliged to respond to the living presence of a Byzantine neighbour

---

[62] S. Gasparri, 'The Aristocracy', in La Rocca (2002), pp. 59–85, p. 68.
[63] *Liutprand*, 83 and 62.
[64] Gasparri (2002), p. 68.
[65] ibid., p. 70.
[66] J.-P. Devroey, *Economie rurale et société dans l'Europe franque (VIe–IXe siècles), Tome I* (Paris, 2003), pp. 224–6.
[67] Everett (2003).

and rival. Thus although the volume of coinage minted by Langobard rulers would appear to have been relatively low compared to the late-Roman period, the Langobards were the last Romano-Germanic rulers to continue to mint mock-Byzantine gold coins. The coinage of the Emperor Justinian II, bearing the image of Christ, for example, was soon copied by Duke Gisulf I of Beneventum (r.689–706).[68] Likewise, legislation from the 660s onwards was increasingly 'Roman' both in form and content, responding to contemporary trends in Byzantine law. The laws of Grimoald, for example, introduced a thirty-year prescription on claims to property derived from imperial law, whilst the prologue to the same laws has much in common with that of the early eighth-century Constantinopolitan law code known as the *Ecloga*.[69] Moreover, even within those parts of Italy that continued to be ruled from Constantinople, a growing militarisation of elite culture is evident, as the besieged Byzantine state found itself progressively dominated by military men (as seen in Chapter Eight).[70] The sort of society that took shape under the Langobards, it should be noted, was capable of great ideological and cultural cohesion, and, especially for the purposes of war, could mobilise manpower and resources to striking effect. So, for example, when—in the late eighth century—the Franks under Charlemagne brought the Langobards under their sway, they were able to leave the political and administrative institutions of the kingdom substantially intact, while drawing on the region's rich cultural heritage to transform intellectual life at the Frankish court.[71] This was a society that worked.

9.3 THE VISIGOTHS AND THE CATHOLIC MONARCHY OF TOLEDO

As we saw in Chapter Five, the reigns of the Visigothic kings Leovigild (r.569–86) and Reccared I (r.586–601) witnessed a major phase of political and territorial reintegration across the Iberian peninsula. To some extent, as in Langobard Italy, this can be linked to a more assertive stance on the part of the Emperor Maurice and his regime, as the East Roman authorities lent their support to Leovigild's rebellious son Hermenegild.[72] Through campaigns of aggressive warfare aimed against the Basques, independent Roman 'senators', Frankish invaders, and Gothic and Suevic warlords to the north, as well as against the imperial authorities to the south-west, Leovigild and Reccared restored the military reputation of the

---

[68] P. Grierson, *Coins of Medieval Europe* (Cambridge, 1991), p. 26; P. Grierson and M. Blackburn, *Medieval European Coinage*, vol. 1: *The Early Middle Ages* (Cambridge, 1986).

[69] *Grimoald*, 2 and 4—mirroring *Codex Theodosianus*, IX, 24.1; both the laws of Grimoald and the *Ecloga* justify themselves in their respective prologues as modifying earlier laws so as to render them more humane.

[70] For Byzantine Italy in this period, see especially T. S. Brown, *Gentlemen and Officers* (Rome, 1984). See also N. Christie, *From Constantine to Charlemagne: An Archaeology of Italy AD 300–800* (Aldershot, 2006).

[71] Wickham (1981), p. 28; Y. Hen, *Roman Barbarians: The Royal Court and Culture in the Early Medieval West* (Basingstoke, 2007).

[72] John of Biclaro, 69.

Visigothic monarchy and amassed substantial reserves of land and treasure with which to win over or reward retainers. Isidore of Seville, writing in c.625, looked back to an age of genuine military achievement: 'After Leovigild had obtained the position of king of Spain as well as Gallia Narbonensis, he set about to enlarge the kingdom through warfare and to increase his riches. With the zeal of his army and the concomitant success of his victories, he brilliantly achieved a great deal . . . he extended his power over the greater part of Spain'.[73]

According to Isidore, this was at least in part achieved by targeting those Gothic noblemen whose authority and wealth threatened to match the king's own. A key concern of the Visigothic monarchy was the comparative standing of the royal demesne and fiscal lands in comparison to the private wealth of the king's leading subjects: 'Leovigild', we are told, 'was also very destructive to some of his own men, for those whom he saw excelling in nobility and power, he either beheaded or sent into exile. He was the first to enrich the fisc and to enlarge the treasury, robbing the citizens and despoiling the enemy.'[74]

As we saw in Chapter Five, Leovigild and Reccared also attempted to convey their authority with greater force to their subjects, Roman and Goth alike, by adopting an increasingly imperial style and also by co-opting the trans-regional structures of the Iberian Church. Although Reccared's conversion to Catholic Christianity led to a series of uprisings and conspiracies on the part of elements of the Gothic palatine nobility and regional aristocracy (the latter receiving Frankish assistance), it won the king powerful new friends. 'A holy synod', we are told, 'of seventy-two bishops from all of Spain, Gallia Narbonensis and Galicia was assembled in the city of Toledo by order of King Reccared. . . . Reccared was present at the holy council, reviving in our own times the image of the ruler Constantine the Great, whose presence illuminated the holy council of Nicaea.'[75] According to the 'Acts' of the council itself, the number of bishops attending was actually sixty-six, but the event was overseen by Leander, Bishop of Seville (and brother of the scholar-bishop Isidore), who had spent time in Constantinople and was no doubt familiar with East Roman conciliar ways.

For much of the seventh century we lack a clear or detailed run of narrative sources for Visigothic Spain, such as we possess with respect to the contemporary East Roman world, thus making it difficult to get to grips with the political evolution of the realm. Such conciliar and royal legal sources as have, however, been read alongside the fragmentary narrative accounts, would suggest that there occurred sporadic bouts of social and political tension within the Visigothic kingdom that acted as a spur towards legislative activity, with periods of conflict being followed by a flurry of law-making.[76] In particular, repeated attempts on the part of Visigothic kings to ensure the dynastic succession of their own sons to

---

[73] Isidore of Seville, *History of the Kings of the Goths*, ch. 49. See ibid., ch. 47, for earlier Byzantine intervention.
[74] ibid., 51.
[75] John of Biclaro, 92.
[76] As argued by Collins (1983).

the throne, irrespective of their age, seem to have been foiled by the royal ambitions of rival Gothic aristocrats and the continuing fundamentally martial nature of Visigothic kingship, which rendered periods of royal minority hard to bear or impossible to sustain.

Upon his death in 601, for example, Reccared was succeeded by his son, Liuva, the fourth of his dynasty to hold the throne, but who came to it, according to Isidore, 'still in the first flower of manhood'.[77] Accordingly, in 603 he was deposed by a certain Witteric, a count of the palace (*comes*) who had formerly conspired against Reccared at the time of his conversion. Seven years later, in 610, Witteric likewise fell victim to a court-centred coup: 'Because he had lived by the sword', Isidore tells us, 'he died by the sword. For Witteric was killed in the midst of a meal as the result of a conspiracy.'[78] Gundemar, who secured the throne as a result, led campaigns against both the Basques and the Byzantines, and established the Bishop of Toledo as head of the Spanish Church, but his life was cut short by natural causes just two years later.[79] His successor, Sisibut, was a remarkable character, who combined high qualities of generalship with something of a reputation as a man of letters. His deep Christian piety, however, fed into a pronounced hostility to the Jews, against whom he passed discriminatory legislation (for which Isidore criticised him).[80] The Jews were not alone in attracting his ire: the king launched campaigns against the Byzantine enclaves to the south, forcing the imperial representative Caesarius to enter into negotiations, and wrote an extraordinary work known as the *Life of Desiderius*, which, whilst presented as a work of hagiography, is in fact a piece of invective aimed at the late sixth-century Frankish king Theuderic and his Visigothic grandmother, Brunhild.[81] The former, we are told, 'was seized by a disease of the bowels [which] ended his vile life', whilst the latter was paraded around on the back of a camel before being ripped apart by horses: 'And so her soul, freed from its mortal flesh, was deservedly cast down to eternal punishment and to burn in seething waves of pitch.'[82] In 621 Sisibut himself died (possibly of poison), leaving 'a small son, Reccared [II] who was recognized as king for a few days after the death of his father until his own death intervened'.[83]

The boy-king Reccared II was succeeded 'by divine grace' by the general (*dux*) Suinthila. If Isidore is to be believed, it was this king who was responsible for driving the Byzantines out of Spain *c*.625, taking full advantage of Heraclius' preoccupation with the East.[84] In order to try to ensure the succession of his son, Riccimir, Suinthila made him co-ruler. 'Even in childhood', Isidore closes his *History* by declaring, 'the spendour of his royal nature shines... may he prove worthy to succeed him [Suinthila] as king!'[85] Isidore's prayers were in vain: in 631 both father and son were deposed by a certain Sisenand, 'having seized the kingship by means of a revolt' in which the Frankish king—and ally of Heraclius—Dagobert, provided military assistance.[86]

---

[77] Isidore of Seville, *History*, 57.   [78] ibid., 57.   [79] ibid., 59.
[80] ibid., 61.   [81] ibid., 61.   [82] *Vita Desiderii*, pp. 9–10.
[83] Isidore of Seville, *History*, 61.   [84] ibid., 62.
[85] ibid., 65.   [86] *Chronicle of 754*, 17; Fredegar, IV, 73.

Both Sisenand (r.631–6) and his successor Chintila (r.636–9) managed to die of natural causes, but not, it would appear, without having to face down revolts on the part of rival claimants to the throne.[87] Chintila's son, Tulga, was overthrown after three years and succeeded by Chindasuinth, who, according to an anonymous mid-eighth-century Spanish chronicle originating from Toledo, 'triumphantly ruled the kingdom of the Goths in Iberia, which he seized by way of a revolt'.[88] The readiness of the Visigothic nobility to depose boy-kings and recently established rulers came to be regarded by Frankish authors as epitomising the *morbus Gothorum quem de regebus degradandum habebant*—'the Gothic weakness for dethroning their kings'.[89] Leovigild was the only ruler of the period to be succeeded on the throne by his son and grandson, a feat largely explicable in terms of his having executed or exiled much of the aristocracy.[90] Under Chindasuinth (r.642–53) and his son Reccesuinth (r.649–72, from 649 as joint-ruler) some stabilisation is again evident, perhaps by virtue of the fact that Reccesuinth likewise is reported to have executed some seven hundred Gothic aristocrats.[91]

In 672 a certain Wamba was elected king by the assembled nobles and bishops of the kingdom, before being formally anointed nineteen days later in the capital of Toledo—the first such ceremony of which we can be certain. That same year, however, he was obliged to face down a rebellion by the count (*comes*) of Septimania and in 680 was forced from the throne in a bloodless but carefully organised coup apparently choreographed by a group of palatine officials and the episcopal leadership, with Wamba 'falling ill' and being sent off to a monastery.[92] The election and consecration of a new king were rapidly set in motion: 'Erwig was consecrated as king of the Goths. He ruled for seven years.'[93]

As already seen, instability of succession was one of the core structural weaknesses of the emergent Romano-Germanic successor kingdoms. The inability of the Visigothic monarchy in Spain to evolve into a hereditary monarchy in the aftermath of the extirpation of the House of Balt, led to rounds of intense military and political competition as a profoundly factionalised aristocracy spotted in the death of each monarch, or any substantial moment of military reversal, the opportunity for a renewed bid for power.[94] The issue was not so much that the elective principle, which members of the palatine aristocracy and episcopal leadership tended to assert against ruling monarchs, was in any sense inherently unstable. Indeed, such a system could be said to carry positive advantages, potentially reducing the incidence of minors sitting on the throne and ensuring that kings were up to the job.[95] Rather, the problem was that the broadly elective framework

---

[87] Collins (1983), p. 120.
[88] *Chronicle of 754*, 22.
[89] The phrase, first used by Sidonius, is repeated in Fredegar, IV, 82.
[90] Banaji (2009), p. 65.
[91] Fredegar, IV, 82.
[92] See discussion in Collins (2004).
[93] *Chronicle of 754*, 37.
[94] Banaji (2009), p. 65.
[95] For a later parallel, see J. Gillingham, 'Elective Kingship and the Unity of Medieval Germany', *German History* 9 (1991), pp. 124–35.

of seventh-century Visigothic kingship was frequently tested to near breaking point by the dynastic ambitions of reigning monarchs on the one hand and the usurpative tendencies of their magnates on the other. By virtue of the resources at the disposal of Visigothic kings—former imperial Crown lands, fiscal lands, personal estates, and the confiscated estates of their opponents—such grabs for the throne were well worth making.

The Visigothic aristocracy, moreover, was acquiring ever greater stratification, with an increasingly visible palatine nobility of families of Gothic 'identity' (but mixed descent) dominating both the court and, presumably, social and economic life in the central heartlands of the kingdom. Certainly, the emergence of this nobility would appear to have coincided with a major programme of Church building in the main areas of Gothic settlement, indicative of the determination of an increasingly self-confident aristocracy to invest its wealth in tangible architectural form, as well as to impress its authority on both the physical and religious landscape.[96]

9.4 KINGS, NOBLES, AND COUNCILS

By the late seventh century, the palatine nobility, which had come to exercise an effective monopoly on the Visigothic kingship, may have consisted of not more than two dozen families.[97] Those families were also coming to dominate not only the royal court but also the Hispano-Gothic Church. *Nobilitas* is something on which one finds growing emphasis in the seventh-century sources, even ecclesiastical and hagiographic ones, indicating a growing aristocratisation of society. The seventh-century *Lives of the Fathers of Merida*, for example, relate an account of a bishop of that city by the name of Renovatus: 'He was a Goth of noble stock, famed for his glorious descent. Tall of stature, handsome to behold, of noble presence, pleasing to look upon, having an attractive expression on his handsome face; he was altogether admirable in appearance.'[98] The emphasis on appearance and breeding is telling: the unfortunate Hispano-Gothic St Nanctus, for example, was murdered by the *servi* of the estate he was given by King Leovigild for not *looking* like a lord.[99]

The smaller the group of noble families that clustered around the king, the more intense and potentially destabilising their jockeying for position is likely to have become. Such tensions were nevertheless rendered to some extent containable by two emergent features of Visigothic political life. First, the court-focused nature of the Gothic nobility appears to have meant that, particularly from the 640s, it was the court (at Toledo), the Crown, and the kingdom that framed political ambitions. Consequently, as in Langobard Italy, there is little evidence of secessionist tendencies save on the part of lower-level, more regionalised lords on the fringes (and

---

[96] Chavarría Arnau (2010).
[97] Collins (2004), pp. 113–14.
[98] *Lives of the Fathers of Merida*, p. 103.
[99] ibid., p. 57.

especially coastal zones) of the kingdom, at some remove from the main areas of Visigothic settlement in the Tierra de Campos (still known in the later Middle Ages as the *Campi Gothorum*—'the fields of the Goths').

Second, through the repeated convening of Church councils, presided over by the king, the decrees of which members of the palatine nobility had to sign in person, a distinct Hispano-Gothic Catholic identity can be seen to have taken shape, separable and distinguishable from that of the imperial Church of Rome and Constantinople, while (as shall be seen) maintaining a measure of theological and ideological communication. Between 589 and 702 some fifteen councils of the Spanish Church are recorded, although of these two were purely provincial and one purely theological.[100] Diversity of custom within the Hispano-Gothic Church was forbidden, and Isidore of Seville gives voice to a strong sense of Hispano-Gothic pride: 'Of all the lands from the West to the Indies', Isidore declares at the start of his *History*, 'you, Spain, O sacred and always fortunate mother of princes and peoples, are the most beautiful. . . . Rightly are you now the queen of all provinces, from which not only the West but also the East borrows its shining light.'[101] At the end of the work, Isidore celebrates the driving out of the Byzantines with the triumphant phrase, 'subjected, the Roman soldier now serves the Goths, whom he sees being served by many people and by Spain itself'.[102] It is hard to imagine Sidonius Apollinaris writing anything as starkly anti-Roman as that.

These ecclesiastical structures and forums were used to advertise royal authority, in a process sometimes described as the 'sacralisation' of Visigothic kingship. In 633, for example, at the Fourth Council of Toledo (IV Toledo), it was decreed that whoever broke their oath of loyalty to the king, which members of the palatine nobility were obliged to make in person, would suffer excommunication. The king, it was declared, was divinely elected. In 636 a subsequent council (V Toledo) threatened with excommunication those who plotted concerning the royal succession. It was perhaps around this time that the tradition of royal 'unction' was first introduced, elevating the person of the king by his being episcopally anointed with holy oil. Although anointing was a rhetorical feature of Byzantine imperial coronations, referred to in the patriarchal prayer, only in Spain, it would appear, was oil actually applied.[103] By the 680s any act in breach of the king's law was supposed to lead to expulsion from the community of the faithful.[104] In the legislation issued by the Visigothic kings in the seventh century, moreover, there is a strong emphasis on there being a single united 'people' (*gens*) and 'homeland' (*patria*).[105] 'Outsiders', by contrast, be they political, religious or moral, were treated with ever greater severity, as we see from the Visigothic legislation against Jews and

---

[100] Barbero and Loring (2005), p. 354, n. 12.
[101] Isidore of Seville, *History*, Prologue.
[102] ibid., 70.
[103] Rapp (2010).
[104] See the excellent discussion of these materials in Collins (1983), pp. 115–21. For excommunication for breach of law see King (1972), p. 127.
[105] *Leges Visigothorum*, II, 1.8, *de his qui contra principem vel gentem aut patriam refugi insolentes*.

homosexuals which, amongst the Romano-Germanic kingdoms, the Visigothic *regnum* pioneered.[106]

The 'sacralisation' of Visigothic kingship is, however, easily overstated. In practice, there is little sign that such measures made any substantive difference to the reality of power relations on the ground or at times of crisis. As an astute critic of the Visigothic conciliar and royal legislation has noted, whilst the canons of the Council of Toledo of 633 (IV Toledo) emphasised the prohibition, on pain of excommunication, on anyone conspiring against the king or seizing the throne, the very king under whose authority the council was being held, Sisenand, had himself come to power three years earlier precisely by means of conspiracy and forceful dethronement.[107] The act of anointing a new king, moreover, essentially served to emphasise his subjection to episcopal scrutiny.[108] Instead of a monarchy growing in authority and might through the concerted actions of kings and bishops, what the Visigothic legislation really portrays is a seventh-century kingship increasingly constrained and controlled by the nobility and the Church leadership. As noted earlier, legislation appears to have been at its most concerted in the aftermath of periods of crisis or struggles for the throne. Accordingly, the councils often reveal strident criticism of past or fallen rulers, and a preoccupation with protecting or restoring the property rights of the nobility, whilst royal legislation itself served to place limitations on the effective power of kings.[109] The Visigothic law codes may look highly Roman; the last of them, the 'Book of Judges' (*Liber Iudicorum*) of 654 (as revised by Erwig in 681), was divided, like the *Codex Iustinianus*, into twelve books, and its language, in its exordium, echoes that of Justinian's constitution on 'Imperial Majesty'.[110] However, in one crucial respect it is fundamentally unlike any legal statement that Justinian would ever have promulgated. For, whereas Justinian, as we have seen, established himself as the one and only source of law, and the person of the Emperor as the *nomos empsychos*, or 'law personified', the Visigothic legislation instead emphasised the status of the ruler as subject to the law and thus answerable to it.

If viewed from the 'top down'—from the perspective of the councils and the court—the Visigothic kingdom of the seventh century can look like a highly ambitious and effective state, and in many ways it clearly was. It is striking, for example, that the earlier recensions of the legislation of Visigothic kings only survive in palimpsest (on manuscripts scratched clean and reused for other purposes): it seems that the Visigothic kings were capable of calling in old copies of legal texts and distributing new, updated ones. This is a feat that only the emperors in Constantinople are likely to have been able to match. Nevertheless, from the 'bottom up', this was still a highly fragmented—and probably fragmenting—

---

[106] For anti-Jewish measures see *Leges Visigothorum*, XII, with excellent discussion in Collins (1983), pp. 129–45. For measures against men for sexual activities with men, see *Leges Visigothorum*, III, 5.4 and III, 5.7.
[107] Collins (1983), pp. 121–2.
[108] J. L. Nelson, *Politics and Ritual in Early Medieval Europe* (London, 1986).
[109] Collins (1983), p. 125.
[110] *Leges Visigothorum*, I, 2.6.

society. For although, if we are to believe the royal legislation, the world of Visigothic Spain was, in theory at least, a remarkably regulated one, with every passing year there was less and less of a public administrative framework capable of achieving the degree of regulation at which the royal and conciliar legislation aimed. There is every indication, for instance, that the fiscal structures of the late-Roman state continued to atrophy over the course of the late sixth and seventh centuries in those areas where they had survived the crisis of the fifth. It is true that some element of royal taxation would continue into the early eighth century, and in 681 Erwig issued a general tax remission. His law makes it clear, however, that it had become common practice for landowners simply to hand over a share of their property to the royal fisc, as a permanent alternative to regular tax payments (from which the Gothic aristocracy was in any case exempt).[111] It is also far from evident what such taxes were for. In the Roman Empire taxes had supported the army and the state bureaucracy. In Visigothic Spain, by contrast, the king raised military levies of arms-bearing men directly from landowners, and all free men had to answer the call to arms if summoned.[112] There are no references to a salaried army in need of support, and only a few to central officials from what might be thought of as 'the state' who were involved in tax collection.[113] Royal, or even 'local', government appears to have been very thin on the ground: in the *Liber Iudiciorum*, a *homo curialis* was no longer a member of the local city council, but rather an attendant at the royal court.[114] Even in the late sixth century, the strongest documentary evidence we have for 'taxation' in the Visigothic kingdom on closer inspection reveals little more than that the king's soldiers or cavalrymen on campaign were able to demand rations for themselves or their mounts; and if such supplies were not forthcoming, they could demand payment in coin at a punitively high rate of exchange so as to be able to purchase supplies on the open market.[115] Isidore of Seville writes expressly of how the higher rates of taxation in the Byzantine enclaves of *Spania* induced many to prefer Visigothic rule, as it was 'better for them to live poor with the Goths than to be powerful among the Romans and bear the heavy yoke of tribute'.[116]

As elsewhere in the post-Roman West, the fading away of late-Roman fiscal structures was associated with an archaeologically visible reduction in the level of material culture and an associated regionalisation of social, economic, and—it might be inferred—political life.[117] Accordingly, what the seventh-century sources effectively reveal at the grass roots of Visigothic society is an increasingly fissiparous world given structure and coherence by ties of dependence between military lords (the grandest of whom focused their political ambitions on the royal court) and

---

[111] Wickham (2005), p. 97.
[112] ibid., p. 98.
[113] King (1972), p. 69.
[114] *Leges Visigothorum*, V, 4.19.
[115] D. Fernández, 'What Is the *De Fisco Barcinonensi* About?' *Antiquité Tardive* 14 (2006), pp. 217–24.
[116] Isidore of Seville, *Historia*, ch. 15 (first redaction).
[117] See Wickham (2005), p. 96, pp. 221–6, and pp. 741–58.

their retainers, clients, and followers. In late-Roman and Justinianic legislation, the patronage (*patrocinium*) of the great landowner was presented as the great enemy of the state, epitomised by such illicit practices as the maintenance of private armed retainers, or *buccellarii*. In the Visigothic legislation, by contrast—especially that of the late seventh century—*patrocinium* is generally presented in morally entirely neutral terms and is omnipresent as the lynchpin of Hispano-Gothic society.[118] In particular, it was central to the functioning of the royal host: freemen summoned to military service could either rally to the muster-call of the local *dux* or *comes* appointed by the king, or instead join the retinue of their own lord, or *patronus*, sometimes described as a lower member of the military aristocracy, or *gardingus*.[119] The laws contain regulations concerning private armed retainers held *in patrocinio* serving a lord in return for a grant of land, which, like the associated military service, was potentially heritable.[120] Other military retainers (*saiones*) were kept in the lord's household and also received arms and armour from him.[121] Armed retainers or clients who, on the orders of their *patronus* committed acts of illicit violence in breach of royal law, could not be held liable for such actions—only their lord could.[122] The personal tie between lord and man informed all social and political relations in the kingdom as revealed in the law codes. All adult males had to swear an oath of loyalty to the king.[123] The palatine nobility, as we have seen, had to do so in person.

The Visigothic nobility stood at the apex of a range of hierarchical ties of dependence that had come to characterise much of the kingdom (beyond, that is, the upland areas, and the tribal zones that had formed in or survived through the fifth century). Beneath the palatine nobility stood lower-ranking aristocrats such as the *gardingi* and the provincial or more peripherally rooted *comites*, *duces*, and lords. At the base of Visigothic society, however, were various free peasantries subject to tribute, tenant farmers, and—most significantly—an undifferentiated mass of servile labourers (*servi*) descended from both slaves (*mancipia*) and Roman *coloni originarii*. These were tightly controlled and ruthlessly exploited agricultural labourers whose flight from estates was a major preoccupation of the Visigothic legislation.[124] The degree of both legal and economic subjugation seems to have been extreme: Erwig's 'army law', for example, 'speaks of slave-owners who, intent on working their fields, thrashed their multitude of slaves'.[125] The Visigothic kingdom inherited from the Roman Empire, and emulated from Constantinople, an especially strong sense of public authority. We see this in the emphasis placed (clearly to very good effect) in the seventh century on the territoriality of law, as also

---

[118] King (1972), p. 107. But see *Leges Visigothorum*, II, 2.8.
[119] King (1972), pp. 58–9.
[120] ibid., pp. 60 and 187.
[121] ibid., p. 188.
[122] ibid., p. 188.
[123] ibid., p. 58.
[124] ibid., pp. 161 and 169.
[125] ibid., p. 169, citing *Leges Visigothorum*, IX, 2.9.

326　　　　　　　　　　　*Empires of Faith*

in the prohibition on private courts organised by landowners with which to discipline their labourers and dependants, and the laws against the extra-judicial execution or mutilation of agricultural workers by their masters.[126] The very existence of such legislation, however, reveals much. This fragmenting world was necessarily becoming harder to hold together.

9.5 THE CRISIS OF THE VISIGOTHIC REALM

There was, therefore, an innate and growing contradiction between the ambitious, shrill, and injunctive tone of the conciliar and royal legislation, exemplifying the integrative ideology and rhetoric of a united Catholic Hispania, and the reality of a society that was becoming ever more localised, fragmented, and, in most cases, dominated by varying forms of aristocratic power.[127] This is not to downplay the sophistication and ambition of the former. When Reccared had announced his conversion to Pope Gregory, the prelate had recommended to him the Biblical figure of David as a model of kingship.[128] Through contacts with the Church, but also perhaps across the diplomatically, economically, and culturally porous Byzantine frontier, Visigothic monarchs had partaken in an increasingly Biblicising culture of kingship that was a marked feature of the seventh century. This was discernible in governing circles in Francia and Constantinople (and, arguably, even the Damascus of Abd al-Malik) at least as much in Spain, and had its roots in Justinian's attempts to harness the Church to his purposes and find ever greater theocratic justification for the imperial office.[129] As we have already seen, not only Visigothic kings, but even Bulgar *khagans* claimed that their royal authority was enhanced by divine grace. The title of *dei gratia rex* had also been appropriated by Agilulf upon the reconstitution of the Langobard monarchy.[130] The 'distribution pattern' of these claims would suggest the radiating ideological influence of Byzantium at work.

Byzantine influence is perhaps similarly discernible in the anti-Jewish legislation of the Visigothic kings, which continued to escalate in severity until, in 694, the Visigothic monarchy effectively reduced all Jews to the status of slaves.[131] There may also, of course, have been very specific and contemporary reasons for this

---

[126] Private courts: *Leges Visigothorum*, II, 1.16; execution of *servi*, VI, 5.12; mutilation VI, 5.13.
[127] P. Diaz and M. R. Valverde, 'The Theoretical Strength and Practical Weakness of the Visigothic Monarchy of Toledo', in Theuws and Nelson (2000), pp. 59–94.
[128] Gregory the Great, *Register*, IX, 228.
[129] For the frontier, see J. Wood, 'Defending Byzantine Spain: Frontiers and Diplomacy', *Early Medieval Europe* 18 (2010), pp. 292–319. For the increasingly Biblicised nature of seventh-century ideology, see Wallace-Hadrill (1971). I am immensely grateful to my pupils Danielle Donaldson of Trinity College, and Michael Humphreys of Pembroke College, Cambridge, for discussion of these points.
[130] W. Ullmann, *Principles of Government and Politics in the Middle Ages* (London, 1961), p. 118.
[131] Collins (1983), p. 135. Again, I owe the point with respect to Byzantine influence to Danielle Donaldson. See also B. Albert, 'Un nouvel examen de la politique anti-juive Wisigothique', *Revue des études juives* 135 (1976), pp. 3–29, 22–5.

particular law. For by the 690s, as we have seen, Byzantine Africa was collapsing before armies preaching an Abrahamic religion that Christians elsewhere had certainly had difficulty distinguishing from Judaism, and which had received active Jewish support in their conquests further afield.[132] The legislation of 694 was issued amid a backdrop of rumours that the Jews were preparing to rise up against the Christians of Spain with support from outside the kingdom, as well as reports of Jewish revolts 'in other parts of the world', probably meaning the Roman Near East.[133] Visigothic kingship clearly continued to engage with, and react to, broader currents of seventh-century Mediterranean religious, political, and legal culture emanating from New Rome.

King Egica, who had succeeded Erwig in 687, reigned until 702, when he was in turn succeeded to the throne by his son Witiza, with whom he had been co-ruler since 693–4.[134] With Carthage now in Arab hands, however, and the forces of *jihad* eager to bear the banners of faith yet further afield, these were dangerous times for a king whose reign elicited starkly conflicting accounts from later authors.[135] His death *c.*710–11 appears to have opened the way to a power struggle between elements of the palatine nobility, apparently including a son of Witiza by the name of Achila, and a certain Roderic. There is numismatic evidence to suggest that each of these ruled different parts of the kingdom simultaneously.[136] It was Roderic, however, who dominated the political heartland of the kingdom around Toledo. Forced to contend with an uprising in the north, presumably by the Basques, however, the new king was suddenly obliged in 711 to make a dash to the south, where Arab armies with their Berber allies had crossed the straits from north Africa and were now active.

There are indications that the arrival of a new military threat raised hopes on the part of rival elements within the Gothic nobility that they too might now have a hope of gaining the throne. According to a mid-eighth-century Toledan chronicle, 'Mustering his forces, he [Roderic] directed armies against the Arabs and Moors . . . who had long been raiding the province. Roderic headed for the Transductine mountains to fight them and in that battle the entire army of Goths, which had come with him fraudulently and in rivalry out of ambition for the kingship, fled, and he was killed. Thus Roderic wretchedly lost not only his rule but his homeland, his rivals also being slain'[137] A second Arab-Berber army now advanced on Toledo. Although the language of our source is highly charged, the Arab tactics described chime with those recorded in the contemporary Syriac accounts for Palestine and in the *Armenian History*, with their emphasis on bouts of intense violence followed by rounds of negotiation:

---

[132] Crone and Cook (1977).
[133] Collins (1983), pp. 135–6 and 141.
[134] *Chronicle of 754*, ch. 44.
[135] ibid., 44 and 47.
[136] Collins (2004), pp. 131–2.
[137] *Chronicle of 754*, ch. 52.

> While Spain was being devastated by the aforesaid forces and was greatly afflicted not only by the enemy but also by domestic strife, [the Arab general] Musa himself approaching this wretched land across the straits of Cadiz... entered the long plundered and godlessly invaded Spain to destroy it. After forcing his way up to Toledo, the royal city, he imposed on the adjacent regions an evil and fraudulent peace. He decapitated on a scaffold those noble lords that still remained, arresting them in their flight from Toledo, with the help of Oppa, king Egica's son. With Oppa's support, he killed them all with sword.... He ruined beautiful cities, burning them with fire, condemned lords and powerful men to the cross.... While he terrorized everyone in this way, some of the cities that remained sued for peace.'[138]

The reference to 'Oppa, king Egica's son' collaborating with the Arab invader against his Gothic noble rivals is telling. For it suggests that rivalries within the upper reaches of the Visigothic nobility may have directly contributed to Arab success in overthrowing the Visigothic kingdom.[139] Certainly, that is what eighth-century Spanish Christians would remember. The 'Gothic weakness for deposing their kings' and the associated intense and bitter rivalry for the throne evident on the part of the Gothic nobility were clearly not entirely a figment of the Frankish imagination.

With Toledo in Arab hands, and the palatine nobility smashed, many of the more regionally focused Visigothic lords would now have had to choose whether to come to terms with the Arabs or fight on. In the rugged north of Galicia and the Basque country resistance was a realistic option, and support was forthcoming from Duke Eudo of Aquitaine, who inflicted a major defeat on the Arabs in 720 near Toulouse as they struck north of the Pyrenees.[140] According to the *Liber Pontificalis*, in the aftermath of this victory, Eudo wrote to Pope Gregory II (r.715–31) claiming, with evident exaggeration, to have slain 375,000 of the enemy in a single day with the loss of only 1,500 of his own men. His warriors had been miraculously aided, he went on to inform the Pope, by eating morsels of the liturgical sponges (sponges dipped in consecrated wine) that had been sent from Rome the previous year.[141] Further south, however, agreeing to pay tribute to the new lords of Toledo arguably made better sense. A certain Theodimir, for example, is recorded to have retained his lordship over seven towns in the south-east (Orihuela, Valencia, Alicante, Mulsa, Bigastro, Eyyo, and Lorca) in return for doing obeisance to the Arabs and paying for peace.[142] There are also indications that the rate of conversion to Islam on the part of members of the Visigothic aristocracy would be high.[143] The concatenation of a concerted Arab threat, a fractious nobility (members of which regarded the throne as their own), and a fragmenting society

---

[138] ibid., 52–4.
[139] Banaji (2009), p. 66; Collins (2004), pp. 133–4.
[140] On whom see P. Fouracre, *The Age of Charles Martel* (London, 2000), pp. 82–7. For the date of the battle, see p. 84.
[141] *Liber Pontificalis*, Gregory, II, ch. 11, p. 8.
[142] Heather (1996), p. 287.
[143] A. Barbero and M. Vigil, *La formación del feudalismo en la Península Ibérica* (Barcelona, 1978), pp. 209 and 229.

thus arguably combined to fatally weaken and then bring down the Catholic Hispania of Reccared and Isidore.

9.6 THE MEROVINGIAN COMMONWEALTH OF KINGDOMS

In many ways the early seventh-century Frankish world to the north of the Pyrenees and to the west of the Rhine bore striking resemblance to that of Visigothic Spain. In each instance we encounter a society increasingly dominated by an ever more visible hereditary nobility that clustered around the royal court.[144] In the Frankish heartland to the north of the Loire, as in the Visigothic heartland around the *Campi Gothorum*, that nobility is likely to have consisted of families of mixed ancestry who had come to regard themselves as united by a common—in this instance Frankish—identity, embodied in a shared military culture, specific traditions of nomenclature, and (in the Frankish case) an inherited body of law.[145] To the south of the Loire, and especially in Aquitaine, a stronger sense of 'Roman' elite identity persisted, just as it did in the Visigothic king's Cantabrian territories; but here too a militarisation of elite culture had taken place, breaking down much of the cultural barrier between 'Roman' and 'barbarian'.[146] In each case the emergence of the nobility can be traced through a range of cultural phenomena; the growing emphasis on 'good birth' and breeding identifiable in seventh-century Visigothic hagiography, for example, is also evident in contemporary Frankish *Saints' Lives*, as members of the Frankish nobility increasingly came to dominate episcopal office, often retiring to the episcopate after years of service in the entourage of their king— just as Gallo-Roman aristocrats such as Sidonius Apollinaris had done after years of service to the Emperor.[147] At times, however, such Frankish bishops seem to have had some difficulty in divesting themselves of the martial identity that had underpinned their status in lay society: it had to be expressly decreed by a Merovingian Church Council, for example, that 'no bishop or priest should take it upon himself to bear arms after the manner of a man of the world'.[148]

The basis of aristocratic wealth (beyond booty) in both Francia and Spain consisted of extensive landed estates, which lords could either build up through their own exertions or expand through royal gift.[149] Such 'private' landed wealth was then in turn often supplemented by means of properties over which members of the nobility were granted control by virtue of the gubernatorial or ecclesiastical

---

[144] Fouracre (2000), p. 19.
[145] Wickham (1981), p. 72.
[146] For the persistence of Roman identity in seventh-century Auvergne, see the *Passio Praeiecti*, ch. 1, p. 272. See also Wickham (2005), p. 177.
[147] Fouracre (2000), pp. 25–7; Hen (2007), pp. 103–4.
[148] *Concilium Latunense* (673–5) 2, in J. Gaudemet and B. Basdevant (eds.), *Les canons des conciles Mérovingiens*, 2 vols. (Paris, 1989), II, p. 577.
[149] For the workings of agrarian society in Francia, the fundamental work is now J.-P. Devroey, *Puissants et misérables—système social et monde paysan dans l'Europe des Francs (VIe–IX siècles)* (Brussels, 2006).

offices that they held.¹⁵⁰ These estates also constituted the foundation of aristocratic military and social power, as lords used their reserves of land to reward their chief military retainers. In Francia these grants were typically made by way of 'precarial tenure' (*in precario*) whereby the land was made available to a retainer or his heirs, but legal ownership remained vested in the lord, who could rescind the grant.¹⁵¹ In Spain retainers were rewarded by way of grants *in stipendio*, which could not be revoked at will but only when the stipendiary was in breach of his obligations.¹⁵² The crucial point in each instance, however, was the role played by land in binding retainers and dependants to their lords. Though different in legal form, such grants were comparable in terms of social effect.

In both Francia and Spain, moreover, the structures of royal government on the ground were broadly similar. The primary royal agent at a local level was the *dux*, or 'duke', who was responsible for assembling the royal host, collecting such dues as were demanded by the king, and resolving legal disputes (often with the assistance of the local bishop). Beneath him stood the *comes*, or 'count', who interacted with the leaders of local society at the level of the city, and whose agents were concerned with smaller administrative subdivisions of the kingdom termed *pagi*. In the Merovingian case, the office of *dux* was primarily associated with members of the Frankish elite, and the greater importance of the *dux* over and above the *comes* can only have been further accentuated by the ongoing ruralisation of Frankish aristocratic culture over the course of the seventh century and the continuing decline of former Roman *civitates*.¹⁵³ Even those southern cities, such as Marseilles, whose economies had been bolstered by contact with the Justinianic Empire in the central Mediterranean, would begin to stagnate from the middle of the seventh century as the Byzantines lost control of the region of Liguria (seized, as we have seen, by the Langobards in 644) and East Roman trade with the West was increasingly diverted up the Adriatic.¹⁵⁴

We should also note that, as suggested earlier, the kings and nobles of the Visigothic and Frankish kingdoms were subject to broadly similar ideological and cultural influences, above all an increasingly Biblicised language of power emanating from Constantinople and associated with the imperial Church. The alliance between kings, aristocrats, and the Catholic Church was at its most evident in Spain with respect to the canons of the councils, convened under royal authority and formally witnessed by the palatine nobility; in the Merovingian case it is revealed above all by the readiness of the royal family and of many aristocratic families to lend their support to a sustained expansion of monasticism and the endowment of monastic estates, initiated by the arrival in Burgundy *c.*590 of the Irish holy man Columbanus and his founding there of the monasteries of Luxeuil and

---

¹⁵⁰ Devroey (2003), pp. 269–74, provides useful discussion.
¹⁵¹ Fouracre (2000), pp. 137–45, for Frankish *precaria*. The institution is probably ecclesiastical in origin.
¹⁵² King (1972), p. 60.
¹⁵³ E. James, *The Franks* (Oxford, 1988), p. 185; Devroey (2003), p. 224.
¹⁵⁴ Devroey (2003), pp. 224–6.

Annegray.¹⁵⁵ Christianity had spread in Columbanus' native Ireland over the course of the fifth century, adjusting itself to the contours of an essentially tribal society that lacked the urban infrastructure of the Roman Empire and the imperial Church. Consequently, whereas imperial Christianity was city-based, and dominated at a local level by the figure of the metropolitan bishop, Irish Christianity had instead evolved networks of rural monastic communities under the charismatic leadership of abbots who were as much men of 'secular' as of religious power, combining monastic, episcopal, and lordly authority, and who, accordingly, were well placed to mediate the transition to a new religion.¹⁵⁶ Moreover, these newly established monastic centres had introduced a vital element to the economic life of Ireland, serving as centres of dense settlement and heightened consumption that gave a spur to the development of specialised agriculture, craft production, and industry.¹⁵⁷

It was this model of rural monasticism, free from metropolitan control, that Columbanus brought with him from Ireland, and which he sought to propagate and popularise through attracting elite patronage. Importantly, in terms of its reception and dissemination, 'Columbanan monasticism' (as it is sometimes termed) was far better suited to the realities and needs of an increasingly ruralised Merovingian world than the more urban-focused monastic traditions that had survived in Gaul from the days of empire. It was also capable of extension to those areas that had never known Roman rule, and where, as a result, there was not even a social or topographical memory of the Roman city. Moreover, it ran with the grain of the land-based interests and kin-focused power structures of both Merovingian kings and their aristocrats. By founding monasteries, endowing them with lands on their royal or private estates, and nominating members of their own families (especially unmarried daughters and nephews, or royal or noble widows) to head them, kings and aristocrats were able to shore up broader dynastic strategies and interests. Although such donations were meant to be perpetual in effect, and kings granted by charter to monastic institutions so-called 'immunities' from public obligations that can only have adversely affected royal income from tallage charges, renders, and such like, land could thus be formally alienated without feeling it was really lost to the family or the Crown.

Moreover, in many ways, such private monastic foundations could potentially serve to bolster and reinforce the interests of their founders and their kin by serving, for example, as a *locus* for the composition and dissemination of hagiographic and other texts glorifying the virtues of the benefactor, or making a contribution to the

---

¹⁵⁵ Wood (1994), pp. 181–204.
¹⁵⁶ T. Charles-Edwards, 'The Pastoral Role of the Church in the Early Irish Laws', in J. Blair and R. Sharpe (eds.), *Pastoral Care Before the Parish* (Leicester, 1992), pp. 63–80, and R. Sharpe, 'Some Problems Concerning the Organization of the Church in Early Medieval Ireland', *Peritia* 3 (1984), pp. 230–70.
¹⁵⁷ J. Bradley, 'Urbanization in Early Medieval Ireland', in C. E. Karkov, K. M. Wickham-Crowley, and B. K. Young (eds.), *Spaces of Living and the Dead: An Archaeological Dialogue*, in *American Early Medieval Studies* 3 (Oxford, 1999), pp. 133–47. See also J. Blair, *The Church in Anglo-Saxon Society* (Oxford, 2005), pp. 246–7.

factional politics of the day by vilifying their opponents. They also helped to imprint royal and aristocratic power on the landscape, with donors and their kin turning private churches and monasteries into noble *mausolea*.[158] In the case of the Merovingian kings themselves, growing emphasis would be placed over the course of the seventh century on seeking to ensure that monastic foundations maintained cycles of 'perpetual praise' (*laus perennis*) in honour of their royal benefactors; and prayers on behalf of the king, to secure his victory in battle, and the stability of the kingdom would eventually become a liturgical feature of the Merovingian Church.[159]

There was, however, one notable difference between Merovingian Francia and the Visigothic kingdom of the seventh century, which is often regarded as having set the two societies on very different paths of political development. The key issue here was the nature of the office of king. As we saw in Chapter Five, the Frankish conquests of the sixth century had led to the emergence of what might be termed a 'Merovingian commonwealth', embracing the Frankish heartlands of Neustria to the north, the eastern territories of Austrasia towards the Rhine, and the former kingdom of the Burgundians. Outlying territories such as Aquitaine had also been brought under a measure of control, and Merovingian authority radiated outwards to north and east over groups such as the Saxons, Thuringians, Bavarians, and Langobards; over the 'Romans' of Aquitaine, and the peoples of Saxony, Thuringia, and Bavaria, the Merovingians appointed dukes who acknowledged Merovingian overlordship, whilst for much of the late sixth and early seventh centuries the Langobards paid considerable sums of tribute. By the end of the sixth century, three core kingdoms had emerged: those of Neustria, Austrasia, and Burgundy, each with its own court and each with its own Merovingian king claiming lineal descent from Clovis; although, as we have seen, the territorial contours of these core kingdoms (often referred to by the German word *Teilreiche*, or 'segmentary kingdoms') were far from fixed, with both kings and their leading subjects owning land that traversed nominal geopolitical divisions.

At the start of the seventh century, therefore, there was no 'Merovingian Toledo', and nor would there be. Even within the core kingdoms, the royal court moved from palace to palace. Within Neustria, the zone of itinerant kingship was not vast: the court moved between a string of around half a dozen palaces located on royal estates within or near the Merovingian heartland of the Paris basin, and Paris itself was a favoured centre of royal authority.[160] In Austrasia, by contrast, the itinerary of the court appears to have been determined to some extent by the long river valleys of the Rhine, the Moselle, and the Meuse, which were the defining geographical features of the region. Here kings moved between royal residences and estates such as Metz, Cologne, and Strasbourg, and there seem to have been more frequent visits made to the residences of the king's leading subjects than in the

---

[158] Blair (2005), pp. 63–5.
[159] Hen (2007), pp. 106–23 and *idem.*, *Culture and Religion in Merovingian Gaul, AD 481–751* (Leiden, 1995).
[160] Wickham (2005), p. 103.

kingdom of the West Franks. As a result, the 'symbolic capital' of kingship, as it is sometimes termed, never came, as it did in Spain, to inhere in control of a specific or fixed centre of authority, city, or palace (although Paris did come to acquire considerable symbolic significance). Rather, as had likewise seemingly been true with respect to the Vandals, or indeed the Visigoths themselves prior to the ideological elevation of Toledo, the true insignia of kingship consisted of control over an inherited, portable, and divisible royal 'treasure' made up of items of exceptional value or historical resonance, which it was the duty of kings to preserve and to augment.[161] So, for example, Gregory of Tours describes how, in 580, the Frankish king Chilperic ordered that the *solidi* he had been sent by the Emperor Tiberius II be melted down, and he had made from them a table of gold, adorned with precious stones, weighing fifty pounds in all. 'I have had this done,' he declared, 'to honour and ennoble the people of the Franks, and should I live long enough, I shall have others made.'[162]

9.7 KINGSHIP AND CONSENSUS

Crucially, across the core kingdoms, what united the emergent Frankish aristocracy was a very un-Visigothic commitment to Merovingian dynastic rule, that is, to having a king of Clovis' bloodline. As mentioned earlier, through a combination of Frankish tradition, military success, and ecclesiastical support, by the end of the sixth century the Merovingians had successfully established themselves as a *stirps regia*—a bloodline royal and true. Merovingians were born royal, and in that sense they were quintessentially unlike any of the noblemen who gathered around them at court.[163] This distinction was accentuated by a tendency on the part of the Merovingian kings and those aspiring to kingship, discernible from the time of Gregory of Tours onwards, to choose brides and concubines either from amongst the princesses of other kingdoms (above all the Visigoths) or from the ranks of the Frankish lower orders.[164] In so marrying, a Merovingian prince or king was able to avoid finding himself tainted by association with any particular noble affinity or aristocratic faction, whilst also intensifying the personal, political (and economic) dependence of his spouse on himself.[165] At the same time, such a queen could perhaps be better trusted by members of the court to act as an impartial arbiter of disputes or a custodian of royal treasure during the absence or illness of a king, or

---

[161] Devroey (2003), pp. 178–83.
[162] Gregory of Tours, *Decem Libri Historiae*, VI, 2.
[163] P. Fouracre and A. Gerberding, *Late Merovingian France: History and Hagiography 640–720* (Manchester, 1996), p. 3.
[164] J. L. Nelson, 'Queens as Jezebels: The Careers of Brunhild and Balthild in Merovingian History', in *Studies in Church History, Subsidia* 1 (1978), pp. 31–77, and I. Wood, 'Deconstructing the Merovingian Family', in R. Corradini, M. Diesenberger, and H. Reimitz (eds.), *The Construction of Communities in the Early Middle Ages: Texts, Resources, and Artefacts* (Leiden, 2003), pp. 149–72.
[165] Nelson (1978), pp. 35–6.

during those periods of royal minority that the dynastic principle rendered inevitable, and when the queen mother was likely to be at her most powerful.

This entrenchment of Merovingian dynastic authority was important. For it meant that rather than being something to which all the nobility (or the more powerful elements within it) felt they could aspire, royal title was to be fought over purely within the family. What partly prevented dynastic monarchy from tipping over into familial tyranny, however, was that (as we noted in Chapter Four) succession to the throne was determined neither by issues of primogeniture nor of legitimacy of birth or marriage. The product of a concubine, a bigamous or overlapping marriage, or even of a 'chance encounter' could make a bid for the throne every bit as legitimate as the son of a publicly acknowledged royal wife. Such wives, in any case, were not necessarily any more chaste than their often promiscuous royal husbands. As a result, who 'was' and who 'was not' a Merovingian with a justifiable claim to power was to some extent open to negotiation within the family and amongst the court nobility.[166] A prince born at court might find his paternity challenged—especially if his mother excited political animosity and he was yet to reach adulthood. Conversely, a hitherto unheard-of 'Merovingian' claimant might emerge from obscurity yet attract considerable support. So, for example, in the late sixth century Gregory of Tours seems to have doubted the paternity of Clothar II, whilst accepting the claims of the shadowy figure of Gundevald, who arrived in Marseilles from Constantinople in 582, and who looks suspiciously like an agent of imperial influence.[167] The fluidity and ambiguity of claims to Merovingian royal authority thus served to enable a broader section of the political community to participate in questions relating to succession to the throne and the future of the kingdom, without rival noble families feeling able to seize the throne for themselves. Struggles between the various recognised Merovingian claimants to royal authority, however, could have the effect of radically recasting the contours of power within the Merovingian world, as the events of the early seventh century would demonstrate.

It was noted earlier that the economic interests of Merovingian kings were not necessarily limited to the confines of the kingdoms over which they ruled. As well as being a force for cohesion, this of itself could also be a cause of war. At the start of the seventh century, the Merovingian core kingdoms were divided between Clothar II, ruling in Neustria to the west, and his cousins Theuderic II in Burgundy and Theudebert II in Austrasia. Of these, Clothar was clearly the weakest. His accession to the throne of Neustria as a minor upon the death of Chilperic in 584 had been engineered by his mother, Fredegundis, in the face of bitter opposition from his rivals, and was only secured by the twelve-year-old king leading an army against his cousins. As the *Chronicle of Fredegar* (probably written in the 660s and our best source for the seventh century) records: 'Clothar and his men hurled themselves upon Theudebert and Theuderic and made great carnage among their forces.'[168]

---

[166] Wood (2003). [167] ibid.
[168] Fredegar, IV, ch. 17 (hereafter all references are to Book IV).

Four years later, however, the kings of Burgundy and Austrasia led a joint campaign against Clothar that obliged him to cede much territory.[169]

In 610 Theudebert II and his Austrasians then launched a raid on Alsace, which had been left to his recent ally Theuderic II by their father Childebert.[170] The two brothers decided to settle the matter by means of what the author of the *Chronicle of Fredegar* tellingly refers to as *Francorum iudicium* ('Frankish judgement')—a euphemism for armed combat. Theudebert had the better of the engagement that ensued, as a result of which 'Theuderic had no option but to cede Alsace by formal agreement [to his brother]. At the same time . . . he lost the Saintois [to the south of Toul], the Thurgau and Champagne which were the subject of frequent disputes.'[171] In retaliation, in 611 Theuderic entered into negotiation with Clothar II to form an alliance against Theudebert: 'He promised that if he were the victor he would restore to Clothar the duchy of Dentelin. . . . The legates worked out the terms of the agreement between Clothar and Theuderic, and the latter proceeded to raise an army.'[172]

In 612 the planned military engagement took place and Theudebert's forces were put to flight first at Toul, then on the approaches to Cologne, where Theudebert's treasury was captured as too, eventually, was the king. 'Theudebert', we are told, 'was sent in chains to Chalon. His little son, Merovech, was seized on Theuderic's orders: a soldier took him by the heels and dashed out his brains on a stone.'[173] Merovingian blood, we should note, may have been royal, but it was never regarded as sacrosanct. As promised, Theuderic now returned Dentelin to his cousin Clothar. Seeking to take advantage of his strong military position, in 613 Theuderic nevertheless launched a military campaign against him. As he headed out towards Neustria, however, Theuderic fell ill and died of dysentery in the royal residence at Metz.[174] Clothar now seized the initiative. Moving against Burgundy, and with the support and assistance of elements of the Burgundian nobility, he seized Brunhild, the late Theuderic's Visigothic grandmother, and the king's three sons. Brunhild, whom both he and his Burgundian supporters despised, was publicly humiliated and tortured to death (described with great glee, as noted earlier, by the pious Visigothic king Sisibert). Two of the royal princes were likewise executed, with Clothar only sparing the third because he was his godson.[175] As a result, the three core Merovingian kingdoms were now once more united under a single ruler.

The readiness of a faction of Burgundian nobles to side with the distant Neustrian Clothar II in 613, and to hand over to him their ruler's sons, is extremely revealing of contemporary political attitudes. What, it might reasonably be asked, bound such aristocrats to the Merovingian system? What prevented them from simply casting off Merovingian claims, or restrained the kings of the 'core kingdoms' from going it alone and establishing completely distinct polities? In terms of the latter, as we have seen, the landed interests of Merovingian kings tended to extend beyond the immediate confines of the territories over which they ruled, and

---

[169] ibid., ch. 20. [170] ibid., ch. 37. [171] ibid., ch. 37. [172] ibid., ch. 37.
[173] ibid., ch. 38. [174] ibid., ch. 39. [175] ibid., ch. 40–42.

the contours of the kingdoms themselves were variable, fluid, and negotiable. As a result, kings of Neustria, Austrasia, and Burgundy were necessarily drawn into contact with a political community broader than that of their own realms and, consequently, could never afford to ignore the activities of their kinsmen reigning elsewhere. Likewise, as a result of inheritance, conquest, and intermarriage, the character of elite landholding in this period—especially at the level of the nobility—appears to have been essentially trans-regional, rather than concentrated into highly localised blocks.[176] To some extent, this was an inheritance from late-Roman patterns of aristocratic landownership, but the shifts in the contours of royal power are also likely to have led to the acquisition on the part of royal retainers of ever more diverse 'property portfolios': Theuderic's gains at the expense of Clothar in 600, for example, may well have resulted in many Burgundian lords acquiring interests in the north. Certainly, Clothar's reunification of the kingdoms in 613 led to a significant expansion of northern landed interests southwards.[177]

Many Merovingian lords in the early seventh century were thus landowners on a grand scale, owning land across regions. It was rare, however, for a single landowner or his family to be locally preponderant. Rather, in the Paris basin and elsewhere, the estates of aristocrats and nobles existed cheek by jowl alongside those of other aristocrats, Merovingian kings and princes, monasteries, and the Church, as well as (in some areas rather more than others) autonomous peasant communities.[178] Faced with such competition for land, authority, manpower, and resources, members of the Frankish nobility needed some means of confirming, consolidating, and defending ownership, of bolstering their authority, of keeping the peace when peace was in their interests, and of legitimising violence when that was expedient. Each of these they found in the person of the king, his court, and at the annual assemblies of magnates that the Merovingian kings summoned on the Kalends of March (1 March). It was by virtue of royal charter, issued by the king, that property rights were enshrined;[179] it was by acquisition of royal office and title, either at court or in the locality, that status was conferred and an edge over one's opponents might be obtained; and it was at the annual assembly that the king sat in judgement, resolving disputes and dispensing justice with the advice of his leading subjects and churchmen.[180] The configuration of Frankish society in the late sixth and early seventh centuries, and the balance of social power in the countryside, thus led landowners to converge on the courts of Merovingian kings who, by virtue of their special status and 'blood royal', were deemed to sit above the fray.[181] As a result, any resistance to the royal will risked unleashing against a magnate the united fury of his peers.

The convergence of royal and aristocratic interest became especially pronounced after Clothar II's victory in 613. For the geographical scale and extent of the

---

[176] Fouracre (2000), pp. 19–20.   [177] Wickham (2005), pp. 186–7.
[178] ibid., p. 193, for the Paris basin.   [179] Fouracre (2000), pp. 14–15.
[180] P. Fouracre, 'Francia in the Seventh Century', in Fouracre (2005), pp. 371–96, p. 393; Fouracre (2000), p. 29.
[181] Fouracre (2000), p. 32.

reunited kingdom was such that, in the absence of the public and fiscal structures of the Roman state, the expression of royal authority at a local or even a regional level could only be effective with the active support of the leading members of local landed society, that is, the landowners, bishops, and lords.[182] As a corollary, however, members of the locally dominant propertied classes could only really feel secure if they bore the badge and stamp of the Merovingian crown.[183] The result was an emphasis on mutually profitable governance by consent, epitomised by the Edict of Paris that Clothar II issued in 614 and through which he asserted his authority over Francia as a whole: a statement of power reinforced by his contemporaneous convening of a Church Council that reiterated the key provisions of the Edict, and which was even attended by a bishop and abbot from the fledgling Christian kingdom of Kent.[184] In the Edict, Clothar swore that he would 'respect the privileges and customs of the provinces', levy no new tax (*census novus*), and only appoint to royal office in the localities men who already owned land there, so that their property could be distrained if they harmed that of others.[185] The policing of local society would remain in local hands, with the 'powerful' in the provinces being made responsible for the apprehending of vagabonds and bandits.[186] The net result was to convey to the locally powerful a strong sense that their interests would not only be left undisturbed but would also be protected at court. In return, a subsequent Church Council would proclaim Clothar to be a prophetic monarch and a New David, and would threaten with excommunication those judges and royal officials who failed to comply with his laws (making explicit reference to those promulgated in Paris in 614), whilst the mint at Marseilles began to issue coins bearing Clothar's name rather than that of the current Emperor in Constantinople.[187] Coinage in the Merovingian world was always primarily a local affair, with royal mints and moneyers issuing coins alongside those of bishops, local potentates, and others.[188] Only by negotiation and conciliation could any degree of even regional standardisation be achieved. Clothar's displacement of the 'pseudo-imperial' coinage of Provence is thus testimony to his ability to appeal to and conciliate local interests.

It has also been suggested that Clothar may have taken advantage of the occasion of the Church Council in 614 to codify and grant written laws to those of his subject peoples who were as yet without them such as the Alamans, Bavarians, and Austrasian ('Ripuarian') Franks—the *Lex Salica* now being thought of as

---

[182] For the fading away of the fiscal structures of the Roman state in sixth- and seventh-century Gaul, see Wickham (2005), pp. 111–17. For the consequent emphasis on the politics of 'consensus', see Fouracre (2005b), pp. 371–2.
[183] ibid., p. 375.
[184] *Clotharii Edictum, Capitularia Regum Francorum* in *MGH Legum*, sectio II, vol. 1, pp. 20–3; *Concilia Galliae 511–695*, pp. 275–82; Fouracre (2000), p. 25.
[185] Fouracre (2000), p. 12.
[186] ibid., pp. 14–15.
[187] *Concilium Clippiacense* (626–7) pr. and ch. 27 in Gaudemet and Basdevant (1989), II, pp. 528–30 and p. 542. On coinage, see Grierson and Blackburn (1986), pp. 117–18. Grierson suggests the coins may have been minted by the administrators of papal estates in the region.
[188] Hendy (1988).

Neustrian.[189] No Merovingian source makes any mention of this, but the law codes that we have for these peoples, whilst clearly codifying 'native' traditions, conform in structure to a common model that bears some resemblance to that of the *Lex Salica*, dealing with laws on the Church, on political authority, on freemen and their injuries, on lower ranks, and on women.[190] Certainly, the *Lex Ribuaria* looks to be early seventh century, whilst both the earliest fragments of the Alamannic law and the extant text of the Bavarian *Lex* preserve the memory of an association with Clothar.[191] By giving these peoples codified versions of their own law, the king would again have been signalling his determination to preserve the rights and customs of his leading subjects.

The sense that Clothar was determined to work with the grain of local society, and in favour of local interests, would have been further conveyed by his decision to appoint a 'mayor of the palace' (*maiordomus*) to both Burgundy and Austrasia in spite of the fact that neither kingdom now had a separate king.[192] The 'mayor of the palace' who, in an earlier age, might have been expected to be a Roman courtier with some experience of bureaucracy or administration, was appointed by the king effectively to run the royal household and to exercise control over Crown land and the granting of office. He was also potentially the main point of contact with the monarch. By maintaining these posts, and keeping them in Burgundian and Austrasian hands, Clothar was sending out a clear message that the reunification of the Frankish monarchy was not simply a Neustrian takeover. In 616, for example, according to the *Chronicle of Fredegar*, Clothar summoned to the villa of Bonneuil, near Paris, his Burgundian mayor Warnachar 'and all the bishops and notables of Burgundy. He then listened to all their just petitions and confirmed them by edict.'[193]

9.8 THE FRANKISH NOBILITY: CONSOLIDATION AND ENTRENCHMENT

As in Visigothic Spain, so too in Merovingian Francia, in addition to dispensing justice, confirming property rights, and acting as arbiter to the nobility, the king also summoned and led the military host in which all free men were liable to serve (although it was increasingly dominated by noble retinues). There are indications that the absence of the king on campaign—irrespective of his age—could lower morale and impair military effectiveness. So, as we have seen, in 600, though only a twelve-year-old, Clothar had personally led his armies against those of Theuderic and Theudebert. The 620s were a period of mounting military pressure on the Austrasian marchlands as Avar expansion led to growing restlessness amongst the Slav tribes. It may have been this fact that induced Clothar II in 622 to appoint his young son Dagobert as king in Austrasia.[194] By contrast, in 626, according to

---

[189] Wormald (1999), p. 43 and pp. 97–100.   [190] ibid., p. 97.
[191] ibid., p. 35 and pp. 43–4.   [192] Fredegar, ch. 42.   [193] ibid., ch. 44.
[194] ibid., ch. 47.

Fredegar, 'Clothar this year assembled the Burgundian nobles and courtiers at Troyes and inquired if they wished to appoint a successor to the position of Warnachar [the *maiordomus*] who had died. But they unanimously decided that they would never again have another mayor of the palace and begged the king earnestly to deal directly with them.'[195] This request again reveals the effectiveness of Clothar's integrative policy.

In 628 Clothar died, drawing to a close a reign of striking, if fortuitous, success. His heir apparent to the kingship of Neustria and Burgundy, Dagobert (already king of Austrasia), was able to secure the throne after a carefully orchestrated show of strength: 'Learning of his father's death', we are told:

> Dagobert ordered all his Austrasian followers to assemble in arms, and sent deputations into Burgundy and Neustria to ensure his choice as king. When he had passed through Rheims and was on the way to Soissons, news reached him that all the bishops and magnates of the kingdom of Burgundy had submitted to him. Most of the Neustrian bishops and magnates were said also to be willing to obey him. His brother Charibert made an attempt to seize the kingdom but his cause made little headway due to his guilessness (*simplicitas*).[196]

Dagobert then proceeded to carve out a territory for his brother in Aquitaine in order to 'provide him with sufficient upkeep for his household'.[197] Within three years, however, Charibert was dead, soon to be followed by his young son. In 628–9 the new king made a visit to Burgundy, dispensing justice and holding audiences with his leading lay and episcopal subjects.[198] The following year he made a similar tour of Austrasia, binding the magnates of the region to him. Thereafter he based himself in the political heartland (and economic powerhouse) of his regime in Neustria and the Paris basin.

The early 630s were once more a period of mounting military pressure on Francia's eastern frontier as relations between the Frankish kingdom and Samo and his Slav (or 'Wendish') followers deteriorated.[199] There are signs that Dagobert's decision to reside in Neustria rather than Austrasia had the effect of demoralising the Austrasian aristocracy, and limiting the effectiveness of Austrasian resistance.[200] Accordingly, in 632, the *Chronicle of Fredegar* records, 'Dagobert came to the city of Metz and there, on the advice of his bishops and lords and with the consent of all the great men of his kingdom, placed his son Sigibert on the throne of Austrasia and allowed him to make Metz his base.'[201] *Fredegar* informs us that thereafter Austrasian resistance stiffened markedly. Sigibert, it should be noted, was only two years old at the time. Again, we are alerted to the totemic significance of 'having a king', no matter how young, in order to be able to summon the royal host. However, it is also worth noting that Dagobert established his son with what *Fredegar* terms 'sufficient treasure' and 'provided him with all that his rank required and confirmed the gifts he had made by separate decrees'.[202] In other words, he

---

[195] ibid., ch. 54. [196] ibid., ch. 56.
[197] ibid., ch. 57. [198] ibid., ch. 58. [199] ibid., ch. 68.
[200] Fouracre (2005b), p. 376. [201] Fredegar, IV, ch. 75.
[202] ibid.. ch. 75.

provided him with the symbolic capital of kingship, a war chest, and a stock of land with which to reward his followers. The appointment of a new mayor of the palace, under the watchful gaze of Bishop Chunibert, together with the re-establishment of a court in Austrasia, may also have helped to give greater cohesion and royal focus to Austrasian aristocratic society.[203]

The following year (633) Dagobert fathered a second son (by a different mother), whom he named Clovis. This necessarily raised questions concerning the royal succession. There are indications that the Neustrian magnates were keen to have their own king (and not necessarily one raised amongst the Austrasians and thus perhaps prone to East Frankish aristocratic influence). Merovingian kingship was nothing if not responsive. Accordingly, we are told, 'Dagobert made an agreement with his son Sigibert *on the advice and at the wish of the Neustrians*', that Clovis should inherit Neustria and Burgundy: 'all the Austrasian magnates, the bishops, and all the warriors of Sigibert swore with hands raised that after Dagobert's death Neustria and Burgundy united should belong to Clovis, while Austrasia, which had the same population and extent of territory, should be entirely Sigibert's'.[204] In 639 Dagobert duly died, leaving a nine-year-old on the throne of Austrasia and a six-year-old on that of Neustria.[205] Each set of magnates, however, had its king.

The reigns of Clothar II and Dagobert I were years of peace and stability, rooted both in a Neustrian dominance of the Frankish world and the consensual basis on which Clothar II had established his rule of the united kingdoms. This dominance made sense economically: as we have seen in Chapter Two, even in the sixth century, the Paris basin had been the preserve of intensively farmed and geographically extensive great estates that were the foundation of both royal wealth and aristocratic power; in economic terms, therefore, the Burgundian and Austrasian elites in *c.*600 are unlikely to have been in a position to compete. Neustrian dominance, however, was never allowed to tip into Neustrian domination. The Burgundian elite was integrated into Neustrian political culture with care and consideration, and twice Austrasian military and political sensibilities had been answered with the appointment of a junior king. Dynastic stability had been reinforced by wise policy and a careful 'pruning back' of the Merovingian bloodline in which the Frankish nobility had been complicit.

The peace and stability of these years were to have long-lasting consequences, for they enabled members of the emergent Frankish nobility to concentrate on the real business of social domination and economic entrenchment at the grass roots of Frankish society without having to dissipate their energies in periodic struggles for the throne on behalf of their Merovingian overlords.[206] From an aristocratic perspective, internal peace meant fewer deaths in battle, greater continuity of lineage, fewer confiscations of patrimony, and thus a greater accumulation of wealth and power from one generation to the next. For those not involved in campaigns on the marchlands, of course, it also meant a diminution in booty, but

---

[203] As argued by Fouracre (2005b), p. 377.   [204] Fredegar, IV, 76.
[205] ibid., IV, 79.   [206] Banaji (2009), p. 65.

that in turn gave aristocrats an incentive to expand their landholdings at the expense of peasants and other neighbours, and to work both their estates and their labourers harder. Already, in the 580s, a Merovingian Church Council had complained of how 'in spite of the canons and laws, those who are close to the king, as well as others, who are puffed up by virtue of their worldly strength, strive after the properties of others, and without proferring any legal procedures or proof, drive the poor not only from their land but even from their homes'.[207] The temptation to behave in such a manner is only likely to have increased in the years that followed. The period thus witnessed a series of developments of crucial significance, which were not only to determine the history of Francia for much of the seventh and eighth centuries but were also to make a fundamental contribution to the crystallisation of a new social and economic order across much of the early medieval West.

First, there are signs of an ongoing integration of networks of elite landholding. Although there was a natural tendency for landowners to seek to concentrate their possessions regionally, extant Merovingian wills reveal a considerable degree of north-to-south integration of property portfolios from Neustria to Aquitaine, linking estates that were two or three hundred kilometres or more apart.[208] This trans-regional pattern of landholding, as noted earlier, and the consequent extension across the kingdoms of aristocratically focused networks and affinities, helped give added cohesion to the inter-regional politics of Neustria and Burgundy.[209]

Second, across and within the same territories, we see an absolute increase in the size of aristocratic (and monastic) estates through purchase and compulsion, and also through the clearance of woodland ('assarting') and an associated growth of peasant holdings (*casatae*) that the expanding estates would later incorporate.[210] The will of Hadoind, Bishop of Le Mans, for example (dating from 643), records how he intended to bequeath to the church of St Victor 'the estate (*villa*) called Aceruco, which I purchased for money, together with the houses, bondsmen, vineyards, forests, meadows and pastures'.[211] The Frankish aristocracy of the seventh century is thus recorded to have made substantial investment in the acquisition of estates, as also in the clearance of land, and the construction of water mills.[212] As a result, larger, more highly capitalised estates emerged. This process had already begun in the late sixth century: Gregory of Tours, for example, mentions a certain Chrodin, whom he described as 'a man of great virtue and piety . . . often creating estates from scratch, laying out vineyards, building houses and clearing the land'.[213] In the late seventh century, Vigilius, Bishop of Auxerre, donated vineyards to his church 'along with the bondsmen (*mancipia*) whom

---

[207] *Concilium Matisconense II* (585), ch. 14, in Gaudemet and Basdevant (1989), I, pp. 472–4.
[208] Wickham (2005), p. 191.
[209] ibid., pp. 196–7.
[210] See Banaji (2009), and F. Theuws, 'Centre and Periphery in Northern Austrasia (6th–8th centuries): An Archaeological Perspective', in J. Besteman, J. Bos, and H. Heidinga (eds.), *Medieval Archaeology in the Netherlands* (Aaasen and Maastricht, 1990).
[211] Banaji (2009), p. 66.   [212] ibid.
[213] ibid., p. 69, citing Gregory of Tours, *Decem Libri Historiae*, IV, 20.

I established there'.²¹⁴ The parcels of land on which estate *mancipia* were settled are referred to in the Merovingian wills as *mansi* (sing. *mansus*)—a term that, by the eighth century, had come to signify the peasant tenure of the bilateral estate increasingly characteristic of aristocratic and institutional landowners.²¹⁵ We thus once more begin to see in clearer outline a bipartite structuring of estates, much as had characterised the late-Roman period, but which, in certain areas, had been occluded by the barbarian settlements and the associated sub-division of properties.²¹⁶

Third, this process of 'manorialisation' was increasingly emulated by members of the Austrasian nobility to the east, as well as in those areas of West Francia (such as the lands to the north of the lower Loire, much of Normandy, Picardy, Flanders, and parts of the north-east) where, in the fifth century, a structural shift had taken place towards pastoralism and mixed farming, or where large estates had never predominated: across northern Gaul, for example, archaeology has revealed a seventh-century reorganisation of the rural settlement landscape, as well as a greater visibility of specialist manufacture on rural sites.²¹⁷ By the early eighth century, manorialisation had extended beyond the Rhine, in the process breaking down the economic distinction between those lands that had known Roman rule (and which, as a result, had inherited a tradition of direct management of land by great landowners) and those areas beyond Roman control where peasant autonomy had been more pronounced.²¹⁸ In Toxandria, in the lower Meuse valley, the testimony of both charters and the archaeological evidence reveals a shift from relatively autonomous peasant farmsteads (*casatae*) to peasant holdings clustered around an estate centre and seigneurial hall (*sala*).²¹⁹ The foundation of monasteries and the expansion of monastic and ecclesiastical landowning to the north and east of the Merovingian realm are also likely to have made a fundamental contribution to this economic reconfiguration, as in Ireland, establishing centres of consumption and thus of specialised agriculture, craft, and industry, in a landscape largely devoid of cities. Through the construction of private churches on the expanding estates of the nobility, and the drawing in of farmers and their families under monastic lordship, here, as elsewhere, the manorialisation of peasant land and the Christianisation of the peasantry are likely to have gone hand in hand.

Crucially, not only was a new social and economic geography emerging, but so too, through an ongoing process of elite formation, was a trans-regional Frankish nobility increasingly taking shape, bound together by 'a culture of power in which were united force, faith, wealth, law and custom'.²²⁰ The cultural cohesion of this

---

²¹⁴ ibid.
²¹⁵ ibid., pp. 69–70; A. Verhulst, *Rural and Urban Aspects of Early Medieval Northwest Europe* (Aldershot, 1992).
²¹⁶ I here modify my argument in Sarris (2004).
²¹⁷ G. Halsall, 'From Roman *fundus* to Early Medieval *grand domaine*: The Crucial Rupture Around 600 AD', *Revue belge d'histoire* (forthcoming).
²¹⁸ As argued by Fouracre (2000), p. 22. See also Blair (2005), p. 41.
²¹⁹ ibid., p. 128, drawing on Theuws (1990).
²²⁰ Fouracre (2000), p. 177.

elite in particular was greatly facilitated by its focus on the royal court and its role as a point of contact and *locus* of acculturation between members of the nobility.[221] Central to this was the 'court school' (*scola*) to which aristocrats from all over the Merovingian world sent their sons to be raised in proximity to the king, and where the young men deported themselves after the manner of the late-Roman imperial bodyguard, whose insignia and gestures they adopted.[222] At the royal *scola* a shared culture was fostered and friendships, affinities, and alliances were forged that could last a lifetime. A young aristocrat from Aquitaine by the name of Desiderius, for example, attended the court of Clothar II and there formed a friendship with the future king Dagobert, whom he went on to serve as treasurer before, in 630, becoming Bishop of Cahors.[223] In a subsequent letter he reminisced with Dagobert over the days they had spent together as boys—'the memory of the camaraderie and the sweetness of youth passed under a cloudless sky'.[224] To another acquaintance he wrote 'may the old affection we had for each other ... remain unchanged just as our close brotherhood used to be. In my silent prayers I beg that we shall be worthy to live together in the palace of the supreme heavenly king, just as we had been friends in the court of the earthly prince.'[225]

Queens could play a particularly important part in nurturing the young aristocrats gathered together. Balthild, the wife of Dagobert I's son Clovis II, for example, is described by her hagiographer as having behaved 'to the great men like a mother, to the bishops like a daughter, and to the young men and boys like the best sort of nurse'.[226] In the century that followed, the culture of power fostered at the Merovingian court was to be exported well beyond the core territories of the Merovingian kingdoms, as Charles Martel, Pippin III, and Charlemagne forcibly subjected to Frankish rule many of the satellite territories to the north, south, east, and west.

9.9 THE MAYORS OF THE PALACE AND THE RISE OF THE NOBLE FACTION

The death of Dagobert I in 639, as we have seen, left two boy-kings on the thrones of Neustria and Austrasia. It is a sign of how court-centred Frankish political culture had become, and how loyal to the Merovingian bloodline it was, that the ensuing period of minority rule elicited no direct attempts at usurpation or secession. The functions of Merovingian kingship and the offices associated with royal government and the palace were simply too central to the workings of

---

[221] ibid., p. 28.
[222] Hen (2007), pp. 101–6.
[223] *Vita Desiderii Episcopi* in *MGH SRM*, IV, pp. 563–93.
[224] Desiderius, *Epistolae*, I, 5. See Hen (2007), p. 105.
[225] Desiderius, *Epistulae*, I, 11. Translation from Hen (2007), p. 105. See also B. H. Rosenwein, *Emotional Communities in the Early Middle Ages* (Ithaca, NY, 2006).
[226] *Vita Balthildis*, ch. 4. Translation taken from Nelson (1978), p. 60, for which see also for discussion of this revealing source. See also Fouracre and Gerberding (1996), pp. 97–118.

aristocratic society for the court and monarchy to be allowed to fall into abeyance. Rather, many of the active responsibilities and duties of kingship necessarily came to be exercised by the figure of the mayor. Predictably, royal mothers also wielded considerable influence: it is striking that upon Dagobert's death, his 'royal treasure' is recorded to have been split three ways between Clovis, Sigibert, and the late king's widow, the queen mother Nantechildis.[227]

Politics at the Neustrian court in the early 640s, therefore, were dominated by Nantechildis, and the mayor of the palace, Aega. Upon Aega's death in *c*.642, the queen mother was able to manoeuvre into the post a kinsman of Dagobert's mother by the name of Erchinoald, who was well regarded by the author of the *Chronicle of Fredegar* ('he lined his own pockets, to be sure, but quite moderately'), whilst in Austrasia the dominant figures at the time of Dagobert's death were Bishop Chunibert and his ally, the mayor of the palace, Pippin.[228] Pippin was head of an already wealthy and powerful Austrasian noble family and upon his death early in Sigibert's reign an attempt was made to ensure that his son, Grimoald, succeed him as mayor of the palace. This was thwarted by a rival aristocratic faction led by a court official and protector of the young king, Uro, who instead ensured that his own son Otto succeeded Pippin in the post.[229] If noble families could not vie for the crown, they could at least eye with ambition and jealousy the office of *maiordomus*, which not only controlled access to the person of the king but also the revenues of the extensive royal estates and the powers of patronage at the king's disposal. Especially at times of royal minority, this was a post worth having and holding onto.

For certain of the Merovingian *duces* established along the frontiers of the kingdom, the demise of the militarily and diplomatically forceful Dagobert may well have opened up opportunities for greater political autonomy. Certainly, it is claimed that shortly after Dagobert's death in 639, the *dux* of Thuringia Radulf, whom Dagobert had appointed to face down the Wends on Austrasia's eastern marchlands, rose up in revolt.[230] In accordance with Merovingian custom, Sigibert led his armies against Radulf in person, for all that he was only nine years old.[231] The crushing of the rebel would be a great act of Merovingian self-affirmation, uniting the king's nobles and retainers in an act of collective judgement upon a pariah in their ranks.

The assault on Radulf in his fortified compound on the banks of the River Unstrut, however, went seriously wrong, partly due to tactical indecision on the part of those in control of the king, and partly due to Radulf's ability to persuade 'certain dukes (*duces*) in Sigibert's army' not to attack him. Rather than being forced to submit to the royal will, the rebel duke 'came through the camp entrance and threw himself and his warriors on Sigibert's and made a carnage to be marveled at.' Radulf, we are informed, 'went back into the camp after his victory while

[227] Fredegar, IV, ch. 85.   [228] ibid., IV chs. 84–5.
[229] ibid., IV, ch. 86.
[230] ibid., IV, ch. 87, and Fouracre (2005b), p. 385.
[231] ibid., IV, ch. 87.

Sigibert, like his followers, was seized with grief and sat there on his horse weeping unrestrainedly for those he had lost.' The following day, the young king sent a delegation to request that he might be allowed to return across the Rhine along with his remaining men. 'Radulf', the *Chronicle of Fredegar* tells us, 'was in transports of pride. He rated himself King in Thuringia (*regem se in Toringia esse cinsebat*) and concluded treaties of alliance with the Wends and made overtures to other neighbouring peoples.'[232]

Radulf's purpose in supposedly rebelling against Sigibert is unclear. The fact that it was he who was the subject of attack in his compound and that, in victory, he did not press home his advantage to seize the king and rout his forces, may indicate that the background to the revolt was an attempt made at court to remove him from the office of *dux* of Thuringia, a move which his power on the ground ultimately precluded. If indeed it was the case that Sigibert's entourage had been attempting to deny Radulf the title that he felt to be his by right, this may help to explain why certain of the *duces* in the royal host held back and would not fight him. In short, there may have been considerable sympathy for his position. Merovingian kings were meant to work with the locally powerful, not against them.

Certainly, it should be noted that the *Chronicle of Fredegar* claims that Radulf 'rated himself king *in Thuringia*', that is to say he *effectively* treated it as his own kingdom. He did not formally proclaim himself king of Thuringia, and indeed the chronicler goes on to note that Radulf in fact continued to acknowledge Merovingian suzerainty: 'He did not however expressly deny Sigibert's overlordship (*in verbis tamen Sigiberto regimini non denegans*)', the *Chronicle* states, 'but in practice did all he could to resist his might (*nam in factis forteter eiusdem resistebat dominacionem*).'[233] The prestige of the Merovingian bloodline clearly continued to retain a palpable hold over the aristocratic world view.

Nevertheless, the debacle that had ensued before Radulf's Thuringian stockade can be seen to have encapsulated certain trends which were potentially quite dangerous from a royal perspective. Foremost amongst these were signs of growing factionalism within the aristocracy, which is reflected for us in the hagiographic literature of the period, generated on behalf of the rival parties. The emergence of a more clearly defined and self-aware nobility at court, clustered around different factions and interests, was arguably introducing into the politics of the Merovingian world an element of political instability that the forceful personality of an assertive adult king such as Dagobert I might have able to contain, but which a boy-king could not. Certainly, these were tensions that no mayor of the palace could resolve, given that this office itself had by now become the preserve and ambition of members of the higher nobility, and was thus itself a factionalising factor.

There are good reasons to suppose that this development was at its most pronounced in Austrasia, where a greater degree of autonomy had long characterised power relations between the Crown and the aristocracy. On one level this was a result of the physical geography of the kingdom itself. As noted earlier,

[232] ibid.   [233] ibid.

stretched out as it was along a series of river valleys, the kingdom lacked the political focus on a single royal heartland that characterised Neustrian politics.[234] The kingdom's extensive and largely open eastern frontier, moreover, necessarily led to the emergence of close relations and affinities between members of the Austrasian aristocracy and the leaders and *duces* of the satellite powers beyond the Rhine—that is to say, men such as Radulf—on whose support Austrasian factions were now willing and able to call just as he could seemingly appeal to them.[235] This, combined with the only intermittent existence of an Austrasian court in an age of Neustrian supremacy, made for an independently minded and locally rooted aristocracy, which, by virtue of the ongoing manorialisation of the eastern territories, was increasingly confident in the material basis of its wealth. Heightened factionalism, intensified ambition for the office of mayor of the palace, and the growing involvement of the peripheral principalities in Austrasian politics are each evident in the events of *c*.641, when conflict broke out between the mayor of the palace, Otto, and Pippin's son, Grimoald, as a result of which 'he [Otto] was slain by Leuthar, duke of the Alamans. The dignity (*honor*) of mayor of Sigibert's palace and control of the whole kingdom of Austrasia was thus decisively assured to Grimoald.'[236] Governance now belonged to the mayor, we should note, not the king. An incipient de-centring of the Merovingian monarchy was underway.

Even within Burgundy, moreover, which had been so effectively integrated into the world of the Neustrian court, there are signs of a destabilising degree of factionalism. It is clear, for example, that after the death of Aega, the office of Burgundian mayor was briefly revived, and that the queen mother Nantechildis had to take great care in order to ensure the acquiescence of the magnates of the region in the appointment of her favoured candidate—a Frank from outside of Burgundy by the name of Flaochad—approaching and convincing each of them in turn.[237] Resistance to the authority of the new mayor, however, was orchestrated by a powerful Burgundian nobleman by the name of Willebad.[238] Tensions ran so high that at a gathering of the magnates, the mayor of the palace hatched a plot to assassinate the troublesome nobleman. Arriving with a large and presumably heavily armed entourage, Willebad refused to enter the palace where the assembly was taking place. Instead Flaochad came out to engage Willebad in single combat. Only the intervention of Willebad's brother and other magnates temporarily defused the situation.

The death of Nantechildis that same year, however, left Flaochad exposed. As a result, rivalry between the two men erupted into open violence on a major scale. Summoned before King Clovis in Autun, Willebad and his military following gingerly made their way towards the city and camped outside its walls. The next day Flaochad and his allies fell upon them and Willebad and his followers were cut down (although Flaochad himself soon died of fever).[239] It is striking, however, that when battle had been joined between the two sides, the Neustrian magnates

---

[234] As noted by Innes (2007), p. 288. [235] ibid., p. 299.
[236] Fredegar, IV, 88. [237] ibid., IV, 89.
[238] ibid., IV, 90. [239] ibid.

present, who, according to the *Chronicle*, had been meant to surround Willebad's forces (*qui undique eodem debuerant circumdare*), had held back. They 'remained spectators', the *Chronicle* states, 'awaiting the outcome with no wish to throw themselves on Willebad'.[240] To the Neustrians, Flaochad may have looked like an interloper, imposed on the world of the Burgundian court from outside, whom Burgundian lords such as Willebad had every right to resist. Certainly, as the events of the late seventh century would reveal, any outsider appointed to the Neustrian mayoralty was likely to receive a frosty reception.

9.10 CONTROLLING THE KING

With the drawing to a close of the *Chronicle of Fredegar*, political events within Francia become increasingly difficult to trace, although a vital Neustrian perspective is provided by a work known as the *Liber Historiae Francorum* (the 'Book of the History of the Franks').[241] By *c.*645 Sigibert had come of age, and, in Neustria, Clovis reached adulthood around 649. Clovis II, however, died in 657, leaving the throne to the eldest of his three sons, the eight-year-old Clothar III, whilst Sigibert predeceased his brother in 656. The events that followed the death of Sigibert in Austrasia are somewhat shadowy.[242] Sigibert left a young son by the name of Dagobert. The mayor of the palace, Grimoald, however, is reported to have seized the boy, had him forcibly tonsured, and then handed him over to the Bishop of Poitiers, who sent him over to Ireland in monastic exile.[243] Grimoald's own son—given the Merovingian name of Childebert—was then put on the throne. Childebert's claims were given a veneer of Merovingian legitimacy (which, as we have seen, was always to some extent negotiable) by his apparent adoption by Sigibert's widow, Himnechild, who would not appear to have been Dagobert's mother, and thus may have borne a grudge against the boy as the product of an earlier marriage. More significantly, she may have been eager to hold on to the position of wealth and power that she enjoyed as queen by aligning herself with Grimoald and Childebert.[244] With the backing of Grimoald and Himnechild, Childebert 'the adopted' (as he is known to historians) seems to have held on to the throne until *c.*662. We have no evidence of any concerted Austrasian resistance to the regime: but then we have almost no evidence. It is perhaps significant, however, that when Grimoald and his son Childebert were brought down, it was as a result of a legitimist intervention on the part of the Neustrian nobility. As the Neustrian *Liber Historiae Francorum* records: 'But the Neustrians, enraged by this, prepared an ambush for Grimoald and removing him they brought him for judgement. . . . In the city of Paris, he was put in prison and bound with painful chains as one worthy

---

[240] ibid.
[241] For discussion, see Fouracre and Gerberding (1996), pp. 79–87.
[242] For the chronological problems posed in particular by historians' attempts to make sense of the events of the late 650s and early 660s, see Fouracre (2005b), pp. 386–7.
[243] *LHF*, ch. 43, p. 87.
[244] Fouracre (2005b), p. 387. Note discussion in Wood (2003).

of death because he had acted against his lord. His death came with terrible torture.'²⁴⁵ Himnechild, however, was left alone. Perhaps as part of a deal to depose Childebert and remove Grimoald, Himnechild's daughter from Sigibert, Bilichild, was married to her first cousin, Clovis II's youngest son, who was placed on the Austrasian throne as Childeric II. Amid the power struggles of the period, Himnechild thus emerged as the great survivor.

In Neustria, the queen mother Balthild, reputedly an Anglo-Saxon slave-girl by origin whose mother-in-law had repeatedly reminded her of the fact that she had once owned her, ruled as regent until Clothar III came of age in 664, whereupon she seems to have been forced into retirement by certain of her son's courtiers.²⁴⁶ She is presented by her hagiographer (almost certainly a monk or nun from a monastic institution of Balthild's founding, such as that of Chelles, to which she ultimately retired) as 'the instrument of divinely-ordained concord between the once warring kingdoms'.²⁴⁷ Evidently, not all agreed.²⁴⁸ The other great powers at court were the mayors of the palace, Erchinoald (who died *c.*658) and his successor, Ebroin—clearly a formidable character who may well have been responsible for a significant overhauling of the monetary system associated with the introduction of a new more plentiful silver coinage, in place of the increasingly scarce gold.²⁴⁹ The office of Burgundian mayor had been abandoned after the difficulties caused by Flaochad. Ebroin, however, emerges from the factional literature generated by his opponents as a still more problematic character, who stirred up mounting resentment amongst the Burgundian nobility by seeking to limit their access to the person of king unless they paid him large bribes. According to one such hostile source, the *Passion of Leudegar* (probably written in Autun in the early 680s, and detailing the suffering and death of the eponymous hero of the work, who was bishop of that city from *c.* 622 to 676): 'Then he [Ebroin] issued this unlawful edict—that no one from the region of Burgundy was to come to the palace unless he had ordered him to come.'²⁵⁰ The mayor is further accused of having seized estates unlawfully, and of having been motivated by a growing sense of insecurity. This allegation receives some external corroboration: according to the Anglo-Saxon monk Bede (born *c.*673), when in 667–8 the Eastern churchman Theodore of Tarsus and his companion Abbot Hadrian made their way across Francia en route for England, they did so under the close scrutiny of Ebroin and his men.²⁵¹ Hadrian was initially prevented from crossing the Channel to Kent from the port town of Quentovic on the grounds that Ebroin 'suspected him of having some mission from the [East Roman] Emperor to the kings of Britain, which might be directed against the kingdom over which

---

²⁴⁵ *LHF*, ch. 43, p. 88. The event is unhelpfully placed under the reign of Clovis II.
²⁴⁶ See the *Vita Balthildis*. It is conceivable that she was in fact an Anglo-Saxon princess.
²⁴⁷ Nelson (1978), p. 51.
²⁴⁸ Fouracre and Gerberding (1996), pp. 112–15.
²⁴⁹ Grierson and Blackburn (1986), pp. 93–5.
²⁵⁰ *Passio Leudegarii*, ch. 4, pp. 220–21. For the provenance, see Fouracre and Gerberding (1996), pp. 193–5.
²⁵¹ Bede, *Ecclesiastical History*, IV, 1.

at that time he held the chief charge'.[252] The arrival of the Emperor Constans II in the West had clearly set even Merovingian nerves on edge.

In 673 Clothar III died, and the magnates of Burgundy prepared to make their way to Neustria to acclaim a new king. Instead, Ebroin seemingly sought to appoint Clothar's brother Theuderic as monarch without any say on the part of the nobles. As the *Passio Leudegarii* relates: 'When the crowd of nobles who were hurrying to meet the new king received Ebroin's order to break off their journey, they took counsel together and, abandoning Theuderic, they all demanded instead his younger brother Childeric who had been assigned the throne in Austrasia.'[253] Members of the Neustrian nobility were equally unhappy. A carefully orchestrated coup ensued, in which Neustrian noblemen took the lead. As the *Liber Historiae Francorum* records: 'The Neustrians formed a conspiracy against Ebroin and they rose up against Theuderic and deposed him from the throne. Dragging them off by force, they cut the hair of both.'[254] Ebroin was exiled to the monastery of Luxeuil in Burgundy, and Childeric was invited to march from the east to take the throne. His brother, King Theuderic III, was placed under house arrest in the royal abbey and Merovingian mausoleum of St Denis, some twelve kilometres to the north of Paris.[255]

Childeric II thus restored the political union of the Frankish kingdoms. The Neustrian nobility now invited him to consolidate his rule by essentially reiterating the terms of the Edict of Paris in which his great-grandfather, Clothar II, had established his *modus vivendi* with the Frankish aristocracy in 614: 'Now that Childeric was king', the *Passio Leudegarii* reports:

> Everyone demanded that he should issue the following edicts throughout the three kingdoms over which he had gained sway: that as of old judges should maintain the law and custom of each kingdom and that rulers from one [province] should not intrude in the others lest one of them should, as Ebroin had done, take up oppressive and unlawful rule and after his example look down on his peers, for, as they acknowledged that access to the highest position should be open to all, nobody was to presume to place himself before another.[256]

Childeric, we are told, acceded to these demands.

The establishment in Neustria of Childeric II and his Austrasian entourage, however, led to rising suspicions and anxieties within the ranks of the Neustrian nobility. The *Passio Leudegarii* blames these on the fact that the king was soon 'corrupted by the advice he took from foolish and nearly pagan people'—an interesting insight into how members of the Austrasian and only recently Christianised trans-Rhenish aristocracy appeared to the Burgundian author of this work.[257] The power wielded at court by these Austrasians was probably deemed

---

[252] ibid.
[253] *Passio Leudegarii*, ch. 5, p. 222.
[254] *LHF*, ch. 45, p. 89.
[255] *Passio Leudegarii*, ch. 6, p. 223.
[256] ibid., ch. 7, p. 224.
[257] ibid.

to be in breach of the terms of the covenants that the king had so recently given. Childeric, for example, had brought with him his Austrasian mayor, Wulfoald, and this certainly would have offended Neustrian sensibilities.[258] It is claimed that the Burgundian Leudegar, as Bishop of Autun, berated the king for having 'so suddenly changed the customs of the kingdoms when he had ordered them to be preserved'.[259] He also instructed the king to set aside his Austrasian wife, Bilichild. The bishop, who had previously conspired against Ebroin, was exiled for his pains.

According to the *Liber Historiae Francorum*, matters came to a head for members of the Neustrian nobility in 675, when Childeric 'ordered one of their number, a Neustrian named Bodilo, to be stretched upon a stake and beaten illegally. Seeing these things, the Neustrians were greatly enraged.' The consequences for Childeric were swift and brutal: 'Ingelbert and Amalbert, along with the other hereditary Neustrian nobility, entered into a plot against Childeric. Bodilo, along with the others who were conspiring against the king, rose up against him and killed him, together with . . . his pregnant queen.'[260] Childeric's mayor, Wulfoald, escaped the murder of the royal party and fled east to Austrasia.

A bitter struggle for power now ensued as Ebroin, Leudegar, and the former king Theuderic all returned from exile or imprisonment. The *Passio Leudegarii* paints an apocalyptic picture of what, from the perspective of both the Burgundian and Neustrian nobility, was the ultimate nightmare: the chaos resulting from a kingless world: 'since no king sat firmly on the throne', the work informs us, 'those who should have been the rulers of the provinces rose up against each other'.[261] Amid the uncertainty, members of the Frankish nobility appointed a certain Leudesius as mayor of the palace and received Theuderic III back as king. Ebroin and his supporters, however, were able to raise an army and seized upon and acclaimed as king a hitherto unheard-of supposed son of Clothar III's bearing the politically resonant name of Clovis.[262] In a decisive move, Ebroin and his host captured the royal treasury and soon thereafter caught and executed Leudesius. Theuderic III then fell into their hands, effectively giving Ebroin control of Neustria. His old enemy Bishop Leudegar was also tracked down and killed.[263] Ebroin evidently still had powerful supporters within the Neustrian elite, including Audoin, Bishop of Rouen, whom the author of the *Liber Historiae Francorum* regarded with evident respect and who was later credited with posthumous miracles.[264] With Theuderic once more under Ebroin's control, the boy-king Clovis was seemingly done away with.

---

[258] *Liber Historiae Francorum*, ch. 42, p. 89 (Wulfoald's appointment in Austrasia), and ch. 45, p. 90 (his flight from Neustria).
[259] ibid., ch. 8, pp. 224–5.
[260] ibid., ch. 45, p. 90.
[261] *Passio Leudegarii*, ch. 15, p. 231.
[262] ibid., chs. 19–20, pp. 235–6.
[263] *Liber Historiae Francorum*, ch. 45, pp. 90–91. See also the *Passio Leudegarii* for more detailed treatment.
[264] *Vita Audoini Episcopi Rotomagensis*, ch. 19, p. 165.

Ebroin now set about attempting to consolidate his position.[265] His leading opponents within the Frankish elite were deliberately targeted and suffered confiscation of estates. Church property associated with his enemies may also have been sequestrated.[266] Allies of the late Bishop Leudegar are recorded as fleeing beyond the Loire into Aquitaine and the Basque country.[267] In Aquitaine itself, the *dux* Lupus, who had supported the initial coup against Ebroin and the accession of Childeric, refused to recognise the new regime. Relations with the magnates of Austrasia, whose king had been killed and whose representatives the Neustrians had chased from the kingdom, had to all intents and purposes broken down.

Within Austrasia itself, concerted efforts were made to find a new king. The Austrasian nobility by this time appears to have been dominated by two related magnates, Martin and Pippin, kinsmen of the former Austrasian mayor of the palace, Grimoald, whose family's fortunes and prestige had evidently survived his fall from grace. These two figures were seemingly instrumental in securing the return from Ireland of the Merovingian prince Dagobert, whom Grimoald had driven from the throne. The Neustrian court, however, refused to acknowledge the legitimacy of Dagobert's appointment as king of Austrasia, and in a major military engagement in the Ardennes, an Austrasian army led by Martin and Pippin suffered a heavy defeat at the hands of Ebroin and the Neustrian host, during the course of which Martin died.[268] In 679 Dagobert II was assassinated, purportedly for failing to consult his magnates and for attempting to levy tribute on his subjects.[269] This left the mayor, Pippin, in sole charge of Austrasian affairs. No new king was acclaimed in Austrasia.

Theuderic III's regime, however, was unwilling to engage with the Austrasian nobility. This situation persisted until 687, when, with the apparent encouragement of Neustrian exiles from Theuderic III's court, Pippin decided to launch a pre-emptive attack on the army of Theuderic and his recently appointed mayor, Berchar, who was aggressively anti-Pippin.[270] The two armies clashed near the villa of Tertry on the Somme. Two highly generalised accounts of the ensuing battle survive in the Neustrian *Liber Historiae Francorum* and a later, pro-Pippin source, the *Annales Mettenses Priores*. What both works agree on is that, as a result of the battle, Berchar and Theuderic III were put to flight and many of their noble followers killed.[271] About a year later Berchar was assassinated, whereupon Pippin proceeded to marry Berchar's widow (thus enabling him to co-opt her, no doubt, powerful political connections and affinities) and succeeded him as mayor of the palace in Neustria, as well as continuing to hold the parallel office in Austrasia.

---

[265] *Passio Leudegarii*, ch. 28, p. 244.
[266] ibid., p. 245.
[267] *Continuation of Fredegar*, 2.
[268] Fouracre (2005b), pp. 390–91.
[269] *The Life of Bishop Wilfrid*, ch. 33, pp. 66–9.
[270] For the political background of the intervening years, see Fouracre (2005b), p. 391. For the role played by Neustrian exiles in inciting intervention, see the *Annales Mettenses Priores*, p. 346. For strife within the Neustrian elite, see *LHF*, ch. 48, p. 92.
[271] *LHF*, ch. 48, pp. 92–3; *Annales Mettenses Priores*, pp. 356–9.

Wisely, Pippin did not attempt to press home his political advantage and thus risk eliciting a backlash on the part of the West Frankish nobility. Rather, he withdrew to Austrasia, where he concentrated on building up his family's martial renown, stock of booty, and string of estates, leading a series of campaigns against the Frisians, Alamans, and other neighbouring peoples.[272] As a result, he was able to forge under his own control a dense network of land, clients, and pro-Pippin monastic foundations, which together constituted a powerbase far surpassing that of any previous Merovingian magnate.[273]

In 691 Theuderic III died and was succeeded by his young son Clovis III.[274] In 695 Clovis himself passed away, and was replaced on the throne by his brother Childebert III, to whom Pippin appointed his son, Grimoald, as mayor.[275] In spite of the violence and turmoil of the 670s, there is every sign that once Childebert reached adulthood, he was able to restore a sense of focus to the Merovingian monarchy. Until his death in 711, the king seems to have made a firm impression on the political scene: 'it is under Childebert that, for the last time in the Merovingian period, we see magnates from the far south attending the court. Childebert was also the last Merovingian whose name appears on coins minted at Marseilles.'[276] It was not for nothing that the *Liber Historiae Francorum* describes him as 'the famous and just lord King Childebert of good memory'.[277]

This having been said, however, it is hard to deny that, beneath the apparent continuities of dynasty and court, the fundamental dynamics of Frankish high politics had altered considerably since the days of Clothar II and Dagobert I. In particular, during the periods of minority rule, matriarchal pre-eminence, and mayoral ascendancy that had ensued since 639, Merovingian kings and claimants to the throne had increasingly become pawns in the escalating factional politics of the day arising from the absence of a strong leader and the burgeoning power of the Frankish nobility, which was itself largely a product of the *pax Merovingorum* of the early seventh century.[278] Nothing reveals this pattern of development so clearly as the readiness of a party of West Frankish nobles to murder their king, Childeric II (675), and the East Frankish assassination of the ruling monarch Dagobert II (679). In the east, moreover, during the period of Neustrian dominance, aristocratic society had steadily grown used to operating without a Merovingian king at all, with the patronage and leadership associated with royalty increasingly exercised by the mayoral family of Pippin and Grimoald. To the south-west, Aquitaine had by 676 fallen outside the orbit of the court altogether, whilst still remaining part of the broader Merovingian commonwealth.[279]

But if the extension and consolidation of noble power can be seen to have caused major political problems for the Merovingians, the effects of this phenomenon on the economic and cultural landscape of the northern and eastern Frankish

---

[272] *Continuation of Fredegar*, 5, and *LHF*, ch. 49, p. 93. For details of Pippin's campaigns, see also Fouracre (2000), pp. 50–53.
[273] Innes (2007), pp. 301–2.
[274] *Continuation of Fredegar*, 6.   [275] ibid.
[276] Fouracre (2000), p. 54.   [277] *LHF*, ch. 50, p. 94.
[278] Wickham (2005), p. 105.   [279] ibid.

territories were still more pronounced. For, at a time when the Mediterranean coastal zone to the south, which had long been the economically most sophisticated and highly developed region under Merovingian control, was suffering the effects of urban decline and the attenuation of trade with the Byzantine East, the expansion of manorialisation and monasticism to the north served to fundamentally reconfigure the material and religious context in which politics took place and lives were lived. Not only was Christianity now able to put down deeper roots amongst the peasantry, but the growth of monastic and lay estates also led to a greater capitalisation and intensification of agriculture, evident in the wider dissemination of watermills, as also, it has been argued, of ploughing technologies better suited to wetter and heavier northern soils.[280] Greater profits from agriculture meant more trade in worked or artisanal goods, as both aristocratic households and monasteries emerged to form great centres of consumption and production, such as had long existed around the Paris basin. This expansion of trade quickened in the late seventh century, as the new silver coinage associated with the figure of Ebroin circulated ever more widely, leading to a more full-blown monetisation of exchange.[281] As the centre of economic gravity in the Frankish world shifted northwards, the Merovingians' northerly neighbours were in turn drawn into the proliferating commercial networks. New trading centres—known as 'wics'—took shape along the Frankish coast of the English Channel and within reach of the North Sea, with similar trading posts emerging on the eastern and southern shores of the kingdoms of the Anglo-Saxons themselves. These new entrepôts—such as Quentovic (to the south of Boulogne), Dorestadt (near Utrecht), and Hamwih (Saxon Southampton)—heralded the rapid maturation of a new economic order no longer primarily driven by the powerhouse of a Mediterranean Roman Empire.[282] This development would both feed off and catalyse political developments in lowland Britain.

9.11 THE AGE OF THE *BRETWALDAS* AND THE ERA OF MARCHLAND EXPANSION

As we saw in Chapters Two and Five, lowland Britain in the late sixth century was a highly fragmented region, dominated by small-scale military lordships in the context of a de-urbanised and de-monetised economy, in which, amid the chronic military insecurity of the age, a structural shift had taken place towards pastoralism and mixed farming very similar to that which can be discerned for parts of the northern Frankish world. The result of this shift was that lordship was loose and kingship highly itinerant, with kings and their retinues traversing the territories

---

[280] J. Henning, 'Revolution or Relapse? Technology, Agriculture, and Early Medieval Archaeology in Germanic Central Europe', in Ausenda, Delogu, and Wickham (2009), pp. 149–64—although note the important caveats of Barnish and Wickham, ibid., pp. 167, 169.

[281] For the possible reasons for this reform, see Hendy (1988).

[282] R. Hodges and D. Whitehouse, *Mohammed, Charlemagne, and the Origins of Europe* (1983), pp. 93–5.

over which they claimed control, demanding renders and supplies (*feorm*) in the form of meat, ale, honey, bread, cheese, and livestock from their 'free' subjects, the menfolk amongst whom they had the right to call to arms.[283] Emergent royal authority thus inhabited 'a landscape of obligation rather than a landscape of ownership', although, as we shall see, this system possessed an economic inner logic of its own that was not without its advantages.[284]

With the withering of contact between the Romano-British kingdoms and Byzantium, which appears to have coincided with and was probably the result of the arrival of the bubonic plague in the mid-sixth century, the economically and politically most developed entities were now the Germanic kingdoms in the east, which were best placed to maintain contact with the continent; kingdoms such as that of Rædwald (?–625), who ruled over the eastern Angles, and whose magnificent grave site is probably that excavated at Sutton Hoo in Suffolk, and the kingdom of the 'men of Kent', or *Cantware*, presided over by Æthelberht. The grave-goods found at Sutton Hoo reveal an East Anglian political culture in which kings and their followers retained close links with Scandinavia and the Baltic. However, the same cache of goods also contains Merovingian gold coins, a Roman-style belt-buckle and helmet, and Byzantine silver, indicative of the on-going appeal of luxury and high-status goods from the Romano-Byzantine world, which were probably reaching Britain via trade routes that stretched through Francia and the Rhineland.[285] Indeed, from the end of the sixth century, a very marked change is discernible in the nature of objects found in Anglo-Saxon burial sites, with Frankish-style jewellery and dress and either imported or copied Roman and Byzatine items coming to replace jewellery 'of a more conspicuously Germanic character'.[286] Likewise, even prior to the king's conversion to Christianity, Æthelberht's Kent appears in many ways to have been a 'sub-Merovingian' kingdom: it is often noted that, as we have seen, the king possessed a Merovingian wife, Bertha, but it is also worth remarking that from around 580 the material culture of the *Cantware* was already drawing much closer to that of Bertha's Christian Frankish kin.[287] Through both political and economic contacts, the eastern kingdoms of lowland Britain were thus forging connections with the Romano-Germanic kingdoms and the Empire of Constantinople beyond. The late sixth century was an age of incipient reintegration.

Moreover, across this fragmented political landscape, there are signs that there had emerged a tradition of 'high kingship' or overlordship which at times was capable of uniting the various Germanic rulers, and which possibly had its origin in phases of cooperation between different war-band leaders in the joint venture of conquest—much as Ammianus Marcellinus describes with respect to the Goths in the fourth century and which Bede records for the continental Saxons in the eighth.

---

[283] R. Faith, *The English Peasantry and the Growth of Lordship* (Leicester, 1997), pp. 1–16.
[284] ibid., p. 10.
[285] Harris (2003), pp. 169–82.
[286] Blair (2005), pp. 39–40.
[287] ibid., p. 40.

Any such tradition is likely to have become increasingly conspicuous as structures of lordship and kingship were consolidated more generally.[288] Completing his *Ecclesiastical History* in 731, the Anglo-Saxon monk Bede looked back to a world of the late sixth and seventh centuries in which dominance (*imperium*) over the various rulers and peoples to the south of the Humber had been achieved by a series of kings. He lists these as Ælle, king of the South Saxons; Ceawlin, king of the West Saxons; Æthelberht of Kent; Rædwald, king of the East Angles; and Eadwine, Oswald, and Oswiu of the 'Northumbrians', ruling from beyond the Humber, but extending their power to the south.[289] In his own day, Bede informs us, all the southern kingdoms 'which reach up to the Humber, together with their various kings, are subject to Æthelbald, king of Mercia'.[290] The later *Anglo-Saxon Chronicle* gives the seven 'high-kings' enumerated by Bede the title of *bretwalda*, or 'ruler of Britain', and in about 700 Adomnán, abbot of Iona, referred to the sixth of Bede's hegemonic rulers, the northern king Oswald, as 'emperor of the whole of Britain' (*totius Britanniae imperator*)—a title suggestive of a measure of imperial emulation.[291]

A broadly similar situation is also discernible in Ireland, and some Irish influence may also have been at work: Adomnán, for example, describes the mid-sixth-century Diarmait, son of Cerbhal, as 'ruler of the whole of Ireland' (*totius Scotiae regnator*).[292] The slightly later Irish legal and literary sources would look back to a world jam-packed with kings (*rí*) or kingdoms (*tuatha*, 'tribes'). Each of these was subordinate to the rule of a 'great king' (*riuri*), who would himself be subject to a 'king of great kings' (*ri riuirech*)—possibly a *rí cóicod* ('king of a fifth'), a ruler of one of the five provinces of Ulster, Leinster, Munster, Connacht, and Meath.[293] Then there were those, such as Diarmait, who claimed to be the *ard rí* ('high king') or *rí Érenn* ('king of Ireland'), inaugurated in the ancient hillfort at Tara in the central province of Meath.[294]

What is clear is that over the course of the seventh century, military and political hegemony in lowland Britain increasingly passed from the eastern kingdoms of Æthelberht and Rædwald to the rulers of the frontier territories of the north and west: namely, the Anglian kingdoms of Bernicia and Deira to the north of the Humber, the Angles of the Midlands known as the *Mierce*, or 'marcher folk' ('Mercians'), and the western Saxons, or *Gewisse*. That is to say, the kings and kingdoms that increasingly gained the upper hand were those best placed to expand their areas of dominance and control at the expense of the Britons and other non-

---

[288] D. P. Kirby, *The Earliest English Kings* (London, 1991), p .16, and C. P. Wormald, 'Bede, the Bretwaldas, and the Origins of the Gens Anglorum', in C. P. Wormald and S. Baxter (eds.), *The Times of Bede* (Oxford, 2006), pp. 106–34, 131–2, and Wormald (2005).
[289] Bede, *Ecclesiastical History*, II, 5.
[290] ibid., V, 23.
[291] See Wormald (2006b), p. 131, n. 1, and Kirby (1991), p. 1. Wormald follows Dumville in preferring the reading *Brytenwalda*. Both *Bretwalda* and *Brytenwalda*, however, he notes, mean the same thing, i.e. 'Britain-ruler'. For Adomnán, see his *Life of St Columba*, I, 1.
[292] Adomnán, *Life of St Columba*, I, 36.
[293] Wormald (2005), pp. 587–8; D. Ó'Corráin, *Early Medieval Ireland 400–1200* (London, 1995).
[294] F. Kelly, *A Guide to Early Irish Law* (Dublin, 1988), p. 18.

Germanic rulers of the British Isles: the Romano-British principalities of the West Country, Cornwall, Wales, the West Midlands; and north, or, beyond the Firth of Forth, the kingdom of the Picts and their westerly neighbours, the Irish of Dál Riata. Through campaigns of aggression against these rivals, the kings of the marchlands were able to acquire a reputation for martial prowess, as well as slaves, booty, and reserves of exploitable terrain with which to attract and reward military retainers, whom they could then turn on their Anglo-Saxon neighbours and foes. Warfare against the Britons and the subjugation and domination of the non-British kingdoms were thus two sides of the same coin. Before elucidating the social and economic ramifications of this phenomenon, however, we must chart (with the aid of Bede's *Ecclesiastical History*) the military and political articulation of marchland expansion.

Foremost amongst those in the ascendant for much of the seventh century were the kings of Bernicia (to the north of the Tees) and Deira (between the Tees and Humber), whose ambitions did much to catalyse the political evolution and military cohesion of the *Mierce*, or Mercians, to their south. The 'Northumbrian' kingdoms as Bede describes them (he has to explain the term, indicating that he had probably coined it himself) were of modest and perhaps relatively recent origin.[295] Both, it should be noted, bear British names.[296] Of the two, Deira is the only part of Northumbria for which there is solid evidence of extensive Germanic settlement in the sixth century, and it was famously the sight of Deiran slave-boys in the marketplace at Rome that had inspired Pope Gregory the Great to send his mission in the 590s.[297] In the late sixth century, by contrast, Bernicia consisted of a small strip of Anglian territory near Lindisfarne and Bamburgh that had supposedly been united some years earlier by a war-band leader called Ida.[298]

What transformed Bernician fortunes was the reign of King Æthelfrith (r. 592–616), who took war to the Britons in a concerted fashion. As Bede records for c.597: 'At this time Æthelfrith ruled the kingdom of the Northumbrians, an exceptionally strong king and one most eager for fame. He ravaged the Britons more extensively than any other English ruler.... For no ruler or king had subjected more land to the English race or settled it, having first either exterminated or conquered the natives.'[299] Æthelfrith's successful campaigns against the Britons to his north aroused the concern of the Irish of Dál Riata, who were also expanding their area of control at British expense. Accordingly, in 603, Áedán mac Gabráin, king of Dál Riata, launched an attack in which the Irish and Bernician armies clashed at the battle of Degsastan. In this engagement the Irish suffered a major defeat, although Æthelfrith's brother, Theobald, was cut down in the melee along with his followers.[300] Æthelfrith next turned his attention to the neighbouring

[295] James (2001), p. 132.
[296] ibid., p. 134.
[297] Charles-Edwards (2003), p. 36.
[298] ibid., p. 36, and A. Williams, *Kingship and Government in Pre-Conquest England* (Basingstoke, 1999), pp. 16–17.
[299] Bede, *Ecclesiastical History*, I, 34.
[300] ibid.

kingdom of Deira, which he conquered around 604, driving into exile the Deiran *ætheling* (or 'prince'), Edwin, son of the first known king of Deira, Ælle. Æthelfrith took Ælle's daughter, Acha, as his second wife. Further expansion at the expense of the Britons then ensued. In 615 Æthelfrith 'won a great victory at Chester, in which a British king, Selyf ap Cynan, was killed and also numerous monks of the great monastery of Bangor-on-Dee'.[301]

In 616, however, Æthelfrith fell in battle against King Rædwald of the eastern Angles, who had given asylum to Edwin, and with whose support the *ætheling* obtained control of both Bernicia and Deira, driving Æthelfrith's sons into exile in Dál Riata and the Pictish lands. Bede, as we have seen, presents Edwin as the fifth king to exercise *imperium* over all the kingdoms to the south, although in Edwin's case he emphasises that the *Cantware* were not subject to his overlordship. Edwin did, however, possess a Kentish wife, indicating a measure of alliance.[302] By 626, Edwin's power was regarded as sufficiently threatening for an attempt to be made by the western Saxons to have him assassinated.[303] Edwin was wounded in the attempt, but once recovered he launched an attack on the *Gewisse* and 'either slew all whom he discovered to have plotted his death or forced them to surrender'.[304] Edwin also extended his power in the north, conquering the British enclave of Elmet.[305]

In many ways it was rivalry between the two royal bloodlines of Bernicia and Deira, and their ambitions to dominate northern Britain, that provided the motivating force behind Northumbrian expansion for much of the early seventh century.[306] The more expansive Northumbrian power became, however, the more reason the enemies of the two Northumbrian kingdoms had to unite against them. In 633 an alliance of Welsh princes under the leadership of Cadwallon, king of Gwynedd, acting with the support of Penda, who had emerged as king of the Mercians, defeated Edwin in battle and slew him. For a year, we are told, it was Cadwallon who was lord of Northumbria, killing the late king's cousin Osric, who had succeeded Edwin in Deira, and Eanfrith, eldest son of Æthelfrith, who had secured the Bernician throne. Eanfrith's half-brother, Oswald, soon avenged his sibling by defeating and killing Cadwallon at the battle of Heavenfield near Hexham. A British revival had perhaps been averted. Extending his control over both kingdoms, it was Oswald who rebuilt Northumbrian power, subjugating, for example, the last remaining territory of the Northumbrian British in Goddodin.[307]

Renewed Northumbrian expansion, however, once more elicited a reaction on the part of the two kingdoms' neighbours. In 642 Bernicia and Deira were again subjected to attack from an alliance of Welsh princes, including the men of Powys, and the

---

[301] Charles-Edwards (2003), p. 38.
[302] Williams (1999), p. 17.
[303] ibid., p. 17.
[304] Bede, *Ecclesiastical History*, II, 9. According to the *Anglo-Saxon Chronicle*, he killed five West Saxon kings in just the one year.
[305] T. Charles-Edwards, 'Wales and Mercia', in M. P. Brown and C. A. Farr, *Mercia: An Anglo-Saxon Kingdom in Europe* (London, 2001), pp. 89–105, p. 93.
[306] Charles-Edwards (2003), p. 38.
[307] Charles-Edwards (2001), p. 93.

Mercian king Penda (the make-up of the alliance conveys a strong sense of the likely focus of Oswald's military ambitions). Unlike in 633, however, Penda would now appear to have been the dominant figure in the coalition.[308] In the battle of Maserfelth, at Oswestry, Oswald and his army were slaughtered; according to Bede, the king's body was then hacked to pieces and his head and hands were stuck on stakes marking the site of the battle.[309] In Bernicia, Oswald's brother Oswiu established himself as king, although there are hints that he may have had some difficulty in doing so, as it was not until a year later that he was able to retrieve the mutilated corpse of his brother.[310] The new king had to face challenges not only from external foes but also rival claimants to the royal title from within his own family. At the same time, he was initially unable to project his power over Deira, where the young prince Oswine, son of Osric, became king.[311] It was not until c.650 that Oswiu felt strong enough to move against Oswine, whose death he arranged in 651.[312]

Even then, however, Oswiu was unable to suppress the Deiran kingship, which passed to Oethelwald, son of Oswald. Although a Bernician, part of Oethelwald's appeal to the lords, or *ealdormen*, of Deira may have lain in the fact that he had opposed his uncle's rule in the neighbouring kingdom. Nevertheless, in the 650s, Oswiu's power and authority were clearly on the rise: his relations with the Irish of Dál Riata and the Britons of Strathclyde seem to have been good, and in 653 his nephew, Talorcan, son of Eanfrith, was made king of the Picts.[313] An interest in Irish alliances and affairs is suggested by the fact that Oswiu was himself married to a princess of the Uí Néill, the principal royal house of Ireland, which, since 637, had held a monopoly on the kingship of Tara that they would maintain down to the end of the tenth century.[314] As a Christian, Oswiu persuaded Sighbert, king of the eastern Angles, to convert, and in 653 he secured the marriage of his daughter to Peada, son of Penda, whom the latter had established as king over the 'Middle Angles'. Peada too soon converted.

Although not included on Bede's list of rulers exercising *imperium*, by the early 650s Penda and his Mercians were clearly the dominant power to the south of the Humber, and had evidently built up a considerable following among the West Britons by virtue of the king's active opposition to Bernician expansion. We can probably explain Bede's omission of him on the grounds that Penda was a pagan whose military focus was repeatedly set on Bernicia and Deira, whereas Bede was both a Christian monk determined to reveal the workings of divine providence and a patriotic Northumbrian. There are hints, however, in the writings of Bede and the (much) later British sources that Penda may even have rendered Oswiu his tributary after besieging the king at Bamburgh, sharing out the spoils with his Welsh allies.[315] Any consolidation of Bernician power, therefore, is likely to have been a cause of concern to the Mercians. Accordingly, in 655 Penda once more summoned his

---

[308] Charles Edwards, (2001), p. 93. [309] Bede, *Ecclesiastical History*, III, 12.
[310] Williams (1999), p. 18. [311] Bede, *Ecclesiastical History*, III, 14.
[312] ibid. [313] Kirby (1991), p. 94; Charles-Edwards (2003), p. 52.
[314] Charles-Edwards (2003), p. 32.
[315] Bede, *Ecclesiastical History*, III, 16–17; *Historia Britonnum*, in D. Whitelock *English Historical Documents: Volume One: c.500-1042* (London, 1979), *English Historical Documents*, I, p. 263.

British allies and clients, as well as those Anglo-Saxon rulers who were subject to him. Bede alludes only to the latter, describing how Penda had at his disposal 'thirty legions of battle-hardened warriors commanded by the royal war-leaders (*duces regii*)', by whom we must assume he means allied or subject kings.[316] According to the *Historia Britonnum*, he was also accompanied by the king of Gwynned and other Welsh princes.[317] Conspicuous amongst Penda's allies was Oethelwald, king of Deira.[318]

In the clash of arms that ensued at Winwæd, near Leeds, in 655, however, it was Oswiu and his warriors who prevailed: 'And Oswiu killed Penda on the field of Gaí [*'the enclosure of the young warrior'*]', our British source records, 'and the kings of the Britons were killed who had gone out with Penda.'[319] It was not necessarily to Oethelwald's credit that just before battle had been joined he and his followers had withdrawn 'and awaited the outcome in a place of safety', presumably so as to claim the Bernician kingship should Oswiu fall.[320]

Oswiu's victory at Winwæd initiated a renewed phase of Bernician expansion. Mercia was taken in hand and Christianity established there. The following year, Penda's son, Peada, was murdered, apparently on the instigation of his wife, Oswiu's daughter Alhflead. According to Bede. 'King Oswiu ruled over the Mercian race, as well as the rest of the southern kingdoms, for three years after King Penda was killed. Oswiu also subjected the greater part of the Pictish race to the dominion of the English.'[321] Oethelwald, we may imagine, was done away with, and after 655 Deira was subjected to the rule of Oswiu's son Ahlfrith, whom, after a dispute, Oswiu replaced with Ahlfrith's half-brother Ecgfrith. Upon Oswiu's death in 670, Ecgfrith (*r.*670–85) succeeded him to the throne of Bernicia, making his younger brother, Ælfwine, the king of Deira. When Ælfwine died in battle in 679, Deira was finally subsumed once and for all under Bernician royal rule. As a result, it has been observed, 'if Bede is right, then Oswiu had a wider power in these islands than any ruler until James I and VI'.[322]

The battle of Winwæd thus heralded the emergence of something approximating to a Bernician *imperium* to the north of the Humber, rooted in the conquest of first Britons and then Picts and the subjugation of the Irish of Dál Riata, from whom, according to Bede, Oswiu was able to extract tribute, a state of affairs that Ecgfrith was able to perpetuate.[323] It was also probably Ecgfrith who subjugated the north British kingdom of Rheged, located to the south of the Solway Firth.[324] To the west, Edwin had already conquered both Anglesey and the Isle of Man, 'offering the Northumbrians the prospect of using sea power along the

---

[316] Bede, *Ecclesiastical History*, III, 34.
[317] Charles-Edwards (2001), p. 93; *Historia Britonnum*, in *EHD*, I, p. 263.
[318] Bede, *Ecclesiastical History*, III, 24.
[319] *Historia Britonnum*, in *EHD*, I, p. 263.
[320] Bede, *Ecclesiastical History*, III, 34.
[321] ibid.
[322] Campbell in Campbell (ed.) (1982), p. 54.
[323] Charles-Edwards (2003), p. 42.
[324] James (2001), p. 135.

coasts of both western Britain and eastern Ireland', and Oswiu and Ecgfrith are likely to have restored control over these territories.[325] Indeed, in 684, Ecgfrith even sent an army into Ireland, led by his military commander, Berht, who attacked the territory of Fínsnechtae Fledach, king of Tara; according to the *Chronicle of Ireland*, Berht 'laid waste the plain of Brega, including many churches'.[326] It has been suggested that this raid may have been conducted to pursue British refugees from the fall of the Rheged, the activities of whose warbands along the east coast of Ireland are possibly recorded in the *Chronicle of Ulster* between 682 and 709.[327] That it was meant, however, as a straightforward projection of power aimed at the territory of a fellow 'high king' is just as likely, with the Irish Sea being turned into a 'Northumbrian lake'. Just as the seventh-century Frankish ascendancy contributed to the breaking down of social and political barriers between territory that had once been Roman and that which had not, so too did Northumbrian hegemony.

The kings of Northumbria had long been characterised by what might be termed 'imperial pretensions'. Bede tells us (as noted in Chapter Five) that Edwin 'would have carried before him the type of standard which the Romans call a *tufa*'.[328] Likewise, the archaeological traces of the king's palace at Yeavering, to the north of Hadrian's Wall, have revealed some interesting Romanising features. Near the great hall, for example, stood a wooden grandstand in the form of a Roman theatre with seating for over three hundred people. The timber hall itself was plastered on the outside and the plaster scored so as to simulate the effects of masonry. This was, to all intents and purposes, what might be termed 'mock-Roman cladding'.[329] Such pretensions reached their height in 664, when Oswiu presided over a Church council convened to consider the dating of Easter. At this synod, Oswiu declared in person in favour of the Roman computation and against 'Celtic' practice, and wrote to Pope Vitalian in Rome, in a quasi-imperial fashion, informing him of his decision.[330] In 680 the chief prelate of the Northumbrian Church, Bishop Wilfrid of York, attended a council in Rome summoned by Pope Agatho at which he claimed to speak on behalf of 'the whole northern part of Britain and Ireland, together with the islands inhabited by the English and British peoples, as well as the Irish and Picts'.[331] If we are looking for a likely point of origin for lofty royal claims and imperial pretensions to the title of *bretwalda* as remembered in the *Anglo-Saxon Chronicle*, then this is it. Only in 685 was Bernician ambition finally checked when, at Dún Nechtain (*Nechtansmere*) Ecgfrith's cousin, Bruide, king of the Picts, defeated his forces and killed him in battle. This engagement effectively marked the end of Northumbrian aspirations to northern *imperium*.[332] The kingdom

---

[325] Charles-Edwards (2003), pp. 41, 43.
[326] ibid., p. 35. See also Bede, *Ecclesiastical History*, IV, 26.
[327] James (2001), p. 135.
[328] Bede, *Ecclesiastical History*, II, 16.
[329] See James (2001), pp. 134–5.
[330] Bede, *Ecclesiastical History*, III, 25 and III, 29.
[331] ibid., V, 19.
[332] Charles-Edwards (2003), pp. 44–5. See also Bede, *Ecclesiastical History*, IV, 26.

nevertheless remained a force to be reckoned with and, under the rule of Ecgfrith's half-Irish half-brother, Aldfrith (r.685–704), its court and monasteries (to which we shall return) pioneered a startling cultural and artistic revival.

To the south of the Humber, Bernician dominance had waned much earlier, primarily due to a rapid Mercian recovery. In 658, Bede tells us, 'the leaders (*duces*) of the Mercian people, Immin, Eafa and Eadberht, rebelled against King Oswiu and set up as their king Wulfhere, Penda's young son, whom they had kept concealed; and having driven out the princes [probably *ealdormen*] of the foreign king, they boldly recovered their land and their liberty at the same time.'[333] Wulfhere and his followers set about restoring the position of political and military dominance to the south of the Humber that his father had built up for the *Mierce* between 633 and 655. By the end of the 650s the area around London (*Lundenwic*) was under Mercian control and by the mid-660s both the East Saxons and the East Angles had been restored to Mercian overlordship.[334]

By the early 670s, there are signs that Mercian power had extended into the Thames Valley, Kent, and the land of the southern Saxons as far the Isle of Wight, applying mounting military pressure on the West Saxons, or *Gewisse*; such that, when Wulfhere arranged for the the baptism of Æthelwealh, the first Christian king of the South Saxons, he was in a position to reward him with the Isle of Wight and parts of Hampshire, territories that the West Saxons would have regarded as their own.[335] Wulfhere appears to have been less successful against the Bernicians: in 675 an attack on his northern neighbour ended in defeat, as a result of which, according to the *Life of Wilfrid*, Ecgfrith was able to exact tribute from the Mercians and, according to Bede, 'ruled in peace for some time more widely'.[336] In 679, however, Wulfhere's brother and successor, Æthelred (r.675–704), defeated the Bernicians at the battle of the Trent, as a result of which Lindsey was returned to Mercian rule and Mercian supremacy over the south confirmed.[337] If much of the seventh century had been characterised by Northumbrian dominance, the eighth century would belong to Mercia.[338]

9.12 THE DYNAMICS OF POWER IN SEVENTH-CENTURY BRITAIN

The period of Mercian ascendancy, we should note, was rooted in an anti-Northumbrian alliance between Penda's *Mierce* and the princes of the Britons.[339] This is important, as it is all too easy when tracing the history of Britain in the sixth and seventh centuries to treat the Britons and Picts as little more than passive sword-

---

[333] Bede, *Ecclesiastical History*, III, 24.
[334] Williams (1999), p. 20.
[335] ibid., pp. 20–21.
[336] *Life of Bishop Wilfrid*, ch. 20, and Bede, *Ecclesiastical History*, II, 5: see Charles-Edwards (2001), p. 98, n. 47.
[337] Williams (1999), pp. 21–3; Charles-Edwards (2001), p. 94.
[338] See Wormald (1982) in Campbell (ed.) (1982), pp. 101–31.
[339] Charles-Edwards (2001), p. 93.

fodder or sullen tributaries boosting the prestige and coffers of active, expansive, and vigorous Anglo-Saxon kings. Certainly, 'Germanic' rulers expanded their realms at British and Pictish expense. In that respect, Penda and his 'marcher folk' were no exception: it was probably during Penda's rule that the Welsh lands in the West Midlands such as Herefordshire, Shropshire, and Cheshire came under Mercian control.[340] But as the events of 633, 642, and 655, and the Pictish victory at Dún Nechtain in 685, remind us, the kings and warriors of the Britons, Picts, and Irish of Dál Riata played an active and often decisive part in the reconfiguration of power in lowland Britain.

What did the overlordship established by the Mercians and confirmed in 679 at the battle of the Trent actually consist of? This question is not entirely pointless; in Ireland, for example, the 'high kingship' of Tara seems to have conferred little more than a primacy of honour, and there are few signs with respect to the Mercians in the late seventh century of the sort of imperial ambitions associated with the Northumbrians and which the term *bretwalda* was probably originally meant to convey. Such evidence as there is points towards varying degrees of domination, subjugation, and control that are perhaps best thought of in terms of concentric rings.[341] At the outer ring (what Charles-Edwards has referred to as 'light domination') was probably the sort of authority that Penda came to exercise over his Welsh allies: an expectation that they would answer a call to arms, and would not give asylum to the king's enemies.[342] Further in, there were those kings from whom tribute could be demanded in treasure, render, or cattle, either in order to buy peace in the aftermath of a defeat or on a more regular basis. As the *Life of Wilfrid* reveals, the payment of tribute (especially if regular or sustained) was a clear marker of dependent status in the sources, whilst the royal Northumbrian site at Yeavering possessed a sort of corrall at which cattle paid as tribute could have been kept.[343] Next were those royal households in whose succession to the Crown the 'overlord' was deemed to have the right to intervene, or the contours of whose boundaries he was able to redraw, as evidenced by Wulfhere's 'gift' of the Isle of the Wight to the king of the South Saxons. Last were those kings whose kingdoms were subsumed within that of their overlord and who, as a result, were reduced to the status of 'sub-kings' (*subreguli*) or *ealdormen*, maintaining something of royal rank but not power; a system of ranked kingship rather more similar at its 'bottom rungs' than its higher ones to that encountered in the Irish sources.[344] In a charter witnessed and confirmed by King Wulfhere c.672, for example, Frithuwald, *subregulus* of the men of Surrey, made over a piece of land to the monastery of Chertsey. Similar charters survive from the 'sub-king' of the *Hwicce*, and the 'men of the Lindsey' appear to have maintained a 'sub-king' under Mercian rule well into the eighth century.[345]

---

[340] James (2001), p. 145.
[341] Charles-Edwards (2001), pp. 94–5.
[342] Charles-Edwards (2003), p. 42.
[343] B. Hope-Taylor, *Yeavering: An Anglo-British Centre of Early Northumbria* (London, 1977).
[344] James (2001), p. 119.
[345] *EHD*, I, p. 479, and James (2001), pp. 118–19. Note, however, the *caveat* of Wormald (2006a), pp. 132–4. See also Campbell (ed.) (1982), pp. 58–9.

The level of 'middling' domination—the exaction of tribute in an organised and regular manner—is probably embedded in a curious document known as the 'Tribal Hidage', which lists the names of over thirty territories and peoples to the south of the Humber, attributing to each a number of taxable land units, or 'hides': so, for example, 'the area first called Mercia—30,000 hides . . . the Elmet dwellers 600 hides . . . the Hwicce 7,000 hides . . . West Saxons 100,000 hides'.[346] That this document is most likely Mercian in origin, although not necessarily Mercian in the form in which we have it, is indicated by its coverage and internal logic: nearly all the peoples listed, it has been noted, lie within an area that had been brought under Mercian control by the end of the seventh century from the Humber to the Thames.[347] Moreover, the thirty or so peoples and regions listed are reminiscent of the thirty *duces regii* ('royal battle-leaders') who, according to Bede, answered Penda's summons in 655.[348] It seems, therefore, that the document most probably originated as a Mercian 'tribute list'. Bede appears to have had access to a similar document when writing his *Ecclesiastical History*, where he too enumerates the number of 'hides' covered by the kingdom of the Mercians, as also of the Isle of Wight.[349]

Kings in seventh-century Britain were still overwhelmingly men of war. As in Merovingian Francia, rulers were expected to lead their armies into battle, and it is striking how many died doing so. Across the forty years of the early to mid-seventh century, of the six kings who ruled over the East Angles, five died violently.[350] Early medieval warfare was always an uncertain business, and the relatively small size of armies in seventh-century Britain made warfare there even more so: as a late seventh-century law of the West Saxon king Ine decreed, 'Up to seven men we call thieves, between seven and thirty-five a war-band, more than thirty-five an army'.[351] Even kings who were victorious in battle might yet fall victim to assassination or plots orchestrated by their rivals. This was a world where, to adapt the words of Thomas Hobbes, no king was so weak he could not kill another.

Crucially, however, the death of a king did not necessarily mean the death, or even eclipse, of his kingdom. As in Merovingian Francia (and in relative contrast to Visigothic Spain), 'royalness' was deemed to inhere in the blood and passed through the male line. Likewise, in seventh-century England there was no assumption of primogeniture (although, under ecclesiastical influence, it would begin to emerge as a factor). As a result, upon the death of a ruler, his kindred or chief retainers (*ealdormen*) could rally behind whoever amongst those eligible to rule was deemed, quite literally, to offer the best fighting chance; a process that can be seen at work in the choice of Wulfhere to rule Mercia in 658. Unlike Merovingian Francia, this was no place for a boy-king. The corollary, however, was that to enjoy

---

[346] See the table in P. Featherstone, 'The Tribal Hidage and the Ealdormen of Mercia', in Brown and Farr (2001), pp. 23–34, p. 24.
[347] Campbell (ed.) (1982), p. 59.
[348] Bede *Ecclesiastical History*, III, 24.
[349] ibid.
[350] Campbell (ed.) (1982), p. 56.
[351] *Ine's Law*, 13.1, in Attenborough (1922), pp. 40–41.

a modicum of security on the throne, kings had to exile their enemies and, in particular, rivals of royal blood with a claim to their title. Thus, during the reign of Æthelfrith over Bernicia and Deira, the young prince Edwin lived as an exile at the courts of King Cadfan of Gwynedd, Rædwald of the East Angles, and Æthelberht of Kent; Oswald and Osric obtained asylum amongst the Irish, and Eanfrith amongst the Picts.

Similar periods of exile are likely to have characterised the experience of these princes' followers, as likewise of those retainers of kings who had died in battle. Indeed, the miserable plight of the lordless man in exile is a major preoccupation of Anglo-Saxon literature. 'So I, often wretchedly anxious', the poem known as *The Wanderer* declares, 'separated from my noble kinsfolk, have had to fasten my heart with fetters ever since, years ago, the darkness of the earth enfolded my generous and loving lord and I, despondent, travelled away, oppressed by wintery anxiety, over the ambit of the waves; full of sorrow I was seeking the hall of a treasure-giving lord where, whether far or near, I might find the one who would acknowledge my love in the mead-hall or would comfort me in my friendlessness and win me over with good things.' 'Often', the poet goes on to relate, 'when grief and sleep combined together enchain the wretched solitary man, it seems to him in his imagination that he is embracing and kissing his lord and laying hands and head on his knee, just as at times previously in days of old he enjoyed the gift-throne.' 'Him', we are told, 'the paths of exile preoccupy, not coiled gold.'[352]

'The paths of exile' were dangerous places: as in Francia and the Langobard kingdom, the basis of Anglo-Saxon justice was the kin-based blood feud. The traveller on the road, distant from home, could not look to the protective embrace of his kinsmen to offer the deterrent of vengeance should he be harmed. One of our earliest Anglo-Saxon law codes, dating from the late seventh century, records that 'if a man from afar, or a stranger, quits the road, and neither shouts, nor blows a horn, he shall be assumed to be a thief, [and as such] may either be slain or put to ransom'.[353] For the young prince ambitious to be king, by contrast, exile offered the chance to make allies, prove his worth in war and attract followers. It was during Edwin's exile at the court of King Rædwald, for example, that the *ætheling* persuaded Rædwald to march against Æthelfrith and help him gain the crowns of Bernicia and Deira. Likewise, Bede reports how in c.685 'Cædwalla, a young and most warlike prince of the *Gewisse*, being an exile from his own land, came with an army and slew King Æthelwealh [of the South Saxons], wasting the kingdom with fierce slaughter and devastation.'[354] Earlier, according to the *Life of Wilfrid*, Cædwalla had 'wandered in the desert places of the Chilterns and the Weald ... until he was powerful enough to overcome his enemies and get a kingdom by slaying or subduing his foes'.[355]

---

[352] *The Wanderer*, tr. Bradley (1982), pp. 322–5.
[353] *Wihtred*, ch. 28, in Attenborough (1922), pp. 30–31.
[354] Bede, *Ecclesiastical History*, IV, 15.
[355] *Life of Bishop Wilfrid*, chs. 40 and 42.

The key to political success, both for a reigning king or a royal exile, was military victory. In order to establish himself as a figure to be reckoned with, therefore, a prince needed to acquire a reputation for martial prowess and for generosity to his companions-in-arms. It was this that would draw to him a loyal following of military retainers whose devotion, commitment, and bravery constituted the surest hope of future success. Seventh-century Anglo-Saxon society was an increasingly aristocratic one whose culture was shaped and determined by the ethos of the warband. Youth (roughly between the ages of fifteen and twenty-five) was a 'testing time' when the young warrior staked his claim to lordship. At the level of the elite, this was also an international (or at least trans-regional) society, in which ambitious warriors of good birth could move from court to court in search of adventure and reward. The early eighth-century *Life of St Guthlac*, for example, records of Peanwealh, a Mercian boy of royal lineage, that 'when therefore his strength had increased in his adolescence, and a noble love of command began to glow in his young breast, remembering the strong deeds of former heroes, he gathered round him bands of followers, and with a changed disposition, as if awakened from sleep, gave himself to arms.... He laid waste the towns and residences, villages and fortresses of his opponents with fire and sword, and brought together comrades from diverse races on all sides and collected immense booty.'[356] Similarly, Bede records of the young King Oswine of Deira (r.642–51) that he 'was tall and handsome, pleasant of speech, courteous in manner and bountiful to nobles and commoners alike; so it came about that he was beloved by all because of the royal dignity which showed itself in his character, his appearance and his actions; and noblemen from almost every kingdom flocked to serve him as retainers.'[357]

As already evident from the language of *The Wanderer*, and as is very clear from the heroic poem *Beowulf*, the emotional and personal bond between lord (especially royal lord) and retainer was celebrated and idealised in the self-glorifying literature of the Anglo-Saxon elite as representing the crux of aristocratic society. Not everybody lived up to that ideal: it was one of his retainers who ultimately betrayed King Oswine to his Bernician rival Oswiu. Nevertheless, the ideal was more than mere fiction. Bede, for example, describes the assassination attempt on King Edwin in c.626. The would-be assassin, we are told, 'suddenly leapt up, drew a sword from beneath his cloak, and made a rush at the king. Lilla, a most devoted royal retainer (*minister Regis*) saw this, but not having a sword interposed his own body to receive the blow.'[358]

The aristocratic nature of seventh-century Anglo-Saxon society comes across very strongly from both the literary and legal evidence. The law codes (to which we shall return) describe a highly ranked world dominated by the king, his attendants, and the *ealdormen* of the kingdom. Bede confirms that by the end of the seventh century an Anglo-Saxon nobility had emerged whose members were recognisable as such by both their peers and their social 'inferiors'. In his account of the battle of

---

[356] Felix, *Life of Guthlac*, chs. 16–17 in *EHD*, I, p. 771.
[357] Bede, *Ecclesiastical History*, III, 14.
[358] ibid., II, 9.

the Trent in 679, Bede relates that a warrior retainer of the Northumbrian king, a young man (*iuvenis*) by the name of Imma, was discovered alive amongst the corpses of his comrades. He was captured by some enemy soldiers, who took him to their lord, who is described as a companion (*comes*) of the Mercian king Æthelred. When asked who he was, Imma pretended to be 'a poor peasant and married' (*rusticus . . . et pauper atque uxureo vinculo conligatus*), thereby attempting to pass himself off as a non-combatant. Eventually, however, his captors 'realized by his appearance, his bearing, and his speech, that he was not of common stock as he had said, but of the nobles' (*ex vultu et habitu et sermonibus eius, quia non erat de paupere vulgo, ut dixerat, sed nobilibus*).[359] As a result, a Mercian royal retainer (*minister regis*) declared that he was minded to kill him as legitimate vengeance for the deaths of his brothers and kinsmen at the hands of the Northumbrians. Fortunately for Imma, the retainer took him to London (*Lundenwic*) instead and sold him to a Frisian slave-trader.

The archaeological evidence for lowland Britain also records growing social stratification over the course of the seventh century, with a return to more structured patterns of settlement and (as we shall see) the re-emergence of estate centres.[360] Although the social hierarchies within these settlements may appear comparatively shallow, the evidence of survey archaeology and rural sites must be placed alongside the extraordinary opulence of the royal burial at Sutton Hoo, or the remarkable collection of what may have been gold stripped from the dead in battle, or 'geld' demanded from a defeated foe, unearthed in Staffordshire in 2009 (Figs. 13 and 14).[361] This was a world in which polarisations of wealth could be stark.

How, one might reasonably ask, were such polarisations of wealth, or assemblages of treasure, achieved in the context of an agrarian economy dominated by pastoral and mixed farming? 'Until the late seventh century', it has been noted, 'there is no sign that cereals were any longer produced for the market, nor of a currency or marketing system that could have put them there.'[362] How could the renders and food rent comprising the *feorm* of the itinerant lord, or the tribute of defeated kings, possibly have been translated into the ostentatious luxury of Sutton Hoo?[363] Was the Anglo-Saxon nobility to which Bede alludes with respect to Imma really comparable to the haughty elite of late seventh-century Francia? Or, in a broader European context, were Imma and his kind simply socially aspirant parvenus?

In order to understand the possible relationship between the 'productive' economy of early Anglo-Saxon Britain and the 'economy of display' we encounter at Sutton Hoo and other high-status sites, it is necessary to return to the situation before the coming of the Saxons. In the first century BC the geographer Strabo had recorded that the Britons exported not only corn but also gold, silver, iron, cattle,

---

[359] Bede, *Ecclesiastical History*, IV, 22.
[360] Wickham (2005), pp. 341–2.
[361] Campbell (1982), pp. 32–3; K. Leahy and R. Bland, *The Staffordshire Hoard* (London, 2009).
[362] Faith (2009), p. 26.   [363] Faith (1997), pp. 1–2.

Fig. 13 Helmet from Sutton Hoo (by kind permission of the British Museum)

animal hides, slaves, and dogs.[364] His contemporary, Pomponius Mela, described the inhabitants of Britain as 'rich in herds and lands'.[365] Even in the late third century AD, when lowland Britain was home to a vibrant villa economy, bustling cities, and intensive arable farming, an imperial panegyricist felt obliged to comment on the 'numerous pasturelands in which it [the island] rejoices'.[366] In post-Roman conditions, as we have seen, the emphasis on stockraising had become still more pronounced. The point is, however, that the climate and ecological resources of the island appear to have been such that it was capable of raising and supporting a great deal of livestock of high quality. In the eighth century, Bede too remarked that Britain was possessed of 'good pasturage for cattle and beasts of burden'.[367]

If *feorm* had begun as an obligation on the part of those subjected to the power of itinerant war-band leaders to feed them, with the stabilisation of lordship and, above all, kingship that is evident in lowland Britain from the late sixth century, the demands made of peasants are likely to have become increasingly regularised. Those peasants in the vicinity brought tribute and renders into royal centres (or 'vills') or more imposing settlements, such as Yeavering, irrespective of the presence or

---

[364] J. R. Maddicott, 'Prosperity and Power in the Age of Bede and Beowulf', *Proceedings of the British Academy* 117 (2002), pp. 49–71, p. 50.
[365] ibid.   [366] ibid.   [367] Bede, *Ecclesiastical History*, I, 1.

Fig. 14 The Staffordshire Hoard (by kind permission of the Birmingham Museum and Art Gallery)

absence of the king.³⁶⁸ Such a regularisation of demands is strongly suggested by the 'Tribal Hidage'. Similarly, in the late seventh-century West Saxon 'Ine's Law' it was decreed that the king could demand 'as food rent from every ten hides' no less than 'ten vats of honey, 300 loaves, twelve ambers of Welsh ale, thirty ambers of clear ale, two full-grown cows or ten wethers, ten geese, twenty hens, ten cheeses, a full amber of butter, five geese, twenty pounds of fodder, and one hundred eels.'³⁶⁹ Crucially, the non-perishable component of such regularised renders and tribute could be turned into storable and exchangeable surplus: in particular, sheep could be sheared and their wool woven or knitted into cloth, and cattle could be skinned and their hides turned into leather for shoes or armour.³⁷⁰ The weaving of cloth or the making of leather could perhaps be demanded of a king's subjects. 'Ine's Law', for example, decreed that 'white cloth paid as rent by each household shall be worth sixpence'.³⁷¹ Such tasks could certainly be imposed on the slaves who feature

---

³⁶⁸ Faith (1997), pp. 15–16.
³⁶⁹ *Ine's Law*, 70.1, in Attenborough (1922), p. 58.
³⁷⁰ See discussion in Maddicott (2002), and also J. Campbell, 'Production and Distribution in Early and Middle Saxon England', in T. Pestell and K. Ulmschneider (eds.), *Markets in Early Medieval Europe: Trading and 'Productive' Sites, 650–850* (Macclesfield, 2003), pp. 12–19.
³⁷¹ *Ine's* Law, 44.1, in Attenborough (1922), p. 50.

prominently in the Anglo-Saxon legal sources, many of whom are likely to have started life as—or to have been descended from—prisoners of war, either captured by conquest or themselves handed over by way of tribute.[372]

Slaves, skins, wool, leather, and cloth were amongst the most significant potential commodities readily extractable from the largely pastoral economy that had developed in post-Roman conditions in lowland Britain. Crucially, these were commodities for which, in the seventh century, there existed an expanding market across the Channel in the northern Frankish world. A market for Anglo-Saxon and British slaves is already apparent from the presence of the Deiran slave-boys whom Gregory supposedly encountered in Rome, and its existence is confirmed by the activities of the Frisian slave-trader to whom Imma was sold. Anglian slaves were certainly on sale in northern Francia in the seventh century, where many of them 'were put to work on the estates of the new monastic foundations'.[373] Moreover, the high value that could be attached to good-quality textiles in Francia is revealed by Gregory of Tours, who describes how King Theuderic I encouraged his men, before a raid on the Auvergne, by declaring to them, 'I will lead you into a country where you may find gold and silver as much as you desire, whence you may take cattle, slaves, and clothing in abundance.'[374] There are indications that, by Bede's day, the Anglo-Saxons may have specialised in the manufacture of purple-dyed cloth, and that, by the end of the eighth century, the high quality of Anglo-Saxon textiles had secured them a significant continental market.[375]

The configuration of the early Anglo-Saxon economy, as also of early Anglo-Saxon lordship and kingship, was thus remarkably well suited to enable rulers to engage with and profit from the commercial expansion and monetisation of the seventh-century north Frankish world. Kings and rulers could draw upon the *feorm* of their subjects and the tribute of their foes to engage in commercialised exchange with Frankish and Frisian traders through the 'wics' that proliferated on the eastern and southern shores of Britain, as well as on the Frankish side of the Channel.[376] In the late seventh century, in *Lundenwic*, the Kentish kings Hlothere and Eadric maintained a *wicgerefa*, or 'wic-reeve', who appears to have imposed tolls on those trading there.[377] Much of the wealth that the Anglo-Saxon elite was able to derive from this expansion of trade is likely to have ended up transformed into jewellery, silver plate, and gold.

As the Anglo-Saxon kingdoms were drawn into the commercialising economy of northern Francia, so too, from the 630s, do we begin to find evidence for the

---

[372] There was also self-sale into slavery by the Anglo-Saxon poor: see Faith (1997), p. 61. For textual and archaeological evidence of royal or aristocratic households as possible centres of production, utilising the labour of slaves, see Campbell (2003), pp. 16–17.

[373] Faith (1997), p. 47.

[374] Gregory of Tours, *Decem Libri Historiae*, III, 11; Maddicott (2002), p. 62.

[375] Maddicott (2002), pp. 55–8.

[376] ibid., p. 50. Note the evidence for livestock being drawn into *wics* in H. Hamerow, 'Agrarian Production and the *Emporia* of Mid-Saxon England ca. AD 650–850', in Henning (ed.) (2007), I, pp. 219–32. See also P. J. Crabtree, 'Agricultural Innovation and Socio-Economic Change in Early Medieval Europe: Evidence for Britain and France', *World Archaeology* 42.1 (2010), pp. 122–36.

[377] Maddicott (2002), p. 65.

minting of Anglo-Saxon coins. Intially, these took the form of golden *tremisses* (worth a third of a *solidus*), modelled on those of the Franks. In the 670s, when the Frankish coinage shifted to silver, so too did the Anglo-Saxon. Continental coinage, however, continued to circulate in the eastern and southern Anglo-Saxon kingdoms.[378] This is important, in that the evidence of coin finds reveals two striking facts that cast into stark relief the extraordinary precocity of the developing Anglo-Saxon commercial economy. First, the Anglo-Saxon silver pennies, or *sceattas*, minted *c.*680–740, and above all those minted *c.*710–40, were clearly produced on a very large scale: thus, it has been noted, they 'constitute the commonest single finds of any pre-Conquest coin series' in England, whilst 'the volume of the currency in these decades was greater than it would ever be again before 1200'.[379] Second, and in spite of that, silver coins minted in Frankish Dorestadt (near Utrecht) have been found in far greater number in England than have Anglo-Saxon *sceattas* in the Low Countries.[380] The clear indication is that, in modern terms, those Anglo-Saxon kingdoms engaged in continental trade enjoyed a significantly positive 'balance of payments'—the Franks bought more from them than they did from the Franks.[381] That the economy of the southern and eastern Anglo-Saxon kingdoms was more highly commercialised than that of northern Francia by the early eighth century is also indicated by the greater density and size of 'wics' along the English coastline.[382] Even the return of the bubonic plague in the late seventh century was not able to reverse the advances that had been made.[383] Indeed—as we see in the fourteenth century—in that depopulation may have resulted in a higher standard of living and increased *per-capita* income for those left behind, the plague may even have served to contribute to a quickening of trade.[384] The convergence of Frankish demand and Anglo-Saxon supply would thus seem to have had startling consequences.

9.13 BISHOPS, 'BOOKLAND', AND THE *GENS ANGLORUM*

The spread of Christianity also had a major role to play in this ongoing process of economic transformation. The Augustinian mission had run into considerable difficulties by the middle of the seventh century, and the evangelisation of the Anglo-Saxons was only really salvaged by an injection of new blood from the Church in Ireland and Dál Riata, especially the monastic centre of Iona. In Ireland, as we have seen, the Church had grown accustomed to dealing with tribal societies,

---

[378] M. Blackburn, 'Money and Coinage', in Fouracre (2005), p. 673; M. Blackburn, 'Productive Sites and the Pattern of Coin Loss in England, 600–1180', in Pestell and Ulmschneider (2003), pp. 20–36.
[379] Maddicott (2002), p. 52, and Blair (2005), pp. 256–7.
[380] Maddicott (2002), pp. 52–3.
[381] Grierson and Blackburn (1986), p. 150.
[382] Maddicott (2002), pp. 50–52.
[383] J. Maddicott, 'Plague in Seventh-Century England', in Little (2007), pp. 171–214.
[384] Campbell (2003), p. 12.

The Princes of the Western Nations 371

and had been able to accommodate itself to the contours of political power as it encountered them on the ground. Irish churchmen were thus arguably in a much stronger position to relate to the essentially tribal politics of seventh-century lowland Britain than were the Roman missionaries of the first generation, with their vision of a Church structured around now defunct and largely abandoned Roman *civitates*. It was whilst in Iona that the Northumbrian exile Oswald had converted to Christianity, and when he obtained the throne of Bernicia in 634, he threw his weight behind the Ionan missionary and monk Aidan, who made great progress amongst his subjects. Under Bernician overlordship, the kings of the West Saxons, or *Gewisse*, the East Saxons, and the 'Middle Angles' converted. Crucially, the death of Penda in 655 marked the demise of the last great pagan king. As we have seen, his son, Peada, was already a Christian, and under Mercian overlordship the South Saxons too embraced the faith. Around 686, the last pagan stronghold of the Isle of Wight gave way when the West Saxon king Cædwalla butchered its inhabitants. Two years later, this pious king gave up his crown and travelled to Rome, where he died a pilgrim.[385] An influx of talent from the Frankish Church also helped to consolidate the faith.[386]

Crucially, the period from *c.*650 was also associated with an expansion of monasteries such as Columbanus and his followers had founded in Francia, closely bound to royal patronage and aristocratic kindreds.[387] 'Monastic settlements and relationships of proprietorship and allegiance centred on them became', in short, 'the framework around which ecclesiastical organization was built.'[388] On a cultural level, these monasteries, such as Whitby (founded in 657), Monkwearmouth (674), and Jarrow (680/1), soon came to serve as centres of Christian learning, helping to reintegrate the Anglo-Saxon kingdoms into a broader Romano-Christian culture. It was at the monastery of St Peter at Monkwearmouth, for example, that the Latin-writing ecclesiastical historian Bede was enrolled as a monk. The proliferation of monasteries also served to disseminate and resurrect Roman and continental traditions in architecture, not least that of building in stone.[389] But above all, on a material level, as in Ireland and Francia, the establishment and expansion of monastic centres served to give a major (and probably decisive) spur to economic development, acting as fixed centres of population, demand, and specialised production.[390] There are signs that around the monasteries areas of directly cultivated arable land emerged, signalling the beginning of a shift away from 'mixed farming' and a return to more intensive (and socially coercive) forms of agriculture under monastic lordship.[391] The highly religious iconography on much early Anglo-Saxon coinage would also suggest that the emergent monasteries played a major role in the

---

[385] Bede, *Ecclesiastical History*, IV, 16.
[386] J. Campbell, 'The First Century of Christianity in England', in *idem., Essays in Anglo-Saxon History* (1986), pp. 49–68, p. 55.
[387] Blair (2005), pp. 70–73.
[388] ibid., p. 73.
[389] Blair (2005), p. 137.
[390] ibid., pp. 251–60.
[391] An argument pioneered by Faith (1997).

minting and circulation of *tremisses* and *sceattas*, with all that that implied in terms of a re-monetisation of exchange. This iconography again signifies the reintegration of the Anglo-Saxons into a broader Romano-Christian world: one (probably early eighth-century) silver penny, for example, displays on its obverse a facing bust of Christ that appears to be derived from the gold coinage of Justinian II, produced in Constantinople at the height of the Emperor's struggle with the Caliph Abd al-Malik (Fig. 15).³⁹²

As in Francia, the association between the newly founded monasteries and royal and noble benefactors served to bolster aristocratic interests, with kings and *ealdormen* appointing either abbots or abbesses from the ranks of their own families. Again, through the intramural burial of founders and founders' kin, the new religious foundations served to monumentalise aristocratic and royal control of the landcape.³⁹³ In the Anglo-Saxon case, however, the impact of monastic expansion on the economic fortunes of the aristocracy was especially pronounced. For, crucially, the agents of the Church introduced Roman law concepts of absolute ownership of land, which appear to have been entirely alien to the mindset of Anglo-Saxon peasants and farmers (who instead tended to conceive of terrain in terms of common-use rights).³⁹⁴ Abbots and priests beseeched kings to grant them land in exclusive possession according to 'church law' (*ius ecclesiasticum*), and to confirm that ownership by written charter. Accordingly, such property would come to be known as 'bookland'.³⁹⁵

Anglo-Saxon aristocrats were quick to discern the advantages of this type of ownership, and were soon to aspire to it themselves. Indeed, one reason why powerful donors were so keen to sign over land to a monastic church of their own founding, but then keep control of that monastery strictly within the family, was seemingly so as effectively to acquire Roman law ownership of that land under ecclesiastical cover. They were, to all intents and purposes, 'giving the land to themselves'.³⁹⁶ As Bede would complain in the 730s: 'under the pretext of founding monasteries, they give money to kings and buy territories for themselves.... Furthermore, they get hereditary rights over these lands ascribed to themselves in royal edicts, and have these documents of their privileges confirmed by the subscriptions of bishops, abbots, and great men of the world.... Having thus engrossed for themselves little estates or villages, they do what they want on them.'³⁹⁷

At the same time, kings and lords began to emulate the forms of estate management, centred upon a directly cultivated demesne, with which the monasteries were associated. The direct cultivation of lay estates by agricultural workers resident on the property of the lord is first alluded to in the late seventh-century

---

³⁹² Lord Stewartby and D. M. Metcalf, 'The Bust of Christ on an Early Anglo-Saxon Coin', *Numismatic Chronicle* 167 (2007), pp. 179–82.
³⁹³ Blair (2005), pp. 63–5.
³⁹⁴ Faith (2009), pp. 32, 39.
³⁹⁵ Blair (2005), pp. 87–9.
³⁹⁶ ibid., p. 90.
³⁹⁷ Bede, *Epistola ad Ecgbertum Episcopum*, tr. taken from Blair (2005), p. 101.

Fig. 15 Anglo-Saxon *sceatta* bearing the image of Christ (by kind permission of Lord Stewartby and the Royal Numismatic Society)

West Saxon 'Ine's Law'.[398] If in receipt of housing from their lord, the law decrees, peasants were obliged to supply labour if he so demanded.[399] Likewise, study of the Mercian landscape has revealed that during the period from c.670 to 840, new blocks of land were carved out and delineated, signifying the emergence of directly exploited core areas of estates.[400] This transformation of the Mercian landscape chimes closely with the archaeologically visible reorientation of settlement patterns encountered with respect to the age of Frankish manorialisation.

In spite of such economic developments, the political structures of the kingdoms of lowland Britain at this time appear to have remained relatively loose, variable, and divisible according to objective military and dynastic circumstance. Kingship could also be held jointly or shared, as the Kentish kings Hlothere and Eadric exemplify in the late seventh century.[401] However, under the growing influence of the Christian Church, there are signs of increased ideological sophistication and an emergent stabilisation of political identities. As we saw in Chapter Six, by adopting 'Catholic' Christianity, Anglo-Saxon kings were more fully drawn into the cultural and ideological orbit of the Roman world: this, indeed, was probably part of the appeal of the faith. It is significant, therefore, that after his conversion, Æthelberht of Kent promulgated a law code for his people. As Bede records: 'Among the other benefits which he [Æthelberht] thoughtfully conferred on his people, he also established enacted judgements for them, following the examples of the Romans (*decreta illi iudiciorum iuxta exempla Romanorum*)'. Unlike the laws of the Franks or

---

[398] *Ine's Law*, 67.
[399] Faith (1997), p. 76. See also T. Aston, 'The Origins of the Manor in England', *Transactions of the Royal Historical Society* 5.8 (1958), pp. 59–83, and T. Charles-Edwards, 'The Distinction Between Land and Moveable Wealth in the Anglo-Saxon Kingdoms', in P. Sawyer (ed.), *English Medieval Settlement* (London, 1976), pp. 97–104.
[400] S. Oosthuizen, 'The Anglo-Saxon Kingdom of Mercia and the Origins and Distribution of Common Fields', *Agricultural History Review* 55 (2007), pp. 153–80, 162–3.
[401] Kirby (1991), pp. 4–9.

the Langobards, these were written in the vernacular of *Anglisc* (*conscripta Anglorum sermone*).[402] As with contemporary Frankish and Langobardic legislation, however, the laws that Æthelberht codified were the customary, feud-based laws of his people. They were not, in that sense, royal law. Nevertheless, the very act of putting law down in writing was clearly regarded as an essentially Roman one. As a result, it is likely to have made the king look more authoritative. It has been argued, indeed, that Æthelberht's legislation may have taken its form and structure from the 'national' laws issued by Clothar II at the Council of Paris in 614, and that its promulgation was meant to signify 'that they [the *Cantware*] had joined the Franks and Romans in the ranks of civilized, because law-abiding, people'.[403] At the same time, as with the Frankish *Lex Salica* or the *Edict of Rothari*, by codifying the customs of his people, the king was able to convey to them a sense that he remained the custodian and guardian of their traditions, in spite of having adopted an alien faith. His decision to codify and promulgate those laws in the vernacular (rather than in Latin) can only have added to that sense.[404] Clearly, there was more to kingship than warfare alone.

As we have seen, Æthelberht was not the only Anglo-Saxon king to legislate in the seventh century. His Kentish successors Hlothere and Eadric (*c*.673–85), and then Wihtred (in 695), all promulgated laws, as did Cædwalla's successor as king of the West Saxons, Ine (*c*.688–94). These texts, however, are fundamentally different from Æthelberht's, in that wheras he had codified established law (Old English *ae*), the later kings issued decrees (*domas*) to supplement that law: 'Hlothere and Eadric, Kings of Kent, extended the laws (*ae*) which their predecessors had made, by the decrees (*domum*) that are stated below'.[405] In the laws of Wihtred, we encounter a more abstract tone, whilst Ine's laws look like responses to specific legal queries or petitions.[406] We also discern amongst Æthelberht's successors a growing interest in profiting from the workings of justice by levying fines, rather than merely determining the levels of compensation required to obviate feud.[407] Under Frankish and Romano-Christian influence, in short, the ambitions of royal government were on the rise.

We also see over the course of the seventh century a process whereby the Church itself began to give greater coherence and cohesion to political identities. This was true at the level of the larger kingdoms of Kent, Wessex, Mercia, Northumbria, East Anglia, and Essex, where we witness the introduction of diocesan structures and bishoprics. As we have already seen, Oswiu's presidency over the synod at Whitby in 664 appears to have been meant as an expression of Northumbrian *imperium*. Likewise, the prologue to the decrees issued by Wihtred of Kent records that they were promulgated at 'a deliberative council of the notables. There were present there Berhtwald, the chief bishop of Britain, and the above-mentioned king; the bishop of Rochester, who was called Gefmund; and every order of the Church of the province

---

[402] Bede, *Ecclesiastical History*, II, 5.
[403] Wormald (1999), pp. 94–7.
[404] For a different perspective on the language issue, see ibid., p. 101.
[405] *Hlothere and Eadric, proemium*; Wormald (1999), pp. 101–2.
[406] ibid., pp. 102–6.   [407] ibid., p. 106.

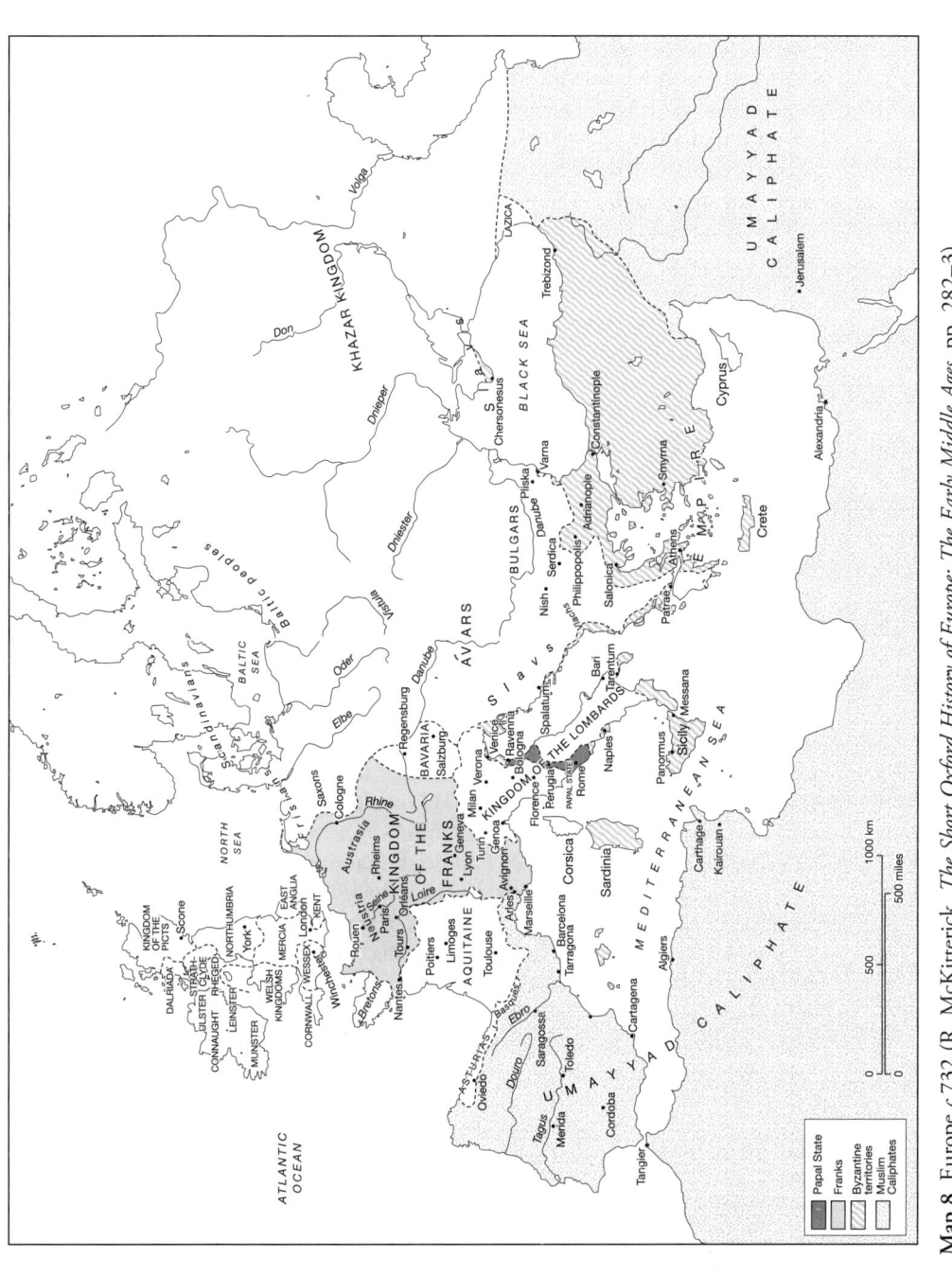

Map 8 Europe c.732 (R. McKitterick, *The Short Oxford History of Europe: The Early Middle Ages*, pp. 282–3)

expressed itself in unanimity with the loyal laity.'⁴⁰⁸ Even the names of kingdoms began to change under ecclesiastical influence. The designations 'East Saxon', 'West Saxon', 'South Saxon', 'East Anglian', and 'Middle Anglian' that we encounter in Bede, and which become increasingly standard from the eighth century onwards, make little sense from the perspective of the kingdoms themselves; but they do make sense from the perspective of the leadership of the Church that Augustine had established at Canterbury. Indeed, they are first encountered in documents emanating from Church councils in the late seventh century.⁴⁰⁹

The ideological influence of the Church, however, may well have extended beyond the level of the kingdom to a higher level of imaginative association. The slave-boys from Deira that Gregory had supposedly encountered in Rome prior to Augustine's mission were Angles (*Angli*); and (as noted in Chapter Five) *Angli* was used by many neighbours of Anglo-Saxons, and by others, to describe the Germanic inhabitants of lowland Britain, drawing upon the Anglo-Saxons' own apparent usage of *Anglisc* to differentiate themselves from the Romano-Britons and continental Saxons.⁴¹⁰ Hence, from the start, the mission was conceived of as being 'to the Angles' (*ad Anglos*) in spite of the fact that, strictly speaking, Æthelberht and his retainers were Jutes—for Angles was what Gregory regarded Æthelberht and his subjects to be. In ecclesiastical useage, therefore, *Angli* became a common term for the Germanic inhabitants of lowland Britain, who were regarded as a single people, or *gens*. Thus, writing in 731, Bede entitled his history the *Historia Ecclesiastica Gentis Anglorum* (*Ecclesiastical History of the People of the Angles*), in spite of the fact that its subject matter was the history of the Anglo-Saxon peoples in general.⁴¹¹

This concept of the existence of a single *gens Anglorum* was given greater structural reality when from the 670s onwards, the bishops of the 'Southumbrian' and Northumbrian kingdoms were summoned together on a regular basis to meet in council under the presidency of the Archbishop of Canterbury, uniting the *gens* in a single *ecclesia*. The first archbishop to do so, at the Council of Hatfield in 670–71, was Theodore, a Greek-speaking refugee from Tarsus in Asia Minor, who arrived in Canterbury in 668 at the age of sixty-six and who remained in office for twenty-two years.⁴¹² As we have seen, there already existed a clearly identifiable community of language and sense of shared core identity across the Germanic kingdoms of lowland Britain, which may have been bolstered by the experience of being ruled by 'high kings' and overlords, at least south of the Humber. This imagined community was now given sharper definition by the trans-regional structures of the Church and the identification of Pope Gregory as the 'Apostle to the English'.⁴¹³ As a result, there are signs that, by the end of the seventh century, the *Anglisc* were on their way to becoming the first 'nation' of Europe (Map 8).

⁴⁰⁸ *Wihtred*, Prologue, in Attenborough (1922) pp. 24–5.
⁴⁰⁹ Kirby (1991), pp. 20–23.
⁴¹⁰ Bede, *Ecclesiastical History*, II, 1; Charles-Edwards (2004).
⁴¹¹ Although note G. Molyneaux, 'The Old English Bede: English Ideology or Christian Instruction?', *English Historical Review* 124 (2009), pp. 1,289–323.
⁴¹² ibid., III, V; Wormald (2006a), p. 120.
⁴¹³ Wormald (2006a), p. 121, revised in light of Molyneaux (2009), p. 1,297, and Charles-Edwards (2004).

Epilogue

Theodore, Archbishop of Canterbury from 668 until 690, is one of the most arresting figures of his age. Born in *c*.602, a subject of the Emperor in Constantinople at the height of the empire's fortunes, but when it was on the very brink of collapse, he was obliged to flee to Rome from his native Tarsus to escape the armies of the Arabs, galvanised by their new faith of Islam. Appointed to the See of Canterbury in 667–8 on the grounds that no Roman cleric was willing to accept the post, he must have departed from Byzantine-controlled Italy as the Emperor Constans II (soon to be assassinated in his bath at Syracuse) was marshalling resources for the great counter-strike against the forces of Antichrist. He and his African companion Hadrian (appointed to accompany Theodore to Britain in order to prevent him from introducing the *Angli* to any untoward 'Greek' customs) had then set sail for Marseilles, from where, as we have seen, they crossed a Francia riven with tension, carefully observed by the *maiordomus* Ebroin, who suspected them of being imperial agents up to no good. Theodore had then sailed across the Channel from the recently founded and newly expanding port town of Quentovic.[1]

Once established at Canterbury, Theodore made a tour of the kingdoms under his charge and brought order and structure to the life of the 'English' Church. As a loyal subject of the Emperor, he ensured that his bishops signed up to the decrees of the Second Council of Constantinople of 553, which had caused Justinian such headaches in the West.[2] In the aftermath of the battle of the Trent in 679, Theodore even managed to broker a deal between the king of Bernicia, Ecgfrith, and the king of the Mercians, Æthelred. Ecgfrith's eighteen-year-old brother had died in the battle, and, in accordance with the custom of the feud, Ecgfrith was thirsting for revenge. Instead, Theodore persuaded him to accept the payment of *wergeld* as compensation—a practice that, until his journey through Francia and arrival in Kent, must have been entirely unknown to him.[3]

Theodore and Hadrian did much to introduce learning to the Anglo-Saxons. As Bede records, 'because both of them were extremely learned in sacred and secular literature, they attracted a crowd of students into whose minds they daily poured the streams of wholesome erudition. They gave their hearers instruction not only in the books of Holy Scripture but also the art of metre, astronomy, and ecclesiastical

---

[1] Bede, *Ecclesiastical History*, IV, I. [2] ibid., IV, 17.
[3] ibid., IV, 21.

computation. As evidence of this, some of their students still survive who know Latin and Greek just as well as their native tongue.'[4] Remarkably, we still have copies of notes taken during Theodore's lectures on Biblical exegesis. As a result, we can hear the elderly Greek, sitting before his audience of puzzled Anglo-Saxon acolytes, attempting to explain curious details of a world once familiar to him but utterly alien to them: 'The race of Ishmael', he tells them in response to a reference in the Old Testament, 'was that of the Saracens, a race which is never at peace with anyone but is always at war with someone.'[5] Later on in the same text 'cucumbers' and 'melons' appear. How was he to explain these to his students in the frozen north? 'They are the same thing', Theodore informs them, 'but cucumbers are called *pepones* when they grow large, and often one *pepon* will weigh thirty pounds. In the city of Edessa they grow so large that a camel can only carry two of them at a time.'[6]

During the course of his journeys, Theodore had left a world that must have seemed to be falling apart. Whether he knew it or not, however, he had made his way through lands and societies that were gradually piecing themselves back together. In Francia, as in Britain, lords were becoming more powerful, and lordships and kingdoms more consolidated. Indeed, across the societies of north-western Europe (with the possible exception of Ireland), there are signs of a growing social stratification associated with the emergence and rise of a military nobility rooted in extensive patterns of landownership and a growing monopoly on violence.[7] On the European continent especially, we can trace a shift from the 'lord-and-king-focused' societies that had taken shape in the fifth and sixth centuries to more straightforwardly lord-focused ones in the seventh and eighth.

This was not necessarily good news for everybody. Across western Europe, iron shackles, used to chain slaves and labourers and bind them to estates, become much more common on excavated rural sites between *c.*500 and 800.[8] But the concentration of wealth in the hands of aristocrats that was underway can be seen to have contributed to the first signs of economic growth that the societies of the West had experienced since the height of Roman economic development in the late fourth century. The signs of growth were to become especially pronounced in the eighth century, as the bubonic plague declined in virulence and eventually faded away, allowing population levels to begin to rise once more.[9] With renewed patterns of aristocratic accumulation, an expansion of the monetary economy is evident, facilitated by the shift from an increasingly scarce gold coinage to a more plentiful

---

[4] ibid., IV, 2.
[5] B. Bischoff and M. Lapidge (eds./trs.), *Biblical Commentaries from the Canterbury School of Theodore and Hadrian* (Cambridge, 1994), p. 325.
[6] ibid., p. 375.
[7] For Ireland, see Wickham (2005), pp. 363–4.
[8] J. Henning, 'Strong Rulers—Weak Economy? Rome, the Carolingians, and the Archaeology of Slavery in the First Millennium AD', in J. D. Davis and M. McCormick (eds.), *The Long Morning of Medieval Europe* (Aldershot, 2008), pp. 33–54.
[9] See Little (2007).

and versatile silver one in Francia in the 670s, and reflected in the renewed minting of coins in lowland Britain from the 630s onwards. Increased inter-regional exchange, generated by the demands of the new elite for luxury and prestige goods, and associated with the expanding monastic centres, is also discernible, with the emergence along the coasts of the Channel and North Sea of new trading centres such as Quentovic in Francia, or Hamwih in the kingdom of the South Saxons. At the end of the day, both the shackles on the slave and the 'wics' on the shore resulted from the same core processes: the rise of the early medieval nobility and the consolidation of lordship.

Abbreviations

EHD	*English Historical Documents*
EHR	*English Historical Review*
JAC	*Journal of Agrarian Change*
J. Edict.	*Justiniani Edicta*
JESHO	*Journal of the Economic and Social History of the Orient*
JHS	*Journal of Hellenic Studies*
J. Nov.	*Justiniani Novellae Constitutiones*
LC	*Liber Constitutionum*
LHF	*Liber Historiae Francorum*
Nov. Val.	*Novellae Divi Valentiniani*
Pan. Lat.	*Panegyrici Latini*
P O	*Patrologia Orientalis*
TRHS	*Transactions of the Royal Historical Society*

Select Bibliography And Further Reading

GENERAL READING

A number of works cover the entirety of the period discussed in this volume. One of the most notable features of the historiography of the early Middle Ages in recent years has been the attempt both to view developments in western Europe in a broader Mediterranean and even West Eurasian context and also to emphasise elements of cultural and ideological continuity (at least on the part of elites) with the late-Roman past. At the same time, much emphasis has been placed on economic discontinuity. Of particular interest to students and general readers will be the following:

P. Brown, *The World of Late Antiquity* (London, 1971).
R. Collins, *Early Medieval Europe*, 3rd ed. (London, 2010).
P. Fouracre (ed.), *The Cambridge Medieval History*, vol. 1: *500–700* (Cambridge, 2005).
M. Innes, *Introduction to Early Medieval Western Europe, 300–900: The Plough, The Sword, and The Book* (London, 2007).
J. Smith, *Europe After Rome: A New Cultural History* (Oxford, 2005).
B. Ward-Perkins, *The Fall of Rome and the End of Civilization* (Oxford, 2005).
C. Wickham, *Framing the Early Middle Ages: Europe and the Mediterranean, 400–800* (Oxford, 2005).
—— *The Inheritance of Rome* (London, 2009).

For the history of the Byzantine and Islamic East in this period, important works of both research and synthesis are available. Note in particular:
J. D. Howard-Johnston, *Witnesses to a World Crisis: Historians and Histories of the Middle East* (Oxford, 2010).
H. Kennedy, *The Great Arab Conquests* (London, 2007).
C. Mango, *Byzantium: The Empire of New Rome* (London, 1980).
C. Morrisson (ed.), *Le monde byzantin: I: L'Empire romain d'Orient, 330–641* (Paris, 2004).

CHAPTER 1 THE WORLD THAT HAD BEEN ROME

The history of the Roman Empire from the second to the fifth centuries has been largely revolutionised since the 1960s, above all in the context of anglophone scholarship, which until that point had been mostly dominated by the perspective of Edward Gibbon's *Decline and Fall of the Roman Empire* (1776–88). Of particular importance in that revolution was A. H. M. Jones, *The Later Roman Empire* (Oxford, 1964), which emphasised the creativity and success of Roman statecraft in the third and fourth centuries. Peter Brown's *The World of Late Antiquity* (Oxford, 1971) recast the cultural history of the period in a similarly sympathetic light. For the eastern provinces of the Roman world, perspectives have been further transformed by examining the empire through sources written in languages other than Latin and Greek (such as Syriac) in order to gain a provincial and local perspective, and so as better to understand relations between cultures: see, for example, F. Millar, *A Greek Roman Empire: Power and Belief Under Theodosius II* (Berkeley, 2007). Much important work has also been produced on the late-Roman economy, emphasising the extraordinarily high levels of monetisation and economic sophistication evident in the fourth century:

382   Select Bibliography and Further Reading

fundamental to this reassessment of late-Roman economic realities is J. Banaji, *Agrarian Change in Late Antiquity: Gold, Labour, and Aristocratic Dominance*, 2nd ed. (Oxford, 2007). The religious history of the era has become more nuanced, as scholars have examined more critically the sources upon which our understanding of the Christianisation of the late-Roman Empire depend (see above all the various works of T. D. Barnes cited below).

Primary Sources in Translation
Ammianus Marcellinus, *Res Gestae*, tr. J. C. Rolfe (Cambridge, Mass., 1935)—also contains the 'Anonymous Valesianus', *Pars Posterior*.
Aurelius Victor, *de Caesaribus*, tr. H. W. Bird (Liverpool, 1994).
Codex Theodosianus = C. Pharr (tr.), *The Theodosian Code* (Princeton, 1952).
De Rebus Bellicis = E. A. Thompson (ed.), and B. Flower (tr.), *A Roman Reformer and Innovator* (Oxford, 1952).
The Digest of Justinian, tr. A. Watson et al., 4 vols. (Philadelphia, 1986).
M. Dodgeon and S. Lieu, *The Roman Eastern Frontier and the Persian Wars, AD 226–336: A Documentary History* (London, 1991).
Eusebius, *Life of Constantine*, tr. A. Cameron (Oxford, 1999).
Eutropius, *Breviarium*, tr. H. W. Bird (Liverpool, 1993).
J. F. Gardner and T. Wiedemann, *The Roman Household: A Sourcebook* (London, 1991).
Lactantius, *De Mortibus Persecutorum*, tr. J. L. Creed (Liverpool, 1984).
M. Maas, *Readings in Late Antiquity: A Sourcebook*, 2nd ed. (London, 2010).
R. A. B. Mynors, C. E. V. Nixon, B. S. Rogers (trs.), *In Praise of the Later Roman Emperors* (1994) (= *Panegyrici Latini*).
Orosius, *History Against the Pagans*, tr. R. Defarri, *Fathers of the Church*, Series 50 (Washington DC, 1964).
R. Rees, *Diocletian and the Tetrarchy* (Edinburgh, 2004).
Salvian, *On the Governance of God*, tr. Fr. O'Sullivan, *Fathers of the Church*, Series 3 (Washington DC, 1947).
Sidonius Apollinaris, *Letters and Poems*, tr. W. B. Anderson, 2 vols. (Cambridge, Mass., 1936–65).
N. P. Tanner, *The Decrees of the Ecumenical Councils*, 2 vols. (Washington DC, 1990).
Virgil, *The Aeneid*, tr. C. Day Lewis (Oxford, 1986).
N. Wilson (ed.), *Saint Basil on Greek Literature* (London, 1975).
Zosimus, *New History*, tr . R. T. Ridley (Canberra, 1982).

Secondary Sources
P. Athanassiadi and M. Frede (eds.), *Pagan Monotheism in Late Antiquity* (Oxford, 1999).
J. Banaji, *Agrarian Change in Late Antiquity: Gold, Labour, and Aristocratic Dominance*, 2nd ed. (Oxford, 2007).
T. Barfield, *The Perilous Frontier: Nomad Empires and China* (Oxford, 1989).
T. D. Barnes, *Constantine and Eusebius* (Cambridge, Mass., 1981).
—— *The New Empire of Diocletian and Constantine* (Cambridge, Mass., 1982).
S. Barnish and F. Marazzi (eds.), *The Ostrogoths from the Migration Period to the Sixth Century* (Woodbridge, 2007).
A. K. Bowman, P. Garnsey, and A. Cameron (eds.), *The Cambridge Ancient History*, 2nd ed., vol. XII: *The Crisis of Empire, AD 193–337* (Cambridge, 2005).
M. Brosius, *The Persians* (London, 2006).
P. Brown, 'Late Antiquity', in Veyne (1987), pp. 239–50.

—— *The Body and Society: Men, Women, and Sexual Renunciation in Early Christianity* (London, 1988).
—— 'Christianization and Religious Conflict', in Cameron and Garnsey (1998), pp. 632–64.
A. Cameron, 'The Reign of Constantine, AD 306–337', in Bowman, Garnsey, and Cameron (2005), pp. 90–109.
A. Cameron and P. Garnsey (eds.), *The Cambridge Ancient History*, vol. XIII: *The Late Empire, AD 337–425* (Cambridge, 1998).
M. P. Canepa, 'Technologies of Memory in Early Sasanian Iran: Achaemenid Sites and Sasanian Ideology', *American Journal of Archaeology* 114.4 (2010), pp. 563–96.
H. Chadwick, *East and West: The Making of a Rift in the Church from Apostolic Times to the Council of Florence* (Oxford, 2003).
G. Clark, *Women in Late Antiquity* (Oxford, 1993).
R. Collins, *Visigothic Spain 409–711* (Oxford, 2004).
M. Corbier, 'Coinage and Taxation: The State's Point of View AD 193–337', in Bowman, Garnsey, and Cameron (2005).
G. E. M. de Ste Croix, *The Class Struggle in the Ancient Greek World* (London, 1981).
F. de Zulueta, 'Patronage in the Later Roman Empire, in P. Vinogradoff (ed.), *Oxford Studies in Social and Legal History* 1 (Oxford, 1909), Part II, pp. 3–78.
J. Drinkwater, 'Maximus to Diocletian and the "Crisis"', in Bowman, Garnsey, and Cameron (2005), pp. 28–66.
J. Durliat, *De la ville antique à la ville byzantine* (Rome, 1990).
G. Fowden, 'Constantine's Porphyry Column: The Earliest Literary Allusion', *Journal of Hellenic Studies* 81 (1991), pp. 119–31.
—— *Empire to Commonwealth: Consequences of Monotheism in Late Antiquity* (Princeton, 1993).
—— 'Polytheist Religion and Philosophy', in Cameron and Garnsey (1998), pp. 538–60.
R. Frye, 'The Sasanians', in Bowman, Garnsey, and Cameron (2005), pp. 461–80.
P. Garnsey, *Social Status and Legal Privilege in the Roman Empire* (Oxford, 1970).
—— *Ideas of Slavery from Aristotle to Augustine* (Cambridge, 1996).
W. Goffart, *Barbarian Tides: The Migration Age and the Later Roman Empire* (Philadelphia, 2006).
J. Goody, *The Development of the Family and Marriage in Europe* (Cambridge, 1983).
G. Greatrex, 'Roman Frontiers and Foreign Policy in the East', in R. Alston and S. Lieu (eds.), *Aspects of the Roman East: Papers in Honour of Professor Fergus Millar*, in *Studia Antiqua Australensia* 3 (Turnhout, 2007), pp. 103–73.
D. Gutas, *Greek Thought, Arab Culture* (London, 1998).
G. Halsall, *Barbarian Migrations and the Roman West 376–568* (Cambridge, 2007).
K. Harper, 'The Greek Census Inscriptions of Late Antiquity', *Journal of Roman Studies* 98 (2008), pp. 83–119.
P. Heather, 'New Men for New Constantines?', in P. Magdalino (ed.), *New Constantines* (Aldershot, 1994), pp. 11–44.
—— 'The Huns and the End of the Roman Empire in Western Europe', *English Historical Review* 110 (1995), pp. 4–41.
—— *The Goths* (Oxford, 1996).
—— (ed.), *The Visigoths: From the Migration Period to the Seventh Century* (Woodbridge, 1999).
—— *The Fall of the Roman Empire: A New History* (London, 2005).

M. Hendy, *Studies in the Byzantine Monetary Economy* (Cambridge, 1985).

G. Hermann, 'The Sasanian Rock Reliefs at Naqsh-i-Rustam: Naqsh-i-Rustam 6, The Triumph of Shapur I', *Iranische Denkmaler* II, 13 (Berlin, 1989).

J. D. Howard-Johnston, 'The Great Powers in Late Antiquity: A Comparison', in A. Cameron (ed.), *The Byzantine and Early Islamic Near East*, vol. III: *States, Resources, and Armies* (Princeton, 1995), pp. 157–226.

H. J. Hummer, 'Franks and Alamanni: A Discontinuous Ethnogenesis', in I. Wood (ed.), *Franks and Alamanni in the Merovingian Period: An Ethnographic Perspective* (Woodbridge, 1998), pp. 9–20.

E. James, *The Franks* (Oxford, 1988).

A. H. M. Jones, *The Greek City from Alexander to Justinian* (Oxford, 1940).

——*The Later Roman Empire*, 3 vols. (Oxford, 1964).

R. A. Kaster, *Guardians of Language: Grammarians and Society in Late Antiquity* (Berkeley, 1988).

M. Kulikowski, *Rome's Gothic Wars* (Cambridge, 2007).

N. Lenski (ed.), *The Cambridge Companion to the Age of Justinian* (Cambridge, 2006).

J. H. W. G. Liebeschuetz, *The Decline and Fall of the Roman City* (Oxford, 2001).

E. Luttwak, *The Grand Strategy of the Roman Empire* (Baltimore, 1976).

C. Mango, *Byzantine Architecture* (London, 1986).

D. Mattingly, *An Imperial Possession: Britain in the Roman Empire* (London, 2004).

J. Matthews, *Western Aristocracies and the Imperial Court AD 384–425* (Oxford, 1976).

F. Millar, *The Roman Empire and Her Neighbours* (London, 1967).

——*The Emperor in the Roman World* (London, 1977).

——*A Greek Roman Empire* (Berkeley, 2006).

A. Poulter, 'Cataclysm on the Lower Danube: The Destruction of a Complex Roman Landscape', in N. Christie (ed.), *Landscapes of Change: Rural Evolutions in Late Antiquity and the Early Middle Ages* (Aldershot, 2004), pp. 223–54.

S. Price, 'Gods and Emperors: The Greek Language of the Roman Imperial Cult', *Journal of Hellenic Studies* 104 (1984), pp. 79–85.

C. Rapp, *Holy Bishops in Late Antiquity: The Nature of Christian Leadership in an Age of Transition* (Berkeley, 2005).

R. Saller, *Patriarchy, Property, and Death in the Roman Household* (Cambridge, 1994).

P. Sarris, 'Is This the Face of Britain's Forgotten Emperor?', *The Times*, Wednesday, 25 February 2004, pp. 1 and 4.

——'Rehabilitating the Great Estate: Aristocratic Property and Economic Growth in the Late Antique East', in W. Bowden, L. Lavan, and C. Machado (eds.), *Recent Research in the Late Antique Countryside* (Leiden, 2004), pp. 55–71.

——*Economy and Society in the Age of Justinian* (Cambridge, 2006).

——'Aristocrats, Peasants, and the State in the Later Roman Empire', in P. Eich, S. Schmidt Hofner, and C. Wieland (eds.), *Der wiederkehrende Leviathan:Staatlichkeit und Staatswerdung in Spätantike und Früher Neuzeit* (Heidelberg, 2011), pp. 377–94.

D. Sinor, 'The Hun Period' in Sinor (1990), pp. 177–205.

——(ed.), *The Cambridge History of Early Inner Asia* (Cambridge, 1990).

A. J. B. Sirks, *Food for Rome: The Legal Structure of the Transportation and Processing of Supplies for the Imperial Distributions in Rome and Constantinople* (Amsterdam, 1991).

——'Reconsidering the Roman Colonate', *Zeitschrift der Savigny Stiftung für Rechtsgeschichte: Romanistische Abteilung* 110 (1993), pp. 330–60.

——'The Farmer, the Landlord, and the Law in the Fifth Century', in R. Mathisen (ed.), *Law, Society, and Authority in Late Antiquity* (Oxford, 2001), pp. 256–71.

—— 'The Colonate in Justinian's Reign', *Journal of Roman Studies* 98 (2008), pp. 120–43.
P. Southern and K. R. Dixon, *The Late Roman Army* (Guildford, 1996).
R. Stoneman, *Palmyra and its Empire: Zenobia's Revolt Against Rome* (Michigan, 1994).
S. Swain and M. Edwards (eds.), *Approaching Late Antiquity: The Transformation from Early to Late Empire* (Oxford, 2005).
E. A. Thompson, 'Peasant Revolts in Late Roman Gaul and Spain', *Past and Present* 2 (1952), pp. 11–23.
M. Todd, *The Early Germans* (Oxford, 1992).
—— 'The Germanic Peoples and Germanic Society', in Bowman, Garnsey, and Cameron (2005), pp. 440–60.
W. Treadgold, *Byzantium and its Army* (Stanford, 1997).
S. Treggiari, *Roman Marriage* (Oxford, 1991).
P. Veyne (ed.), *A History of Private Life*, vol. 1: *From Pagan Rome to Byzantium* (Cambridge, Mass., 1987).
B. Ward-Perkins, 'The Cities', in Cameron and Garnsey (1998), pp. 371–410.
—— *The Fall of the Roman Empire and the End of Civilization* (Oxford, 2005).
C. Wickham, *Framing the Early Middle Ages: Europe and the Mediterranean, 400–800* (Oxford, 2005).
R. Williams, *Arius: Heresy and Tradition*, 2nd ed. (London, 2001).
S. Williams, *Diocletian and the Roman Recovery* (London, 1985).
I. Wood, 'The Barbarian Invasions and First Settlements', in Cameron and Garnsey (1998), pp. 516–37.
—— (ed.), *Franks and Alamanni in the Merovingian Period: An Ethnographic Perspective* (Woodbridge, 1998), pp. 9–20.
G. Woolf, *Becoming Roman* (Cambridge, 1999).
C. P. Wormald, 'The Decline of the Western Roman Empire and the Survival of its Aristocracy', *Journal of Roman Studies* 66 (1976), pp. 217–26.

CHAPTER 2 THE FORMATION OF POST-ROMAN SOCIETY

The historiography of post-Roman society in the fifth and sixth centuries has become considerably more polarised in recent years, divided as it is between military and economic historians (to whom significant ruptures, turmoil, and change are apparent) and cultural historians (who are more inclined to emphasise cultural continuities and longer-term, less violent processes of social and cultural evolution). Leading examples of the former are B. Ward-Perkins, *The Fall of Rome and the End of Civilization* (Oxford, 2005), and P. Heather, *The Fall of the Roman Empire: A New History* (London, 2006). Continuity and the rhetorical character of many of the sources on which our knowledge of the 'barbarian invasions' depends have been most trenchantly argued for by Walter Goffart (see below). Cultural historians of the period have placed particular emphasis on the mutability, fluidity, and constructed character of 'barbarian' identities in this period—a field associated with the names of Wenskus, Wolfram, and Pohl (see below), and dominated by the so-called 'Vienna School'. A sensible 'middle way' through such issues of identity, as well as of continuity and discontinuity in governmental structures and administrative mechanisms, is to be found in G. Halsall, *Barbarian Migrations and the Roman West 376–568* (Cambridge, 2007).

Primary Sources in Translation

Ammianus Marcellinus, *Res Gestae*, tr. J. C. Rolfe (Cambridge Mass., 1935)—also contains the 'Anonymous Valesianus', *Pars Posterior*.

R. C. Blockley, *The Fragmentary Classicising Historians of the Later Roman Empire*, 2 vols. (Liverpool, 1981–3).

Cassiodorus, *Variae*, tr. S. Barnish (Liverpool, 1992), contains a selection. Abbreviated translations of the Latin of the complete collection can be found in T. Hodgkin, *The Letters of Cassiodorus* (1896).

Chronicle of 452—see Murray (1998). See also S. Muhlberger, *The Fifth-Century Chroniclers: Prosper, Hydatius, and the Gallic Chronicler of 452* (Leeds, 1990).

Chronicle of Theophanes, tr. C. Mango and R. Scott (Oxford, 1998).

Codex Theodosianus = C. Pharr, *The Theodosian Code* (Philadelphia, 1952).

Gildas, *de Excidio Britanniae* = M. Winterbottom, *Gildas: The Ruin of Britain and Other Works* (London, 1978).

Gregory of Tours, *Decem Libri Historiae* = L. Thorpe, *Gregory of Tours: History of the Franks* (London, 1974).

Hydatius = R. W. Burgess, *The Chronicle of Hydatius and the Consularia Constantinopolitana* (Oxford, 1993).

Jordanes, *Getica* = C. C. Mierow, *The Gothic History of Jordanes* (Princeton, 1915, repr. 2006).

Leges Burgundionum: Constitutiones Extravagantes—see Fischer Drew (1972).

Lex Visigothorum, tr. in S. P. Scott, *The Civil Law* (Boston, 1932)—not entirely reliable.

Liber Constitutionum = K. Fischer Drew, *The Burgundian Code* (Pennsylvania, 1972).

A. C. Murray, *From Roman to Merovingian Gaul* (Peterborough, Ontario, 1998).

Olympiodorus—see Blockley (1981–3).

Pactus Legis Salicae = see T. J. Rivers, *Laws of the Salian and Ripuarian Franks* (New York, 1986).

Paulinus of Pella, *Eucharisticon*, in vol. 2 of *Ausonius: Works*, tr. Evelyn White, 2 vols. (Cambridge, Mass., 1921).

Procopius, *Secret History*, tr. G. Williams and P. Sarris (London, 2007).

—— *Wars* = *Procopius: History of the Wars, Secret History, Buildings*, tr. H. B. Dewing and G. Downey, 7 vols. (Cambridge, Mass., 1914–40).

Prosper—see Murray (1998).

Querolus, tr. C. Jacquemard Le Saos (Paris, 1994).

Sidonius Apollinaris, *Letters and Poems*, tr. W. B. Anderson, 2 vols. (Cambridge, Mass., 1936–65).

Victor of Vita, *History of the Vandal Persecution*, tr. J. Moorhead (Liverpool, 1992).

Zosimus *New History*, tr . R. T. Ridley (Canberra, 1982).

Secondary Sources

R. Alston, *The City in Roman and Byzantine Egypt* (London, 2002).

B. S. Bachrach, *Merovingian Military Organization 481–751* (Minneapolis, 1972).

J. Banaji, 'Precious-metal Coinages and Monetary Expansion in Late Antiquity', in F. De Romanis and S. Sorda (eds.), *Dal denarius al dinar: l'oriente e la monetà romana* (Rome, 2006), pp. 265–303.

—— *Agrarian Change in Late Antiquity: Gold, Labour, and Aristocratic Dominance*, 2nd ed. (Oxford, 2007).

—— 'Aristocrats, Peasantries, and the Framing of the Early Middle Ages', *Journal of Agrarian Change* 9.1 (2009), pp. 59–91.

—— 'Late Antiquity to the Early Middle Ages: What Kind of Transition?', in *idem.*, *Theory as History* (Leiden 2001).
—— *Theory as History* (Leiden, 2010).
S. J. B. Barnish, 'Taxation, Land, and Barbarian Settlement in the Later Roman Empire', *Papers of the British School at Rome* 54 (1986), pp. 170–95.
—— 'Transformation and Survival in the Western Senatorial Aristocracy, *c.* AD 400–700', *Papers of the British School at Rome* 65 (1988), pp. 120–55.
—— 'The Transformation of Classical Cities and the Pirenne Debate', *Journal of Roman Archaeology* 2 (1989), pp. 385–400.
G. Berndt and R. Steinacher, 'Minting in Vandal Africa: Coins of the Vandal Period in the Coin Cabinet of Vienna's Kunsthistorisches Museum', *Early Medieval Europe* 16 (2008), pp. 252–98.
P. Brown, *The World of Late Antiquity* (London, 1971).
T. Charles-Edwards, *After Rome* (Oxford, 2003).
A. Chavarría Arnau, 'Churches and Aristocracies in Seventh-Century Spain: Some Thoughts on the Debate on Visigothic Churches', *Early Medieval Europe* 18 (2010), pp. 160–74.
F. L. Cheyette, 'The Disappearance of the Ancient Landscape and the Climatic Anomaly of the Early Middle Ages: A Question To Be Pursued', *Early Medieval Europe* 16 (2008), pp. 127–65.
E. Chrysos and A. Schwarz (eds.), *Das Reich und Die Barbaren* (Vienna, 1989).
R. Collins, *Early Medieval Europe* (London, 1999).
—— *Visigothic Spain 409–711* (Oxford, 2004).
M. Crusafont, *El sistema monetario visigodo: cobre y oro* (Barcelona and Madrid, 1994).
K. Dark, *Britain and the End of the Roman Empire* (Stroud, 2000).
M. Decker, *Tilling the Hateful Earth: Agriculture in the Late Antique East* (Oxford, 2009).
G. E. M. de Ste Croix, *The Class Struggle in the Ancient Greek World* (London, 1981).
J. Durliat, *De la ville antique à la ville byzantine* (Rome, 1990).
A. England et al., 'Historical Landscape Change in Cappadocia (Central Turkey): A Palaeoecological Investigation of Annually Laminated Sediments from Nar Lake', *The Holocene* 18 (2008), pp. 1,229–45.
R. Faith, *The English Peasantry and the Growth of Lordship* (Leicester, 1997).
—— 'Forces and Relations of Production in Early Medieval England', *Journal of Agrarian Change* 9.1 (2009), pp. 23–41.
P. Fouracre (ed.), *The Cambridge Medieval History*, vol. 1: *500–700* (Cambridge, 2005).
W. Goffart, *Barbarians and Romans: The Techniques of Accommodation 418–584* (Princeton, 1980).
—— *Barbarian Tides: The Migration Age and the Later Roman Empire* (Philadelphia, 2006).
M. Grant, *The Fall of the Roman Empire* (London, 1976).
P. Grierson and M. Blackburn, *Medieval European Coinage: The Early Middle Ages (5th–10th c.)* (Cambridge, 1986).
G. Halsall, 'The Barbarian Invasions', in P. Fouracre (ed.), *The New Cambridge Medieval History, Volume I, c.500–700* (Cambridge, 2005), pp. 35–55.
—— *Barbarian Migrations and the Roman West 376–568* (Cambridge, 2007).
—— 'The Techniques of Barbarian Settlement in the Fifth Century: A Reply to Walter Goffart', *Journal of Late Antiquity* 3.1 (2010), pp. 99–112.
S. Hawkes, 'Soldiers and Settlers in Roman Britain', *Medieval Archaeology* 5 (1961), pp. 1–70.

P. Heather, *The Fall of the Roman Empire: A New History* (London, 2006).
—— *Empires and Barbarians: Migration, Development, and the Birth of Europe* (London, 2009).
M. F. Hendy, 'From Public to Private: The Western Barbarian Coinages as a Mirror of the Disappearance of Late Roman State Structures', *Viator* 19 (1988), pp. 29–78.
J. Hines, 'Society, Community, and Identity', in Charles-Edwards (2003), pp. 61–102.
M. Innes, 'Land, Freedom, and the Making of the Medieval West', *Transactions of the Royal Historical Society*, Sixth Series, 16 (2006), pp. 39–74.
E. James, *The Franks* (Oxford, 1988).
J. Jarnut, H.-G. Goetz, and W. Pohl (eds.), *Gentes and Regna* (Leiden, 2002).
A. H. M. Jones, *The Later Roman Empire*, 3 vols. (Oxford, 1964).
J. Lafaurie and C. Morrisson, 'La penetration des monnaies byzantines en Gaule', *Revue Numismatique* VI (29) (1987), pp. 38–98.
E. Levy, *West Roman Vulgar Law* (Philadelphia, 1951).
M. Lombard, *L'Islam dans sa première grandeur* (Paris, 1971).
D. Mattingly, *An Imperial Possession: Britain in the Roman Empire* (London, 2004).
A. H. Merrills and R. Miles, *The Vandals* (Oxford, 2010).
J. Morris, 'Pelagian Literature', *Journal of Theological Studies* 16 (1965), pp. 26–60.
C. Morrisson, 'The Re-Use of Obsolete Coins: The Case of Roman Imperial Bronzes Revived in the Late Fifth Century', in C. N. L. Brooke, B. H. I. H. Stewart, J. G. Pollard, and T. R. Volk (eds.), *Studies in Numismatic Method Presented to Philip Grierson* (Cambridge, 1983), pp. 95–112.
—— 'La Sicile byzantine: un lueur dans les siècles obscurs', *Numismatica e antichità classiche* 27 (1998), pp. 307–34.
W. Pohl, 'Conceptions of Ethnicity in Early Medieval Studies', in L. K. Little and B. H. Rosewnwein (eds.), *Debating the Middle Ages* (Oxford, 1998), pp. 15–24.
—— and H. Reimitz (eds.), *Kingdoms of the Empire: The Integration of Barbarians in Late Antiquity* (Leiden, 1997).
A. Rovelli, 'La circulazione monetaria a Roma nei secoli VII e VIII. Nuovi dati per la storia economica di Roma bell'alto medioevo', in P. Delogu (ed.), *Roma medievale. Aggiornamenti* (Florence, 1998), pp. 79–91.
—— 'Coins and Trade in Early Medieval Italy', *Early Medieval Europe* 17 (2009), pp. 45–76.
P. Sarris, 'The Origins of the Manorial Economy: New Insights from Late Antiquity', *English Historical Review* 119 (2004), pp. 279–311.
—— *Economy and Society in the Age of Justinian* (Cambridge, 2006).
—— 'Continuity and Discontinuity in the Post-Roman Economy', *Journal of Agrarian Change* 6.3 (2006), pp. 400–13.
—— 'Introduction: Aristocrats, Peasants, and the Transformation of Rural Society, c.400–800', *Journal of Agrarian Change* 9.1 (2009), pp. 3–22.
—— 'Aristocrats, Peasants, and the State in the Later Roman Empire', in P. Eich, S. Schmidt Hofner, and C. Wieland (eds.), *Der wiederkehrende Leviathan:Staatlichkeit und Staatswerdung in Spätantike und Früher Neuzeit* (Heidelberg, 2011), pp. 377–94.
O. Schipp, *Der weströmische Kolonat von Konstantin bis zu den Karolingern (332 bis 861)* (Hamburg, 2009).
J. Teall, 'The Byzantine Agricultural Tradition', *Dumbarton Oaks Papers* 13 (1959), pp. 35–59.
B. Ward-Perkins, 'Why Did the Anglo-Saxons Not Become More British?', *English Historical Review* 115 (2000), pp. 513–33.

—— *The Fall of the Roman Empire and the End of Civilization* (Oxford, 2005).
R. Wenskus, *Stammesbildung und Verfassung: Das Werden der frühmittelalterlichen Gentes* (Cologne, 1961).
C. Wickham, 'The Fall of Rome Will Not Take Place', in L. K. Little and B. H. Rosenwein (eds.), *Debating the Middle Ages: Issues and Readings* (Oxford, 1998), pp. 45–57.
—— *Framing the Early Middle Ages: Europe and the Mediterranean, 400–800* (Oxford, 2005).
H. Wolfram and W. Pohl (eds.), *Typen der Ethnogenese* (Vienna, 1990).
H. Wolfram and A. Schwarcz (eds.), *Anerkennung und Integration* (Vienna, 1988).
I. Wood, 'Appendix: The Settlement of the Burgundians', in Wolfram and Pohl (1990).
—— 'The Barbarian Invasions and First Settlements', in A. Cameron and P. Garnsey (eds.), *The Cambridge Ancient History*, vol. XIII, *The Late Empire, A.D. 337–425* (Cambridge, 1998), pp. 516–37.
—— (ed.), *Franks and Alamanni in the Merovingian Period: An Ethnographic Perspective* (Woodbridge, 1998).
C. P. Wormald, 'The Decline of the Western Roman Empire and the Survival of its Aristocracy', *Journal of Roman Studies* 66 (1976), pp. 217–26.
—— 'Lex Scripta and Verbum Regis', in P. Sawyer and I. Wood (eds.), *Early Medieval Kingship* (Leeds, 1977).
—— *The Making of English Law*, vol. 1 (Oxford 1999), pp. 29–51.
—— 'Kings and Kingship', in Fouracre (2005), pp. 571–604.

CHAPTER 3 THE ROMANO-GERMANIC KINGDOMS: THE ERA OF THEODERIC AND CLOVIS

Much important research has been conducted of late with respect to the Romano-Germanic kingdoms of the sixth century. The general tendency has been to emphasise the cultural and ideological sophistication of many of the regimes that emerged in post-Roman conditions (see Amory and Hen below) and, more controversially, the fluidity of identities on the part of local Roman elites and the leaders of the barbarians themselves. With respect to identity, the towering figures are again Wolfram and Pohl. Insightful studies of the literary authors on whom much of our knowledge of the period depends have also had far-reaching consequences, with Ian Wood's work on Gregory of Tours, in particular, fundamentally recasting our understanding of Merovingian politics. The most interesting work, however, has resulted from examining these societies and regimes in their archaeological setting, and attempting to marry the archaeological and textual materials. For Italy, the work of Bryan Ward-Perkins is again important here, and admirable use of the archaeology is also evident in G. Halsall, *Settlement and Social Organization: The Merovingian Region of Metz* (Cambridge, 1995), and in A. H. Merrills and R. Miles, *The Vandals* (Oxford, 2010). It is through advances in archaeology that our understanding of this world is most likely to be transformed in the years ahead. The archaeology of all the post-Roman societies is discussed in detail (and used to elucidate historical reality to excellent effect) in Wickham, *Framing the Early Middle Ages: Europe and the Mediterranean, 400–800* (Oxford, 2005).

Primary Sources in Translation
'Anonymous Valesianus', *Pars Posterior: Historia Theodericiana*, Ammianus Marcellinus, *Res Gestae*, tr. J. C. Rolfe (Cambridge, Mass., 1935).
Boethius, *Tractates: The Consolation of Philosophy*, tr. H. F. Stewart, E. K. Rand, and S. J. Tester (Cambridge, Mass., 1918).

Cassiodorus, *Variae*, tr. S. Barnish (Liverpool, 1992), contains a selection. Abbreviated translations of the Latin of the complete collection can be found in T. Hodgkin, *The Letters of Cassiodorus* (1896).

Cosmas Indicopleustes, *Christian Topography* = *La Topographie chrétienne de Cosmas Indicopleuste*, tr. W. Wolska-Conus, 3 vols. (Paris, 1968–73).

Decem Libri Historiae = L. Thorpe, *Gregory of Tours: History of the Franks* (Toronto, 1974).

P. J. Geary, *Readings in Medieval History* (Peterborough, Ontario, 1989), contains useful material from Tacitus' *Germania*, Jordanes' *Getica*, the *Hildebrandlied*, letters addressed to Clovis from Bishops Remigius of Rheims and Avitus of Vienne, and Gregory of Tours.

Jordanes, *Getica* = C. C. Mierow, *The Gothic History of Jordanes* (Princeton, 1915, repr. 2006).

Liber Pontificalis = *The Book of Pontiffs (Liber Pontificalis): The Ancient Biographies of the First Ninety Roman Bishops to AD 715*, tr. R. Davis (Liverpool, 2000).

J. Matthews and P. Heather, *The Goths in the Fourth Century* (Liverpool, 1992).

Pactus Legis Salicae = see T. J. Rivers, *Laws of the Salian and Ripuarian Franks* (New York, 1986).

Procopius, *Secret History*, tr. G. Williams and P. Sarris (London, 2007).

—— *Wars* = Procopius, *History of the Wars, Secret History, Buildings*, tr. H. B. Dewing and G. Downey, 7 vols. (Cambridge, Mass., 1914–40).

Tacitus, *Germania*, tr. M. Winterbottom (Oxford, 1986).

Victor of Vita, *History of the Vandal Persecution*, tr. J. Moorhead (Liverpool, 1992).

Secondary Sources

P. Amory, *People and Identity in Ostrogothic Italy* (Cambridge, 1998).

S. J. B. Barnish, 'The *Anonymous Valesianus II* as a Source for the Last Years of Theoderic', *Latomus* 42 (1983), pp. 472–96.

—— 'Maximian, Cassiodorus, Boethius, Theodahad: Literature, Philosophy, and Politics in Ostrogothic Italy', *Nottingham Medieval Studies* 34 (1990), pp. 16–31.

G. Berndt, *Konflikt und Anpassung. Studien zu Migration und Ethnogenese der Vandalen* (Husum, 2007).

—— and R. Steinacher (eds.), *Das Reich der Vandalen und Seine (Vor)Geschichten* (Vienna, 2008).

S. Bjornlie, 'What Have Elephants to Do with Sixth-Century Politics? A Reappraisal of the "Official" Governmental Dossier of Cassiodorus', *Journal of Late Antiquity* 2.1 (2009), pp. 143–71.

A. K. Bowman, P. Garnsey, and A. Cameron (eds.), *The Cambridge Ancient History*, 2nd ed., vol. XII: *The Crisis of Empire, AD 193–337* (Cambridge, 2005).

T. S. Burns, *A History of the Ostrogoths* (Bloomington, Indiana, 1984).

C. P. Caratelli (ed.), *Magistra barbaritas: I barbari in Italia* (Milan, 1984).

E. Chrysos and A. Schwarz (eds.), *Das Reich und Die Barbaren* (Vienna, 1989).

R. Collins, *Law, Culture, and Regionalism in Early Medieval Spain* (Aldershot, 1992).

J. Conant, 'Literacy and Private Documentation in Vandal North Africa', in Merrills (2004), pp. 199–224.

F. Clover, *The Late Roman West and the Vandals* (Aldershot, 1993).

C. Courtois, *Les Vandales et l'Afrique* (Paris, 1955).

W. M. Daly, 'Clovis: How Barbaric? How Pagan?', *Speculum* 69 (1994), pp. 619–64.

S. Dick, *Der Mythos vom 'Germanischen' Königtum* (Berlin, 2008).

J. F. Drinkwater and H. Elton (eds.), *Fifth-Century Gaul: A Crisis of Identity?* (Cambridge, 1992).
W. H. C. Frend, 'From Donatist Opposition to Byzantine Loyalism', in Merrills (2004), pp. 259–70.
J. W. George, 'Vandal Poets in Their Context', in Merrills (2004), pp. 133–44.
M. Gibson (ed.), *Boethius: His Life, Thought, and Influence* (Oxford, 1981).
W. Goffart, *The Narrators of Barbarian History (AD 550–800): Jordanes, Gregory of Tours, Bede, and Paul the Deacon* (Princeton, 1988).
G. Greatrex, 'Roman Identity in the Sixth Century', in S. Mitchell and G. Greatrex (eds.), *Ethnicity and Culture in Late Antiquity* (Swansea, 2001), pp. 267–92.
D. H. Green, *The Carolingian Lord* (Cambridge, 1965).
P. Grierson and M. Blackburn, *Medieval European Coinage: The Early Middle Ages (5th–10th c.)* (Cambridge, 1986).
G. Halsall, *Settlement and Social Organization: The Merovingian Region of Metz* (Cambridge, 1995).
—— *Barbarian Migrations and the Roman West 376–568* (Cambridge, 2007).
P. Heather, 'Cassiodorus and the Rise of the Amalic Genealogy and the Goths under Hun Domination', *Journal of Roman Studies* 78 (1988), pp. 103–28.
—— 'Theoderic, King of the Goths', *Early Medieval Europe* 4.2 (1995), pp. 145–73.
—— *The Goths* (Oxford, 1996).
—— 'Christianity and the Vandals in the Reign of Geiseric', in J. Drinkwater and B. Salway (eds.), *Wolf Liebeschuetz Reflected: Bulletin of the Institute of Classical Studies, Supplement 91* (2007), pp. 22–47.
Y. Hen, *Roman Barbarians: The Royal Court and Culture in the Early Medieval West* (Basingstoke, 2007).
J. D. Howard-Johnston, 'The Great Powers in Late Antiquity: A Comparison' in A. Cameron (ed.), *The Byzantine and Early Islamic Near East*, vol. III: *States, Resources, and Armies* (Princeton, 1995), pp. 157–226.
H. J. Hummer, 'The Fluidity of Barbarian Ethnic Identity: The Ethnogenesis of Alemanni and Suebi, AD 200–500', *Early Medieval Europe* 7.1 (1998), pp. 1–27, 9–10.
E. James, *The Franks* (Oxford, 1988).
A. H. M. Jones, 'The Constitutional Position of Odoacer and Theoderic', *Journal of Roman Studies* 52 (1962), pp. 126–30.
M. Kulikowski and K. Bowes (eds.), *Hispania in Late Antiquity: Current Perspectives* (Leiden, 2005).
E. Luttwak, *The Grand Strategy of the Byzantine Empire* (Cambridge, Mass., 2009).
M. McCormick, *Eternal Victory: Triumphal Rulership in Late Antiquity, Byzantium, and the Early Medieval West* (Cambridge, 1986).
A. H. Merrills, 'The Perils of Panegyric', in Merrills (2004), pp. 145–62.
—— *History and Geography in Late Antiquity* (Cambridge, 2005).
—— 'The Secret of My Succession: Dynasty and Crisis in Vandal Africa', *Early Medieval Europe* 18 (2010), pp. 135–59.
—— (ed.), *Vandals, Romans, and Berbers: New Perspectives on Late Antique North Africa* (Woodbridge, 2004).
—— and R. Miles, *The Vandals* (Oxford, 2010).
A. Momigliano, 'Cassiodorus and the Italian Culture of His Time', *Proceedings of the British Academy* 41 (1955).
J. Moorhead, *Theoderic in Italy* (Oxford, 1993).

C. Morrisson, 'The Re-Use of Obsolete Coins: The Case of Roman Imperial Bronzes Revived in the Late Fifth Century', in C. N. L. Brooke, B. H. I. H. Stewart, J. G. Pollard, and T. R. Volk (eds.), *Studies in Numismatic Method Presented to Philip Grierson* (Cambridge, 1983), pp. 95–112.

W. Pohl, 'The Vandals: Fragments of a Narrative', in Merrills (2004), pp. 31–48.

—— and M. Diesenberger (eds.), *Integration und Herrschaft* (Vienna, 2002).

P. Sarris, 'The Origins of the Manorial Economy: New Insights from Late Antiquity', *English Historical Review* 119 (2004), pp. 279–311.

D. Shanzer, 'Dating the Baptism of Clovis: The Bishop of Vienne vs. The Bishop of Tours', *Early Medieval Europe* 7.1 (1998), pp. 29–57.

—— 'Intentions and Audiences', in Merrills (2004), pp. 271–90.

M. Spencer, 'Dating the Baptism of Clovis', *Early Medieval Europe* 3.1 (1994), pp. 97–116.

G. Tabacco, *The Struggle for Power in Medieval Italy: The Structures of Political Rule* (Cambridge, 1989).

Teoderico il Grande et I Goti d'Italia, Atti del XIII Congresso internazionale di studi sull'alto medioevo, Milan 1992 (Spoleto, 1993).

E. A. Thompson, *The Visigoths in the Time of Ulfila* (Oxford, 1966).

J. M. Wallace-Hadrill, *The Long-Haired Kings* (Oxford, 1953).

—— *Early Germanic Kingship* (Oxford, 1971).

B. Ward-Perkins, *From Classical Antiquity to the Middle Ages: Urban Public Building in Northern and Central Italy AD 300–850* (Oxford, 1984).

—— *The Fall of the Roman Empire and the End of Civilization* (Oxford, 2005).

R. Wenskus, *Stammesbildung und Verfassung: Das Werden der frühmittelalterlichen Gentes* (Cologne, 1961).

H. Wolfram, 'The Shaping of the Early Medieval Kingdom', *Viator* 1 (1970), pp. 1–20, 4–5.

—— 'Athanaric the Visigoth: Monarchy or Judgeship?', *Journal of Medieval History* 1 (1975), pp. 259–78.

—— *History of the Goths* (Berkeley, 1988).

—— *The Roman Empire and the Germanic Peoples* (Chicago, 1998).

—— and A. Schwarcz (eds.), *Anerkennung und Integration* (Vienna, 1988).

I. Wood, 'Gregory of Tours and Clovis', *Revue Belge de Philologie et d'Histoire* 63 (1985), pp. 249–72.

—— 'The "Secret Histories" of Gregory of Tours', *Revue Belge de Philologie et d'Histoire* 71 (1993), pp. 253–70.

—— *The Merovingian Kingdoms 450–751* (London, 1994).

—— (ed.), *Franks and Alamanni in the Migration Period* (Leiden, 1999).

C. P. Wormald, 'Kings and Kingship', in Fouracre (2005), pp. 571–604.

CHAPTER 4 THE VIEW FROM THE EAST: CRISIS, SURVIVAL, AND RENEWAL

The history of the early Eastern Roman (or 'Byzantine') empire of the fifth and sixth centuries has been most obviously transformed in recent years by the extent and quality of late-antique archaeology that has been undertaken, much of which is ably summarised in M. Decker, *Tilling the Hateful Earth: Agricultural Production and Trade in the Late Antique East* (Oxford, 2009), and in the chapters by Bryan Ward-Perkins in volumes XIII and XIV of the *Cambridge Ancient History*. Close attention to the economic history of the period is also evident in J. Banaji, *Agrarian Change in Late Antiquity: Gold, Labour, and Aristocratic*

Dominance, 2nd ed. (Oxford, 2007), and P. Sarris, *Economy and Society in the Age of Justinian* (Cambridge, 2006). The works of James Howard-Johnston and Geoffrey Greatrex have cast important light on the military and diplomatic contexts in which imperial politics took place (see below), and our chief literary source for the reign of Justinian—the historian Procopius—has been the subject of studies of fundamental importance by Averil Cameron and Anthony Kaldellis. The best overall narrative of the period is to be found in C. Morrisson (ed.), *Le monde byzantin: I: L'Empire romain d'Orient, 330–641* (Paris, 2004), and those able to read German should turn to the voluminous works of Mischa Meier. New perspectives on life in the empire (and especially the problems caused by religion) have been gleaned from closer attention to sources in Syriac and Coptic, and by current and forthcoming work by Richard Payne on the neighbouring Sasanian Empire of Persia. For the significance of the Syriac sources, see Philip Wood, *'We Have No King But Christ': Christian Political Thought in Greater Syria on the Eve of the Arab Conquest* (Oxford, 2010). M. Maas (ed.), *The Cambridge Companion to the Age of Justinian* (Cambridge, 2005), also contains much that is useful.

Sources in Translation

The *Codex Iustinianus* and Justinian's post-codificatory 'novels' are not currently available in print in a reliable English translation, although translations of both works are forthcoming from Cambridge University Press. Translations by Justice Fred H. Blume are available online, however, on the website of the University of Wyoming ('Annotated Justinian Code').

Acts of the Council of Chalcedon, tr. R. Price and M. Gaddis, 3 vols. (Liverpool, 2005).
Acts of the Council of Constantinople of 553, tr. R. Price, 2 vols. (Liverpool, 2009).
Agathias, *Histories*, tr. J. D. Frendo (Berlin, 1975).
'Anonymous Valesianus', *Pars Posterior: Historia Theodericiana*, Ammianus Marcellinus, *Res Gestae*, tr. J. C. Rolfe (Cambridge, Mass., 1935).
Anthologia Graeca (The Greek Anthology), tr. W. Paton, 5 vols. (Cambridge, Mass., 1916–18).
P. Bell, *Three Political Voices from the Age of Justinian: Agapetus' Advice to the Emperor, Dialogue on Political Science, Paul the Silentiary's Description of Hagia Sophia* (Liverpool, 2009).
Chronicon Paschale, tr. M. and M. Whitby (Liverpool, 1989).
Corippus = *Flavius Cresconius Corippus, in Laudem Iustini Minoris Libri Quattor*, tr. A. Cameron (Oxford, 1976).
Cosmas Indicopleustes, *Christian Topography* = *La Topographie chrétienne de Cosmas Indicopleuste*, tr. W. Wolska-Conus, 3 vols. (Paris, 1968–73).
Cyril of Scythopolis, *Life of John* = R. Price and J. Binns, *The Lives of the Monks of Palestine* (Kalamazoo, 1991).
Evagrius Scholasticus, *Ecclesiastical History*, tr. M. Whitby (Liverpool, 2005).
G. Greatrex and S. Lieu, *The Roman Eastern Frontier and the Persian Wars: Part II AD 363–630* (London, 2002).
John of Ephesus, *Ecclesiastical History* = *The Third Part of the Ecclesiastical History of John Bishop of Ephesus*, tr. R. Payne Smith (Oxford, 1860).
John Lydus, *On the Magistracies of the Roman State*, tr. A. C. Bandy (Philadelphia, 1983).
John Malalas, *Chronicle*, tr. E. Jeffreys, M. Jeffreys, and R. Scott (Melbourne, 1986).
Justinian, *Digest*, trs. A. Watson et al., 4 vols. (Philadelphia, 1986).
——*Institutes*, trs. P. Birks and G. McLeod (1987).
M. Maas, *Readings in Late Antiquity: A Sourcebook*, 2nd ed. (London, 2010).

Marcellinus Comes, *Chronicle*, tr. B. Croke (Sydney, 1995).
Maurice, *The Strategikon of the Emperor Maurice*, tr. G. T. Dennis (Pennsylvania, 1984).
Menander the Guardsman = *The History of Menander the Guardsman*, tr. R. C. Blockley (Cambridge, 1985).
The Oracle of Baalbek, tr. P. J. Alexander (Washington DC, 1967).
Procopius, *Secret History*, tr. G. Williams and P. Sarris (London, 2007).
—— *Wars* = *Procopius: History of the Wars, Secret History, Buildings*, tr. H. B. Dewing and G. Downey, 7 vols. (Cambridge, Mass., 1914–40).
Pseudo-Dionysius of Tel Mahre, *Chronicle: Part Three*, tr. W. Witakoski (Liverpool, 1996).
K. P. Wesche, *On the Person of Christ* (New York, 1991).
Zacharias of Mitylene, *Historia Ecclesiastica* = F. J. Hamilton and E. W. Brooks, *The Syriac Chronicle Known as That of Zachariah of Mitylene* (1899).

Secondary Sources
P. Amory, *People and Identity in Ostrogothic Italy* (Cambridge, 1997).
J. Banaji, *Agrarian Change in Late Antiquity: Gold, Labour, and Aristocratic Dominance*, 2nd ed. (Oxford, 2007).
—— 'Precious Metal Coinages and Monetary Expansion in Late Antiquity', in F. De Romanis and S. Sorda (eds.), *Dal denarius al dinar: l'oriente et la moneta romana* (Rome, 2006), pp. 265–303.
P. Bell, 'Social Tensions in the Early Byzantine Empire' (Oxford University, D.Phil. dissertation, 2006).
M. Boyce, *The Zoroastrians* (London, 1979).
S. Brock, 'The Nestorian Church: A Lamentable Misnomer', *Bulletin of the John Rylands Library* 78.3 (1996), pp. 23–36.
A. Cameron, *Circus Factions: Blues and Greens at Rome and Byzantium* (Oxford, 1976).
—— 'Images of Authority: Elites and Icons in Late Sixth-Century Byzantium', in M. Mullett and R. Scott, *Byzantium and the Classical Tradition* (Birmingham, 1981), pp. 205–34.
—— *Procopius and the Sixth Century* (London, 1985).
—— (ed.), *The Byzantine and Early Islamic Near East*, vol. III: *States, Resources, and Armies* (Princeton, 1995), pp. 157–226.
J. F. Coakley and K. Parry Bull (eds.), *The Church of the East: Life and Thought* (Bulletin of the John Rylands Library, 78.3, 1996).
P. Crone, 'Kavad's Heresy and Mazdak's Revolt', *Iran* 29 (1991), pp. 21–42.
M. Decker, *Tilling the Hateful Earth: Agriculture in the Late Antique East* (Oxford, 2009).
J. A. S. Evans, *The Age of Justinian: The Circumstances of Imperial Power* (London, 1996).
W. Goffart, *Rome's Fall and After* (Princeton, 1989).
G. Greatrex, *Rome and Persia at War, 502–32* (Leeds, 1998).
—— and S. Lieu, *The Roman Eastern Frontier and the Persian Wars: Part II AD 363–630* (London, 2002).
F. Haarer, *The Reign of the Emperor Anastasius* (Aldershot, 2006).
A. M. Honoré, *Tribonian* (London, 1978).
J. D. Howard-Johnston, 'The Two Great Powers in Late Antiquity: A Comparison', in Cameron (1995), pp. 157–226.
A. H. M. Jones, *The Later Roman Empire*, 3 vols. (Oxford, 1964).
W. Kaegi, *Byzantium and the Decline of Rome* (Princeton, 1968).
H. Kaimian, 'Cities and Social Order in Sasanian Iran: The Archaeological Potential', *Antiquity* 84 (2010), pp. 453–66.

Select Bibliography and Further Reading 395

A. Kaldellis, *Procopius of Caesarea: Tyranny, History, and Philosophy at the End of Antiquity* (Pennsylvania, 2004).
M. Kaplan, *Les Hommes et la Terre à Byzance* (Paris, 1992).
H. Karmian, 'Cities and Social Order in Sasanian Iran: The Archaeological Potential', *Antiquity* 84 (2010), pp. 453–66.
D. Keys, *Catastrophe: An Investigation into the Origins of the Modern World* (London, 1999).
A. Kolesnikov, *Denezhnoe Khozaistvo v Irane v VII Veke* (Moscow, 1998).
J. H. W. G. Liebeschuetz, *The Decline and Fall of the Roman City* (Oxford, 2001).
C. S. Lightfoot, 'Armenia and the Eastern Marches', in Bowman, Garnsey, and Cameron (2005), pp. 481–97.
L. K. Little (ed.), *Plague and the End of Antiquity: The Pandemic of 541–750* (Cambridge, 2007).
E. N. Luttwak, *The Grand Strategy of the Byzantine Empire* (Cambridge, Mass., 2009).
M. Maas, 'Roman History and Christian Ideology in Justinianic Reform Legislation', *Dumbarton Oaks Papers* 40 (1986), pp. 17–31.
——*John Lydus and the Roman Past* (London, 1992).
——(ed.), *The Cambridge Companion to the Age of Justinian* (Cambridge, 2005).
M. McCormick, *Eternal Victory: Triumphal Rulership in Late Antiquity, Byzantium, and the Early Medieval West* (Cambridge, 1986).
M. Meier, *Das anderer Zeitalter Justinians* (Göttingen, 2003).
——*Justinian: Herrschaft, Reich und Religion* (Munich, 2004).
——*Anastasios I* (Stuttgart, 2009).
J. Meyendorff, 'Justinian, the Empire, and the Church', *Dumbarton Oaks Papers* 22 (1968), pp. 43–60.
R. E. Payne, 'Christianity and Iranian Society in Late Antiquity, ca. 500–700 CE' (Princeton, D.Phil. dissertation, 2010).
R. Price and M. Whitby (eds.), *Chalcedon in Context: Church Councils 400–700* (Liverpool, 2009).
Z. Rubin, 'The Mediterranean and the Dilemma of the Roman Empire in Late Antiquity', *Mediterranean Historical Review* 1.1 (1986), pp. 13–62.
——'The Reforms of Khusro Anushirwan', in Cameron (1995), pp. 227–98.
P. Sarris, 'The Justinianic Plague: Origins and Effects', *Continuity and Change* 17.2 (2002), pp. 169–82.
——*Economy and Society in the Age of Justinian* (Cambridge, 2006).
——'Aristocrats, Peasants, and the State in the Later Roman Empire', in P. Eich, S. Schmidt Hofner, and C. Wieland (eds.), *Der wiederkehrende Leviathan:Staatlichkeit und Staatswerdung in Spätantike und Früher Neuzeit* (Heidelberg, 2011), pp. 377–94.
——'The Early Byzantine Economy in Context', *Early Medieval Europe* (forthcoming).
S. Sears, 'Monetary Revision and Monetization in the Late Sasanian Empire', in R. Gyselen and M. Szuppe (eds.), *Matériaux pour l'histoire économique du monde iranien* (Paris, 1999), pp. 149–65.
I. Shahid, *Byzantium and the Arabs in the Fifth Century* (Washington DC, 1989).
——*Byzantium and the Arabs in the Sixth Century* (Washington DC, 1995).
E. Stein, *L'histoire du Bas Empire*, 2 vols. (Paris, 1949).
J. Teall, 'The Barbarians in Justinian's Armies', *Speculum* 40 (1965), pp. 294–322.
A. Weir, 'Two Great Legislators', *Tulane European and Civil Law Forum* (New Orleans, 2006), pp. 35–51.

CHAPTER 5 BYZANTIUM, THE BALKANS, AND THE WEST: THE LATE SIXTH CENTURY

The historiography of the early medieval Balkans has been dogged by debates concerning the medieval origins of modern 'nations', very similar to those which once beset study of the kingdoms of the early medieval West; see P. Geary, *The Myth of Nations: The Medieval Origins of Europe* (Princeton, 2002). Questions relating to the origins of the Slavs, the nature of Slav migration, and the extent of Slavonic settlement in Greece were thus bedevilled by issues of ideology, as well as by the limited number of written sources. In recent years, however, considerable advances have been made through adopting more sophisticated models and concepts of identity, and by paying closer attention to the archaeological evidence—each of which tendencies are exemplified by the writing of Florin Curta (see below). Greater attention to early medieval archaeology, by historians of many nationalities, has also added much to our understanding of life in town and country in Langobard Italy, Merovingian Gaul, and Visigothic Spain, as also of changing settlement patterns in lowland Britain (see, for example, the work of Hamerow, Henning, Lewit, Loseby, Olma Enciso, and Reynolds). Again, the archaeological record is ably integrated with the historical in C. Wickham, *Framing the Early Middle Ages: Europe and the Mediterranean, 400–800* (Oxford, 2005). For the nature of royal politics in this period, fundamental are the works of Ewig and Wood with respect to the Merovingian world, and as regards Spain those of Collins and Sánchez-Albornoz. With respect to Britain, important advances in our understanding have been made by placing the development of the Anglo-Saxon kingdoms in a broader British context, for which one should turn to the writings of Thomas Charles-Edwards.

Primary Sources in Translation
Agathias, *Histories*, tr. J. D. Frendo (Berlin, 1975).
Bede, *Ecclesiastical History of the English People*, ed. and trs. B. Colgrave and R. Mynors, 2 vols. (Oxford, 1969).
R. C. Blockley, *The Fragmentary Classicising Historians of the Later Roman Empire*, 2 vols. (Liverpool, 1981–3).
Chronicon Paschale, trs. M.and M. Whitby (Liverpool, 1989).
Codex Theodosianus = C. Pharr (tr.), *The Theodosian Code* (Princeton, 1952).
Corippus = *Flavius Cresconius Corippus, in Laudem Iustini Minoris Libri Quattor*, tr. A. Cameron (Oxford, 1976).
Felix, *Life of Guthlac*, ed. P. Colgrave (Cambridge, 1956).
Fredegar = *The Fourth Book of the Chronicle of Fredegar and its Continuations*, ed. and trs. J. M. Wallace-Hadrill (London, 1960).
Gildas, *de Excidio Britanniae* = M. Winterbottom, *Gildas: The Ruin of Britain and Other Works* (London, 1978).
Gregory of Tours, *Decem Libri Historiae* = L. Thorpe, *Gregory of Tours: History of the Franks* (London, 1974).
Isidore of Seville, *History of the Goths* = see Wolf (1999).
John of Biclaro = see Wolf (1999).
John of Ephesus, *Ecclesiastical History* = *The Third Part of the Ecclesiastical History of John Bishop of Ephesus*, tr. R. Payne Smith (Oxford, 1860).
Jordanes, *Getica* = C. C. Mierow, *The Gothic History of Jordanes* (Princeton, 1915, repr. 2006).

Lex Visigothorum, tr. in S. P. Scott, *The Civil Law* (Boston, 1932)—not entirely reliable.
Maurice, *The Strategikon of the Emperor Maurice*, tr. G. T. Dennis (Pennsylvania, 1984).
Menander the Guardsman = *The History of Menander the Guardsman*, tr. R. C. Blockley (Cambridge, 1985).
Miracula Sancti Demetrii = P. Lemerle, *Les plus anciens receuils des miracles de S. Demetrius*, 2 vols. (Paris, 1979)—contains French summaries of the Greek text.
Paul the Deacon, *History of the Langobards*, tr. W. D. Foulke (London, 1907).
Procopius, *Secret History*, tr. G. Williams and P. Sarris (London, 2007).
—— *Wars* = *Procopius: History of the Wars, Secret History, Buildings*, tr. H. B. Dewing and G. Downey, 7 vols. (Cambridge, Mass., 1914–40).
Theophylact Simocatta, *History*, trs. M. and M. Whitby (Oxford, 1985).
Venantius Fortunatus, *Personal and Political Poems*, tr. J. George (Liverpool, 1995).
K. B. Wolf, *Conquerors and Chroniclers of Early Medieval Spain* (Liverpool, 1990).

Secondary Sources
C. J. Arnold, *An Archaeology of the Early Anglo-Saxon Kingdoms* (London, 1988).
A. Barbero and M. I. Loring, 'The Formation of the Sueve and Visigothic Kingdoms in Spain' in Fouracre (2005), pp. 162–92.
S. Bassett, *The Origins of the Anglo-Saxon Kingdoms* (Leicester, 1989).
C. Behr, 'The Origins of Kingship in Early Medieval Kent', *Early Medieval Europe* 9 (2000), pp. 25–52.
E. Campbell and C. Bowles, 'Byzantine Trade to the Edge of the World', in M. Mundell Mango (ed.), *Byzantine Trade 4th–12th Centuries* (Farnham, 2009), pp. 297–314.
J. Campbell, 'The Lost Centuries', in Campbell (ed.) (London, 1982), pp. 20–44.
T. Charles-Edwards, *After Rome* (Oxford, 2003).
—— 'The Making of Nations in Britain and Ireland in the Early Middle Ages', in R. Evans (ed.), *Lordship and Learning: Studies in Memory of Trevor Aston* (Woodbridge, 2004), pp. 11–38.
A. Chavarría Arnau, 'Churches and Aristocracies in Seventh-Century Spain: Some Thoughts on the Debate on Visigothic Churches', *Early Medieval Europe* 18 (2010), pp. 160–74.
N. Christie and S. T. Loseby (eds.), *Towns in Transition: Urban Evolution in Late Antiquity and the Early Middle Ages* (Aldershot, 1996).
R. Collins, *Early Medieval Spain: Unity in Diversity* (London, 1983).
—— *Visigothic Spain 409–711* (Oxford, 2004).
F. Curta, *The Making of the Slavs: History and Archaeology of the Lower Danube Region c.500–700* (Cambridge, 2001).
—— *Southeastern Europe in the Middle Ages 500–1200* (Cambridge, 2006).
A. Dooley, 'The Plague and its Consequences in Ireland', in L. K. Little (ed.), *Plague and the End of Antiquity* (Cambridge, 2007), pp. 215–30.
N. Everett, *Literacy in Lombard Italy c.568–774* (Cambridge, 2003).
E. Ewig, 'Volkstum und Volkbewusstein im Frankenreich des 7. Jahrhunderts', in *idem.*, *Spätantikes und frankisches Gallien*, 2 vols. (Stuttgart, 1976–9).
P. Fouracre (ed.), *The Cambridge Medieval History*, vol. 1: *500–700* (Cambridge, 2005).
P. Geary, *Before France and Germany: The Making and Transformation of the Merovingian World* (repr. New York, 1998).
H. Hamerow, 'The Earliest Anglo-Saxon Kingdoms', in Fouracre (2005).
A. Harris, *Byzantium, Britain, and the West* (Stroud, 2003).

P. Heather, *Empires and Barbarians: Migration, Development, and the Birth of Europe* (London, 2009).
J. Henning (ed.), *Post-Roman Towns, Trade, and Settlement in Europe and Byzantium*, 2 vols. (Berlin, 2007).
J. Hines, 'Society, Community, and Identity', in Charles-Edwards (2003), pp. 61–102.
E. James, *Britain in the First Millennium* (London, 2001).
D. Keys, *Catastrophe: An Investigation into the Origins of the Modern World* (London, 1999).
P. D. King, *Law and Society in the Visigothic Kingdom* (Cambridge, 1992).
T. Lewit, 'Vanishing Villas: What Happened to Elite Rural Habitation in the West in the 5th–6th c?', *Journal of Roman Archaeology* 16 (2003), pp. 260–74.
S. T. Loseby, 'Marseille: A Late Antique Success Story', *Journal of Roman Studies* 82 (1992), pp. 165–85.
J. Maddicott, 'Plague in Seventh-Century England' in L. K. Little (ed.), *Plague and the End of Antiquity* (Cambridge, 2007), pp. 171–214.
H. Mayr-Harting, *The Coming of Christianity to Anglo-Saxon England*, 3rd ed. (London, 1991).
A. H. Merrills and R. Miles, *The Vandals* (Oxford, 2010).
J. Moorhead, 'The Byzantines in the West in the Sixth Century', in Fouracre (2005), pp. 118–39.
R. Niblett, 'Why *Verulamium?*', in M. Henig and P. Lindley (eds.), *Alban and St Albans: Roman and Medieval Architecture, Art, and Archaeology* (Leeds, 2001), pp. 1–12.
D. Obolensky, *The Byzantine Commonwealth* (New Haven, 1971).
L. Olmo Enciso, 'The Royal Foundation of *Recopolis* and the Urban Renewal in Iberia During the Second Half of the Sixth Century', in Henning (ed.) (2007), I, pp. 181–96.
W. Pohl, 'The Empire and the Lombards: Treaties and Negotiations in the Sixth Century', in W. Pohl (ed.), *Kingdoms of the Empire: The Integration of Barbarians in Late Antiquity* (Leiden, 1997), pp. 75–134.
A. Poulter, 'Cataclysm on the Lower Danube: The Destruction of a Complex Roman Landscape', in N. Christie (ed.), *Landscapes of Change: Rural Evolutions in Late Antiquity and the Early Middle Ages* (Aldershot, 2004), pp. 223–54.
K. Randsborg, *The First Millennium* A.D. *in Europe and the Mediterranean: An Archaeological Essay* (Cambridge, 1991), pp. 28–9.
P. Reynolds, *Hispania and the Roman Mediterranean*, AD *100–700: Ceramics and Trade* (London, 2010).
C. Salter, 'Early Tin Extraction', in M. Mundell Mango (ed.), *Byzantine Trade 4th–12th centuries* (Farnham, 2009), pp. 315–22.
C. Sánchez-Albornoz, *Investigaciones y documentos sobre las instituciones hispanas* (Santiago, 1970).
F. M. Stenton, *Anglo-Saxon England* (Oxford, 1943).
J. M. Wallace-Hadrill, *Early Germanic Kingship* (Oxford, 1971), pp. 12–13.
M. Whitby, *The Emperor Maurice and his Historian* (Oxford, 1988).
C. Wickham, *Framing the Early Middle Ages: Europe and the Mediterranean, 400–800* (Oxford, 2005).
K. P. Witney, *The Kingdom of Kent: A History from c. 450–825* (Chichester, 1982).
K. B. Wolf, *Conquerors and Chroniclers of Early Medieval Spain* (Liverpool, 1999).
I. Wood, *The Merovingian North Sea* (Alingsas, 1983).
—— 'The Code in Merovingian Gaul', in J. Harries and I. Wood (eds.), *The Theodosian Code* (London, 1993), pp. 159–77.
—— *The Merovingian Kingdoms 450–751* (London, 1994).

—— 'Deconstructing the Merovingian Family', in R. Corradini, M. Diesenberger, and H. Reimitz (eds.), *The Construction of Communities in the Early Middle Ages: Texts, Resources, and Artefacts* (Leiden, 2003), pp. 149–72.
J. Wood, 'Defending Byzantine Spain: Frontiers and Diplomacy', *Early Medieval Europe* 18 (2010), pp. 292–319.
P. Wormald, *The Making of English Law: King Alfred to the Twelfth Century*, vol. I: *Legislation and its Limits* (Oxford, 1999).
F. E. Wozniak, 'East Rome, Ravenna, and Western Illyricum, 454–536 AD', *Historia* 30.3 (1981), pp. 351–82.
B. Yorke, 'The Kingdom of the East Saxons', *Anglo-Saxon England* 14 (1985), pp. 1–36.

CHAPTER 6 RELIGION AND SOCIETY IN THE AGE OF GREGORY THE GREAT

The study of religious history in the late antique and early medieval periods has become something of a discipline unto itself, cut off from broader discussion of military and economic contexts. This was always true on the European continent, where it formed part of the broader study of theology and doctrine. In the English-speaking world, however, the concentration is less theological, and more dominated by the figure of Peter Brown, whose work in the 1970s on the 'rise and function of the Holy Man in late antiquity' continues to exercise a decisive influence on much scholarship. In recent years, however, Brown has himself reacted against his earlier 'functionalism', and there is a greater tendency now to view the accounts we possess of the lives of early medieval saints more as literary products, rather than necessarily reflecting or directly recording reality (as Brown's essay of 1971 presupposed). More significantly, greater attention has been paid in the latest work to resistance to Christianisation and to elements of Church doctrine, and to scepticism as to the claims made by holy men and priests. The works of Philip Booth and Matthew Dal Santo are of central significance to this reorientation.

Primary Sources in Translation
Athanasius, *Life of Anthony and Letter to Marcellinus*, tr. R. C. Gregg (Mahwah, New Jersey, 1980).
Augustine, *Confessions*, tr. W. Watts, 2 vols. (Cambridge, Mass., repr. 1989).
Bede, *Ecclesiastical History of the English People*, ed. and trs. B. Colgrave and R. Mynors, 2 vols. (Oxford, 1969).
—— *Life of Cuthbert* = B. Colgrave (ed.), *Two Lives of St Cuthbert* (Cambridge, 1940).
Benedict, *Rule*, tr. C. White (2008).
E. Dawes and N. H. Baynes, *Three Byzantine Saints: Contemporary Biographies of St Daniel the Stylite, St Theodore of Sykeon, and St John the Almsgiver* (Oxford, 1948).
Gregory of Tours, *Decem Libri Historiae* = L. Thorpe, *Gregory of Tours: History of the Franks* (London, 1974).
—— *Glory of the Confessors*, tr. R. Van Dam (Liverpool, 1988).
—— *Life of the Fathers*, tr. E. James (Liverpool, 1985).
—— *Glory of the Martyrs*, tr. R. Van Dam (Liverpool, 1988).
Gregory the Great, *Dialogues*, tr. O. J. Zimmermann (Washington DC, 2002).
—— *Pastoral Care*, tr. H. Davis (Mahwah, New Jersey, 1950).
J. N. Hillgarth, *Christianity and Paganism 350–750: The Conversion of Western Europe* (Pennsylvania, 1988)—useful collection of sources.

Hydatius = R. W. Burgess, *The Chronicle of Hydatius and the Consularia Constantinopolitana* (Oxford, 1993).
Life of Nicholas of Sion, trs. I and N. Sevcenko (Brookline, Mass., 1984).
Procopius, *Secret History*, tr. G. Williams and P. Sarris (London, 2007).
—— *Wars* = Procopius, *History of the Wars, Secret History, Buildings*, tr. H. B. Dewing and G. Downey, 7 vols. (Cambridge, Mass., 1914–40).
H. Waddell, *The Desert Fathers* (1936).

Secondary Sources
P. Booth, 'John Moschus, Sopronius Sophista, and Maximus Confessor Between East and West' (Cambridge University, Ph.D. dissertation, 2007).
P. Booth, M. Dal Santo, and P. Sarris, *An Age of Saints? Hagiography and Society in the Early Middle Ages* (Leiden, 2011).
J. Boswell, *Christianity, Social Tolerance, and Homosexuality* (Chicago, 1981).
P. Brown, *Augustine of Hippo* (London, 1967).
—— *The Cult of the Saints* (London, 1981).
—— *Authority and the Sacred* (Cambridge, 1995).
—— *Power and Persuasion in Late Antiquity* (Madison, 1998).
—— 'Asceticism: Pagan and Christian', in A. Cameron and P. Garnsey (eds.), *The Cambridge Ancient History*, vol. XIII (Cambridge, 1998), pp. 601–31.
—— *The Rise of Western Christendom* (repr. Oxford, 2003).
—— 'Christendom c.600', in T. F. X. Noble and J. M. Smith (eds.), *The New Cambridge History of Christianity: Early Medieval Christianities c.600–c.1100* (Cambridge, 2008), pp. 1–20.
J. Campbell and C. P. Wormald, *The Anglo-Saxons* (London, 1981).
A. Cameron, 'Images of Authority: Elites and Icons in Late Sixth-Century Byzantium', in M. Mullett and R. Scott (eds.), *Byzantium and the Classical Tradition* (Birmingham, 1981), pp. 205–34.
G. Clark, *Women in Late Antiquity: Pagan and Christian Lifestyles* (Oxford, 1993).
R. Collins, *Early Medieval Spain: Unity in Diversity* (1983).
M. Dal Santo, 'Gregory the Great and Debate Concerning the Cult of the Saints in the Early Byzantine Mediterranean and its Hinterland During the Late Sixth and Seventh Centuries' (Cambridge University, Ph.D. dissertation, 2008).
—— 'Gregory the Great and Eustratius of Constantinople: The Dialogues on the Miracles of the Italian Fathers as a Justification of the Cult of the Saints', *Journal of Early Christian Studies* 17.4 (2009), pp. 421–58.
—— *Debating the Saints' Cult in the Age of Gregory the Great* (Oxford, forthcoming).
N. de Lange, 'The Jews in Justinian's Empire', in M. Maas (ed.), *The Cambridge Companion to the Age of Justinian* (Cambridge, 2005).
B. Dumézil, *Conversion et liberté dans les royaumes barbares d'Occident* (Paris, 2005).
G. R. Evans, *The Thought of Gregory the Great* (Cambridge, 1986).
P. Fouracre, 'Why Were So Many Bishops Killed in Merovingian Francia?' in N. Fryde and D. Reitz (eds.), *Bishofsmord im Mittelalter: Murder of Bishops* (Göttingen, 2003), pp. 13–36.
E. R. Hardy, *The Large Estates of Byzantine Egypt* (New York, 1931).
J. Herrin, *The Formation of Christendom* (Oxford, 1987).
E. John, *Orbis Britanniae* (Leicester, 1949).
C. Mango, *Byzantium: The Empire of New Rome* (London, 1983).
—— 'Saints', in G. Cavallo (ed.), *The Byzantines* (Chicago, 1997), pp. 255–80.

R. A. Markus, 'Gregory the Great and a Papal Missionary Strategy', in Markus (1983), XI.
—— 'Gregory the Great's Europe', in Markus (1983), XV.
—— *From Augustine to Gregory the Great* (London, 1983).
—— *Gregory the Great and His World* (Cambridge, 1997).
—— *The End of Ancient Christianity* (Cambridge, 1998).
C. Rapp, *Holy Bishops in Late Antiquity: The Nature of Christian Leadership in an Age of Transition* (Berkeley, 2005).
—— 'Old Testament Models for Emperors in Early Byzantium', in P. Magdalino and R. Nelson (eds.), *The Old Testament in Byzantium* (Washington DC, 2010), pp. 175–98.
J. Richards, *Consul of God* (London, 1980).
M. Rouche, 'Violence and Death', in P. Veyne (ed.), *A History of Private Life from Pagan Rome to Byzantium* (Cambridge, Mass., 1992), pp. 485–518.
P. Sarris, *Economy and Society in the Age of Justinian* (Cambridge, 2006).
—— 'Introduction', in *Procopius: Secret History*, tr. Williamson and Sarris (2007).
R. D. Scott, 'Malalas, *The Secret History*, and Justinian's Propaganda', *Dumbarton Oaks Papers* 39 (1985), pp. 99–110, p. 104.
F. M. Stenton, *Anglo-Saxon England* (Oxford, 1943).
E. A. Thomson, 'Peasant Revolts in Late Roman Gaul and Spain', *Past and Present* 2 (1952), pp. 11–23.
J. R. R. Tolkien, 'Beowulf, the Monsters, and the Critics', *Proceedings of the British Academy* 22 (1936), pp. 245–95.
J. M. Wallace-Hadrill, *Early Germanic Kingship* (Oxford, 1971).
D. Whitelock, *The Audience of Beowulf* (Oxford, 1951).
I. Wood, 'The Conversion of Barbarian Peoples' in G. Barraclough (ed.), *The Christian World* (London, 1981).
C. P. Wormald, 'Bede, Beowulf, and the Conversion of the Anglo-Saxon Aristocracy', in C. P. Wormald and S. Baxter (eds.), *The Times of Bede* (Oxford, 2006a), pp. 30–105.

CHAPTER 7 HERACLIUS, PERSIA, AND HOLY WAR *AND* CHAPTER 8 THE AGE OF DIVISION

The history of the early Byzantine Empire of the late sixth and early seventh centuries has been the subject of much excellent military history in recent years. Foremost amongst the works produced are M. Whitby, *The Emperor Maurice and His Historian* (Oxford, 1988), and the various publications of James Howard-Johnston, culminating in his *Witnesses to a World Crisis* (Oxford, 2010). The history of early Islam has been subject to even greater revision, and has produced some of the most thought-provoking and exciting research in any field of the Humanities and Social Sciences. In broad terms, debate has been dominated by those (such as Patricia Crone) who are sceptical as to the extent of the historicity of many of the Arabic sources, and so who are inclined to turn to the more contemporary accounts of early Islam written by Greek, Coptic, or Syriac-speaking authors, and those (such as Hugh Kennedy) who hold that early Islamic history is best written with the grain of the Arabic sources themselves. Such differences have at times scaled polemical heights, but important work by Robert Hoyland, Petra Sijpesteijn, and others has sought to tread a middle path, drawing on the best scholarship of all those concerned. As with other parts of the late-antique world, important advances have been made through the integration of new archaeological discoveries. In particular, careful study of the early Byzantine-Arab and Islamic coinage, and of the documentary evidence that survives on papyrus from Egypt, are currently revolutionising our understanding of the first century of Arab rule (see Foss and Sijpesteijn below). Similarly exciting conclusions are emerging with respect to the world of Iraq and Iran in the writings of Richard Payne.

Primary Sources in Translation
Acts of the Council of Constantinople of 553, tr. R. Price, 2 vols. (Liverpool, 2009).
Agathias, *Histories*, tr. J. D. Frendo (Berlin, 1975).
Armenian History = *The Armenian History Attributed to Sebeos*, tr. R. W. Thomson with historical commentary by J. D. Howard-Johnston, 2 vols. (Liverpool, 1999).
Bibliotheca Vaticana, Barberini, gr. 336, fols. 176v–177r, eds. S. Parenti and E. Velkovska, *L'Euchologio Barberini gr.336 (ff.1–263)* (Rome, 1995).
Chronicon Paschale, trs. M. and M. Whitby (Liverpool, 1989).
Doctrina Iacobi, tr. V. Déroche, *Travaux et Mémoires* 11 (1991), pp. 69–219 (into French).
Evagrius Scholasticus, *Ecclesiastical History*, tr. M. Whitby (Liverpool, 2005).
Fredegar = *The Fourth Book of the Chronicle of Fredegar and its Continuations*, ed. and trs. J. M. Wallace-Hadrill (London, 1960).
G. Greatrex and S. Lieu, *The Roman Eastern Frontier and the Persian Wars: Part II* AD *363–630* (London, 2002).
Ibn Ishaq = *The Life of Muhammad: A Translation of Ibn Ishaq's Sirat Rasul Allah*, tr. A Guillaume (Karachi, 1955).
John of Ephesus, *Ecclesiastical History* = *The Third Part of the Ecclesiastical History of John Bishop of Ephesus*, tr. R. Payne Smith (Oxford, 1860).
John of Nikiu = *The Chronicle of John, Bishop of Nikiu*, tr. R. H. Charles (London, 1916).
Liber Pontificalis = *The Book of Pontiffs (Liber Pontificalis): The Ancient Biographies of the First Ninety Roman Bishops to* AD *715*, tr. R. Davis (Liverpool, 2000).
Menander the Guardsman = *The History of Menander the Guardsman*, tr. R. C. Blockley (Cambridge, 1985).
Movses Dasxuranci, *History of the Caucasian Albanians*, tr. C. F. J. Dowsett (London, 1961).
A. Palmer and S. Brock, *The Seventh Century in the West-Syrian Chronicles* (Liverpool, 1993).
Paul the Deacon, *History of the Langobards*, tr. W. D. Foulke (London, 1907).
Procopius, *Secret History*, tr. G. Williams and P. Sarris (London, 2007).
—— *Wars* = *Procopius: History of the Wars, Secret History, Buildings*, tr. H. B. Dewing and G. Downey, 7 vols. (Cambridge, Mass., 1914–40).
Qur'an = *The Koran*, tr. N. J. Dawood (1999).
Shahnameh = Ferdowsi, *Shahnameh*, tr. D. Davis (London, 2007).
Theophanes = *Chronicle of Theophanes*, tr. C. Mango and R. Scott (Oxford, 1998).
Theophylact Simocatta, *History*, tr. M. and M. Whitby (Oxford, 1985).

Secondary Sources
J. Banaji, 'Precious-metal Coinages and Monetary Expansion in Late Antiquity', in F. De Romanis and S. Sorda (eds.), *Dal denarius al dinar: l'oriente e la moneta romana* (Rome, 2006), pp. 265–303.
—— 'Late Antique Legacies and Muslim Economic Expansion', in J. F. Haldon (ed.), *Money, Power and Politics in Early Islamic Syria* (Farnham, 2010), pp. 165–80.
T. Barfield, *The Perilous Frontier: Nomad Empires and China* (Oxford, 1989).
S. Bashear, 'Apocalyptic and other Materials on Early Muslim-Byzantine Wars: A Review of Arabic Sources', *Journal of the Royal Asiatic Society* Series 3.1 (1991), pp. 173–207.

J. M. Blázquez Martínez, 'Religión y Estado en el monacato oriental. Muhammad', *Gerión* 25.1 (2007), pp. 501–34.

S. Borgehammar, 'Heraclius Learns Humility: Two Early Latin Accounts Composed for the Celebration of the *Exaltatio Crucis*', *Millennium* 6 (2009), pp. 145–202.

W. Brandes, *Finanzverwaltung in Krisenzeiten: Unterchungen zur byzantinischen Administration im 6–9. Jahrhundert* (Frankfurt, 2002).

L. Brubaker and J. Haldon, *Byzantium in the Iconoclast Era, c. 680–850: A History* (Cambridge, 2010).

F. Carlà, *L'oro nella tarda antichità: aspetti economici e sociali* (Turin, 2009).

L. I. Conrad, 'The Conquest of the Arwad: A Source-Critical Study in the Historiography of the Early Medieval Near East', in A. Cameron and L. I. Conrad (eds.), *The Byzantine and Early Islamic Near East*, vol. 1: *Problems in the Literary Source Materials* (Princeton, 1992), pp. 317–401.

M. Cook, *Muhammad* (Oxford, 1983).

P. Crone and M. Cook, *Hagarism and the Making of the Islamic World* (Cambridge, 1977).

J. W. Dijvers, 'Heraclius and the *Restitutio Crucis*—Notes on Symbolism and Ideology', in G. R. Reinink and B. H. Stolte (eds.), *The Reign of Heraclius (610–41): Crisis and Confrontation* (Leuven, 2002), pp. 175–90.

F. M. Donner, 'The Background to Islam', in M. Maas (ed.), *The Cambridge Companion to the Age of Justinian* (Cambridge, 2005), pp. 210–35.

——*Muhammad and the Believers: At the Origins of Islam* (Cambridge, Mass., 2010).

A. England et al., 'Historical Landscape Change in Cappadocia (Central Turkey): A Palaeoecological Investigation of Annually Laminated Sediments from Nar Lake', *The Holocene* 18 (2008), pp. 1,229–45.

C. Foss, 'The Persians in Asia Minor and the End of Antiquity', *English Historical Review* 90 (1975), pp. 721–47.

——*Ephesus After Antiquity* (Cambridge, 1979).

——*Arab-Byzantine Coins: An Introduction, with a Catalogue of the Dumbarton Oaks Collection* (Washington DC, 2008).

——'Egypt under Mu'awiyya, Part I: Flavius Papas and Upper Egypt', *Bulletin of the School of Oriental and African Studies* 72.1 (2009), pp. 1–24.

——'Egypt under Mu'awiya, Part II: Middle Egypt, Fustat and Alexandria', *Bulletin of the School of Oriental and African Studies* 72.2 (2009), pp. 259–78.

G. Frantz-Murphy, 'The Economics of State Formation in Early Islamic Egypt', in P. Sijpesteijn, L. Sundelin, S. Torallas Tovar, and A Zomeno (eds.), *From al-Andalus to Khurasan: Documents from the Medieval Muslim World* (Leiden, 2007), pp. 101–14.

W. H. C. Frend, *The Rise of the Monophysite Movement* (Cambridge, 1972).

P. Golden, 'The Peoples of the South Russian Steppes' in D. Sinor (ed.), *The Cambridge History of Early Inner Asia* (Cambridge, 1990), pp. 256–84, p. 265.

P. Grierson, 'The Monetary Reforms of Abd al Malik: Their Metrological Basis and their Financial Repercussions', *JESHO* 3.3 (1960), pp. 241–64.

——*Byzantine Coinage in the Dumbarton Oaks Collection*, vol. II: *Phocas to Theodosius III 602–717* (Washington DC, 1968), pp. 568–70.

——and M. Blackburn, *Medieval European Coinage*, vol 1: *The Early Middle Ages* (Cambridge, 1986).

J. F. Haldon, *Byzantium in the Seventh Century: The Transformation of a Culture* (Cambridge, 1983), pp. 186–91.

J. F. Haldon, 'The Fate of the Late Roman Senatorial Elite', in J. F. Haldon and L. I. Conrad (eds.), *The Byzantine and Islamic Near East*, vol. 6: *Elites Old and New* (Princeton, 2004), pp. 179–234.

—— 'Greek Fire: Recent and Current Research', in E. Jeffreys (ed.), *Byzantine Style, Religion, and Civilization: In Honour of Sir Steven Runciman* (Cambridge, 2006), pp. 290–326.

—— 'Social Elites, Wealth, and Power' in J. F. Haldon (ed.), *A Social History of Byzantium* (Oxford, 2009), pp. 168–211.

C. Head, *Justinian II of Byzantium* (Wisconsin, 1972).

M. Hendy, *Studies in the Byzantine Monetary Economy* (Cambridge, 1985).

J. Herrin, *The Formation of Christendom* (Oxford, 1987).

J. D. Howard-Johnston, 'Thema', in A. Moffatt (ed.), *Maistor: Classical, Byzantine and Renaissance Essays for Robert Browning* (Canberra, 1984), pp. 189–97.

—— 'The Great Powers in Late Antiquity: A Comparison', in A. Cameron (ed.), *The Byzantine and Early Islamic Near East*, vol. III: *States, Resources, and Armies* (Princeton, 1995), pp. 157–226.

—— 'Heraclius' Persian Campaigns and the Revival of the Eastern Roman Empire', *War in History* 6 (1999), pp. 1–44.

—— 'Social Change in Early Medieval Byzantium', in R. Evans (ed.), *Lordship and Learning: Studies in Memory of Trevor Aston* (Woodbridge, 2004), pp. 39–50.

—— *East Rome, Sasanian Persia, and the End of Antiquity* (Aldershot, 2006).

—— 'The Siege of Constantinople in 626', in Howard-Johnston (2006), VII.

—— 'The Official History of Heraclius' Persian Campaign', in Howard-Johnston (2006), IV.

—— 'Al-Tabari on the Last Great War of Antiquity', in Howard-Johnston (2006), VI.

—— 'Pride and Fall: Khusro II and his Regime, 626–8', in Howard-Johnston (2006), IX.

—— *Witnesses to a World Crisis: Historians and Histories of the Middle East* (Oxford, 2010).

R. Hoyland, *Seeing Islam as Others Saw It: A Survey and Evaluation of Christian, Jewish, and Zoroastrian Writings on Early Islam* (Princeton, 1997).

—— *Arabia and the Arabs from the Bronze Age to the Coming of Islam* (London, 2003).

—— 'New Documentary Texts and the Early Islamic State', *Bulletin of SOAS* 69.3 (2006), pp. 395–416.

E. A. Ivison, 'Amorium in the Byzantine Dark Ages (Seventh to Ninth Centuries)', in J. Henning (ed.), *Post-Roman Towns, Trade, and Settlement in Europe and Byzantium*, 2 vols. (Berlin, 2007), II, pp. 25–60.

W. E. Kaegi, *Heraclius: Emperor of Byzantium* (Cambridge, 2003).

V. Kalas, 'The 2004 Survey of the Byzantine Settlement at Selime-Yaprakhisar in the Peristrema Valley, Cappadocia, *Dumbarton Oaks Papers* 60 (2006), pp. 271–93.

H. Kennedy, *The Prophet and the Age of the Caliphates* (London, 1987).

—— *The Great Arab Conquests* (London, 2007).

J. H. W. G. Liebeschuetz, *The Decline and Fall of the Roman City* (Oxford, 2001).

M. Lombard, *L'Islam dans sa première grandeur* (Paris, 1971).

J. Maddicott, 'Plague in Seventh-Century England' in L. K. Little (ed.), *Plague and the End of Antiquity* (Cambridge, 2007), pp. 171–214.

W. Madelung, *The Succession to Muhammad: A Study of the Early Caliphate* (Cambridge, 1997).

P. Magdalino, *The Empire of Manuel I Komnenos, 1143–80* (Cambridge, 1993).

C. Mango, *Byzantium: The Empire of New Rome* (London, 1983).

T. F. and A. C. D. Matthews, 'Islamic-Style Mansions in Byzantine Cappadocia and the Development of the Inverted T-Plan', *Society of Architectural Historians* 56.3 (1997), pp. 294–315.

F. Millar, *The Roman Near East* (Cambridge, Mass., 1993).

—— 'Hagar, Ishmael, Josephus, and the Origins of Islam', *Journal of Jewish Studies* 44 (1993), pp. 23–45.

M. Morony, *Iraq after the Muslim Conquests* (Princeton, 1984).

G. Nedungatt and M. Featherstone, *The Council in Trullo Revisited* (Rome, 1995).

L. Neville, *Authority in Byzantine Provincial Society* (Cambridge, 2004).

P. Niewöhner, 'Archaeologie und die Dunkeln Jahrhunderte im byzantinischen Anatolien', in J. Henning (ed.), *Post-Roman Towns, Trade and Settlement in Europe and Byzantium*, 2 vols. (Berlin, 2007), vol. 1, pp. 119–58.

D. Obolensky, *The Byzantine Commonwealth* (New Haven, 1971).

D. M. Olster, *The Politics of Usurpation in the Seventh Century: Rhetoric and Revolution in Byzantium* (Amsterdam, 1993).

G. Ostrogorsky, *History of the Byzantine State*, tr. J. Hussey (Oxford, 1956).

—— 'Byzantine Cities in the Early Middle Ages', *Dumbarton Oaks Papers* 13 (1959), pp. 47–66.

—— 'Agrarian Conditions in the Byzantine Empire in the Middle Ages', in M. M. Postan (ed.), *The Cambridge Economic History of Europe*, vol. 1: *The Agrarian Life of the Middle Ages* (Cambridge, 1966), pp. 205–34.

R. E. Payne, 'Christianity and Iranian Society in Late Antiquity, *ca.* 500–700 CE', (Princeton, D.Phil. dissertation, 2010).

P. Pourshariati, *Decline and Fall of the Sasanian Empire: The Sasanian-Parthian Confederacy and the Arab Conquest of Iran* (London, 2009).

C. Robinson, *Empire and Elites after the Muslim Conquest: The Transformation of Northern Mesopotamia* (Cambridge, 2000).

—— *Islamic Historiography* (Cambridge, 2003).

P. Sarris, *Economy and Society in the Age of Justinian* (Cambridge, 2006).

—— 'Introduction: Aristocrats, Peasants, and the Transformation of Rural Society, *c.* 400–800', *Journal of Agrarian Change* 9.1 (2009), pp. 3–22.

—— 'Large Estates and the Peasantry in Byzantium, *c.* 600–1100', in *Revue Belge de Philologie et d'Histoire* (forthcoming).

I. Shahid, *Byzantium and the Arabs in the Fifth Century* (Washington DC, 1989).

P. Sijpesteijn, 'Landholding Patterns in Early Islamic Egypt', *Journal of Agrarian Change* 9.1 (2009), pp. 120–33.

D. Stathokopoulos, *Famine and Pestilence in the Late Roman and Early Byzantine Empire* (Birmingham, 2004).

—— 'Crime and Punishment: The Plague in the Byzantine Empire, 541–749, in L. K. Little, *Plague and the End of Antiquity* (Cambridge, 2007), pp. 99–118.

A. Toynbee, *Constantine Porphyrogenitus and His World* (Oxford, 1973).

W. Treadgold, *A History of the Byzantine State and Society* (Stanford, 1997).

H. Vanhaverbeke, F. Martens, M. Waelkens, and J. Poblome, 'Late Antiquity in the Territory of Sagalassos', in L. Lavan and C. Machado (eds.), *Recent Research on the Late Antique Countryside* (Leiden, 2004), pp. 247–80.

A. K. Vionis, J. Poblome, and M. Waelkens, 'The Hidden Material Culture of the Dark Ages: Early Medieval Ceramics at Sagalassos (Turkey). New Evidence (*c.* AD 650–800)', *Anatolian Studies* 59 (2009), pp. 147–66.

M. Whitby, 'The Occasion of Paul the Silentiary's *Ekphrasis* of S. Sophia', *Classical Quarterly* 35 (1985), pp. 215–28.

—— *The Emperor Maurice and His Historian* (Oxford, 1988).

M. Whittow, *The Making of Orthodox Byzantium* (London, 1996).

—— 'Early Medieval Byzantium and the End of the Ancient World', *Journal of Agrarian Change* 9 (2009), pp. 134–53.

C. Wickham, *Early Medieval Italy* (London, 1981).

—— 'The Other Transition: From the Ancient World to Feudalism', *Past and Present* 103 (1984), pp. 3–36.

—— *Framing the Early Middle Ages: Europe and the Mediterranean, 400–800* (Oxford, 2005).

C. Zuckerman, 'Learning from the Enemy and More Studies in "Dark Centuries" Byzantium', *Millennium* 2 (2005), pp. 79–135, pp. 114–17.

CHAPTER 9 THE PRINCES OF THE WESTERN NATIONS

The historiography of the early medieval kingdoms of the seventh century is still largely divided up by region and dominated by essentially local concerns. To some extent, an exception in this regard is the world of Visigothic Spain, where concerted efforts have been made by Spanish historians to place Visigothic developments in a broader context of the development of early medieval 'feudal' or 'proto-feudal' social relations. As Roger Collins has noted, however, these are not debates that currently attract the attention of many scholars outside of Spain, who also tend to be unaware of the Spanish historiography. Rather, questions concerning the impact of Langobard rule on the Italian peninsula, or of when the political decline of the Merovingian monarchy set in, still tend to dominate. With respect to England, much emphasis has been placed on the impact of Christianisation on political identities and ideologies (Wormald) and the precocious economic development of the Anglo-Saxon world (led by the doyen of Anglo-Saxon economic historians and of the history of the Anglo-Saxon state, James Campbell). As C. Wickham's *Framing the Early Middle Ages: Europe and the Mediterranean, 400–800* (Oxford, 2005) reveals, it will probably be through advances in archaeology that historians will be drawn beyond these regional historiographical preoccupations to engage in historical study of a more inter-regional and comparative sort. It is to be hoped, for example, that Guy Halsall's seventh-century project will lead to such a study. Within the area studies, however, the writings of Wormald on Britain, Fouracre and Innes on Francia, and Collins on Spain are especially thought provoking, and should be the first point of reference for any anglophone reader. Much excellent research has also been published in Spanish, Catalan, French, Italian, and German, especially in the field of archaeology (to which the reader should turn to Wickham for the references). For the social and economic historian, the writings of J. P. Devroey are of particular interest: although their focus is Frankish, the author's gaze spans the world of the early medieval West as a whole.

Primary Sources in Translation

Adomnan of Iona, *Life of St Columba*, tr. R. Sharpe (1995).

Annales Metenses Priores = Fouracre and Gerberding (1996).

F. L. Attenborough, *The Laws of the Earliest English Kings* (Cambridge, 1922, repr. 2000).

Bede, *Ecclesiastical History of the English People*, ed. and trs. B. Colgrave and R. Mynors, 2 vols. (Oxford, 1969).

Beowulf = Bradley (1982).

Select Bibliography and Further Reading

V. Besevliev, *Die Protobulgarische Inschriften* (Berlin, 1963).
B. Bischoff and M. Lapidge (eds./trs.), *Biblical Commentaries from the Canterbury School of Theodore and Hadrian* (Cambridge, 1994).
S. A. J. Bradley, *Anglo-Saxon Poetry* (London, 1982).
Cassiodorus, *Variae*, tr. S. Barnish (Liverpool, 1992), contains a selection. Abbreviated translations of the Latin of the complete collection can be found in T. Hodgkin, *The Letters of Cassiodorus* (1896).
Chronicle of 754 = Wolf (1999).
Constantine VII, *De Administrando Imperio*, tr. R. J. H. Jenkins (Washington DC, 1967).
Continuation of Fredegar = see under Fredegar.
Einhard, *Vita Karoli* = *The Life of Charlemagne*, tr. E. S. Firchow and E. H. Zeydel (Coral Gables, 1985).
A. T. Fear, *Lives of the Visigothic Fathers* (Liverpool, 1997).
Felix, *Life of Guthlac*, ed. P. Colgrave (Cambridge, 1956).
K. Fischer Drew, *The Lombard Laws* (Philadelphia, 1983).
P. Fouracre and A. Gerberding, *Late Merovingian France: History and Hagiography 640–720* (Manchester, 1996).
Fredegar = *The Fourth Book of the Chronicle of Fredegar and its Continuations*, ed. and tr. J. M. Wallace-Hadrill (London, 1960).
Hlothere and Eadric = Attenborough (2000).
Ine's Law = Attenborough (2000).
Isidore of Seville, *Historia Gothorum* = *History of the Goths*; see Wolf (1990).
John of Biclaro = see Wolf (1999).
Laws of Aethelberht = Wormald (2005).
Lex Visigothorum, tr. in S. P. Scott, *The Civil Law* (Boston, 1932)—not entirely reliable.
Liber Historiae Francorum = Fouracre and Gerberding (1996).
Liber Pontificalis = *The Book of Pontiffs (Liber Pontificalis): The Ancient Biographies of the First Ninety Roman Bishops to AD 715*, tr. R. Davis (Liverpool, 2000).
Life of Bishop Wilfrid by Eddius Stephanus, tr. B. Colgrave (Cambridge, 1927).
Life of Fructuosus of Braga = Fear (1997).
Lives of the Fathers of Merida = Fear (1997).
Nicephorus, Patriarch of Constantinople, *Short History*, tr. C. Mango (Washington DC, 1990).
Passio Leudegarii = Fouracre and Gerberding (1996).
Passio Praiecti = Fouracre and Gerberding (1996).
Paul the Deacon, *History of the Langobards*, tr. W. D. Foulke (London, 1907).
The Chronicle of Ireland, tr. T. Charles-Edwards (Liverpool, 2006).
Theophanes = *Chronicle of Theophanes*, tr. C. Mango and R. Scott (Oxford, 1998).
The Wanderer = Bradley (1982).
Vita Audoini Episcopi Rotomagensis = Fouracre and Gerberding (1996).
Vita Balthildis = Fouracre and Gerberding (1996).
Vita Desiderii = Fear (1997).
D. Whitelock, *English Historical Documents I: 500–1042* (London, 1979).
Wihtred = Attenborough (2000).
K. B. Wolf, *Conquerors and Chroniclers of Early Medieval Spain* (Liverpool, 1999).
Zacharias of Mitylene, *Historia Ecclesiastica* = F. J. Hamilton and E. W. Brooks, *The Syriac Chronicle Known as That of Zachariah of Mitylene* (1899).

Secondary Sources

B. Albert, 'Un nouvel examen de la politique anti-juive Wisigothique', *Revue des études juives* 135 (1976), pp. 3–29, 22–5.

T. Aston, 'The Origins of the Manor in England', *Transactions of the Royal Historical Society* 5.8 (1958), pp. 59–83.

G. Ausenda, P. Delogu, and C. Wickham (eds.), *The Langobards Before the Frankish Conquest: An Ethnographic Perspective* (San Marino, 2009).

J. Banaji, 'Aristocrats, Peasantries, and the Framing of the Early Middle Ages', *Journal of Agrarian Change* 9.1 (2009), pp. 59–91.

A. Barbero and M. Vigil, *La formación del feudalismo en la Península Ibérica* (Barcelona, 1978).

A. Barbero and M. I. Loring, 'The Catholic Visigothic Kingdom', in Fouracre (2005), pp. 346–70.

J. Blair, *The Church in Anglo-Saxon Society* (Oxford, 2005).

M. Blackburn, 'Productive Sites and the Pattern of Coin Loss in England, 600–1180', in Pestell and Ulmschneider (2003), pp. 20–36.

—— 'Money and Coinage', in Fouracre (2005), pp. 660–74.

J. Blair, *The Church in Anglo-Saxon Society* (Oxford, 2005), pp. 246–7.

J. Bradley, 'Urbanization in Early Medieval Ireland', in C. E. Karkov, K. M. Wickham-Crowley, and B. K. Young (eds.), *Spaces of Living and the Dead: An Archaeological Dialogue*, in *American Early Medieval Studies* 3 (Oxford, 1999), pp. 133–47.

M. P. Brown and C. A. Farr, *Mercia: An Anglo-Saxon Kingdom in Europe* (London, 2001).

T. S. Brown, *Gentlemen and Officers* (Rome, 1984).

—— 'Lombard Religious Policy in the Late Sixth and Seventh Centuries: The Roman Dimension', in Ausenda et al. (eds.) (2009), pp. 289–308.

J. Campbell, 'The First Century of Christianity in England', in *idem.*, *Essays in Anglo-Saxon History* (1986), pp. 49–68, p. 55.

—— 'Production and Distribution in Early and Middle Saxon England', in T. Pestell and K. Ulmschneider (eds.), *Markets in Early Medieval Europe: Trading and 'Productive' Sites, 650–850* (Macclesfield, 2003), pp. 12–19.

—— (ed.), *The Anglo-Saxons* (London, 1982).

T. Charles-Edwards, 'The Distinction Between Land and Moveable Wealth in the Anglo-Saxon Kingdoms', in P. Sawyer (ed.), *English Medieval Settlement* (1976), pp. 97–104.

—— 'The Pastoral Role of the Church in the Early Irish Laws', in J. Blair and R. Sharpe (eds.), *Pastoral Care Before the Parish* (Leicester, 1992), pp. 63–80.

—— 'Wales and Mercia', in Brown and Farr (2001), pp. 89–105.

—— *After Rome* (Oxford, 2003).

—— 'The Making of Nations in Britain and Ireland in the Early Middle Ages' in R. Evans (ed.), *Lordship and Learning: Studies in Memory of Trevor Aston* (Woodbridge, 2004), pp. 11–38.

A. Chavarría Arnau, 'Churches and Aristocracies in Seventh-Century Spain: Some Thoughts on the Debate on Visigothic Churches', *Early Medieval Europe* 18 (2010), pp. 160–74.

N. Christie, *The Lombards* (Oxford, 1995).

—— *From Constantine to Charlemagne: An Archaeology of Italy* AD *300–800* (Aldershot, 2006).

—— 'Pannonia: Foundation of Langobardic Power and Identity', in Ausenda et al. (eds.) (2009), pp. 6–29.

R. Collins, *Early Medieval Spain: Unity in Diversity* (London, 1983).

―― *Law, Culture, and Regionalism in Early Medieval Spain* (Aldershot, 1992).
―― *Visigothic Spain 409–711* (Oxford, 2004).
M. Costambeys, *Piety and Property in Early Medieval Italy* (Cambridge, 2007).
P. J. Crabtree, 'Agricultural Innovation and Socio-Economic Change in Early Medieval Europe: Evidence from Britain and France', *World Archaeology* 42.1 (2010), pp. 122–36.
P. Crone and M. Cook, *Hagarism and the Making of the Islamic World* (Cambridge, 1977).
F. Curta, *Southeastern Europe in the Middle Ages 500–1200* (Cambridge, 2006).
P. Delogu, 'Kingship and the Shaping of the Lombard Body Politic', in Ausenda et al. (eds.) (2009), pp. 251–88.
J.-P. Devroey, *Economie rurale et société dans l'Europe franque (VIe–IXe siècles), Tome I* (Paris, 2003), pp. 224–6.
―― *Puissants et misérables: système social et monde paysan dans l'Europe des Francs (Ve–IX siècles)* (Brussels, 2006).
P. Diaz and M. Valverde, 'The Theoretical Strength and Practical Weakness of the Visigothic Monarchy of Toledo', in J. Nelson and F. Theuws (eds.), *Rituals of Power from Late Antiquity to the Early Middle Ages* (Leiden, 2000), pp. 59–92.
N. Everett, *Literacy in Lombard Italy c.568–774* (Cambridge, 2003).
R. Faith, *The English Peasantry and the Growth of Lordship* (Leicester, 1997).
―― 'Forces and Relations of Production in Early Medieval England', *Journal of Agrarian Change* 9.1 (2009), pp. 23–41.
P. Featherstone, 'The Tribal Hidage and the Ealdormen of Mercia', in Brown and Farr (2001), pp. 23–34.
D. Fernández, 'What Is the *De Fisco Barcinonensi* About?' *Antiquité Tardive* 14 (2006), pp. 217–24.
P. Fouracre, *The Age of Charles Martel* (London, 2000).
―― 'Francia in the Seventh Century', in Fouracre (2005), pp. 371–96.
―― (ed.), *The Cambridge Medieval History*, vol. 1: *500–700* (Cambridge, 2005).
―― and A. Gerberding, *Late Merovingian France: History and Hagiography 640–720* (Manchester, 1996), p. 3.
S. Gasparri, 'Kingship Rituals and Ideology in Lombard Italy', in F. Theuws and J. L. Nelson (eds.), *Rituals of Power from Late Antiquity to the Early Middle Ages* (Leiden, 2000), pp. 95–114.
―― 'The Aristocracy', in C. La Rocca (ed.), *Italy in the Early Middle Ages* (Oxford, 2002), pp. 59–85.
J. Gaudemet and B. Basdevant (eds.), *Les canons des conciles Mérovingiens*, 2 vols. (Paris, 1989), II.
P. Geary, *Aristocracy in Provence: The Rhone Basin at the Dawn of the Carolingian Era* (Stuttgart, 1985).
J. Gillingham, 'Elective Kingship and the Unity of Medieval Germany', *German History* 9 (1991), pp. 124–35.
D. Green, 'Linguistic and Literary Traces of the Langobards', in Ausenda et al. (eds.) (2009), pp. 174–94.
P. Grierson, *Coins of Medieval Europe* (Cambridge, 1991).
P. Grierson and M. Blackburn, *Medieval European Coinage*, vol. 1: *The Early Middle Ages* (Cambridge, 1986).
G. Halsall, *Settlement and Social Organization: The Merovingian Region of Metz* (Cambridge, 1995).
―― 'From Roman *fundus* to Early Medieval *grand domaine*: The Crucial Rupture Around 600 AD', *Revue belge d'histoire* (forthcoming).

H. Hamerow, 'Agrarian Production and the *Emporia* of Mid Saxon England *ca.* AD 650–850', in Henning (ed.) (2007), I, pp. 219–32.

A. Harris, *Byzantium, Britain, and the West* (Stroud, 2003).

P. Heather, *The Goths* (Oxford, 1996).

Y. Hen, *Culture and Religion in Merovingian Gaul, AD 481–751* (Leiden, 1995).

——*Roman Barbarians: The Royal Court and Culture in the Early Medieval West* (Basingstoke, 2007).

M. F. Hendy, 'From Public to Private: The Western Barbarian Coinages as a Mirror of the Disappearance of Late Roman State Structures', *Viator* 19 (1988), pp. 29–78.

J. Henning, 'The Metropolis of Pliska, or, How Large Does an Early Medieval Settlement Have to be in order to be Called a City?', in Henning (ed.) (2007), II, pp. 209–40.

——'Strong Rulers—Weak Economy? Rome, the Carolingians, and the Archaeology of Slavery in the First Millennium AD', in J. D. Davis and M. McCormick (eds.), *The Long Morning of Medieval Europe* (Aldershot, 2008), pp. 33–54.

——'Revolution or Relapse? Technology, Agriculture, and Early Medieval Archaeology in Germanic Central Europe', in Ausenda et al. (eds.) (2009), pp. 149–64.

——(ed.), *Post-Roman Towns, Trade, and Settlement in Europe and Byzantium*, 2 vols. (Berlin, 2007).

J. N. Hillgarth, *Visigothic Spain, Byzantium, and the Irish* (London, 1985).

R. Hodges and D. Whitehouse, *Mohammed, Charlemagne, and the Origins of Europe* (London, 1983).

B. Hope-Taylor, *Yeavering: An Anglo-British Centre of Early Northumbria* (London, 1977).

J. D. Howard-Johnston, 'Urban Continuity in the Balkans in the Early Middle Ages', in A. Poulter (ed.), *Ancient Bulgaria*, 2 vols. (Nottingham, 1983), I, pp. 242–55.

M. Innes, *State and Society in the Early Middle Ages: The Middle Rhine Valley 400–1000* (Cambridge, 2000).

——*Introduction to Early Medieval Western Europe, 300–900: The Plough, The Sword, and The Book* (London, 2007).

E. James, *Britain in the First Millennium* (London, 2001).

F. Kelly, *A Guide to Early Irish Law* (Dublin, 1988).

P. D. King, *Law and Society in the Visigothic Kingdom* (Cambridge, 1972).

D. P. Kirby, *The Earliest English Kings* (London, 1991).

K. Leahy and R. Bland, *The Staffordshire Hoard* (London, 2009).

L. K. Little (ed.), *Plague and the End of Antiquity* (Cambridge, 2007), pp. 171–214.

J. Maddicott, 'Two Frontier States: Northumbria and Wessex *c.*650–750', in J. Maddicott and D. Palliser (eds.), *The Medieval State: Essays Presented to James Campbell* (London, 2000), pp. 25–46.

——'Prosperity and Power in the Age of Bede and Beowulf', *Proceedings of the British Academy* 117 (2002), pp. 49–71.

——'Plague in Seventh-Century England', in L. K. Little (ed.), *Plague and the End of Antiquity* (Cambridge, 2007), pp. 171–214.

M. McCormack, *Origins of the European Economy* (Cambridge, 2001).

G. Molyneaux, 'The Old English Bede: English Ideology or Christian Instruction?', *English Historical Review* 124 (2009), pp. 1,289–323.

J. L. Nelson, 'Queens as Jezebels: The Careers of Brunhild and Balthild in Merovingian History', *Studies in Church History, Subsidia* 1 (1978), pp. 31–77.

——*Politics and Ritual in Early Medieval Europe* (London, 1986).

D. Ó'Corráin, *Early Medieval Ireland 400–1200* (London, 1995).

S. Oosthuizen, 'The Anglo-Saxon Kingdom of Mercia and the Origins and Distribution of Common Fields', *Agricultural History Review* 55 (2007), pp. 153–80.

T. Pestell and K. Ulmschneider (eds.), *Markets in Early Medieval Europe: Trading and 'Productive' Sites, 650–850* (Macclesfield, 2003).

W. Pohl, 'The Empire and the Lombards: Treaties and Negotiations in the Sixth Century', in W. Pohl (ed.), *Kingdoms of the Empire: The Integration of Barbarians in Late Antiquity* (Leiden, 1997), pp. 75–134.

——'Invasions and Ethnic Identity', in C. La Rocca (ed.), *Italy in the Early Middle Ages* (Oxford, 2002), pp. 11–34.

——and M. Diesenberger (eds.), *Die Langobarden: Herrschaft und Identität* (Vienna, 2006).

G. Prinzing, 'Pliska in the View of Protobulgarian Inscriptions and Byzantine Writers', in Henning (ed.) (2007), pp. 241–52.

B. H. Rosenwein, *Emotional Communities in the Early Middle Ages* (Ithaca, NY, 2006).

M. Rouche, *L'Aquitaine des Wisigoths aux Arabes* (Paris, 1979).

A. Rovelli, 'Coins and Trade in Early Medieval Italy', *Early Medieval Europe* 17 (2009), pp. 45–76.

P. Sarris, 'The Origins of the Manorial Economy: New Insights From Late Antiquity', *English Historical Review* 119 (2004), pp. 279–311.

R. Sharpe, 'Some Problems Concerning the Organization of the Church in Early Medieval Ireland', *Peritia* 3 (1984), pp. 230–70.

A. J. B. Sirks, 'The Colonate in Justinian's Reign', *Journal of Roman Studies* 98 (2008), pp. 120–43.

Lord Stewartby and D. M. Metcalf, 'The Bust of Christ on an Early Anglo-Saxon Coin', *Numismatic Chronicle* 167 (2007), pp. 179–82.

R. Stocking, *Bishops, Councils, and Consensus in the Visigothic Kingdom, 589–633* (Michigan, 2000).

F. Theuws, 'Centre and Periphery in Northern Austrasia (6th–8th Centuries): An Archaeological Perspective', in J. Besteman, J. Bos, and H. Heidinga (eds.), *Medieval Archaeology in the Netherlands* (Aaasen and Maastricht, 1990).

W. Ullmann, *Principles of Government and Politics in the Middle Ages* (London, 1961).

A. Verhulst, *Rural and Urban Aspects of Early Medieval Northwest Europe* (Aldershot, 1992).

J. M. Wallace-Hadrill, *Early Germanic Kingship* (Oxford, 1971).

B. Ward-Perkins, 'The Lombard City and Urban Economy', in Ausenda et al. (eds.) (2009), pp. 95–117.

D. Whitelock, *English Historical Documents, Volume One: c.500–1042* (London, 1979).

C. Wickham, *Early Medieval Italy* (London, 1981).

——*Framing the Early Middle Ages: Europe and the Mediterranean, 400–800* (Oxford, 2005).

——(ed.), *The Lombards from the Migration Period to the Eighth Century* (London, 2008).

A. Williams, *Kingship and Government in Pre-Conquest England* (Basingstoke, 1999).

K. B. Wolf, *Conquerors and Chroniclers of Early Medieval Spain* (Liverpool, 1990).

I. Wood, *The Merovingian North Sea* (Alingsas, 1983).

——*The Merovingian Kingdoms 450–751* (London, 1994).

——'Deconstructing the Merovingian Family', in R. Corradini, M. Diesenberger, and H. Reimitz (eds.), *The Construction of Communities in the Early Middle Ages: Texts, Resources, and Artefacts* (Leiden, 2003), pp. 149–72.

J. Wood, 'Defending Byzantine Spain: Frontiers and Diplomacy', *Early Medieval Europe* 18 (2010), pp. 292–319.

C. P. Wormald, *The Making of English Law: King Alfred to the Twelfth Century*, vol. 1: *Legislation and its Limits* (Oxford, 1999).
—— *The First Code of English Law* (Canterbury, 2005).
—— 'Bede, Beowulf, and the Conversion of the Anglo-Saxon Aristocracy', in C. P. Wormald and S. Baxter (eds.), *The Times of Bede* (Oxford, 2006a), pp. 30–105.
—— 'Bede, the *Bretwaldas*, and the Origins of the *Gens Anglorum*', in Wormald and Baxter (eds.) (2006b), pp. 106–34.
—— 'The Venerable Bede and the Church of the English', in Wormald and Baxter (eds.) (2006c), pp. 207–28.
—— and S. Baxter (eds.), *The Times of Bede* (Oxford, 2006).

Index

Aachen 170
Abd Allah b. al-Zubayr 294–6, 299
Abd al-Malik 295–6, 298–302, 326, 372
Abd al-Rahman 291
Abraham (Old Testament Patriarch) 261, 264, 284
Abu Bakr 263, 268, 272, 286
Acha 357
Achila 327
Adaloald 311, 313
Adomnán 355
Adrianople, battle of (Constantine) 21
Adrianople, battle of (Valens) 34, 58, 85, 172, 246
Adriatic Sea 117, 211, 330
Áedán mac Gabráin 356
Aega 344, 346
Aegean Sea 172, 173, 248, 291, 303, 304
Aegidius 45, 120
Ælfwine 359
Ælle (Northumbrian king) 357
Ælle (South Saxon king) 355
Aeneas 4
Aeneid 4
Æthelbald 355
Æthelberht 203–4, 205, 223, 354, 355, 364, 373–4, 376
Æthelfrith 356–7, 364
Æthelred 361, 366, 377
Æthelwealh 364
Aetius 42–3, 51, 52–3, 64, 196, 197
Africa 14, 20, 27, 36–7, 42–3, 50, 54, 59, 65, 67, 87, 158, 169, 191, 223, 243–4, 260, 280, 282, 289, 292, 297, 327
    Arab conquest 297
    Byzantine conquest 95–7, 191
    Vandal conquest 37, 42–3, 50, 51, 58, 89
    Vandal kingdom 58, 67, 78, 89–97, 145
Africa Proconsularis 8, 11, 43, 57, 89, 243, 244
Africa Tripolitania 89, 215, 244
Agatho, Pope 360
Agila 190, 191
Agilulf 310–11, 312, 313, 326
agriculture 29–30, 75–6, 79, 126, 129, 160, 303, 353, 367, 372–3
Ahlfrith 359
Aidan 371
Aisha 286, 287
aldii 312, 315
al-Dahhak 295
al-Harith 143, 154
al-Hira 259, 270, 276

al-Mundhir 231, 233
al-Nu'man 233
al-Qadisiyya 270, 302
al-Walid 297
al-Zubayr 286, 287
Alamanni/Alamans 9, 98, 104, 121, 337, 338, 346, 352
Alans 36, 37, 38, 43, 46, 48, 49, 50, 51, 58, 59, 87, 97, 171, 188
Alaric I 36, 41–2, 48, 49
Alaric II 104, 191
Alban, saint 200
Albania (Caucasian) 234, 252, 255, 295
Albinus 110–11
Alboin 178, 179, 180, 204
Aldfrith 361
Alexander (bishop) 24
Alexander the Great 5–6, 248
Alexander (praetorian prefect) 253
Alexandria 17, 24, 123, 143, 158, 190, 241, 244, 248, 271, 276, 281, 282, 283, 285
    patriarch 163–4, 217, 271
Ali 286–7
Alid party 286–8, 295
Alps 37, 104
Alsace 335
Alypius 213
Amal dynasty 88, 113, 119
Amalaric 105, 189, 192
Amalasuntha 85, 104, 111, 112, 114
Amalfrida 95, 104, 113
Amantius 135
Ambrosius Aurelianus 199–200
Amida 133, 134, 135, 140, 270
amir al-mu'minin 269, 277, 282
Ammianus Marcellinus 31, 32, 34, 73, 87, 196, 354
Amorium 291
Amr ibn al-As 271, 276, 282
Anastasius 102, 104, 105, 109, 122, 126, 127, 128, 130, 132, 134, 135, 137, 138, 141, 145, 151, 162, 173, 207, 209, 228, 229, 243, 253
Anatolia 76, 245, 248, 252, 253, 259, 272, 275, 291, 297
Anchises 4
Ancyra 248
Angles 46, 197, 198, 356, 376
Anglesey 359
Anglisc 73 *see also* Old English
Anglo-Saxon Chronicle 202, 355, 360

Anglo-Saxons 56, 71, 197–204, 205–8, 223, 225, 315, 353–76
  see also Angles; Jutes; Saxons
Anatolikon theme 282
Annegray 331
'Anonymous Valesianus' 98, 100, 102, 103, 105, 107, 108, 109, 111
Antae 175–82 *see also* Sclavenes; Slavs
Anthemiolus 55
Anthemius 39, 54, 55
Antioch 10, 11, 13, 15, 17, 18, 143, 154, 155, 212, 238, 241, 245, 246, 294, 295
  patriarch 164, 217
Antony, saint 211–12, 213–4
Apamea 245
apocalypse, apocalypticism 218–9, 258, 260, 266, 267–8, 272, 274, 298, 300–302
Apocalypse of Pseudo-Methodius 301–2
Apollinaris (son of Sidonius) 73
Apollo 23
Apulia 49, 289
Aquitaine 38, 46, 50, 57, 59, 61, 64, 65, 187, 328, 329, 332, 339, 343, 351, 352
Arabia 140, 152, 221, 229, 230, 261–8, 287, 294, 295, 296
Arabic (language) 264–5, 267, 299
Arabs 133, 135, 137, 140, 142, 143, 154, 213, 229, 231–2, 237, 246, 252, 259–74, 275–305, 309, 310, 377, 378
Aradus (Arwad) 283, 284
Arbogast 57, 71, 120
Arcadius 27, 126
Ardashir (third-century) 10, 235
Ardashir (seventh-century) 256
Ardennes 351
Arianism 24, 86, 88, 105, 110, 193, 194, 313
  see also Arius
Arichis I 311
Arioald I 313
Aripert I 315,
aristocracy, Bulgar 308
aristocracy, Persian 146, 234
aristocracy, Roman 8, 14, 29–30, 41–2, 67–8, 73–4, 84, 123, 160, 162, 224–5, 237–8, 302–6
aristocracy, senatorial 8, 14, 15, 18, 29–30, 73–4, 84, 134, 162, 177–8, 224–5, 237–8, 249, 302–6
aristocracy of service, Persian 146, 234–5, 258
aristocracy of service, Roman 19, 29–30, 129–31, 224–5, 237–8, 302–6
Aristomachus 237
Aristotle 222
Arius 24, 86
Arles 55, 69, 183, 185
Armenia 10, 125–6, 132, 133, 135, 137, 138, 140, 143, 144, 153, 158, 230–34, 236, 237, 242–3, 245, 251–2, 270, 271, 275–6, 279, 284, 285, 286, 289, 295, 296, 297

Armenia Inferior 133, 153
Armeniakon theme 282, 291
Armenian History 235–7, 241, 243, 246–7, 260, 265, 268, 270, 272, 273, 275, 279, 281, 285, 287, 293, 327
Armorica (Brittany) 50, 54, 56, 195
armies, Anglo-Saxon 363
armies, barbarian 48–9, 87
armies, private 56, 152–3, 237, 325
army, Arab 258–74, 275–304
army, Frankish 45, 123, 338
army, Persian 15, 146, 234, 253–5, 258, 259, 270, 271
army, Roman 8, 10, 14, 15, 18, 19, 45, 55, 234, 236, 239, 242, 249, 250, 270, 271, 272, 281–2, 287–8, 296
army, Visigothic 324, 325
Arsacids 9–10, 234, 236
Arvandus 39, 54
ascetics, asceticism 210–215, 225, 266, 267
  see also monks, monasticism
Asia Minor 66, 126, 160, 238, 247, 248, 255, 259, 275, 284, 285, 291, 292, 294, 304
Asidona 191
Asparukh 308
assemblies, royal 336
Assyria 140, 146, 234, 235
Astorga 188
Asturias 46
Atacotti 195 *see also* Ireland, Irish
Athalaric (Visigothic king) 49, 66
Athalaric (Ostrogothic king) 79, 85, 111–4,
Athanagild 190, 191, 192
Athanaric 87
Athanasius 211
Athaulf 36, 42, 46, 49, 50, 57
Athens 172, 221, 289, 309
Atlas Mountains 96
Atropatene 229, 252, 255
Attila 39, 40, 52–3, 54, 99, 126, 131
Augustine of Canterbury 203–4, 370–71, 376
Augustine of Hippo 55, 213–4, 220, 250, 301
augustus (imperial title) 8
Augustus (Octavian) 4, 34, 109
Audefleda 104
Audoin 204
Aurelian 12, 13, 14, 15, 16, 22, 26
Aurelius Victor 18
Austrasia 332, 333, 334, 335–53
Authari 182, 310, 311, 312
Autun 346–7, 348
Auvergne 55, 56, 64–5, 68, 184, 369
Avars 170–71, 177–82, 183, 228–9, 250, 251, 252, 253–5, 258, 294, 307, 315, 338
Avitus 54, 56, 188
Avitus of Vienne 122, 127
Axum (Ethiopia) 140, 158, 260
Azov, Sea of 308

Babylon (Egyptian) 271, 282
bacaudae 12, 37, 49, 50, 224
  see also resistance, peasant
Badr 263
Baduila (also known as Totila) 118–20
Baetica 58, 191, 192
Baian 177, 182, 253–5
Balash 132
Balearic Islands 89, 191
Balkans 4, 11, 14, 15, 18, 21, 27, 34, 43, 53, 60, 99, 119, 126, 131, 145, 171–82, 191, 228, 232, 236, 239–40, 250, 258, 259, 307–10
Balt dynasty 189, 192, 320
Balthild 343, 348
Baltic Sea 84, 202, 354
Bamburgh 202, 356, 358
Bangor-on-Dee 357
bankers 225
Banu Ijl 259
Banu Shayban 259
Barcelona 194
Barsanuphius 212, 219
Basiliscus 127–8
Basilius 68
Basina 199, 204
Basques 46, 317, 319, 327, 328
Basra 277
Basti 191
Batnae 135
Bavaria 313, 332, 337, 338
Bede 197–8, 200, 205, 206, 220, 221, 224, 225, 348, 354, 355, 356, 357, 358, 359, 361, 363, 364, 365, 366, 367, 369, 371, 372, 373–4, 376
Bedouin 269
Belgica Secunda 120
Belisarius 96–7, 115, 117–8, 143–4, 150–51, 169, 210
Benedict of Nursia, saint 219
Beneventum 179, 289, 310, 311, 315, 317
Beowulf 202, 206, 365
Berbers 93, 95, 244, 327
Berchar 351
Berht 360
Bernicia 202, 203, 355, 356–61, 364, 371, 377 *see also* Northumbria
Bertha 204, 207, 354
Bertram of Le Mans 184
Berytus 147
Bestam 236
Bethlehem 269
Bible 6, 28, 210, 218, 258, 264, 268, 287, 297, 300, 326, 330, 378
Bible, Gothic 85
Bilichild 348, 350
bishops 23, 24, 26, 84, 92, 121, 123, 164, 167, 184, 185, 186, 194, 208–10, 215, 217, 228, 237, 277–8, 297, 309, 311, 316, 318, 320, 329, 338, 374–6
Bithynia 250, 303, 304
Bitlis Pass 235
Blachernae 255
Black Sea 138–9, 152, 252
Bleda 52
blood-feud 186–7, 314, 364, 366, 377
blood-money 71, 186–7, 202, 314, 377
blood, royal 87, 88, 94–5, 187, 199, 333, 363
Blues 148–51, 241–2 *see also* circus factions
Boethius 110–11, 112, 222
Boniface 207
Bonosus 244
'bookland' 372
Boran 256
Bordeaux 64, 184
Boructari 198
Bosphorus 21, 254
Bosporus 232
Bostra 246
Bourges 55
Brescia 180
bretwaldas 355, 360, 362
Britain 4, 8, 12, 20, 37, 44, 45–6, 51, 56, 75–6, 77, 158, 159, 195–204, 218, 223, 225, 295, 353–76, 377–9
Brittonic, language 196, 198, 203
Bruide 360
Brunhild 183, 187, 319, 335
Bulgars 104, 175, 177, 307–10, 326
Burgundians 38, 46, 50, 51, 52, 55, 57, 58, 59–68, 87, 104, 121, 182, 184, 311
Burgundy, Burgundian kingdom 78, 184, 330, 332, 333, 334, 335–53
Busta Gallorum 119
Byzacena 43, 57, 89
Byzantium, Byzantion (city) 21

Cadfan 364
Cadiz 328
Cadwallon 357
Cædwalla 364, 371, 374
caesar (imperial deputy) 15, 17
Caesar, Julius 4
Caesarea (Cappadocian) 246, 252
Caesarea (maritime) 246, 260, 271, 276
Calabria 49, 290
caliphate, caliphs, caliphal title 300–302
Callinicum 155
Calminius 69
Cambrai 121
Campania 49, 98, 223
Canterbury 204, 376, 377, 378
capitals, imperial 15, 18, 26, 69
capitals, royal 332–3
Cappadocia 152–3, 243, 246, 252, 285, 304
Caprara 120

Caputvada 96
Carinus 15
Carpathian Mountains 175, 258–9, 307
Cartagena 78, 190, 191
Carthage 37, 43, 89, 93, 96, 113, 260, 297, 327
Carthaginiensis 58, 188
Carus 15, 17
Caspian Gates 131, 140, 157
Cassiodorus 60, 98, 100, 107, 108, 111, 112, 117
Catalaunian Plains 45, 52–3
Ceawlin 355
Central Asia 157
ceremonial, imperial 16, 18, 88, 167, 209–10
ceremonial, royal 193, 311, 318, 320
Ceuta 189
Chalcedon 247, 253, 254, 281, 285, 291
 Council of, 109, 128, 164, 210, 215, 224
 see also councils, ecumenical
Champagne 335
Channel, English 197, 204, 348, 369, 377, 379
Charibert I 183, 184, 339
Charlemagne 308, 317, 343
Charles-Edwards, Thomas 362
Charles Martel 343
Chelles 348
Cherson 283, 293
Chertsey 362
Chester 357
Chichester 197
Childebert I 121–2, 182, 183, 189, 204
Childebert II 183, 186, 187, 335
Childebert III 352
Childebert 'the Adopted' 347
Childeric I 55, 71–2, 80, 120–21, 185, 187, 199, 204
Childeric II 348, 349–50, 351, 352
Chilperic I 78, 183, 184, 333
Chilterns 200, 364
China 33, 170, 230, 242, 257, 279–80, 306
Chindasuinth 320
Chintila 320
Chlodomer 121–2, 183
Chunibert 340, 344
Chramnesind 186–7
Christianity 21–4, 138–40, 143, 146, 194, 205–225, 256–8, 263–4, 279, 296–7, 307, 309, 342, 353, 354, 358, 370–76
 Arian 86, 207 *see also* Arianism; Arius
 Catholic (Imperial Orthodox) 122–3, 193, 204, 205–225
Christology 109, 128, 160–8, 222, 237, 257–8, 266, 279, 280, 283, 301
 duophysite 160–8
 miaphysite 160–8, 224
Chronicle of Fredegar 308, 334, 335, 338, 339, 344, 345, 347
Chronicle of Ireland 360

Chronicle of Theophanes 241–2, 249, 252, 255, 269, 289, 291, 292, 293, 294, 295, 296, 307–8
Chronicle of Ulster 360
Chronicle of Zuqnin 298
Chronicon Paschale 149–51, 240, 241, 243, 244–5, 247, 253, 254, 255
Chrysopolis 21, 253, 254, 255
Church, Albanian 255
Church, Anglo-Saxon 370–76, 377–8
Church, Arian 89, 90, 91, 108, 193
Church, Armenian 138, 230, 250, 251, 279, 284
Church, Frankish 186, 260, 329, 330–32, 371
Church, imperial 91, 105, 163–8, 237, 249, 296–7, 303, 304, 307, 322, 326, 330
Church, Irish 223, 331, 370–71
Church, Miaphysite 224, 237, 257, 277–8, 279, 280, 296
Church, Nestorian (Church of the East) 230, 257–8
Church, Visigothic 318, 319, 320, 321, 322–3, 330
Church councils 24 *see also* councils, ecumenical
Cilicia 11, 238, 246, 247, 270, 292
circus factions 136–8, 148–51, 238–9, 240–42
Circus Maximus 6
cities, urbanism 4–6, 27, 79, 146, 172, 181, 193–5, 209, 221, 242, 249–50, 259, 288, 302–3, 304, 308–9, 310, 316, 330, 331, 353
citizenship, Roman 6, 28
city councillors 4–6, 12, 25, 114, 130, 160, 195, 324
city councils 4–6, 19, 25, 26, 238
Cividale 180
civitas 105–6, 108
clarissimi 30
Claudius II 14, 16
Cleph 182, 311
Clermont 56
climate change 76, 80, 158, 170–71, 197–8
Clothar I 121–2, 183
Clothar II 334, 335, 336, 337–9, 340, 343, 374
Clothar III 347–9, 350
Clovis I 45, 69, 80, 94, 104, 105, 121–2, 139, 182, 185, 186, 206, 207, 332
Clovis II 340, 343, 344, 346
Clovis III 352
Clovis (prince) 350
Codex Argenteus 108
Codex Euricianus 59, 61, 69
Codex Iustinianus 147–8, 323
Codex Theodosianus 62, 69, 147, 186
coinage 11, 26, 75, 76–8, 238, 278, 288, 298–300, 317, 348, 378
 see also economy, monetary
 Anglo-Saxon 370, 371–2, 379
 Byzantine-Arab 278, 298–300

copper 78, 126, 160, 239, 249, 288
Frankish 185, 337, 348, 352, 353, 354, 370, 379
gold 26–7, 75–8, 159, 160, 239, 348 370, 378 *see also* solidus
Langobard 317
Roman 11, 26, 74–5, 126, 159–60, 278, 288, 300, 301, 303, 317
silver 11, 249–51, 348, 353, 370, 379 *see also* hexagram
Ostrogothic 106
Sasanian 146, 278
Vandal 92–3
Visigothic 190, 193
Cologne 121, 332, 335
coloni adscripticii/originarii 30, 60, 62, 66, 80–82, 118, 130, 214, 223–4, 312, 315, 325
Columbanus, saint 330–31, 371
Connacht 355
Constans I 24, 222
Constans II 276, 280–93, 309, 315, 349, 377
Constantia 248
Constantina 241
Constantine I 20–25, 29, 91, 127, 146, 147, 186, 204, 205–6, 209, 222, 230, 240, 299, 306, 318
Constantine II 24
Constantine III 44, 56
Constantine IV 289, 293–5, 308
Constantine VII 309
Constantinople 21, 27, 39, 41, 53, 57, 76, 77, 78, 91, 96–7, 99, 104, 105, 110, 114, 122, 123, 125–6, 135, 143, 148–51, 158–9, 170, 172, 173, 175, 176, 177, 179, 183, 190, 193, 199, 200, 208, 212, 214–5, 216, 217, 218, 219, 221, 224–5, 237, 238, 239–42, 243–5, 247, 248, 253–5, 255, 269, 271, 276, 280–82, 283, 284, 289, 302, 303, 304, 307, 326, 334, 354, 372, 377
Arab siege 284–6
Augustaeum 149
Avar siege 253–5, 258
Council of (first), 163 *see also* councils, ecumenical
Council of (second), 165–8, 224–5, 280, 277 *see also* councils, ecumenical
Forum of Constantine 241
Forum of Theodosius 249
Golden Gate 240
Hagia Sophia 151, 152, 169, 210, 248, 253
Hippodrome 137, 148–51, 245
Land Walls 52, 53, 126, 171, 174, 177, 253, 254, 285
Mese 240, 241, 244
patriarch 164, 217, 225, 248, 253
praetorium 149, 241

Senate 30, 112, 130, 134, 137, 148–51, 171, 226–8, 236, 241, 243, 244–5, 248, 249, 281, 304
Senate House 137, 149
Treasury buildings 241
Constantius I 17, 20
constitutio Antoniana 6, 29, 31
consulate 105, 200, 207
Coptic, language 278, 299
Córdoba 190, 191, 193
Corinth 172
Cornwall 356
coronation, imperial 227
Cos 285
councils, Church (Anglo-Saxon) 208, 360, 374–6
councils, Church (Frankish) 186, 329, 337, 341
councils, Church (Visigothic) 208, 318, 322–3, 330
councils, civic 130
councils, ecumenical 24, 163–8, 208
Council *in Trullo* 296–7, 304
counts, (*comites*), Frankish 330
counts (*comites*), Visigothic 319, 325, 330
court, Roman imperial 16, 18, 19, 44, 209–10, 281, 291
court, Sasanian 156, 234
courts, royal 68–9, 72–3, 88, 108, 332–3, 336, 340, 342–3
Cremona 101
Crete 285
Crimea 232, 308
Croats 258, 307
Ctesiphon 10, 13, 17, 125, 138, 156, 229, 242, 247, 255, 270, 271–2
culture, Frankish 342–3
culture, Greek 4–6, 28, 221–2, 303
culture, martial 71–3, 84–9
culture, non-Roman (barbarian) 71–3, 84–9
culture, Roman 4–6, 70, 84, 221–2
Cunicpert 315
Cunimund 178, 180
Cuthbert, saint 224–5
Cyprian 91, 110
Cyprus 173, 248, 271, 276, 282, 283, 284, 296, 297
Cyriacus 240
Cyril of Alexandria 163–5
Cyrus (patriarch) 271, 276

Dacia 36
Dagobert I 260, 307, 319, 338, 339–40, 343, 352
Dagobert II 347, 351, 352
Dalmatia 115
Dál Riata 356, 357, 358, 359, 370–71
Damascus 246, 270, 284, 290, 292, 295, 299, 326

Danes 198
Danube, River (also known as the Ister) 4, 8–9, 33, 34, 44, 101, 104, 126, 171, 173, 177, 185, 236, 239, 308
Danubian basin 170, 175, 181
  see also Pannonian plain
Dara 134, 135, 140, 142, 143, 144, 154, 155, 231, 232, 233, 235, 242, 270
David (Old Testament king) 227, 258, 300, 326, 337
defensor civitatis 25, 151, 209
Degsastan 356
Deira 355, 356–61, 364, 365, 376
  see also Northumbria
Dentelin 335
Desiderius 343
Dhu Nuwis 140, 264
Dhu Qar 259
Digest of Justinian 147–8
  see also Justinian, legal reforms
Diocletian 11, 17–20, 21, 22, 26, 41, 91, 146
diplomacy, Arab 292
diplomacy, Avar 171, 177–8, 229, 251
diplomacy, Ostrogothic 104–5
diplomacy, papal 115, 207, 216–7
diplomacy, Roman 9, 88, 89–90, 95–6, 131, 135, 138–40, 144, 156–7, 171, 176, 177, 179, 180, 181, 220–21, 228–9, 230–32, 235–6, 248, 250, 251, 252, 255, 256, 258–9, 287, 289, 296, 307–8, 310
diplomacy, Sasanian 125–6, 131, 141, 235–6, 248, 259
diplomacy, Turk 230–32, 255
diplomacy, Visigothic 191
Diarmait 355
Doctrina Iacobi 241, 260–61, 267–8
Domitian (bishop) 237
Domitius Alexander 20
donatists 91
Dorestadt 353, 370
duces 25, 87–8, 135, 180, 310, 319, 325, 330, 332, 344
duchies, Langobard 180, 182, 308, 310–17
Dún Nechtain (Nechtansmere) 360, 362
Dvin 252, 284

Eadbald 205, 223
Eadric 369, 373, 374
Eadwine 355
ealdormen 362, 363, 365, 372
Eanfrith 357, 364
earthquakes 143
East Angles, East Anglia 202, 354, 355, 358, 361, 363, 364, 374, 376
East Saxons, Essex 202, 361, 371, 374, 376
Ebroin 348–51, 353, 377
Ecdicius 56–7, 64
Ecgfrith 359, 360, 361, 377
Ecloga 317

economy, monetary 11–12, 20, 26–7, 74–8, 84, 126, 129, 194, 238–9, 249–51, 278, 303, 369–70
economy, post-Roman 73–82
economy, Roman 11–12, 74–5
Edessa 134, 135, 155, 234, 242, 245, 250, 270, 378
Edict of Rothari 312, 313–5, 316, 374
Edictum Theoderici 70, 81
education 28, 85, 93, 112–3, 148, 342–3, 377–8
Edwin 205, 206, 207, 223, 357, 359, 360, 364, 365
Egica 327, 328
Egypt 4, 11, 13, 17, 27, 62, 77, 81, 109, 126, 128, 129, 130, 152–3, 158, 164, 165, 173, 221, 224, 237, 241, 244, 248, 259, 271, 277–8, 279, 281, 282, 286, 287, 289, 295, 301
Einhard 308
elites, Germanic 9
elites, military 57
elites, provincial 4–6, 12, 16, 19, 44, 56, 67–8, 72–3, 84, 92, 123, 189–90, 209, 277, 301
Elmet 357, 363
Emesa 245, 270
emperor, imperial office, Roman 8, 11, 14, 27, 207, 224–5, 258
empire, Gallic 12, 15
Ephesus 247
Ephesus, Council of, 164
  see also councils, ecumenical
Erchinaold 344, 348
Erwig 320, 323, 324, 325, 327
estates 26, 43, 73–4, 80–2, 84, 90–91, 128–9, 160, 184, 237–8, 243, 303–4, 312, 321, 325–6, 329–30, 331–2, 336, 340–42, 348, 351, 353, 366, 371–2, 372–3, 378–9
  ecclesiastical 223–4, 290, 336, 342, 371–2
  imperial 59, 76, 80
  management 74, 81–2, 129, 342, 372–3
  papal 216, 223–4, 290
  royal 59, 80, 90–91, 121, 312, 317, 331–2, 335–6, 372–3
ethnicity 71, 84–86, 188, 198, 202, 314
Euchaita 135
Eucherius 69
Eudo 328
Eudocia 43
Euphrates, River 140, 154, 242, 243, 245, 252, 257, 270, 287
Euric 39, 54, 55, 57, 65, 67, 68, 69
Eusebia 240
Eusebius 22
Eustratius 222
Eutharic 104, 111
Eutychius 216
Evagrius 159, 225, 238
exile 315, 364

familia 28
farae 180, 310
faramanni 60, 63, 70
Faustus of Lérins 197
feasting 108, 206
Felix of Nantes 195
Felix IV, Pope 110
feorm 354, 366, 367, 369
Festus 102, 105
finance, military (Roman) 11, 51, 65, 234, 249, 281–2, 287–8, 290
finance, state (Roman) 19–20, 27, 37–8, 128–9, 237–8 *see also* taxation, Roman
Fínsnechtae Fledach 360
Firth of Forth 356
fitna, first 286–9
fitna, second 294–6, 298, 301
Flaochad 346–7
Flavius Apion (early sixth-century) 134
Flavius Apion (early seventh-century) 240
Flavius Apion, aristocratic household 223, 277
Flavius Constantius 50, 51
foederati 46, 57, 62, 66, 197
Francia 326, 329–53, 354, 363, 364, 369, 370, 372, 377, 378–9 *see also* Gaul
Frankish, language 188
Franks 9, 36, 44–6, 52, 55, 57, 67, 71, 72–3, 98, 104, 107, 119, 120–24, 170, 178, 179, 182–8, 191, 192, 204, 207, 258, 307, 310, 311, 315, 317
Fredegundis 333
Frisians 122, 198, 199, 352, 366
Frithuwald 362
Fritigern 34
Friuli, 169
Fustat (Cairo) 277, 278

Gabriel, archangel 261
gairthinx 311
Galata 253
Galerius 20
Galicia 38, 328
Galilee 246
Gallaecia 51, 58, 188
Gallia Ulterior 38, 50, 51, 65
Gallienus 13, 14, 16
Gallipoli 174
Ganzak 235
gardingi 325
Garibald 315
Garonne valley 59, 64
gastaldi 294, 312
Gaul 11, 12, 17, 27, 36, 44, 45, 46, 50, 52, 54, 55, 59, 76, 77, 78, 79, 104, 113, 120–24, 158, 170, 182–8, 194, 203, 209, 212, 223 *see also* Francia
Gaza 259, 269
Geiseric 37, 42–3, 89, 90, 94, 96, 97, 207
Gelimer 95–7, 154, 169

George of Pisidia 250, 252
Gepids 52, 101, 104, 172, 173, 174, 177, 178–9, 185
Germanus 119
Gesalic 191
Gewisse see West Saxons
Ghittia of Pisa 316
Gildas 46, 196, 197, 199, 203
Gisulf I of Beneventum 317
Gisulf II of Friuli 310
Godas 95–6
Godegisel (Vandal leader) 94
Godigisel (Burgundian leader) 121
Goddodin 357
Golden Horn 253
Gospels 211, 212
Gosuintha 192
Gothic, language 85, 103
Goths 9, 12, 34–40, 41, 44–55, 58, 64, 69, 84–5, 107, 171, 172, 175, 354
Gourgenes 139–42
government, Roman 4–5, 10–11, 18–20, 25, 237–8
governors, provincial (Roman) 4–5, 10–11, 19, 25, 26, 151–3, 209, 237–8
Greece 57, 172, 309
Greek fire 294
Greek, language 28, 278, 299, 308–9, 378
Greens 148–51, 240, 241 *see also* circus factions
Gregory (exarch) 282
Gregory I, Pope 204, 207, 215–220, 222, 223, 240–41, 266, 310, 326, 356, 369, 376
Gregory II, Pope 328
Gregory Thaumaturgus 12,
Gregory of Tours 45, 73, 78, 123, 124, 159, 183, 184–5, 186–7, 188, 199, 204, 206, 207, 208, 209, 215, 216, 225, 333, 334, 341, 369
Greuthungi 49 *see also* Goths
Grimoald (Langobard king) 315
Grimoald (son of Pippin) 344, 346, 347–8, 352
Grimoald II (Mayor of the Palace) 352
Gubazes 155, 156
Gundemar 319
Gundevald 183, 184, 187, 334
Gundioc 63
Gundobad 61–4, 67, 69, 121
Gunthamund 94
Guntram 183, 184, 187
Guthlac, saint 203, 365
Gwynedd 200, 357, 359, 364

Hadoind 341
Hadrian (abbot) 348, 377–8
Hadrian's Wall 360
Hadrumentum (Unericopolis) 193
Hagar 264, 298
hagiography, saints' lives 213, 329, 330–31
hajj 286

Hamazasp Mamikonean 289
Hampshire 361
Hamwih 353, 379
Harran 270
Hasding dynasty 94–5
Hassan 287
Hassan ibn Thabit 159
Hatfield, council of 376
Hawran plain 269–70
Heavenfield 357
Hebdomon 244
Helenopontus 135
Heliopolis 294
Hellenistic kings 5–6
henotheism 16, 22
henotikon of Zeno 109
Heraclius 243–58, 260, 266–7, 272, 273, 275, 278, 280, 289, 290, 295, 301, 302, 307, 319
Heraclius the Elder 243–4, 251
Heraclius Constantine 280
Heraclonas 280–81
Hercules 18
heresy 23, 309
heretics 167
Hermenegild 192–3, 194, 317
Hermeric 188
Herminafrid 104
Heruls 85, 88, 97, 104, 107, 108, 144
hexagram 249–51 *see also* coinage, silver
Hexham 357
hijra 267
Hilderic 94–5, 112
Himnechild 347
Himyar (Yemen) 140, 230, 263, 283
Historia Britonnum 359
History of the Caucasian Albanians 291–2
Hlothere 369, 373, 374
holy war 138, 250–53, 258, 266–7
homosexuals 167, 221–2, 323
honestiores 29
honorati 30 *see also* aristocracy, senatorial
Honorius 27, 32, 45, 46, 48, 50, 56
Hormizd IV 233–5
hospitalitas 59–68, 311
households, aristocratic (Roman) 73–4, 130, 141, 152, 277, 302–6
humiliores 29
Humber, River 355, 356, 361, 363
Huneric 43, 89, 91, 92, 94, 113, 193
Huns 34, 36, 39, 40, 43, 44, 45, 49, 51, 52–4, 58, 72, 125–6, 131, 171, 172, 175, 198, 292
 Hephthalite 131, 132, 140, 145, 157, 170–71
 Sabir 137, 156, 177
hunting 93
Husayn 287
Hydatius 37, 58, 59, 224
Hypatius 141, 150–51

hypostasis 164–8
Hwicce 362, 363

Ibas 165
Iberia (Caucasian) 138, 139–42, 155, 156, 229, 230, 234, 255, 284, 285, 289, 291–2, 295, 296
Ibn Ishaq 265, 267
icons 209–10, 300
identity, Alan 94
identity, Anglo-Saxon 198–9, 202–3, 376
identity, Arab 264–5, 267
identity, barbarian 31–2, 68, 70–71, 84–9
identity, civilian 56
identity, Frankish 72–3, 123–4, 187–8, 329
identity, gendered 28, 214–5, 221–2, 225
identity, Gothic 85, 107–8, 321
identity, Langobard 313–5
identity, military 14, 57, 70–71, 225, 314, 329
identity, Roman 5–6, 14, 31–2, 55–6, 68
ideology, Roman 18, 31–2, 55–6, 138, 148, 258, 297, 299–300, 304, 326, 330
ideology, Sasanian 18, 133, 157
ideology, Umayyad 299–300
Ildebad 118
Illyricum 17, 27, 100, 147, 158, 171, 173, 180, 239
Imma 366
imperialism, Roman 4–8
indiction, fiscal 20
Ine 363, 374
Ine's Law 363, 368, 373
Institutes of Justinian 147–8 *see also* Justinian, legal reforms
invasions, Arab 77, 268–74, 275–305, 327–9
invasions, barbarian 9–11, 36–40, 44–55, 76
Iona 370–71
Iran 133
Iraq 138, 154, 236, 259, 270, 278, 286, 287, 295, 296
Ireland, Irish 86, 158, 170, 195, 203, 223, 331, 347, 351, 355, 358, 360, 364, 378
Isauria 119, 127, 284
Isfahan 249
Ishmael 261, 264, 378
Isidore of Seville 192, 193, 208, 318, 319, 320, 324, 329
Isis 221
Islam 258–74, 275–302, 328
Isle of Man 359
Isle of Wight 361, 362, 371
Isonzo bridge (*pons Sontii*) 101
Italy 6–7, 14, 20, 37, 39, 45, 48–9, 51, 54, 56, 59–60, 85, 97–120, 122, 158, 159, 169, 170, 17, 179–80, 182, 183, 185, 190, 204, 223, 280, 281, 289–90, 293, 295, 308, 310–17
 Byzantine 315, 316, 317, 377
 kingdom of Odoacer 79, 82, 97–102

Langobard 179–80, 182, 310–17, 326, 364
Ostrogothic 66, 78, 79, 85, 102–20, 145, 175, 193
Iustiniana Prima 173
Iyad 271

Jafnids 143, 154, 155, 231–2, 233, 259
Jarrow 371
Jerome 36, 42
Jerusalem 6, 241, 246–7, 249, 250, 252, 256, 258, 259, 269, 280, 294, 299, 300, 301
  patriarch 164–5, 217, 269
Jesus Christ 21, 163, 209, 211, 212, 258, 261, 266, 280, 284, 297, 299, 300, 301, 317, 372, 373
Jews, Judaism 6, 140, 165, 221, 241, 245–6, 257–8, 259, 260–1, 264, 265, 273, 297, 300, 319, 322–3, 326–7
jihad 266–7, 284, 291, 297–8
John of Antioch 244
John the Baptist 211
John of Biclaro 192, 194
John the Cappadocian 149–51, 162, 222
John of Damascus 266, 276–7
John of Damietta 276
John of Ephesus 158, 159, 176, 178, 181, 228–9
John the Lydian 135, 162, 222
John Malalas 135, 138
John Moschus 266
John of Nikiu 237, 241, 245, 276, 279
John Philoponus 222
John, Pope 110
Jordan, River 269–70
Jordanes 52–3, 54, 55, 85, 88, 98, 100, 109, 192
Joshua the Stylite 132
Juanshir 289, 291–2
Judgement, Last 168
Julian 24, 57, 134
Jupiter 18, 22
jurisprudence, Roman 69, 71
Justin I 110, 135–42, 143, 146, 173, 229, 243
Justin II 162, 177–80, 209, 227–32, 235, 237, 239, 257
Justinian I 96, 114, 115–23, 137, 141, 142–68, 169–70, 171–7, 185, 190, 200, 204, 209, 210, 221, 222, 223, 224–9, 242, 243, 244, 258, 280, 296–7, 304, 307, 314, 315, 323, 325, 326, 377
  legal reforms 147–8, 162, 224–5
  provincial reforms 151–3, 162
  religious policy 163–8
Justinian II 295–7, 300, 301, 304, 309, 317, 372
Jutes 46, 122, 197, 198, 376
Jutland 197

Kallinikos 294
Kandikh 171
Karin 284
kastra 288
Kavadh 132–44, 234
Kavad-Shiroe 255
Kent, Kentings, *Cantware* 203–4, 205, 218, 223, 337, 348, 354, 355, 357, 361, 364, 369, 373, 374, 377
khagan, khaganate, Avar 177–82, 251, 253–5, 289, 307–8
khagan, khaganate, Bulgar 307–10, 326
khagan, khaganate, Khazar 279–80, 295, 297
khagan, khaganate, Turk 157, 170–1, 229, 230, 242, 249, 252, 255–7, 279–80
  strategic objectives 232, 242, 256–7
Khalid ibn al-Walid 259, 268
Kharijites 287
Khazars 279–80, 292, 295, 297
Khorasan 298
Khusro I 141, 144–6, 229, 232–3
Khusro II 235–6, 237, 240, 242–3, 245–58, 259, 270, 272, 301
kings, kingship 71, 84–9, 106–8, 330
  Anglo-Saxon 199, 206, 353–5, 362–6, 373–4
  cultic/totemic 86–7
  Frankish 184–5, 332–53
  Gothic 87, 107–8
  Irish 86, 355, 362
  itinerant 108, 332–3, 353–4
  Langobard 310–15
  military aspects 71, 86, 107–8, 120, 199, 353–4, 363–4, 365
  nomothetic functions 69–71
  Old Testament 205–6, 210
  Vandal 94–7
  Visigothic 191–4, 317–33
Kirder 11
Koubrat 307–8
Kufa 277
Kutrigurs 175, 177
Lactantius 20

landholdings, military 66, 288–9
landowners, Roman 57, 73–4, 152–3, 167, 228, 311–12
landownership, Roman patterns of 29–30, 57, 73–4, 121, 336
Langobardic, language 315
Langobards 119, 122, 124, 170, 173, 174, 178–9, 204, 241, 281, 294, 308, 330, 332
Laodicea 143
Latin, language 5, 70, 72, 73, 121, 147, 185, 188, 314, 378
law, canon 296–7
law, legislation 69–71, 92, 105–6, 185, 186, 193, 202, 313–5, 316, 317, 318–9, 322–3, 326, 326–7, 337–8, 364, 365, 373–6
Laws of Grimoald 315, 317
Lazica 137–41, 143, 153, 155–8, 171, 229, 252, 253, 255, 283, 297

Leander 318
Lebanon 152, 276, 296
Lebanon, Mount 276, 294
Leeds 359
Leinster 355
Le Mans 121
Leo of Narbonne 70
Leo (emperor) 131
Leovigild 192, 193, 194, 317, 318, 320, 321
Leudegar 348–51
Leudes 183, 184
Leudesius 350
Leuthar 346
Lex Ribuaria 338
Lex Romana-Burgundionum 69
Lex Salica 69–71, 121, 185, 337–8, 374
Liber Constitutionum 59, 61–4, 81
Liber Historiae Francorum 347, 349, 350, 352
Liber Iudicorum 323, 324
Liber Pontificalis 290
Liberius 60, 115, 190
Libya 244, 282
Licinius 21, 24
Liguria 108, 281, 330
Lilla 365
limestone massif, Syrian 126
limitanei 66
Limoges 78
Lindisfarne 202, 356
Lindsey 388
literature, Anglo-Saxon 206–8, 364–5
literature, Greek 28, 303
literature, Latin 6, 28, 72
liturgy, Christian 250, 260, 332
Liutprand 316
Liuva 192, 319
Lives of the Fathers of Merida 321
Loire, River 46, 183, 212, 329, 342, 351
London (*Lundenwic*) 361, 366, 369
lords, lordship 84–9, 108, 202, 205–6, 314, 324–5, 330, 353–4, 364–5, 378–9
Lorraine 184
Lusitania 58, 188, 190
Luxeuil 330–31, 349
Lycia 160, 215, 292, 294

magister militum 26, 32, 57
  per Armeniam 143, 243, 282
  per orientem 143, 231, 282
magister officiorum 111
Majorian 25, 45, 54, 89
Malaga 78, 190
malaria 54
Manchuria 157, 170, 230, 232, 257
mancipia 61–4, 80–82, 325, 341, 378
mandylion of Edessa 234, 250
Mango, Cyril 214
mansus 81–2, 342
Manuel 271, 282

Marcellinus (count) 127
Marcian (emperor) 164
Marcian (*magister militum*) 231
Marcus Aurelius 6, 14, 236
Mardaites 276, 294, 295, 296
Mardin 270
Marmara, Sea of 253–4, 304
Marseilles 55, 78, 84, 194, 330, 334, 337, 352, 377
Martin I, Pope 283, 293
Martin of Tours, saint 185
Martina 280–81
martyrdom 210–15, 250–53, 266–7
Martyropolis 234, 235
Marwan ibn al-Hakam 295
Mary, Blessed Virgin 209, 254, 266, 299, 300
Matasuntha 119
Matrona, saint 214–5
Mauretania 93
Maurice 204, 217, 233–41, 242, 248, 249, 250, 251, 257, 310, 317
Maxentius 20
Maximian 12, 17, 18, 20, 22
Maximus Confessor 283, 293
mayors of the palace 338, 339, 343–53
Mazdakites 133, 141, 144, 146
Meath 355
Mecca 261, 263, 267, 268, 286, 294, 296, 299
Media 236, 271, 286, 295
Medina (Yathrib) 259, 261, 263, 267, 268, 269, 271, 277, 286, 294
  constitution of 267–8
medicine, Galenic 28, 222
Mediterranean Sea 4, 76, 145, 154, 172, 223, 248, 279, 353
Melitene 135, 233, 234, 291
Menander the Guardsman 170–71, 177, 178, 180, 230
Mercia, *Mierce* 202, 208, 223, 355, 356–61, 362, 363, 366, 371, 373, 374, 377
Merida 78, 190, 194
Merobaudes 43, 48
Merovech (father of Childeric I) 122, 187
Merovech (Frankish prince, sixth-century) 183
Merovech (Frankish prince, seventh-century) 335
Merovingian dynasty 67, 77, 80, 120–24, 182–8, 329–53
Meseta 46, 189
Mesopotamia 13, 133–5, 137, 140, 142, 144, 146, 153, 155–6, 230, 231–6, 237, 238, 242–3, 259, 263, 270, 271, 276
Metz 332, 335, 339
Meuse, River 332, 342
Michael the Syrian 230
Milan 15, 18, 37, 57, 101, 118, 122, 311
Milvian bridge 20–21, 205
Miracles of Saint Demetrius 238–9
missionaries, Christian 86, 203–4, 205–6, 220, 263–4, 370–71, 376

Moesia Inferior 173
monasticism, monks 210–25, 219–20, 223, 225, 330–32
   Frankish 330–32
   Irish 223, 331
monasteries, 'minsters' 330–32, 342, 353, 361, 370–73, 379
Mongolia 242, 249
Monkwearmouth 371
Monocarton 234, 250
monoergism 280
monotheism 21–2, 264, 265
monothelitism 280, 282
Mons Badonicus 199
Monte Cassino 169
Moselle, River 71, 332
Moses (Old Testament patriarch) 211, 215, 261
Mu'awiya I 271, 283, 284–7, 290–92
Mu'awiya II 295
Muhammad 259–74, 275, 286, 299
Munster 355
Musa 328
Myra 160, 215
Mzez (Mizezios) 292, 293

Nanctus, saint 321
Nantechildis 344, 346
Naples 115, 117, 118, 289
Narbonne 42, 50, 189, 192
Narses (sixth-century general) 119, 150, 173, 179
Narses (seventh-century general) 242
Nasrids 137, 140, 142, 144, 154, 157, 233, 243, 259, 270
navy, Arab 283, 284–5, 290, 294
navy, Ostrogothic 112
navy, Roman 43, 89, 105, 122, 180, 254, 279, 282, 285, 290, 294
navy, Vandal 89
Negev desert 126
Nestorius 163–4
Neustria 332, 335–53
Nicaea, council of, 24, 163, 318
   see also councils, ecumenical
Nicephorus 307
Nicetas 244
Nicholas of Sion, saint 160, 215
Nicomedia 18, 21, 24, 248
Nihawand 271
Nika riot 148–51, 162, 173, 210
Nikiu 282
Nile Delta 271, 276, 282
Nineveh 255
Nisibis 132, 134, 135, 140, 142, 143, 155, 229, 230–32, 235
nobility, Anglo-Saxon 365–6, 372–3
nobility, Armenian 138, 143, 153, 156, 230, 251, 286
nobility, Frankish 329, 338–53, 366

nobility, Gothic 85, 112–3, 318, 320, 321, 327–9
nobility, Parthian/Persian 146, 154, 234–5, 255, 258
nomads, nomadism 33, 58, 93, 158, 170–71, 213, 232
Noricum 179
Normandy 198, 342
Northumbria, Northumbrians 206, 207, 223, 355, 356–61, 362, 364, 366, 371, 374
notables, civic 130, 146
Notitia Dignitatum 45
Numerian 15
Numidia 43, 89
nuns, nunneries 214–5

Odenathus 13, 14
Olybriones 45, 52
Odoacer 39, 55, 60, 66, 79, 97–102, 115, 117, 179, 190
Oethelwald 358, 359
Offa 208
Old English 73, 86, 88, 198–9, 203, 374
Old Testament 206, 210, 211, 215, 300, 378
Olympiodorus of Thebes 64, 74, 81
Oppa 328
Opsikion theme 282, 289, 296
order, equestrian 16, 18, 28
order, plebeian 28
order, senatorial 4–8, 15, 18, 28
Orestes 97, 99
origo 19, 30
Orleans 184
Orosius 38, 41–2, 48
orthodoxy 23
Osrhoene 137
Osric 357, 364
Ostrogotho 104
Ostrogoths 40, 85, 88, 99–120, 122, 169, 172, 189
Oswald 223, 355, 357–8, 364, 371
Oswestry 358
Oswine 358, 365
Oswiu 355, 358–61, 365, 374
Otto 344, 346
Ottoman Turks 126
Oxus, River 249
Oxyrhynchus 223, 271, 277

paganism, Anglo-Saxon 205
paganism, pagans, Graeco-Roman 21–22, 24, 25, 167, 221
Palestine 126, 131, 142, 143, 158, 219, 239, 244, 246–7, 248, 259, 260, 268, 269, 271, 272, 279, 291, 294, 296
Palladius 225
Palmyra 13, 15, 142, 143, 273
Pannonia 98, 100, 104, 175, 179
Pannonian plain 170, 175, 307–8

papacy, popes 105, 109, 164, 215–220, 223, 240–41, 280, 283
Papak 10
Paris 184, 332, 338, 349
Paris basin 77, 80, 84, 121, 184, 332, 336, 339
Paris, council of, 337, 374
Paris, edict of, 337, 349
Parthenius 186
Parthia 4
pastoralism 75–6, 342, 353, 369–70
Patras 309
patronage 30–31, 38, 64, 129–31, 145, 325
Paul the Deacon 169–70, 179, 182, 289–90, 292, 295, 310, 311, 312
Paulinus of Pella 55, 57, 61, 64, 67, 69
Pavia 108, 118, 312, 315
Peada 358, 371
Peanwealh 365
peasants 27, 30, 79–82, 84, 159–60, 192, 197, 223–5, 228, 238, 304, 325–6, 336, 340–42, 367, 378
Pelagius, pelagianism 47, 220
Peloponnese 174, 181, 309
Pelusium 158, 244
Penda 223, 357–9, 362, 363, 371
Pentapolis 282
Perctarit 315
Peroz 132
Persarmenia 137, 229–32, 233, 252
Persia 6, 9–10, 13, 18, 31, 39–40, 219, 228, 229–32, 234, 252, 270, 271, 301, 302
Peter the Patrician 156
Peter, saint 164, 217
Petra (Caucasian) 153, 155, 156
Pharangium 144
Philae 221
Philippikos Bardanes 304
philosophy, philosophers 213, 218–9, 221, 222
Phocas 239–45, 248, 249, 281
Phoenix 285
physis 163–8
Picardy 198, 342
Picenum 108
Picts 20, 50, 196, 356, 357, 358, 359, 360, 361–2, 364
Pippin I 344, 352
Pippin II 351–2
Pippin III 343
Pityus 155
plague, bubonic 158–60, 162, 178, 179, 200–1, 219, 283, 295–6, 354, 370, 378
Pliska 308–9
Po, River 98, 103, 117, 124, 310
Pompeius 150
Pomponius Mela 367
Pontus 11, 12, 252
population levels 31, 126, 129, 158–60, 201, 378
Postumus 12, 14, 44

Powys 357–8
precarial tenure 330
prefect, praetorian 26, 48
Priscus (general) 234
Priscus (prefect) 244
Probus 15, 16
Procopius 59, 60, 61, 82, 85, 88, 90, 91, 93, 95, 96, 97, 109, 111, 112, 115, 119, 123, 132, 139, 141, 143, 144, 148, 150, 154, 158–9, 174, 185, 199, 200, 204, 222, 228, 303, 307
Prosper 62
Provence 105, 121, 122, 184, 190, 194, 337
provinces, Roman 4–5, 18–19, 26
Prudentius 41
Pudentius 95
Pyrenees 184, 189, 328, 329

quaestor 141, 147
Quaestura Exercitus 173, 180
queens, queenship 333–4, 343
Quentovic 348, 353, 377, 379
Querolus 46–7, 49
Qur'an 261, 264, 266–7, 300
Quraysh 286

Radagaisus 36, 49
Radulf 344–5
Rædwald 354, 355, 357, 364
Raetia 98
Ravenna 37, 43, 51, 57, 99, 101–2, 105, 108, 115, 117–8, 119, 180, 182, 186
Rayy 249
Reccared I 192, 193, 195, 206, 208, 313, 317, 318, 326, 329
Reccared II 319
Reccesuinth 320
Rechiarius 188, 207
Rechila 188
Recitach 99
Recopolis 193
Red Sea 140, 158
Remigius of Rheims 121
Reptila 179
resistance, peasant 12, 37, 49, 223–5
Rheged 359, 360
Rheims 184
Rhine, River 4, 8–9, 27, 33, 36, 44, 45, 122, 196, 329, 332, 342, 345
Rhineland 120, 197, 354
Rhodes 248, 285
ri, riuri 355 *see also* kings, kingship, Irish
Ricimer 55, 57
Riothamus 54–5
Ripuarian Franks 337
Rochester 374
Roderic 327
Rodolf 104
Roman Empire 5–40

eastern 39–40, 125–68, 209–10, 279–306, 307–10, 315, 377
  strategic geography 8–9, 33–4, 145, 170, 173, 273, 279, 307
  western 36–8, 44–55
Romanitas 69, 206–7, 209 *see also* identity, Roman
Romano-Britons 71, 195–202, 355–60, 361–2
Rome 8, 11, 20, 27, 36, 39, 41–2, 46–7, 49, 51, 56, 78, 89, 101, 117, 118, 119, 216, 281, 289–90, 310, 328, 356, 369, 371
  Caelian Hill 216
  Forum 240
  monastery of St. Andrew 216
  Pantheon 240, 290
  Senate 8, 14, 15, 30, 98, 105, 107, 112, 113, 114, 118
  urban prefect 56, 216
Romuald 289, 315
Romulus Augustulus 39, 55, 97, 99, 103, 107, 127, 289
Rosamund 179, 180
Rothari 313–5
Rugi 52, 98, 100, 101, 107, 198
Rushtam 270
Rusticiana 240
Rutilius Namatianus 50, 51

sacrum consistorium 30
St. Denis, abbey of 349
saiones 108, 113, 323
Salian Franks 121 *see also* Franks
Salvian of Marseilles 32, 37, 38, 48, 61
Samaritans 143, 165, 259
Samnium 108
Samo 207, 339
San Apollinare Nuovo, church of 108
Sapaudia 38, 46, 50
Sardinia 89, 95–6, 216, 290
Sarmatians 9, 52, 175
Sasanian dynasty 10, 132, 133, 233, 234, 271
Sasanian empire 9–10, 39–40, 125, 146
  see also Persia
  strategic geography 125–6, 133, 138–9, 146, 153–4, 157, 251, 256–7
Satala 144, 243
Savoy 38, 46, 50, 51, 57, 59, 60, 61–4
  see also Sapaudia
Saxons, *Seaxisc* 32, 37, 46, 50, 52, 122, 196–204, 315, 332, 354–5
Scandinavia 84, 151, 354
Scandza 85
sceattas see coinage, Anglo-Saxon
scepticism, religious 218–9, 220–5, 266
Schemarion 283
Sciri 52, 97
Sclavenes 175–82 *see also* Slavs; Antae
Scotti 195 *see also* Ireland, Irish
Scythia Inferior 173

Sebastopolis 155
Secundus of Non 310, 311
Seine, River 184
Seleucia 154
Selyf ap Cynan 357
Septimania 320
Serbs 258, 307
Serena 32
Sergiopolis 135, 237
Sergius (patriarch) 245, 254
Sergius, saint 237
Seronatus 64, 70
settlement, barbarian 39, 50–52, 58–68, 77–82, 90–91, 98, 103, 179, 181, 189, 201, 259, 289, 309–10, 310–12
Septimus Severus 91
Severus 20
Severus Alexander 11, 16
Seville 78, 190, 191, 193
shahs, Sasanian 10, 17
Shahin 247–8
Shahnameh 271–2
Shahvaraz 245, 246, 252, 254–5, 256
Shapur I 10, 11,
Shapur (general) 291
Sichar 186–7
'Sicilian Briton' 47, 49–50
Sicily 78, 89, 113, 115, 190, 216, 225, 240, 289, 290, 291, 292
Sidonius Apollinaris 52, 55, 56, 57, 64–5, 68, 70, 71, 72, 73, 322, 329
Siffin 287
Sighbert 358
Sigibert 178, 183, 184, 225, 339–40, 344–5, 347
Sirmium 15, 18, 101, 104, 172, 173, 174, 178–9, 182
Sigismund 59, 60, 104
Sisenand 319–20, 323
Sisibut 319
Sizabul 230
sklaviniai 309, 310 *see also* Slavs
Slavs 175–82, 228, 236, 250, 253–5, 259, 296, 297, 307–10, 338, 339
slaves, slavery 28, 31, 80–81, 118, 214, 222, 312, 325–6, 356, 366, 368–9, 378
Smyrna 291, 292
social structures, Germanic 9, 84–9,
social structures, Roman 25–32
social structures, Slav 175–7
society, rural 29–3, 73–82, 90, 92, 126, 195, 302–6, 312, 340–42
Soissons 45, 120, 183, 184
Sol Invictus 16, 22, 23
solidus 26–7, 75, 106–7, 159, 160, 239
  see also coinage, gold
Solomon (Old Testament king) 151, 210, 300
Solway Firth 359
Sophia 232

Sophronius (patriarch) 247, 269, 280
Sornegau 224
South Saxons, Sussex 197, 355, 361, 362, 364, 371, 376, 379
Spain 12, 36, 46, 50, 51, 55, 56, 58, 59, 78, 87, 105, 119, 158, 162, 188–95, 208, 224, 247, 317–33
   Byzantine (*Spania*) 190–91, 208, 247, 290, 319, 322, 324
   Visigothic 105, 188–95, 221, 290, 313, 317–33, 363
Spoleto 179
Sri Lanka 107
'Staffordshire Hoard' 366, 368
status, social 28–30, 71, 72–3, 202–3
Stephen (Iberian king) 255
steppe, Arabian 14, 143
steppe, Eurasian 33, 125–6, 138, 157, 170–71, 232, 252, 257, 271, 279, 295
steppe, Ukrainian 170, 171, 177, 232, 307–8
Stilicho 32, 33, 57
stipendiary tenure 330
stipends, military 234, 239, 250, 277, 288
Strabo 366
Strasbourg 332
stratêgiai 288
Stratêgikon of Maurice 170, 175–6
stratêgoi 288
Strathclyde 358
Suania 156, 157, 229, 233, 235
succession, royal 94, 111, 184, 318–9, 320–21, 333–4, 363
Sudan 298
Sueves 36, 38, 48, 51, 58, 188, 189, 197, 206, 317
Suinthila 319
Susa 155
Sutton Hoo 354, 366, 367
Sweden, Swedes 85, 202
Syagrius (correspondent of Sidonius Apollinaris) 70, 73
Syagrius (king of the Romans) 45, 120, 121
Sycaminum 260
Symeon Stylites the Elder, saint 212, 213, 214
Symmachus (fourth-century) 32
Symmachus (sixth-century) 110–11
Synesius 58, 215
Syracuse 290, 292, 293, 377
Syria 4, 10, 11, 13, 109, 126, 129, 131, 133, 135, 142, 155–6, 158, 159, 212, 214, 224, 245, 259, 261, 270, 271, 277, 279, 282, 284, 287, 294, 295, 296
Syriac, language 259, 278, 299

Tacitus 31, 87
Talorcan 358
T'ang 257, 279–80 *see also* China
Takht-i-Sulaiman 252
Tara 355, 358, 360, 362
Tardu 242
Tarentum 289
Tarraconensis 190
Tarragona 55
Tarsus 246, 377
Taurus Mountains 243, 246, 272
tax evasion 38, 129–30, 145
taxation, Arab 277–8, 298–9, 301
taxation, post-Roman (western) 66–7, 77–8, 90, 117, 186, 312, 324
taxation, Roman 19–20, 26, 27, 30, 74–7, 152–3, 159, 173, 238, 290, 324
taxation, Sasanian 146
Tees 356
Teia 120
Tella 270
Tertry 351
Tervingini 34, 49 *see also* Goths
'Tetrarchy' 17
Tetricus 12
Thames valley 202, 361, 363
Thannuris 143
themes, *themata* 282, 287–8, 305
Themistius 34
Theobald 356
Theocritus 135
Theodahad 61, 100, 111, 114, 115, 119, 311
Theodelinda 311, 313, 315
Theoderic I (Visigothic king) 53–4, 57
Theoderic II 54, 68, 188
Theoderic 'the Ostrogoth' 40, 60, 66, 79, 82, 88, 92, 94, 95, 99–112, 121, 122, 124, 126, 127, 128, 172, 179, 189, 190, 207, 311
Theoderic Strabo 99
Theodisc 73
Theudisclus 189, 190, 192
Theodora 114, 149–51, 155, 162, 210
Theodore (Archbishop of Canterbury) 348, 376, 377–8
Theodore (brother of Heraclius) 269
Theodore Calliopas 283
Theodore of Mopsuestia 165
Theodore Rshtuni 275–6, 284, 286
Theodore of Sykeon, saint 214, 224
Theodoret of Cyrrhus 165
Theodosiopolis 133, 135, 243, 252, 284
Theodosius I 27, 36, 58, 78
Theodosius II 52, 69, 126, 130, 141, 163
Theodosius (son of Maurice) 240, 243
theology, pastoral 219
theology, speculative 219
theology, Trinitarian 24, 266
Theophylact Simocatta 234, 235–6, 239
Thessalonica 21, 104, 171, 172, 181–2, 238, 250, 251, 309
Theudebert I 118, 122, 183, 185, 186
Theudebert II 183, 311, 333, 334, 335, 338
Theuderic I 121–2, 183, 184, 369

Theuderic II 183, 319, 334, 335, 336, 338
Theuderic III 349, 350
Theudis 119, 189
Thiudigotho 104
Thiudimer 99
Thrace 40, 99, 171–2, 173, 177, 237, 289, 296, 308, 309
Thrakesion theme 282
Thrasamund 94, 95
Thraustila 101
'Three Chapters' controversy 165, 280, 283
Thrutpert, saint 224
Thurgau 335
Thuringia, Thuringians 104, 122, 199, 332, 344–5
Tiberius I 21
Tiberius II 180, 182, 232–3, 237, 333
Ticenum 123
Tiflis 255
Tigris, River 140, 255
Tiridites IV 138
Tivoli 13
Toledo 193, 195, 208, 318, 319, 320, 321, 322, 323, 327, 328
Tolkien, J.R.R. 206
Torcilingi 100
Toul 335
Toulouse 38, 59, 68, 101, 104, 189, 190, 328
Tours 55, 123, 186–7
Toxandria 342
trade 9, 27, 74–7, 78, 93, 106–7, 153, 172, 190–91, 200–1, 261, 298, 353, 354, 369–70
Transcaucasus 4, 133–5, 137–8, 143, 153, 154, 155–158, 159, 229–37, 242–3, 250–53, 255–8, 263, 275–6, 279–80, 284, 286, 289, 295, 296, 297
treasure, treasury, royal 117, 179, 190, 233, 270, 333, 335, 339, 344
Trebizond 243
Trent, battle of the, 361, 366, 377
Trento 180
'Tribal Hidage' 363, 368
tribes, Arab 259, 264–5, 267
tribes, Germanic 8–9, 48, 84–7
Tribonian 147–8, 149–51, 162
Tricamarum 96
Trier 15, 18, 27, 120, 186, 215
Tripoli (Africa) 95
Tripoli (Syria) 284–5
Troyes 339
True Cross 247, 250, 251, 255, 256, 258, 260, 269, 289, 301, 302
tuatha see kingship, Irish
Tulga 320
Turan 133, 157, 249, 257, 271
Turin 180
Turks 157, 158, 170–71, 229, 230, 232, 234, 249, 252, 279–80

Tuscany 49, 61, 311
Tyne, River 224
Typos of Constans II 283
Tyrrhenian Sea 211
Tzanica 143
Tzath 138–9
Tzazo 96

Uí Néill 358
Ukraine 9, 172, 175
Ulfila 86
Ulpian 12
Ulster 355
Umar 263, 268, 269, 272, 277
umma 261, 267, 277, 284, 286–8, 295, 298
Unstrut, River 344
unction, royal 227, 320, 322–3
Unigurs 177
Uro 344
Uthman 277, 282, 286, 287

Vaballathus 13
Vahram 234–6
Valence 50
Valencia 78, 190
Valens 34, 85, 246
Valentinian III 37, 38, 43, 54, 57
Valentine 281
Valerian 10, 91
Van, Lake 284, 286
Vandals 36, 37, 38, 39, 46, 48, 49, 50, 56, 57, 58, 84, 85, 87, 88–9, 112, 169, 188, 297
Vardan 230
Veneto 118, 122, 124
Verenianus 56
Verona 108, 118, 120
Verulamium (St. Albans) 75, 200
Victor of Vita 58, 90–91, 92, 93
Victorinus 12
Vienne 27, 57
Vigilius (bishop) 341–2
Vigilius, Pope 166, 224, 283
Virgil 4, 6
Visigoths 34–40, 50–51, 53–7, 59, 61, 65, 68–71, 87, 101, 121, 311, 317–29
see also Goths; Tervingini
Vitalian, Pope 289–90, 360
Vortigern 196
Vouillé 105, 121, 188, 191
Vulfolaic 215

Wales 356
Wamba 320
The Wanderer 364, 365
war-band (*comitatus posse*) 86, 88, 183, 184, 365
Warnachar 338, 339
Warni 104
Wealsc, Wilisc (Welsh) 71, 202, 357–8

Wends 207, 339, 345
West Saxons, Wessex 355, 357, 361, 363, 364, 368, 371, 374, 376
Whitby, council of, 360, 374
Whitby (monastery) 371
'wics' 353, 369, 370, 379
Widsith 204, 208
Wihtred 374
Wilfrid 360, 361, 362, 364
Willebad 346–7
Winwæd 359
Witigis 117–8, 154, 311
Witiza 327
Witteric 319
Woden 199
Wulfhere 361, 362, 363
Wulfoald 350

Yarmuk 269–70
Yazdgerd I 126, 141
Yazdgerd II 138
Yazdgerd III 270, 271–3, 289
Yazid 291, 294
Yeavering 360, 362, 367
York 20, 360

Zacharias (patriarch) 247
Zagros Mountains 255, 257, 271, 276
Zamasp 132
Zeno 97, 99, 100, 101, 102, 109, 127, 131, 132, 137, 140
Zenobia 13
Ziebel 255, 257
Zoroastrianism 18, 125, 133, 138, 139, 229, 252, 264, 301
Zosimus 21, 41, 49, 55, 127